# the Unofficial Guide® to Chicago

## 3rd Edition

## Also available from Macmillan Travel

*Mini-Mickey: The Pocket-Sized Unofficial Guide to Walt Disney World*, by Bob Sehlinger

*The Unofficial Disney Companion: The Untold Story of Walt Disney World and the Man Behind the Mouse*, by Eve Zibart

*The Unofficial Guide to Branson, Missouri*, by Bob Sehlinger and Eve Zibart

*The Unofficial Guide to California with Kids*, by Colleen Dunn Bates and Susan LaTempa

*The Unofficial Guide to Cruises*, by Kay Showker and Bob Sehlinger

*The Unofficial Guide to Disneyland*, by Bob Sehlinger

*The Unofficial Guide to Florida with Kids*, by Pam Brandon

*The Unofficial Guide to the Great Smoky and Blue Ridge Region*, by Bob Sehlinger and Joe Surkiewicz

*The Unofficial Guide to Las Vegas*, by Bob Sehlinger

*The Unofficial Guide to Miami and the Keys*, by Bob Sehlinger and Joe Surkiewicz

*The Unofficial Guide to New Orleans*, by Bob Sehlinger and Eve Zibart

*The Unofficial Guide to New York City*, by Eve Zibart and Bob Sehlinger with Jim Leff

*The Unofficial Guide to San Francisco*, by Joe Surkiewicz and Bob Sehlinger with Richard Sterling

*The Unofficial Guide to Skiing in the West*, by Lito Tejada-Flores, Peter Shelton, Seth Masia, and Bob Sehlinger

*The Unofficial Guide to Walt Disney World*, by Bob Sehlinger

*The Unofficial Guide to Washington, D.C.*, by Bob Sehlinger and Joe Surkiewicz with Eve Zibart

# the Unofficial Guide® to Chicago

## 3rd Edition

Joe Surkiewicz
and
Bob Sehlinger

Macmillan • USA

Every effort has been made to ensure the accuracy of information through-out this book. Bear in mind, however, that prices, schedules, etc., are constantly changing. Readers should always verify information before making final plans.

**Macmillan Travel**
A Pearson Education Macmillan Company
1633 Broadway
New York, New York 10019-6785

Produced by Menasha Ridge Press

MACMILLAN is a registered trademark of Macmillan, Inc.
UNOFFICIAL GUIDE is a registered trademark of Ahsuog, Inc.

ISBN 0-02-862779-2

ISSN 1083-1452

Manufactured in the United States of America

10 9 8 7 6 5 4 3 2 1

Third edition

To the brides: Shane, Rachel, and Grace; and the grooms: Jason, Curt, and Steve. May you all grow prosperous and support your parents in grand style.

—B. S.

To Dennis Coello and that rolling two-lane blacktop in the Valley: There's no such thing as a coincidence.

—J. S.

# Contents

List of Illustrations   ix
Acknowledgments   x

**Introduction**
The Most "American" of American Cities   1
About This Guide   3

**1  Understanding the City**
A Brief History of Chicago   31
Skyscrapers and the Prairie School: Chicago Architecture   39
Sculpture in the Loop   43

**2  Planning Your Visit to Chicago**
When to Go: Seasons of the Windy City   45
Getting to Chicago   48
*Calendar of Special Events*   49

**3  Hotels**
Deciding Where to Stay   55
Getting a Good Deal on a Room   56
Chicago Lodging for Business Travelers   66
Hotels and Motels: Rated and Ranked   67

**4  Visiting Chicago on Business**
Convention Central, U.S.A.   79
*Convention and Trade Show Calendar*   89

**5  Arriving and Getting Oriented**

Coming into the City    95
Getting Oriented    103
Things the Natives Already Know    108
How to Avoid Crime and Keep Safe in Public Places    114

**6  Getting around Chicago**

Driving Your Car: A Really Bad Idea    121
Public Transportation    123

**7  Entertainment and Night Life**

Chicago Night Life    129
Night Club Profiles    140

**8  Exercise and Recreation**

Handling Chicago's Weather    161
Indoor Sports    161
Outdoor Sports    163
Spectator Sports    171

**9  Shopping in Chicago**

Nothing Like It Back Home    176
Where to Find . . .    185
Suburban Shopping Centers and Discount Malls    218

**10  Sight-Seeing Tips and Tours**

Touring Chicago    221
Exploring Chicago's Neighborhoods    229
Chicago for Children    243
Helpful Hints for Tourists    245

**11  Attractions in Chicago**

The Loop . . . and Beyond    249
Sights: Zone 1—The North Side    252
Sights: Zone 2—North Central/O'Hare    255
Sights: Zone 3—Near North    263
Sights: Zone 4—The Loop    272
Sights: Zone 5—South Loop    285
Sights: Zone 6—South Central/Midway    292

Sights: Zone 7—South Side   293
Sights: Zone 8—Southern Suburbs   299
Sights: Zone 9—Western Suburbs   300
Sights: Zone 11—Northern Suburbs   302

## 12 Dining and Restaurants

Dining in Chicago   304
The Restaurants   312
Restaurant Profiles   326

### Appendix

Hotel Information Chart   452

Index   463
Reader Survey   483

## List of Illustrations

The Midwest   2
Chicago Touring Zones   8–9
Zone 1: North Side   10–11
Zone 2: North Central/O'Hare   12–13
Zone 3: Near North   14–15
Zone 4: The Loop   16–17
Zone 5: South Loop   18–19
Zone 6: South Central/Midway   20–21
Zone 7: South Side   22–23
Zone 8: Southern Suburbs   24–25
Zone 9: Western Suburbs   26–27
Zone 10: Northwest Suburbs   28–29
Zone 11: Northern Suburbs   30
Downtown Hotels   58–59
McCormick Convention Center   83
McCormick Convention Center Numbering System   86
Rosemont Convention Center   92
O'Hare International Airport   97
Midway Airport   101

# Acknowledgments

It isn't that Chicagoans are just crazy about their town; first-time visitors must be converted into believers, too. And that's very good news for anyone putting together a guidebook to a city as multifaceted, hectic, and astonishingly large as Chicago. We'd like to thank the folks who shared their intimate knowledge of the city, gave us heads-up practical advice, and charged us with their enthusiasm as we researched and wrote this book.

Dining diva Camille Stagg, author of *The Cook's Advisor, The Best of the Cook's Advisor, Cooking with Wine,* and *The Eclectic Gourmet Guide to Chicago,* is the former award-winning food editor for the *Chicago Sun-Times* and *Cuisine* magazine; she wrote our section on restaurants and dining in the Windy City. Ms. Stagg has more than 28 year's experience in the journalism and consulting professions. She has directed a cooking school, continues to teach numerous seminars and classes, and conducts food and wine tastings. She develops recipes for "A Taste of California," a wine of the month club in fourteen states, and conducts food and wine tastings with that organization. Ms. Stagg has also served as dining critic for Pulitzer-Lerner Newspapers, *Inside Chicago* magazine, *Talking to the Boss, Chicago Social,* and currently for Copley Chicago Newspapers' *Fox Valley Villages 60504.* She has been a regular contributor to the "Food" section of the *Chicago Sun-Times* and continues to contribute to a variety of national publications. She holds a B. S. in food science and journalism from the University of Illinois and has studied cooking with experts here and abroad.

Frequent *Outside* magazine contributor Debra Shore took a Sunday to show us around some of Chicago's ethnic enclaves—and then wrote our wit- and insight-infused section on neighborhoods. Her son, Ben Smith, chipped in with a kid's-eye view of what's *really* cool in Chicago.

Laurie Levy, who wrote our shopping section, contributes to the *Chicago Tribune, Mademoiselle, McCall's, Travel & Leisure,* and the *Christian Science Monitor.* Her handbook on child safety for parents and teachers, *The Safe and Sound Child,* is published by Good Year Books; she's also an award-winning short story writer and a novelist.

*Chicago Sun-Times* staff writer and columnist Dave Hoekstra penned our section on entertainment and night life. He won a 1987 Chicago Newspaper Guild Stick-O-Type Award for Column Writing for outstanding commentary on Chicago night life. He's also a contributing writer for *Playboy* and has been a contributing editor for *Chicago* magazine.

Mike Steere, a frequent contributor to *Outside* magazine, gave us invaluable insights into Chicago's outdoors scene that only a native could know, such as pointing out the least-crowded stretches of the Lakeshore Trail and the best spots to windsurf on Lake Michigan. Robert Feder at the *Chicago Sun-Times* tuned us in to the latest on the Chicago TV talk show scene, while the folks at Performance Bike Shop on North Halsted Street loaned us a mountain bike (*and* a helmet) for a blustery cruise along the lakefront.

To fulfill her task as hotel inspector, Diane Kuhr endured sore feet and hasty, high-cholesterol lunches as she zipped around the Windy City.

Finally, many thanks to Brian Taylor, Tim Krasnansky, Laura Poole, Caroline Carr, Chris Mohney, Allison Jones, Holly Cross, and Ann Cassar, the pros who managed to transform all this effort into a book.

# Introduction

## The Most "American" of American Cities

When you think of great American cities, it's no wonder that Chicago is not the first to spring to mind. Chicago, it seems, has an image problem. You could say it's the Rodney Dangerfield of American cities.

The *Second* City? The *Windy* City?

Chicago gets no respect.

Funny thing, though—the people who live in Chicago get along very well without the external validation that fires and sustains New Yorkers. Chicago is big, brash, independent, and, most important, self-confident. With a magnificent lakefront park for a front yard, stunning architecture, a rich and colorful history, world-class cuisine and shopping, and a thriving arts and culture scene, Chicagoans don't require constant reassurance. They're just happy to be there.

Yet many of Chicago's charms remain a secret to outsiders; even worse, over the years some folks have nurtured decidedly unflattering notions about the town. Maybe it was the devastating fire of 1871 that leveled the center city, or the reeking, mile-square stockyards—a notorious Chicago landmark for more than a century. It could be the city's sinister reputation for gangsters, tough guys, and hardball politicians. Or perhaps it's the plight of the hapless Chicago Cubs, the National League club that hasn't won a World Series since 1908.

But out-of-towners who write Chicago off as a layover at O'Hare are missing a lot. Brassy and blowsy, Chicago is a place where people speak their minds and aren't reluctant to talk to strangers—especially about sports and politics. With a score of major museums, an impressive collection of public sculpture, thriving regional theaters, a frenetic night life scene, and hundreds of first-rate restaurants, Chicago is a city where people come to have a good time. Chicago is a blues and jazz town without compare, but it also boasts one of the finest symphony orchestras in the world. Additionally, it's a city with a no-holds-barred literary tradition,

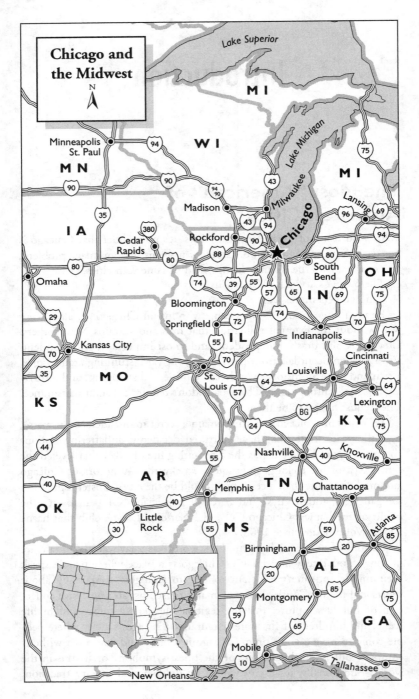

Chicago and the Midwest

from the muckraking of Upton Sinclair to the machine-gun dialogue of Pulitzer Prize–winning playwright David Mamet.

Chicagoans know their town as a city of strength, bold visions, and decisive action. In a remarkably short time, Chicago sprang from flat prairies and swampland and grew into an international trade center whose financial markets and commercial enterprises influence economies all over the world. There are miles of public beaches, three of the world's ten tallest buildings, a river that runs backward, "Da Bears," the world's largest indoor aquarium, Oprah Winfrey, Michael Jordan . . . and the ever-popular deep-dish pizza. Yet for all that, Chicago has never been regarded as particularly cosmopolitan or "international" in the manner of, say, European capitals or waterfront American cities such as San Francisco or New Orleans. Chicago derives its identity from within, from its energy and from its diversity. Chicago is the melting pot. Chicago is a metaphor for America.

# About This Guide

## How Come "Unofficial"?

Most "official" guides to Chicago tout the well-known sights, promote the local restaurants and hotels indiscriminately, and leave out a lot of good stuff. This guide is different.

Instead of pandering to the tourist industry, we'll tell you if a well-known restaurant's mediocre food is not worth the wait. We'll complain loudly about overpriced hotel rooms that aren't convenient to the Loop or the airport, and we'll guide you away from the crowds and congestion for a break now and then.

Chicago's crush of world-class traffic jams and staggering size can bewilder first-time visitors. We sent in a team of evaluators who toured downtown and its outlying neighborhoods and popular attractions, ate in the area's best restaurants, performed critical evaluations of its hotels, and visited Chicago's best nightclubs. If a museum is boring, or a major attraction is overrated, we say so—and, in the process, hopefully make your visit more fun, efficient, and economical.

## Creating a Guidebook

We got into the guidebook business because we were unhappy with the way travel guides make the reader work to find any usable information. Wouldn't it be nice, we thought, if we were to make guides that are easy to use?

Most guidebooks are compilations of lists. This is true regardless of whether the information is presented in list form or artfully distributed through pages of prose. There is insufficient detail in a list, and prose can present tedious helpings of nonessential or marginally useful information. Not enough wheat, so to speak, for nourishment in one instance, and too much chaff in the other. Either way, these types of guides provide little more than departure points from which readers initiate their own quests.

Many guides are readable and well researched, but they tend to be difficult to use. To select a hotel, for example, a reader must study several pages of descriptions with only the boldface hotel names breaking up large blocks of text. Because each description essentially deals with the same variables, it is difficult to recall what was said concerning a particular hotel. Readers generally must work through all the write-ups before beginning to narrow their choices. The presentation of restaurants, clubs, and attractions is similar except that even more reading is usually required. To use such a guide is to undertake an exhaustive research process that requires examining nearly as many options and possibilities as starting from scratch. Recommendations, if any, lack depth and conviction. These guides compound rather than solve problems by failing to narrow travelers' choices down to a thoughtfully considered, well-distilled, and manageable few.

## How *Unofficial Guides* Are Different

Readers care about the author's opinion. The author, after all, is supposed to know what he is talking about. This, coupled with the fact that the traveler wants quick answers (as opposed to endless alternatives), dictates that authors should be explicit, prescriptive, and, above all, direct. The *Unofficial Guide* tries to do just that. It spells out alternatives and recommends specific courses of action. It simplifies complicated destinations and attractions and helps the traveler feel in control in the most unfamiliar environments. The objective of the *Unofficial Guide* is not to have the most information or all of the information; it aims to have the most accessible, useful information, unbiased by affiliation with any organization or industry.

An *Unofficial Guide* is a critical reference work; it focuses on a travel destination that appears to be especially complex. Our authors and research team are completely independent from the attractions, restaurants, and hotels we describe. *The Unofficial Guide to Chicago* is designed for individuals and families traveling for the fun of it, as well as for business travelers and conventioneers, especially those visiting the Windy City for the first time. The guide is directed at value-conscious, consumer-oriented adults who seek a cost-effective, though not Spartan, travel style.

## Special Features

The *Unofficial Guide* incorporates the following special features:

- Friendly introductions to Chicago's vast array of fascinating ethnic neighborhoods.

- "Best of" listings giving our well-qualified opinions on bagels to baguettes, four-star hotels to best night views of Chicago.

- Listings that are keyed to your interests, so you can pick and choose.

- Advice to help sight-seers avoid crowds; advice to business travelers on avoiding traffic and excess expense.

- A zone system and maps that make it easy to find places you want to go and avoid places you don't.

- Expert advice on avoiding Chicago's street and highway crime.

- A hotel chart that helps narrow your choices fast, according to your needs.

- Shorter listings that include only those restaurants, clubs, and hotels we think are worth considering.

- A detailed index to help you find things quickly.

What you won't get:

- Long, useless lists where everything looks the same.

- Insufficient information that gets you where you want to go at the worst possible time.

- Information without advice on how to use it.

## HOW THIS GUIDE WAS RESEARCHED AND WRITTEN

While a lot of guidebooks have been written about Chicago, very few have been evaluative. Some guides practically regurgitate hotel and tourist office promotional material. In preparing this book, nothing was taken for granted. Each museum, monument, art gallery, hotel, restaurant, shop, and attraction was evaluated and rated by a team of trained observers according to formal criteria. Interviews were conducted to determine what tourists of all ages enjoyed most *and least* during their Chicago visit.

While our observers are independent and impartial, they do not claim to have special expertise. Like you, they visited Chicago as tourists or business travelers, noting their satisfaction or dissatisfaction.

The primary difference between the average tourist and the trained evaluator is the evaluator's skills in organization, preparation, and observation. The trained evaluator is responsible for much more than simply observing and cataloging. While the average tourist is gazing in awe from the observation deck at the Sears Tower, for instance, the professional is rating the attraction in terms of pace, how quickly crowds move, the location of rest rooms, and how well children can see over the railing in front of the big plate glass windows. The evaluator also checks out nearby attractions, alternatives if the line at a main attraction is too long, and where to find the best local lunch options. Observer teams used detailed checklists to analyze hotel rooms, restaurants, nightclubs, and attractions. Finally, evaluator ratings and observations were integrated with tourist reactions and the opinions of patrons for a comprehensive quality profile of each feature and service.

In compiling this guide, we recognize that tourists' ages, backgrounds, and interests will strongly influence their taste in Chicago's wide array of activities and attractions. Our sole objective is to provide the reader with sufficient description, critical evaluation, and pertinent data to make knowledgeable decisions according to individual tastes.

## LETTERS, COMMENTS, AND QUESTIONS FROM READERS

We expect to learn from our mistakes, as well as from the input of our readers, and to improve with each book and edition. Many of those who use the *Unofficial Guides* write to us to ask questions, make comments, or share their own discoveries and lessons learned in Chicago. We appreciate all such input, both positive and critical, and encourage our readers to continue writing. Readers' comments and observations will frequently be incorporated in revised editions of the *Unofficial Guide* and will contribute immeasurably to its improvement.

### How to Write the Authors

Bob Sehlinger, Joe Surkiewicz
*The Unofficial Guide to Chicago*
P.O. Box 43059
Birmingham, AL 35243

When you write, be sure to put your return address on your letter as well as on the envelope—sometimes envelopes and letters get separated. And remember, our work takes us out of the office for long periods of time, so forgive us if our response is delayed.

### Reader Survey

At the back of the guide you will find a short questionnaire that you can use to express opinions concerning your Chicago visit. Clip the questionnaire along the dotted line and mail it to the above address.

## HOW INFORMATION IS ORGANIZED: BY SUBJECT AND BY GEOGRAPHIC ZONES

To give you fast access to information about the *best* of Chicago, we've organized material in several formats.

**Hotels**   Because most people visiting Chicago stay in one hotel for the duration of their trip, we have summarized our coverage of hotels in charts, maps, ratings, and rankings that allow you to quickly focus your decision-making process. We do not go on page after page describing lobbies and rooms which, in the final analysis, sound much the same. Instead, we concentrate on the variables that differentiate one hotel from another: location, size, room quality, services, amenities, and cost.

**Restaurants**   Because you will probably eat a dozen or more restaurant meals during your stay, and because not even *you* can predict what you might be in the mood for on Saturday night, we provide detailed profiles of the best restaurants in and around Chicago.

**Entertainment and Night Life**   Visitors frequently try several different clubs during their stay. Because clubs and nightspots, like restaurants, are usually selected spontaneously after arriving in Chicago, we believe detailed descriptions are warranted. The best nightspots and lounges are profiled by category under Chicago's Night Life in the same section (see pages 129 – 160).

**Geographic Zones**   Once you've decided where you're going, getting there becomes the issue. To help you do that, we have divided the Chicago area into geographic zones and created maps of each zone.

| | |
|---|---|
| Zone 1. | North Side |
| Zone 2. | North Central/O'Hare |
| Zone 3. | Near North |
| Zone 4. | The Loop |
| Zone 5. | South Loop |
| Zone 6. | South Central/Midway |
| Zone 7. | South Side |
| Zone 8. | Southern Suburbs |
| Zone 9. | Western Suburbs |
| Zone 10. | Northwest Suburbs |
| Zone 11. | Northern Suburbs |

All profiles of hotels, restaurants, and nightspots include zone numbers. For example, if you are staying at the Westin Hotel on Chicago's Magnificent Mile and want to sample the latest in the new Southwestern cuisine, scanning the restaurant profiles for those in Zone 3 (Near North) will provide you with the best choices.

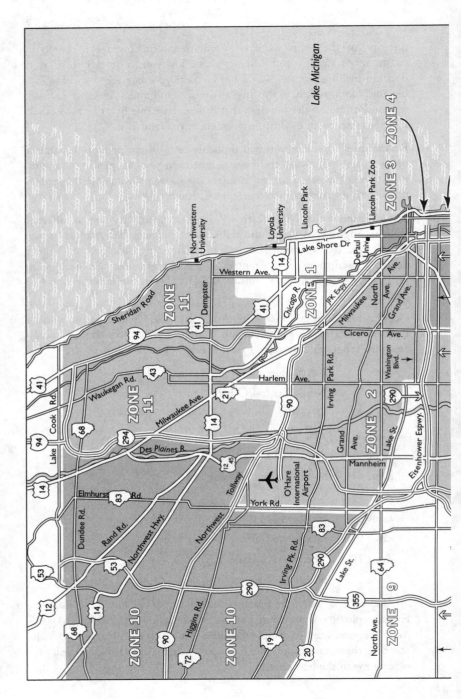

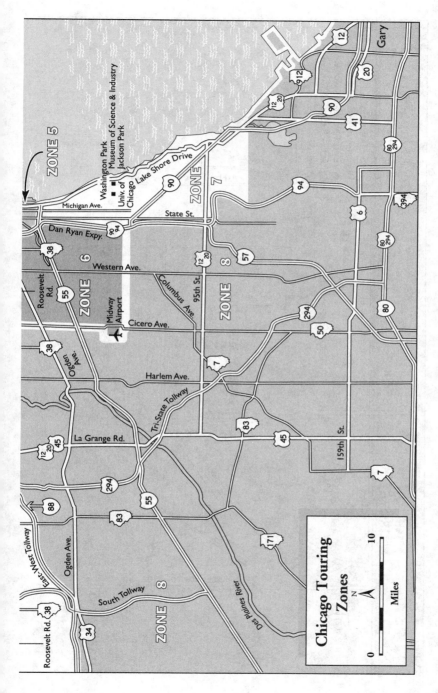

Chicago Touring Zones

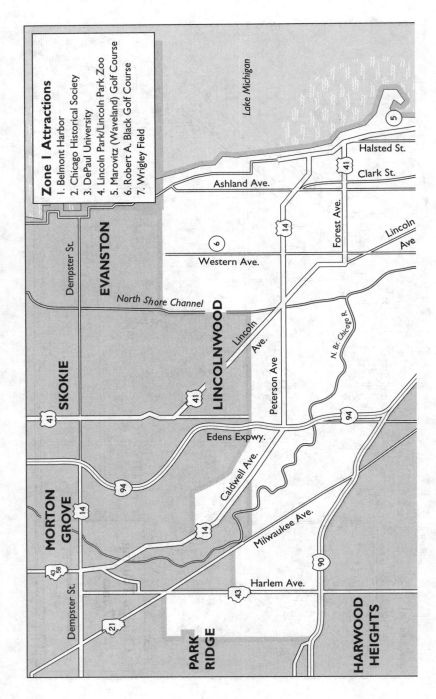

**Zone I Attractions**
1. Belmont Harbor
2. Chicago Historical Society
3. DePaul University
4. Lincoln Park/Lincoln Park Zoo
5. Marovitz (Waveland) Golf Course
6. Robert A. Black Golf Course
7. Wrigley Field

Lake Michigan

Halsted St.

Clark St.

Ashland Ave.

Forest Ave.

Lincoln Ave.

EVANSTON

Dempster St.

Western Ave.

North Shore Channel

LINCOLNWOOD

Lincoln Ave.

Peterson Ave

N. Br. Chicago R.

SKOKIE

Edens Expwy.

Caldwell Ave.

Milwaukee Ave.

MORTON GROVE

Dempster St.

Harlem Ave.

PARK RIDGE

HARWOOD HEIGHTS

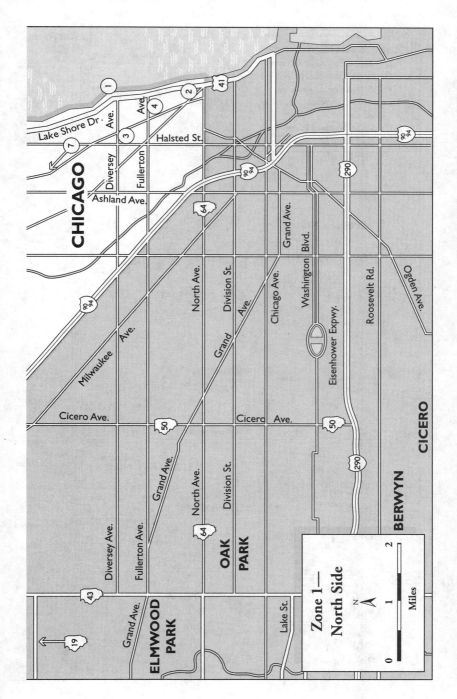

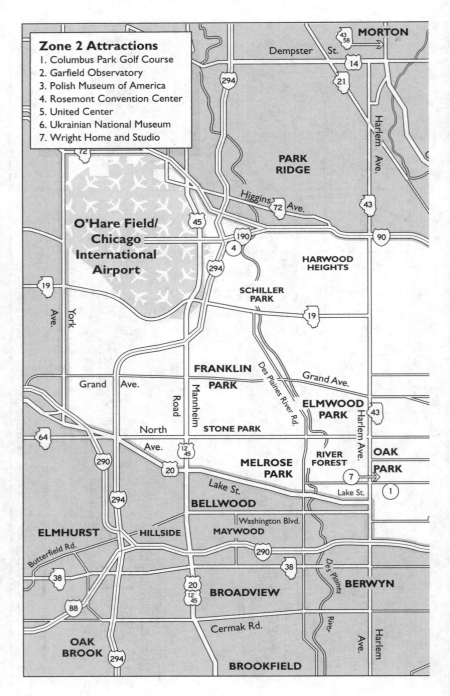

**Zone 2 Attractions**
1. Columbus Park Golf Course
2. Garfield Observatory
3. Polish Museum of America
4. Rosemont Convention Center
5. United Center
6. Ukrainian National Museum
7. Wright Home and Studio

MORTON

Dempster St.

PARK RIDGE

Higgins 72 Ave.

O'Hare Field/ Chicago International Airport

HARWOOD HEIGHTS

SCHILLER PARK

York Ave.

Grand Ave.

FRANKLIN PARK

Des Plaines River Rd.

ELMWOOD PARK

Harlem Ave.

Grand Ave.

Mannheim

Road

STONE PARK

North

Ave.

MELROSE PARK

RIVER FOREST

OAK PARK

Lake St.

Lake St.

BELLWOOD

Washington Blvd.

ELMHURST

HILLSIDE

MAYWOOD

Butterfield Rd.

BROADVIEW

Des Plaines

BERWYN

Cermak Rd.

River

Harlem

OAK BROOK

BROOKFIELD

Harlem Ave.

Zone 2—
North Central/
O'Hare

N

0          1          2
Miles

GROVE

SKOKIE

Dempster St.

EVANSTON

Shore Channel

North

Edens Expwy.

Western Ave.

Ashland Ave.

Lake
Michigan

Caldwell Ave.

LINCOLNWOOD

Lincoln

Ave.

Peterson Ave.

North Br.

Chicago River

Foster

Ave.

Ashland Ave.

Lincoln Ave.

Clark St.

Halsted St.

CHICAGO

Milwaukee

Ave.

Diversey Ave.

Diversey Ave.

Fullerton Ave.

Fullerton Ave.

Halsted St.

Milwaukee Ave.

North Ave.

Grand

Ave.

Division St.

Cicero

Ave.

Chicago Ave.

Grand Ave.

Washington

Blvd.

Eisenhower

Expwy.

Roosevelt Rd.

Ogden Ave.

Ashland

Ave.

Michigan

CICERO

Cermak Rd.

Archer Ave.

Halsted Ave.

Ave.

MLK, Jr. Dr.

13

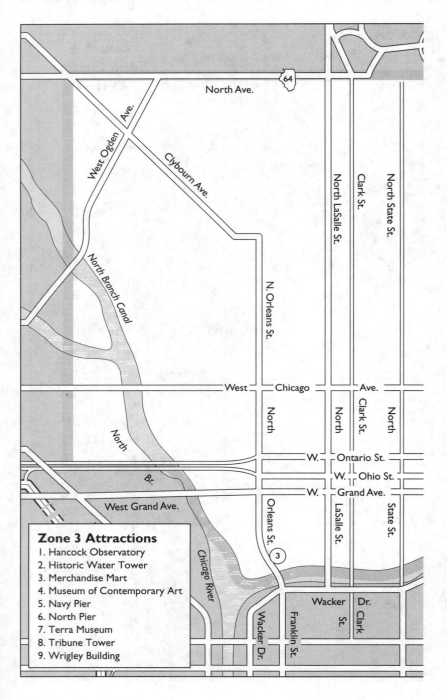

Zone 3 Attractions
1. Hancock Observatory
2. Historic Water Tower
3. Merchandise Mart
4. Museum of Contemporary Art
5. Navy Pier
6. North Pier
7. Terra Museum
8. Tribune Tower
9. Wrigley Building

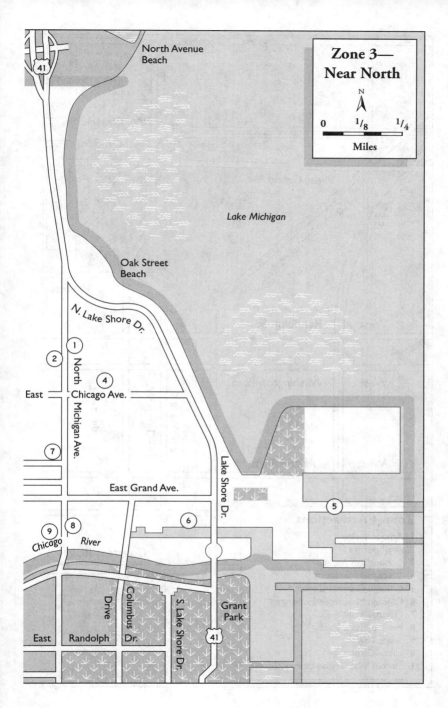

North Avenue
Beach

**Zone 3—
Near North**

N

0    1/8    1/4

Miles

Lake Michigan

Oak Street
Beach

N. Lake Shore Dr.

① 1

② 2

East | Chicago Ave.

North Michigan Ave.

④ 4

⑦ 7

East Grand Ave.

Lake Shore Dr.

⑤ 5

⑨ 9  ⑧ 8

⑥ 6

Chicago    River

Drive

Columbus Dr.

S. Lake Shore Dr.

Grant
Park

East | Randolph

41

15

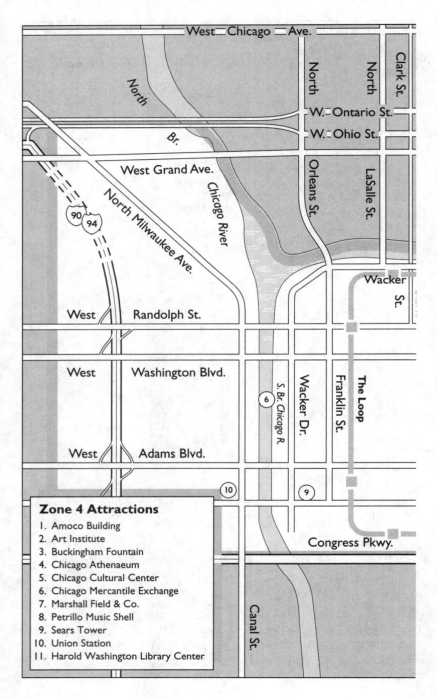

Zone 4 Attractions

1. Amoco Building
2. Art Institute
3. Buckingham Fountain
4. Chicago Athenaeum
5. Chicago Cultural Center
6. Chicago Mercantile Exchange
7. Marshall Field & Co.
8. Petrillo Music Shell
9. Sears Tower
10. Union Station
11. Harold Washington Library Center

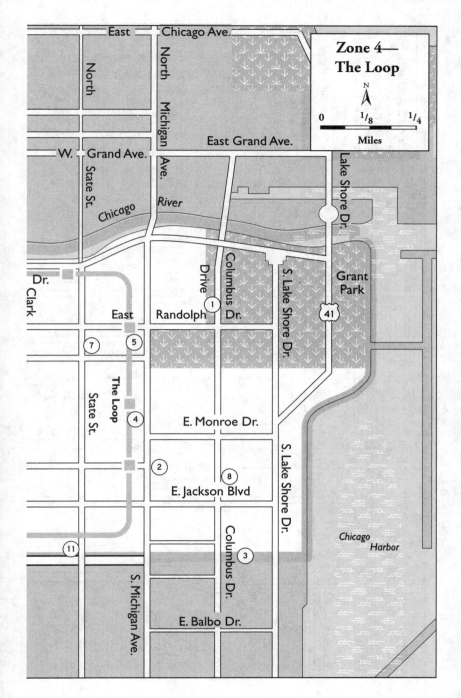

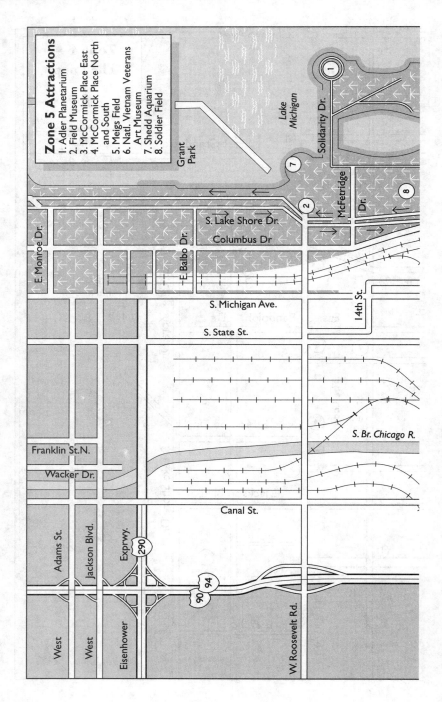

**Zone 5 Attractions**
1. Adler Planetarium
2. Field Museum
3. McCormick Place East
4. McCormick Place North and South
5. Meigs Field
6. Natl. Vietnam Veterans Art Museum
7. Shedd Aquarium
8. Soldier Field

Grant Park

Lake Michigan

Solidarity Dr.

McFetridge

Dr.

S. Lake Shore Dr.

Columbus Dr

E. Monroe Dr.

E. Balbo Dr.

S. Michigan Ave.

S. State St.

14th St.

S. Br. Chicago R.

Franklin St.N.

Wacker Dr.

Canal St.

Adams St.

Jackson Blvd.

Exprwy.

290

90 94

West

West

Eisenhower

W. Roosevelt Rd.

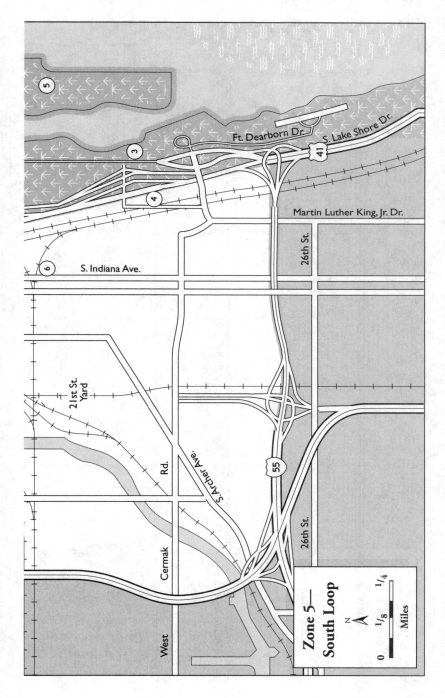

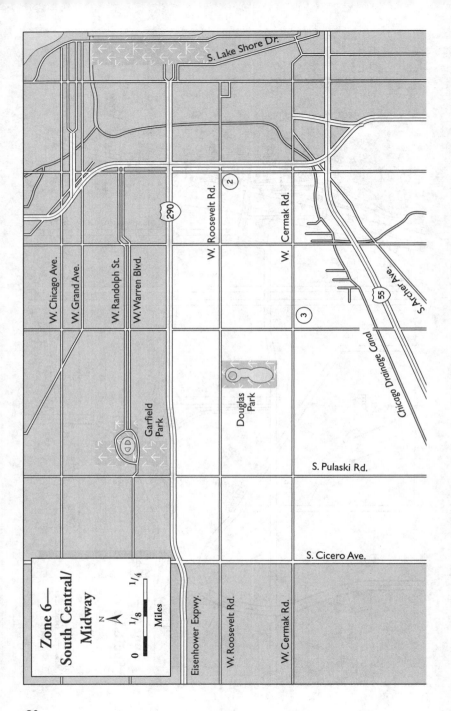

Zone 6—
South Central/
Midway

N

0   1/8   1/4
Miles

S. Lake Shore Dr.

290

W. Roosevelt Rd.

2

W. Cermak Rd.

W.

S. Archer Ave.

55

3

W. Chicago Ave.

W. Grand Ave.

W. Randolph St.

W. Warren Blvd.

Garfield
Park

Douglas
Park

Chicago Drainage Canal

S. Pulaski Rd.

S. Cicero Ave.

Eisenhower Expwy.

W. Roosevelt Rd.

W. Cermak Rd.

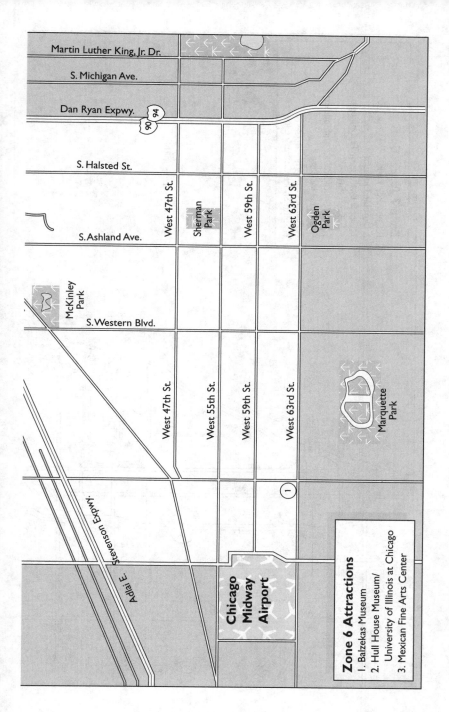

Martin Luther King, Jr. Dr.

S. Michigan Ave.

Dan Ryan Expwy. 90 94

S. Halsted St.

West 47th St.

Sherman Park

West 59th St.

West 63rd St.

Ogden Park

S. Ashland Ave.

McKinley Park

S. Western Blvd.

West 47th St.

West 55th St.

West 59th St.

West 63rd St.

Marquette Park

Adlai E. Stevenson Expwy.

Chicago Midway Airport

## Zone 6 Attractions
1. Balzekas Museum
2. Hull House Museum/
   University of Illinois at Chicago
3. Mexican Fine Arts Center

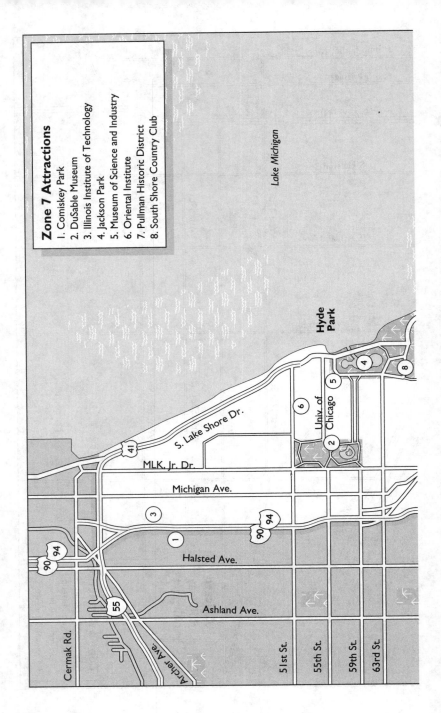

**Zone 7 Attractions**
1. Comiskey Park
2. DuSable Museum
3. Illinois Institute of Technology
4. Jackson Park
5. Museum of Science and Industry
6. Oriental Institute
7. Pullman Historic District
8. South Shore Country Club

Lake Michigan

Hyde Park

S. Lake Shore Dr.

Univ. of Chicago

MLK. Jr. Dr.

Michigan Ave.

Halsted Ave.

Ashland Ave.

Archer Ave.

Cermak Rd.

51st St.

55th St.

59th St.

63rd St.

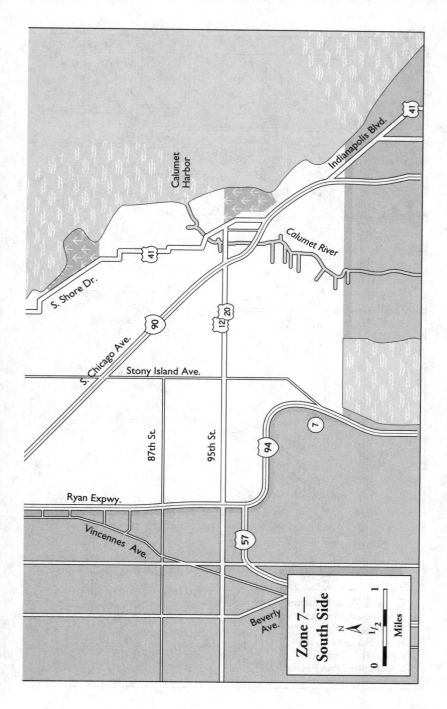

Calumet Harbor

Indianapolis Blvd.

41

Calumet River

41

S. Shore Dr.

90

12 20

S. Chicago Ave.

Stony Island Ave.

87th St.

95th St.

94

7

Ryan Expwy.

Vincennes Ave.

57

Beverly Ave.

## Zone 7—
## South Side

N

0   ¹/₂   1

Miles

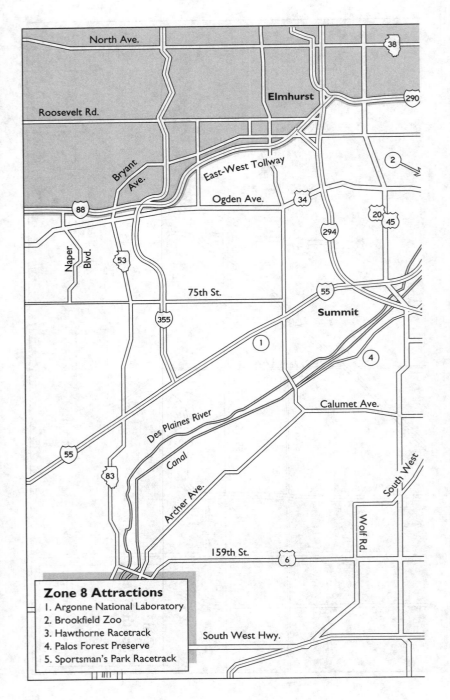

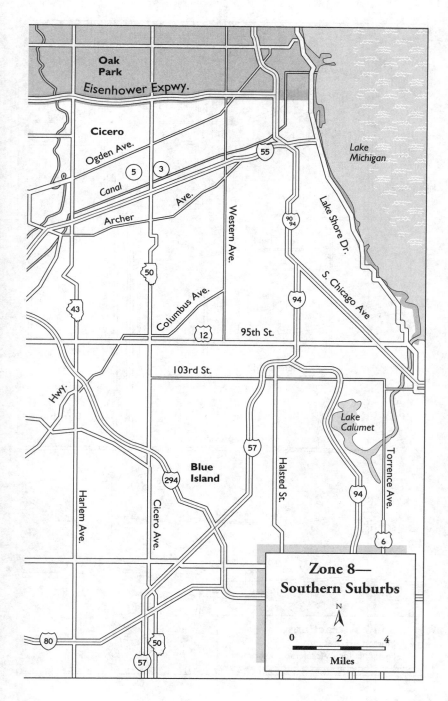

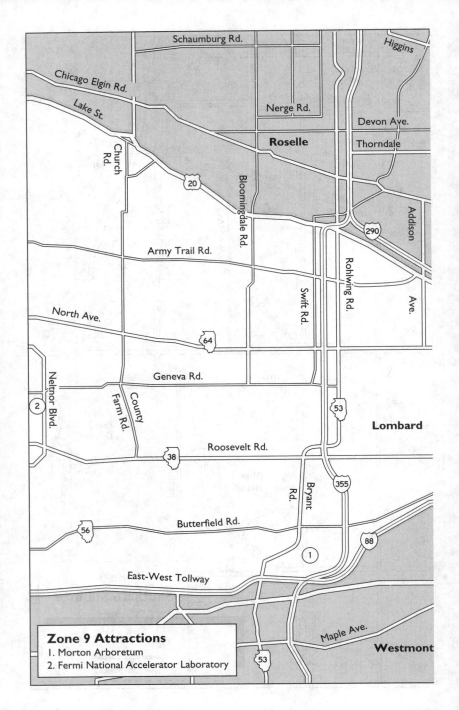

Zone 9 Attractions
1. Morton Arboretum
2. Fermi National Accelerator Laboratory

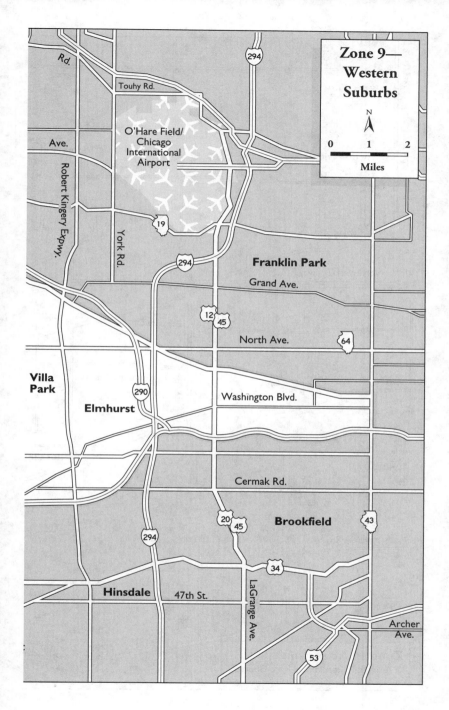

Zone 9—
Western
Suburbs

N

0    1    2
Miles

Rd.

294

Touhy Rd.

O'Hare Field/
Chicago
International
Airport

Ave.

19

Robert Kingery Expwy.

York Rd.

294

Franklin Park

Grand Ave.

12
45

North Ave.

64

Villa
Park

290

Washington Blvd.

Elmhurst

Cermak Rd.

20
45

Brookfield

43

294

34

Hinsdale

47th St.

LaGrange Ave.

53

Archer
Ave.

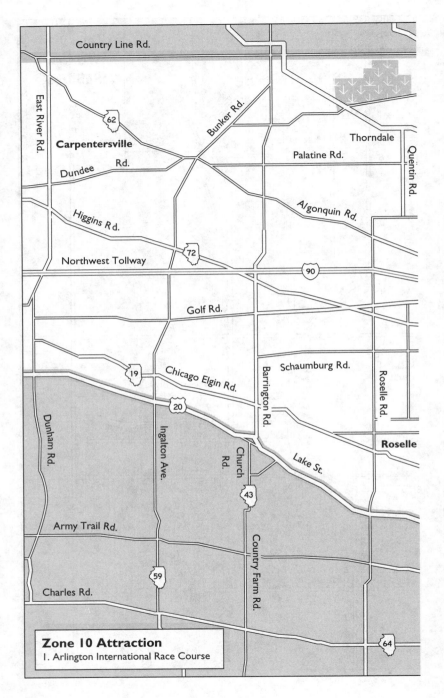

**Zone 10 Attraction**
1. Arlington International Race Course

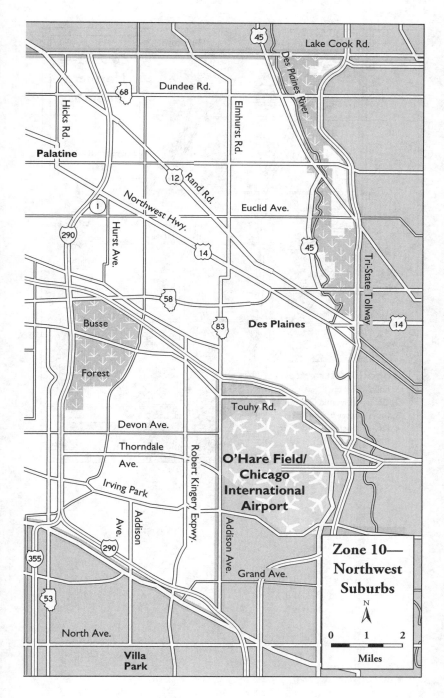

Zone 10—
Northwest
Suburbs

0    1    2
Miles

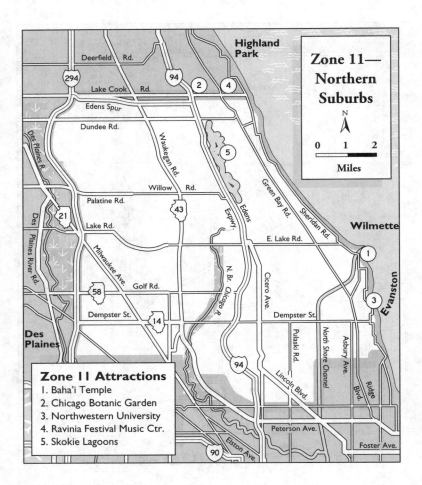

Zone 11—
Northern
Suburbs

N

0   1   2
Miles

Highland
Park

Deerfield Rd.

294

Lake Cook Rd.

Edens Spur

Dundee Rd.

Waukegan Rd.

94

2   4

5

Willow Rd.

Palatine Rd.

43

21

Lake Rd.

Milwaukee Ave.

Des Plaines R.

Des

Des Plaines River Rd.

58

Golf Rd.

Dempster St.

14

94

Lincoln Blvd.

Edens Espwy.

Edens

N. Br. Chicago R.

N. Br. Chicago R.

E. Lake Rd.

Green Bay Rd.

Sheridan Rd.

Wilmette

1

3

Evanston

Cicero Ave.

Dempster St.

Pulaski Rd.

North Shore Channel

Asbury Ave.

Ridge Blvd.

Des
Plaines

**Zone 11 Attractions**
1. Baha'i Temple
2. Chicago Botanic Garden
3. Northwestern University
4. Ravinia Festival Music Ctr.
5. Skokie Lagoons

Peterson Ave.

Elston Ave.

Foster Ave.

90

# Understanding the City

## A Brief History of Chicago

New York has always leaned toward Europe, and Los Angeles toward the Pacific Rim. But Chicago stands on its own: a freshwater port, a mid-continental city of Big Shoulders. The city was founded on a swamp and later rebuilt itself from the ashes of a tremendous fire into the nation's third-largest city. With a lakefront skyline recognized around the world, it's a town that owes its verve to generations of strong backs. Chicago is a true American city.

It's also a cauldron of bubbling contrasts: Shimmering skyscrapers on Michigan Avenue and the squalor of Cabrini-Green; a growing city beset by post-industrial urban decay; a town whose long-suppressed black minority points with pride to Chicagoan Carol Moseley-Braun, the first black woman U.S. senator. Chicago is Al Capone and Michael Jordan, Jane Addams and Hugh Hefner, perennial losers the Chicago Cubs and Nobel Prize winner Saul Bellow.

Chicago is a city of legends, of a few precious visionaries and quite a few scoundrels. Built on swampland at the edge of a prairie, the city has endured cycles of booms and busts. As the nation grew westward, Chicago found itself in a unique geographical position to supply the raw materials that fed the expansion. The city was incorporated on March 4, 1837.

### Beginnings

Twelve thousand years ago, Lake Chicago was a larger version of Lake Michigan that covered much of what is now the Midwest. As this great glacial lake receded, it left behind a vast prairie and a shoreline swamp that linked North America's two great waterways: the Mississippi (via the Des Plaines and Illinois rivers) and the Great Lakes.

The area's first residents were Native Americans who called it Checa-gou or Checaguar, which probably meant something like "wild onion" or "swamp gas"—no doubt a reference to the pungent smell of decaying marsh vegetation that permeated the swamp. Either way, the name implied great strength. The Potawatomi tribe, able to traverse the swamp in shallow-bottomed canoes during spring rains, was the first to take advantage of Chicago's bridge between the two waterways. It was about eight miles from the Des Plaines River to Lake Michigan; traders in those days dealt in furs and skins.

## First Settlers

In 1673 two French explorers were the first Europeans to set eyes on what is now Chicago: Louis Jolliet, who was searching for gold, and Father Jacques Marquette, who was searching for souls. When their Native American allies showed them the portage trail linking the Mississippi Valley and the Great Lakes, Jolliet saw Chicago's potential immediately. He predicted to Marquette, "Here some day will be found one of the world's great cities."

In the late eighteenth century, the flat prairies stretching west were as empty and primeval as when the last glacier had retreated thousands of years before. Chicago's first nonnative resident, Jean Baptist Point du Sable, arrived in 1779 and erected a rough-hewn log house on the north bank of the Chicago River. A tall, French-speaking son of a Quebec merchant and a black slave, du Sable established a trading post at what is now Michigan Avenue. As the local Native Americans noted, "The first white man to live here was a black man."

After du Sable pulled up stakes and moved to Missouri in 1800 (leaving a handful of other traders at the mouth of the river), Chicago's first boom began. But first the frontier outpost had to endure a massacre. The Indians had been run out in 1795, ceding huge tracts of Midwestern land—including "six miles square at the mouth of the Chickago River." The swamp turned into a speculator's dream almost overnight.

Soldiers of the fledgling United States Republic arrived from Detroit in 1803 and erected Fort Dearborn near what is now the corner of Lower Wacker Drive and Michigan Avenue. After evacuating the fort during the War of 1812 against the British, settlers and soldiers fleeing the fort were ambushed by Indians in league with the enemy; 52 men, women, and children were slain in the Fort Dearborn Massacre.

## Boom ...

Illinois became a state in 1818—a time when Chicago was still a struggling backwater far north of southern population centers—and in 1829 the state legislature appointed a commission to plot a canal route between

Lake Michigan and the Mississippi River. Chicago was poised for a population explosion.

The pace of westward development from bustling Eastern Seaboard cities was accelerating in the early nineteenth century, and pioneers surged into the Midwest. Fort Dearborn was rapidly rebuilt and in 1825 the Erie Canal opened, creating a new water route between Chicago and the East. Pioneer wagons rolled in daily and Chicago's population swelled from around 50 in 1830 to over 4,000 in 1837. As waves of Irish and German immigrants arrived, the town's population increased by another 100,000 in the following 30 years.

Speculators swooped in and lots that sold for $100 in 1830 changed hands for as much as $100,000 in 1837 during a real estate frenzy fueled by visions of wealth to be made from the planned canal. Fort Dearborn closed in 1836, symbolizing the end of Chicago's frontier era, and the town started taking on the trappings of civilization. The first newspaper, the *Chicago Democrat,* was launched in 1833, the first brewery was opened in 1836, and the first policeman was hired in 1839—and no doubt had his hands full in a town overflowing with saloons.

### ... and Bust

The boom went bust, however, in the Panic of 1837, one of the nation's first economic depressions. Work on the canal ground to a halt, and many local investors went broke. Slowly, a recovery set in, work on the canal resumed, and Chicago spawned its first ethnic neighborhood.

Originally called Hardscrabble, it was an enclave of Irish laborers digging the waterway. By the time it was annexed in 1863, the South Side neighborhood was known as Bridgeport, later famous as the wellspring for generations of Irish-American politicians—including Mayor Richard J. Daley (aka Hizzoner) and his son, current mayor Richard M. Daley.

### A Transportation Hub

While the waterway was a boon to commerce when it opened in 1848, it was quickly overshadowed by a new form of transportation—railroads. Soon, locomotives were hauling freight along the tracks of the Galena and Chicago Union line and the newly opened Chicago Board of Trade brokered commodities in what was to become the world's greatest rail hub. German and Scandinavian immigrants swelled the city's population, and horse-drawn street railways stimulated growth of the suburbs.

Before growth could proceed much farther, however, the swamp-bound city first had to elevate itself; streets were a quagmire most of the year. In the years prior to the Civil War street grades were raised as many as a dozen feet and first floors became basements. It was an impressive technological feat—the first of many to come.

By 1856 Chicago was the hub of ten railroad trunk lines. Lumber from nearby forests, iron ore from Minnesota, and livestock and produce from the fertile Midwest were raw materials shipped to the city and manufactured into the products that fueled the nation's rapid growth. Passenger rail service from New York began in 1857, cutting travel time between the cities from three weeks to two days. The population soared to 28,000 in 1850 and to 110,000 in 1860. Economically, Chicago was the national middleman between the East and West, a role it has never ceased to play.

## Innovative Marketing and a Presidential Nomination

Just as the city mastered transportation and manufacturing, it spawned a generation of marketing geniuses. Mail-order giants Montgomery Ward & Co. and Sears, Roebuck & Co. were founded in Chicago. Other legendary names of Chicago merchandising include Marshall Field, Potter Palmer, Samuel Carson, and John Pirie.

By 1860 Chicago was the ninth-largest city in the United States and hosted the nominating convention of the fledgling Republican Party. A jerry-built convention hall with a capacity of 10,000 was thrown up at Lake and Market Streets on the fringe of today's Loop, where the Republicans nominated Abraham Lincoln on the third ballot. The city would host another 23 major-party nominating conventions, including the bruising 1968 Democratic Convention. In 1996 the Democrats returned after an absence of nearly 30 years.

One of Chicago's most famous—and odorous—landmarks opened in 1865: the Union Stockyards. The yards were Chicago's largest employer for half a century. By 1863 the city had earned the moniker "Porkopolis" by processing enough hogs to stretch snout-to-tail all the way to New York. Gustavus Swift of meatpacking fame boasted, "We use everything but the squeal." The darker sides of the yard—abysmal sanitation problems and horrific working and living conditions for its laborers—were brought to light in 1906 in Upton Sinclair's *The Jungle*.

## Industrial Might

More growth: In the years following the Civil War, Chicago ranked as the world's largest grain handler and the biggest North American lumber market. The North Side's huge McCormick plant churned out reapers and other farm equipment that were shipped around the globe. George Pullman built his first sleeping car in 1864, the nation's first steel rails came out of the North Side in 1865, and the number of sea vessels docked at

Chicago in 1869 exceeded the combined number calling on New York and five other major United States ports.

While knee-deep mud was a thing of the past, the city was still steeped in quagmires of different sorts. Cholera and typhoid struck regularly as Chicago fouled its Lake Michigan drinking water via the dangerously polluted Chicago River. Corruption at City Hall became rampant and the city was notorious for its gambling, saloons, and 400 brothels. Hundreds of thousands of poor Chicagoans were jammed into modest pine cottages on unpaved streets without sewers. Some observers warned of dire consequences unless the city cleaned up its act.

### The Great Chicago Fire of 1871

They were right. Chicago in 1871 was a densely packed city of 300,000 whose homes were built almost entirely of wood. A lengthy drought had turned the town tinder-dry, setting the stage for the most indelibly mythic event in the city's history: the Great Fire of 1871.

Legend has it that Mrs. O'Leary's cow kicked over a lantern and started the conflagration, probably a myth created by a journalist of the era. But the fire spread rapidly from the O'Leary barn in the West Side and burned its way north and east through the commercial center and residential North Side. More than 17,000 buildings were destroyed, 100,000 people were left homeless, and 250 were killed. The city lay in ashes.

So they built it again—this time with fireproof brick. Architects, sensing unlimited opportunity, flocked to Chicago. In five years the city's commercial core was restored with buildings erected to meet stringent fire codes and a tradition of architectural leadership was established. In 1889 the city annexed a ring of suburbs and was crowned America's Second City in the census of 1890.

Chicago was emerging from an era of cutthroat Social Darwinism into an age of social reform. Jane Addams's Hull House became a model for the nation's settlement house movement. Addams and her upper-class cohorts provided fresh, clean milk for babies, taught immigrants English, and set up day-care centers for the children of working mothers.

The Columbian Exposition of 1893 was a fabulously successful world's fair that left indelible cultural marks on the city, including the Art Institute of Chicago and the Field Museum. The era ushered in the skyscraper, a distinctly urban form created in Chicago that has reshaped skylines around the world. The University of Chicago, one of the world's great research institutions, was founded in 1892 with funds from the Rockefellers.

In 1900, another technological feat: The flow of the Chicago River was reversed, much to the relief of a population in desperate need of safe drinking water from Lake Michigan—and to the consternation of populations downstream.

In 1909 architect Daniel H. Burnham left his mark on the city by pursuing a plan to preserve Chicago's pristine lakefront through creation of a series of parks and the acquisition of a green belt of forest lands on the city's periphery. "Make no little plans," Burnham urged, and the city heeded his words. Today, with the exception of massive McCormick Place, the lakefront is an uncluttered recreational mecca.

## Labor Troubles

Yet around the turn of the century Chicago seethed with labor unrest and the threat of class warfare. Nascent labor movements argued for better working and living conditions for the city's laborers. Seven policemen were killed in the 1886 Haymarket Riot and four anarchists were hanged; the Pullman Strike of 1894 was crushed by United States Army troops after wages were sharply cut by the sleeping-car magnate.

The lowest rung in Chicago's pecking order was reserved for blacks, who started to arrive from the South in substantial numbers, reaching 110,000 by 1920. Segregation formed a "black belt" ghetto with buildings in poor repair—often without indoor toilets—and substantially higher rents than white housing. A six-day riot in July 1919 left 23 blacks and 15 whites dead; the governor had to send in troops to quell the uprising. Yet the underlying causes of the unrest weren't addressed.

Carl Sandburg celebrated the city and its tradition of hard work in verse ("Hog Butcher for the World / Tool Maker, Stacker of Wheat / Player with Railroads and the Nation's Freight Handler; / Stormy, husky, brawling / City of Big Shoulders"). Other pre-Depression literary lights from Chicago include Theodore Dreiser and Ben Hecht; later came James T. Farrell, Nelson Algren, Richard Wright, and Saul Bellow.

## The Roaring Twenties

Following World War I, the focus of power shifted from industrialists to politicians; crooked pols and gangsters plundered the city. The smoke-filled room was invented in Chicago at the 1920 Republican National Convention when Warren G. Harding's nomination was sewn up in Suite 804–805 at the Blackstone Hotel.

A baby-faced crook from New York named Alphonse Capone hit town in 1920, right after Prohibition became law. It wasn't a coincidence. Chicago was soon awash in bootleg hooch—much of it illegally imported by Capone and his mob. The short, pot-bellied gangster nicknamed Scarface still holds the world record for the highest gross income ever accumulated by a private citizen in a year—$105 million in 1927, when he was 28 years old.

Alas, Capone didn't pay his taxes and was put away by a group of Feds, known as the Untouchables, led by Eliot Ness. The gangster, probably Chicago's best-known historical figure, served eight hard years in Alcatraz and died of syphilis in his bed in 1947.

### Another Depression ... and Another Fair

In the 1930s, the Great Depression hit Chicago hard. Out-of-work men and women marched down State Street. Businessmen went bust. Nearly 1,400 families were evicted from their homes in the first half of 1931 alone. Hardest hit were Chicago's blacks, whose population then totaled about 250,000.

Yet in 1933 the city hosted another world's fair: the Century of Progress exposition, which occupied 47 acres of lakefront south of the Loop. The show attracted about 39 million visitors and actually made money. The star of the show was fan dancer Sally Rand, who went on stage nude with large props—not only fans but feather boas and large balloons. Like Little Egypt at the Columbian Exposition 40 years before, she drew mobs of men to her shows and further embellished the city's notorious reputation.

### The Second World War

World War II and an unparalleled surge in defense spending lifted Chicago—and the rest of the country—out of the Depression. The $1.3 billion spent to build war plants in the city was unmatched anywhere else in the country.

In 1942, a team at the University of Chicago under the direction of physicist Enrico Fermi built the world's first nuclear reactor under the stands of Stagg Field. The feat provided critical technology for the development of nuclear power and allowed the nation to embark on the ambitious Manhattan Project, which led to the manufacture of the atomic bomb. Today the portentous site is marked by a brooding sculpture by Henry Moore.

### A New Era

The city reached its peak population of 3.6 million in 1950, a year that marked the beginning of a long slide as Chicago's population drained off into surrounding suburbs. Following eras of settlement, growth, booms, busts, depression, and war, Chicago moved into one last period: the 21-year rule of Mayor Richard J. Daley, "da Boss." He was a powermonger who left yet another indelible mark on the city.

Elected in 1955, Daley bulldozed entire neighborhoods, built segregated walls of high-rise public housing, and constructed an elaborate system of freeway exchanges in the heart of the city. Critics noted with dismay that the maze of highways cut the hearts out of flourishing neighborhoods and provided handy corridors for suburban flight.

Daley was also a kingmaker for presidents; he delivered the winning—though slim—margin to John F. Kennedy in 1960. In 1968, at the peak of the Vietnam conflict, Daley unleashed his police on anti-war protesters at the Democratic Convention; some called it a "police riot." Hizzoner pugnaciously scowled at news cameras and growled, "Duh policeman isn't dere to create disorder, duh policeman is dere to *preserve* disorder." The whole world was watching.

## Post-Industrial Chicago

Daley passed away in 1976, computer operators now outnumber steel mill workers, and post-industrial Chicago shuffles along. The Gold Coast and the Magnificent Mile are glitzier than ever, and Chicago's work force—what's left of it, anyway—is learning to survive in a service economy. More and more people have fled for greener horizons beyond the city limits, trading deteriorating schools and racial strife for safer neighborhoods.

Yet Chicago hangs on. In the 1970s and 1980s a forest of new skyscrapers shot up on the city's skyline, including the Sears Tower, the world's third-tallest office building. Since Daley's death the city has seen its first woman mayor (Jane Byrne) and its first black mayor (Harold Washington, a beloved figure who died in office in 1987). The city entered the '90s with Mayor Richard "Richie" Daley, son of Hizzoner, solidly in office with his roots still embedded in the South Side. Although Chicago has been leaking population for decades, nearly three million people still live here.

## "A Real City"

So what is Chicago today? It is 228 square miles stretching 30 miles along Lake Michigan's shore. It is 550 parks, 8 forest preserves, 29 beaches, 200 good restaurants, 2,000 lousy restaurants, and dozens of stands selling the best hot dogs in the world. Chicago is a city where football is a serious business and politics is a game. It's heaven for symphony lovers and nirvana for jazz buffs.

Come to Chicago and within half an hour someone will tell you it's "a city of neighborhoods." Sprinkled with curiosities, the city's ethnic neighborhoods offer visitors a flavor of the Old World and a chance for discovery.

And the Loop? Walk downtown along busy Michigan Avenue late on a Friday afternoon, watch the lights wink on in the skyscrapers overhead, feel the city's vitality, and you'll agree with what Rudyard Kipling wrote a century ago: "I have struck a city—a real city—and they call it Chicago."

# Skyscrapers and the Prairie School: Chicago Architecture

While no one seriously argues Chicago's status as the Second City—even the most avid boosters concede New York's status as America's leading city in population, culture, and finance—the Windy City lays claim to one superlative title that remains undisputed: the world capital of modern architecture.

And it's not just that the skyscraper was born here. A visit to Chicago is a crash course in the various streams of architecture that have helped shape the direction of twentieth-century building design. Even folks with an otherwise casual interest in architecture are bedazzled by the architectural heritage displayed here. Chicago is the world's largest outdoor museum of modern architecture.

## A Bovine Beginning

A substantial amount of the credit for Chicago's status in the world of architecture can be laid at the feet of a cow—if it's true that Mrs. O'Leary's cow kicked over a lantern, starting an inferno of mythic proportions. The Great Chicago Fire of 1871 destroyed four square miles of the central city, and architects from around the world flocked to Chicago—not unlike Sir Christopher Wren, who rushed to London after a great fire leveled much of that city in the late seventeenth century.

Several other factors figured in Chicago's rise to preeminence in building design in the decades after the fire. The rapidly rising value of real estate in the central business district motivated developers to increase building heights as much as they could. Advances in elevator technology freed designers from vertical constraints; easily rentable space no longer needed to be an easy climb from street level.

But most important was the development of the iron and steel skeletal frame, which relieved the walls of the burden of carrying a building's weight. For the first time, a structure's exterior walls didn't need to grow thicker as the building grew taller. New technology also allowed for larger windows.

## The Chicago School

As new technology took hold, many architects felt a building's external form should be equally innovative. The result was a style of architecture with a straightforward expression of structure. A masonry grid covered the steel structure beneath, while projecting bay windows created a lively rhythm on the facade. Any ornamentation was usually subordinated to the overall design and often restricted to the top and bottom thirds of the building, creating a kind of classical column effect. Collectively, the style came to be known as the Chicago School of Architecture.

Early skyscrapers that flaunt the technological innovations that made Chicago famous include the 15-story **Reliance Building** (32 North State Street; Burnham and Root; 1890) and the 12-story **Carson Pirie Scott & Company** department store (1 South State Street; Adler and Sullivan; 1899). These show-off buildings, held up by thin tendons of steel, are close in spirit to the modernist architecture that was to follow.

## Classical Designs by the Lake

Daniel Burnham, who developed Chicago's urban plan and designed some of its most innovative buildings, also organized the 1893 World's Columbian Exposition. Yet the formal Beaux Arts style used in the major structures that remain were designed by East Coast architects. As a result, cultural institutions such as the **Art Institute** (Michigan Avenue at Adams Street; Shepley, Rutan & Coolidge; 1892) and the **Chicago Cultural Center** (78 East Washington Street; Shepley, Rutan & Coolidge; 1897) have their underlying structures disguised in white, neoclassical historical garb.

## The Prairie School

Yet not all of Chicago's architectural innovations pushed upward or aped the classical designs of the past. In the early 1900s Frank Lloyd Wright and his contemporaries were developing a modern style that's now called the Prairie School. The break from historically inspired Victorian house designs is highlighted by low, ground-hugging forms, hovering roofs with deep eaves, and bands of casement windows. Interiors feature open, flowing floor plans, centrally located hearths, natural woodwork, and uniform wall treatments.

Truly shocking in their day, Wright's designs now dot Chicago and its suburbs. The flowing horizontal planes sharply contrast with the upward thrust of skyscrapers in the Loop and convey a feeling of peace and calm. The largest groups of Prairie School houses are found in Oak Park, where Forest Avenue and nearby streets are lined with houses designed by Wright and his disciples.

## 1920s Prosperity and Art Deco

The prosperity of the 1920s resulted in a building boom; the construction of the Michigan Avenue Bridge encouraged developers to look for sites north of the Chicago River. It was the "heroic age" for the city's skyline and designers borrowed heavily from European sources. The **Wrigley Building** (400 North Michigan Avenue; Graham, Anderson, Probst & White; 1922) is a dazzling white, terra cotta–clad lollipop of a building that's strikingly well lighted from the opposite shore of the river; the clock tower remains one of Chicago's most distinctive landmarks.

The **Tribune Tower** (435 North Michigan Avenue; Hood & Howells; 1925) is a neo-Gothic tower (considered "retro" when built) that soars upward like a medieval cathedral. At **333 North Michigan Avenue** stands Chicago's first Art Deco skyscraper, designed by Holabird & Root in 1928. More of the Art Deco impulse is displayed south of the river at the **Chicago Board of Trade Building** (141 West Jackson Boulevard; Holabird & Root; 1930), which anchors LaSalle Street's financial canyon and is topped with a 30-foot aluminum statue of Ceres, the Roman goddess of grain.

### The International Style

When the Depression hit, most construction ground to a halt and didn't resume until after World War II. But after the post-war economic recovery arrived, German-born Ludwig Mies van der Rohe (who fled Nazi persecution before the war and later taught architecture at the Illinois Institute of Technology) found Chicago a receptive canvas for his daring designs.

Mies's motto was "Less is more," and the result was the sleek and unadorned International Style (often called the Second Chicago School). He was concerned with structural expression and the use of new technology as much as his predecessors in the 1890s, and Chicago boasts some of his most famous designs: the **Federal Center Complex** (Dearborn Street between Jackson Boulevard and Adams Street; 1964–75), the **Illinois Institute of Technology** (State Street between 31st and 35th Streets; 1940–58), and his last major design, the **IBM Building** (330 North Wabash; 1971).

Mies's signature style is the high-rise with an open colonnaded space around a solid shaft; the glass-and-steel skin is carefully detailed to represent the steel structure within. The designs are macho, strong and sinewy, with great care given to proportion, play of light, and simplicity. Detractors sniff and call them "glass boxes."

### Postmodernism

Inevitably, rebellion began, and the result was postmodernism, a catchall term describing anything outside mainstream modernist design. Often, the postmodernists overturned modernist beliefs while echoing the Chicago aesthetic of the past in new, often graceful, designs. Macho and cold is out; whimsy and colorful are in. The starkness of Mies-inspired architecture gave way to purely decorative elements in designs that are still unmistakably modern.

Arguably the most graceful of the new buildings in Chicago, **333 North Wacker Drive** (Kohn Pedersen Fox/Perkins and Will; 1983) features a curved facade of glass that reflects the Chicago River in both shape and color. Another stunner is **150 North Michigan Avenue** (A. Epstein & Sons; 1984), whose sloping glass roof slices diagonally through the top ten floors.

Tipping its hat to the past is the **Harold Washington Library Center** (400 South State Street; Hammond, Beeby & Babka; 1991), which references numerous city landmarks. A red-granite base and brick walls pay tribute to the Rookery and Manadnock buildings (two Burnham and Root gems), while the facade and pediments along the roof recall the Art Institute. Even more retro is the **NBC Tower** (455 North Cityfront Plaza; Skidmore, Owings & Merrill; 1989), a 38-story Art Deco tower that successfully mines the architectural past.

One of Chicago's most controversial buildings is the **State of Illinois Center** (100 West Randolph Street; C. F. Murphy/Jahn Associates and Lester B. Knight & Associates; 1983). It's a 17-story, glass-and-steel interpretation of the traditional government office building created by the bad boy of Chicago architecture, Helmut Jahn. Inside, 13 floors of balconied offices encircle a 332-foot central rotunda that's topped with a sloping glass skylight 160 feet in diameter. You've got to see it to believe it. The controversy? Some people loathe it—and state employees often endure blistering heat in the summer and freezing cold in the winter.

### Three of the World's Ten Tallest Buildings

Another hard-to-ignore element in recent downtown Chicago designs is height: Chicago claims three of the world's ten tallest buildings, including the 1,454-foot **Sears Tower** (233 South Wacker Drive; Skidmore, Owings & Merrill; 1974). The world's third-tallest office building is a set of nine square tubes bundled together to give strength to the whole; seven tubes drop away as the building ascends, and only two go the distance.

Yet the 1,127-foot **John Hancock Center** (875 North Michigan; Skidmore, Owings & Merrill; 1969) usually gets higher marks from critics for its tapered form that's crisscrossed by diagonal wind-bracing; locals say the view from the top is better, too. The 80-story **Amoco Building** (200 East Randolph Street; E. D. Stone/Perkins and Will; 1974) is the city's third-tallest building; new white-granite cladding replaced a Carrara marble skin that couldn't stand up to Chicago's wind and temperature extremes.

**An Outdoor Museum**

Most of Chicago's landmark buildings—and we've only described a handful—are located in and around the Loop, making a comfortable walking tour the best way to explore this outdoor museum of modern architecture. If you've got the time and the interest, we strongly recommend taking one of the Chicago Architectural Foundation's two-hour walking tours of the Loop (see page 224). It's by far the best way to gain a greater appreciation of one of the world's great architectural mosaics.

# Sculpture in the Loop

Chicago, the world leader in modern architecture, also boasts one of the finest collections of public art in the United States. Major pieces by such twentieth-century greats as Picasso, Chagall, Calder, Miró, Moore, Oldenburg, Nevelson, and Noguchi are scattered throughout the Loop.

It's a cornucopia of postmodern masterpieces—although some might take a little getting used to. After Picasso's untitled abstract sculpture in the Civic Center plaza was unveiled by Mayor Richard J. Daley in 1967, one Chicago alderman introduced a motion in the city council that it be removed and replaced by a monument to Cubs baseball hero Ernie Banks. Nothing came of the motion, and now the sculpture is a beloved city landmark. Here's an informal tour of some of the Loop's best:

1. *Untitled Picasso Sculpture* (1967, Pablo Picasso); Richard J. Daley Plaza (West Washington Street between North Dearborn and North Clark Streets); Cor-Ten steel.

2. *Flamingo* (1974, Alexander Calder); Federal Center (219 South Dearborn Street between West Adams Street and West Jackson Boulevard); painted steel.

3. *Miró's Chicago* (1967, Joan Miró; installed 1981); Chicago Temple (69 West Washington Street at North Clark Street); bronze, concrete, tile.

4. *The Four Seasons* (1975, Marc Chagall); First National Plaza (West Monroe Street between South Clark and South Dearborn Streets); hand-chipped stone, glass fragments, brick.

5. *Monument with Standing Beast* (1985, Jean Dubuffet); State of Illinois Center (100 West Randolph Street at North Clark Street); fiberglass.

6.  *Ceres* (1930, John Storrs); Chicago Board of Trade (141 West Jackson Boulevard at South LaSalle Street); aluminum.

7.  *Being Born* (1983, Virginio Ferarri); State Street Mall (at East Washington Street in front of Marshall Field's); stainless steel.

8.  *Batcolumn* (1977, Claes Oldenburg); Social Security Administration Building Plaza (600 West Madison Street at North Clinton Street); painted steel.

9.  *Dawn Shadows* (1983, Louise Nevelson); Madison Plaza (200 West Madison Street at North Wells Street); steel.

10. *Universe* (1974, Alexander Calder); Lobby, Sears Tower (233 South Wacker Drive); painted aluminum.

# Part Two

# Planning Your Visit to Chicago

## When to Go: Seasons of the Windy City

### FOUR DISTINCT SEASONS

Chicago is a town that boasts four distinct seasons. Arrive on a blustery winter day—when pedestrians battle fierce winds off Lake Michigan that rake North Michigan Avenue—and you may assume Chicago is called "the Windy City" because of the weather. (It's not. The moniker was earned by long-winded nineteenth-century Chicago pols.) In January and February, Chicago's climate is often distinguished by a bone-chilling combination of sub-freezing temperatures and howling winds. And the white stuff? The average winter snowfall is 40 inches.

The summer months of June, July, and August, on the other hand, are noted for high temperatures and high humidity that frequently approach triple digits. While the combination can make for miserably hot and sticky summer afternoons, breezes off Lake Michigan are often a mitigating factor that can make a stroll through Lincoln Park (or an afternoon at the Taste of Chicago festival) bearable.

Temperature-wise, spring and fall are the most moderate times of the year; many people say autumn is their favorite Chicago season. While evening temperatures in October and November may dip into the 40s, the days are usually warm. Starting in mid-October, the fall foliage creates a riot of color that tempts thousands of folks to jump in their cars for day trips north of the city along scenic Sheridan Road.

One common cliché applies in Chicago: If you don't like the weather, just wait a while . . . it may change. In any season, the city's lakefront setting and location in a major west-to-east weather path make atmospheric conditions highly changeable (and, as you'll discover during your stay, difficult to predict). Plan accordingly on all-day outings by bringing along appropriate rain gear and/or extra clothing.

For visitors in town enjoying Chicago's museums, galleries, shopping, restaurants, and other attractions, any season is okay. The city goes full-blast all year. In fact, while winter may be the least desirable time of year to hit town, it's the cultural season; theater, music, and special programs at museums are running at full steam.

| Chicago's Average Temperatures and Precipitation | | |
|---|---|---|
| Month | Avg Daily Temperature (Minimum/Maximum in Fahrenheit) | Avg Monthly Precipitation |
| January | 18°/34° | 1.6" |
| February | 20°/36° | 1.3" |
| March | 29°/45° | 2.6" |
| April | 40°/58° | 3.7" |
| May | 49°/70° | 3.2" |
| June | 59°/81° | 4.1" |
| July | 65°/86° | 3.6" |
| August | 65°/85° | 3.5" |
| September | 56°/76° | 3.4" |
| October | 45°/65° | 2.3" |
| November | 32°/49° | 2.1" |
| December | 22°/36° | 2.1" |

## AVOIDING CROWDS

In general, the summer months (mid-June through mid-August, when school is out) are the busiest times at most tourist attractions. Popular tourist sites are busier on weekends than weekdays, and Saturdays are busier than Sundays. Many major Chicago attractions offer free admission one day a week; it's usually the most crowded day.

On weekdays during the school year places such as the Art Institute of Chicago, the Field Museum, and the Lincoln Park Zoo are besieged by yellow school buses. If you'd rather tour when things are a little quieter, come back in the afternoon: The kids are whisked back to class by 1:30 p.m. because the buses are needed at the end of the school day.

Driving during Chicago's rush hour—for that matter, driving in Chicago at any time for out-of-town visitors—should be avoided. Massive tie-ups are routine on the main arteries leading in and out of the city, as well as on the major highways that connect the suburbs. If you must drive, stay off the road before 9 a.m. and after 4 p.m. so you'll miss the worst rush hour traffic. Generally, getting around by car on weekends and holidays is a breeze, although you may run into an occasional backup on the Eisenhower or Kennedy expressways, the two major highways that lead in and out of downtown Chicago.

By the same token, if you're driving to Chicago or planning to get from the airport to downtown by car or cab, avoid arriving during rush hour— especially on Friday afternoons. The drive from O'Hare to the Loop can take up to four hours as all those high-rise office buildings disgorge legions of office workers focused on getting home for the weekend. Don't get in their way.

### Warning: Population Explosion

Be forewarned that Chicago is home to some of the largest conventions and trade shows in the world. If you attempt to visit the Windy City while one of these monsters is in progress, you will find hotel rooms scarce and expensive, restaurants crowded, and empty cabs impossible to find. This population explosion is often compounded between Thanksgiving and the third week in December when shoppers and conventioneers converge on Chicago simultaneously. To help you avoid the crowds, we have included a calendar of those conventions and trade shows large enough to affect your visit (see pages 89– 91).

## HOW TO GET MORE INFORMATION ON CHICAGO BEFORE YOUR VISIT

For additional information on entertainment, sight-seeing, maps, shopping, dining, and lodging in the Chicago area, call or write:

Chicago Office of Tourism
Chicago Cultural Center
78 East Washington Street
Chicago, Illinois 60602
(312) 744-2400, (312) 744-2964 (TDD)

In addition, three visitor information centers are centrally located: in the Historic Water Tower on the Magnificent Mile (on North Michigan Avenue across from the Water Tower Place shopping mall); in the Chicago Cultural Center (downtown on South Michigan at Washington Street); and in the Illinois Market Place Visitor Information Center (at Navy Pier). All are open daily, offer help planning an itinerary, make suggestions about things to do, and feature plenty of free information and maps.

# Getting to Chicago

Folks planning a trip to the Windy City have several options when it comes to getting there: plane, train, or automobile. Your distance from Chicago—and your tolerance for hassles such as traffic congestion and interminable waits in holding patterns—will probably determine which mode of transportation you ultimately choose.

## FLYING

If you're coming to Chicago from the east, west, Gulf coast, Europe, Asia, South America, or any other place that's more than a 12-hour drive away, you'll probably arrive the way most folks do: by plane into O'Hare International Airport, the world's busiest—and often, most frustrating—airfield.

Yet many domestic flyers can avoid the hassles of O'Hare by flying into Midway, an airport with architecture right out of the '50s that's conveniently located about ten miles southwest of the Loop. Midway is a one-level airport that's considerably less congested than O'Hare, located on a subway line, and only about 20 minutes from downtown (longer during rush hour). Our advice: If you can, fly into Midway. (See Part Five for maps of O'Hare and Midway.)

## TAKING THE TRAIN

Just as O'Hare is a major air hub between the east and west coasts of the United States, Chicago's Union Station is the major rail station between the two coasts. While long-distance travel by train can be tedious, people who live in the Midwest can travel by rail into Chicago without fear of getting stuck in a holding pattern over O'Hare or trapped in a traffic snarl on the Eisenhower Expressway.

The closest cities to Chicago with Amtrak passenger train service are Milwaukee (1.5 hours one-way) and Indianapolis (4.5 hours). Other cities offering daily rail service to Union Station include St. Louis (5 hours), Detroit (5 hours), Cincinnati (7 hours; three days a week), Cleveland (6 hours), Kansas City (8.5 hours), Toronto (12 hours), Omaha (9 hours), and Minneapolis (8 hours). For schedules and reservations, call Amtrak at (800) 872-7245.

## DRIVING

If you live close to Chicago and driving is an option, think again. Why? Chicago traffic congestion never lets up. Backups, accidents, and delays occur perpetually throughout the metropolitan area. And parking? Not a chance. Convenient, affordable, and/or secure places to leave your car are rare luxuries. Instead of enduring traffic and parking crises, try using

Chicago's extensive public transportation systems and abundance of taxis to get around town, and airport vans to get to and from downtown hotels. For more information about travel in Chicago without a car, see page 123.

But what if, in spite of our advice, you drive to Chicago? Here's the short list of things to do (and avoid) when driving around town: make sure your hotel offers on-site or nearby off-street parking, don't arrive during rush hour, and be flexible about using public transportation throughout your stay. Often, it's less expensive and a lot less hassle to leave the car parked and to take a bus, the El, or a cab. For more information on getting around Chicago by car, see page 121.

## Calendar of Special Events

Chicago hosts a variety of special events throughout the year, including the internationally renowned Taste of Chicago food festival, which draws millions each summer to Grant Park. For exact dates, times, locations, and admission fees (if any), call the phone numbers provided below before your visit.

### January

**Chicago Park District Holiday Flower Show**   Garfield Park Conservatory and Lincoln Park Conservatory. Through the first week of January. Free. (312) 746-5100 (Garfield Park), (312) 742-7737 (Lincoln Park).

**Chicago Boat, Sports, and RV Show**   McCormick Place. Hands-on displays of sporting goods, boats, motor homes, and recreational vehicles. Admission fee. (312) 946-6262.

**Zooperbowl Cafe Brauer at the Lincoln Park Zoo**   A fundraiser for the zoo on Super Bowl Sunday features a big-screen TV and unlimited food and drink. Admission fee. (312) 742-2000.

### February

**Chinese New Year Parade**   Chinatown. A parade, firecrackers, and a paper dragon dance through the streets of Chinatown. Free. (312) 225-6198.

**Chicago Park District Azalea Flower Show**   Garfield Park Conservatory and Lincoln Park Conservatory. Thousands of spring flowers on display from mid-February to early March. Free. (312) 746-5100 (Garfield Park), (312) 742-7737 (Lincoln Park).

**Chicago Auto Show**   McCormick Place. The largest commercial auto show in the world, featuring new models, classics, and race cars. Admission fee. (630) 791-7000.

**Medinah Shrine Circus**    Medinah Temple, 600 North Wabash Avenue. The Shriners' one-ring circus comes to town for three weeks to benefit children's hospitals; a Chicago tradition. Admission fee. (312) 266-5050.

**National African-American History Month**    Various locations. A month-long, city-wide celebration of black Americans' lives, times, and art. Free. (312) 747-2536 (South Shore Cultural Center).

## March

**South Side Irish St. Patrick's Day Parade**    Western Avenue from 103rd to 114th Streets the weekend before St. Patty's Day. Free. (773) 239-7755.

**St. Patrick's Day Parade**    Dearborn Street from Wacker Drive to Van Buren Street. Forty pounds of vegetable dye turns the Chicago River green and everyone is Irish for the day. The parade starts at 11 a.m. and features floats, marching bands, and hundreds of thousands of spectators. Free. (312) 942-9188.

**Chicago Park District Spring Flower Show**    Garfield Park Conservatory and Lincoln Park Conservatory. An eyeful of spring. Free. (312) 746-5100 (Garfield Park), (312) 742-7737 (Lincoln Park).

## April

**Cinco de Mayo Festival**    McCormick Place. A two-day festival celebrating Mexican independence featuring food, drink, and more. Free. (312) 751-5560.

**Chicago Latino Film Festival**    Various locations. (312) 663-1600.

## May

**Art Chicago**    Navy Pier. Art, both past and present, offered for sale by prestigious art galleries. Admission fee. (312) 587-3300.

**Polish Constitution Day Parade**    Dearborn Street from Wacker Drive to Van Buren Street. Free. (773) 889-7125.

**Wright Plus**    Oak Park. The only chance to tour the interiors of ten homes designed by Frank Lloyd Wright and his contemporaries. Admission fee; tickets go on sale on March 1, and the event usually sells out by mid-April. The all-day tour is held on the third Saturday in May. (708) 848-1976.

## June

**Chicago Blues Festival**   Petrillo Music Shell, Grant Park. Fabulous music, food, and dozens of artists from Chicago and beyond. Free. (312) 744-3370.

**57th Street Art Fair**   57th Street and South Kimbark Avenue. Oldest juried art fair in the Midwest. Free. (773) 684-8383.

**Chicago Gospel Festival**   Petrillo Music Shell, Grant Park. Free. (312) 744-3315.

**Celebrate on State Street Festival**   State Street from Wacker Drive to Van Buren Street. Free. (312) 782-9160.

**Gay and Lesbian Pride Parade**   Starts at Halsted Street and Belmont Avenue. Free. (773) 348-8243.

**Midsummer Festival in Andersonville**   Neighborhood festival on Clark Street from Foster to Catalpa avenues. Free. (773) 728-8111.

**Chicago Country Music Festival**   Petrillo Music Shell, Grant Park. Free. (312) 744-3315.

**Taste of Chicago**   Grant Park. In the week preceding Independence Day more than 100 restaurants serve Chicago-style and ethnic cuisine at this alfresco food festival; musical entertainment. (312) 744-3315.

**Ravinia Festival**   Highland Park from late June to late August. A 12-week season of the Chicago Symphony Orchestra, dance, jazz, ballet, folk, and comedy in a picnic setting. Admission fee. For information, call (847) 266-5000; for travel information, call (847) 266-5100.

**Taste of River North**   Superior Street, between LaSalle and Wells Streets. Two days of food tastings from up to 40 restaurants located in this trendy Chicago neighborhood. Free. (312) 645-1047.

## July

**Concerts in the Parks**   Various locations. More than 80 concerts performed in 64 Chicago parks in July and August. Free. (312) 747-0816.

**Independence Day Concert and Fireworks**   Petrillo Music Shell, Grant Park. A classical concert kicks off Chicago's traditional Fourth of July celebration. Free. (312) 294-2420.

**Sheffield Garden Walk and Festival**   Corner of Sheffield Avenue and Webster Street at St. Vincent's Church. Self-guided walking tour of private gardens, garage sales, food, and entertainment. Admission fee. (773) 929-9255.

**Black Harvest Film Festival**   Film Center of the Art Institute, Columbus Drive and Jackson Boulevard. Admission fee. (312) 443-3733.

**Taste of Ireland Festival**   Irish American Heritage Center, 4626 North Knox Avenue. Two days of continuous entertainment, 40 Irish bands, food, Irish step dancing, and museum and art gallery tours. Admission fee. (773) 282-7035.

**Newberry Library Annual Book Fair**   60 West Walton Place. Free. (312) 255-3501.

**Venetian Night**   Chicago's lakefront, from Navy Pier to the planetarium. The Grant Park Symphony and a parade of animated floats and illuminated yachts. Free. (312) 744-6068.

## August

**Concerts in the Parks**   Various locations. More than 80 concerts performed in 64 Chicago parks in July and August. Free. (312) 747-0816.

**Bud Billiken Parade**   King Drive to Washington Park. The South Side black community's fun-filled event for kids and grownups. Free. (312) 225-2400.

**Chicago Air and Water Show**   North Avenue Beach. The largest free air and water show and one of the largest spectator events in the United States attracts two million people each year; powerboat racing and a dazzling aerial display in the sky over Lake Michigan. Free. (312) 744-3370.

**Ginza Holiday**   Midwest Buddhist Temple, 435 West Menomonee Street. A celebration of Japanese culture featuring food, dance, mime, martial arts, music, origami, painting, and sculpture. Admission fee. (312) 943-7801.

**National Antique Show & Sale**   Rosemont Convention Center (near O'Hare). A large semiannual show of antiques and collector's items. Admission fee. (847) 692-2220.

**Gold Coast Art Fair**   Between Ontario, Huron, Franklin, and State Streets. For three days 400 artists display and sell high-quality paintings, photographs, and hand-crafted fine art. Free. (312) 787-2677.

**Oz Festival**   Lincoln Park. Family-oriented fun featuring arts and crafts, entertainment for children, and food. Admission fee. (773) 868-3010.

**New East Side ArtWorks Festival**   Michigan Avenue and Lake Street. Free. (773) 404-0763.

**Chicago Jazz Festival** Petrillo Music Shell, Grant Park. A jazz marathon over Labor Day weekend; the world's largest free jazz festival featuring the greats from traditional and swing to bebop, blues, and avant garde. Free. (312) 744-3370.

## September

**Berghoff Oktoberfest** Adams Street between State and Dearborn Streets. Street party featuring beer tents, bands, and dancing. (312) 427-3170.

**"Viva Chicago" Latin Music Festival** Petrillo Music Shell, Grant Park. Free. (312) 744-3315.

## October

**Chicago International Film Festival** Screenings at various theaters throughout the city. Exciting new international films, directors, and stars. Admission fee. (312) 425-9400.

**Columbus Day Parade** Dearborn Street from Wacker Drive to Congress Parkway. Free. (312) 828-0010.

**Historic Pullman District's Annual House Tour** Historic Pullman Center, 614 East 113th Street. Annual fall tour of homes and historic buildings; refreshments available. Admission fee. (773) 785-8181.

**Edgar Allan Poe Reading** Clarke House Museum. Listen to an actor read Poe stories in a candlelit setting. Admission fee. (312) 326-1480.

**Spooky Zoo Spectacular** Lincoln Park Zoo. Kids (with their parents) are encouraged to dress up in costumes and trick-or-treat at the animal houses; more than a million pieces of candy are given away on the Saturday before Halloween each year. Free. (312) 742-2246.

## November/December

**Annual Polish Film Festival in North America** Various movie theaters. Admission fee. (773) 486-9612.

**Historic Pullman District's Candlelight Tour** Historic Pullman Center, 614 East 113th Street. Candlelight tour of Historic Pullman Center and five homes, with dinner; $50 per person; reservations only. (773) 785-8181.

**Chrysanthemum Show** Lincoln Park Conservatory and Garfield Park Conservatory. Mum's the word. (312) 746-5100 (Garfield Park), (312) 742-7737 (Lincoln Park).

**Veteran's Day Parade**   Dearborn Street from Wacker Drive to Van Buren Street. Free. (312) 744-7582.

**Magnificent Mile Festival of Lights**   North Michigan Avenue from the Chicago River to Oak Street. The kickoff of Chicago's traditional holiday shopping season features stage shows, a parade, fireworks, and 300,000 lights on Michigan Avenue and Oak Street. Free. (312) 642-3570.

**Brach's Kids' Holiday Parade**   Michigan Avenue from Balbo Drive to Wacker Drive. Held the Saturday after Thanksgiving every year. Free. (773) 935-8747.

**Christmas around the World**   Museum of Science and Industry. A grand ethnic festival, plus entertainment. Admission fee. (773) 684-1414.

**Caroling to the Animals**   Lincoln Park Zoo. Chicago's traditional kick-off of the holiday season (held on the first Sunday in December) features children's choirs stationed around the zoo, complimentary cider and song-books, and Santa feeding the sea lions. Free. (312) 742-2283.

**Candlelight Tours of Prairie Avenue Houses**   Near McCormick Place. Authentic period Christmas decorations; docents talk about the history of Christmas traditions in Chicago. Admission fee. (312) 326-1480.

**Chicago Park District Holiday Flower Show**   Garfield Park Conservatory and Lincoln Park Conservatory. Free. (312) 746-5100 (Garfield Park), (312) 742-7737 (Lincoln Park).

## Part Three

# Hotels

## Deciding Where to Stay

Though Chicago sprawls for miles north and south along Lake Michigan, and threatens on the west side to realize some suburban manifest destiny by creeping all the way to the Iowa border, the city is as focused and anchored as Manhattan. Chicago is defined by its city center. Downtown Chicago is not simply the heart of the city, it is the heart of the Midwest. As American as Valley Forge and as foreign as Warsaw, downtown Chicago is a magnet. If you visit Chicago, downtown is where you want to be.

The Chicago hotel scene reflects the dynamism and power of the city's bustling core. By and large Chicago hotels are big, huge even, soaring 20, 30, and more stories above the lake. Although there are hotels near Midway and O'Hare airports and in smaller towns that have expanded to surround the great city, the majority of Chicago's nearly 70,000 rooms are situated in a narrow strip bordered by Lake Michigan on the east, Clark Street on the west, North Avenue on the north, and Roosevelt Road on the south. All told, the area is about three miles north to south and less than a mile wide.

Though some of the finest hotels in the world are in Chicago, finding comfortable lodging for less than $100 a night is easier here than in New York. Chicago is not cheap, but the quality standards for hotels are generally high. Also in Chicago, unlike in Boston, Atlanta, or Washington D.C., the option of booking a less expensive hotel in the suburbs and commuting to downtown is impractical. The commute is long, the suburban hotels few, and the savings insignificant to nonexistent.

Finally, Chicago is the busiest convention city in the United States. If your visit to Chicago coincides with one or more major conventions or trade shows, hotel rooms will be both scarce and expensive. If on the other hand, you are able to schedule your visit to avoid big meetings, you will have a good selection of hotels at suprisingly competitive prices. If you happen to be attending one of the big conventions, book early and use some of the tips listed below to get a discounted room rate. To assist in timing your visit, we have included a convention and trade show calendar in the chapter "Visiting Chicago on Business" (see page 79).

## SOME CONSIDERATIONS

1. When choosing your Chicago lodging, make sure your hotel is situated in a location convenient to your recreation or business needs, and that it is in a safe and comfortable area. Please note that while it is not practical to walk to McCormick Place (the major convention venue) from any of the downtown hotels, larger conventions and trade shows provide shuttle service.

2. Find out how old the hotel is and when the guest rooms were last renovated. Request that the hotel send you its promotional brochure. Ask if brochure photos of guest rooms are accurate and current.

3. If you plan to take a car, inquire about the parking situation. Some hotels offer no parking at all, some charge dearly for parking, and a few offer free parking.

4. If you are not a city dweller, or perhaps are a light sleeper, try to book a hotel on a more quiet side street. Ask for a room off the street and high up.

5. The Chicago skyline is quite beautiful, as is the lake. If you are on a romantic holiday, ask for a room on a higher floor with a good view.

6. If shopping is high on your agenda, try to book a hotel near Michigan Avenue between Oak Street and East Wacker Drive.

7. When you plan your budget, remember that Chicago's combined room and sales tax is a whopping 14.9%.

# Getting a Good Deal on a Room

## Special Weekend Rates

Although well-located Chicago hotels are tough for the budget conscious, it's not impossible to get a good deal, at least relatively speaking. For starters, most downtown hotels that cater to business, government, and convention travelers offer special weekend discount rates that range from 15% to 40% below normal weekday rates. You can find out about weekend specials by calling individual hotels or by consulting your travel agent.

## Getting Corporate Rates

Many hotels offer discounted corporate rates (5–20% off rack). Usually you do not need to work for a large company or have a special relationship with the hotel to obtain these rates. Simply call the hotel of your choice and ask for their corporate rates. Many hotels will guarantee you the discounted rate on the phone when you make your reservation. Others may make the rate conditional on your providing some sort of bona fides, for instance a fax on your company's letterhead requesting the rate, or a company credit card or business card on check-in. Generally, the screening is not rigorous.

## Half-Price Programs

The larger discounts on rooms (35–60%), in Chicago or anywhere else, are available through half-price hotel programs, often called travel clubs. Program operators contract with an individual hotel to provide rooms at deep discounts, usually 50% off rack rate, on a "space available" basis. Space available in practice generally means that you can reserve a room at the discounted rate whenever the hotel expects to be at less than 80% occupancy. A little calendar sleuthing to help you avoid city-wide conventions and special events will increase your chances of choosing a time when the discounts are available.

Most half-price programs charge an annual membership fee or directory subscription charge of $25 to $125. Once enrolled, you are mailed a membership card and a directory listing participating hotels. Examining the directory, you will notice immediately that there are many restrictions and exceptions. Some hotels, for instance, "black out" certain dates or times of year. Others may only offer the discount on certain days of the week, or require you to stay a certain number of nights. Still others may offer a much smaller discount than 50% off rack rate.

Programs specialize in domestic travel, international travel, or both. More established operators offer members between 1,000 and 4,000 hotels to choose from in the United States. All of the programs have a heavy concentration of hotels in California and Florida, and most have a very limited selection of participating properties in New York City or Boston. Offerings in other cities and regions of the United States vary considerably. The programs with the largest selections of Chicago hotels are *Encore, Travel America at Half Price* (Entertainment Publications), *International*

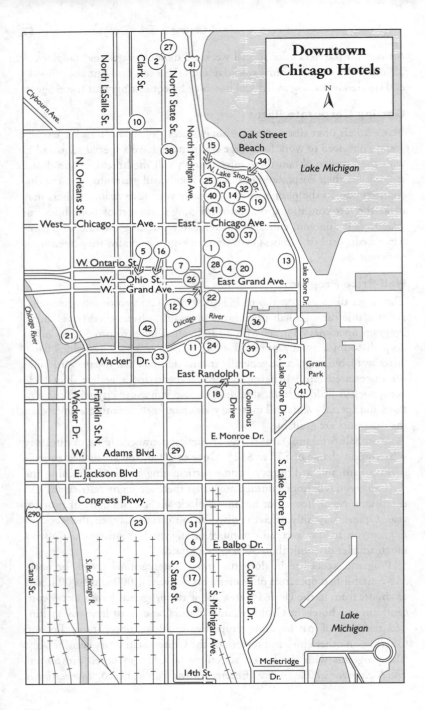

**Downtown Chicago Hotels**

N

Oak Street Beach

Lake Michigan

West Chicago Ave. East Chicago Ave.

W. Ontario St.
W. Ohio St.
W. Grand Ave.

East Grand Ave.

Chicago River

Wacker Dr.

East Randolph Dr.

E. Monroe Dr.

Adams Blvd.

E. Jackson Blvd

Congress Pkwy.

E. Balbo Dr.

Lake Michigan

McFetridge Dr.

14th St.

North LaSalle St.
Clybourn Ave.
Clark St.
North State St.
North Michigan Ave.
N. Orleans St.
N. Lake Shore Dr.
Lake Shore Dr.
Wacker Dr. W.
Franklin St. N.
Canal St.
S. Br. Chicago R.
S. State St.
S. Michigan Ave.
Drive
Columbus
S. Lake Shore Dr.
Columbus Dr.
Grant Park

# Downtown Chicago Hotels

1. Allerton Hotel
2. Ambassador West
3. Best Western Grant Park Hotel
4. Best Western Inn of Chicago
5. Best Western River North
6. Blackstone
7. Cass Hotel
8. Chicago Hilton and Towers
9. Chicago Marriott Hotel
10. Claridge Hotel
11. Clarion Executive Plaza
12. Courtyard
13. Days Inn Lake Shore Drive
14. Doubletree Guest Suites
15. The Drake
16. Embassy Suites
17. Essex Inn
18. Fairmont Hotel
19. Four Seasons Hotel
20. Holiday Inn Chicago City Centre
21. Holiday Inn Mart Plaza
22. Hotel Inter-Continental
23. Hyatt on Printers Row
24. Hyatt Regency
25. The Knickerbocker
26. Lenox House Suites
27. Omni Ambassador East
28. Omni Chicago Hotel
29. Palmer House Hilton
30. Radisson Hotel and Suites
31. Ramada Congress Hotel
32. The Raphael
33. Renaissance Hotel
34. Residence Inn
35. Ritz-Carlton
36. Sheraton Hotel and Towers
37. Summerfield Suites
38. The Sutton Place Hotel
39. Swissôtel
40. The Talbott
41. The Westin Hotel
42. Westin River North Chicago
43. The Whitehall Hotel

*Travel Card,* and *Quest.* Each of these programs lists between 4 and 50 hotels in the greater Chicago area.

| | |
|---|---|
| Encore | (800) 638-0930 |
| Entertainment Publications | (800) 285-5525 |
| International Travel Card | (800) 342-0558 |
| Quest | (800) 638-9819 |

One problem with half-price programs is that not all hotels offer a full 50% discount. Another slippery problem is the base rate against which the discount is applied. Some hotels figure the discount on an exaggerated rack rate that nobody would ever have to pay. A few participating hotels may deduct the discount from a supposed "superior" or "upgraded" room rate, even though the room you get is the hotel's standard accommodation. Though hard to pin down, the majority of participating properties base discounts on the published rate in the *Hotel & Travel Index* (a quarterly reference work used by travel agents) and work within the spirit of their agreement with the program operator. As a rule, if you travel several times a year, your room rate savings will easily compensate for program membership fees.

A noteworthy addendum: Deeply discounted rooms through half-price programs are not commissionable to travel agents. In practical terms this means that you must ordinarily make your own inquiry calls and reservations. If you travel frequently, however, and run a lot of business through your travel agent, he or she will probably do your legwork, lack of commission notwithstanding.

## Preferred Rates

If you cannot book the hotel of your choice through a half-price program, you and your travel agent may have to search for a lesser discount, often called a preferred rate. A preferred rate could be a discount made available to travel agents to stimulate their booking activity, or a discount initiated to attract a certain class of traveler. Most preferred rates are promoted through travel industry publications and are often accessible only through an agent.

We recommend sounding out your travel agent about possible deals. Be aware, however, that the rates shown on travel agents' computerized reservations systems are not always the lowest rates obtainable. Zero in on a couple of hotels that fill your needs in terms of location and quality of accommodations, and then have your travel agent call the hotel for the latest rates and specials. Hotel reps almost always respond more to travel agents because travel agents represent a source of additional business. As discussed earlier, there are certain specials that hotel reps will disclose only to travel agents. Travel agents also come in handy when the hotel you want is supposedly booked. A personal appeal from your agent to the hotel's director of sales and marketing will get you a room more than 50% of the time.

## Wholesalers, Consolidators, and Reservation Services

If you do not want to join a program or buy a discount directory, you can take advantage of the services of a wholesaler or consolidator. Wholesalers and consolidators buy rooms, or options on rooms (room blocks), from hotels at a low, negotiated rate. They then resell the rooms at a profit through travel agents, tour packagers, or directly to the public. Most wholesalers and consolidators have a provision for returning unsold rooms to participating hotels, but are not inclined to do so. The wholesaler's or consolidator's relationship with any hotel is predicated on volume. If they return rooms unsold, the hotel may not make as many rooms available to them the next time around. Thus wholesalers and consolidators often offer rooms at bargain rates, anywhere from 15–50% off rack, occasionally sacrificing their profit margins in the process, to avoid returning the rooms to the hotel unsold.

When wholesalers and consolidators deal directly with the public, they frequently represent themselves as "reservation services." When you call, you can ask for a rate quote for a particular hotel, or alternatively ask for their best available deal in the area where you prefer to stay. If there is a maximum amount you are willing to pay, say so. Chances are the service will find something that will work for you, even if they have to shave a dollar or two off their own profit. Sometimes you will have to pay for your room with a credit card when you make your reservation. Other times you will pay as usual, when you check out. Listed below are several services that frequently offer substantial discounts:

| | |
|---|---|
| Hotel Reservations Network | (800) 964-6835 |
| Hot Rooms | (773) 468-7666 |
| Illinois Reservations | (800) 978-7890 |

## Alternative Lodging

**B&Bs**   Bed & Breakfast Chicago at (800) 375-7084 or (773) 248-0005 is a reservation service for guest houses and furnished apartments primarily in the downtown area. Rates usually range from $85–185 for guest houses and $105–325 for furnished apartments.

**Condos**   If you want to rent a condo for a week in Chicago, you are out of luck. Local law stipulates a minimum rental period of 30 days. If you are planning an extended stay and are interested in a condo, your best bet is to shop realtors in the area of town where you prefer to stay. If they don't handle rentals, they can refer you to someone who does.

**Dorm Programs**   Located three blocks from the lake and Lincoln Park, the Eleanor Residence offers guest accommodations for up to 28 days for women who will be working, attending courses, or just visiting in Chicago. Rooms are available at a rate of $60–95 per night (including a full, hot breakfast and dinner). All rooms are fully furnished with private phone lines and daily maid service. They also offer the use of a kitchenette, so you can prepare all your meals if you like. TV lounges, 24-hour front desk services, exercise rooms, and study rooms are also available.

Eleanor Residence for Women
1550 North Dearborn Parkway (at the corner of North Avenue)
(312) 664-8245

Within walking distance of Northwestern University and a 20–25 minute El ride to the Loop, Kendall College offers suite-style, air-conditioned dorm rooms. Regular rates: single, $27.30 per night; double, $38.25 per night (linens are included). Group rates: single, $20.60 per night; double, $10.65 per person per night ($10 per week linen charge). There is a $75 key deposit. Guests are welcome to eat in the cafeteria for $5.40. The college is also home to a famous culinary school that makes its dining room available (lunch, $14.95; dinner, approximately $25–30 per person). Kendall College is located at 2408 Orrington in Evanston. Call (847) 866-1391 for dorm reservations, and (847) 866-1399 ext. 1276 for dining.

## How to Evaluate a Travel Package

Hundreds of Chicago package vacations are offered to the public each year. Packages should be a win/win proposition for both the buyer and the seller. The buyer only has to make one phone call and deal with a single salesperson to set up the whole vacation: transportation, rental car, lodging, meals, attraction admissions, and even golf and tennis. The seller, likewise, only has to deal with the buyer once, eliminating the need for separate sales, confirmations, and billing. In addition to streamlining sales, processing, and administration, some packagers also buy airfares in bulk on contract like a broker playing the commodities market. Buying a large number of airfares in advance allows the packager to buy them at a significant savings from posted fares. The same practice is also applied to hotel rooms. Because selling vacation packages is an efficient way of doing business, and because the packager can often buy individual package components (airfare, lodging, etc.) in bulk at discount, savings in operating expenses realized by the seller are sometimes passed on to the buyer so that, in addition to convenience, the package is also an exceptional value. In any event, that is the way it is supposed to work.

All too often, in practice, the seller cashes in on discounts and passes none on to the buyer. In some instances, packages are loaded additionally with extras that cost the packager next to nothing, but inflate the retail price sky-high. As you may expect, the savings to be passed along to customers remain somewhere in Fantasyland.

When considering a package, choose one that includes features you are sure to use. Whether you use all the features or not, you will most certainly pay for them. Second, if cost is of greater concern than convenience, make a few phone calls and see what the package would cost if you booked its individual components (airfare, rental car, lodging, etc.) on your own. If the package price is less than the à la carte cost, the package is a good deal. If the costs are about the same, the package is probably worth buying just for the convenience.

If your package includes a choice of rental car or airport transfers (transportation to and from the airport), take the transfers unless you are visiting Chicago for the weekend. During the weekend, with the exception of some sections of Michigan Avenue, it is relatively easy to get around. During the week, forget it. Also, if you take the car, be sure to ask if the package includes free parking at your hotel.

## HELPING YOUR TRAVEL AGENT HELP YOU

When you call your travel agent, ask if he or she has been to Chicago. If the answer is no, be prepared to give your travel agent some direction. Do not accept any recommendations at face value. Check out the location and rates of any suggested hotel and make certain that the hotel is suited to your itinerary.

Because some travel agents are unfamiliar with Chicago, your agent may try to plug you into a tour operator's or wholesaler's preset package. This essentially allows the travel agent to set up your whole trip with a single phone call and still collect an 8–10% commission. The problem with this scenario is that most agents will place 90% of their Chicago business with only one or two wholesalers or tour operators. In other words, it's the line of least resistance for them, and not much choice for you.

Travel agents will often use wholesalers who run packages in conjunction with airlines, like Delta's Dream Vacations or American's Fly-Away Vacations. Because of the wholesaler's exclusive relationship with the carrier, these trips are very easy for travel agents to book. However, they will probably be more expensive than a package offered by a high-volume wholesaler who works with a number of airlines in a primary Chicago market.

To help your travel agent get you the best possible deal, do the following:

1. Determine where you want to stay in Chicago, and if possible choose a specific hotel. This can be accomplished by reviewing the hotel information provided in this guide, and by writing or calling hotels that interest you.

2. Check out the hotel deals and package vacations advertised in the Sunday travel sections of the *Chicago Tribune* and *Chicago Sun-Times* newspapers. Often you will be able to find deals that beat the socks off anything offered in your local paper. See if you can find specials that fit your plans and include a hotel you like.

3. Call the hotels, wholesalers, or tour operators whose ads you have collected. Ask any questions you have concerning their packages, but do not book your trip with them directly.

4. Tell your travel agent about the deals you find and ask if he or she can get you something better. The deals in the paper will serve as a benchmark against which to compare alternatives proposed by your travel agent.

5. Choose from the options that you and your travel agent uncover. No matter which option you select, have your travel agent book it. Even if you go with one of the packages in the newspaper, it will probably be commissionable (at no additional cost to you) and will provide the agent some return on the time invested on your behalf. Also, as a travel professional, your agent should be able to verify the quality and integrity of the deal.

## IF YOU MAKE YOUR OWN RESERVATION

As you poke around trying to find a good deal, there are several things you should know. First, always call the specific hotel as opposed to the hotel chain's national 800 number. Quite often, the reservationists at the national 800 number are unaware of local specials. Always ask about specials before you inquire about corporate rates. Do not be reluctant to bargain. If you are buying a hotel's weekend package, for example, and want to extend your stay into the following week, you can often obtain at least the corporate rate for the extra days. Do your bargaining, however, before you check in, preferably when you make your reservations.

## Chain Hotel Toll-Free Numbers

| | |
|---|---|
| Best Western | (800) 528-1234 U.S. & Canada |
| | (800) 528-2222 TDD (Telecommunication Device for the Deaf) |
| Comfort Inn | (800) 228-5150 U.S. |
| Courtyard by Marriott | (800) 321-2211 U.S. |
| Days Inn | (800) 325-2525 U.S. |
| Doubletree | (800) 528-0444 U.S. |
| Doubletree Guest Suites | (800) 424-2900 U.S. |
| Econo Lodge | (800) 424-4777 U.S. |
| Embassy Suites | (800) 362-2779 U.S. & Canada |
| Fairfield Inn by Marriott | (800) 228-2800 U.S. |
| Hampton Inn | (800) 426-7866 U.S. & Canada |
| Hilton | (800) 445-8667 U.S. |
| | (800) 368-1133 TDD |
| Holiday Inn | (800) 465-4329 U.S. & Canada |
| Howard Johnson | (800) 654-2000 U.S. & Canada |
| | (800) 654-8442 TDD |
| Hyatt | (800) 233-1234 U.S. & Canada |
| Loew's | (800) 223-0888 U.S. & Canada |
| Marriott | (800) 228-9290 U.S. & Canada |
| | (800) 228-7014 TDD |
| Quality Inn | (800) 228-5151 U.S. & Canada |
| Radisson | (800) 333-3333 U.S. & Canada |
| Ramada Inn | (800) 228-3838 U.S. |
| | (800) 228-3232 TDD |
| Residence Inn by Marriott | (800) 331-3131 U.S. |
| Ritz-Carlton | (800) 241-3333 U.S. |
| Sheraton | (800) 325-3535 U.S. & Canada |
| Stouffer | (800) 468-3571 U.S. & Canada |
| Wyndham | (800) 822-4200 U.S. |

# Chicago Lodging for Business Travelers

The primary considerations for business travelers are affordability and proximity to the site or area where you will transact your business. Identify the zone(s) where your business will take you, and then use the Hotel Chart to cross-reference the hotels located in that area. Once you have developed a short list of possible hotels that are conveniently located, fit your budget, and offer the standard of accommodation you require, you (or your travel agent) can make use of the cost-saving suggestions discussed earlier to obtain the lowest rate.

## LODGING CONVENIENT TO MCCORMICK PLACE

If you are attending a meeting or trade show at McCormick Place, the most convenient lodging is downtown Chicago, though none of the hotels, practically speaking, are within walking distance. From most downtown hotels, McCormick Place is a 5–14 minute cab or 10–30 minute shuttle ride away. Parking is available at the convention center, but it is expensive and not all that convenient. We recommend that you leave your car at home and use shuttles and cabs. The Hyatt Regency McCormick Place has 800 rooms and is connected to McCormick's Grand Concourse.

Commuting to McCormick Place from the suburbs or the airports during rush hour is something to be avoided if possible. If you want a room downtown, book early . . . very early. If you screw up and need a room at the last minute, try a wholesaler or reservation service, or one of the strategies listed below.

## CONVENTION RATES: HOW THEY WORK AND HOW TO DO BETTER

If you are attending a major convention or trade show, it is probable that the meeting's sponsoring organization has negotiated "convention rates" with a number of hotels. Under this arrangement, hotels agree to "block" a certain number of rooms at an agreed upon price for conventioneers. Sometimes, as in the case of a small meeting, only one hotel is involved. In the event of a large "city-wide" convention at McCormick Place, however, almost all downtown and airport hotels will participate in the room block.

Because the convention sponsor brings a lot of business to the city and reserves a large number of rooms, it usually can negotiate a volume discount on the room rates, a rate that should be substantially below rack rate. The bottom line, however, is that some conventions and trade shows have more bargaining clout and negotiating skill than others. Hence, your convention sponsor may or may not be able to obtain the lowest possible rate.

Once a convention or trade show sponsor has completed negotiations with participating hotels, it will send its attendees a housing list that includes all the hotels serving the convention, along with the special convention rate for each. When you receive the housing list, you can compare the convention rates with the rates obtainable using the strategies covered in the previous section. If the negotiated convention rate doesn't sound like a good deal, you can try to reserve a room using a half-price club, a consolidator, or a tour operator. Remember, however, that many of the deep discounts are available only when the hotel expects to be at less than 80% occupancy, a condition that rarely prevails when a big convention is in town.

### Strategies for Beating Convention Rates

There are several tactics for getting around convention rates:

1. Reserve early. Most big conventions and trade shows announce meeting sites one to three years in advance. Get your reservation booked as far in advance as possible using a half-price club. If you book well ahead of the time the convention sponsor sends out the housing list, chances are good that the hotel will accept your reservation.

2. Compare your convention's housing list with the list of hotels presented in this guide. You may be able to find a suitable hotel that is not on the housing list.

3. Use a local reservations agency or consolidator. This is also a good strategy to employ if, for some reason, you need to make reservations at the last minute. Local reservations agencies and consolidators almost always control some rooms, even in the midst of a huge convention or trade show.

# Hotels and Motels: Rated and Ranked

## WHAT'S IN A ROOM?

Except for cleanliness, state of repair, and decor, most travelers do not pay much attention to hotel rooms. There is, of course, a discernible standard of quality and luxury that differentiates Motel 6 from Holiday Inn, Holiday Inn from Marriott, and so on. In general, however, hotel guests fail to appreciate the fact that some rooms are better engineered than others.

Contrary to what you might suppose, designing a hotel room is (or should be) much more complex than picking a bedspread to match the carpet and drapes. Making the room usable to its occupants is an art, a planning discipline that combines both form and function.

Decor and taste are important, certainly. No one wants to spend several days in a room whose decor is dated, garish, or even ugly. But beyond the decor, several variables determine how "livable" a hotel room is. In Chicago, for example, we have seen some beautifully appointed rooms that are simply not well designed for human habitation. The next time you stay in a hotel, pay attention to the details and design elements of your room. Even more than decor, these will make you feel comfortable and at home.

It takes the *Unofficial Guide* researchers quite a while to inspect a hotel room. Here are a few of the things we check that you may want to start paying attention to:

**Room Size**    While some smaller rooms are cozy and well designed, a large and uncluttered room is generally preferable, especially for a stay of more than three days.

**Temperature Control, Ventilation, and Odor**    The guest should be able to control the temperature of the room. The best system, because it's so quiet, is central heating and air conditioning, controlled by the room's own thermostat. The next best system is a room module heater and air conditioner, preferably controlled by an automatic thermostat, but usually by manually operated button controls. The worst system is central heating and air without any sort of room thermostat or guest control.

The vast majority of hotel rooms have windows or balcony doors that have been permanently sealed. Though there are some legitimate safety and liability issues involved, we prefer windows and balcony doors that can be opened to admit fresh air. Hotel rooms should be odor free, smoke free, and not feel stuffy or damp.

**Room Security**    Better rooms have locks that require a plastic card instead of the traditional lock and key. Card and slot systems allow the hotel, essentially, to change the combination or entry code of the lock with each new guest. A burglar who has somehow acquired a conventional room key can afford to wait until the situation is right before using the key to gain access. Not so with a card and slot system. Though larger hotels and hotel chains with lock and key systems usually rotate their locks once each year, they remain vulnerable to hotel thieves much of the time. Many smaller or independent properties rarely rotate their locks.

In addition to the entry lock system, the door should have a deadbolt, and preferably a chain that can be locked from the inside. A chain by itself is not sufficient. Doors should also have a peephole. Windows and balcony doors, if any, should have secure locks.

**Safety**    Every room should have a fire or smoke alarm, clear fire instructions, and preferably a sprinkler system. Bathtubs should have a nonskid surface, and shower stalls should have doors that either open outward or slide side to side. Bathroom electrical outlets should be high on the wall and not too close to the sink. Balconies should have sturdy, high rails.

**Noise**  Most travelers have been kept awake by the television, partying, or amorous activities of people in the next room, or by traffic on the street outside. Better hotels are designed with noise control in mind. Wall and ceiling construction are substantial, effectively screening routine noise. Carpets and drapes, in addition to being decorative, also absorb and muffle sounds. Mattresses mounted on stable platforms or sturdy bed frames do not squeak, even when challenged by the most acrobatic lovers. Televisions enclosed in cabinets, and with volume governors, rarely disturb guests in adjacent rooms.

In better hotels, the air conditioning and heating system is well maintained and operates without noise or vibration. Likewise, plumbing is quiet and positioned away from the sleeping area. Doors to the hall, and to adjoining rooms, are thick and well fitted to better block out noise.

If you are easily disturbed by noise, ask for a room on a higher floor, off main thoroughfares, and away from elevators and ice and vending machines.

**Darkness Control**  Ever been in a hotel room where the curtains would not quite meet in the middle? Thick, lined curtains that close completely in the center and extend beyond the edges of the window or door frame are required. In a well-planned room, the curtains, shades, or blinds should almost totally block light at any time of day.

**Lighting**  Poor lighting is an extremely common problem in American hotel rooms. The lighting is usually adequate for dressing, relaxing, or watching television, but not for reading or working. Lighting needs to be bright over tables and desks, and beside couches or easy chairs. Since so many people read in bed, there should be a separate light for each person. A room with two queen beds should have individual lights for four people. Better bedside reading lights illuminate a small area, so if one person wants to sleep and another to read, the sleeper will not be bothered by the light. The worst situation by far is a single lamp on a table between beds. In each bed, only the person next to the lamp will have sufficient light to read. This deficiency is often compounded by weak light bulbs.

In addition, closet areas should be well lit, and there should be a switch near the door that turns on room lights when you enter. A seldom seen, but desirable, feature is a bedside console that allows a guest to control all or most lights in the room from bed.

**Furnishings**    At bare minimum, the bed(s) must be firm. Pillows should be made with nonallergenic fillers and, in addition to the sheets and spread, a blanket should be provided. Bedclothes should be laundered with fabric softener and changed daily. Better hotels usually provide extra blankets and pillows in the room or on request, and sometimes use a second topsheet between the blanket and spread.

There should be a dresser large enough to hold clothes for two people during a five-day stay. A small table with two chairs, or a desk with a chair, should be provided. The room should be equipped with a luggage rack and a three-quarter- to full-length mirror.

The television should be color and cable-connected; ideally, it should have a volume governor and remote control. It should be mounted on a swivel base, and preferably enclosed in a cabinet. Local channels should be posted on the set and a local TV program guide should be supplied. The telephone should be touchtone, conveniently situated for bedside use, and should have on or near it easy-to-understand dialing instructions and a rate card. Local white and yellow pages should be provided. Better hotels install phones in the bathroom and equip room phones with long cords.

Well-designed hotel rooms usually have a plush armchair or a sleeper sofa for lounging and reading. Better headboards are padded for comfortable reading in bed, and there should be a nightstand or table on each side of the bed(s). Nice extras in any hotel room include a small refrigerator, a digital alarm clock, and a coffeemaker.

**Bathroom**    Two sinks are better than one, and you cannot have too much counter space. A sink outside the bath is a great convenience when one person bathes as another dresses. Sinks should have drains with stoppers.

Better bathrooms have both a tub and shower with a nonslip bottom. Tub and shower controls should be easy to operate. Adjustable shower heads are preferred. The bath needs to be well lit and should have an exhaust fan and a guest-controlled bathroom heater. Towels and washcloths should be large, soft, and fluffy, and generously supplied. There should be an electrical outlet for each sink, conveniently and safely placed.

Complimentary shampoo, conditioner, and lotion are a plus, as are robes and bathmats. Better hotels supply bathrooms with tissues and extra toilet paper. Luxurious baths feature a phone, a hair dryer, sometimes a small television, or even a Jacuzzi.

**Vending**    Complimentary ice and a drink machine should be located on each floor. Welcome additions include a snack machine and a sundries (combs, toothpaste) machine. The latter are seldom found in large hotels that have restaurants and shops.

| Room Star Ratings | | |
|---|---|---|
| ★★★★★ | Superior Rooms | Tasteful and luxurious by any standard |
| ★★★★ | Extremely Nice Rooms | What you would expect at a Hyatt Regency or Marriott |
| ★★★ | Nice Rooms | Holiday Inn or comparable quality |
| ★★ | Adequate Rooms | Clean, comfortable, and functional without frills (like a Motel 6) |
| ★ | Super Budget | |

## ROOM RATINGS

To distinguish properties according to relative quality, tastefulness, state of repair, cleanliness, and size of standard rooms, we have grouped the hotels and motels into classifications denoted by stars. Star ratings in this guide apply to Chicago area properties only and do not necessarily correspond to ratings awarded by Mobil, AAA, or other travel critics. Because stars carry little weight when awarded in the absence of commonly recognized standards of comparison, we have linked our ratings to expected levels of quality established by specific American hotel corporations.

Star ratings apply to room quality only, and describe the property's standard accommodations. For most hotels and motels a "standard accommodation" is a hotel room with either one king bed or two queen beds. In an all-suite property, the standard accommodation is either a one- or two-room suite. In addition to standard accommodations, many hotels offer luxury rooms and special suites that are not rated in this guide. Star ratings for rooms are assigned without regard to whether a property has restaurant(s), recreational facilities, entertainment, or other extras.

In addition to stars (which delineate broad categories), we also employ a numerical rating system. Our rating scale is 0–100, with 100 as the best possible rating, and zero (0) as the worst. Numerical ratings are presented to show the difference we perceive between one property and another. Rooms at the Ambassador West Hotel, Marriott Chicago Downtown, and the Regal Knickerbocker Hotel are all rated as three and a half stars (★★★½). In the supplemental numerical ratings, the Ambassador West is rated an 82, the Marriott is rated an 80, and the Regal Knickerbocker a 77. This means that within the three-and-a-half-star category, the Ambassador

West and Marriott are comparable, and both have slightly nicer rooms than the Regal Knickerbocker.

The location column identifies the greater Chicago area where you will find a particular property.

## How the Hotels Compare

Cost estimates are based on the hotel's published rack rates for standard rooms. Each "$" represents $60. Thus a cost symbol of "$$$" means a room (or suite) at that hotel will cost about $120 a night.

Below is a hit parade of the nicest rooms in town. We've focused strictly on room quality, and excluded any consideration of location, services, recreation, or amenities. In some instances, a one- or two-room suite can be had for the same price or less than that of a hotel room.

If you use subsequent editions of this guide, you will notice that many of the ratings and rankings change. In addition to the inclusion of new properties, these changes also consider guest room renovations or improved maintenance and housekeeping. A failure to properly maintain guest rooms or a lapse in housekeeping standards can negatively affect the ratings.

Finally, before you begin to shop for a hotel, take a hard look at this letter we received from a couple in Hot Springs, Arkansas:

> *We cancelled our room reservations to follow the advice in your book [and reserved a hotel room highly ranked by the* Unofficial Guide]. *We wanted inexpensive, but clean and cheerful. We got inexpensive, but [also] dirty, grim, and depressing. I really felt disappointed in your advice and the room. It was the pits. That was the one real piece of information I needed from your book! The room spoiled the holiday for me aside from our touring.*

Needless to say, this letter was as unsettling to us as the bad room was to our reader. Our integrity as travel journalists, after all, is based on the quality of the information we provide our readers. Even with the best of intentions and the most conscientious research, however, we cannot inspect every room in every hotel. What we do, in statistical terms, is take a sample: we check out several rooms selected at random in each hotel and base our ratings and rankings on those rooms. The inspections are conducted anonymously and without the knowledge of the management. Although unusual, it is certainly possible that the rooms we randomly inspect are not representative of the majority of rooms at a particular hotel. Another possibility is that the rooms we inspect in a given hotel are representative, but that by bad luck a reader is assigned a room that is inferior. When we rechecked the hotel our reader disliked, we discovered our rating was correctly representative, but that he and his wife had unfortunately been assigned to one of a small number of threadbare rooms scheduled for renovation.

The key to avoiding disappointment is to snoop around in advance. We recommend that you ask for a photo of a hotel's standard guest room before you book, or at least get a copy of the hotel's promotional brochure. Be forewarned, however, that some hotel chains use the same guest room photo in their promotional literature for all hotels in the chain; a specific guest room may not resemble the brochure photo. When you or your travel agent call, ask how old the property is and when your guest room was last renovated. If you arrive and are assigned a room inferior to that which you had been led to expect, demand to be moved to another room.

## How the Hotels Compare

| Hotel | Zone | Star Rating | Quality Rating | Cost |
|---|---|---|---|---|
| Omni Chicago Hotel | 3 | ★★★★★ | 96 | $$$$$– |
| Four Seasons Hotel | 3 | ★★★★½ | 95 | $$$$$$$$– |
| The Drake | 3 | ★★★★½ | 93 | $$$$$$– |
| The Fairmont Hotel | 4 | ★★★★½ | 93 | $$$$$$– |
| The Ritz–Carlton Chicago | 3 | ★★★★½ | 92 | $$$$$$$ |
| Hotel Sofitel Chicago | 2 | ★★★★½ | 91 | $$$+ |
| House of Blues Hotel | 3 | ★★★★½ | 91 | $$$$– |
| The Westin River North Chicago | 3 | ★★★★½ | 91 | $$$$$ |
| Hyatt Regency McCormick Place | 5 | ★★★★½ | 90 | $$$$$$– |
| Chicago Hilton & Towers | 5 | ★★★★ | 89 | $$$$$ |
| Hyatt on Printer's Row Chicago | 4 | ★★★★ | 89 | $$$– |
| Doubletree Guest Suites | 3 | ★★★★ | 88 | $$$$+ |
| Hotel Allegro | 4 | ★★★★ | 88 | $$$+ |
| The Westin Hotel O'Hare | 2 | ★★★★ | 88 | $$$$+ |
| Hyatt Regency O'Hare | 2 | ★★★★ | 87 | $$$+ |
| Marriott Suites O'Hare | 2 | ★★★★ | 87 | $$– |
| Swissôtel Chicago | 4 | ★★★★ | 87 | $$$$$– |
| Hotel Inter–Continental Chicago | 3 | ★★★★ | 86 | $$$$$$+ |
| Residence Inn by Marriott | 2 | ★★★★ | 86 | $$$– |

## How the Hotels Compare (continued)

| Hotel | Zone | Star Rating | Quality Rating | Cost |
|-------|------|-------------|----------------|------|
| Sheraton Gateway Suites O'Hare | 2 | ★★★★ | 86 | $$$$+ |
| Hyatt Regency Chicago in Illinois Center | 4 | ★★★★ | 85 | $$$+ |
| Marriott Suites Downers Grove | 8 | ★★★★ | 85 | $$– |
| Palmer House Hilton | 4 | ★★★★ | 85 | $$$$$– |
| The Sutton Place Hotel | 3 | ★★★★ | 85 | $$$$$– |
| The Whitehall Hotel | 3 | ★★★★ | 85 | $$$$– |
| Embassy Suites Chicago | 3 | ★★★★ | 84 | $$$$+ |
| Hilton Suites Oak Brook Terrace | 8 | ★★★★ | 84 | $$$+ |
| Marriott Residence Inn Downtown | 3 | ★★★★ | 84 | $$$– |
| Radisson Suites Downers Grove | 8 | ★★★★ | 84 | $$$– |
| Renaissance Chicago Hotel | 4 | ★★★★ | 84 | $$$$ |
| The Westin Hotel Chicago | 3 | ★★★★ | 83 | $$$$$+ |
| Ambassador West Hotel | 3 | ★★★½ | 82 | $$$$$ |
| Claridge Hotel | 3 | ★★★½ | 82 | $$$$– |
| Omni Ambassador East | 3 | ★★★½ | 82 | $$$$$– |
| Renaissance Hotel Oak Brook | 8 | ★★★½ | 82 | $$$+ |
| Rosemont Suites O'Hare | 2 | ★★★½ | 82 | $$$+ |
| Sheraton Chicago Hotel & Towers | 3 | ★★★½ | 82 | $$$$– |
| Hyatt at University Village | 6 | ★★★½ | 81 | $$$+ |
| Hyatt Regency Oak Brook | 8 | ★★★½ | 81 | $$$$– |
| Marriott Oak Brook | 8 | ★★★½ | 81 | $$+ |
| O'Hare Hilton | 2 | ★★★½ | 81 | $$$+ |
| Summerfield Suites Chicago | 3 | ★★★½ | 81 | $$$$+ |
| Courtyard by Marriott Downtown | 3 | ★★★½ | 80 | $$$+ |
| Marriott Chicago Downtown | 3 | ★★★½ | 80 | $$$$– |
| O'Hare Marriott | 2 | ★★★½ | 80 | $$$+ |
| Residence Inn by Marriott O'Hare | 2 | ★★★½ | 80 | $$$– |
| Courtyard by Marriott Oak Brook Terrace | 8 | ★★★½ | 79 | $$+ |
| Courtyard by Wood Dale | 10 | ★★★½ | 79 | $$– |
| Regal Knickerbocker Hotel | 3 | ★★★½ | 77 | $$$$$– |
| Radisson Hotel & Suites Chicago | 3 | ★★★½ | 75 | $$$$$– |
| Holiday Inn Mart Plaza | 3 | ★★★ | 74 | $$$$$– |
| Surf Hotel | 1 | ★★★ | 74 | $$+ |

| How the Hotels Compare (continued) | | | | |
|---|---|---|---|---|
| Hotel | Zone | Star Rating | Quality Rating | Cost |
| The Drake Oak Brook | 8 | ★★★ | 74 | $$$– |
| The Midland Hotel | 4 | ★★★ | 74 | $$$$ |
| Omni Orrington Hotel Evanston | 11 | ★★★ | 73 | $$$– |
| The Talbott Hotel | 3 | ★★★ | 73 | $$$$– |
| Clarion Executive Plaza | 4 | ★★★ | 72 | $$$$$– |
| Lenox House Suites | 3 | ★★★ | 71 | $$$+ |
| Club Hotel by Doubletree | 10 | ★★★ | 70 | $$+ |
| Holiday Inn Chicago City Center | 3 | ★★★ | 69 | $$$$+ |
| Holiday Inn O'Hare International | 2 | ★★★ | 69 | $$$$$– |
| Days Inn Lakeshore | 3 | ★★★ | 68 | $$– |
| Four Points Sheraton | 2 | ★★★ | 68 | $$$ |
| The Blackstone Hotel | 5 | ★★★ | 68 | $$– |
| The Carleton of Oak Park | 2 | ★★★ | 67 | $$+ |
| Days Inn Lincoln Park North | 1 | ★★★ | 66 | $$– |
| Hampton Inn Midway Bedford Park | 6 | ★★★ | 66 | $$+ |
| The Raphael Chicago | 3 | ★★★ | 66 | $$$$$ |
| Hampton Inn O'Hare | 2 | ★★★ | 65 | $$ |
| Best Western River North | 3 | ★★½ | 64 | $$$– |
| Comfort Inn O'Hare | 2 | ★★½ | 64 | $$– |
| Howard Johnson Express O'Hare | 2 | ★★½ | 64 | $$– |
| Radisson O'Hare | 2 | ★★½ | 64 | $$+ |
| Best Western Grant Park Hotel | 5 | ★★½ | 63 | $$+ |
| Holiday Inn Evanston | 11 | ★★½ | 63 | $$$– |
| Radisson O'Hare | 2 | ★★½ | 63 | $$+ |
| The Ramada Congress Hotel | 4 | ★★½ | 63 | $$– |
| Holiday Inn Express Downers Grove | 8 | ★★½ | 62 | $$– |
| Quality Inn Downtown | 2 | ★★½ | 62 | $$$– |
| Sleep Inn Midway Airport | 6 | ★★½ | 62 | $$– |

## How the Hotels Compare (continued)

| Hotel | Zone | Star Rating | Quality Rating | Cost |
|-------|------|-------------|----------------|------|
| Best Western Inn of Chicago | 3 | ★★½ | 61 | $$$+ |
| La Quinta Motor Inn Oak Brook | 8 | ★★½ | 61 | $$− |
| Ramada Plaza Hotel O'Hare | 2 | ★★½ | 61 | $$+ |
| Comfort Inn Downers Grove | 8 | ★★½ | 60 | $+ |
| Essex Inn | 5 | ★★½ | 60 | $$+ |
| Best Western O'Hare | 2 | ★★½ | 59 | $$+ |
| Days Inn O'Hare South | 2 | ★★½ | 59 | $$− |
| Motel 6 Chicago Downtown | 3 | ★★½ | 58 | $$− |
| Holiday Inn Chicago O'Hare | 2 | ★★½ | 57 | $$$− |
| Travelodge Chicago O'Hare | 2 | ★★½ | 57 | $+ |
| Red Roof Inn Downers Grove | 8 | ★★ | 55 | $ |
| Days Inn Gold Coast | 1 | ★★ | 54 | $$$ |
| Comfort Inn Lincoln Park | 1 | ★★ | 53 | $$ |
| Ohio House Motel | 3 | ★★ | 48 | $+ |
| Cass Hotel | 3 | ★½ | 42 | $$− |

## GOOD DEALS AND BAD DEALS

Having listed the nicest rooms in town, let's reorder the list to rank the best combinations of quality and value in a room. As before, the rankings are made without consideration of location or the availability of restaurant(s), recreational facilities, entertainment, and/or amenities. Once again, each lodging property is awarded a value rating on a 0–100 scale. The higher the rating, the better the value.

A reader recently complained to us that he had booked one of our top-ranked rooms in terms of value and had been very disappointed in the room. We noticed that the room the reader occupied had a quality rating of ★★½. We would remind you that the value ratings are intended to give you some sense of value received for dollars spent. A ★★½ room at $30 may have the same value rating as a ★★★★ room at $85, but that does not mean the rooms will be of comparable quality. Regardless of whether it's a good deal or not, a ★★½ room is still a ★★½ room.

Listed below are the best room buys for the money, regardless of location or star classification, based on averaged rack rates. Note that sometimes a suite can cost less than a hotel room.

| The Top 30 Best Deals in Chicago | | | | |
|---|---|---|---|---|
| Hotel | Zone | Star Rating | Quality Rating | Cost |
| 1. Marriott Suites Downers Grove | 8 | ★★★★ | 85 | $$– |
| 2. Courtyard by Marriott Wood Dale | 10 | ★★★½ | 79 | $$– |
| 3. Residence Inn by Marriott | 2 | ★★★★ | 86 | $$$– |
| 4. Hyatt on Printer's Row Chicago | 4 | ★★★★ | 89 | $$$– |
| 5. Hotel Sofitel Chicago | 2 | ★★★★½ | 91 | $$$+ |
| 6. Marriott Oak Brook | 8 | ★★★½ | 81 | $$+ |
| 7. Marriott Residence Inn Downtown | 3 | ★★★★ | 84 | $$$– |
| 8. Radisson Suites Downers Grove | 8 | ★★★★ | 84 | $$$– |
| 9. Courtyard by Marriott Oak Brook Terrace | 8 | ★★★½ | 79 | $$+ |

## The Top 30 Best Deals in Chicago (continued)

| Hotel | Zone | Star Rating | Quality Rating | Cost |
|---|---|---|---|---|
| 10. Days Inn Lakeshore | 3 | ★★★ | 68 | $$– |
| 11. Comfort Inn Downers Grove | 8 | ★★½ | 60 | $+ |
| 12. The Blackstone Hotel | 5 | ★★★ | 68 | $$– |
| 13. Hotel Allegro | 4 | ★★★★ | 88 | $$$+ |
| 14. Hyatt Regency Chicago in Illinois Center | 4 | ★★★★ | 85 | $$$+ |
| 15. Red Roof Inn Downers Grove | 8 | ★★ | 55 | $ |
| 16. House of Blues Hotel | 3 | ★★★★½ | 91 | $$$$– |
| 17. Hilton Suites Oak Brook Terrace | 8 | ★★★★ | 84 | $$$+ |
| 18. Days Inn Lincoln Park North | 1 | ★★★ | 66 | $$– |
| 19. Travelodge Chicago O'Hare | 2 | ★★½ | 57 | $+ |
| 20. Howard Johnson Express O'Hare | 2 | ★★½ | 64 | $$– |
| 21. Residence Inn by Marriott O'Hare | 2 | ★★★½ | 80 | $$$– |
| 22. Hyatt Regency O'Hare | 2 | ★★★★ | 87 | $$$+ |
| 23. Surf Hotel | 1 | ★★★ | 74 | $$+ |
| 24. Days Inn O'Hare South | 2 | ★★½ | 59 | $$– |
| 25. Hampton Inn O'Hare | 2 | ★★★ | 65 | $$ |
| 26. Marriott Suites O'Hare | 2 | ★★★★ | 87 | $$$$– |
| 27. The Ramada Congress Hotel | 4 | ★★½ | 63 | $$– |
| 28. Holiday Inn Express Downers Grove | 8 | ★★½ | 62 | $$– |
| 29. La Quinta Motor Inn Oak Brook | 8 | ★★½ | 61 | $$– |
| 30. Hampton Inn Midway Bedford Park | 6 | ★★★ | 66 | $$+ |

# Part Four

# Visiting Chicago on Business

## Convention Central, U.S.A.

Chicago, the gateway to the Midwest and the third-largest city in the United States, attracts more than six million overnight pleasure visitors a year. Tourists from all over the world come to enjoy the city's fabled attractions, ogle the legendary skyline, and enjoy the summer season's free lakefront festivals. The numbers? The Shedd Aquarium and the Museum of Science and Industry, Chicago's most popular fee-charging attractions, drew 1.8 million and 1.7 million visitors, respectively, in 1997, while the Taste of Chicago attracts 3.4 million outdoor fun-seekers each summer.

Yet not everyone visiting the Windy City comes with a tourist agenda. Chicago bills itself as the Convention Capital of the World, hosting more top trade shows than any other city in the country. The town's central geographical location, 7,000 restaurants, and 67,000 hotel rooms make it a natural destination for nearly five million trade show and convention visitors annually.

The Windy City also boasts an unparalleled location to house all those exhibitions (more than 1,500 in 1994): **McCormick Place Convention Center**, the largest convention hall in North America. Located on the shores of Lake Michigan a mile or so south of downtown, McCormick Place is a sprawling, 27-acre venue with 2.2 million square feet of exhibit space, a 4,000-seat theater, and ceilings up to 50 feet high.

In May 1993 ground was broken on a $987 million expansion of McCormick Place. Now completed, the project included the construction of the 840,000-square-foot South Building (near the intersection of the Stevenson Expressway and Lake Shore Drive), a glass-enclosed Grand Concourse linking the three buildings that comprise the convention center, a five-acre landscaped park, and renovations to existing facilities.

## OTHER BUSINESS VISITORS

In addition to conventioneers and trade show attendees bound for McCormick Place or another convention hall, other people come to conduct business at the city's wide array of manufacturing and financial firms (many of which are located in Chicago's suburbs). In addition to Chicago's four major financial exchanges (Chicago Mercantile Exchange, Chicago Stock Exchange, Chicago Board of Trade, and Chicago Board Options Exchange), the Windy City is also home to many blue-chip public companies, including Sears, Amoco, Motorola, Allstate, Sara Lee, and Caterpillar.

The city's large number of higher learning institutions (including the University of Chicago, Northwestern University, the University of Illinois at Chicago, DePaul University, the Illinois Institute of Technology, and Loyola University) attract a lot of visiting academics, college administrators, and students and their families.

## HOW THE *UNOFFICIAL GUIDE* CAN HELP

In many ways, the problems facing business visitors and conventioneers on their first trip to Chicago don't differ much from the problems of tourists intent on seeing Chicago's best-known attractions. Business visitors need to locate a convenient hotel, want to avoid the worst of the city's traffic, face the same problems of navigating a huge city, must figure out the public transportation system, and want to pinpoint Chicago's best restaurants. This book can help.

For the most part, though, business visitors aren't nearly as flexible about the timing of their visit as people who pick Chicago as a vacation destination. While we advise that the best times for visiting the city are spring and fall, the necessities of business may dictate that you pull into the Windy City in hot and humid August—or even worse, January, a month when cold temperatures and stiff winds off Lake Michigan often create double-digit minus-zero windchill readings.

Yet much of the advice and information presented in the *Unofficial Guide* is as valuable to business visitors as it is to tourists. As for our recommendations on seeing the city's many sights . . . who knows? Maybe you'll be able to squeeze a morning or an afternoon out of your busy schedule, grab this book, and spend a few hours exploring some of the attractions that draw more than six million tourists each year.

## McCORMICK PLACE CONVENTION CENTER

### It's Big . . .

Chicago's McCormick Place (2301 South Lake Shore Drive, Chicago, IL 60616; phone (312) 791-7000; fax (312) 791-6356; Web site: www.

mccormickplace.com) stands today as the largest exhibition and meeting facility in North America. With 2.2 million square feet of exposition space (1.3 million on one level), 170,000 square feet of meeting room, banquet, and ballroom space, and four theaters (including the 4,300-seat Arie Crown Theater), McCormick Place is the 800-pound gorilla of Chicago convention venues.

The original McCormick Place was the brainchild of Colonel Robert R. McCormick, a former owner of the *Chicago Tribune*. It opened in 1960 and enjoyed seven years of success before being destroyed by fire in 1967. A new, more comprehensive structure (today's East Building, soon to be renamed Lakeside Center) replaced it in 1971 and, along with the North Building added in 1986 and the South Building (completed in late 1996), comprises today's McCormick Place.

### ... and It Has Its Drawbacks

While McCormick Place is huge, its drawbacks are varied. The convention center's location on Lake Michigan destroys any vestiges of an open, uncluttered Chicago lakefront; a formidable tangle of ramps and viaducts connects the Stevenson Expressway (I-55) to Lake Shore Drive. For weary conventioneers looking for a respite from crowded exhibition halls, there is nothing, repeat nothing, within walking distance of the huge complex that can provide distractions—with the possible exception of a stroll along the bike path that follows the shoreline of placid Lake Michigan.

As one spokesman for the giant hall once commented, McCormick Place is "totally business-oriented. There is no lounge area in the lobby. There aren't even any clocks in this place. The reason this place is popular with exhibitors is once a guy is here, he's stuck." While we spotted a few clocks in the recently renovated East Building, the rest of the statement remains essentially true: The closest hotels and restaurants (with the exception of eating places inside the center) are a $5 cab ride away. Even the new food court in the South Building offers relatively few dining options—and with $7 hamburgers and $2.25 fries, it's overpriced.

McCormick Place also garnered a notorious reputation over the years for scandals and union problems. Recently, however, the trade unions involved with moving in, assembling, and moving out trade shows have agreed to some modifications of work rules to allow exhibitors to work on their own equipment. How liberal are the new rules? You be the judge. For example, full-time employees of the exhibiting company with verifiable documentation may screw in their own light bulbs if neither tools nor ladders are needed. At the American Booksellers Association show in June 1995, a certain travel publisher had a display that could be erected without any tools whatsoever. Employees of the publisher who were familiar with the design of the display could easily set the whole thing up in 45 minutes. Union representatives halted erection of the display and insisted that the task be turned over to a union carpenter. The carpenter required two hours to set up the display, one of which was considered double overtime.

## The Layout

McCormick Place is, in fact, three separate convention venues (the East Building/Lakeside Center, the North Building, and the new South Building). The three buildings are connected by the Grand Concourse, which serves as a unified entrance to McCormick Place and a link between the three structures. The spectacular, 100-foot-high, 900-foot-long pedestrian walkway includes visitor lobbies, a business center, cafes, coffee shops, specialty shops, and fountains. The glass-enclosed, multilevel concourse also crosses Lake Shore Drive to provide a seamless connection with the East Building/Lakeside Center and allows the South and North buildings' exhibit halls to be combined for a total of 1.3 million square feet of exhibition space on one level.

## Finding Your Way

Exhibit halls are named by consecutive letters. The South Building contains exhibit hall A; the North Building houses exhibit halls B (level 3) and C (level 1); and the East Building/Lakeside Center contains exhibit halls D (level 3), E (level 2), and F (level 1). Sometimes halls may be divided, for example: D1 and D2.

All meeting room numbers begin with either E, N, or S, and stand for East Building/Lakeside Center, North Building, and South Building. The next numeral (1, 2, 3, or 4) indicates the level, and the last two digits specify the exact room. To avoid confusion, no room numbers are duplicated between the three buildings. Rooms 1–25 are located in the South Building, 26–49 are in the North Building, and 50–75 are found in the East Building/Lakeside Center. Some meeting rooms with divider walls can create several smaller meeting rooms; these will have an "a," "b," "c," or "d" suffix following the number. Thus, meeting room N126b is located on the first level of the North Building, room 26.

## Parking at McCormick Place

Our advice to Chicago visitors is the same whether you're vacationing or attending a convention at McCormick Place: don't drive. Not only is the traffic congestion of epic proportions but finding a place to put your car is equally frustrating—and expensive. While McCormick Place has 8,000 adjacent parking spaces and an underground parking garage ($10 a day for

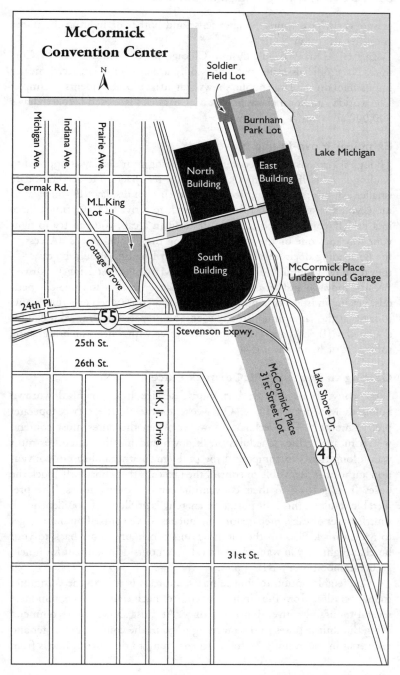

private cars), save yourself the expense and bother of fighting the traffic and leave the car at home.

In fact, so many people fly into Chicago for conventions that McCormick Place officials claim parking is only a major problem (read: nearly impossible) during large public shows that attract local residents. Example: The world's largest car show, held at McCormick Place each January, draws 900,000 auto buffs.

## Exhibitor Move-In and Move-Out

Though it's expensive, we recommend shipping your display as opposed to hauling it yourself. McCormick Place is not really set up to accommodate smaller exhibitors who want to bring in their own displays. If you elect to move yourself in and out, the easiest way is to arrive at McCormick Place in a cab. If you have too much stuff to fit in a cab, you can try to fight your way into one of the tunnels servicing the loading docks. (Access to the 65 loading docks serving the new South Building should be easier— they're above ground and accessible from Martin Luther King Jr. Drive.) Because move-in and set-up usually take place over two- to three-day periods, getting in is less of a problem than getting out (when everyone wants to leave at the same time). In any event, be prepared to drag your exhibit a long way. Try to pack everything into cases with wheels or bring along some sort of handcart or dolly.

## Getting to and from McCormick Place

Large conventions provide bus shuttle service from major downtown hotels to McCormick Place. On weekends the shuttle service operates pretty smoothly. On weekdays, however, when the buses must contend with Chicago traffic, schedules break down and meeting attendees must wait a long time. To compound the problem, neither police nor convention authorities seem able to control the taxi cabs that constantly block the buses from getting to their convention center loading zones. The predictable result of this transportation anarchy is gridlock. If you depend on shuttle buses or cabs, prepare for long queues. Give yourself an hour to get to McCormick Place in the morning and two hours to get back to your hotel at night. If you want to take a cab to an outside restaurant for lunch, go before noon or after 1:30 p.m.

A preferable option to shuttle buses and cabs is to take the commuter train, accessible from the Grand Concourse. Each train can accommodate several thousand conventioneers at once. At most shows, we recommend using the shuttle buses in the morning to go to the convention center and returning in the evening by train. To commute to downtown hotels from

McCormick Place, take the northbound train three stops to the Randolph Station at the end of the line. You will emerge from the station in the Loop area, a reasonably safe part of Chicago just south of the Chicago River. From here you can take a cab or walk to most downtown hotels in about 15 minutes. On weekdays the trains run frequently enough that you don't really need to consult a schedule. On weekends, however, the trains run up to 45 minutes apart.

## Getting to and from the Airport

**Airport Express** offers van service to and from McCormick Place and O'Hare and Midway airports. The vans depart from the main entrance at the new Grand Concourse. The fare to O'Hare is $13.75 one-way; the ride to Midway is $9.75. For reservations and more information, call (312) 454-7800.

Cab fare to O'Hare is about $30, and $23 to Midway; actual fares vary depending on traffic conditions and don't include a tip. However, the cost will be the same regardless of the number of passengers.

## Lakeside Center (The East Building)

Located east of South Lake Shore Drive on the shores of Lake Michigan, the East Building underwent a $34 million renovation and reopened in late 1997. Upgrades include new carpeting, walls, ceilings, and lighting. The renovated building also features a new business center, cafe/bar, and gift shop.

Lakeside Center is able to operate independently of the rest of McCormick Place, separating smaller and midsized events from the huge shows taking place in the North and South buildings across Lake Shore Drive. The building contains more than a half-million square feet of exhibit area and a 2,100-space underground parking garage.

Level 2, the lobby and mezzanine level, features the 283,000-square-foot Hall E1, the building's second-largest major exhibit area (which has its own loading docks). Also located on this level is the Arie Crown Theater, a site for major entertainment productions, corporate meetings, and convention keynote addresses; it's the largest theater in Chicago. Upgrades to the theater include reupholstered seats, improved acoustics, a new sound system, and theatrical lighting.

The 75,000-square-foot lobby on Level 2 accommodates registration and includes private show management offices and a press facility. The **McCormick Place Business Center** offers a wide array of services, including faxing, photocopying, equipment rentals, shipping, secretarial services,

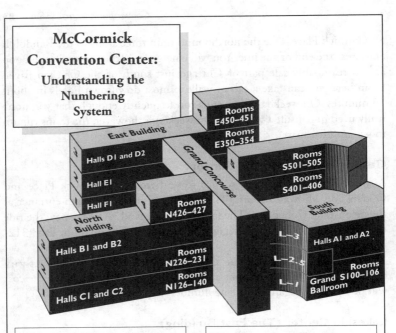

## McCormick Convention Center:
### Understanding the Numbering System

Rooms E450–451
Rooms E350–354
East Building
Halls D1 and D2
Hall E1
Hall F1
Grand Concourse
Rooms S501–505
Rooms S401–406
South Building
Rooms N426–427
North Building
Halls B1 and B2
Rooms N226–231
Rooms N126–140
Halls C1 and C2
L-3
L-2.5
L-1
Halls A1 and A2
Grand Ballroom
Rooms S100–106

---

## The McCormick Place Numbering System makes it easy to find your Exhibit Hall.

All Exhibit Halls are named alphabetically:
A, B, C, D...

The East Building has
   Hall D—Level 3
   Hall E—Level 2 and
   Hall F—Level 1

The North Building has
   Hall B—Level 3
   Hall C—Level 1

The South Building has
   Hall A—Level 3

## Finding your Meeting Room is just as simple.

All meeting rooms begin with either N, S, or E.
The Letters stand for North Building, South Building, or East Building.

The first numeral in the meeting room is 1, 2, 3, 4, or 5. This number stands for the level number.

The last two digits of the room number specify the exact room.

Some rooms have divider walls which create smaller rooms. These have an "a, b, c, or d" after the room number.

E271b

office supplies, foreign currency exchange on show management request, and more; the phone number is (312) 791-6400 and the fax number is (312) 791-6501. There's also an additional 10,000 square feet of meeting rooms on this level.

Level 3 contains a new 45,000-square-foot Grand Ballroom and Lobby that's divisible into two 22,500-square-foot rooms. Hall D, with a new north-south divider wall, can be divided into two 150,000-square-foot exhibition spaces for midsized shows. Two meeting rooms add another 58,000 square feet of space. The Grand Concourse connects Lakeside Center with the North and South buildings across Lake Shore Drive. Loading docks are located at the north end of the building.

Level 1 offers Hall F1, a 60,000-square-foot room for extra exhibits, meetings, or registration; restaurants; two meeting rooms totaling nearly 5,000 square feet; and a coffee shop. Also located on this level are the McCormick Place administrative offices and an office of the Chicago Convention and Tourism Bureau. Level 4, the small upper level, contains three meeting rooms totaling 35,000 square feet.

## The North Building

Completed in the mid-1980s and recently expanded, the North Building boasts 188,000 square feet of new exhibit space, additional escalators, a business center, and a gift shop. Level 1, the lower level, contains Hall C1, a 148,500-square-foot exhibition space that can be used independently or in conjunction with the larger upper level hall; Hall C2, a 61,000-square-foot extension area can be used for additional exhibit space or crate storage. The lower-level lobby has dedicated taxi and bus loading/unloading areas, 15 meeting rooms, and direct access to 4,000 outside parking spaces.

Level 3, the upper level, contains Hall B1, a 369,000-square-foot exhibition hall with an adjoining 127,000 square feet of space (Hall B2) that can be used for exhibits or crate storage; both halls can be combined with exhibition space in the South Building for a total of 1.3 million square feet of space on one level. A suspended roof design provides virtually column-free exhibition space and allows for clear ceiling heights of up to 40 feet. Loading docks are located at the north end of the building. The Grand Concourse connects the North Building with the South Building and the East Building (Lakeside Center).

Level 2, the mezzanine level, provides easy access to both the upper- and lower-level exhibition halls, as well as eight meeting rooms, two restaurants, and service areas. Over 50,000 square feet of lobby space is available for registration. Level 4 has two meeting rooms totaling 14,555 square feet.

## The South Building

Completed in December 1997, at a cost of $675 million, the new South Building provides an additional 840,000 square feet of exhibition space and 45 meeting rooms totaling another 170,000 square feet. It also boasts the 22,000-square-foot Vista Room and the 33,000-square-foot Grand Ballroom. Behind the scenes, the new building has 170,000 square feet of indoor crate storage and full in-floor utilities.

The new South Building has 65 concealed truck docks and a special ramp for oversized exhibits. The new weather-protected west entrance faces five-acre McCormick Square, featuring lighted, 75-foot pylons, fountains, and landscaping.

Level 3 contains Hall A1 and Hall A2, which when combined total 840,000 square feet. Loading docks are located on the east and south ends of the building. Across the Grand Concourse is Level 3 of the North Building and another half-million square feet of exhibition space.

Level 1 features the main entrance and lobby, the Grand Ballroom, and six meeting rooms; Level 2.5 contains a food court, a restaurant, a business center, a first-aid station, access to Metra commuter trains, and retail stores; Level 4 has five meeting rooms totaling about 24,000 square feet and the two-story, 22,000-square-foot Vista Room; Level 5 contains five meeting rooms with nearly 19,000 square feet of space.

## Lunch Alternatives for Convention and Trade Show Attendees

Eating at McCormick Place is a real hassle. There are too few food service vendors for the size of the facility, and even fewer table areas where you can sit and eat your hard-won victuals. Almost without exception, you must wait in one queue to obtain your food and in another to pay for it. We waited 35 minutes to get a turkey croissant sandwich and a lemonade, and then stood in line an additional 15 minutes to pay. How much? About $6 for two of us.

If you are an exhibitor, a small cooler should be an integral part of your booth. Ice frozen in a gallon milk jug lasts for days to keep drinks cold. Both exhibitors and non-exhibitors should eat breakfast before going to the show. After breakfast, but before you catch your shuttle, stop at one of the many downtown delis and pick up a sandwich, chips, fruit, and some drinks for lunch as well as for snacking throughout the day. If you want to leave campus for lunch, get in the cab queue before 11:30 a.m. or after 1:30 p.m. Getting back to McCormick Place by cab after lunch will not be a problem. For a rundown on the best restaurants for a quiet business lunch, see our section on dining and restaurants (page 304).

## Convention and Trade Show Calendar

Business visitors have a huge impact on Chicago when, say, 70,000 exhibitors and trade show attendees come into town and snatch up literally every hotel room within a 100-mile radius of the Loop. Finding a place to sleep can be nearly impossible when most of the practicing radiologists in the United States converge on Chicago for their national convention.

The good news: The large trade shows register no discernible effect on the availability of cabs and restaurant tables, or on traffic congestion; it seems that only hotel rooms and rental cars become scarce when a big convention hits town. Use the following list of major 1999 and 2000 conventions and trade shows when planning your trip to Chicago.

## Convention and Trade Show Calendar

| Dates 1999 | Convention Event | Location | Estimated Attendance |
|---|---|---|---|
| Mar. 4–7 | Big Ten Conference | United Center | 20,000 |
| Mar. 6–8 | Midwest Beauty and Trade Show | Rosemont | 65,000 |
| Mar. 15–18 | National Manufacturing Week | McCormick | 65,000 |
| Mar. 21–23 | National Assoc. for the Specialty Food Trade | McCormick | 20,000 |
| Mar. 26–30 | Transworld Housewares and Variety | Rosemont | 40,000 |
| Mar. 27–29 | GlobalShop | McCormick | 20,000 |
| April 12–15 | Converting Machinery and Materials | McCormick | 35,000 |
| April 19–22 | Comdex | McCormick | 110,000 |
| May 2–4 | Supermarket Conv. | McCormick | 33,000 |
| May 22–25 | National Restaurant Hotel-Motel Show | McCormick | 105,000 |
| May 26–28 | Data Warehousing | Navy Pier | 40,000 |
| June 7–9 | World's Trade Fair | Merchandise Mart | 45,000 |
| June 14–16 | National Cable Television Association | McCormick | 27,000 |

| Dates | Convention Event | Location | Estimated Attendance |
|-------|------------------|----------|----------------------|
| June 24–27 | International Collectible Exposition | Rosemont | 20,000 |
| July 8–12 | Transworld Housewares and Variety | Rosemont | 50,000 |
| July 9–11 | World Sports Expo | McCormick | 86,000 |
| July 16–18 | Chicago Comicon | Rosemont | 30,000 |
| July 23–27 | Chicago Gifts and Decorative Accessories | Merchandise Mart | 30,000 |
| Aug. 15–18 | National Hardware Show | McCormick | 70,000 |
| Sept. 21–23 | The Motivation Show | McCormick | 36,000 |
| Oct. 3–5 | National Association of Convenience Stores | McCormick | 30,000 |
| Oct. 13–15 | International Sanitary Supply Association | McCormick | 20,000 |
| Oct. 17–20 | Graph Expo | McCormick | 40,000 |
| Oct. 21–25 | Transworld Housewares and Variety | Rosemont | 50,000 |
| Oct. 28–31 | National Model and Hobby Show | Rosemont | 22,000 |
| Oct. 28–31 | Worldwide Food Expo | McCormick | 30,000 |
| Nov. 15–18 | Society of Mfg. Engineers | McCormick | 30,000 |
| Nov. 28– Dec. 3 | Radiological Society of North America | McCormick | 61,000 |
| Dec. 7–9 | Data Base World | Navy Pier | 40,000 |

**2000**

| Dates | Convention Event | Location | Estimated Attendance |
|-------|------------------|----------|----------------------|
| Jan. 16–19 | International Housewares Show | McCormick | 60,000 |
| Jan. 29– Feb. 2 | Chicago Gift Show | McCormick | 21,000 |
| Feb. 24–27 | Chicago Dental Society | McCormick | 35,000 |
| Mar. 13–16 | National Manufacturing Week | McCormick | 65,000 |
| Mar. 25–27 | GlobalShop | McCormick | 22,000 |
| April 7–9 | Multi Housing World | McCormick | 30,000 |
| April 17–20 | Comdex | McCormick | 110,000 |
| April 29– May 2 | American Association of Orthodontists | McCormick | 20,000 |

| Dates | Convention Event | Location | Estimated Attendance |
|-------|------------------|----------|---------------------|
| May 7–9 | Supermarket Convention | McCormick | 35,000 |
| May 20–24 | National Restaurant Hotel-Motel Show | McCormick | 105,000 |
| June 3–5 | Book Expo America | McCormick | 26,000 |
| June 19–23 | NPE—The Plastics Exposition | McCormick | 75,000 |
| July 8–11 | American Library Association | McCormick | 19,000 |
| July 14–16 | World Sports Expo | McCormick | 86,000 |
| July 29– Aug. 2 | Chicago Gift Show | McCormick | 20,000 |
| Aug. 13–16 | Nat'l Hardware Show | McCormick | 70,000 |
| Sept. 6–14 | International Mfg. Technology | McCormick | 115,000 |
| Sept. 24–27 | Graph Expo | Lakeside Center | 40,000 |
| Oct. 10–12 | The Motivation Show | McCormick | 20,000 |
| Oct. 14–17 | American Dental Association | McCormick | 30,000 |
| Oct. 22–27 | American College of Surgeons | McCormick | 19,000 |
| Nov. 5–9 | Pack Expo | McCormick | 80,000 |
| Nov. 26– Dec. 1 | Radiological Society of North America | McCormick | 61,000 |

## NAVY PIER

In the summer of 1995 Navy Pier, a Chicago landmark jutting out nearly a mile into Lake Michigan, was reopened after a nearly $200 million facelift. (The pier first opened in 1916.) Today, it's a year-round tourist attraction and convention center for exhibitions, meetings, and special events. Festival Hall, located near the east end of the pier, contains 170,000 square feet of exhibit space and 65,000 square feet of meeting rooms designed for small- and medium-sized shows. The hall is surrounded by dining spots, cruise boats, a 150-foot Ferris wheel, a shopping mall, and a drop-dead view of Chicago's skyline.

Unlike visitors to McCormick Place, conventioneers and trade show attendees at Festival Hall have access to 13,000 hotel rooms located within a few blocks, enclosed parking for 1,900 cars (which still isn't enough; we recommend either walking, public transportation, or cabs to reach Festival

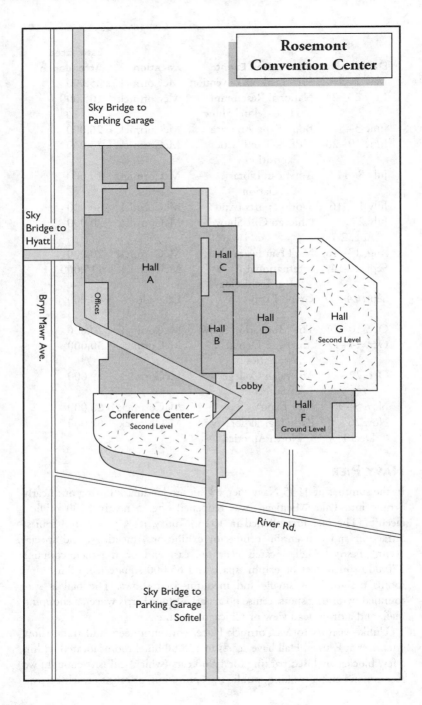

Sky Bridge to
Parking Garage

Sky
Bridge to
Hyatt

Bryn Mawr Ave.

Offices

Hall
A

Hall
C

Hall
B

Hall
D

Lobby

Hall
F
Ground Level

Hall
G
Second Level

Conference Center
Second Level

River Rd.

Sky Bridge to
Parking Garage
Sofitel

**Rosemont
Convention Center**

Hall), and on-the-pier restaurants and catering providing choices ranging from fast food to elegant dining with skyline and waterfront views. Plus, Chicago's best hotels, shopping, and restaurants are only a few blocks away. Navy Pier is literally within walking distance of the Magnificent Mile and the Loop. For more information on tourist attractions at Navy Pier, see page 268 in Part Eleven.

## Convention Facilities

Festival Hall features more than 170,000 square feet of exhibit space divisible into two areas of 113,000 square feet (Hall A) and 56,000 square feet (Hall B). Taking maximum advantage of the pier's lakefront setting, the halls boast ceiling heights of up to 60 feet (30 feet minimum) and a full range of electrical and telecommunication amenities for exhibitors' needs.

The main halls are located on the second level; small exhibitors can carry or roll show material from the public parking area on the first level. Loading docks are located on the second (main hall) level at the west end of Festival Hall. The ramp to the loading docks is reached from the drive along the north side of Navy Pier.

Meeting rooms divisible into as many as 36 separate areas total more than 48,000 square feet and are located on a mezzanine overlooking the exhibition floor and on the exhibition level. The 18,000-square-foot Grand Ballroom, featuring an 80-foot domed ceiling and panoramic water views, continues to serve banquet, performance, and special exhibit functions as it has since the pier first opened in 1916.

# ROSEMONT CONVENTION CENTER

Located northwest of downtown Chicago and five minutes from O'Hare International Airport, the Rosemont Convention Center (9301 West Bryn Mawr, Rosemont, IL 60018; phone (847) 692-2220, fax (847) 696-9700) is an exhibition venue offering convenience for fly-in exhibitors and trade show attendees—but not much else. Unfortunately, the location on the far fringe of Chicago's suburbs is strictly nowheresville in terms of easy access to the attractions, restaurants, night life, and ethnic diversity that make the Windy City a world-class destination.

Rosemont is, however, a clean, modern facility offering 600,000 square feet of flexible convention space that can accommodate a continuous 250,000-square-foot space containing up to 1,150 booths. A 5,000-space parking garage and more than 3,000 nearby hotel rooms (in the Hotel Sofitel and Hyatt Regency O'Hare) are connected by a 7,000-linear-foot, enclosed pedestrian Skybridge Network. Heated in the winter and air conditioned in the summer, it's very nice when the weather is nasty outside and you want to get to your car or one of the nearby hotels.

Rosemont handles a wide variety of both public and trade shows, ranging from the Chicago Midwest Bicycle Show (trade) to public ski shows. The center's six halls feature ceiling heights ranging from 16 to 26 feet and five drive-in freight doors. The conference center offers an additional 52,000 square feet of floor space in 34 meeting rooms located on two levels.

Other hotels close to Rosemont include the Westin Hotel O'Hare (527 rooms), Ramada Hotel O'Hare (723 rooms), Clarion International/Quality Inn at O'Hare (468 rooms), Holiday Inn O'Hare International (507 rooms), and Sheraton Gateway Suites O'Hare (300 suites). For places to eat that rise above standard hotel dining rooms, see our section on dining and restaurants (page 304).

Getting to downtown Chicago from Rosemont takes about 20 minutes by car (except during rush hours) and about 45 minutes by train. To drive, take I-90 (the Kennedy Expressway) east. You can board the CTA O'Hare Line train to downtown at either O'Hare or River Road in Rosemont (which has parking).

# Part Five
# Arriving and Getting Oriented

## Coming into the City

### BY CAR

The major route into Chicago from both the south and the north is Interstate 90/94 (better known locally as the Dan Ryan Expressway south of the Loop and the Kennedy Expressway to the north). The busy highway runs roughly north to south through Chicago (paralleling Lake Michigan) and features both express lanes (without exits) and local lanes (with exits); it's a setup guaranteed to exasperate first-time visitors.

South of the city, I-90/94 links with I-80, a major east-west route that connects Chicago to South Bend, Toledo, Cleveland, and New York City to the east, and Davenport, Des Moines, Omaha, and other points to the west. It also joins I-57, which continues south through Illinois to Kankakee and Champaign.

North of the Loop, I-90/94 changes names to become the recently expanded Kennedy Expressway; it veers northwest toward O'Hare International Airport before splitting. I-90 (now called the Northwest Tollway) continues northwest past the airport to Madison, Wisconsin, where it meets I-94.

The Stevenson Expressway (I-55) enters Chicago near McCormick Place from the southwest; this interstate begins in New Orleans and goes north through Memphis and St. Louis before crossing I-80 and passing Midway Airport to its terminus in the city at Lake Shore Drive. From the west, the Eisenhower Expressway (I-290) comes into the Loop from I-88 (the East-West Tollway) and DeKalb.

West of the city limits, two highways run north and south through Chicago's suburbs to link the major roads coming into Chicago from the south, west, and north; the highways serve as de facto "beltways" in beltwayless Chicago. I-294 (the Tri-State Tollway) starts at I-80 south of the city and crosses I-55 (the Stevenson Expressway), I-290 (the Eisenhower

Expressway), and I-90 (the Kennedy Expressway) near O'Hare. North of Chicago it merges with I-94, which goes to Milwaukee.

A few miles west of I-294, US 355 (the North-South Tollway) connects I-55 and I-88 (the East-West Tollway) to I-290 west of O'Hare; I-290 goes north to I-90, the Northwest Tollway that links Madison and Chicago.

US 41, the Edens Expressway, links I-90/94 in Chicago's North Side (north of the Chicago River) with the northern suburbs of Skokie, Highland Park, and Lake Forest before merging with I-94 south of the Wisconsin state line. Farther south in the city, US 41 becomes Lake Shore Drive, which follows Lake Michigan south past downtown and into Indiana.

## BY PLANE

O'Hare International Airport is famous (or, as some cynics snort, infamous) as the busiest airport in the world. More than 70 million people a year fly in and out of the airport located 17 miles northwest of downtown Chicago. That means there are usually enough travelers on hand to turn the huge facility into a refugee camp when lousy weather snarls air traffic and strands travelers by the thousands.

Yet O'Hare isn't the only game in town. Midway Airport, located eight miles southwest of downtown, handles about one-tenth of the passenger traffic of its big brother to the north, making it a more hassle-free point of arrival and departure for many visitors to the Windy City.

### O'Hare International Airport

Opened in 1955 and named for Congressional Medal of Honor winner Edward O'Hare (a navy pilot killed in the Battle of Midway), this sprawling airport includes four terminals connected by passenger walkways, moving sidewalks, and a "people mover" (a new, automated transit system that covers 2.7 miles of airport property).

Statistics on O'Hare are impressive. For 30 years it has been the commercial aviation capital of the world, providing service to all 50 states and many foreign countries. The mammoth airport handles more passengers and aircraft than any other field in the world; about 190,000 travelers pass through O'Hare each day and an average of 100 aircraft arrive or depart each hour. The complex covers nearly 7,700 acres and the airport serves nearly 60 commercial, commuter, and cargo airlines on a regular basis.

The airport is also connected to Chicago's subway system and is close to I-90 (the Kennedy Expressway), which goes downtown to the Loop. While O'Hare is renowned for its headache-inducing holding patterns in the air, on the ground this modern airport boasts a new international terminal, is

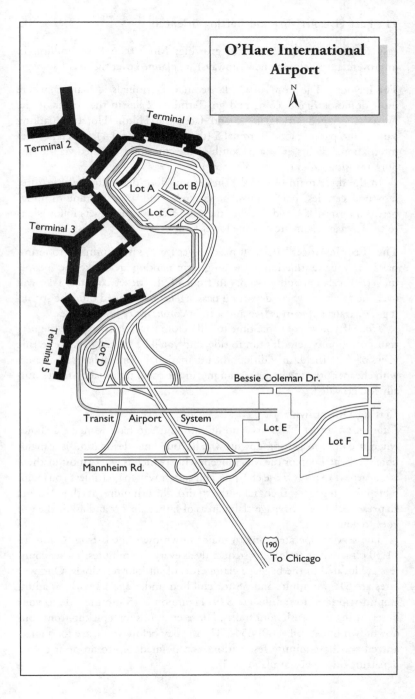
O'Hare International Airport

easy to get around, and is still growing. More than $700 million in improvements (including new runways) are planned over the next few years.

**The Layout**   The "core" of O'Hare contains terminals 1, 2, and 3, where most domestic flights come and go. Terminal 2 lies in the center of the horseshoe-shaped arrangement and faces the Hilton Hotel, a parking garage, and parking lots. Terminal 5 (there's no terminal 4), which handles international flights, is located south of the core and is reached via the Airport Transit System (or "people mover").

In the three main terminals, the second-floor departure level features fast-food eateries, bars, shops, newsstands, and a "restaurant rotunda" between terminals 2 and 3. From the gate, arriving passengers follow signs to the baggage claim area on the lower level.

**The "People Mover"**   If you need to get from, say, terminal 1 to terminal 3, or your destination is the long-term parking area, take the "people mover." Escalators and elevators in front of the ticket counters take you over the roadway where departing passengers are dropped off. The spanking new transit system is free and a train comes every few minutes.

*Hint:* If you've got some time to kill before your flight, explore the new transportation system. It's fun to ride, and you'll be treated to some terrific views of the airfield. In addition, the international terminal has a food court with cheaper prices than the restaurants in the other terminals. And it's usually less crowded.

### Getting Downtown

*Cabs and Shuttles*   Visitors who fly into Chicago have to make a choice when it comes to getting downtown. If your final destination is a major hotel near the Loop or the Magnificent Mile (which is where most of them are), Airport Express is the cheapest and easiest way to go (unless you're not schlepping luggage; then take the train). Just inquire at the **Airport Express** desk in the baggage claim areas of either airport and ask if the van goes to your hotel.

The service operates vans to major downtown hotels from 6 a.m. to 11:30 p.m. daily that leave as frequently as every five minutes. Ticket counters are located in the baggage claim areas of all four terminals. One-way fares are $16 for adults and $8 for children under age 12 with an adult. Round-trip fares for adults are $29. Figure on a 45-minute ride to your hotel during non–rush hour traffic. For reservations for a pickup from your downtown hotel, call (800) 654-7871 the day before you leave for a guaranteed seat; last-minute reservations can be made up to an hour before departure on a space-available basis.

If your hotel isn't served by Airport Express, taxis, buses, hotel vans, and rental car pickups are located outside the lower-level baggage areas. Cab fares to downtown run about $28 one-way for the normal travel time of 30 minutes; share-the-ride cabs cost $15 per person for a taxi shared between two to four passengers headed downtown. Allow at least an hour and a half during rush hour and expect to pay a higher fare for the longer cab ride.

*Public Transportation*  If you're traveling light, the Chicago Transit Authority (CTA) Blue Line train terminal is located in front of and beneath Terminal 2 (follow signs that read "Trains to Downtown"); it's about a 40-minute trip to the Loop that costs $1.50 one-way. Trains leave about every 10 minutes weekdays and about every 15 minutes early evenings and weekends. Unfortunately, there's no place to store luggage on the rapid-transit trains (although one piece of luggage is usually manageable, as many airline employees attest). For more information, call (312) 836-7000.

*Driving*  If you're renting a car and driving, getting to the Loop is pretty easy. Follow signs out of the airport to I-90 east, which puts you on the recently revamped Kennedy Expressway; it's a straight, 18-mile ride to downtown that takes about a half hour (longer during rush hour—and Friday afternoons are the worst). As you approach the city, Chicago's distinctive skyline, anchored by the John Hancock Center on the left and the Sears Tower on the right, comes into view—if it's not raining.

If you're headed for the Loop, move into the right lane as you approach the tunnel (just before the city center) and get ready to exit as you come out of the tunnel. Take the Ohio Street exit to get to the north downtown area. The last of four exits to downtown is the Congress Parkway (where I-290 west, the Eisenhower Expressway, meets the Kennedy Expressway) to South Loop; miss it and you're on your way to Indiana. Taking the Congress Parkway exit scoots you *through* the U.S. post office building to the south edge of the Loop; South Michigan Avenue and South Lake Shore Drive lie straight ahead. For more information on getting around Chicago, see Part Six (page 121).

*Visitor Services*  Twenty-six multilingual information specialists are on hand to provide information and translation assistance to travelers. Four **airport information** booths are located throughout the airport: on the lower levels of terminals 1, 2, and 3, and outside the lower-level customs area in terminal 5. The booths are open daily from 8:15 a.m. to 8 p.m. For more information, call the main airport number at (773) 686-2200.

The **U.S. Postal Service** operates an office in terminal 2 on the upper level. Hours are 7 a.m. to 7 p.m. weekdays. **Teletext phones for the hearing impaired** are located next to the airport information booths in the three domestic terminals (lower level) and outside the customs area in the international terminal. More teletext phones are located in phone banks throughout the airport.

A **foreign currency exchange** is located in terminal 5 on the lower level near McDonald's. Hours are 9 a.m. to 8 p.m. daily. A second exchange is located on the upper level, past the security checkpoint across from gate M9. Hours are 8 a.m. to 6 p.m. daily. A satellite facility is located in terminal 3 across from gate K11; hours are 10 a.m. to 7:30 p.m. daily.

A **duty free shop,** located in terminal 5 in the center court on the upper level, offers a wide range of merchandise free of export duties and taxes. Hours are 7 a.m. to 8 p.m. daily; the shop frequently stays open beyond regular hours to serve other international flights. Satellite shops are also located in terminal 1 near gate C18 and in terminal 3 across from gate K11; hours vary according to flight times.

**Automatic teller machines** are located on the upper levels of terminals 1, 2, and 3 near the concourse entrances (airside) and on the upper and lower terminals of terminal 5.

**Kids on the Fly** is an exhibit for youngsters operated by the Chicago Children's Museum. Centrally located in Terminal 2 (near the security checkpoint), the 2,205-square-foot interactive playground lets children ages 1–12 burn off excess energy as they explore a kid-sized air traffic control tower, a ceiling-high model of the Sears Tower, a cargo plane, and a fantasy helicopter. It's free and open to all visitors during regular flight hours and to ticketed passengers after 10 p.m.

**Parking**   O'Hare provides more than 10,000 spaces in short- and long-term parking lots and a garage. Short-term parking in the parking garage and in outside lots B and C costs $3 for an hour or less, with a maximum fee of $18 for 24 hours. Rates in short-term lot D (next to the international terminal) are $3 for an hour or less, and $2 for each additional hour. The maximum fee for 24 hours is $18.

Long-term parking in lots E (served by the "people mover") and F costs $2 for an hour or less and $1 for each additional hour; the maximum fee per day in lot E is $9. Current parking lot status and information can be heard on ParkNet, 800 AM on the radio dial. For more information, call (800) 54-PK-ORD.

## Midway Airport

Located in a bungalow community eight miles southwest of downtown Chicago, this airport is everything O'Hare isn't: small, convenient, and uncongested. It's an airport right out of the '50s. Our advice: If you can get a direct flight into Midway, take it. Why fight the hassles of the world's busiest airport?

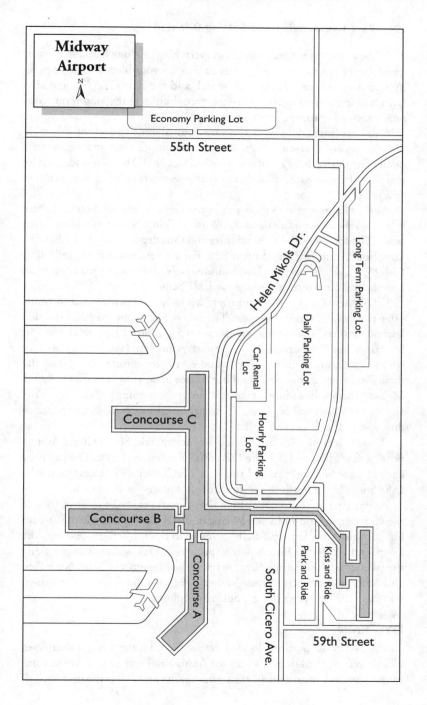

Midway
Airport

N

Economy Parking Lot

55th Street

Helen Mikols Dr.

Long Term Parking Lot

Daily Parking Lot

Car Rental Lot

Concourse C

Hourly Parking Lot

Concourse B

Kiss and Ride

Park and Ride

Concourse A

South Cicero Ave.

59th Street

Midway has three concourses, and everything's on one level. From your gate follow signs to the baggage area to pick up your bags. Passenger pick-up and drop-off, taxis, buses, car rental, and the new CTA Orange Line train station are right outside the door. Free shuttles to the long-term economy parking lot arrive every 15 minutes.

Cab fares from Midway to downtown run about $18 and the ride takes 20 minutes (in non–rush hour traffic; allow more time and figure on a higher fare during heavy traffic and/or bad weather). Share-the-ride cabs let you split the ride with up to three other passengers going downtown; the cost is $10 per person.

Airport Express offers van service to and from downtown hotels; the fare is $11 one-way for adults and $7.75 for children under age 12 with an adult. The trip takes about 30 minutes and vans depart every 15 to 20 minutes. Round-trip fare for adults is $20. For a return reservation, call (800) 654-7871 a day in advance. Last-minute reservations can be made up to an hour before departure on a space-available basis.

CTA's new Orange Line connects Midway to downtown, and trains offer plenty of room for luggage. The fare is $1.50 one-way and the ride lasts 30 minutes. Trains run every day from 5 a.m. to 11 p.m. weekdays and Saturdays, and 7:30 a.m. to 11 p.m. Sundays and holidays. Trains run every six to eight minutes in rush hours and every ten minutes the rest of the time. Weekday *morning* rush hour bus service to downtown is via the #99M Midway Express bus (do *not* take this bus in the evening). Pick it up at the airport's center entrance. The #62 Archer bus provides 24-hour service to downtown. Bus fares are $1.50.

If you're renting a car and driving downtown, take South Cicero Avenue north a few miles to I-55 (the Stevenson Expressway) east. The highway ends at Lake Shore Drive and the huge McCormick Place complex; take Lake Shore Drive north to get downtown or places farther north.

As you bear left onto Lake Shore Drive, you're treated to a great view of the Chicago skyline and Lake Michigan. After passing the Field Museum on the right, turn left onto Balbo Avenue to reach Michigan Avenue, the Loop, and I-290 (the Eisenhower Expressway). Or continue straight along the lake across the Chicago River to reach the Magnificent Mile, Navy Pier, and other points north. From Midway, the 10-mile drive to downtown takes about 20 minutes (longer during rush hour).

## BY TRAIN

Chicago's **Union Station,** located across the Chicago River a couple of blocks west of the Loop, is a hub for Amtrak rail service and Metra commuter service. Unfortunately, the train station's location is inconvenient—

it's not particularly close to anything (say, major hotels, tourist attractions, or subway stations)—and its layout is confusing.

Amtrak trains arrive on the concourse level of the station. After picking up your baggage, head for the taxi stand near the north concourse (Adams Street exit). Alas, Chicago's fabled "El" is several blocks to the east—too far to walk if you're carrying luggage. The only public transportation option is the #151 bus—also not a good idea if you're lugging a suitcase or two—which you can catch outside on Canal Street. The bus goes through the Loop and up North Michigan Avenue. To sum up: If you're not being picked up by someone in a car, a cab is your best option for getting out of Union Station.

# Getting Oriented

The operative word for Chicago, currently the nation's third-largest city, is "big."

Located a third of the way between the east and west coasts of the United States, the Windy City covers 227 square miles and stretches 33 miles along the southwestern coastline of Lake Michigan (the second-largest of the five Great Lakes, after Lake Superior). With a population of just under three million—in a metropolitan area of over six million—Chicago is not only the largest city in Illinois, it's the de facto economic and cultural capital of the Midwest. (But not the state capital; the state house is 200 miles away in Springfield.)

## A Geography Lesson

Chicago is located in the northeast corner of Illinois, a large Midwestern state bordered by (starting clockwise southeast of the city) Indiana, Kentucky, Missouri, Iowa, and Wisconsin; Michigan is to the east and north across the eponymous lake. Most of the land that surrounds the city is flat—just like most of the Midwest—a fact, theorists say, that may explain the city's passion for tall buildings and the dizzying, easily recognized skyline (which includes Sears Tower, the tallest office building in the western hemisphere).

To the southeast, just past the city line on the southern tip of Lake Michigan, lies the gritty industrial town of Gary, Indiana. North along the lake the city merges with the comfortable suburban enclave of Evanston (home of Northwestern University); farther north, but still within commuting range of Chicago, are Highland Park and Waukegan. The Wisconsin state line lies about 40 miles north of the Loop, the heart of downtown Chicago.

The closest major city is Milwaukee, a blue-collar town on Lake Michigan 90 miles to the north. Other big Midwestern cities arrayed around Chicago are Detroit (290 miles to the east), Indianapolis (180 miles to the southeast), St. Louis (300 miles to the southwest), Des Moines (360 miles to the west), and Minneapolis/St. Paul (410 miles to the northwest).

## CHICAGO'S LAYOUT

### River and Lake

The other major geographic feature of Chicago is the narrow Chicago River, which meets Lake Michigan downtown along the carefully preserved lakefront (which is lined with parks and a wildly popular bike and jogging trail, not factories and wharves). The direction of the river was reversed around 1900 and today flows away from Lake Michigan downstate to the Illinois River; it's a major shipping route to the Gulf of Mexico. Boat tours on the Chicago River provide some of the best views of the city's fabled architecture.

### The Loop and Grant Park

Tucked south and east of a bend in the river is the Loop, Chicago's downtown core of skyscrapers, government buildings, financial and trading institutions, office buildings, hotels, and retail establishments. The name comes from the elevated train (the "El") that circles the downtown business district.

A couple of blocks east of the Loop and hugging Lake Michigan is Grant Park, a barrier of green where millions of Chicagoans and visitors flock each summer to enjoy a variety of outdoor events and music festivals. Grant Park also provides a campus-like setting for some of the city's largest museums, colorful Buckingham Fountain, and many softball fields. The view of the Chicago skyline from the park is spectacular.

### Lake Shore Drive

Running north and south through Grant Park and along Lake Michigan is Lake Shore Drive. Although the multilane road's high speeds and congestion usually result in a white-knuckled driving experience for first-time visitors, a cruise along the venerable highway provides spectacular vistas of the Chicago skyline, yacht basins, parks full of trees and greenery, beaches, and ocean-like Lake Michigan stretching east to the horizon. (The views at night are even more mind-boggling.) It's also a major north-south corridor through the city, which is longer than it is wide.

In late 1996 Lake Shore Drive was relocated to the west of the Field Museum and Soldier Field. In 1997, the old lanes to the east were demolished and transformed into ten acres of new parkland, creating a traffic-free museum campus for the Field Museum, the Adler Planetarium, and the Shedd Aquarium. With its paths, bikeways, a pedestrian concourse under Lake Shore Drive serving as a gateway to the Museum Campus, and extensive landscaping, this new lakefront park provides Chicagoans and visitors with another place to stroll, bike, run, and relax as they take in the views. For drivers, an extensive system of new directional signs was installed.

## Near North

North of the Chicago River are two areas popular with out-of-town visitors: the Magnificent Mile (a glitzy strip of North Michigan Avenue full of the city's toniest shops and galleries) and River North (Chicago's premier night club and restaurant district). Renovated and reopened in 1995 and jutting out into Lake Michigan is Navy Pier, featuring amusement rides, a shopping mall, clubs and restaurants, and a convention center. Farther north are the Gold Coast, an enclave of exclusive homes (and a great walking destination), and Lincoln Park, often called Chicago's "Central Park." It's surrounded by a residential neighborhood full of high-rises offering spectacular lake views and is home to the most visited zoo in the United States.

## South and West of the Loop

South of the Loop along the lake is McCormick Place, North America's largest (and recently expanded) convention venue. Farther south is where visitors will find the huge Museum of Industry and Science, and Hyde Park, home of the beautiful University of Chicago campus (and more museums).

Some sections of the city west of downtown encompass the most economically distressed—and for out-of-town visitors, unsafe—neighborhoods. Yet not-to-be-missed attractions west of the Loop include Hull House (where Nobel Prize winner Jane Addams gave turn-of-the-century Chicago immigrants a leg up on the American dream), ethnic restaurants in Greektown and Little Italy, huge Garfield Park Conservatory, and, just beyond the city line, Oak Park (hometown of famed architect Frank Lloyd Wright and Nobel-laureate novelist Ernest Hemingway).

Scattered throughout the city to the north, west, and south of downtown are a wide array of urban neighborhoods featuring shops, museums, and dining that reflect the ethnic diversity of the Windy City; see page 229 for descriptions and locations. Beyond the city limits are more attractions worth the drive: Brookfield Zoo, Chicago Botanic Garden, and the Morton

Arboretum are all less than an hour from downtown Chicago (allow more time in rush hour traffic).

## THE MAJOR HIGHWAYS

The major interstate routes to Chicago's Loop are I-90/94 (better known to Chicagoans as the Dan Ryan Expressway south of downtown and the Kennedy Expressway to the north and west), I-290 (the Eisenhower Expressway), and I-55 (the Stevenson Expressway, which ends about a mile south of downtown at McCormick Place).

West of the city, I-294 (the Tri-State Tollway) parallels Lake Michigan through Chicago's suburbs as it heads north and links I-80 (a major transcontinental route south of the city) to I-90 (which goes to Milwaukee). I-294 also skirts O'Hare International Airport, where it intersects with I-90 (which links Chicago and Madison, Wisconsin).

## A WORD ABOUT DRIVING: DON'T

With four major interstates converging downtown at or near the Loop, entering the city on one of them makes for a very, uh, *interesting* driving experience, especially if it's your first visit to Chicago . . . and it's rush hour.

Our advice: If you're staying in a downtown hotel, don't drive. Why? The congestion in America's third-largest city is unrelenting: morning and evening rush hour traffic reports endlessly list backups, accidents, and delays occurring throughout the metropolitan area. And parking? Forget it. Chicago is notorious for its lack of convenient and/or affordable places to park.

Whether you're in town for business or pleasure, spare yourself the frustration of battling traffic, lanes that change direction depending on the time of day, and a tangle of highways. Instead, ride Chicago's extensive public transportation systems, take airport vans to and from downtown hotels, and take advantage of an abundance of taxis to get around town. (For more information on how to negotiate Chicago without a car, see page 121.)

## FINDING YOUR WAY AROUND CHICAGO

Chicago's sheer size can be overwhelming, but here's some good news for visitors: The city is a relentlessly "right-angle" town, a characteristic that's invaluable in finding your way around. Except for the rare diagonal street, Chicago is laid out numerically on a grid, with State and Madison Streets (in the Loop) intersecting at the zero point.

It works like this: North Side Chicago is north of Madison Street and South Side is south of it. The West Side, logically enough, is west of State Street. And the East Side? It hardly exists; most of what could be termed "East Side" is Lake Michigan, since State Street is only a few blocks west of the lakefront.

Street numbers run in increments of 100 per block, with eight blocks to the mile. (Folks who like mental arithmetic can have fun figuring distances using street addresses.) Generally speaking, North Side streets and north-south streets on the South Side have names (Michigan Avenue, Erie Street), while east-west streets on the South Side usually are numbered (for example, the popular Museum of Science and Industry is at 57th Street and Lake Shore Drive).

After you've tried it a few times, navigating Chicago's grid gets to be fun (at least on weekends, when traffic is light). Locating, say, the Balzekas Museum of Lithuanian Culture is a snap. The address, 6500 South Pulaski Road, tells you the museum is at the corner of South Pulaski and 65th Street. It also helps that many (but not all) major avenues traverse the entire city from north to south. Like old friends, names such as Western, Cermak, Halsted, and Clark crop up over and over as you explore the city.

One last note that will help you stay oriented when exploring Chicago: Keep in mind that if the street numbers are going up, you're headed away from downtown; if they're going down, you're moving toward the center of the city.

## WHERE TO FIND TOURIST INFORMATION IN CHICAGO

If you're short on maps or need more information on sight-seeing, hotels, shopping, or other activities in and around Chicago, there are several places to stop and pick up maps and brochures:

- In downtown Chicago, the Visitor Information Center located in the Randolph Lobby of the **Chicago Cultural Center** dispenses literature and advice to tourists. Just off the lobby, the Welcome Center provides orientation with videos and displays. Open Monday through Friday 10 a.m. to 6 p.m., Saturday 10 a.m. to 5 p.m., and Sunday 11 a.m. to 5 p.m. Closed on major holidays. 78 East Washington Street (at Michigan Avenue), Chicago, IL 60602; phone (312) 744-2400.

- On the Magnificent Mile north of the Loop, the **Water Tower Welcome Center** at Chicago and Michigan avenues (you can't miss it; the tower is one of two structures that survived the Great Fire of 1871) provides tourist information, maps, hotel reservations, and advice. In addition, the Center stocks plentiful information on tourist attractions throughout Illinois. The Center is open Monday through Friday 9:30 a.m. to 6 p.m., Saturday 10 a.m. to 6 p.m., and Sunday 11 a.m. to 5 p.m.

■ At Navy Pier, 700 East Grand Avenue, the **Illinois Market Place Visitor Information Center** is open Monday through Thursday 10 a.m. to 8 p.m., Friday and Saturday 10 a.m. to 11 p.m., and Sunday 10 a.m. to 7 p.m.

■ In suburban Oak Park, visitors interested in touring the former residences of hometown heros Frank Lloyd Wright and Ernest Hemingway should make their first stop at the **Oak Park Visitor Center,** 158 Forest Avenue, phone (708) 848-1500. Visitors can park for free in the adjacent parking garage on weekends and can purchase tickets and pick up free maps in the visitor center. Open daily 10 a.m. to 4 p.m.

# Things the Natives Already Know

## CHICAGO CUSTOMS AND PROTOCOL

Chicagoans have earned a well-deserved reputation for friendliness and often display a degree of forwardness that can put off foreigners and visitors from more formal parts of our country. Sometimes Chicago natives come off as brash or blunt, since many value getting directly to the point. And that's mostly good news for tourists, who can count on plenty of help finding a destination when, say, riding a crowded rush hour bus. The moral is, don't hesitate to ask the natives for assistance.

**Eating in Restaurants**    By and large, casual is the byword when dining in the Windy City. Only the most chichi Chicago eateries require men to wear a jacket or prohibit ladies from wearing shorts or tank tops. Even swank places such as the Ritz-Carlton have dropped any requirement that men wear a tie at dinner.

Although people tend to get more dressed up for dinner downtown, you'll still find plenty of casual restaurants (the ones at North Pier, for example). Just about all ethnic restaurants beyond downtown have relaxed (read: nonexistent) dress codes. If in doubt, call ahead—or dress "chic casual": nice looking, but no T-shirts or running shoes.

**Tipping**   Is the tip you normally leave at home appropriate in Chicago? The answer is yes. Just bear in mind that a tip is a reward for good service. Here are some guidelines:

*Porters and Skycaps*   A dollar a bag.

*Cab Drivers*   A lot depends on service and courtesy. If the fare is less than $8, give the driver the change and a dollar. Example: If the fare is $4.50 give the cabbie 50 cents and a buck. If the fare is more than $8, give the driver the change and $2. If you ask the cabbie to take you only a block or two, the fare will be small, but your tip should be large ($3 to $5) to make up for his or her wait in line and to partially compensate him or her for missing a better-paying fare. Add an extra dollar to your tip if the driver handles a lot of luggage.

*Parking Valets*   $2 is correct if the valet is courteous and demonstrates some hustle. A dollar will do if the service is just OK. Pay only when you check your car out, not when you leave it.

*Bellmen and Doormen*   When a bellman greets you at your car with a rolling luggage cart and handles all of your bags, $5 is about right. The more luggage you carry yourself, of course, the less you should tip. Add another $1 or $2 if the bellman opens your room. For calling a taxi, tip the doorman 50 cents to a dollar.

*Waiters*   Whether in a coffee shop, an upscale eatery, or ordering room service from the hotel kitchen, the standard gratuity ranges from 15–20% of the tab, before sales tax. At a buffet or brunch where you serve yourself, leave a dollar or two for the person who brings your drinks. Some restaurants, however, are adopting the European custom of automatically adding a 15% gratuity to the bill, so check before leaving a cash tip.

*Cocktail Waiters/Bartenders*   Here you tip by the round. For two people, a dollar a round; for more than two people, $2 a round. For a large group, use your judgment. Is everyone drinking beer, or is the order long and complicated? Tip accordingly.

*Hotel Maids*   On checking out, leave a dollar or two per day for each day of your stay, provided the service was good.

**How to Look and Sound Like a Native**   Good news: Chicagoans, by and large, are unpretentious, down-to-earth realists who, for example, take perverse pride in their city government's legendary corruptness. This town shuns phoniness, so visitors who want to blend in only need to be themselves. Yet, if it's important to you not to look like A Visitor on Holiday in the Windy City, we offer the following advice:

1. Don't crash diet. Except for razor-thin fashion victims haunting the over-priced boutiques along the Magnificent Mile, Chicagoans disdain the frou-frou svelteness that's the norm in New York or Los Angeles. Being overweight in Chicago isn't a social faux pas—this is, after all, a town renowned for its pizza, Italian beef and sausage sandwiches, and other artery-clogging, waistband-expanding "hand food."

2. Be obsessive, if not maniacal, about the Cubbies, White Sox, Bears, Bulls, and Blackhawks.

3. Talk through your nose. Master the flat phonetics of the Midwest: give the letter "a" a harsh sound and throw in a few "dem's" and "dose's" when conversing with natives.

4. Occasionally, for no apparent reason, erupt in your best attempt at a Chicago accent, "Yah, but the city works."

5. Never, under any circumstances, put ketchup on a Chicago-style hot dog.

6. Never eat in Michael Jordan's restaurant.

## PUBLICATIONS FOR VISITORS

Chicago has two major daily newspapers, the *Chicago Tribune* and the *Chicago Sun-Times*. Both are morning papers that cover local, national, and international news, and have Friday editions with up-to-the-minute information on entertainment for the weekend. The *Trib* is home turf of movie reviewer Gene Siskel; the other half of TV's ubiquitous movie duo is Roger Ebert at the *Sun-Times*. Grab a Friday edition of both papers at a hometown newsstand before coming to Chicago for the weekend.

An even better source for entertainment and arts listings is the weekly *Reader,* a free tabloid that starts showing up on downtown newsstands (as well as a wide variety of clubs, bars, bookstores, coffee cafes, and shops) on Thursday afternoons. *New City,* another "alternative" weekly published on Thursdays, irreverently examines Chicago news, art, and entertainment.

*Chicago* is a monthly magazine that's strong on lists (top 20 restaurants, etc.) and provides a calendar of events, dining information, and feature articles. *Windy City Sports* is a free monthly guide to fitness and outdoor recreation that highlights seasonal sports such as skiing, bicycling, running, inline skating, and sailboarding. Pick up a copy at bike shops and outdoors outfitters.

*Chicago Social* highlights Chicago's beautiful people and visiting celebs as they scarf canapés at the town's top fund-raising social events; the free monthly also contains articles on dining and fashion. Pick up a copy at swank shops, hair salons, and cafes up and down the Gold Coast. At the other end of the social spectrum, *StreetWise* is published twice monthly and is sold by homeless and formerly homeless men and women for a dollar (look for identifying vendor badges). The tabloid paper includes features, a calendar of events, local sports, poetry, and film reviews.

## CHICAGO ON THE AIR

Aside from the usual babble of format rock, talk, easy listening, and country music stations, Chicago is home to a few radio stations that really stand out for high-quality broadcasting. Tune in to what hip Chicagoans listen to, as listed below:

| Chicago's High-Quality Radio Stations | | |
| --- | --- | --- |
| **Format** | **Frequency** | **Station** |
| Jazz | 95.5 FM | WNUA |
| NPR, News, Jazz | 91.5 FM | WBEZ |
| Classical | 98.7 FM | WFMT |
| Progressive Rock | 93.1 FM | WXRT |
| Classical | 97.1 FM | WNIB |

## ACCESS FOR THE DISABLED

Like most large U.S. cities, Chicago tries to make itself accessible to folks with physical handicaps. Most museums and restaurants, for example, feature wheelchair access. At the **Art Institute of Chicago,** wheelchair access is through the Columbus Drive (east) entrance, and a limited number of wheelchairs and strollers are available for free at both main entrances. Most public areas associated with the **Chicago Historical**

**Society** are accessible to the disabled, and a limited number of wheelchairs are also available. Parking for disabled visitors is provided in the parking lot adjacent to the building.

The **Field Museum** has wheelchairs available on the ground level near the West Entrance and first-floor North Door, and the **Adler Planetarium** has wheelchair-accessible rest rooms on the first floor (down the vending machine hallway). Elevators are available for folks in wheelchairs, with strollers, or with other special needs.

**Chicago Botanic Garden** has wheelchairs available at the Information Desks in the Gateway and Education Centers. Accessible parking is located in parking lots #1, #2, and #3. The Orientation Center is equipped with assistive listening devices, closed caption monitors, and raised letters. **Brookfield Zoo** provides assistive listening devices in the Administration Building near South Gate and in the Discovery Center near the North Gate. A telecommunication device for the deaf (TDD) is also available in the Administration Building.

## Services for Disabled People

The **City of Chicago Department on Disability** offers information and reference: (312) 746-5773 and (312) 744-6777 (TDD only). The city also provides a 24-hour information hotline for the hearing impaired: (312) 744-8599 (TDD).

Handicapped visitors can arrange door-to-door transportation from the airport or train station to their hotel, as well as transportation anywhere in the city in special vans; the rate is $1.50 each time you board. Call the Chicago Transportation Authority Special Services Division at (312) 432-7025 (432-7116, TTY) for more information.

The **Chicago Transit Authority** operates 79 routes with lift-equipped buses; look for the blue wheelchair symbol displayed in the first bus/last bus chart on the Chicago Transit map. For routes, fares, schedules, and a copy of the latest Chicago Transit map, call (312) 836-7000 from 5 a.m. to 1 a.m. The TDD number is (800) 439-2202. Some, but not all, train stations are handicapped accessible. Here's the list; call (312) 836-7000 for hours of operation:

- Blue Line (O'Hare-Congress-Douglas): O'Hare, Rosemont, Cumberland, Harlem/Higgins, Clark/Lake (Lake transfer), Jackson, Polk, 18th, Cicero/Cermak, and Forest Park.

- Red Line (Howard-Dan Ryan): Loyola, Granville, Addison, Jackson, Roosevelt, and 79th.

- Orange Line (Midway): All stations between Midway Airport and Roosevelt; also Clark/Lake and Washington/Wells.

- Brown Line (Ravenswood): Kimball, Western, Clark/Lake, Washington/Wells, and Merchandise Mart.

- Purple Line (Evanston): Linden, Davis, Merchandise Mart, Clark/Lake, and Washington/Wells.

- Yellow Line (Skokie).

- Green Line (Lake Street/Jackson Park): East 63rd–Cottage Grove, 51st, 47th, 43rd, 35-Bronzeville-ITT, King Drive, Roosevelt, Clark/Lake, California, Kedzie, and Central.

## TIME ZONE

Chicago is located in the Central Time Zone, which puts Windy City clocks one hour behind New York, two hours ahead of the West Coast, an hour ahead of the Rocky Mountains, and six hours behind Greenwich Mean Time.

## PHONES

The Chicago area is served by five area codes: (312) in the Loop and downtown, (773) for the rest of the city, (630) for the far western suburbs, (708) for the near western and southern suburbs, and (847) for the northern suburbs. Calls from pay phones are 35 cents. To dial out of Chicago to the suburbs, dial 1, then the appropriate area code followed by the phone number you want to reach. While the initial call to the suburbs costs the same as an intra-city call, keep some change handy. On longer calls you may have to plug in more coins or get disconnected. If you're calling into the city from the suburbs, dial 1, then (312) or (773), followed by the number.

## LIQUOR, TAXES, AND SMOKING

In Chicago the legal drinking age is 21, and no store may sell alcoholic beverages before noon on Sundays. The local sales tax is 8%, and the combined sales and hotel room tax is 14.9%. City laws require all restaurants to offer nonsmoking sections. In addition, smoking is prohibited in theaters, public buildings, and on public transportation.

# How to Avoid Crime and Keep Safe in Public Places

## CRIME IN CHICAGO

For most folks, Chicago and crime are synonymous. It's mostly left over from the Prohibition era, when bootlegger Al Capone and arch-gangster John Dillinger earned Chicago worldwide notoriety. Go almost anyplace in the world and mention Chicago and the response will likely be a pantomimed machine gun and a "rat-a-tat-tat" flourish.

The truth is, Chicago wasn't all that dangerous for John Q. Public in the 1920s. History shows that only 75 hoodlums went down in gang warfare in 1926—about 10% of today's annual murder count. Sadly, although metropolitan Chicago has about the same population as it did in the Roaring Twenties, the average person today is much more likely to become a crime statistic.

## PLACES TO AVOID

Like virtually all large U.S. cities, Chicago has its ghettoes, including the nation's most infamous: the Cabrini-Green projects, a series of high-rises that stand as a monument to the failure of mid-twentieth-century urban planning. Located in Chicago's West Side, the housing project is an island of chronically unemployed and underemployed tenants, a segregated slum that is regularly regarded as one of America's worst neighborhoods.

Much of the South Side and Near West Side contain areas that most visitors should avoid; exceptions include Chinatown, Hyde Park, and Pullman. On the North Side, glitzy neighborhoods are often next door to areas of high crime, so don't wander too far afield. Often in Chicago, relative safety is a question of day or night; the lakefront, public parks, Loop, and River North are active during the day, but except around restaurants and clubs, are deserted at night. Take a cab or drive directly to nighttime destinations in these areas.

Safe areas at virtually any time of the day or night include the Magnificent Mile and Oak, Rush, and Division Streets in the Gold Coast community. Just stay within well-lighted areas, and keep your eyes peeled for shady-looking characters who may have designs on your purse or billfold. Pickpockets, by the way, are especially active in downtown shopping crowds during the holiday season and on subway trains to and from O'Hare.

While we recommend that visitors stay away from unsafe public housing projects and other economically deprived areas, keep in mind that crime can happen anywhere. And Chicago, unfortunately, is an innovator when it comes to new ways of victimizing people; this is where carjacking and "smash and grab"—breaking a car window and snatching a purse off the seat—first gained national notoriety. Here are some security procedures that can help you avoid becoming a crime victim.

## CRIME PREVENTION PLANNING

Random violence and street crime are facts of life in any large city. You've got to be cautious and alert, and plan ahead. Police are rarely able to actually foil a crime in progress. When you are out and about you must assume that you must use caution because you are on your own; if you run into trouble, it's unlikely that police or anyone else will be able to come to your rescue. You must give some advance thought to the ugly scenarios that might occur, and consider both preventive measures that will keep you out of harm's way and an escape plan just in case.

Not being a victim of street crime sort of parallels the survival of the fittest theory. Just as a lion stalks the weakest member of the antelope herd, muggers and thieves target the easiest victims. Simply put, no matter where you are or what you are doing, you want potential felons to think of you as a bad risk.

**On the Street** For starters, you seldom represent an appealing target if you are with other people. Second, if you must go out alone, act alert, and always keep at least one arm and hand free. Felons gravitate toward the preoccupied, the kind found plodding along staring at the sidewalk, with both arms encumbered by briefcases or packages. Visible jewelry (on either men or women) attracts the wrong kind of attention. Men, keep your billfolds in your *front* trouser or coat pocket, or in a fanny pack. Women, keep your purses tucked tightly under your arm; if you're wearing a jacket, put it on *over* your shoulder bag strap.

Here's another tip: Carry two wallets. Include one inexpensive one, carried in your hip pocket, containing about $20 in cash and some expired credit cards. This is the one you hand over if you're accosted. Your real credit cards and the bulk of whatever cash you have should be in either a money clip or a second wallet hidden elsewhere on your person. Women can carry a fake wallet in their purses, and keep the real one in a pocket or money belt.

*If You're Approached* Police will tell you that a felon has the least amount of control over his intended victim during the first few moments of his approach. A good strategy, therefore, is to short-circuit the crime as quickly as possible. If a felon starts by demanding your money, for instance, quickly take out your billfold (preferably your fake one), and hurl it in one direction while you run shouting for help in the opposite direction. Most likely, the felon would rather collect your billfold than pursue you. If you hand over your wallet and just stand there, the felon will likely ask for your watch and jewelry next. If you're a woman, the longer you hang around, the greater your vulnerability to personal injury or rape.

*Secondary Crime Scenes*   Under no circumstances, police warn, should you ever allow yourself to be taken to another location—a "secondary crime scene" in police jargon. This move, they explain, provides the felon more privacy and consequently more control. A felon can rob you on the street very quickly and efficiently. If he tries to remove you to another location, whether by car or on foot, it certainly indicates that he has more in mind than robbery. Even if the felon has a gun or knife, your chances are infinitely better running away. If the felon grabs your purse, let him have it. If he grabs your jacket, slip out of it. Hanging onto your money or jacket is not worth getting mugged, raped, or murdered.

Another maxim: Never believe anything a felon tells you, even if he's telling you something you desperately want to believe, for example, "I won't hurt you if you come with me." No matter how logical or benign he may sound, assume the worst. Always, *always,* break off contact as quickly as possible, even if that means running.

**In Public Transportation**   When riding a bus, always take a seat as close to the driver as you can; never ride in the back. In fact, many Chicagoans who depend on public transportation don't ride buses at night (they take a cab). Likewise, on the subway or elevated train, sit near the driver's or attendant's compartment. These people have a phone and can summon help in the event of trouble.

*In Cabs*   When hailing a cab, you are somewhat vulnerable. Particularly after dusk, call a reliable cab company and stay inside while it dispatches a cab to your door. When your cab arrives, check the driver's certificate, which must, by law, be posted on the dashboard. Address the cabbie by his last name (for example, Mr. Jones) or mention his cab number. This alerts the cab driver that you are going to remember him and/or his cab. Not only will this contribute to your safety, it will keep your cabbie from trying to run up the fare.

If you are comfortable reading maps, familiarize yourself with the most direct route to your destination ahead of time. If you can say, "Pipers Alley movie theater on North Wells via State Street, please," the driver is less likely to take a longer route so he can charge you for extra mileage.

If you need to catch a cab at the train station or at one of the airports, always use the taxi queue. Taxis in the official queue are properly licensed and regulated. Never accept an offer for a cab or limo made by a stranger in the terminal or baggage claim area. At best, you will be significantly over-charged for the ride. At worst, you may be abducted.

## PERSONAL ATTITUDE

While some areas of every city are more dangerous than others, never assume that any area is completely safe. Never let down your guard. You can be the victim of a crime—anywhere. If you go to a restaurant or night spot, use valet parking or park in a well-lighted lot. Women leaving a restaurant or club alone should never be reluctant to ask to be escorted to their car.

Never let your pride or sense of righteousness and indignation imperil your survival. This is especially difficult for many men, particularly for men in the presence of women. It makes no difference whether you are ap-proached by an aggressive drunk, an imbalanced street person, or an actual felon, the rule is the same: forget your pride and break off contact as quickly as possible. Who cares whether the drunk insulted you, if everyone ends up safely back at the hotel? When you wake up in the hospital with a concus-sion and your jaw wired shut, it's too late to decide that the drunk's filthy remark wasn't really all that important.

## SELF-DEFENSE

In a situation where it is impossible to run, you'll need to be prepared to defend yourself. Most police officers insist that a gun or knife is not much use to the average person. More often than not, they say, the weapon will be turned against the victim. Additionally, concealed firearms and knives are illegal in most jurisdictions. The best self-defense device for the aver-age person is Mace. Not only is it legal in most states, it is nonlethal and easy to use.

When you shop for Mace, look for two things: it should be able to fire about eight feet, and it should have a protector cap so it won't go off by mis-take in your purse or pocket. Carefully read the directions that come with your device, paying particular attention to how it should be carried and stored, and how long the active ingredients will remain potent. Wearing a rubber glove, test-fire your Mace, making sure that you fire downwind.

When you are out about town, make sure your Mace is someplace easily accessible, say, attached to your keychain. If you are a woman and you keep your Mace on a keychain, avoid the habit of dropping your keys (and your Mace) into the bowels of your purse when you leave your hotel room or your car. *Mace will not do you any good if you have to dig around in your purse for it.* Keep your keys and your Mace in your hand until you have safely reached your destination.

## MORE THINGS TO AVOID

When you do go out, walk with a minimum of two people whenever possible. If you have to walk alone, stay in well-lighted areas that have plenty of people around. And don't walk down alleys. It also helps not to look too much like a tourist when venturing away from places such as North Michigan Avenue and the Loop. Don't wear a camera around your neck, and don't gawk at buildings and unfold maps on the sidewalk—or thumb through guidebooks, including this one. Be careful about whom you ask for directions. (When in doubt, shopkeepers are a good bet.) Don't count your money in public, and carry as little cash as possible. At public phones, if you must say your calling card number to make a long-distance call, don't say it loud enough for strangers around you to hear. Avoid public parks and beaches after dark.

## CARJACKINGS

With the recent surge in carjackings, drivers also need to take special precautions. Keep alert when driving in traffic and keep your doors locked, with the windows rolled up and the air conditioning on. Leave enough space in front of your car so that you're not blocked in and can make a U-turn if someone approaches your car and starts beating on your windshield. Store your purse or briefcase under your knees or seat when you are driving, rather than on the seat beside you.

## THE HOMELESS

If you're not from a big city or haven't been to one in a while, you're in for a shock when you come to Chicago. It seems like every city block in the Loop is filled with shabbily dressed people asking for money. Along beaches on Lake Michigan, in Grant Park, and near large public buildings in the Loop, you will see people sleeping in blankets and sleeping bags, their possessions piled up next to them.

**Who Are These People?**  "Most are lifelong . . . residents who are poor," responds Joan Alker, Assistant Director of the National Coalition for the Homeless, an advocacy group headquartered in Washington, D.C. "The people you see on the streets are primarily single men and women. A disproportionate number of them are minorities and people with disabilities—they're either mentally ill or substance abusers or have physical disabilities."

**Are They a Threat to Visitors?**  "No," Alker says. "Studies . . . show that homeless men have lower rates of conviction for violent crimes than the population at large. We know that murders aren't being committed by the homeless. I can't make a blanket statement, but most homeless people you see are no more likely to commit a violent crime than other people."

**Should You Give the Homeless Money?**  "That's a personal decision," Alker says. "But if you can't, at least try to acknowledge their existence by looking them in the eyes and saying, 'Sorry, no.'" While there's no way to tell if the guy with the Styrofoam cup asking for a handout is really destitute or just a con artist, no one can dispute that most of these people are what they claim to be.

**Ways to Help**  It's really a matter for your own conscience. We confess to being both moved and annoyed by these unfortunate people; moved by their need and annoyed that we cannot enjoy Chicago without facing a gauntlet of begging men and women. In the final analysis, we found that it is easier on the conscience and spirit to get a couple of rolls of quarters at the bank and carry a pocket full of change at all times. The cost of giving those homeless who approach you a quarter really does not add up to all that much, and it is much better for the psyche to respond to their plight than to deny or ignore their presence.

There is a notion, perhaps valid in some instances, that money given to a homeless person generally goes toward the purchase of alcohol or other drugs. If this bothers you excessively, carry granola bars for distribution or, alternatively, some inexpensive gift certificates for McDonald's or other fast-food restaurants for coffee or a sandwich.

We have found that a little kindness regarding the homeless goes a long way, and that a few kind words delivered along with your quarter or granola bar brightens the day for both you and someone in need. We are not suggesting a lengthy conversation or prolonged involvement, but something simple like, "Sure, I can help a little bit. Take care of yourself, fella."

You'll also see homeless people in Chicago selling *StreetWise,* a $1 a copy newspaper published to create a way for street people to make some money. The vendors keep a portion of the proceeds, and editorially the paper supports programs for the homeless.

Those moved to get more involved in the nationwide problem of home-lessness can send inquiries—or a check—to the National Coalition for the Homeless, 1012 Fourteenth Street, NW, #600, Washington, D.C. 20005.

**Keep It Brief**    Finally, don't play psychologist. All the people you encounter on the street are strangers. They may be harmless, or they may be dangerous. Either way, maintain distance. Be prepared to handle street people in accordance with your principles, but mostly, just be prepared. If you have a druggie in your face wanting a handout, the last thing you want to do is pull out your wallet and thumb through the twenties looking for a dollar bill. As the sergeant on *Hill Street Blues* used to say, be careful out there.

# Part Six

# Getting around Chicago

## Driving Your Car: A Really Bad Idea

Four major interstates and rush-hour traffic jams of mythic proportions are some of the unfortunate realities faced by drivers who venture into downtown Chicago on weekdays. Throw in a dearth of on-street parking, astronomical rates at most parking garages, and the in-your-face driving style of most Chicago drivers, and you've got a recipe for driver meltdown.

Yet as the traffic congestion attests, lots of people continue to brave the streets of the Windy City by car every day—and that includes some out-of-town visitors. What if you're one of them?

### TIME OF DAY

First-time Chicago drivers who are staying downtown should map out their routes in advance, avoid arriving or departing during rush hour (weekdays 7–9:30 a.m. and 4–7 p.m.), and then plan on leaving the car parked in their hotel garage during most of their stay. Exceptions to the don't-drive rule are weekday evenings and on weekends and holidays.

### PARKING

Chicago's lack of on-street parking is legendary. If you decide to try your luck at finding a space, however, bring lots of quarters—most meters demand two for 15 minutes, with a two-hour limit (which isn't much time for sight-seeing or attending a business meeting). The fine for parking at an expired meter, by the way, is $30. Be careful and read signs that may restrict parking—Chicago traffic cops are notoriously efficient at handing out tickets and towing illegally parked cars.

While the chances of finding an on-street spot in the Loop on weekdays are virtually nil, you'll have better luck east of the Loop on Congress Parkway between Lake Shore Drive and South Michigan Avenue (behind the Art Institute, facing the lake). Just be prepared to do a lot of circling before snagging a space.

A better idea: Head south of the Loop for one of the many outside commercial parking lots located along State and Wabash Streets south of Congress Parkway. After about 9:30 a.m. you can park the car for about $6 a day. On weekends, finding on-street parking in and around the Loop is usually easy.

Another option that's popular with savvy Chicago drivers is Field Harbor Parking Garage (165 North Field Boulevard at East Randolph Street), an underground parking garage located between the Loop and Lake Michigan, just south of the Chicago River. Parking is cheap ($5 for up to an hour, $7 for up to 10 hours, and $9 for up to 12 hours) and the location is particularly convenient for festivals in Grant Park. Call (312) 938-8989 for directions.

Parking near the Magnificent Mile is another headache-inducing experience; street parking is virtually impossible near this shopping mecca—and that includes evenings and weekends. Most major area hotels have under- or above-ground parking garages; be sure to check when making a reservation.

Farther from downtown it is generally easier to find a parking spot, although exceptions abound. For example, in popular and hip Old Town, forget about finding street parking on a Friday or Saturday night; even the parking garages fill up. In addition, many neighborhoods have resident-only permit parking that prohibits nonresidents from grabbing scarce parking spaces in the evenings. A final note: When you do find a space, don't leave valuables in your car or trunk.

## INSIDER TIPS FOR DRIVERS

Many native Chicagoans who own cars routinely use public transportation or taxis to get downtown. They say the hassle and expense of parking just aren't worth it. It's especially true during the holidays, when out-of-towners and suburbanites converge on the city to shop—and parking the car for a long evening of shopping and enjoying the lights can cost $12–15.

Yet because Chicago is relatively easy to navigate and traffic levels drop off significantly after rush hour and on weekends, sometimes driving makes sense—at least, if you've already got a car. For example, if you're going out to dinner, call ahead and see if the restaurant offers valet parking (as more and more Chicago eateries do) or is close to a commercial parking lot. In addition, some out-of-the-way museums provide convenient parking; the Museum of Science and Industry in Hyde Park is the best example.

## SUBTERRANEAN CHICAGO

Adventurous drivers can explore subterranean Lower Wacker Drive and Lower Michigan Avenue. (Actually, they're at lake level; Chicago's downtown streets were elevated before the Civil War.) They're generally less congested than their surface counterparts, but are a bit scary for drivers making the descent for the first time. Drawbacks include lots of truck traffic, poor signage, and underground murkiness; pluses include quick access to the Eisenhower Expressway and views of locations used in popular films such as *The Untouchables* and *Code of Silence.*

# Public Transportation

## THE CTA

While Chicagoans may grouse about bus, subway, and train service, out-of-towners are usually impressed by the extensive public transportation system operated by the **Chicago Transit Authority** (CTA). So are we.

True, much of the system's infrastructure is aging, but many CTA routes run 24 hours a day, crisscrossing the city and providing service to a number of bordering suburbs. And consider the alternative: battling Chicago's epic traffic jams in a car.

For the most part CTA service is clean and dependable, even though it's an uneven mix of the sleek and seedy as some routes get upgraded while others are bypassed. Most routes take visitors to the places they want to be—or at least within a few blocks. (A notable exception is the lack of train service to McCormick Place.) *Warning:* After evening rush hour, for safety's sake don't use public transportation. Either drive or take a cab.

## THE EL

For visitors, the most important and easiest-to-master segment of CTA service is rapid transit—what is usually called "the subway" in other cities. But in Chicago, it's called "the El" (for "elevated"), although large parts of the train system run underground or down the middle of expressways. Never mind: The entire train system is known as the El.

Chicago currently boasts seven train routes that run north, northeast, east, southeast, and south from downtown. The Brown (Ravenswood), Purple (Evanston), and Orange (Midway) lines are elevated, while the Red (Howard-Dan Ryan), Blue (O'Hare-Congress-Douglas), and Yellow (Skokie) line trains run underground or on the surface. The new Green Line is an elevated line linking Jackson Park (south), the Loop, and Lake Street (east).

Downtown, the El defines the Loop as it circles Chicago's core financial and retail district; it's obvious that this part of the system is more than 100 years old as the trains rattle, shake, and roar overhead. The aging, peeling structures that hold the trains up don't inspire much confidence in most first-time visitors. Just think of the rickety system as a Chicago landmark and a bit of nineteenth-century charm.

## Fares

Cash fares for the train are $1.50 ($0.75 for children ages 7–11). Don't worry about exact fare; attendants are on hand (except at stations on the Orange Line on the Southwest Side, where token vending machines accept $1, $5, and $10 bills). Attendants, however, won't change a $20 bill. Transfers cost 30 cents (10 cents for children), must be purchased when you pay your fare, and allow two more rides within two hours—but not on the route you started on. They also allow transfers to a bus route (and vice versa).

If you plan to use the El or buses a lot during your stay in Chicago, consider purchasing a one-, two-, three-, or five-day visitor pass that allows unlimited rides. The passes range in price from $5 (one day) to $18 (five days) and are sold at both airports, Amtrak at Union Station, visitor information centers, Hot Tix, and most museums and major attractions.

Another option: In mid-1997, the CTA introduced a new electronic fare card system that allows you to purchase $3–100 worth of rides on the system's trains and buses. You can buy the fare cards at Transit Card machines installed in the stations as well as from the locations mentioned above.

## Train Line Names

The six El lines currently in operation are color coded, such as the Red Line. Watch out, though—some signs at stations and on the trains themselves have not yet been changed to show the new color names. So it's good to know that the Red Line is also called the Howard-Dan Ryan line (the names identify the two ends of the line).

Trains run every 3 to 12 minutes during rush hours; every 6 to 15 minutes midday, early evening, and weekends; and every 6 to 20 minutes in the later evening. From 1:30 a.m. to 4:30 a.m. only four lines operate: the Red Line (every 15 minutes), the Purple Line (every 30 to 45 minutes), and the Blue and Green Lines (every 30 to 60 minutes). Late at night, you should take a cab.

## Riding the El

In the Loop, finding the stations is easy: just look up. Then climb the rickety stairs up to the platform, pay the fare, and enjoy the weather as you await the next train—the elevated stations are partially covered, but not enclosed. To determine the direction of the train you want, use the maps displayed and the signs posted overhead and on columns.

## Taking the Plunge in the Loop

Figuring out which lines are elevated and which lines are underground—and how they all interconnect—is a headache-inducing experience in the Loop, where all the El lines converge. Here's some help: On the elevated lines circling the Loop, as you face north, the Orange Line to Midway runs counterclockwise and the Brown Line to Ravenswood runs clockwise; at the Clark/Lake, State/Lake, Adams/Wabash, and LaSalle/Van Buren stations riders can transfer to other lines (at no extra charge), including the underground Blue Line to O'Hare and the Red Line to the North Side.

Our advice: To get familiar with the system, take the plunge and board the elevated Brown (Ravenswood) El in the Loop. The views as you circle the downtown area are spectacular. Next, the train passes the Merchandise Mart and continues northwest.

If it's a nice day, continue north to, say, the Diversey station; get off the train and reboard the next one south. The drop-dead view of the approaching Chicago skyline that unfolds as you go back downtown shouldn't be missed. At $1.50, the ride is one of the best tourist bargains in town. If you haven't had your fill of aerial views of Chicago, board the Orange Line and take the elevated train to Midway Airport and back (a half-hour ride one-way).

To reach the platform at underground stations, riders descend a set of narrow stairs to the (often) seedy stations; the first time feels much like a descent to Hades as you sink below sidewalk level into a grungy, dilapidated station. After paying the fare, descend to the next level and the platform, which is usually narrow, littered, not climate-controlled, and very noisy when a train comes through. The trains themselves, however, are usually clean and litter- and graffiti-free (but not carpeted).

## BUSES

Chicago's bus system is massive and complicated—and better left to commuters. Buses are also slower than trains, especially in Chicago's dense traffic. Yet a few bus lines that follow relatively unconvoluted routes are invaluable to visitors staying downtown—particularly those visitors lodging in a hotel along the subway-less Magnificent Mile. We don't recommend that visitors on vacation use the bus system exclusively when in town, but we do think judicious use of buses can save tourists, business travelers, and conventioneers a lot of shoe leather, not to mention cab fares or parking fees.

Examples: While it's not a long walk to the below-ground Red Line train station at State and Chicago Streets from hotels on North Michigan Avenue, it's often more convenient to grab one of the many buses going up and down the Magnificent Mile. That's especially true when it is cold, raining, windy, snowing, or any combination of the above.

Buses #145, #146, and #151 (among others) provide easy, quick access south to the Loop and attractions such as the Field Museum along Lake Michigan. The #36 bus that goes north along State and Clark Streets provides easy access to Lincoln Park and Old Town. The #6 express bus, which can be boarded at State and Lake Streets in the Loop, quickly traverses the South Side to the Museum of Science and Industry (which doesn't have a convenient El station). The #56 bus heads out Milwaukee Avenue through Chicago's extensive Polish neighborhoods; think of it as an ethnic field trip. Buses #29, #56, #65, and #66 stop at Navy Pier, Chicago's most popular attraction.

### Which Bus?

To get exact, efficient directions for the bus and El routes, check with your hotel concierge or call 836-7000 from anywhere in the Chicago area between 5 a.m. and 1 a.m. every day. CTA personnel who answer the phones are polite and helpful; just tell them where you are and where you want to go and they'll give you exact directions on routes and transfers (if any). Make sure you've got pencil and paper handy to write down the directions.

### More Information on Buses

Bus fares are $1.50 ($0.75 for children 7–11); a transfer is $0.30. Unlike the El, you need either exact change or a token to ride the bus; dollar bills are OK, but the drivers don't make change. If you need a transfer, purchase it when you board. (You can use the transfer to enter the El system or board a bus on a different route twice within two hours.) In our experience, Chicago bus drivers are friendly and will answer any questions you have about reaching your intended destination.

Two warnings, though, about riding Chicago's buses: First, rush-hour crowds, especially along hectic Michigan Avenue, are mind-boggling, and often you'll have to wait for a bus to come along that's not packed full. Second, after the evening rush hour, for safety's sake either drive or take a cab.

# TAXIS

In Chicago, taxis are plentiful and constitute one of the primary modes of transportation in this spread-out city. Along major thoroughfares it's easy to hail a cab, with the possible exception of rush hours and when the weather has just turned nasty (and you most need one). Stands in front of major hotels are another place to find a taxi.

Chicago's taxi fare system is straightforward and similar to New York City's. The fare is based on both distance and time—which means a $3.50 fare at non–rush hour can double when traffic is slow and heavy. The base charge is $1.50 and a three-mile jaunt downtown from, say, a hotel along the Magnificent Mile or from McCormick Place typically will run about $5 (non–rush hour). If you need to summon a cab, ask your hotel door-man or call a major cab company that offers 24-hour service.

| Chicago's Major Cab Companies | |
| --- | --- |
| Checker and Yellow Cab | (312) 829-4222 |
| American United Cab | (773) 248-7600 |
| Flash Cab | (773) 561-1444 |

# WALKING

While Chicago is a huge city stretching about 30 miles north and south along Lake Michigan and 15 miles to the west, the major areas of interest to visitors are concentrated in a few fairly compact areas: the Loop, the Magnificent Mile along North Michigan Avenue (also called Streeterville), Grant Park (a campus-like setting that's home to some of the city's best museums), and the Near North Side (with a wide range of shopping, dining, and night life options). Plus, there isn't a hill for miles around. Given good weather and a relaxed schedule, walking is the primary mode of discovering the city.

Great places to take a walk or a stroll include the Loop; Grant Park (great views of the skyline, the lake, and many museums), anywhere along the bike and jogging path that follows the Lake Michigan shoreline; the Gold Coast (where Chicago's richest citizens have lived since the 1890s); the Magnificent Mile (nearly peerless window shopping); and, just west of the city line, Oak Park (with 25 homes, churches, and fountains designed by Frank Lloyd Wright). Chicago's varied ethnic neighborhoods such as

Andersonville (a charming mix of Swedish and Middle Eastern) are also great walking destinations.

## Pedways

In addition, downtown is honeycombed with an underground system of pedestrian walkways that makes the Windy City a lot easier to negotiate for walkers when the weather is, well, windy. The "pedways" link train stations and major buildings (such as the State of Illinois Center, Marshall Field's, the Chicago Cultural Center, and the Prudential Building). Visitors seeking a mole's-eye view of the city will even find an occasional shop or cafe as they explore the still-growing underground walkway. Hours are 6:30 a.m. to 6 p.m., Monday through Friday.

# Part Seven

# Entertainment and Night Life

## Chicago Night Life

It's a mistake to attack Chicago after-hours with an overly specific agenda. The city's nocturnal landscape is made up of so many characters and neighborhoods, sticking to a game plan can be difficult.

Chicago is about humanity, and humanity can move in peculiar ways.

Natives are passionate about their pursuit of happiness, which is why an edgy spirit pervades alternative rock rooms, dance clubs, country-western joints, neighborhood jazz clubs, and local theater.

As contemporary culture grows more homogenous, Chicago proudly flaunts diversity. And denizens of the city's night culture guard its variety as closely as old-line Chicago precinct captains watch a ballot box.

Before the immigration laws of the 1920s, Chicago offered respite for fruit peddlers, meat packers, shopkeepers, and jacks-of-all-trades. They worked hard and played hard. Their playful pursuits still live in the city; a great number of entertainment venues have been around for years. Much of Chicago's night life lives in venerable shadows.

An eclectic ethic is the heartbeat of Chicago's live entertainment scene, which can be divided into seven categories: live rock, jazz, country music, live blues, comedy, theater, and classical music. Chicago is the home of American blues and demands a category of its own. The profiles of clubs that follow focus on live music, dance clubs, and the classic neighborhood taverns that define the city.

Nightly schedules of live music clubs, comedy clubs, and theatrical productions, as well as comprehensive listings of movie show times and other events, are printed in the *Chicago Sun-Times* Friday "Weekend Plus" section, the *Chicago Tribune* "Friday" section, and the free *New City, Chicago Reader,* and *Barfly* alternative newspapers.

## LIVE ROCK

The Wicker Park neighborhood at Milwaukee, Damen, and North avenues on the city's Near Northwest Side has received national attention for producing alternative rockers Liz Phair and Urge Overkill. The neighborhood's once-affordable rents attracted artists, musicians, writers, and slackers; now, its growing profile accounts for weekend congestion from young suburban voyeurs.

Wicker Park hot spots include the **Rainbo Club** (1150 North Damen Avenue, (773) 489-5999) where Phair has been known to have a quiet drink when she is in town. In an earlier incarnation, the Rainbo was also a favorite watering hole for author Nelson Algren. There are occasional unannounced live sets and lots of musicians hang here.

For some of the most passionate local live alternative music in the neighborhood, check out **Phyllis' Musical Inn** (1800 West Division Street, (773) 486-9862). Portions of the Michael J. Fox–Joan Jett film *Light of Day* were filmed in this sweet, ramshackle, 100-seat family-run bar. After World War II and through the early 1960s, West Division Street was known as "Polish Broadway" because more than a dozen night clubs on the strip featured live polka music. Open since 1954, Phyllis' is the last remnant of that era. One of the newer live music rooms in Wicker Park is the **Double Door** (1572 North Milwaukee Avenue, (773) 489-3160), which features an assortment of national alternative rock acts and up-and-coming local bands.

Whereas Wicker Park's rock scene is relatively new, the Wrigley Field neighborhood, 3600 North Clark Street at Addison Street, holds a more storied and eclectic tradition. **Metro** (3730 North Clark Street, (773) 549-0203) is the rock 'n' roll catalyst for the upscale neighborhood. A transformed theater-cabaret with a balcony, Metro is heavy into alternative and grunge with an occasional exploration into the offbeat, such as Tom Jones and even an ABBA tribute band. Owner Joe Shanahan (who also owns the Double Door) has been a long-time champion of local rock. He gave Smashing Pumpkins their big break, allowing them to open for bands like Jane's Addiction at Metro.

The **Cubby Bear Lounge** (1059 West Addison Street, (773) 327-1662) stands directly across the street from the historic home of the Chicago Cubs. Like most bars in what real estate speculators coined "Wrigleyville," the Cubby Bear is packed after games. But an eclectic booking policy has brought rock, country, and reggae through the Cubby Bear in past years. The proximity of the ballpark brings out weird things in people. One time, just before midnight in the middle of a guitar solo, Tex-Mex new wave rocker Joe "King" Carrasco ran out of the Cubby Bear, across the intersection of Clark and Addison, and continued his jam directly in front of the ballpark entrance.

Wrigleyville is also the home of one of America's oldest live reggae clubs, **The Wild Hare: A Singing Armadillo Frog Sanctuary** (3530 North Clark Street, (773) 327-4273). Co-owned by former members of the Ethiopian band Dallol, who toured behind reggae superstar Ziggy Marley, this cozy nightclub has presented live reggae seven nights a week since it opened in 1979. It has evolved into a cultural mecca for transplanted Jamaicans and Africans.

Just a few blocks south of Wrigleyville is **Schubas Tavern** (3159 North Southport Avenue, (773) 525-2508), a comfortable restaurant-bar-music room whose entertainment policy is heavy on acoustic music, small jazz outfits, and weekly hoot nights. American roots artists such as Steve Earle, Joe Ely, and Jimmie Dale Gilmore have performed in the pristine 100-seat music room.

Other essential (and deeply intimate) rooms to hit on the live alternative rock/pop circuit include **Lounge Ax** (2438 North Lincoln Avenue (773) 525-6620, parking can be a problem), **Empty Bottle** (1035 North Western Avenue, (773) 276-3600), and the **Elbo Room** (2871 North Lincoln Avenue, (773) 549-5549).

The mega- and middle-sized rock concert venues in the Chicago area are in a constant state of flux. Chicagoans love summer, due to the temperamental nature of the other three seasons. The big outdoor sheds are very popular. There are three major sites. The 28,000 seat **World Music Theatre** (Ridgeland Avenue and Flossmoor Road in south suburban Tinley Park) is one of the largest outdoor concert facilities in the country. Acts like Bruce Springsteen and Peter Gabriel play here. Bring binoculars. Even pavilion seats can be far away.

The **Ravinia Festival** in the northern suburb of Highland Park is older, prettier, and more intimate. The focus is generally on classical music and jazz, although light rock and roots acts pop up. Ravinia has a capacity for 15,000 fans on lawn seating and 3,500 in a rustic pavilion. The city's newest outdoor venue is the one-year-old **Skyline Stage** at Navy Pier, located east of downtown and just off Lake Michigan. And don't let someone send you to the **Poplar Creek Music Theatre** in Hoffman Estates. It closed down in the winter of 1994 after a 14-year run.

The city and suburbs are sprinkled with diverse indoor live music venues. The new home of the Chicago Bulls and Chicago Blackhawks, the 22,000-seat **United Center** (1901 West Madison Street) books superstars like Frank Sinatra, Billy Joel, and the Eagles. Built in 1980, the **Rosemont Horizon** (6920 North Mannheim Road in Rosemont, right next to

O'Hare Airport) also features superstar-caliber acts with a spin on arena country music. The Horizon holds up to 18,500 folks for music events.

Middle-range rock venues include the **Park West** (322 West Armitage Avenue), a former strip club turned into an elegant 800-seat music room; the 1,200-seat **Vic Theatre,** a vaudeville house built in 1912 at 3145 North Sheffield Avenue; and the crazy **Aragon Ballroom,** 1106 West Lawrence Avenue. A popular spot for big band dancing in the 1940s, the Aragon (capacity 5,500) now almost exclusively features head-banging metal music, in which acoustics really don't matter. Tickets for all these shows are usually available by phone from TicketMaster at (312) 559-1212, but be on guard for "service" charges and handling fees.

## JAZZ

Chicago's live jazz scene has made a lively migration from downtown clubs and hotels into the neighborhoods. One of the best bets is the historic jazz speakeasy, the **Green Mill Jazz Club** (4802 North Broadway, (312) 878-5552).

For authentic ambience head to the **Velvet Lounge** (2128½ South Indiana Street, (312) 791-9050), which since 1982 has been owned by powerful Chicago tenor saxophonist Fred Anderson. He conducts jam sessions between 5 p.m. and 9 p.m. every other Sunday. Anderson is a founding member of the South Side's respected Association for the Advancement of Creative Musicians.

The most dependable downtown jazz spots are **Andy's** (11 East Hubbard Street, (312) 642-6805), a soulful bar and grill that's known for vibrant after-work sets featuring top local players, and the historic **Jazz Showcase** (59 West Grand, (312) 670-2473). Irrepressible owner Joe Segal books many prestigious national acts into his intimate room, which features a blessing from a blown-up, black-and-white photograph of Duke Ellington that hangs between velvety blue curtains behind the stage. In almost 50 years of operation, Segal and his Jazz Showcase have moved through several Chicago locations; the newest spot is well served by a tie-in with the adjacent Zinfandel's restaurant for beer, snacks, and dinner-show packages.

A little farther north, **Green Dolphin Street** (named for the classic tune "On Green Dolphin Street," 2200 North Ashland, (773) 395-0066) is the newest jazz club on the block, featuring straight-ahead local jazz with occasional salsa and funk-inspired acid jazz bookings. A cool decor is defined by a lofty ceiling, wood paneling, blinds, and white cloth–covered tables. The club seats around 120 and serves appetizer-type snacks and drinks. There is also an adjacent restaurant.

## COUNTRY AND WESTERN

While most veteran nightcrawlers are hip to Chicago's strong jazz lines, the city has developed more of a country-western scene than one might expect. Just as the blues migrated north to Chicago, the traditional country music tastes of industrial transplants from Kentucky and Tennessee have moved in, too.

There are typical boot scooter places like **Sundance Saloon** (Routes 176 and 83 in far north suburban Mundelein, (847) 949-0858). Despite its orientation to line dancing, the club still presents periodic live entertainment.

But the most authentic country-western bar in the Chicago area is the appropriately named **Nashville North** (101 East Irving Park Road, Bensenville, (630) 595-0170). Located since 1975 in the long, tall shadow of O'Hare International Airport, this live music room mixes "hot new" country with deep-frozen old country character. There's an elaborate western boutique that customers must walk through before entering the music room. Local live bands play four nights a week, but in an earlier time young whippersnappers like Garth Brooks and surf guitarists the Ventures performed here.

## LIVE BLUES

An essential live blues experience still reflects the city's segregated tradition. A great majority of whites and tourists go to North Side clubs and most African Americans go to South Side clubs. It has been that way since the Hoochie Coochie Man was a kid.

Still, there is not as much difference between North and South Side shows today as there was in the 1960s and 1970s. All South Side (and West Side) shows are casual, and there is more sitting-in on sets. South Side artists hang out in the street with their friends. The North Side clubs are more structured, have better sound, and in general, feature higher quality musicianship because artists are paid better.

Here are the best of the Chicago blues clubs:

**Checkerboard Lounge** (423 East 43rd Street on the south side, (773) 624-3240). Chicago blues guitarist Buddy Guy owned this club between 1972 and 1986, when it became known for jam sessions whenever blues-influenced guitarists such as Eric Clapton and Jimmy Page came to town. Guy cut his chops along 43rd Street listening to legends such as slide guitarist Earl Hooker and Muddy Waters before much of the neighborhood was gutted during the late-1960s riots. The Checkerboard is the last bastion of that precious history, which you can still get a feel for through black-and-white promotional photos of blues stars, a humble stage decorated by blue and silver rayon curtains, and a loud blues jukebox. Live music is featured Thursday through Monday nights. Take a cab.

Today, Guy has moved to the South Loop where he owns **Buddy Guy's Legends** (754 South Wabash Avenue, (312) 427-0333). Guy periodically plays to sold-out crowds in the spacious, but spirited room, which mixes local and national bookings. The late Stevie Ray Vaughan, Jeff Beck, and Eric Clapton have performed at Legends. This is the only Chicago blues bar with a full kitchen, wide-screen television sets, and ample pool tables.

**Rosa's Lounge** (3420 West Armitage Avenue, (773) 342-0452) celebrates traditional values in the middle of a transitional Hispanic neighborhood. The 150-person-capacity club is owned by Italian blues drummer Tony Manguilo and his mother Rosa. Their passionate approach to American blues stretches from a tenderly refurbished mahogany bar to a spacious stage and impeccable sight lines. Live blues start at 9:30 p.m., seven nights a week. Street parking all around.

The B.L.U.E.S. organization presents live music 365 days a year at two locales: **B.L.U.E.S.** (2519 North Halsted Street, (773) 528-1012) and **B.L.U.E.S., Etc.** (1124 West Belmont Avenue, (773) 525-8989). Because of its intimate and storied setting, the original B.L.U.E.S. on Halsted will always overshadow its little brother on Belmont. B.L.U.E.S. on Halsted is the longest-running North Side club with the same location and ownership. You can arrive at any time of the night (or morning) at the Halsted Street joint and be assured of a good shot at the stage, even though the room, which holds 100 people max, usually is crowded. B.L.U.E.S. features live local bands every night of the year, while B.L.U.E.S., Etc. leans more toward middle-range national acts. And don't fret. B.L.U.E.S. doesn't stand for anything in particular.

Finally, **Kingston Mines** (2548 North Halsted Street, (773) 477-4646) draws hard-core fans from B.L.U.E.S. across the street because of its late license (4 a.m. Saturday, 5 a.m. Sunday). Local blues acts alternate on two stages, so there's rarely any dead time. This club has been around for 25 years in various North Side locations.

## COMEDY/INTERACTIVE THEATER

A funny thing happened to Chicago comedy while crossing the punch line. It became theater.

The big yuks have shifted to interactive theater. *Shear Madness* is a goofy, particapatory whodunit that opened September 1982 in the Mayfair Theatre of the Blackstone Hotel (636 South Michigan Avenue, (312)

786-9120). Weighing in with more than 6,000 performances, it holds the record as the longest running non-musical play in Chicago history.

Set in a wacky unisex hair salon, the audience not only shapes and curls the outcome of the *Shear Madness* plot but also jumps into the action. As hard-nosed detectives attempt to solve the murder of eccentric concert pianist Isabelle Czerny, the audience shouts out hints or screams with complaints when something is clearly overlooked.

The play also absorbs local color, right down to local product placement, which means *Shear Madness* in Chicago and *Shear Madness* in Boston (where it debuted in 1980) can be two different experiences. *Shear Madness* is dark on Tuesday; performances are Monday and Wednesday–Friday nights, with two shows on Saturday evening, and a Sunday matinee and evening show. Tickets are $28 per person; $32 per person on Friday and Saturday.

***Tony n' Tina's Wedding*** is slightly more cutting edge than *Shear Madness*. Now in its fourth year at the Pipers Alley Theater (230 West North, directly behind Second City, (312) 664-8844), *Tony n' Tina's Wedding* is a two-hour-and-45-minute production with 32 cast members, a huge set, and buffet dinner. Audience members/"guests" enter a beautiful chapel for a wedding ceremony, which is followed by a dinner and dance reception (complete with a live band) that goes haywire. The wedding ceremony is scripted, but the rest of the show is free-form improvisation.

Like *Shear Madness, Tony n' Tina's Wedding* features lots of hometown nuance, right down to local celebrities. Many media and sports figures (they're the biggest celebrities Chicago has to offer) have appeared in *Tony n' Tina's Wedding,* and the New York production has featured everyone from ex–New York Met Lee Mazzilli to big-name NYPD narcotics agent Robert Cea. The Chicago version of *Tony n' Tina's Wedding* does such a good job of meshing actors with the audience, you can't always tell who is who. No weddings on Monday and Tuesday; performances are Wednesday through Sunday nights. Tickets are $47 per person Wednesday and Thursday, $55 per person Friday and Sunday, and $60 per person Saturday.

## DANCE CLUBS

College- and postcollege-age Chicago club goers have reshaped the urban dance scene as "The Swing Set." The late alto-saxophonist Louis Jordan was the father of swing. As early as 1938 Jordan meshed small combo jazz, blues, calypso, country, and even African American vaudeville into swing. Jordan was a profound influence on Chuck Berry as well as bandleaders like Amos Milburn and Wynonie Harris, but local, young hipsters know far more about Michael Jordan than Louis Jordan.

Picking up on a trend that began in Los Angeles, Chicago club goers use swing dancing as a way to meet members of the opposite sex and to dress up in wacky 1950s suits and gowns. The music and its sources are secondary.

**Liquid Nightclub** (1997 North Clybourn, (773) 528-3400) bills itself as the city's swing capital: live bands perform Thursday–Saturday nights from 6 to 9 p.m.; Sunday is all-ages night and the club even offers swing and jitterbug dance lessons. Liquid used to be a country music club, back when they offered line dance lessons. Can't wait for the limbo craze to come back!

**Frankie's Blue Room** (16 West Chicago, Naperville, (630) 416-4898) is more authentic, with classic 1940s–50s black-and-white dance videos appearing on dance floor monitors and wall murals featuring the likenesses of swingers like Frank Sinatra. Frankie's live booking policy mixes national swing bands with roots music and blues acts. Also, **Olive** (tucked away at 1115 North Branch on the Near North side of Chicago, (312) 280-7997) features big bands, swing, and jazz from 7 p.m. to 2 a.m. Thursday–Saturday. Likewise, the **Beat Kitchen** (2100 West Belmont, (773) 281-4444) includes a Monday night swing session in its appetizing live booking policy of rock and rhythm and blues. Lessons start at 8 p.m., and music starts at 9 p.m.

## LOOKIN' FOR LOVE

Chicago is a predominately Catholic/puritan city, which means the sex and singles situation can get temperamental. After all, this is the place where Frank Sinatra actually "saw a man dance with his wife."

Nevertheless, the city's legendary singles bars include **Butch McGuire's** (20 West Division Street, (312) 337-9080) and across the street, a more diminutive **The Lodge** (21 West Division Street, (312) 642-4406). Both these places have been around since the early 1960s, and on a clear night you can almost see the path through the two establishments. And don't miss Butch's during the holiday season, when more than 200,000 Christmas lights twinkle in two rooms.

Not far off Division Street, or what veterans call "The Street of Dreams," is the **River Shannon,** a cozy neighborhood tap (425 West Armitage Avenue, (312) 944-5087) in the DePaul University neighborhood. The jam-packed Friday night crowds consist of fewer outsiders and more local folks. The demographics are heavy on attorneys and law students. After last call, the bravest and boldest customers head down the street to **Gamekeepers** (1971 North Lincoln Avenue, (773) 549-0400), a late-night *Animal House*–type establishment.

The Wicker Park neighborhood is known for its live rock 'n' roll and slacker bars, but a singles oasis is **Nick's** (1516 North Milwaukee Avenue, (773) 252-1155). Formerly located in the DePaul neighborhood, Nick's has found a niche in Wicker Park. And it boasts one of the best jukeboxes in the city, with ample Memphis soul, Chicago blues, and Carolina beach music.

Nick's owner, Nick Novich—a former high school football coach— also runs **The Note** (1901 West Armitage Avenue, (312) 489-0011), a dark, hip, and too-cool-for-school tavern that's very popular with Wicker Park artists and musicians on the sex trail. The 100-CD jukebox here leans more toward jazz and moody soul, and the crowd is not as diverse as it is a few blocks south at Nick's. Translated: wear black and slap on a ponytail.

To meet in a more subtle setting, the city offers some classy piano bars. Buddy Charles is the king of local piano men. He's been gigging in legendary North Side rooms for more than 40 years. Charles, who teaches Sunday school after a late Saturday night set, performs from 9:30 p.m. to 1:30 a.m. Tuesday through Saturday at the piano bar of the elegant **Coq d' Or** room in the Drake Hotel (140 East Walton, (312) 787-2200). Expect Charles to play things like the *West Side Story* medley and Fats Waller's "Your Feet's Too Big" as well as attending to a dream world of requests.

Another dean of the piano bar scene is the cagey Bob Freitag, going on his 22nd year at **Orso's** (1401 North Wells Street, (312) 787-6604), an Italian restaurant in the heart of the Near North Old Town neighborhood. Freitag is different from most piano men because he rarely sings. Instead, he brings a graceful style to such classics as Irving Berlin's "I Love a Piano" and "I Got It Bad (And That Ain't Good)." Freitag plays between 6:30 and 10:30 p.m. every night except Monday.

Other grand piano bars (without restaurants) include the dark and tiny **Zebra Lounge** (1220 North State Street, (312) 642-5140) and the subterranean **Redhead Piano Bar** (16 West Ontario Street, (312) 640-1000).

And for guys who have struck out, or simply choose to sit out, in the last few years, the strip club has made a comeback in Chicago. This time around they're called "gentlemen's clubs," which follow a nationwide trend toward posh nightclubs where scantily clad or nude women are the entertainment attraction.

The more mainstream gentlemen's clubs are: **The Admiral Theater** (3940 West Lawrence Avenue on the city's far northwest side, (312) 478-8111) and **Heavenly Bodies** (1300 South Elmhurst Road, (847) 806-1120) in Elk Grove Village, about ten miles from O'Hare International Airport.

Collars, shirt, and/or nice sweater are required at Heavenly Bodies after 7 p.m. Just so you're not totally surprised: only the Admiral offers full nudity, because it does not serve alcohol or full-course meals (snacks are available).

## LEGITIMATE THEATER

In recent years Chicago theater has been a fertile arena of actors and directors for casting directors, agents, and producers from the East and West coasts. While the Loop (downtown) theater enjoys success with safe straight-from-Broadway touring companies, a cutting-edge off-Loop scene has flourished.

Chicago features more than 1,000 theatrical venues, which range from established institutions to mid-level professional companies to smaller and younger troupes.

The **Goodman Theater** is the oldest and largest resident theater in Chicago, working out of the rear portion of the Art Institute since its founding in 1925. The Goodman pioneered regional theater in America. Under artistic director Robert Falls, shows have ranged from experimental Shakespeare to Bertolt Brecht to August Wilson. The main theater seats 700, a cutting-edge studio seats 135. The Goodman is located at 200 South Columbus Drive, (312) 443-3800.

The **Steppenwolf Theater** is one of the pioneers in the off-Loop movement. Steppenwolf is unique for the consistency of its ensemble; audiences have been able to watch a group of actors develop over the years. The original 1976 ensemble included actors John Malkovich and Laurie Metcalf. Steppenwolf received international acclaim for *The Grapes of Wrath;* it has also portrayed works by Sam Shepard and Tennessee Williams. The immaculate 500-seat main stage and 100-seat experimental theater are at 1650 North Halsted Street, (312) 335-1888.

Some people perceive **Second City** as a comedy club, but it is a legitimate local theatrical institution that started in 1959. Major talent like Ed Asner, John Belushi, Valerie Harper, Bill Murray, and George Wendt cut their teeth here. The original founding format is still used. With minimal costuming and props, six or seven actors lampoon life in a torrid series of topical skits.

Following every show, the troupe draws ideas from the audience from which they improvise new sketches. There is no charge for these late-night sets. And producer emeritus Joyce Sloane has always pledged to keep the theater admission charge ($10) in the same ballpark as a movie ticket. The original 350-seat location at 1616 North Wells Street, (312) 337-3992 also features a 180-seat back room for Second City E.T.C., sometimes regarded as more rebellious than its big brother. Another Second City is in northwest suburban Arlington Heights.

The last of the established groups is the **Northlight Theater,** whose office is at 9501 Skokie Boulevard, but which mounts shows in various north suburban locations. For just over 20 years, Northlight has been one of the largest and most innovative theaters in the Chicago area and is an artistic anchor of the northern suburbs. Northlight has won critical acclaim for its productions of a wide range of new and contemporary plays and several original chamber-size musicals. Call (847) 679-9501 for more information.

Quality mid-level theaters include **Body Politic** (2261 North Lincoln Avenue, (773) 348-7901); **Organic Theater** (3319 North Clark Street, (773) 327-5588); **Victory Gardens** (2257 North Lincoln Avenue, (773) 871-3000); and **Wisdom Bridge** (750 West Wellington at the Ivanhoe Theater, (312) 975-7171), one of the oldest off-Loop companies. Wisdom Bridge Theater is the place where Robert Falls, now artistic director of the Goodman Theater, first made his mark.

The best of the younger and smaller theaters are **Annoyance Theater** (3747 North Clark Street, (773) 929-6200), which presents offbeat fare like "Coed Prison Sluts" and "The Real Live Brady Bunch"; **Live Bait** (3914 North Clark Street, (773) 871-1212), named because the founders felt that attempting to attract an audience was like being bait on a line; the empathetic **Latino Chicago Theater Company** (at the Firehouse, 1625 North Damen Avenue, (773) 486-5120); the **Griffin Theater Company at the Calo Theater** (5404 North Clark Street, (773) 769-2228); The **Famous Door Theater Company,** which presents world premiere works with a spin on political pieces (at the Jane Addams theater, 3212 North Broadway, (773) 404-8283); and **Eclipse** (2074 North Leavitt, (773) 862-7415).

Apart from the young and experimental spaces, most of these shows can be expensive and many often sell out. The League of Chicago Theatres offers a Hot Tix program where theater tickets are half-price the day of the performance. Hot Tix booths are at 108 North State Street in Chicago, the Metra train station, 700 North Michigan in Chicago Place, and 1616 Sherman Avenue in Evanston. There are also a few dinner theaters in Chicago suburbs. Check the listings in the *Chicago Sun-Times* "Weekend Plus" section on Fridays or the *Chicago Tribune* "Friday" insert. The monthly *Chicago Magazine* also does a good job of covering local theater.

The general dress code for Chicago theater is casual. Men need not wear ties, and women don't have to overdress. Jeans, slacks, and nice shirts are perfectly acceptable.

## THE CLASSICS

The world-renowned **Chicago Symphony Orchestra** is the touchstone of the Chicago classical music landscape. Since 1960, the CSO has won 51 Grammy awards, 23 of them between 1972 and 1991 when the great music director Georg Solti was conductor. Overall, Solti won 31 Grammies, more than any other artist including Michael Jackson. Solti's tradition is consistently celebrated in the CSO's glorious clarity and logic.

The 104-year-old Chicago Symphony Orchestra is based in Orchestra Hall, 220 South Michigan Avenue. Visiting American orchestras also appear at Orchestra Hall as part of an "Orchestra Hall Presents" season (phone (312) 294-3000). Be sure to call ahead. Subscriptions account for roughly 80% of tickets sold for CSO concerts and 1994 attendance filled 94% of Orchestra Hall's capacity. Orchestra Hall recently underwent a $100 million renovation and restoration project.

On a smaller scale, the 12-year-old **Newberry Consort** is the city's premiere early music ensemble. Their season begins in the fall in various locations in Chicago, Lake Forest, and Oak Park (phone (312) 943-9090, ext. 391).

The **Music of the Baroque** chorus and orchestra offers concerts in River Forest, Hyde Park, the DePaul area of Chicago, and Evanston (phone (312) 551-1414). In the fall, Alan Heatherington's innovative **Chicago String Ensemble** kicks in with performances in Chicago and suburban Evanston and LaGrange (phone (312) 332-0567).

## ADMIRAL THEATRE

Women without clothes, men with desire
*Who Goes There:* If you need to ask, you shouldn't go. This upscale strip club draws young professionals, businessmen, some Northwest Side neighborhood voyeurs, and, of course, classically lonely sailors

3940 West Lawrence Avenue; (773) 478-8111
Zone 2 North Central/O'Hare

Cover: $15
Minimum: Two drinks, no alcohol
Mixed drinks: Soft Drinks, $3.50
Dress: Casual, no ripped jeans. Anything goes for women on stage.

Specials: Amateur night on Thursdays
Food available: Personal pizza, hot dogs

**Hours:** Monday–Thursday, noon–3 a.m.; Friday and Saturday, noon–4 a.m.; Sunday, 6 p.m.–2 a.m. Movie theater open 24 hours.

**(Admiral Theatre)**

**What goes on:** Stripping in a sophisticated setting. The classic Chicago movie house opened in 1948 and became a strip club in 1970. For 20 years it was known for cellulite strippers, funky old men, and anxious vice cops. The Admiral underwent an ambitious nine-month renovation in 1991, becoming something you'd be more likely to see on the Las Vegas strip rather than in a sin strip. Couples are welcome, although they're in the minority.

**Setting & atmosphere:** Circuit stars like Venus DeLight, Nikki Knockers, and adult film legend Tori Welles make regular stops at the Admiral. The 200-seat Centerfold Show Lounge has a bright contemporary texture defined by purple pillars and blue and pink neon. The Admiral's old vaudeville stage is framed by 25-foot-tall gold-leaf statues of naked women. Tuxedoed maître d's usher people to their seats. An 88-seat movie theater is open 24 hours. The $15 admission includes free entry for the skin flicks. If you only want to see the movies, there is a $10 admission.

**If you go:** The Admiral is the only "gentlemen's club" in the city that presents full nudity. The Chicago Adult Use Ordinance, enacted in 1987, says that "topless dancers, strippers, male or female impersonators, or similar entertainers" cannot perform with "less than completely and opaquely covered" private parts in clubs where alcohol is served. So pick your poison. At other clubs, you can have alcohol and see partially clad strippers. At the Admiral, you can't drink alcohol, but the dancers are nude.

## BROTHER JIMMY'S

Frat party in a North Carolina sports bar setting
*Who Goes There:* 25–35, lots of Atlantic Coast Conference poseurs and/or frathouse beer buddies, wayward neighborhood people, DePaul University students; not for the faint of heart

2909 North Sheffield Avenue; (773) 528-0888
Zone 1 North Side

Cover: $5 admission charge after 10 p.m. weekends
Minimum: None
Mixed drinks: $3.25
Wine: $4
Beer: $3–3.50
Dress: Casual

Food available: Brother Jimmy's bills itself as a Southern restaurant that happens to have a great barbecue. The *Chicago Tribune* ranked the restaurant's ribs third best in the Midwest. Classic sides include mashed potatoes and collard greens

### (Brother Jimmy's)

**Hours:** Monday–Friday, 5 p.m.–midnight; Saturday, noon–3 a.m.; Sunday, noon–10 p.m.

**What goes on:** Eating, drinking, and televised Atlantic Coast Conference (ACC) sports in an often rambunctious setting. A down-home jukebox is heavy on old soul, Carolina beach music, and Texas blues. High-quality local roots, rock, and blues acts play Thursday through Saturday nights. Special events include outdoor pig pickin's (roast pig parties), an ACC tradition. A $16.95 Sunday special covers all the ribs you can eat and draft you can drink.

**Setting & atmosphere:** The 450-capacity room looks like a funky tobacco warehouse, replete in tobacco baskets and house drinks served in Mason jars. But, besides Michael Jordan's apprenticeship at North Carolina, what does the Atlantic Coast Conference have to do with Chicago? Owner Jim Goldman attended Duke University. Goldman is also principal owner of Brother Jimmy's and Manny's Car Wash in New York City.

**If you go:** Make eating a priority. The food is great, you can get a seat, and on weekends the post–10 p.m. $3 live entertainment charge is removed from your meal ticket. The noise can get intense, and in Illinois, the Atlantic Coast Conference remains an acquired taste.

## BUDDY GUY'S LEGENDS

Live blues in a downbeat, rec room–type setting
*Who Goes There:* International tourists, more of a racial mix than North Side blues clubs, and sometimes even Buddy Guy, the dramatic Chicago-based guitar great

754 South Wabash Avenue; (312) 427-0333
Zone 5 South Loop

Cover: $5–15
Minimum: None
Mixed drinks: $3.25
Wine: $3.50
Beer: $2.75–3.50
Dress: Everything from tees and sweats to after-work attire
Specials: Local record release parties, spur-of-the-moment bookings

such as Eric Clapton and occasional live recordings, like owner Buddy Guy playing with G. E. Smith of the "Saturday Night Live" band
Food available: Southern Louisiana cuisine: ribs, red beans and rice, and "Peanut Buddy Pie," a Buddy Guy–endorsed peanut butter pie

**(Buddy Guy's Legends)**

**Hours:** Monday–Friday, 5 p.m.–2 a.m.; Saturday, 5 p.m.–3 a.m.; Sunday, 6 p.m.–2 a.m.

**What goes on:** A stately approach to booking live local, national, and international blues acts seven nights a week. From 1972–86, local guitar hero Buddy Guy (who influenced Eric Clapton and Stevie Ray Vaughan) ran the Checkerboard Lounge, a South Side blues club that still stands today. In 1989, he reopened in a bigger and safer location as part of Chicago's developing South Loop. The sprawling storefront club is popular with tourists because of Guy's international reputation and its prime location.

**Setting & atmosphere:** Urban roadhouse. Four pool tables are almost always occupied at stage left. Portraits of blues greats like Muddy Waters, Lightin' Hopkins, and Howlin' Wolf hang throughout the museum-like space. Near the club entrance there's a display case featuring Guy's awards; guitars from the likes of Eric Clapton and Muddy Waters hang above the bar.

**If you go:** Don't request "Achy Breaky Heart." This is a blues sanctuary. It's also best to arrive early as all shows are general admission and often sell out. The Southern Louisiana kitchen serves better than average bar food. And periodically check out the far west end of the bar. That's Guy's favorite spot.

## CHARLIE'S

Chaps, young and old—it's a gay country-western dance club
*Who Goes There:* Predominantly gay men, some gay women; about ten percent of the crowd are straight country-western fans; lots of neighborhood boot scooters

3726 North Broadway; (773) 871-8887
Zone 1 North Side

| | |
|---|---|
| Cover: None | Dress: No dress code; leather chaps |
| Minimum: None | and cowboy hats are okay |
| Mixed drinks: $2.75–4 | Specials: None |
| Wine: $2.75 | Food available: Occasional Sunday |
| Beer: $2.75 | afternoon barbecue |

**Hours:** Sunday–Thursday, 3 p.m.–2 a.m.; Friday, until 4 a.m.; Saturday, until 5 a.m.

**What goes on:** Charlie's is one of the friendliest clubs in the city, gay or straight. Lots of line dancing on a floor lit up by a big mirrored boot, a

**(Charlie's)**

Charlie's trademark. The gay country-western club chain kicked off in the early 1980s in Denver, Colorado, and has expanded to Phoenix and Chicago. The Saddle Swingers, a nine-member gay men's country line dance troupe, appear one Saturday night a month at Charlie's, and the Chi-Town Squares, a gay square dance club, practice at Charlie's on Sunday evenings.

**Setting & atmosphere:** Clean, dark, and with a great sound system for listening to Brooks & Dunn hits like "Boot Scootin' Boogie" and "My Maria," Alan Jackson's "Chattahoochee," and other house favorites. At late night/early morning, the deejay throws in some progressive dance tunes to mix things up. The club holds between 300–350 people, and the ample dance floor gives people room to boogie.

**If you go:** Be sensitive to the fact that Charlie's tackles two extreme American stereotypes: country-western music and the gay lifestyle. Charlie's makes the evening a memorable experience with a sincere staff and keen musical programming. And Charlie's gives back to the community: the club's monthly "Mr. Charlie's" program (an award bestowed to the man who brings in the most money that night in the bar) has raised more than $224,000 for AIDS-related charities since it was organized in 1982.

## CHICAGO FOLK CENTER

I'd like to teach the world to sing; the country's premiere resource center for folk and world music idioms

*Who Goes There:* Everyone between 8 and 88; people who have either attended or taught here include John Prine, Roger McGuinn of the Byrds, Billy Corgan of Smashing Pumpkins, and Jeff Tweedy of Wilco

4544 North Lincoln Avenue; (773) 728-6000
Zone 1 North Side

Cover: Varies
Minimum: None
Mixed drinks: None
Wine: $2
Beer: $2–3
Dress: No code; flannel welcomed

Specials: Latin Festival in October; Do-It-Yourself Chanukah in December
Food available: Sandwiches and snacks, $1–5

**Hours:** Monday–Thursday, 9 a.m.–11 p.m.; Friday and Saturday, 9 a.m.–5 p.m. (for concerts, the center closes at 1 a.m.); Sunday, 10 a.m.–4 p.m.

**What goes on:** The Chicago Folk Center services more than 3,500 adult and youth students weekly in classes as eclectic as Bulgarian singing, fla-

**(Chicago Folk Center)**

menco guitar playing, and Hawaiian hula dancing. Nearly 30,000 people attend Old Town School concerts annually. Folk singer Joni Mitchell christened the Chicago Folk Center in the fall of 1998. Other concert regulars include singer-songwriter Guy Clark, Peter Yarrow of Peter, Paul, and Mary, and rhythm and blues singer Charles Brown. The Chicago Folk Center's previous home (909 West Armitage) remains open as the Old Town School of Folk Music Children's Center.

**Setting & atmosphere:** The Chicago Folk Center was restored from the 43,000-square-foot Hild Library, an art deco treasure built in 1929. The acoustically perfect $2 million concert hall is the crown jewel of the center. With 275 seats on the main floor and 150 in the balcony, no audience member is more than 45 feet from the procenium stage. The $150,000 sound system features 38 speakers that ring throughout the intimate hall. Vintage acoustic instruments are hung on the hall's 14 pillars to absorb sound. The center also includes 31 teaching spaces. The Different Strummer music store sells instruments and rare recordings—instruments are also rented and repaired.

**If you go:** This can be one of the most rewarding musical experiences in Chicago. During the day, the concert hall transforms into a cafe area where folk music fans can relax, talk, and hear impromptu concerts by students. The Old Town School of Folk Music began in 1957 as an offshoot of the humanist movement in folk music—a notion of bringing people together under the belief that music belongs to the masses. The warmth of the Chicago Folk Center embodies and nurtures that unifying spirit.

## EXCALIBUR

Royal order of endless nights in a real North Side castle
*Who Goes There:* 25 and over, big hair from the 'burbs, the office party circuit, some tourists

632 North Dearborn Street; (312) 266-1944
Zone 3 Near North

**Cover:** $4 Friday and Saturday and you get a free drink. $5–9 (Wednesday, Friday and Saturday) for upstairs dance Club X
**Minimum:** None
**Mixed drinks:** $3.75–5.50
**Wine:** $4.50
**Beer:** $3–4.25

**Dress:** Nothing tattered, torn, or soiled
**Specials:** Discount drinks on Wednesday, free pool for women
**Food available:** Full menu from Cajun chicken to steak sandwiches. Late night breakfast served until 4 a.m., Saturday until 5 a.m.

**(Excalibur)**

**Hours:** Sunday–Friday, 5 p.m.–4 a.m.; Saturday, 5 p.m.–5 a.m. Open 365 nights a year.

**What goes on:** Everything for the MTV generation. A downstairs game room features nearly 100 state-of-the-art video, pinball, and pseudo–virtual reality games. Pool tables are all over the place, eight in one billiard room. An upstairs dance club called Club X holds 1,500 people, and a main-floor cabaret features live rock and pop for over-30 geezers.

**Setting & atmosphere:** Party in a historic building. Resembling a castle, this rambling 40,000-square-foot building is one of the few nineteenth-century Gothic buildings to survive the Chicago Fire, designed by American architect Henry Ives Cobb. It's been the home of the Chicago Historical Society, the Chicago Institute of Design, and before Excalibur, the hoity-toity Limelight nightclub.

**If you go:** You won't get bored. And if you do, the adjacent Dome Room features metal bands on Friday and Saturday nights, along with unique special events like "Bondage Night/Love Hurts" when ladies and couples in chains, handcuffs, and leashes get in free. There is a separate entrance and $5 cover to get into the Dome Room.

## FITZGERALD'S

Live American roots music in a roadhouse club
*Who Goes There:* Music lovers of all ages, a hearty portion of Lake Woe-begone characters, Near West suburban folks; slacker factor very low

6615 West Roosevelt Road, Berwyn; (708) 788-2118
Zone 9 Western Suburbs

| | |
|---|---|
| Cover: $2–15 | Dress: Casual |
| Minimum: None | Specials: No drink specials, but special holiday events |
| Mixed drinks: $3–4.50 | |
| Wine: $3.50 | Food available: Occasional event related fare |
| Beer: $2.50–4 | |

**Hours:** Tuesday–Thursday, 7 p.m.–1 a.m.; Friday and Saturday, 7 p.m.–3 a.m.; Sunday, 4 p.m.–1 a.m.

**What goes on:** A family-run operation since it opened in 1980, FitzGerald's is one of the most passionately booked rooms in the Chicago area. Blues legend Stevie Ray Vaughan played the intimate 300-seat club in 1981, long before he hit it big. Other landmark shows that remain indicative of the club's musical mission include appearances from the late zydeco

**(FitzGerald's)**

king Clifton Chenier and the Neville Brothers. Ample attention is also given to Chicago blues and folk, and Sunday night sets are generally reserved for traditional and big band jazz.

**Setting & atmosphere:** Totally roadhouse. The backwoods feel has even attracted Hollywood. The Madonna jitterbug scene from *A League of Their Own* was filmed here as well as the pool hall shots in the Paul Newman flick *The Color of Money*. During the latter shooting a local family pointed out that the room's origins go back to the early 1900s when it was a men's sport club. Sound and sight lines are top-notch and space for a dance floor is cleared when appropriate.

**If you go:** Respect the experience. Over the years, FitzGerald's has cultivated fans who love roots music as well as the roots texture of the room. Rarely do you hear an acoustic performance drowned out by audience chatter. And don't be intimidated by the suburban location. Berwyn is a ten-minute drive from the Loop and the Congress El goes to Berwyn. Get off at Oak Park Avenue, walk three blocks south and then three blocks east. Or call co-owner Bill FitzGerald and ask him to pick you up. If he has time, he probably will. It's that type of touch that makes FitzGerald's a local treasure.

## GREEN MILL JAZZ CLUB

Hep cat speakeasy with quality live jazz
*Who Goes There:* Sincere jazz fans, local poets, romantic couples on the last stop before home, 25–ageless

4802 North Broadway; (773) 878-5552
Zone 1 North Side

**Cover:** $3–7
**Minimum:** None
**Mixed drinks:** $3–5
**Wine:** $2.50–3.75
**Beer:** $1.75–4
**Dress:** Casual and hip

**Specials:** The Uptown Poetry Slam 7–10 p.m. on Sundays. The Green Mill is a literary landmark for the frenetic poetry slams, which began here in July 1986
**Food available:** Bar snacks

**Hours:** Monday–Friday, noon–4 a.m.; Saturday, noon–5 a.m.; Sunday, 11 a.m.–4 a.m.

**What goes on:** Top-notch local jazz artists and a steady influx of New York musicians who aren't heard anywhere else in town. The Mill also is the city's premiere joint for late-late jam sessions.

## (Green Mill Jazz Club)

**Setting & atmosphere:** Can't be beat. The dark, seductive Mill opened in 1907 and enjoyed its first run of popularity in the 1920s during the neighborhood's vaudeville heyday. Proprietor Dave Jemilo purchased the club in 1986 and instead of gutting it, he lovingly restored it to its earlier splendor. The only additions were a dance floor and a new stage. The piano behind the bar has always been there, and it's still used on Sunday nights.

**If you go:** Listen to the music. It's rare that quality jazz can be heard at affordable prices in a neighborhood setting.

## HALA KAHIKI

Tiny bubbles—lots of them
*Who Goes There:* 21–60, Chicagoans suffering from intense cabin fever, Jimmy Buffett fans, visitors on layovers from O'Hare International Airport—less than ten minutes north of the Chicago area's biggest tiki bar

2834 North River Road, River Grove; (708) 456-3222
Zone 2 North Central/O'Hare

| | |
|---|---|
| Cover: None | Dress: Casual; no hats or tank tops; |
| Minimum: None | a Hawaiian shirt and hula skirt are |
| Mixed drinks: $3.50–7.50 (for two) | fine |
| Wine: $3.25 a glass | Food available: Pretzels—they make |
| Beer: $3.50 | you thirsty |

**Hours:** Monday and Tuesday, 7 p.m.–2 a.m.; Wednesday and Thursday, 4 p.m.–2 a.m.; Friday and Saturday, 4 p.m.–3 a.m.; Sunday, 6 p.m.–2 a.m.

**What goes on:** Located in near west suburban River Grove since 1967, Hala Kahiki (meaning "House of Pineapple") serves almost 75 different tropical drinks, including bizarre concoctions like Dr. Funk of Tahiti (licorice-flavored Pernod and rum), Skip and Run Naked (a gut-wrenching gin and beer mix), and the house favorite, the Zombie, a potent mix of fruit juice and three rums—including 151.

**Setting & atmosphere:** The tiki hut holds more than 200 people in three separate, dimly lit rooms and the bamboo-dominated front bar. The back room features a romantic light blue water fountain, while the front bar's innocent 1950s feel is accented by seashell-covered lamp shades and a dash of incense. In the back of the nightclub, there is a Hala Kahiki Gift Shop,

**(Hala Kahiki)**

complete with leis, tropical drink glasses, and cardboard hula dancers. There are even Don Ho cassette tapes for those who really want to catch a wave. With the exception of the Kahiki in Columbus, Ohio, this is really the only full-tilt tropical bar and South Sea shop in the Midwest.

**If you go:** Don't order beer. Do consider a designated driver. The drinks pack a punch, and getting pulled over wearing a green Hawaiian shirt, a yellow lei, and listening to Don Ho will not help your case.

## HARD ROCK CAFE

It's only rock 'n' roll, but they like it.

*Who Goes There:* Golden oldies, conventioneers, cabbies, confused sailors; all ages

63 West Ontario Street; (312) 943-2252
Zone 3 Near North

Cover: None
Minimum: None
Mixed drinks: $3.50–5.25
Wine: $3.25–4.25 (glass),
 $10.95–19.50 (bottle)
Beer: $3–3.75 (bottles only)
Dress: Haphazard at best: short-sleeved dress shirt–clad business-man style, even in winter. Fringy leather jacket and tees on teen-agers, plus the usual preps and Gappers
Specials: Hard Rock Hurricane for $10 and keep the glass
Food available: Americanized classics: burgers, nachos, and health-conscious sandwiches

**Hours:** Monday–Thursday, 11:30 a.m.–midnight; Friday, 11:30 a.m.–1 a.m.; Saturday, 11 a.m.–1 a.m.; Sunday, 11:30 a.m.–10 p.m.

**What goes on:** Go-go gawking at the self-dubbed "Self-Guided non-nuclear powered drug free tour of the most extensive collection of rock 'n' roll memorabilia ever assembled." Everyone does laps around the circular bar to ensure they don't miss a thing. HRC Chicago's free New Year's Eve shows from the cafe balcony are a city favorite.

**Setting & atmosphere:** Authentic rock 'n' roll archives get classy in rustic trappings. In the world of assembly-line HRC's, Chicago's claims to fame are John Hiatt's autographed perfectly smashed guitar and the motorcycle from The Who's film "Quadrophenia." Everything is PC down to the recycled paper menus printed with soy ink.

**(Hard Rock Cafe)**

**If you go:** Time is not on your side. There's a long wait to sit down for service, and an even longer wait for a Hard Rock T-shirt, baseball cap, or one of the dozens of other items from the in-store boutique. But once you're situated, the waitstaff is prompt and courteous, just like Pat Boone.

## THE HIDEOUT

An urban roadhouse in the middle of nowhere, surrounded by everything
*Who Goes There:* Local musicians and music industry folks ages 25–35, older blue-collar workers, people trying to maintain a low profile

1354 West Wabansia; (773) 227-4433
Zone 1 North Side

**Cover:** Occasionally; never more than $5
**Minimum:** None
**Mixed drinks:** $2.50–3
**Beer:** $1.50, Pabst Blue Ribbon; $3, others

**Dress:** Very cas
**Specials:** Free bag of pretzels or a shot of Hot Damn! if you mention *The Unofficial Guide to Chicago*
**Food available:** Chips and peanuts

**Hours:** Monday, 2 p.m.–8 p.m.; Tuesday–Friday, 2 p.m.–2 a.m.; Saturday, 2 p.m.–3 a.m.

**What goes on:** If Chicago is the capital of the nation's punky alternative-country scene, then The Hideout is the White House. Although the tiny building's first deed dates back to 1890 and the club has been called The Hideout since 1934, only recently has the joint been discovered by an edgy, younger crowd. On most weekends live music is presented in the comfortable back room. Adorned with Christmas lights and an efficient stage, the concert space seats about 100 people. The Honky Tonk Living Room series is held every other Thursday night. It features local and national country and old-timey folk artists. The Devil in a Woodpile acoustic blues quartet performs every Tuesday in the low-ceilinged front bar space.

**Setting & atmosphere:** Friendly. Black-and-white pictures of Chicago Cubs, circa 1969, hang behind the bar, as well as a goofy picture of former Chicago Bears coach Abe Gibron. Owners Tim and Katie Tuten found the pictures when they were cleaning up the bar. Tuten is also a history teacher at a Chicago public high school. There's seating for about 18 people along the bar, and the staff is personal. No jukebox, house tapes. And this may be the only bar in Chicago that offers free lollipops at the door before you depart.

**(The Hideout)**

**If you go:** Follow directions. The Hideout is in a hard-to-find industrial neighborhood. Known only by its crooked old-style sign out front, The Hideout is directly west of the City of Chicago Fleet Management parking lot, two blocks north of North Avenue and a block east of Elston Avenue. There's ample free parking, and any decent cab driver can find the place.

## THE HOUSE OF BEER

Brewskies/Blues/Hopped-up jukebox
*Who Goes There:* 21–35, wannabe fishermen, weeknight frequent flyers, cigar lovers, brewmasters, and residue singles from neighboring bars

16 West Division Street; (312) 642-2344
Zone 3 Near North

**Cover:** $3.50 for live blues on Friday nights, otherwise no cover
**Minimum:** None
**Mixed drinks:** $3.25–7 (for fine scotch)
**Wine:** None
**Beer:** $3.25–8.50
**Dress:** Anything goes

**Specials:** Cigar tasting sessions twice a month, Wednesday night combination scotch and cigar specials
**Food available:** High-cholesterol heartland stuff like nachos, Damn Hot Wings, Ostrich Burgers, and Char-Burgers

**Hours:** Monday–Friday, 4 p.m.–4 a.m.; Saturday, 11 a.m.–5 a.m.; Sunday, 11 a.m.–4 a.m.

**What goes on:** Beer drinking and cigar smoking. This is one of the newest spots on the city's most popular singles strip. It is also the most idiosyncratic. Division Street has always been known for pick-up lines. Designed like a northwoods fishing tavern, this place is known for lures. Tastings from 100 microbrewed bottled beers from around the world.

**Setting & atmosphere:** Exposed brick, bartenders in plaid shirts, and 99 bottles of beer on the wall (literally), creating an authentic Wisconsin escapism. It's completely different from anything else in the neighborhood. Jukebox is adventurous, including traditional Chicago blues, classic country, and alternative.

**If you go:** Check attitudes at the door. The waitstaff is friendly and knowledgeable. Be prepared to like sports, as events are beamed in via satellite. Also, take a cab if you can. Parking is at a premium in this neighborhood.

## HOUSE OF BLUES

The blues as a tap root for a colorful musical tree
*Who Goes There:* 21 and way over; very few blues fans; the audience
demographic depends on the booking; always a smattering of tourists
and a hard-core group of Chicago roots music listeners

329 North Dearborn Street; (312) 923-2000
Zone 3 Near North

**Cover:** $10–50, depending on the act; none in restaurant
**Minimum:** None
**Mixed drinks:** $3.75–6
**Wine:** $4.25 by the glass
**Beer:** $2.75–4
**Dress:** Anything from Bourbon Street to State Street
**Specials:** Monday SIN (Service Industry Night); last Sunday of every month is gay night, featuring dance and house music
**Food available:** A 300-seat House of Blues restaurant serves Creole-Southern cuisine under the watchful eye of executive chef Samuel McCord, formerly executive chef of the House of Blues in New Orleans and with the Rainbow Room in New York City. The restaurant is open: Monday–Thursday, 11:30 a.m.–midnight; Friday and Saturday, 11:30–2 a.m.; and Sunday, 5 p.m.–midnight. Local blues acts perform on a front porch stage within the restaurant. Sunday gospel brunch seatings in the music hall are at 10:30 a.m. and 1:30 p.m.

**Hours:** Sunday–Friday, 8 p.m.–2 a.m.; Saturday, an hour before show time until 3 a.m.

**What goes on:** Live music seven nights a week. No American concert venue is booked with the adventure and passion of the House of Blues. The Chicago club opened Thanksgiving weekend 1996, and in the first three months of operation, acts as diverse as Soul Brother #1 James Brown, Johnny Cash, jazz guitarist Les Paul, rocker-hunter Ted Nugent, and Cuban salsa singer Celia Cruz all graced the HOB (as locals call it) stage. The 400-room House of Blues hotel with 30 suites is adjacent.

**Setting & atmosphere:** House of Blues owner-founder Isaac Tigrett calls his Chicago music hall a "juke-joint opera house," and it is actually designed from the Tyl Theatre opera house in Prague, Czechoslovakia, where Mozart debuted *Don Giovanni* in 1787. The 1,465-capacity music room is the largest of the House of Blues chain (Cambridge, MA; West Hollywood, CA; Myrtle Beach, SC; and New Orleans, LA). The four-tiered music hall is adorned with hundreds of pieces of eclectic Southern

**(House of Blues)**

folk art and closed-circuit television monitors where fans can watch the live music while waiting for a drink. The music room is framed by 12 gold-plated private opera boxes that are sold for House of Blues–related charities. Sound is impeccable, and sight lines are clear. If you want to sit down, arrive very early. There are a limited number of bar stools near serving areas. Otherwise, it truly is standing room only.

**If you go:** It took a long time for musically provincial Chicagoans to get over the fact this is not a "blues" bar. *Hello?* Check your attitude at the door and you'll discover this club oozes with warmth and spirit. House of Blues is Chicago's showcase live music venue.

## JILLY'S BISTRO

Come fly with me

*Who Goes There:* 30–55, Sinatraphiles, Chicago jocks, Steve Lawrence and Eydie Gorme; lots of singles—the second, third, or fourth time around

1007 North Rush Street; (312) 664-1001
Zone 3 Near North

Cover: None
Minimum: None
Mixed drinks: $6
Wine: $5
Beer: $4–5

Specials: Sing and swing with piano man Nick Russo (until 1:30 a.m. Tuesday–Saturday). Extensive cigar selection
Food available: Only for thought

**Hours:** Sunday–Friday, 3 p.m.–2 a.m.; Saturday, until 3 a.m.

**What goes on:** Jilly Rizzo was Frank Sinatra's best friend and bodyguard. In 1992, Rizzo was killed on his 75th birthday by a drunk driver in Palm Desert, CA. Sinatra was devastated. Jilly's Bistro lives on as a tribute to Rizzo. The cozy 100-seat nightclub is a splendid Near North spot for sophisticated conversation and, quite frankly, a stiff drink. The Bistro opened on May 6, 1995 (Rizzo's birthday), and became so popular the owners quickly expanded into a separate downstairs '70s dance club called Jilly's Retro. The 400-capacity disco is open Tuesday–Friday, 8 p.m.–2 a.m.; Saturday, until 3 a.m. The disco is closed on Sunday and Monday. Covers vary between $5–10. But for intense intimacy, stick with the Bistro.

**Setting & atmosphere:** Ring-a-ding-ding. A seductive setting is accented by ornate walls filled with Sinatra and Rat Pack photographs. A model train chugs around the top of the Bistro's long cherry-oak bar. Sinatra, of course, was a train fanatic. Even bar receipts say "My Favorite Bistro—

**(Jilly's Bistro)**

Frank Sinatra." Hanging in the hallway into the bistro is the tender eulogy delivered by Las Vegas comic Joey Villa at Rizzo's funeral. Celebrities like Don Rickles, Kevin Costner, Michael Jordan, and metal-head Ozzy Osbourne have dropped in, and Steve Lawrence and Eydie Gorme stop in every time they are in town.

**If you go:** Pretend it's 1960 all over again. A Kennedy kind of Camelot has been reborn on Rush Street.

## THE LODGE

In-yo-face drinking and schmoozing in a neighborhood tavern
*Who Goes There:* Jocks, aging jocks, wannabe jocks, real jocks like Charles Barkley, and conventioneers; curious suburban invasion on weekends

21 West Division Street; (312) 642-4406
Zone 3 Near North

| | |
|---|---|
| Cover: Only for St. Patrick's Day and New Year's throngs | Dress: Anything goes |
| Minimum: None | Specials: Occasional liquor company promotions |
| Mixed drinks: $3.50–5.50 | Food available: Shelled peanuts on the floor, chili bar until 7 p.m. |
| Wine: $3.75–6.50 | |
| Beer: $3.25–4 | |

**Hours:** Monday–Friday, 2 p.m.–4 a.m.; Saturday, noon–5 a.m.; Sunday, noon–4 a.m.

**What goes on:** Open since 1957, this is the longest-running act on Division Street, or what locals call "The Street of Dreams." One of the area's premiere singles bars, the Lodge has held its own against evil influences such as disco, punk, and herpes. Its late-night license and 1:1 male-female ratio makes it a popular stop for pro athletes winding down after a game. NBA superstar Charles Barkley and ex–Kansas City Royals infielder George Brett have made the Lodge a regular stop when they're in town.

**Setting & atmosphere:** Less is more. The charm comes in a shoebox-size room resplendent in refined cedar and pseudo-antique paintings, accented by three tottering chandeliers and one of the loudest oldies jukeboxes in Chicago. You can't help but meet someone in this setting.

**If you go:** Stock up on breath mints, cologne, and perfume. On a busy night, it's like riding an El train at rush hour. And know all the words to Meat Loaf's "Paradise by the Dashboard Light." It's a traditional Lodge sing-a-long.

## MARIE'S RIP TIDE

A neighborhood bar looking for a neighborhood
*Who Goes There:* Artists, musicians, working-class neighborhood
people, and folks who swing in memory of Bobby Darin

1745 West Armitage Avenue; (773) 278-7317
Zone 1 North Side

Cover: None
Minimum: None
Mixed drinks: $3.50–4.50
Wine: $3
Beer: $2.50–3

Dress: Hello sailor
Specials: None
Food available: Chips, peanuts, hard-
boiled eggs, package liquor

**Hours:** Monday–Friday, 3 p.m.–4 a.m.; Saturday, 6 p.m.–5 a.m.; Sunday,
6 p.m.–4 a.m.

**What goes on:** People get ripped. People slow dance to the Sinatra–Elvis–
Patsy Cline jukebox. People contemplate other people in a driftwood world.

**Setting & atmosphere:** Unpretentious in a psychedelic Wisconsin way. A
long main bar is sourly accented by '50s-style diner booths. Even the regulars slip off the slick vinyl barstools. The staff redecorates the room in elementary school motif according to most approaching holidays. Rip Tide
was included on the set of *Crime Story* television series. And the back bar
features the smallest bidet on the North Side.

**If you go:** Notify your next of kin. Marie's is directly west of the Kennedy
Expressway at the Armitage Avenue exit, so it's safe and well lighted at
night. Neighborhood parking is available. Parking spaces open up as the
night goes on.

## METRO

Alternative city concert venue with an attitude
*Who Goes There:* 18–30, anybody who knows anything about music or
happens to have a friend in the band

3730 North Clark Street; (773) 549-0203
Zone 1 North Side

Cover: $5–20
Minimum: None
Mixed drinks: $3.50–5
Wine: $3
Beer: $2.75–3.50
Dress: A potpourri of flannel, Doc

Martens, leopard coats, Dr. Seuss
hats (yuck!), and anything in
black leather
Specials: Occasional record release
parties
Food available: None

**(Metro)**

**Hours:** 7 p.m.–4 a.m. nights of concerts, jam on Saturday

**What goes on:** Local and national alternative rock bands love playing this former cabaret theater because of the appreciative crowds. Metro presents all-ages shows and over-21 concerts. The downstairs Smart Bar is a dark and brooding dance club for concertgoers and people watchers. It is open 9 p.m.–4 a.m. Wednesday through Sunday. There's a separate $5 cover on Friday and Saturday, unless you attend the concert, in which case admission is waived.

**Setting & atmosphere:** With body surfing and moshing in the concert hall upstairs and blue-hazed zebra motif in the Smart Bar, there's something for every nonconformist. People come to Metro strictly to hear the music, therefore the aesthetics are underplayed.

**If you go:** You can say you knew them when. Metro has been the launching pad for breakout alternative bands from Chicago like Smashing Pumpkins and Urge Overkill. Even superstars like Axl Rose of Guns n' Roses like to hang around Metro/Smart Bar.

## MICHAEL JORDAN'S RESTAURANT

High-flying sports bar/restaurant popular with down-to-earth tourists
*Who Goes There:* Tourists, including a sizable international population, 21–40 locals who can't get tickets to Bulls games, and occasionally M.J. himself

500 North LaSalle Street; (312) 644-3865
Zone 4 The Loop

**Cover:** None
**Minimum:** None ·
**Mixed drinks:** $3.95–4.95
**Wine:** $4–4.50
**Beer:** $3–3.75
**Dress:** Casual to business attire; no baggy shorts
**Specials:** Gift shop with more than 200 Jordan memorabilia items, including T-shirts, beer mugs, and autographed basketballs. For a really wacky touch, Jordan himself answers the phone on tape and leads customers through voice mail options
**Food available:** Michael Jordan's favorites, notably his wife Juanita's macaroni and cheese, which has become something of a legend. Also, ribs, burgers, chicken, crab cakes, and Jordan's own pregame tradition of steak and potato. Dinner $20–25 per person; lunch $12–14

**Hours:** Monday–Friday, 11:30 a.m.–10:30 p.m.; Saturday and Sunday, 11 a.m.–10 p.m.

**(Michael Jordan's Restaurant)**

**What goes on:** Despite the international celebrity status of the owner, Michael Jordan's Restaurant maintains an approachable air. The clientele is less obnoxious than at the traditional Chicago (i.e., Chicago Bears) sports bars and the wait staff is friendly. Perhaps the only arrogance comes from Jordan's glassed-in private dining room, which overlooks the main floor. When His Airness is in town, he comes to the restaurant two or three times a week, but the segregation still kind of elevates him to Pope status.

**Setting & atmosphere:** Basketball nirvana. A $350,000 6-by-20-foot "video wall" for televised basketball and other sports events. You'll recognize the restaurant with a 250-foot-diameter basketball on the roof. Originally a horse and trolley car stable, the bar/restaurant is slam-jammed with jerseys, bronzed sneakers, archival photos, and 20 *Sports Illustrated* covers depicting Jordan—with the exception of his minor league baseball exploits. Kids love it. A main-floor sports bar seats 150. The second-floor restaurant offers another 200 seats, and there is a 250-person capacity for banquet facilities on the third floor.

**If you go:** This is Chicago's answer to Disney World. When Jordan's first opened in 1993, people waited for up to two hours to gain entry for dinner. Reservations are not taken for dinner, but lunch reservations are accepted. The rumble has been tempered over time, although with more than 1,100 customers a day, locals still regard Jordan's as one of the world's busiest restaurants. Be patient and hang loose.

## OLD TOWN ALE HOUSE

From Bach to Bukowski
*Who Goes There:* Whoever dares, 25–70, but a sanctuary for artists, journalists, Second City actors, and late-night waitresses and bartenders

219 West North Avenue; (312) 944-7020
Zone 3 Near North

| | |
|---|---|
| Cover: None | Dress: Old raincoated; funky; cigars |
| Minimum: None, nor is there a maxi-     mum | are welcome |
| | Specials: None |
| Mixed drinks: $3–5 | Food available: Snacks, but it's okay |
| Wine: $2.25–2.75 | to bring in fast food |
| Beer: $1.75–3.25 | |

**Hours:** Sunday–Friday, noon–4 a.m.; Saturday, noon–5 a.m. Open 365 days a year.

**(Old Town Ale House)**

**What goes on:** Serious talking and serious drinking. Classic Chicago writers like Studs Terkel and the late Mike Royko used to pound a few here. The original Ale House opened across the street in 1958. It burned down in 1970, maybe due to a negative karma. The original Ale House was run by a German who owned a pack of German sheperds named after Nazi generals. Only the long bar was salvaged from across the street. The Ale House's late-night license makes it a popular stop for nightcrawlers getting off work late.

**Setting & atmosphere:** Sleazy, which is a word even the proprietors use. The jukebox is heavy on jazz, soul, classical, and opera. A cornucopia of crazy artifacts include a gorilla bust that is decorated for appropriate seasons, a crooked "Jurassic Park" sign, and strange newspaper clippings bartenders cut and paste on the wall. Chicago folk singer–humorist Larry Rand best summed up the Ale House as "A fern bar where the customers are often more potted than the plants."

**If you go:** You won't be sorry. This is as authentic as a Near North Side drinking experience can get. Just don't cross the stray punch lines from the Second City folks, still winding down from their late-night sets across the street.

## POPS FOR CHAMPAGNE

Cozy, classy, and cleverly understated
*Who Goes There:* Upper echelon, 30–50, well-dressed connoisseurs of fine bubbly, young urban professionals, fancy neighborhood folks

2934 North Sheffield Avenue; (773) 472-1000
Zone 1 North Side

**Cover:** No cover Sunday and Monday, $6 Tuesday–Thursday, $9 Friday and Saturday. Live jazz every night
**Minimum:** None
**Mixed drinks:** $4.50–12
**Wine:** $5–10 (glasses), $14–160 (bottles)

**Beer:** $3.25–7.75
**Dress:** After-work garb
**Specials:** Champagne tasting parties, classes
**Food available:** Nightly appetizers including osetra caviar

**Hours:** Every day, 5 p.m.–2 a.m.

**What goes on:** Although the ambience can be intimidating, the easygoing staff and patrons could be found in any neighborhood pub. Conversation flows from the newest plays in town to the latest imports in champagne. The sophistcated jazz club opened in 1986 and entertains nightly to crowds that generally pour in around 11 p.m. Private parties can be arranged.

**(Pops for Champagne)**

**Setting & atmosphere:** This once-Spanish grocery store envelops you in a highly elegant world. Vaulted ceilings, two-story windows, and marbleized walls accent the cozy lounge with 25 small tables and an elevated stage (complete with a black baby grand piano) behind the bar. Art deco accents and burgundy curtains add a nice touch. Weather permitting, customers can adjourn to a small back patio lined with beautiful evergreen and relax under the evening sky.

**If you go:** Don't order a beer. Prepare yourself for the prices; this is no cheap route. Bring a date to make a good impression, bring a boss to ask for a raise. Patrons run next door to the attached, more casual Star Bar— also owned by Pops—but always return for a touch of real class.

## WEEDS

Cultural anarchy for a new Beat Generation
*Who Goes There:* Lovable riffraff between 21–65, artists and/or slackers, newspaper people, cab drivers, and strippers

1555 North Dayton; (312) 943-7815
Zone 1 North Side

| | |
|---|---|
| Cover: None | Dress: Grateful Deadish |
| Minimum: None | Specials: A free shot of tequila if it's |
| Mixed drinks: $2.50–3.50 | late enough |
| Wine: $3 | Food available: Chips, etc. |
| Beer: $2.50–3.25 | |

**Hours:** Monday–Friday, 4 p.m.–2 a.m.; Saturday, 4 p.m.–3 a.m.; Sunday, closed.

**What goes on:** Just about anything. Monday is poetry night, hosted by Gregorio Gomez, artistic director of the Chicago Latino Theater. Tuesdays and Wednesdays are "Comfort Nights," which means there are no scheduled activities. Some of the city's top jazz players jam on Thursday nights, featured rock bands play on Friday nights, and Saturday nights are reserved for open stage. There are bizarre special events like Lawrence Welk Bubble Day and Birth Control Day (where customers wear IUDs as earrings). Never a cover.

**Setting & atmosphere:** Twisted Bohemian. Old bras and unused condoms hang from the ceiling along with the year-round Christmas lights thing. Most of the bar's furnishings were gathered from neighborhood dumpsters. Sabbath candles and incense burn along the bar, and a funky beer garden is utilized in season. The bar gets its name from being at the corner of Dayton and Weed Streets.

**(Weeds)**

**If you go:** Owner-proprietor-poet Sergio Mayora—who once ran for mayor of Chicago—wrote of his bar: "A place with a difference; where what you are or who you are is only as important as where you are." Be prepared to rub shoulders with all walks of life, hell-raisers, hillbillies, chicks, and tricks. A once-in-a-lifetime experience.

## WRIGLEYVILLE TAP

Rock 'n' baseball is the soundtrack for this classic neighborhood bar
*Who Goes There:* The most knowledgable Chicago Cubs fans in the city, musicians and rock fans, regulars like Eddie Vedder of Pearl Jam (a Chicago-area native) and Jewel, when she's in town

3724 North Clark; (773) 528-4422
Zone 1 North Side

| | |
|---|---|
| Cover: Never | Dress: Day: baseball caps and T-shirts; Night: body piercings, eyeshadow, paint it black |
| Minimum: None | |
| Mixed drinks: $3.25 | |
| Wine: $3.50 | Specials: End of season pig roast |
| Beer: $2.50, $3.50 for imports | Food available: A 20-item menu |

**Hours:** Monday–Thursday, 3 p.m.–2 a.m.; Friday and Sunday, 11 a.m.–2 a.m.; Saturday, 11 a.m.–3 a.m.

**What goes on:** During the baseball and even the basketball season this is the place to congregate before and after games. You never know who you will run into. The Smashing Pumpkins live in the neighborhood, and they've been known to stop in for a libation when they're in town. The Tap is in an ideal location, next door to the alternative rock club Metro and a block north of Wrigley Field, the home of the beloved Chicago Cubs.

**Setting & atmosphere:** The Tap has two cozy rooms. The 50-seat back room is a pool hall and (real steel-tipped) dart room, the 60-seat front area is full of sports autographs and memorabilia donated by Chicago Cubs personnel and the occasional ballplayer. Rock 'n' roll items include autographed pictures from Tap visitors like Hootie and the Blowfish, the BoDeans, and the Smithereens. The bar's GoliathTapper features 25 microbrews, imports, and domestics—the largest draught beer selection in the neighborhood.

**If you go:** Don't worry, be happy. The Tap's diverse clientele will rub off on you. This is one of the last neighborhood bars in this trendy northside area. Look no further than Carmella, a 95-year-old bleacher bum who has been known to accompany the Tap regulars on their annual summer road trips to watch the Cubs play in Milwaukee.

## Part Eight

# Exercise and Recreation

## Handling Chicago's Weather

Most of the folks on our *Unofficial Guide* research team work out routinely. Some bike, some run, some lift weights, while others play tennis or do aerobics. We discovered that Chicago is a city of extremes when it comes to climate. In the summer, humidity is intense and temperatures often climb above 90° by mid-afternoon, making outdoor exercise and recreation problematic unless you plan to lounge on a Lake Michigan beach or go for a swim. Winter, on the other hand, can be positively arctic in intensity, especially in January and February, when cold temperatures and icy blasts off the lake plunge windchill factors to well below zero.

The solution in the summer is to exercise early, before the sun and humidity make conditions outdoors too hot and muggy. In the winter, only hearty outdoor types such as cross-country skiers will want to brave the cold and wind; everyone else should plan to exercise indoors. The good news is that spring and fall are usually delightful for enjoying the outdoors.

Regardless of the season, however, keep in mind that Chicago's weather is highly variable. As the locals like to say, if you don't like the weather, just wait a while; it'll change.

Keep that in mind before setting out on an all-day outing, and take along appropriate rain gear and/or warm clothing.

## Indoor Sports

### FREE WEIGHTS AND NAUTILUS

Many of the major hotels in Chicago have either a spa or fitness room with weight-lifting equipment on-site, or have reciprocity with a nearby health club that extends privileges to hotel guests. For an aerobic workout, most of the fitness rooms offer a Lifecycle, a Stairmaster, or a rowing machine.

## FITNESS CENTERS AND AEROBICS

Many Chicago fitness centers are coed and accept daily or short-term memberships. The **Chicago Fitness Center,** located at 3131 North Lincoln Avenue (at Belmont) offers a weight room with 50 pieces of equipment, including free weights, and Nautilus and Universal fixed-weight machines. Aerobic equipment includes Stairmasters, treadmills, and exercise bikes. The daily fee is $7; bring a lock. For more information, call (773) 549-8181.

**World Gym and Fitness Center,** located at 909 West Montrose (at Sheridan), offers free weights and Nautilus fixed-weight machines, Stairmasters, exercise bikes, Nordic Track, and steam and sauna rooms. The cost is $15 a day; for more information, call (773) 348-1212.

## EXERCISING IN YOUR HOTEL

You work out regularly, but here you are stuck on a rainy day in a hotel without an excercise room. Worse, you're out of sorts from overeating, sitting in airplanes, and not being able to let off steam. Don't despair. Unless your hotel is designed like a sprawling dude ranch, you have stairs to play on. Put on your workout clothes and find a nice interior stairwell, which all hotels are required to have in case of fire. Devise a step workout consistent with your fitness level.

Bob's Plan (for a ten-story hotel): From your floor, descend to the very bottom of the stairwell. Walk up ten flights and down again to get warmed up. Then, taking the stairs two at a time, bound up two floors and return to the bottom quickly, but normally (i.e., one step at a time). Next, bound up three floors and return. Add a floor after each circuit until you get to the top floor. Then reverse the process, ascending one less floor on each round trip: 9-, 8-, 7-, floors etc. You get the idea. Tell somebody where you'll be in case you fall down the stairs or something. Listen to your body and don't overdo it. If your hotel has 30 stories, don't feel compelled to make it to the top.

Joe's Plan (for a ten-story hotel): Sit in the stairwell on the fourth-floor landing with a sixpack of Bud and laugh at Bob every time he chugs past. Thank God that you are not a Type-A obsessive-compulsive.

If steps aren't your gig, you might consider buying a Reebok Slide exerciser. Self-contained, compact, and weighing less than 12 pounds, the slide can be spread out on your hotel room floor for a great workout. Take it with you wherever you travel.

# Outdoor Sports

## WALKING

While not as compact as, say, most European cities, Chicago is still a great town for getting around by foot. After all, the city is as flat as an Illinois corn field. If you mentally break the city up into discrete chunks—the Loop, River North, the Magnificent Mile, etc.—and don't overextend yourself, walking is the best way to explore Chicago. Folks who are fit and enjoy using their own two feet should bring comfortable walking shoes and regularly give themselves a rest by occasionally taking a taxi, a bus, or the El.

### Along the Lake

Serious walkers and people in search of great scenery and primo people-watching as they stretch their legs should head for Chicago's premier walking destination, the **Lakefront Trail** along Lake Michigan. The 20-mile paved path is flat, clean, well lighted—and usually crowded with people who have the same idea as you. You really haven't done Chicago unless you've experienced the Lakefront Trail.

Some safety notes: The stretch of path from McCormick Place south to Hyde Park is considered bandit turf; stay to the north in daylight hours and you'll be OK. Pedestrian tunnels under Lake Shore Drive make it possible to reach the trail without getting killed on the busy roadway.

### City Walks

Other great destinations for a scenic stroll include the **Gold Coast** (a neighborhood of sumptuous mansions and townhouses located just above the Magnificent Mile), **Lincoln Park** (featuring 1,200 acres of greenery, three museums, and a zoo), and **Oak Park** (where strollers can explore a shady neighborhood full of homes designed by Frank Lloyd Wright).

In late 1996 the northbound lanes of Lake Shore Drive were relocated to the west of the Field Museum. New landscaping created a new, traffic-free **Museum Campus** comprising the Field Museum, the Shedd Aquarium, and the Adler Planetarium. Other pedestrian friendly amenities planned for the ten-acre park include rows of elm trees; a large, sloping lawn in front of the Field Museum and to the west of the Shedd Aquarium; and a series of decorative plazas linked by walkways between the museums. A new pedestrian concourse underneath Lake Shore Drive at Roosevelt Road will serve as an entranceway to the Museum Campus.

The planetarium, by the way, sits on a former island in Lake Michigan that's now linked to the shore by a half-mile peninsula. The view of

Chicago's skyline, as you can imagine, is stupendous, and it's a great place to watch private planes landing and taking off at Meigs Field. It's one of Chicago's top make-out spots.

Another outstanding place to walk is the Gothic—and beautiful— campus of the **University of Chicago** in Hyde Park. Don't miss the unmistakable 12-ton abstract sculpture, *Nuclear Energy,* by Henry Moore; it's located on the spot where Enrico Fermi and other University of Chicago scientists achieved the first self-sustained nuclear chain reaction in 1942.

Farther afield, more great walking destinations include **Brookfield Zoo** (14 miles west of the city), the **Morton Arboretum** (25 miles west of the Loop; 1,500 acres of native woodlands and 25 miles of trails), and the **Chicago Botanic Garden** (300 acres of landscaped gardens and islands located 18 miles north of downtown Chicago).

## RUNNING

The Big Enchilada of Chicago running routes is the **Lakefront Trail** along Lake Michigan. And runners, without handlebars sticking out or the need to weave like in-line skaters, have it easier when it comes to penetrating the throngs that choke the path in nice weather. And this is where you'll routinely see the Windy City's most serious runners working out.

Folks looking for more elbow room can go a little north of downtown and run on the section of trail between Belmont Harbor and the northern neighborhood of Edgewater. While the same holds true for the six-mile stretch starting below McCormick Place, it's not nearly as safe.

Good news for runners who prefer training on a soft surface instead of asphalt: Chicago is surrounded by a network of forest preserves that are easy to reach by car. To run in a sylvan setting, head to **Palos Forest Preserve District** in southwest Cook County, about 20 miles from downtown. The nation's largest forest preserve (nearly 14,000 acres) features 80 miles of multipurpose trails, which are ten feet wide and covered with gravel or grass. For more information on Palos and other forest preserves, call (773) 261-8400.

## TENNIS

The Chicago Park District has close to 700 outdoor tennis courts and some of them are convenient to visitors staying downtown. The nets go up in mid-April and usually stay up through October. Reservations aren't required for most courts; just put your racquet by the net and the players using the court will know you want to use it next. Other courts require phone reservations; see below.

**Daley Bicentennial Plaza,** located downtown at 337 East Randolph Street (between Columbus and Lake Shore drives), features 12 lighted courts. For reservations, call (312) 742-7650 after 10 a.m. the day before you plan to play. Hours are 7 a.m. to 10 p.m. weekdays and 8 a.m. to 7 p.m. weekends; the fee is $5 an hour.

Another 12 lighted courts are available in **Grant Park** at 900 South Columbus Drive; reservations aren't accepted, courts are free during the day, and there's a nominal charge after 5 p.m. **Lake Shore Park,** 808 North Lake Shore Drive (across from Northwestern University), has two lighted courts; no reservations are accepted, hours are 7 a.m. to 11 p.m. daily, and they can be used for free. **Waveland,** located in Lincoln Park, features 20 lighted courts. Reservations are required and fees are charged; call (773) 868-4132.

**McFetridge Sports Center,** located at 3843 North California Avenue in northwest Chicago, has six indoor tennis courts. Hours are 7 a.m. to 10 p.m. daily; rates are $10.50 per person/per hour during the day and $18 in the evening and on weekends. Call (312) 742-7586 for reservations.

## GOLF

The Chicago Park District boasts six public golf courses managed by Kemper Golf Management. The courses are open mid-April through November from dawn to dusk. Make reservations at least a week in advance on Kemper's helpful automated phone tee-time reservation system, which provides directions to, and descriptions of, all six courses. Have a credit card handy and keep in mind that no rain checks or refunds are issued; call (312) 245-0909.

The **Sydney R. Marovitz Golf Course** (usually called "Waveland," the course's former name) is the *crème de la crème* of Chicago's public courses. Located close to the ritzy Gold Coast and Lake Michigan, the course features great views, a location close to downtown, and a design modeled on Pebble Beach. Not a lot of trees, but the fairways are fairly long (3,290 yards) compared to other municipal courses.

It's the place to go to impress a client—and you won't be alone. The nine-hole course handles about 400 golfers a day; figure on three hours to play a round. Fees for nonresidents are $14.50 on weekdays, $16.50 on weekends, and $8 for seniors and kids. The course is located at the lakefront in Lincoln Park.

**South Shore Golf Course,** located at 7059 Lake Shore Drive, is a nine-holer that's fairly short (2,903 yards). But the holes are well designed and moderately challenging, and South Shore is considered an undiscovered gem. The setting on the lake means that every hole is a visual feast, whether it's waves of Lake Michigan crashing along the fairway or spectacular views of the city. It's also the only municipal course that rents driving carts ($16 per round). Fees for nonresidents are $10.50 on weekdays, $11.50 on weekends, and $7.50 for seniors and kids.

**Robert A. Black Golf Course,** located at 2045 West Pratt Street (near the lakefront and the city's northern boundary), is a nine-hole, 3,200-yard course with no water hazards. But it does have 21 bunkers (sand traps), making it a challenging course. Nonresident fees are $12.50 weekdays, $13.50 weekends, and $8 for seniors and kids.

Chicago's only 18-hole municipal course is at **Jackson Park,** located near the southern terminus of Lake Shore Drive at 63rd Street and Stony Island Avenue. It's a moderately difficult, 5,538-yard course with a lot of trees, but not much sand or water. Fees for nonresidents are $16.50 week-days, $17.50 weekends, and $9 for seniors and kids.

**Marquette Park Golf Course,** a nine-holer located at 6700 South Kedzie Avenue (at 67th Street near Midway Airport), offers wide fairways and water on seven holes. The 3,300-yard course is rated pretty easy. Non-resident fees are $11 weekdays, $12 weekends, and $8 for seniors and kids.

Located west of downtown near Oak Park, **Columbus Park Golf Course** (5700 West Jackson Boulevard) is recommended for novices. The 2,832-yard course offers wide, open fairways and large greens. Fees for nonresidents are $10.50 weekdays, $11.50 weekends, and $7.50 for seniors and kids.

## ROAD BICYCLING AND IN-LINE SKATING

With the exception of hardened urban cyclists and former bike messen-gers, recreational riders should stay off Chicago's mean streets. And that goes double for weaving in-line skaters.

So where's the best place to ride a skinny-tire bike or skate the black ice? That's easy—the **Lakefront Trail,** which hums with throngs of the Lycra-clad and sportif, is the Windy City's primo riding and Rollerblading desti-nation. Any excursion on the paved path along Lake Michigan is an out-and-back endeavor, so try to figure out which way the wind blows before starting out. Then ride or skate out into a head wind, which becomes a helpful tail wind on the way back. If you want to avoid the worst of the crowds, try riding or 'blading north of downtown between Belmont Har-bor and the neighborhood of Edgewater.

The six-mile stretch of trail south of McCormick Place is considered unsafe, in spite of beefed-up bike-mounted police patrols. "Gangs use two-way radios to spot riders on bikes with suspension forks, beat the shit out of them and steal their bikes," reports Chicago cyclist Ron Bercow, former manager of the Performance Bike Shop on North Halsted Street. Ride with a friend and go early, and you should be alright.

### Renting Bikes and In-Line Skates

**Bike Chicago** rents bikes at four locations along the Lakefront Trail and offers free maps, group guided tours, and delivery to your hotel. Call (800) 915-BIKE for more information.

For rental of high-quality in-line skates, your best bet is **Windward Sports,** located at 3317 North Clark Street. Rates are $10 a day; the shop is only three blocks from the Lakefront Trail. For more information, call (773) 472-6868.

### Road Rides

Local roadies who like to go the distance say the best road riding is out Sheridan Road and north to Kenosha, Wisconsin—a 115-mile round-trip ride, if you're up for it. A shorter option is to drive to Evanston, park at Northwestern University, and ride north on **Sheridan Road** to Fort Sheridan, about 30 miles round-trip. While Sheridan Road is scenic and even has a couple of hills (!), it's not very bicycle-friendly—there's no bike lane, often not much shoulder, and traffic is heavy—so it's a route best left to experienced road cyclists.

## MOUNTAIN BIKING

Even though it's paved, the **Lakefront Trail** is Chicago's number one fat-tire route. But what if you want the feel of mud between your knobbies? While mountain biking has taken the Windy City by storm (just like everywhere else), we're sad to report that challenging single-track trails are scarce around Chicago.

The **Palos Forest Preserve District** in Cook County has restricted bicycles to designated single-track trails in the immensely popular 14,000-acre Palos Preserve. It's a ravine-sliced forest located 20 miles southwest of the city and the best place around for dedicated fat-tire fanatics to rock 'n' roll in the dirt. Call Palos at (708) 771-1330 for a free map showing the trails that are okay to ride.

### For the Hard-Core

Local hammerheads report the most adventurous, varied, and accessible single-track action is found at **Kettle Moraine** in Wisconsin, about a 90-minute drive from Chicago. A system of trails originally cut for hikers (and now legal for mountain bikes) features some steep and narrow stuff that will thrill experienced mountain bikers, but might put off first-time riders. For more information, call (414) 594-6200.

To get there, take I-94 to Wisconsin Highway 50 to US 12. Park at the LaGrange General Store and pick up sandwiches and maps; then head down County Road H a mile to the main parking area. The parking fee is $7 and there's a $3 per person trail-use fee.

## Easy Riding

Other off-road options close to Chicago are considerably tamer than the challenging trails in Palos. Forty miles west of Chicago, the **Fox River Trail** provides relative solitude and easy pedaling on a 37-mile stretch of asphalt and crushed limestone that follows the eponymous river between the Wayne's Worldian suburbs of Aurora and Elgin. **Mill Race Cyclery,** located in the western suburb of Geneva at 11 East State Street, rents hybrid and mountain bikes for use on the trail. Rates are $6 an hour (two-hour minimum) and $20 a day on weekdays, and $25 a day on weekends. For more information, call the shop at (630) 232-2833.

The **Busse Woods Bicycle Trail** is an 11-mile scenic bike path weaving through the woods and meadows of the 3,700-acre Ned Brown Preserve, located in northwestern Cook County about 20 miles from the Loop. The **North Branch Bicycle Trail** starts at Caldwell and Devon avenues in Chicago and continues north 20 miles along the North Branch of the Chicago River to the Chicago Botanic Garden. Pack a lunch and picnic at the gardens; fresh-water wells are located along the trail.

## SWIMMING

The Lake Michigan shore is lined with 31 sand beaches for sunning and swimming. These public beaches are manned with lifeguards from June to mid-September daily from 9 a.m. to 9 p.m., and are free. Lockers are available at the major beaches.

**Oak Street Beach,** the closest to downtown and only a credit card's throw away from Bloomingdale's, is called the St. Tropez of the Midwest. It's also the most crowded of the lakefront beaches; the young and the beautiful, perfect-10 models, jet-setting flight attendants, all-American Frisbee-tossing frat brothers and sorority sisters, Eurotrash, ordinary folk, and voyeurs blanket the sand on steamy summer weekends. Pedestrians can get there safely via the underpass across from the Drake Hotel at Michigan Avenue and Oak Street.

**North Avenue Beach** is more family-oriented than hip Oak Street Beach and stretches north for a mile, from just above North Avenue to

Fullerton Avenue. Farther north, **Montrose Avenue Beach** offers great views of the Chicago skyline.

Rule of thumb: The crowds at the popular beaches tend to thin out the farther north you go. Example: Unabashed bare-it-all types flock to **Pratt Boulevard Beach** for illegal skinny-dipping in the wee hours. Separated by a seldom-used park, a wide beach, no spotlights, no high-rises, no search-lights, and even a little hill to block joggers' views, the dark sandy beach near Morse Avenue may be the perfect place to take it all off and dive into the surf. A practical note: Lake Michigan water can be chilly, even in August.

## PADDLING

For folks in search of a touch of wilderness solitude, the best bet in lake-bound Chicago is by water. While powerboat traffic on Lake Michigan can make the lake a misery of chop, noise, and exhaust on summer afternoons, tranquility in a canoe or sea kayak can be found early in the morning or late at night. On the main branch of the Chicago River, canoeing may be the best way of enjoying the architectural delights of the city, while a canoe trek on the North Branch of the river reveals an astounding amount of wildlife for an urban stream.

Headquarters for paddling information and rentals in the Windy City is **Chicagoland Canoe Base,** located at 4019 North Narraganset Avenue (phone (773) 777-1489). Vic Hurtowy points clients toward some of the Midwest's best-kept paddling secrets, such as the Skokie Lagoons, a nearby urban jewel where boaters can sneak up on deer, coyote, fox, great blue heron, egrets, and other fish-eating birds.

Canoe rentals are $35 the first day and $15 each additional day, and include a car-top carrier, paddles, personal flotation devices, and plenty of advice. The shop also schedules more than 100 organized trips a year; they're free. Give Vic a call to find out what's on tap.

## WINDSURFING

The Windy City earns its epithet with nine-mile-an-hour average winds on Lake Michigan. Hey, it ain't Oregon's Columbia River Gorge, but Chicago boardsailors aren't complaining. **Montrose Beach** is rated Chicago's safest launch point, with the **South Side Rainbow Beach** next in popularity.

Never tried windsurfing? **Windward Sports** offers a two-day certification course that will teach you all you need to know for $120. Lessons are given at Wolf Lake, south of Chicago near the Indiana state line; it's a controlled environment that's safe and lets novices concentrate on learning skills. Board rentals, offered June through August by Windward Sports at Montrose Beach, are $35 a day. For more information, call the shop at (773) 472-6868.

To get a **marine weather forecast** before setting out, call the National Weather Service at (815) 834-0675. Keep in mind that Chicago's quick-change weather can leave novices stranded far from shore.

## ICE SKATING

**Daley Bicentennial Plaza,** located at 337 East Randolph, features an out-door, 80-foot by 135-foot rink with stunning views of Lake Michigan and the Loop. The season on the prepared rink (which is equipped with chillers) starts in November and runs through mid-March. Hours are 10 a.m. to 10 p.m. daily. Admission is $2 for adults and $1 for children age 14 and under; figure-skate rentals are the same price as admission. For more information, call (312) 742-7650.

At **Skate on State** (in the Loop at State and Randolph Streets) skating admission is $1 during a season that lasts from November through mid-March. During the week, two-hour sessions run 9 to 11:15 a.m., noon to 2 p.m., 2:30 to 4:30 p.m., and 5 to 7:15 p.m. On weekends, shorter sessions run 9 to 11 a.m., 11:30 to 1 p.m., 1:30 to 3 p.m., and 3:30 to 7:15 p.m. Skate rentals per session are $3 for adults and $2 for children. For more information, call (312) 744-3315.

## DOWNHILL SKIING

The closest ski resort to Chicago is **Wilmot Mountain,** about an hour's drive north of O'Hare, just over the Wisconsin state line. The resort features 25 runs with a 230-foot vertical, snowmaking, night skiing until 11 p.m., a pro shop, rentals, instruction, cafeteria, and bar. Weather permitting, Wilmot is open from December 1 through mid-March; call their local snow information line at (773) 736-0787. For directions and a list of local motels, call (414) 862-2301.

## CROSS-COUNTRY SKIING

When Mother Nature lays down a blanket of the white stuff, a lot of Chicagoans strap on skinny skis and head for the nearest park or forest preserve to enjoy a day of kicking and gliding.

**Camp Sagawau,** located about 20 miles southwest of the Loop in the Cook County Palos Forest Preserve District, features a system of groomed cross-country ski trails that traverse a scenic landscape of forest and prairie. The Sag Trail is gentle and ideal for novices, while rolling Ridge Run accommodates intermediate and advanced Nordic skiers.

The trails are open whenever there's enough snow on the ground to ski; ski rentals and lessons are also available. Camp Sagawau is on Route 83 east of Archer Avenue at 12545 West 111th Street in Lemont. For more information, a snow report, and directions, call (630) 257-2045.

# Spectator Sports

## A SPORTS-CRAZY TOWN

Chicago is quite possibly the most sports-crazy town in the United States, a city famous for its teams that win frequently . . . and those that don't. Either way, Chicago sports fans are renowned for their tenacity, whether it's for the oft-winning Bears, Bulls, or Blackhawks or those perennial losers, the Chicago Cubs.

The enthusiasm is fueled by a sports culture steeped in tradition and folklore. Consider this: In 1876, the same year General George Custer was shut out by Sitting Bull at Little Big Horn, the team that would evolve into today's Chicago Cubs won the National League championship in its first season of baseball. Since then, Chicagoans have shown an unwavering passion for pro sports. Other notable events and personalities from Chicago's sports past include the "Black Sox" betting scandal of 1919, Hall of Fame TV and radio sports announcer Harry Caray singing an off-key "Take Me Out to the Ballgame" during the seventh-inning stretch at Wrigley Field, the glorious Bears triumph of 1986, and Michael Jordan, the world's most famous athlete, leading the Chicago Bulls to consecutive NBA championships.

For visitors, the quintessential Chicago sporting experience is an afternoon baseball game at Wrigley Field, home of the Cubs. It's a place where fans feel like they've stepped back in time to the days before World War II. Spectators love the ivy-covered walls, the way errant breezes can turn pop-ups into home runs, and the opportunity for some first-rate people-watching as all sizes, shapes, and classes of Chicagoans root for the Cubs.

Chicago is also blessed with many colleges and universities, which provide a wide array of spectator sports. For current listings and goings-on of both pro and amateur events, check the sports sections of the *Chicago Tribune* and the *Chicago Sun-Times*.

## PRO TEAMS

### Baseball

Chicago is home to two professional baseball teams: The **Chicago Cubs** (National League), who play at venerable Wrigley Field on the North Side (1060 West Addison) and the **Chicago White Sox** (American League), who play at the new Comiskey Park on the South Side (333 West 35th Street). The season starts around the first week of April and continues through early October.

The Cubs, as most baseball fans know, are a testament to Chicago's unstoppable allegiance in the face of adversity; the team hasn't won a World Series since 1908. No matter—like the New York Mets of yesteryear, the Cubbies are affectionately embraced by Chicago fans and picture-perfect Wrigley Field draws more than two million fans each year for a taste of baseball history. Although lights were added to the stadium in 1988, most games are still played during the day; aficionados insist it's still the only way to see a game at the park.

For schedule information, call (773) 404-2827; tickets can be ordered by calling (312) 831-CUBS (in Illinois) or (800) 347-CUBS (outside Illinois). Get tickets as far in advance as possible, but you can try your luck at the ticket window or outside the gates before game time; some gracious souls occasionally sell or even give away extra tickets. Scalpers are another source.

Street parking is restricted during day games in the neighborhood around Wrigley Field; public transportation is the best way for visitors to reach the park. Take the Englewood/Howard El line to the Addison Street station.

While geography divides the fans of the North Side Cubs from the South Side White Sox, they're at least joined together by a long tradition of championship futility; the Sox last won the World Series in 1917. Today the White Sox play in spanking-new Comiskey Park, which replaced the old stadium of the same name in 1991. The new facility features unobstructed views of the action and TV monitors in the walkways so fans don't miss a thing. Warning: The upper-deck seats should be avoided by folks who are prone to nose bleeds or scared of heights.

To find out when the White Sox are playing at home, call (312) 674-1000; for tickets, call (312) 831-1769. Forget about parking at Comiskey; on-street parking is virtually nonexistent and the official lots are a nightmare to get in and out of. Take the train: El service runs along the Dan Ryan Expressway two blocks to the east; get off at 35th Street. Large crowds flocking to and from the game virtually eliminate the chance of getting mugged on the short walk, but watch out for pickpockets working the throngs.

### Football

Sports tradition in Chicago isn't restricted to baseball. The **Chicago Bears** can point to a football history that goes back to the 1930s. Yet like their baseball counterparts, "da Bears" suffer from an inability to pull off championships. Only once, in 1986, has the team won the Super Bowl—a game that made William "Refrigerator" Perry a household name.

Pro gridiron action takes place at Soldier Field, where a colonnade of paired 100-foot concrete Doric columns rise majestically behind fans brave enough to endure icy blasts off Lake Michigan. Glassed-in skyboxes added in 1981 to shelter corporate hotshots cost about $7,500 a game; the price is negotiable if rented for the season. Soldier Field is located at 425 East McFetridge Drive (at South Lake Shore Drive, just south of the Field Museum).

For tickets and information on Bears games, call (847) 615-2327 Monday through Friday from 9 a.m. to 4 p.m. Alas, subscription sales account for most tickets. Your best bet is to locate a subscriber trying to unload a ticket before the game. Parking is relatively plentiful and nearby. Public transportation: By bus, take the #146 State Street/North Michigan Avenue downtown, or the Red or Orange Line train to the Roosevelt Road station and walk east.

## Basketball

The NBA **Chicago Bulls** always sell out. Currently, the team plays in the United Center, a $170 million arena that seats 21,500 and is adorned with 217 luxury skyboxes. For game times, call (312) 455-4000. To purchase tickets, call (312) 559-1212; the season starts in October and runs through April.

Tickets go on sale in September for the season and some games sell out in a few weeks. Scattered single tickets are sometimes available two weeks before a game, but day-of-game tickets are never available. The United Center is located at 1901 West Madison Street, west of the Loop; take the #20 Madison Street bus.

## Hockey

Loud, gregarious fans like to watch the NHL **Chicago Blackhawks** mix it up on the ice as much as they like to mix it up in the stands. They're also fiercely devoted to the team, which has claimed three National Hockey League championship trophies—in 1934, 1938, and 1961.

The Blackhawks share quarters with the Chicago Bulls in the United Center, located at 1901 East Madison Street; take the #20 Madison Street bus. For schedules and game times, call (312) 455-4500; for tickets, call (312) 559-1212. The season runs October through April.

## Soccer

For fast indoor soccer action, watch the **Chicago Power** play at the Rosemont Horizon near O'Hare. Order tickets by calling (312) 559-1212. To get there, take the Blue Line train to the River Road station. The season starts in November and ends in April.

## COLLEGE SPORTS

Chicago's only Division I conference (Big Ten) football/basketball representatives are the **Northwestern University Wildcats,** who play in nearby Evanston. Gridiron action takes place in Dyche Stadium, 1501 Central Avenue; call (847) 491-7503 for information. Basketball is played at McGaw Hall, 2705 Ashland Avenue; phone (847) 491-7887.

Other college basketball teams include the **DePaul Blue Demons,** who play at DePaul University, 1011 West Belden (phone (312) 362-8000); the **Loyola Ramblers,** who provide on-the-court action at Loyola University, 6525 North Sheridan Road (phone (773) 508-2560); and the **University of Illinois at Chicago Flames,** who play ball at the University of Illinois Pavilion, 1150 West Harrison Street (phone (312) 413-5700).

## HORSE RACING

Out of the ashes of the old Arlington Park Race Track (which burned in 1985) has risen **Arlington International Race Course,** rated as an even bigger and better thoroughbred racing/entertainment venue. The horses run May through October; the track is located at Euclid and Wilkie roads in Arlington Heights (about 25 miles northwest of the Loop). For more information, call (847) 255-4300.

**Hawthorne Race Course** in Cicero features harness-racing excitement in January and February, and thoroughbred racing September through December. The track is located at 3501 South Laramie Avenue, about five miles southwest of the Loop. For post times and more information, call (708) 780-3700. **Sportsman's Park,** next to Hawthorne in Cicero, features thoroughbred racing from late February through late May and harness racing from early May through October. Call (708) 652-2812 for more information.

## OFF-TRACK BETTING AND RIVERBOAT CASINOS

Folks allergic to real horses and mud can still play the ponies at off-track betting locations downtown. There are two locations: State Street OTB at 177 North State Street (phone (312) 419-8787) and Jackson OTB at 223 West Jackson (phone (312) 427-2300).

Riverboat gambling is as close as an hour away from downtown Chicago. **Hollywood Casino Aurora** features slots, table games, dining, Las Vegas–style entertainment, and movie memorabilia. Hollywood's boats depart every 90 minutes from 8:30 a.m. to 9:30 p.m. (often later on weekends) daily for three-hour sessions on the Fox River. Admission is free. Patrons must be age 21 or older and a photo ID may be required. For more information and directions, call (800) 888-7777.

**Empress River Casino** offers more than 1,000 slots and more than 60 table games, plus Empress Off-Track Betting. Fourteen gaming sessions are offered daily; gaming and boarding begin 30 minutes prior to departure. Reservations are suggested on Friday and Saturday. Express bus service is available from downtown hotels; call (888) 436-7737 for more information.

Harrah's **Northern Star** and **Southern Star** cruise the Des Plaines River with three levels of gaming, entertainment, and dining. **Harrah's Joliet Casino** operates daily from 8 a.m. to 2:15 a.m. Cruises are free. Reservations are suggested on Friday and Saturday. Call (800) HARRAHS for more information.

# Part Nine

# Shopping in Chicago

## Nothing Like It Back Home

Visitors who come here expecting second (or third) city are overjoyed. Time was, fashion was the resultant mélange of trends that blew in from The Coast (either one). No more. Said mélange floated down Boul Mich, blew west across the Loop, fanned north and south, and became Chicago Style. Suddenly, the world sat up and took notice.

The City of Big Shoulders still takes the best of the West, combines it with the best of the East, imports every possible plum from abroad, adds the dash that is all its own, and comes up with the formula that puts the chic in Chicago. As a clever copywriter for Marshall Field's said so succinctly long ago: "There's nothing like it back home."

The savviest locals will tell you style has nothing to do with how much you spend; it's how you spend it. Chic, elan, verve, and all those natty synonyms are rooted in curiosity and vitality, indigenous to Chicago. Style has nothing to do with what's In or Out, and everything to do with aesthetics (and fun). Great taste means it would be nice to own an original Cézanne, but you can still stir the senses with a stunning litho created by a local artist and purchased at a local gallery.

The question is, in a city this size, where should you look? There's always the obvious Michigan Avenue, but what *about* those neighborhood boutiques that are the natives' well-kept secrets? Sorry, natives, it's time to divulge the where's and how-to-find-it's.

### THE WHERE OF IT

Chicago shopping is centered downtown. First, bordered by the Chicago River on both the north and west is the Loop, a 35-block cornucopia of retail action circumscribed by elevated train tracks and home of the giant Marshall Field's and Carson Pirie Scott department stores. Moving north of the river is the so-called Magnificent Mile where grand malls and opulent boutiques flank both sides of Michigan Avenue. The Near North Side (Zone 3) (known for streets that fan east and west of the Magnificent Mile, including the "tree streets": Maple, Chestnut, Oak, etc.) is home to small pockets of eclectic shopping pleasures. Off the north end of Michigan Avenue, heading west, is Oak Street, a shopping venue in its own right. Ritzy, upscale, exclusive, and generally expensive, Oak's single block is designer fashion headquarters. River North, on the west side of Near North, is the epicenter of Chicago's art, antique, and designer furniture scene.

Moving beyond Near North and River North and away from downtown are Lincoln Park and the Clybourn Avenue corridor. This area is filled with great shopping (great dining, too, since some of the city's best restaurants are nearby). The parallel streets of Webster and Armitage are such fun they warrant time of their own, though neither is all that long. Because most of these shops are "Mom and Pop" operations, with the owners usually on site, they provide an antidote to any impersonality you might find on Boul Mich. In this same area, the north-south streets of Halsted and Clark amble for miles, sometimes in a drab fashion, sometimes glowing with shops and restaurants to rival top areas in the city. Lincoln Avenue, slanting northwest from Lincoln Park, is less likely to glow, but has some surprising charmers that refute that theory.

One of the newer shopping/gallery neighborhoods west of downtown is Wicker Park, offering some junque and a lot of fun. Cut east and head north along the lake into Evanston. When you're finished trooping the Northwestern campus, avail yourself of some of the town's good shopping. North of Evanston are affluent and shopping-rich communities such as Wilmette, Glencoe, Winnetka, Highland Park, and Lake Forest. To the north is Milwaukee (Wisconsin), but before you get there, stop at Gurnee Mills in Gurnee for your Ph.D. in outlet shopping.

## THE HOW OF IT

Because people shop Michigan Avenue as if it's one huge consolidated shopping center, that is the way we have described it. Block by block, we describe the malls and the stores in and between them without attempting to organize what's available into specific categories of goods and services. As much an attraction as a repository of goods, Michigan Avenue is a browser's paradise. No shopping list or agenda is required. Simply set off to walk the Magnificent Mile and some article or item will thrust itself upon you and insist you buy it. The aggregation of merchandise is so vast that you generally don't need to concern yourself with its availability. If it can be sold in a store, you'll find it on Michigan Avenue.

In discussing the other downtown and Greater Chicago shopping venues, however, the territory is immense and the stores geographically dispersed. Off Michigan Avenue it's more important, and sometimes necessary, to define what you are shopping for. When we talk about shopping in the myriad stores of the Loop, Oak Street, Near North, River North, and beyond, we organize our discussion around specific genres of merchandise. Some Michigan Avenue stores not incorporated in malls are also included in these categories.

## MICHIGAN AVENUE: THE MIRACLE MILE

From the Chicago River north along Michigan Avenue is America's largest concentration of upscale shopping, known collectively as the "Miracle" or "Magnificent" Mile. Leading department stores anchor a dazzling array of chain stores, boutiques, and malls. It is a place where department stores are grander and boutiques more specialized, and where even chain habitués of suburban malls are enticingly fashioned (Gap, take a bow). Many stars in this shopping galaxy are neatly integrated into malls tucked away inside huge buildings. Imagine ducking into a streetside shop that opens unexpectedly into canyons of retail concourses. To shopping junkies, the discovery of these merchandise cities is akin to passing through the looking glass. And the malls are fairly gorgeous: Chicago Place, Water Tower Place, and 900 North Michigan, for three.

It is no secret that Oprah loves Michigan Avenue (and Chicago shopping, in general). Another talk-show host, Jenny Jones, who arrived from L.A. to set up in Chicago, confided that she was dazzled by the proximity of so many great stores. "Everything in L.A.," she lamented, "is a car ride away."

True. Add the three B's (Bloomingdale's, Barneys, and Bulgari) to the likes of Field's, Lord & Taylor, Chanel, Escada, and more within a two-block area, and it's shopper's paradise.

### Michigan Avenue's Grand Malls

While there is some shopping on Michigan Avenue between the river and Ohio Street, most of the primo shops are concentrated in the nine blocks from Ontario north to Oak. However, this may change when the mall housing **Nordstrom,** located to the south, is completed.

**540 North Michigan**   This block now houses a **Virgin Megastore** and **Kenneth Cole** accessories.

**600 North Michigan**   Located at 600 North Michigan, this mall houses **Eddie Bauer** and features stores with separate addresses. Here, you'll find outdoor goods and gear for men and women, with everything from parkas to stainless steel lunch bottles. At the **Original Levi's** store, women can buy "customized" Levi's (thanks to the store's unique Personal Pair, jeans-that-fit service). Also in this mall are **Marshalls, Linens & Things,** and **Cineplex Odeon** theaters (entrance at the corner of Rush and Ohio Streets).

**Chicago Place**   The eight-level shopping center at 700 North Michigan is known as Chicago Place, with one of the nation's prettiest **Saks Fifth Avenue** stores and some 45 specialty stores, including **Ann Taylor, Talbots** (their flagship store), a hugely expanded **Room & Board** (home furnishings) and its new concept store **Retrospect,** and **Williams-Sonoma.** There are also decorative arts galleries, such as famed **Chiaroscuro,** where the wares of 300 artists and artisans are shown (including jewelry, glass, furniture, and mixed media).

If you can't jet to County Cork, **Joy of Ireland** imports gifts and goodies to compensate. Another attraction is **Tutti Italia,** where authentic Italian housewares, food items, and books are sublime. A recent traveler to Deruta, home of Umbrian ceramics, returned from her Italian trip and soon after dropped into Tutti Italia to find the same up-to-the-minute pasta bowl she'd been sure *no one* had in the United States.

700 also houses bath and body products at **The Body Shop,** gifts for your dog at **Arf ! Inc.,** and coffee blends at **Torrefazione Italia.** A favorite here is **The Real Nancy Drew** (8th level). The real Nancy Drew is a Michigan artist/cartoonist, whose distinctively naive, colorful drawings appear on everything from lamps and vases to clothing and furniture. In the store, prices range from a $1.50 card to her $2,500 fine art paintings. (She does custom work, too.)

Finally, give the last word to glossy **Saks Fifth Avenue:** The retailer has been on the Avenue since 1929, and this is one of their showcase stores; across the street at 717 North Michigan Avenue, the **Saks Men's Store** will open in autumn of 1999. There are also Saks stores at Oakbrook Shopping Center, Old Orchard, and a new beauty in Highland Park. The low-end (one hesitates to say "cut-rate" about anything Saks-ish) **Saks Off Fifth Avenue** stores are in Schaumberg and Gurnee Mills.

**Neiman Marcus**   Just down the Avenue from 700 is a non-malled titan, Neiman Marcus, at 737 North Michigan. Suburbanites (who adore the NM at Northbrook Court in Northbrook) swear that NM is the only reason they trek into the city. Says one, firmly: "This is Michigan Avenue's best store. I can find evening wear there and costume jewelry I can't find anywhere else." You have been warned. (Note also great gift wrapping, a zippy gourmet foods section, and unique home decor items.)

**Water Tower Place**   At.875 North Michigan is the marble palace known as Water Tower Place, anchored by **Marshall Field's** and **Lord & Taylor.** Once past the beautiful entrance (the waterfall is soothing), you may think this is chainville, but some of the retailers may surprise you. Take **Dunhill** (an outpost far from London), where men can spend a *lot* on clothes, small leather goods, and cigars (Viscount David Linley's architectural humidors, as well as his $14,000 jewelry cases, are gorgeous). Of the more than 100 specialty shops, some are exclusive to Chicago, some to the area. Far indeed from its Italian antecedents is the fine **Rizzoli** bookstore, perhaps the only place in the Midwest where you can find Italian newspapers and magazines in *Italiano*. **Michael Jordan Golf** is here, too, with MJ golf logo apparel, equipment, and gifts.

One of the more interesting aspects of this fun shopping center is the vast food court called **foodlife,** where you can dig into (or take out) almost anything, from tacos to freshly baked pies. Ensconced here, lounging amid the fake greenery while forking good pasta, it may become easy to forget you're in the middle of a huge city. (Tucked into a space behind the food court is a restaurant called **Mity Nice Grill;** calm and filled with delicious menu items, it's one of the mall's best-kept secrets.)

The children's paradise, FAO Schwarz, opened its luscious free-standing candy store, **FAO Schweetz,** on level two here, delighting families with a giant gumball machine, a lollipop forest, and over 250 bulk candy bins. **FAO Schwarz,** the stunning toy emporium, is no longer in this mall. (It reappears across the street at 840 North Michigan, where adults have as much fun gawking at the stuffed animals, toys, and games as the diminutive shoppers).

**Plaza Escada**   On this block is Plaza Escada, 840 North Michigan, a smaller four-floor mall that offers Escada, Escada Sport, Margaretha Ley, Laurel, a full line of accessories (including leather goods), a shoe salon, and Escada Beaute fragrance. The shoes are particularly good here, and the director of special services can arrange for same-day delivery to homes, offices, and hotels; the director will also provide gratis gift wrap and car service if needed. Atop Michigan Avenue with a view of the action is Escada's fourth floor coziest-cafe-in-town; have pasta for lunch, or, if you're dieting, a salad.

**900 North Michigan**   Close by is the formidable 900 North Michigan, which houses **Bloomingdale's,** gorgeous **Gucci,** silvery **Christofle,** and a city mall of elegant laidback charm that makes it easy to shop. Bloomie's is full of surprises, offering a range of prices. Find shoes that are divine ripoffs of styles attempted by only top designers right along with shoes by the latter; housewares (bedding, kitchen, and tabletop items) are superb. Soon after you've found inexpensive jeans, you can go up a floor or two and find the priciest of import gowns. Cosmetics on the first floor offers extraordinary abundance.

Two neighbors on the fifth floor have the same name: **Pavo Real.** One is a boutique (with sweaters handknit in Peru and Bolivia), and the other is the Pavo Real Gallery of animal arts and sculptures, featuring artist Todd Warner's magical menagerie (including zebras, birds, and a sprawling frog). **Gallery Lara** has unusual art pieces; **Galt Toys** has items for kids who have a lot (but would always like a little more); and **Oilily** has their clothes. A new "Chanel for children" is **Tartine Et Chocolat,** 5th floor fantasies of country-French fashions and furnishings for kids. Tiny **Glove Me Tender** is the place to buy (natch) gloves, and they have hats, too. Among other clothing stores is **Yolanda Lorente,** the designer whose exquisite gowns have long adorned local fashionables. New additions here include **Linda Campisano Millenery** (6th level), featuring custom-designed hats for women (and men); **Club Monaco; Mario Tricoci Hair Salon and Day Spa;** and even more special, the fifth U.S. location of **Lalique,** where you can pick up crystal, along with perfume, scarves, leather accessories, and porcelain. This store will be known for its commitment to Lalique's accessories collection.

You can't help but love 900 for its chic occasional pianist and its charm; the escalators are rather awkwardly spaced, but elevators make getting around easier.

**One Mag Mile**   Across the street from the Drake Hotel is another marble palace, dubbed "One Mag Mile" by the developer, but it didn't stick (so don't expect a cabbie to know what you're talking about if you drop the name on him). **Barry Bricken** (the entire women's collection) is at 940 North Michigan, as is the exquisite **Revillon** furs showroom. At 970 North (corner of Oak Street) is one of the best Italian cashmere houses, **Manrico Cashmere.** After you've finished your fashion spending, go upstairs and have a glass of pinot grigio at **Spiaggia,** one of the city's best Italian restaurants.

## EAST OF MICHIGAN

East of Michigan Avenue (don't go too far, or you'll wind up in the lake) is another shopping enclave, **River East Plaza Shops and Food Court** (formerly North Pier Marketplace), 435 East Illinois Street. Located between Michigan Avenue and Navy Pier, this is a fun place for eclectic shopping, waterfront dining, live music, and entertainment. River East was restucturing at press time, so shops are as yet unannounced.

At **Navy Pier,** 700 East Grand Avenue, you'll find one of the best places in the city to take the kids: the **Chicago Children's Museum,** with hands-on exhibits. Afterward, take them for a ride on the pier's Ferris wheel or to the **Crystal Gardens** for a snack. Call (312) 595-PIER for hourly information on cruise ships that depart from Navy Pier.

## THE LANDMARK DEPARTMENT STORES OF THE LOOP

South of the Chicago River and just west of Michigan Avenue is The Loop, circumscribed by elevated train tracks. As concerns shopping, this area falls into the obvious category. Nevertheless, even many locals don't realize just how interesting the Loop's two treasure houses *are*. And there might be more to come (Macy's is rumored). The cliché for tourists, you see, is to avoid them, so, do the opposite. Even though these great stores can't obscure the fact that the Loop's glory comes and goes, visitors to the city, influenced by locals who shop *only* boutiques (whether they be Armani or thrift shops), may pass up a chance to investigate, and thus fail to bask in the light of these stars. So don't listen. Tell naysayers you know the stars are supposed to be Out, but you know they're In. Go see.

### Marshall Field's

Star One is Marshall Field's, 111 North State Street. The 7¾-ton clocks (at Randolph and Washington corners) that tower over this granddaddy of Chicago stores signal your arrival. After a five-year renovation, the block-long wonder is gorgeous—from the Walnut Room (wood-paneled, of course) for dining on the seventh floor, all the way down to The Market-place in the "basement" (all basements should look like this) where you can grab a sandwich. In between are floors chock-full of everything from cosmetics (first floor) to teapots (housewares), and try the basement, lower level. Their high-fashion "28 Shop" is a renovated stunner.

Marshall Field's is, arguably, the most beautiful department store in the country. It is also a source of firsts: first to establish a European buying office (in England in 1871); first to open a dining room in a department store; first to delight customers with lavish store window displays; and first United States store to start a bridal registry. Field's is home of the largest department store candy kitchen (Frango chocolates are shipped all over the world). Also in the notable category are galleries for antique furniture, silver, and jewelry, and their Christmas season "Great Tree," towering 45 feet, has delighted patrons for more than 83 yuletide seasons.

Architecturally, Field's is awesome. The State Street Tiffany dome is the largest glass mosaic of its kind and the first ever built of iridescent glass. A 1992 addition—an 11-floor, 165-foot-high atrium—is another knockout.

Field's is probably the only store of its kind that burned down *twice* in its history (once, when it was Field & Leiter, during the great Chicago Fire of 1871, and again, in 1873). Leiter retired in 1881, and the store became Marshall Field & Co., reigning in this fashion almost a century until it became part of the Department Store Division of the Dayton Hudson

Corporation in 1990. Field's owns 24 stores in Illinois, Wisconsin, Ohio, and Indiana.

But, back to *this* one. Perhaps the best way to shop Field's is to pretend you're exploring a small village.

There's a huge store for men (the largest selection of shirts and ties in the Midwest). On two are men's suits and coats, with designer separates, Tommy Hilfiger, and Polo Shop. The remodeled men's area includes a business center where Field's guests (that's what they call their customers) can watch CNN, send faxes, and get their shoes shined. Women enjoy designer wares on three as well as Select (free personal shopping). Also on three is the Country shop. On four are petites, moderate sportswear, designer and moderate shoes, and Women's Way (larger-sized fashions).

Five is for kid stuff, as well as intimate apparel and the beauty salon.

The highlight of six is the home store, with crystal galleries, antique silver, a shop for designer bed linens, and more than 12,000 china patterns. The hot new gallery in crystal, joining huge collections of Hoya, Orrefors, Baccarat, Waterford, Swarovski, and Lalique, is Steuben. Field's Oakbrook store also features a state-of-the-art Steuben gallery. Tiffany and Christofle join in offering flatware patterns, china, and crystal, and there are also departments here for quilts and corporate gifts. This is the only department store in the country that has Pickard china; they're known for doing embassy china.

The newly renovated seventh floor (State Street) is largely dedicated to food. A recent renovation has created and updated some fine attractions. The famed **Walnut Room** has a center fountain, and the plates here feature the Norman Rockwell painting of Field's famous Great Clock. (Both natives and tourists make a point to come to the Walnut Room at Christmas to gape at the Great Tree.) The **Frango Cafe,** replacing the Crystal Palace, is a 140-seat cafe featuring soups, salads, sandwiches, ice cream delights, a children's menu, bakery, and dessert bar. An open atrium area houses the "7 on State Gourmet Food Stations," seating 450 people, with goodies that range from soups and noodles to crêpes and skewers. A new Visitor Services Center has been relocated to the seventh floor as well.

On the lower level of State are the Marketplace Food Court (including a deli, a bakery, and "Marketplace Lite" foods for calorie counters), Hinky Dink Kenna's pub (on the pedway, which connects you underground to other Loop addresses), and Cafe Gio.

The eighth floor is earmarked for furniture, one source of which is the Ralph Lauren furniture gallery, with designs by the ubiquitous Ralph and production by Henredon. The Trend House rooms are here, and what Field's people claim (who knows?) is the largest Oriental carpet collection of any United States department store.

## Carson Pirie Scott

Heading south on State, shoppers find another Loop star, Carson Pirie Scott. When the great architect Louis H. Sullivan designed the building at State and Madison, he utilized the most modern construction technology available at the time, ensuring the store's place in the history of retailing. This flagship store was named a Chicago landmark in 1970 (and it's listed in the National Register of Historic Places). Today, having passed its 140th year, CPS deserves its status for its ever-innovative direction. The 1994 first-floor State renovation revitalized the original Sullivan floor plan and the columns. And 1999 brings more remodeling.

You can find the best here, from fashion to furniture. Beginning on the lower level are men's career apparel, men's outerwear, luggage, optical, shoe repair, and a Wall Street Deli franchise. The fur salon and Juniors are also here.

On the main level are cosmetics, handbags, and accessories (the hosiery store has its own entrance for a quick exit).

On first-floor Wabash look for the first NFL Concept Shop in the United States, designed to commemorate the League's 75th anniversary, and the original Chicago Bulls' team shop (the decor features the legs of basketball players, 20 times life size). First-floor Wabash is also home to men's furnishings, fragrance, a Dockers' shop, and the only Sharper Image shop within a department store.

On remodeled level two, women find better sportswear, bridge and moderate update sportswear, and petites, while men find a Big & Tall shop, better sportswear, young men's, and men's shoes. A busy TicketMaster ticket center is also on this floor, plus a small post office, dry cleaner, and Wardrobe Consulting, housed in the historic Rotunda. On level three are women's shoes, coats, an Elizabeth Arden Salon and Day Spa, and Women's Studio (sizes 16–24). On level four are intimate apparel and The Bride's Room, while level five houses a collectors' Sports Memorabilia Shop (rare coins, signed footballs), plus stationery, a 40,000-square-foot furniture gallery with an interior design studio, and a new Office Essentials shop.

Level six features the Home Store, with a computerized gift registry (you type in the giftees' names to see what they've registered for). Level seven is home to the children's departments and a magical Trim-A-Home Shop (open mid-September through early January).

Hungry? The Cream City Cafe is open at 7:30 a.m. Grab coffee, muffins, and other goodies; you'll also find birthday cards, postcards, Chicago-themed T-shirts, local crafts, and candy in this section.

The Corporate Gifts division enables one-stop shopping to enhance a corporate image; for company gifts and awards, call (800) 945-GIFT.

Carson's also has the ability to assist disabled customers. Full-time shoppers serve this clientele, but you must call in advance for an appointment (whether single or group).

There are 24 CPS stores and 3 furniture galleries in the Chicago area, including ones at Harlem-Irving Plaza on the north side and at 120 South Riverside Plaza (near the train station). They're also at suburban malls: Chicago Ridge, Ford City, Stratford Square, Spring Hill, Hillside, Lincoln Mall (Matteson), Randhurst, North Riverside, Orland Square, and Edens Plaza (take the Lake East exit on the Edens Expressway).

# Where to Find . . .

If you choose not to shop in a Michigan Avenue mall or in one of the huge department stores in the Loop, there is a distinct possibility that you are looking for something specific. We have, therefore, chopped the remainder of the Chicago shopping iceberg into neat little categories to make it easy to find what you want.

## ART AND FINE CRAFTS

**In the Loop**    Be sure to stop at **The Chicago Athenaeum Museum of Architecture and Design,** 6 North Michigan Avenue (at Madison), known for its fabulous **Good Design** store, purveying architectural books and decorative design objects from candle holders and picture frames to vases and jewelry. The 30,000-square-foot museum is dedicated to international design arts, and there are fine art exhibits here.

Don't leave the Loop without a thorough look-see at one of the city's most tasteful (and too-little-known) galleries: the **Illinois Artisans Shop,** 100 West Randolph Street (Suite 2–200). Everything here is handmade by an Illinois artist. Into this category fall jewelry, glass, ceramics, handwoven wearable art, quilts, baskets, dolls, woodworking, ironwork, prints, paintings, sculpture, and photographs. Trust us on this: 9 a.m.–5 p.m., Monday through Friday.

**On North Michigan Avenue**    There was a time when Michigan Avenue not only was the retail repository of the Midwest's best but also was dotted with a parcel of some of the city's best art galleries. Many have moved to the River North area, but among those remaining are the **Richard Gray Gallery,** one of Chicago's outstanding dealers in fine art (875 North Michigan Avenue, the John Hancock Building, level 25), and **R. S. Johnson Fine Art** (Suite 234, 645 North Michigan). **Stephen Solovy Fine Arts** joins only a few others still on the Avenue at 980 North Michigan. Over a year ago, the **Wally Findlay Galleries** moved from its longtime home on Michigan Avenue to 188 East Walton Place, but it remains a prized source of fine art.

When you say "art in Chicago," your number one thought should be the **Art Institute of Chicago,** the magnificent institution south of the Chicago River (Michigan Avenue at Adams—Zone 4) that consistently outpaces the finest museums in the world. Also extraordinary is the Art Institute Museum Shop, which was one of Chicago's best-kept secrets for too long; it helped when several branches of the Museum Shop were opened in malls (gasp) and people began to see what delectables were available. You can find the Midwest's best art books, posters, T-shirts, and notecards, everything from a Monet-inspired paperweight to Impressionist-inspired scarves, unique designs of Baltic amber jewelry, Monet prints, even umbrellas ($39 each), such as one imprinted with a Parisian scene ("Paris Street, Rainy Day") by "urban impressionist" Gustave Caillebotte. And more, more, more.

Another gorgeous store, generously trimmed in oak, is a highlight of the **Museum of Contemporary Art,** 220 East Chicago Avenue. The MCA store is on the first level, with the bookstore on the second floor; a sweeping two-story winding staircase under a skylight centers this light, bright, and airy backdrop for art and gifts. You'll find such items as rare and fine contemporary art books, compact discs (they shine in experimental music), wonderful animal masks, mobiles (HFU and Hotchkiss designs are $23–300), interesting jewelry, and candles. The **M-Cafe** is the place for lunch. Dine al fresco in good weather on the granite deck off the sculpture garden. It's just a few feet from the shops on Michigan Avenue, but it feels like a world away.

At the **Terra Museum of American Art,** 666 North Michigan, which concentrates on American art and exhibitions, a bright museum store features a wide variety of collectible art prints, books, paper goods, children's interactive games, and crafts; all are suffused with Americana. A recent exhibit here featured the photography of Robert Capa.

The **Chicago Cultural Center,** 78 East Washington Street, has ongoing exhibits that are original, usually intriguing, new to the city, and feature both emergent and recognized artists. The exhibits are free of charge and a real attraction.

**Near North** One of the most unique galleries was owned by **Joy Horwich,** but she has closed it and become an art consultant who runs wonderful tours to art-filled places (from the Getty Museum in California to Bilbao, Spain, her first European trip in early summer 1999). She also takes individuals and families on personalized offbeat and conventional artistic and cultural jaunts in Chicago (such as a trip to an auction house or to an artist's studio). Call (773) 327-3366 for information. **Accents Studio,** 611 North State Street, should be filed under wearable art. It has accessories, both funky and refined: artist-designed jewelry (including sterling silver), gifts, and collectibles. Some of the 100 artists and craftsmen featured here are local. Several galleries brighten Oak Street. One is **Aaron Art Gallery,** second floor, 50 East Oak, where you'll find nineteenth- and early-twentieth-century American paintings and master prints.

**River North**    Van Gogh might have given his other ear to stroll the hugely expanded **Pearl Art & Craft Supply,** 225 West Chicago Avenue. The mostly discount store provides an incredibly wide supply of materials for artisans. Making jewelry? Beads overflow. Want a choice of brushes? Options abound. Staffers get a feel for what you want, whether you're a professional or a hobbyist. Hundreds of new handmade papers come from around the world.

To begin our discussion of the gallery district, we'll attempt a quick summation (then you can go and make up your own mind).

**Robert Henry Adams Fine Art,** 715 North Franklin, features American and European Impressionist and modern (prior to 1945) paintings. The **Douglas Dawson Gallery,** 222 West Huron, is known for ancient and historic ethnic arts from Asia, Africa, and the Americas (textiles, ceramics, furniture, and sculpture); and at 325 West Huron is the **Zolla/Lieberman Gallery** (contemporary painting, sculpture, works on paper). **Habitat Galleries** has moved to 222 West Superior, and you'll now find **Aldo Castillo Gallery** (specializing in Latin American art) at 233 West Huron. Once on Huron but now to the west of River North is **Rhona Hoffman,** 312 North May; the gallery is recognized internationally for contemporary art in all media.

When you hit Superior Street, the galleries come a little thicker and faster. It's fun to wander Superior and stop when the feeling (or the gallery) moves you. New here is **Portia Gallery,** 207 West, where we saw contemporary glass by international artists. Several galleries in the 300 Building are **Catherine Edelman** (contemporary photography), **Belloc Lowndes** (twentieth-century British art including paintings, drawings, and sculpture), and the **Judy A. Saslow Gallery** (outsider, self-taught, folk, and visionary art from all parts of the globe, plus African art, primitive objets, and American folk and contemporary works). **Printworks,** with contemporary prints, drawings, photographs, and artists books, is at 311 West, as is **Michael Fitzsimmons. Carl Hammer,** 200 West, is a specialist in self-taught and contemporary artworks; and **Perimeter Gallery,** 210 West, is home to contemporary fine art (also ceramics, fiber, and metalwork) by internationally recognized artists.

You may also want to drop into **Carol Ehlers Gallery, Ltd.,** 750 Orleans Street, suite 303 (she specializes in twentieth-century master and contemporary photography).

One of the best galleries in this area is **Roy Boyd,** 739 North Wells Street. Exhibits here tend not to disappoint, and they're likely to be contemporary. At 706 North Wells is **Primitive Art Works,** featuring one of the city's largest tribal and ethnic displays of authentic international textiles, rugs, jewelry, and artifacts. At 1551 North Wells hang the goods at **Vintage Posters International, Inc.** Here, owner Susan Cutler not only displays fashion and Euro advertising posters but also furniture (circa 1880–1960), costume/vintage jewelry, and twentieth-century vintage objects of art.

**Wicker Park**    Again, to the west, in the Wicker Park area, is the **Aron Packer Gallery,** 1579 North Milwaukee Avenue, featuring paintings and sculpture.

**Lincoln Park/Clybourn Corridor/and Farther North**    At 1022 West Armitage, **Fortunate Discoveries** purveys ethnic art accessories such as Swat (Pakistan) windows; wonderful Kilim rugs from Turkey, Afghanistan, Persia, and Russia; and interesting, one-of-a-kind pillows and artifacts from around the world.

At 651 West Armitage Avenue is **Art Effect,** one of the first stores to feature wearable art, and that's still one of its strong points. National artists' works are displayed here, with attention paid to clothes, jewelry, and items for the home. The art effect is dazzling.

The busy marketplace area at 2121 North Clybourn Avenue houses **A Unique Presence,** where Judy Harris and Ellen Royce sell carefully selected artisan crafts and gifts. Twenty percent of their artists are local, and a sign posted there says it best: "One should either be a work of art or wear a work of art" (Oscar Wilde). Works of art here include clocks, candlesticks, picture frames, flower pots, and the like. Their suburban store now graces Old Orchard Shopping Center. And you can find them on the Web at www.auniquepresence.com.

A find to the north in an area that is blooming with galleries lately is the **Judith Racht Gallery,** 3737 North Southport Avenue in the Music Box (theater) building. Known for her appeal in her Harbert (Michigan/Indiana Dunes) country gallery, Racht features a mélange of contemporary art, outsider art, furniture, and even antique quilts.

## BABY FURNITURE

**Bellini,** 2001 North Halsted Street, is a synonym for beautiful furniture for baby. From cribs to dressing tables to first beds for tots, they're here, along with rocking chairs, high chairs, strollers, clothing (up to toddler 4), and fun bedroom furnishings such as colorful crib linens and mobiles. Many of these pieces are imports; few are bargain priced, but all are unusual and will make baby sit up and take notice. They also do teen beds and bedding.

## BEAUTY ITEMS

**Near North**   On Oak Street, lined with really beautiful stores, the jewel-box salon of international perfume/cosmetic creator **Marilyn Miglin,** 112 East Oak Street, is right up there at the top for any woman. For one thing, this immaculate salon sparkles divinely, and it *smells* so good. Marilyn's perfumes include Pheromone ("the world's most precious perfume"), Goddess, Nirvana Destiny, and Mystic, her latest—these and more are available here. And if you've seen her on TV and she's in town when you visit, she'll autograph her photo for you.

**Face & Facial,** 104 East Oak Street, features internationally known facialist Mila Bravi. There are manicurists here, too, who are among the best (and *not* the most expensive) in the city. Another trained esthetician with a soothing touch is **Kathleen Peara,** a bit to the north at 154 West Schiller, Studio 2D, where indulgence in an aromatherapy facial will have you purring with satisfaction.

Hair salons in Near North aren't likely to indulge you with bargain prices, but they *produce.* At 106 East Oak is **Charles Ifergan** hair salon; he's a trendsetting hair designer who wins national awards for his styles for men and women. The **Russum Waters Studio,** 8 East Delaware Place, is an oasis of tranquility, where hair colorist Anita Russum works her magic. Again, no bargain prices, but the artistry performed by Russum (plus the skill of other staffers) will win your heart.

Spas are proliferating in Chicago, and followers of the **Elizabeth Arden Red Door Salon** will be pleased with the beautiful, large environs at 919 North Michigan Avenue (the entrance is on the side at Walton Street). Then there's **Urban Oasis,** 12 West Maple, specializing in stress-freeing massage, and **Spa Thira,** 840 North Michigan Avenue (again, the entrance is on the side at Chestnut), where the action seems to center more on hair removal. Newest is **Kiva,** with its Am-I-in-Santa Fe? ambience. No, you're at 196 East Pearson, adjacent to the Ritz-Carlton hotel, enjoying an oasis for body/mind/spirit nurturing, with every type of treatment, from aromatherapy and massages at the spa to pedicures and scalp analysis at the salon. Have breakfast, lunch, and dinner here, too (even treats such as low-fat brownies!).

## BIKES

Many find their way to **Turin Bicycle Store** in Evanston (at 1027 Davis Street), but let's stay in the city. If we start at North Avenue and work our way north on Halsted, we'll encounter a bike shop, **Quick Release,** 1623 North Halsted Street. They sell mostly mountain bikes, 26"-wheel type; Ross and Canadian Peugeot brands are sold here, among others; full-service repair shop. Beloved to others: **Kozy's Cyclery** at 3712 North Halsted, 1451 West Webster at Clybourn, and 601 South LaSalle Street in the South Loop. Voted #1 bike shop in Chicago by *Windy City Sports,* Kozy's carries Cannondale, Specialized, Gary Fisher, Schwinn, and Trek. **Cycle Smithy,** 2468½ North Clark Street, is popular, too (you'll see a lot of Lincoln Park's Yups hanging out here to get air in their tires).

## BOATS, YACHTS, AND SAILING CRAFT

Chicago has a limited boating season, but serves as headquarters for **Brunswick,** the biggest marine manufacturer in the world. Numerous marine dealerships in the area, particularly in the far north suburbs, including Fox Lake and Grayslake, sell Brunswick boats, including Sea Rays, Bayliners, and Masums. Most are powered by Mercury Marine engines, another Brunswick company. **Outboard Marine Corporation** is based in Waukegan. It is a leading manufacturer of internationally known boat brands including ChrisCraft, Four Winns, Sea Swirl, Hydra Sports, Stratos, Javelin, Lowe, Prince Craft, marine engines under the brand name of Johnson and Evinrude, Ficht Fuel injection (the industry's premier low-emission, two-stroke engine technology), and marine accessories. Chicago has powerboat retailers in the suburbs, though none in the city proper.

A spokesman for the **National Marine Manufacturers' Association** claims that Chicagoland is an active area for purchasing and selling pleasure boats. People buy boats where they live, and Illinois reports $250 million in annual pleasure boat sales (these are combined boat, motor, trailer, and marine accessory purchases), the seventh largest in the country. Where you buy (or sell) a yacht, motorboat, or other watercraft depends on what you want. See the Yellow Pages; sail and power boat dealers are listed. If you want a specific brand name, you also can consult the boating magazines for an 800 number and they'll tell you where to go. You might also want to check out the following Chicago-area boat shows: the must-see **Chicago Boat Show** in January (all the boats are under one roof at McCormick Place, Zone 5); the (all-sailboat) **Strictly Sailboat Show** at Navy Pier also in January; and the **Midwest Boat Show** held mid-February in Rosemont, IL (Zone 10). People really do buy at boat shows locally, notes our NMMA spokesman.

## BOOKS, CARDS, AND STATIONERY

**On Michigan Avenue** The national chain titans continue to battle the small independent booksellers around the city, but even among the giant discounters there are favorites. One of the best is **Borders,** 830 North Michigan Avenue, which has won over many readers with a caring staff, a vast supply of tomes (some 200,000 titles), a coffee cafe (featuring live jazz on Friday evening), children's story hours, and exciting author appearances.

The son of legendary bookseller Stuart Brent, whose store stood on Michigan Avenue for 50 years, is Adam Brent. Adam first opened a store in the Loop and won success with his dedication to personal service. He has recently opened **Brent Books & Cards, Ltd.,** 316 North Michigan Avenue, and plans to continue offering a well-read staff with a reverence for books, author appearances, a huge selection of titles (including a wide selection of children's books), and a coffee cafe. He's also out to "match and exceed discounts at the megabookstores," with 10% off hardcovers and 30% off retail *New York Times* best-sellers. The table where Adam plans to seat his authors for lectures and signings has a lot of history: Saul Bellow, Tom Wolfe, Nelson Algren, Truman Capote, Gore Vidal, and hundreds of others sat at that table with Stuart Brent.

More should be said about **Rizzoli,** 835 North Michigan Avenue at Water Tower Place, a beloved 21-year-old outpost of the Italian giant's American division. Note the impressive art books, a children's department, and a large reduced-cost book section. There are also international magazines and newspapers and internationally oriented CDs and language and music tapes.

**Near North** Rush Street, which once housed cabarets, now is home to several fine, unique shops. Noteworthy for custom papers and leather goods is **d b Pineider,** 1003 North Rush, the third U.S. store of this distinguished Italian firm that also specializes in bookbinding. At 909 North Rush is **Children in Paradise Bookstore,** a kids-only first in Chicago, where both children and their parents can browse among the tomes in happy-making surroundings. They sell kids' software in a complete section called Children in Technology. Older readers (11–15 years of age) might be found upstairs in an art supplies and activities section, separating them from the tots. A carpeted reading pit with pillows is used for weekly story hours (mornings, twice weekly).

**On Oak Street** Oak isn't all fashion. For instance, you can find custom stationery and gifts at **The Watermark,** 109 East Oak.

**River North**   At 211 West Huron Street is **Write Impressions,** a source of paper goods (invitations are good here). At the corner of Franklin and Chicago Avenue is **Paper Source,** where we've noticed handmade rag papers (in fact all manner of unusual and special papers and notebooks), specialty books, ribbons, and wax seals. There are great gifts here, such as glass pens.

**Lincoln Park/Clark/Clybourn Corridor**   A bookstore that has scored high with much of literary Chicago is **Barbara's Bookstore,** headquartered at 1350 North Wells Street. (Barbara's has been based in Old Town since 1963.) Readings and author signings are regularly scheduled; staffers know their stuff; and the store pays attention to local authors. (**Barbara's** kiosks for downtown readers are located at Sears Tower and Navy Pier; two suburban stores are in Oak Park and Evergreen Park.)

**The Lincoln Park Book Shop,** 2423 North Clark Street, is one of the city's best. One reason: owner Joel Jacobson *reads.* "Our idea is to have in stock selected literature, cookbooks, travel guidebooks, all of very good quality," he says. "We know the material and we're not afraid to say this is good and this is not so good. It's the old concept of a neighborhood store; we want people to come in as friends as well as customers."

**Hyde Park   57th Street Books,** 1301 East 57th Street, is an exemplary store.

## Used Books

For used books, try **Bookseller's Row,** 408 South Michigan Avenue. It is the only used bookstore in the Loop and offers review copies and a wide collection (three floors). The books here all have been gently used, and are thus discounted; the savings can really add up. Farther up Lincoln Avenue at 2850 is another good used bookstore, **Powell's,** which can also be found at 828 South Wabash (Zone 4) and at 1501 East 57th Street in the Hyde Park neighborhood (Zone 7). We prefer the Lincoln Park location, though, because it's usually so quiet it's almost ghostly.

## CAMERAS

Looking for a camera? Check out **Helix Camera & Video,** where prices are fair and the selection is great (over 100 types of film). They have several locations: 2 Illinois Center, 3 First National Plaza, and the main store at 310 South Racine Avenue. **Central Camera Company** at 230 South Wabash is an old-timer and dependable. They carry a large, varied selection of cameras, lenses, flashes, and other equipment, plus darkroom items. Another top choice is **Calumet Photographic,** 520 West Erie, and don't forget the national biggies, **Wolf Camera** and **Moto Photo.**

## CANOES AND KAYAKS

West and north of Wicker Park (4000 north and 6400 west, Zone 1) is a street called Narragansett, and at 4019 may be the largest (it certainly is the most unusual) dealer in the country for canoes and kayaks. **Chicagoland Canoe Base** retails over 150 models of canoes and kayaks, and builds canoes from 14½ feet long to 34 feet long. Owner Ralph Frese, in business over 50 years, says his full-fledged blacksmith shop comes in handy for designs and repairs on everything from fittings to boat trailers. He not only makes custom canoes for films (birchbark models for Universal Studios) but also sells accessories from clothing to paddles to camping gear to trailers. See Frese, too, for restoration of antique canoes.

## CLOTHING AND SHOES

**In the Loop**   Pick up flannel shirts at **Pendleton Products Store,** 119 South State, in the Palmer House Hotel arcade. The store has been there for 75 years, offering goods from Pendleton woolen mills in Oregon. But here they go beyond woolens for men and women to cotton knit sweaters, sweatshirts, jewelry, umbrellas, tote bags, and more. In woolens there are scarves, blankets, men's sport coats and slacks, and coats aplenty in winter. (Note: If you're visiting the western suburbs, there's a Pendleton at 777 North York Road, Gateway Square Shopping Center, in Hinsdale.)

LaSalle Street houses an enclave of men's stores (some of the best in the country) and emporiums dedicated to business accessories. About those men's stores: no doubt the reason there are so many is because the men (shoppers) involved in law and finance in this area outnumber the women. You'll find a men's store called **The Leading Man,** 32 East Adams Boulevard (there's another at Evergreen Plaza, 9506 South Western Avenue). And the suits you buy at **Syd Jerome Men's Wear,** 2 North LaSalle Street, will also make you someone's leading man.

**Brooks Brothers** (209 South LaSalle Street) is the menswear powerhouse now beloved by both men and women. The BB many prefer is at 713 North Michigan Avenue, and BB is big in the suburbs (Northbrook Court, Old Orchard, Woodfield, and Oak Brook Center Mall).

A popular men's retailer is **Men's Wearhouse,** with a Loop location at 25 East Washington Boulevard. The action here is discounted name brand menswear, plus personal service. Other branches are in Near North at 48 East Walton Place and at 2070 North Clybourn Avenue, as well as in the suburbs.

Another menswear supplier is **Jos. A. Bank Clothiers,** 25 East Washington (also with stores in Oakbrook, Vernon Hills, and Wilmette). A final men's outfitter is **Duru's,** known for custom-tailoring shirts and suits at 221 North LaSalle Street.

**Bridal Magic,** 25 East Washington Street, is a salon catering to the re-marrying bride (or the bride who's a little older), with semiformal gowns, cocktail suits, and accessories. Owner Mary Gerace also features semifor-mal plus sizes, such as designs by Chicagoan Regina Hunter, and simple Afro-centric gowns. Gerace works by appointment; call (312) 984-0427.

**On Michigan Avenue**   Let's begin with an old-time custom tailor recog-nized for his expertise with hand-tailored suits, **Lawrence Pucci,** 333 North Michigan Avenue. And, while you're cruising the Magnificent Mile, peruse the premises at **Nike Town,** 669 North. If you don't, people won't believe you've been to Chicago.

Speaking of shoes, **Hanig's** shoes get around: a large emporium at 660 North Michigan Avenue, one less traditional, **Hanig's Slipper Box,** at 2754 North Clark, and, when we last looked, even a **Hanig's Birkenstock Shop** at 847 West Armitage.

At 633 North Michigan you'll see the beauteous **Burberry's,** where men and women seek the instantly recognizable camel-and-cream (with a touch of black) icon check that enhances so many raincoats, scarves, and other fashion items, which are becoming less traditional and more mod-ern. At 645 North Michigan is the local outpost of the great Italian design house of **Ermenegildo Zegna.** The clothing is carried at several other stores, but the boutique housing this exclusive menswear is here. As for that huge **Gap** store at 679 North, the sales help are really friendly, and they have Gap shoes and Gap kids' clothes here, too. (There are, of course, other Gap stores around town, one notably at Water Tower Place.)

One of the newest big names to hit the Avenue is **Ralph Lauren** at 750 North Michigan. This 37,000-square-foot Chicago flagship is said to be the largest Polo Ralph Lauren store in the world. Here you'll find the designer's men's, women's, and children's clothing and accessories, plus home furnishings; there's even (the first) Ralph Lauren restaurant. Within the Georgian facade is everything from White Label sheets and towels to Polo Golf to a women's equestrian shop (fourth floor). Things for the home are presented in unique lifestyle environments.

**Banana Republic,** 744 North Michigan (and other locations), started as a repository for clothes you wished you could afford to buy to go camp-ing, and has graduated into providing really nice sportswear and acces-sories, but you already knew that.

If we had a separate category in this section for girls age seven and up, the following would be number one: **American Girl Place,** 111 East Chicago Avenue (across from the water tower), is chock-full of the American Girl collection of books, dolls, dresses, and other delights, including the latest fashions from A.G. Gear. There's a cafe here for lunch, tea, or dinner, and a theater, too (call (877) AG-PLACE for tickets).

Another titan, **Rochester Big & Tall,** 840 North Michigan Avenue, echoes its name with top fashions for larger men (notable clients include most of the Chicago Bulls). The emphasis is on the best of Italian designers (from Zanella dress trousers to cashmere coats from Movimento), as well as Donna Karan, Levi, Timberland, Izod, and much more.

At 875 North Michigan is the stunning nearly-100-story-high John Hancock Building, which houses the veddy chic men's clothiers, **Paul Stuart,** which came west from Manhattan; they carry women's clothing, too. While you're there, check out the Hancock's newsy restaurants, little shops (such as Aveda), and, of course, the view.

A word (or more) about **Bloomingdale's** belongs here: Lyman and Joseph Bloomingdale set up a little notions shop in New York, and by 1872 it had become an east side bazaar. It took until the 1980s for the big B to hit Chicago at 900 North Michigan Avenue. Bloomie's was first to feature in-store boutiques for Calvin Klein, St. Laurent, Montana, and Mugler, and they introduced the first designer shopping bag. Of the current 23 stores, Chicago has one of the most beautiful. There are also stores in Old Orchard and Oakbrook Center.

At 919 North Michigan, there's a **Mark Shale** (men's and women's fashions).

This end of the avenue is shoe paradise, with **Bally** at 919 North Michigan (briefcases and small leather goods, too), Water Tower Place's **Brown's** (women's and Doc Martens for men), and **Avventura** (men's) footwear. **Salvatore Ferragamo** has a sparkling store at 645 North Michigan (the company's first in the Midwest), housing women's and men's shoes (ready-to-wear), handbags, luggage, ties, knitwear, silk, and leather accessories.

At 935 North Michigan Avenue is **Chanel,** a lush store filled with awesome, internationally known clothes, accessories, and cosmetics.

An interesting shop with staying power is **Giovanni,** on the Avenue for 20 years, the last dozen at 140 East Walton. The accent is on special occasion clothing—gowns for balls, mothers of the bride, and nontraditional brides, plus ready-to-wear (suits, separates, leathers, suedes) and accessories (handbags, scarves, hats, costume jewelry). Among other design talents here is Chicago favorite and national comer **Maria Pinto,** who does gorgeous evening wear.

**On Oak Street**  World-class shopping begins on (no, not Rodeo Drive) Oak Street (Zone 3). Early Oak Street ambience was strictly beads and wampum. Then the settlers descended. By 1850, Oak was a residential street, among the first to turn to ashes in the Chicago Fire of 1871. By the 1880s, chic mansions gave new meaning to the words "Gold Coast," and this probably set Oak on its lifelong mission to cross sophistication with cozy hospitality. Now, the low-rise, high-fashion city block rimmed by Rush Street and the northernmost end zone of Michigan Avenue has come into its own, evolving into the style center it is today.

In most major cities, visions of the world's most exotic bazaars suddenly crystalize into one prototypical street, teeming with treasures arrayed before the eyes of dazzled shoppers. Surrounded by urban canyons, that single special avenue stands apart, its unique charm inviting, delighting. Such is Oak, Chicago's blockbuster block of fabulous fashion. The Oak Street council carefully keeps the 38 art deco street lights new, the 33 trees replaced if winter has been particularly rough, and even its sidewalks colored a distinctive charcoal grey.

What's in store? The ultimate by the world's most prestigious designers, presented with hometown flair. You can go crazy spending money on Oak, as you waltz the long block from the Michigan Avenue end to the corner of Rush and Oak Streets (where you'll find the newly expanded **Barneys New York**). Designers love it here, including locals such as the principals of **Hino & Malee** at 50 East Oak, whose sleek contemporary clothes are now carried throughout the world. Another star favorite is **Sansappelle** at 34 East Oak. Founded in 1976, this is a top manufacturer of late-day, evening, and special occasion fashions for women.

Oak's most uniquely homegrown high-fashion treasure is **Ultimo** at 114 East, known internationally for the ultimate in designer clothing for men and women as well as their tomorrow-flavored accessories. Under the direction of Joan Weinstein, the store paved the way for the roster of international stars that now dot Oak: **Georgio Armani,** 113, **Sonia Rykiel,** 106, and **Jil Sander,** 46, for three.

A giant step for couture came with the entrance of **Gianni Versace,** at 113; the late maestro's clothes and accessories for men and women are now under the direction of his sister Donatella, bringing joy to Midwestern aficionados. **Luca Luca,** 59, presents more Italian women's wear (the colors are lush); **Hermes of Paris,** 110, sends us its exclusive scarves, ties, leather goods, and other goodies à la Française; and **The Wolford Boutique** brings imported fun and fashionable hosiery and bodywear to 54 East Oak. Wolford is an international chain (originating in Austria); the hosiery, bodywear, and swimwear are pricey, but women like them because they fit, last longer, and are so incredibly luxe.

A new shop is **Hana K,** 72 East Oak, where luxury outerwear for men and women reigns. Here are lightweight shearlings, gorgeous rainwear (cashmere-, flannel-, or fur-lined), coats of precious cashmere and baby alpaca, and much more.

Among other Oak shops to peruse are the **Nicole Miller Boutique,** 61 East, with a full line of the New York designer's often whimsical prints; the exquisitely tailored fashions at **St. John Boutique,** 51; maternity fashions at **A Pea in the Pod,** 46; and superb men's fashions at **Sulka,** 55, and **Tessuti,** 50. One of the most right-now bridal salons (specializing in couture gowns) in the country is at 106, **Ultimate Bride.** And, juniors make a bee-line for hot fashions and accessories at **Sugar Magnolia,** 34 East.

One of the newer stores is **Chacok,** a bright outpost of style at 47 East Oak, with fashions for women brought from Paris by owner Barbara Travers. The boutique is the first in the United States, and the flavor is fresh, imaginative, and bursting with gorgeous color, whether the clothes are knits for winter or gauzy silks for summer. Another Euro gift to Oak Street is **Chasalla,** a German-based store opened by Marc Engel and Richard Settlemire at 70 East Oak, with clothing, shoes, and accessories for men and women from Hugo (the designer line of the Hugo Boss label), D&G (from Dolce & Gabbana), JOOP!, Cinque, and J&ANS (D&G's casual line).

Because parking is such a nuisance, choose from two solutions: valet parking with an attendant (stationed mid-block in front of 101) or the 1 East Oak garage (corner of Oak and State Streets, where you'll receive a small discount).

**Near North**   At 724 North Wabash Avenue is **Biba Bis,** where you'll find cutting-edge fashion design for the professional woman (we've seen great suits here) and unique home accessories and gifts. Customers are aged 20–60; Oprah, Madonna, and Kim Basinger have come to call. Clothes are primarily for women ("but we'll do custom for men and larger sizes").

Newly located amid Rush Street's unique shops is **Diesel,** 923 North Rush, the third of eight U.S. stores (they're also in New York City and Washington, D.C.). Here you'll find men's and women's clothes and accessories (including tons of five-pocket jeans) and a cafe on the second floor.

At 46 East Walton Place is one of 90 exclusive, worldwide boutiques set up by Parisian designer **agnes b.** The look is spare, sleek, simple, luxe, and classique.

Back at 946 North Rush Street is an improbable boutique (**Tender Buttons,** by name), which no doubt has that missing button you'd love to re-sew on your favorite jacket. Here are men's blazer buttons and imports (including gold buttons from France). Button, button, who's got the button? They do.

The address of the new **Bottega Veneta** is listed as 840 North Michigan Avenue, but the entrance is on Chestnut Street. Go see the gorgeous Italian imported shoes, handbags, small leather goods, and other accessories that are shaking up the fashion world with their fine design and materials. You can also order hot (but not inexpensive) clothes from their "look book."

At 54 East Chestnut Street is **Material Possessions,** a haven for fans of wearable art (from wovens to jewelry). This is also the place to find the most unusual items for your table (pottery, glasses, and serving pieces). See Home Furnishings for more information (page 207).

**Realta,** 1 East Delaware Place, is an elegant store housing sophisticated Italian suitings for men. The look here is ultra urbane; find handmade suitings by Redaelli and Sartori, Bill Kaiserman suits and sportcoats, sportswear from Spain and Italy, and neckwear by such designers as Gianfranco Ferre, Christian LaCroix, and Jon Marco Venturi, among others.

A source for gently used women's fashions is **Shabby Chic,** 46 East Superior. But everything's new for women at **Emli Marrero,** 19 East Chestnut, with exclusive Joan Vass designs.

Fashion for the career woman is the focus at **Mary Walter,** 650 North Dearborn Street (at Erie). In this attractive store, removed from hectic Avenue shoppers, you can browse among beautifully chosen suits, jackets, and other items for work and leisure hours, such as hand-painted scarves and Heather on the Hill jewelry (a lot of one-of-a-kind pieces). There's also a full-time tailor here.

**River North**    At 678 North Wells Street are the French sportswear creations of **Marithe + François Girbaud;** a sample of Girbaud innovation is the unisex Freedom pant, a "peaceful commando cargo pant incorporating a rucksack practicality with eight ample hold-everything pockets." 200 West Superior Street serves as somewhat off-the-beaten-track headquarters for **June Blaker,** the last word in Chicago high fashion (Blaker is *so* high, she looks down on most others who call themselves avant-garde). *This* is where you go to see the latest created by the Japanese designers; this is where you find tomorrow's accessories. They're usually eclectic: watches, semiprecious jewelry, silver, shoes. You can find Comme des Garcons socks as well as slacks. And, if you like Yohji Yamamoto, come here. There's even a bridal registry (so many gifts, from flasks to handblown vases to sunglasses).

At 704 North Wells Street is **Mongerson Wunderlich,** a store for western wear (indeed, many think a good pair of handmade cowboy boots is art of a sort). Here too are jackets, wonderful blankets, and even furniture. Also on Wells, but farther north at 1706, is **Handle with Care,** famous for up-to-the-second women's fashions.

**Lincoln Park/Clybourn Corridor**    Fronting the edge of Lincoln Park, at 1750 North Clark Street, is Chicago's interesting menswear duo, **Bigsby & Kruthers.** B&K is, in reality, two brothers named Silverberg, who've been in several locations and are now concentrating on expanding this flagship store, adding women's wear soon. There's also a terrific below-ground restaurant named **Trocadero.**

859 West Armitage Avenue houses one of the reasons area fashionables don't always have to dash to Michigan Avenue or the Loop. The name is **Celeste Turner,** a contemporary clothing boutique that serves the best in brand names (particularly good in sportswear).

If you're desperate for something new (if used), note **Cynthia's Consignments,** at 2218 Clybourn Avenue, and investigate **Cactus Trade,** at 2040 North Halsted.

**The Kangaroo Connection,** 1113 West Webster, carries goods and gear from Australia and New Zealand, including some cuddly toy koala bears that are indicative of the land from whence they came. They sell Beanie Babies here, too.

After 50 years in business, **Davis for Men,** 824 West North Avenue (there's also a store at 900 North Michigan, third level of Bloomingdale's), offers menswear for both business and leisure, for classic and avant-garde tastes.

One of the most outstanding shops on Webster is **Krivoy,** 1145 West. It's not a big place, and with the walls lined with home furnishings, you may not focus at first on the fashion. Then it hits you: this is the place to find a *hat* (they're made by the owner). There are also clothes and bags, and everything here is as tasteful as it is desirable. Also on Webster, pull up to **Underthings,** 804 West. Don't be embarrassed; this is a store for lingerie, and it's wonderfully complete, from robes to bras.

At 808 West Armitage Avenue you'll find clothes by the inventive Chicago designer **Cynthia Rowley,** and there are more handmade wearables by national artisans at **Isis on Armitage,** at 823 West Armitage. Another outpost for handmade wearables is **Elle Jae,** 2204 North Clybourn Avenue.

At 1115 West Armitage, **Jane Hamill** plies her trade, which is creating women's clothes that are both chic and affordable. With each season, her design talents grow; her accessories are always well chosen, too.

At 2229 North Clybourn is the **A Arsenault Designer Cooperative,** where some 18 designers sell clothing, millinery, accessories, and jewelry. One of the delightful advantages of shopping here is that there's always something to like among all these talented artisans.

**On Halsted, Clark, and Lincoln** Young women love to shop in the 2100 block of North Halsted Street; here are **Baby Gap,** 2108, **The Gap,** 2128 (with **Gap Kids** at the rear of the store), **Banana Republic,** 2104 North, and **Fitigues,** 2130 North (the Chicago-based cotton knit sportswear worn by kids and their mothers). Just past Armitage at 2202 North Halsted, **Chia** has very kicky fashions for young women, and across the street at 2217 is **All Our Children,** a lovely store that attracts many grandparents, looking for fashions for their little darlings (parents can come, too). There are clothes for newborns up to preteens.

Clark street fashion stores mostly for women include: trendsetting sportswear and edge-y accessories (handbags and jewelry, especially) at **Panache,** 2252. A sleek store nearby that fits its Italian name (it looks like a shop you might encounter in Milan), is **Palazzo,** 2262. Designs here are unruffly, what you think of when you hear the words *urban chic.* An **Express** (women's fashions) and a **Structure** (men's sportswear) are on the corner of Clark and Belden. Across the street is **Nonpareil,** 2300, where you're likely to see incredibly eclectic goods: fashions as well as vases and table treasures, silk jackets, trinkets, expensive imported jewelry, and more. There's also a large **Urban Outfitters,** 2352 North Clark, purveying clothing as well as home designs.

Pass The Gap at Fullerton and head north to **Hubba-Hubba,** 3338 North Clark Street, for vintage fashions, and since we've arrived at that subject, more may be found in the area a bit north of Belmont. Shoppers at **Flashy Trash,** 3524 North Halsted Street, usually like to skate over to **The Alley,** 858 West Belmont Avenue, where one teen shopper told us, "they have really neat jewelry and those hard-to-find Chicago cop leather jackets." They also have a vast number of T-shirts emblazoned with the name of your favorite rock 'n' roll band. **Tragically Hip,** 931 West Belmont, carries mostly (new) junior sizes. A huge golden retriever belonging to owner Kathleen Jamieson guards the premises, and you'll find cutting-edge fashions at ultra-reasonable prices, though styles are, notes one young shopper, "not as fancy as **Toshiro.**" The latter is at 3309 North Clark Street and purveys all-new (and lovely) fashions for women. (And they offer parking in back.)

To finish our brief youngish wrapup, **The Pink Frog,** 857 West Belmont Avenue, has relatively inexpensive items, and **Strange Cargo,** 3448 North Clark Street, is a thrift shop crossed with a vintage store (some '70s shoes were here when we last looked). The trendy young women who like all of the above will also like shoes by **Alternatives,** 1969 North Halsted (they're also at 942 Rush Street).

Let's let a truly elegant store have the last word on Clark Street: **Robave,** 3270 North, where two designers create their own unique, sleek, and chic fashions for the sophisticated woman.

At **Blake Women's Apparel,** 2448 North Lincoln Avenue, don't be put off by the storefront aspect. It's only one of the best high fashion sources. Here are very selective designer clothing and accessories—the *outré* designers, some Gaultier, some British notables. There are always a few accessories you *must* have.

Go way west to 1800 West Fullerton Avenue, and you'll find **Chicago Tennis & Golf,** where you can pick up great tennis and golf sportswear, including warmups, shoes, headbands, vests, hats—everything you need for tennis and golf. (This membership club also has services for restringing racquets and same-day regripping of golf clubs.)

Finally, not far from the Clybourn area near North Avenue in Wicker Park, at 1629 North Milwaukee Avenue, is a charming shop called **Pentimento,** filled with clothes and accessories (everything from earrings to hats) by designers (some local, some national) who create unique, one-of-a-kind pieces. There are a lot of small gift items, and everything is handmade. It's well worth the trip. And the area is rife with new shops, so take a long look around.

**Beyond Wicker Park**   Do costumes belong in the clothing category? Why not? **Fantasy Headquarters,** 4065 North Milwaukee Avenue, is *the* place to buy and rent costumes and wigs (both crazy and serious), makeup, and party props. This is the largest costume store in the Midwest. If you're in need of a Santa Claus suit or an Easter Bunny outfit, don't say we didn't tell you.

**In Glencoe and Winnetka**   When it comes to women's clothes, people from the city drive to **Shirise** for shoes and to **Scarboro Fair** for gladrags in Glencoe, and while they're in that suburb they never miss **Nicchia** for gorgeous sportswear (great knits) for men and women. Then it's off to **Perlie** in Hubbard Woods (Winnetka). Many, in fact, prefer the **Neiman Marcus** at **Northbrook Court** (in the suburbs of Northbrook, bordering Highland Park and Deerfield) to the NM downtown; there's a huge parking lot, for one thing, and the sales force tends to be the shoppers' neighbors, dedicated to the fine art of Finding Something. Northbrook Court is perhaps more fun to shop than most malls, thanks to its size (not too large) and goods (upscale, but not desperately pricey).

## Clothing and Shoes Discount Outlets
**In the Loop**   Actually, this is a bit south of the Loop, but among several discounters is **I.B. Diffusion,** 5020 West Roosevelt Road (between Cicero and Laramie), where we hear all women's apparel is 40–80% off. This company specializes in sportswear, and this is their warehouse outlet store. At Franklin and Randolph Streets (160 North Franklin) is **Eurodirect,**

which advertises its menswear (Italian suits, slacks, and sportcoats, for example) at 40–70% off.

By the way Chicagoans have taken to heart the Boston biz **Filene's Basement,** 1 North State, you'd think it was a native operation. Clothes here sometimes surprise you: rakeoff DKNY and Calvin Klein, shoes, wedding dresses. There are FB stores out north and west in the suburbs, one at 2838 North Broadway (in The Broadway at Surf), as well as the one in Designerland (Michigan Avenue).

Discount hunters may also want to peek into **Group USA,** 12 North Wabash Avenue. Women's fashion labels include Laundry, BCBG, and Kenar, and there are shoes by Sacha Too. Accessories such as jewelry, scarves, bags, and more are very affordable.

**On Michigan Avenue**    Above Borders Bookstore at 830 North Michigan is the first "discount" store to hit the Avenue, and the powers that be determined it couldn't open on the ground floor. Therefore, **Filene's Basement** opened on the third and fourth floors in a 50,000-square-foot shop that's a bit glossier than most FBs (as befits Michigan Avenue). They offer a variety of bargains.

**Lincoln Park/Clybourn Corridor**    On Clybourn, there are a parcel of boutiques both pricey and not (some assure you of really good bargains). There's a **Land's End Outlet** (first-quality sportswear catalog overstocks, 20–40% off). They have men's, women's, and children's clothing, but because it's an outlet store, it won't have everything you see in their catalog. If you're hunting for menswear, head west (5–10 minutes) to Elston Avenue, then just north to Fullerton (east of I-94). At 2593 North Elston Avenue is **Mark Shale Outlet.** (Shale does women's wear, too, rather on the tailored side.) Here: 30–70% off, much of it private label Shale merchandise; men can find Calvin Klein, Joseph Abboud, and dozens more designers. Look for summer and winter blowouts 20–50% off already marked-down goods.

**Lori's Discount Designer Shoes,** 824 West Armitage Avenue, does exactly what it says: gives you discount prices on shoes sold elsewhere for more (can we put it any more boldly?). They're always up to the minute, with a vast stock; the emphasis is on variety, with a shoe for every style. We've seen great-looking bags in here, jewelry, hosiery, and socks, too. (There's a Northfield store, too.)

**On Halsted, Clark, and Lincoln**    A standout in the roster of bargain fashion stores (it's as big as a warehouse) is **Chernin's,** 2665 North Halsted Street. All kinds of affordable footwear here: boots, shoes for dancing, jogging, you name it. There are two consignment boutiques to visit: **Buy Pop-**

**ular Demand,** 2629 North Halsted, with clothes (some new) for women to buy and sell; and **Selections,** 2152 North Clybourn Avenue; low, low prices.

Finally, it's reported that you can save 20–50% off department store regular prices at **DSW Shoe Warehouse,** in Lincoln Park at the Pointe (where Clark and Halsted Streets meet).

**In the Suburbs**   A number of outlet malls are described in our coverage of suburban shopping centers (page 218).

## CRYSTAL, CHINA, AND KITCHEN ITEMS

**On Michigan Avenue**   You don't want to miss a lovely little shop that specializes in Waterford (world-renowned crystal) and Wedgwood (world-famous china). **Waterford/Wedgwood** is at 636 North Michigan.

"Major" is the word for **Crate & Barrel**'s flagship store, 646 North; it's as luminous at night as an ocean liner. Contemporary home furnishings are provided at mostly moderate prices. You may run across Mexican glass, Danish teak, Italian pottery, you name it. The store also purveys furniture.

**Lalique** is a new crystal palace at 900 North. While you can find Lalique pieces all over town, this is the one place that gathers them all together. You can spend under $100 for a tabletop item or find a crystal dining table for $100,000—and everything in between.

**Near North**   One of Rush Street's pleasures is **Belvedere,** 948 North Rush Street. It dazzles with a range of goods and gifts, everything from Victorian antique salt and pepper shakers to sterling silver trays. Specialty items here include antique and vintage porcelains, new and old tabletop pieces, and linens.

Among the nation's first "paint-your-own-pottery" shops, the **PotHead Store,** 6 West Maple, is a fun way to turn adults and children onto do-it-yourself ceramics.

**Lincoln Park/Clybourn Corridor**   If you're looking for houseware bargains, it may pay to drive north to 2829 North Clybourn Avenue (Damen and Diversey area) to browse at **Krasny & Company.** There's everything for the tabletop (miles of glassware and professional cookware, plus some spices and herbs). Calphalon can be found here below retail. At 1800 North Clybourn is **Bed, Bath, & Beyond,** loaded with exactly what it says. There are some good values here in bedding, towels, and accessories.

On the northeast corner of Clybourn and Webster is **Samples.** The name says it: samples of everything from Copco to Bodum coffee pots. Walk in and find nothing one day; the next day, there's gold in them thar aisles. At 2525 North Elston Street is the **Edward Don Outlet,** where they sell everything you need for your kitchen and dining room thanks to "at cost" prices. Not everything is great, but if your tastebuds are in bloom, you can find good bargains; some china is swell, some glassware is less than $2 per piece. Commercial cookware is here, as well as a back room for closeouts.

Two finds are **Tabula Tua,** 1015 West Armitage Avenue, and **Faded Rose,** 1017 West Armitage Avenue. Tabula Tua (which means "your table") has the logo "beautiful wares," and that's the truth. Half of the tablewares are imported, such as pottery from Provence, and half are American, such as a handpainted pear dish. There are tables, picture frames, and other home accessories; prices are mixed.

The big news in a convenient mall at 800 West North Avenue is the **Crate & Barrel Outlet.** As one of Chicago's own housewares successes (see Michigan Avenue), C&B here offers goods more gently priced than at their other stores, making it worth a shopping stop. Usually, prices are 20–70% off discontinued and sample C&B merchandise. However, since Crate & Barrel has opened a gigantic new (non-outlet) store at 850 West North, this nearby (right across the street) store might have a new address in the future.

Another find on Armitage is **Findables, Inc.** at 907, a treasure trove of items past, present, and future. You're as likely to find antique beads or a piece of antique crystal or silver as a new woolen throw from Italy or table linens from France. Here, too, are unique books, decorative dinnerware and home furnishings, and luxe bath items, including body lotions and scented soaps. Findables is truly a find.

Those searching for kitchenware, woks, electric rice cookers, bread makers, knives, and other implements used to cook Oriental foods will find the **J. Toguri Mercantile Company,** 851 West Belmont Avenue, a treasure. (Here, too, are nonperishable foods, as well as goods from kimonos to CDs of hard-to-find Japanese music.)

**In Wilmette   The Crystal Cave,** 1141 Central, features a master artisan who repairs crystal and designs crystal pieces (they've done several award pieces for the Olympics). They also carry dozens of china and crystal patterns.

## FLORISTS

One of Chicago's most unique florists is **A New Leaf** at 1675 North Wells Street, packed with posies to adorn your hotel room or take to a lucky hostess. We've seen things here that nobody else seems to stock. (See Home Furnishings for news of their second store, page 207.)

In a city where many floral designers seem to create look-alike pieces, **That Flower Shop,** 537 South Dearborn Street (in the Printer's Row area) truly shines. Owner Geneva Currin uses fresh-cut Holland flowers to do natural designs (she did Michael Jordan's Mother's Day flowers). The shop also has dried flowers, candles, unusual French wire baskets, and an all-natural line of bath products called Mon Jardinet.

In the Wicker Park area at 2117 North Damon is an art gallery *cum* flower shop named **Robin Brisker** (he's the artist). The flowers here are arranged by creative Miki Herman.

## FOOD AND WINE

**In the Loop**   If you miss the Rue Cler in Paris, now is your moment. Just be in the Loop in the summer months, and shop at the City of Chicago **Farmer's Market,** usually held at Daley Plaza. The city sponsors these merry markets (overflowing with trucked-in *fleurs,* fruits, and vegetables) at some 24 locations during various times weekly. The Saturday market on Armitage (off Halsted) is one of our favorites. Call (312) 744-9187 for details on where and when.

Chocoholics should know about a fulfilling **Godiva Chocolatier** at 10 South LaSalle Street. (There's another at Water Tower Place.)

**Near North**   The place to find fresh mozzarella is **L'Appetito,** 30 East Huron Street, along with many imported Italian goodies; there's a second L'Appetito on the ground floor of the John Hancock Building. The divine breads from **The Corner Bakery,** 516 North Clark Street, are much praised. There are actually eight Corner Bakeries in the city and two in the suburbs, plus two outside of Illinois in Atlanta and McLean, Virginia. All have delish sandwiches, pizzas, and muffins.

In addition to Chicago's multiple **Starbucks** and **Seattle's Best** coffee bars, a cozy cafe (both coffee and food) with a hometown flavor is **The 3rd Coast,** 1260 North Dearborn Street, with another location at 29 East Delaware Place.

**Lincoln Park/Clybourn Corridor**   At 2121 Clybourn Avenue is Market Square. The "market" refers to a huge **Treasure Island;** some consider this food store chain the city's best, and this particular one best of all. To the west, take Elston south till you reach North Avenue; at 1558 North Elston, you'll bump into **Stanley's,** notable for good fruits and veggies. Some prefer the huge **Whole Foods** shopping mall, 1000 West North Avenue. Here you'll find everything from health aids to top-notch meats and poultry, and many rave about their huge salad bar (it's one of few places to find diced celery). There's a cafe here called **Eden**—big on healthy foods, and everything's tasty.

At 1720 North Marcey (across the street from Whole Foods) look for **Sam's Liquors.** This is a place beloved by many Chicagoans, who know they can pick up the best wines for the best prices. Staffers here know how to advise you, so *listen*. You may come in for a California Cabernet Sauvignon and walk out with a Piemontese Barolo. You won't be sorry. Also check out **The House of Glunz,** wine merchants at 1206 North Wells Street, with a very broad range thanks to their extensive wine cellar. If you are from certain (very few) states, you may order your selections by mail and your wines will be shipped to you sans Illinois sales tax.

Back on North Avenue, **Burhop's** has opened, to the delight of Lincoln Parkers and Near North neighbors who crave the freshest fish and seafood, ready-to-heat-and-serve entrees, great crab cakes, party trays, and such pleasures as good soups and key lime tarts.

**In Evanston and Wilmette** For those with a sweet tooth: **Belgian Chocolatier,** 509 Main Street, Evanston. And, if you hate to cook, stop at **Foodstuffs,** 2106 Central Avenue, Evanston (or in Glencoe at 338 Park). Both stores have huge delis, bake their own pastries, feature fish (Glencoe) and meats and fish (Evanston), and offer gift baskets and catering—both are outstanding. In Wilmette, the best take-out place is **À La Carte,** 111 Green Bay Road. All the foods are marvelous, but special raves go to their soups, salads, and desserts. (You can also eat here, too, in the small lunchroom and, in summer, outdoors.)

## FORMALWEAR

Formalwear is well represented in the Loop. For men, there's **Seno** (rental tuxes) at 6 East Randolph Street, and the ever-popular hometown favorite, **Gingiss Formalwear** (to buy and to rent), 151 South Wabash Avenue. There are three more far-flung Gingiss city stores (including an outlet store at 542 West Roosevelt Road, south of the Loop) and umpteen (21, actually) suburban outlets.

## FURS

The **Chicago Fur Mart,** after a tremendous remodeling, is now in it's permanent location at Summerfield Hotel, 166 East Superior. On the edge of the Lincoln Park area is a satisfying new and "gently used" fur shop called **Chicago Fur Outlet** ("home of the furry godmother") at 777 West Diversey Parkway. They have furs for both men and women, as well as shearlings and leathers. Of course, if you're interested in higher-end furs, see **Maximilian** at Bloomingdale's, 900 North Michigan Avenue, or **Revillon Paris,** 940

North Michigan Avenue. One of the city's best fur departments is **Marshall Field's Fur Salon** (opened in 1859, this is perhaps the oldest fur business in Chicago and the first in a Chicago department store). This is a very large, very pretty full-service fur salon on third floor State Street, offering sales, remodeling, repair, cleaning, and storage. Mink (lately, the sheared variety) comprises the bulk of their sales, but they have everything from beaver to sable and chinchilla (tsk! Not too practical, except as trim). And if you can't find what you want, they'll make it for you.

## GARDEN AND LANDSCAPING

At 1006 West Armitage Avenue is another "world" in itself; at **Urban Gardener** the backdrop is the home garden, and an eclectic variety of related items are spread throughout two floors. The two owners have a grasp of both architecture and landscaping, and they display architectural salvage (fragments for the garden, including old metal gates and coach lanterns). There are dried flowers, housewares with floral themes, books, baskets, floral soaps, and pillows. Speaking of fab "salvage," note **Architectual Artifacts,** way out north at 4325 North Ravenswood, where you're as likely to find a gorgeous garden bench as you are a magnificent fireplace mantel.

Near Diversey, at 2760 North Lincoln Avenue, **Fertile Delta** is a source for plants and trees (to put it mildly; the place is huge). It's probably one of the few places in the city where you can find both real and artificial Christmas trees.

## HOME FURNISHINGS, LINENS, AND BATH SUPPLIES

**On Michigan Avenue**   See the section on Crystal, China, and Kitchen Items for more details on **Crate & Barrel** stores (page 203).

**West of the Loop**   This discounter advertises itself as "locationally challenged," as it's indeed off-the-beaten-path, but if you happen to be driving while looking for furniture bargains, trek to 2145 West Grand to **EFW** (European Furniture Warehouse). One customer found an Italian marble cocktail table for an outstanding $299 (it was, of course, a one-time-only sale).

**On Oak Street**   One of the city's top home furnishings emporiums is **Elements,** at 102 East Oak. Tabletop accessories can be found here, along with everything from picture frames to men's and women's jewelry and wedding gifts. The owners have been on the *avant* scene for years and buy with wisdom; what you buy here will be knockout. Luxe bed, bath, and table linens come with love (and great taste) from Italy at **Pratesi Linen Co.,** 67 East Oak. They're not inexpensive, but the quality is high.

**Near North**    New and impressive, **The Morson Collection,** 100 East Walton Street, has European contemporary furniture, area rugs, lighting, and accessories. The interior design atelier known as **Atelier Branca,** 1325 North State Street, is no longer a retail shop, but the great taste of Alessandra Branca is available (by appointment only) to those seeking her exclusive lines of dinnerware, antique prints, lamps, and topiaries, as well as custom-made furniture, including faux finishes and antiquing. Call (312) 787-6123.

At 54 East Chestnut Street is **Material Possessions,** where eclectic spirit is combined with a sense of humor in showcasing a unique selection of original home furnishings, specializing in tabletop. The display of custom-made dinnerware, glassware, and linens complements other areas of the store where contemporary items are sold alongside antiques. This is a must-see for the discerning shopper. There's another MP in the suburbs (Winnetka).

A bit west of Michigan Avenue: If you're into "faded, classical slip-covered furniture," slip into **Shabby Chic,** 46 East Superior Street. On Walton (66 East) is an enchanting boutique with a French accent: **La Maison de Nicole.** The latter features a mélange of gifts, home accessories, antiques, even furniture. Quel chic.

Another Near North must-visit is **Pimlico Road, L.P.,** 940 North Rush Street, with its fine eighteenth- and nineteenth-century reproductions of English furnishings and decorative objects. Maitland-Smith is a featured manufacturer here.

**River North**    Along with most of the city's best galleries are some of its most cherished home decor emporiums. There are, in fact, so many of them, it's not easy to pick and choose. The problem is, of course, that what one person detests another will adore. We'll try to give you a quick summary; then you can go and make up your own mind.

One more necessary disclaimer: stores, like galleries, come and go; at this writing, everything's in place. Who knows about tomorrow? We've tried to include the enduring ones, but, just to be sure, call to check before you go shopping.

The scene here began with a few furniture and antiques galleries that first moved west from LaSalle to cluster around Superior and Huron Streets (wags named it SuHu, after New York's Soho, but it didn't take). Today, the area is larger, extending in spots to Clark Street on the east, and south of Grand Avenue as far as Illinois, Hubbard, and Kinzie, in some cases. The cut-off point is usually Chicago Avenue to the north, but . . . rules are made to be broken.

At 65 West Illinois Street is **Champagne Furniture Gallery,** and on Clark at 72 West Hubbard Street is **The Golden Triangle.** Imports here are often dazzling, such as a teak/cane plantation chair from Thailand and Burmese wooden puppets. **Sawbridge Studios,** 406 North Clark Street, is a gallery of custom-made designs by craftspeople from around the world. Furniture (from Shaker to traditional to Prairie) is predominant, and, considering the high cost for custom-made pieces, it's affordable. Many other craft items are also here, including pottery, glass, quilts, and handpainted rugs. One of their latest exhibits details the cottage furniture by Indiana artisan Michael O'Shea. There is also a suburban gallery in Winnetka.

At 220 West Kinzie Street is **The Antiques Centre at Kinzie Square.** This is an exciting enclave for shoppers to enjoy more than 500 selections in furniture, lighting, decorative objects, rugs, fine art, and estate jewelry. There are vendors who purvey everything from vintage Miriam Haskell pearl pins to antique rocking chairs to sterling flatware with inlaid mother-of-pearl handles. There's no musty attic feeling here, either; everything's bright and light.

Also on Kinzie (159 West) is **Asian House,** boasting a complete line of Oriental furniture and accessories, such as cloisonné vases and animals, bronze statues, porcelain fishbowls, Korean furniture, antique Chinese furniture, coromandel screens, and more.

On Hubbard Street, furniture reigns at **Roche-Bobois,** 222 West, and also at the **Kreiss Collection** showroom, 415 North LaSalle Street. The Kreiss family designs and manufactures its own elegant pieces; you can pick out the finishes, fabrics, and accessories right here.

In a city blessed with tabletop treasure troves, one of distinction is **Table of Contents,** 444 North Wells Street, where brides- and grooms-to-be go to indulge pottery and flatware dreams; there are so many giftables on these amply stocked shelves, you'll probably not leave here empty-handed.

**Rita Bucheit,** 449 North Wells Street (use the Illinois Street entrance), is *the* major Biedermeier expert and importer for the Midwest. She searches for furniture made by the Austrian master after 1840; at Christmastime, she has small silver pieces, small furniture items (such as accent chairs for additional seating), and ornaments.

At 500 North Wells Street and Illinois is **Mario Villa,** home to unique lamps and other antiques. Across the street at 501 is the place to go if you're looking for exquisite floor tiles; the name is **Ann Sacks,** where you'll also see stone flooring that is gorgeous, but not necessarily expensive.

215 West Ohio Street is home to **Leslie Hindman,** known as a national auction authority and an expert on antiques, which can be found here. On the corner of 549 North Wells Street at Ohio is **Mig & Tig,** with a fine

furniture mix: upholstered pieces, some wood, wrought iron from Mexico, and other imports. They're pieces that would fit in all settings, from contemporary to country.

Nearby at 445 North Wells Street is **Arrelle Fine Linens.** This is not the place to come if you're looking for Fieldcrest on sale. No. This is where you'll find an Italian sheet as silky as gelato that might set you back $100 or more. At least go in and look at the table linens and gorgeous bed settings (maybe you can afford pillowcases).

We passed Erie Street and didn't mention **Jan Cicero Gallery** (221 West), so we will now. Another outlet for furniture, **Phoenix Design** (368 West Huron Street), is a "street version of a Merchandise Mart showroom," one shopper told us. (Incidentally, **The Mart Store** at 153 West Ohio Street also shows things you'd see at the Merchandise Mart, but you have to know what you want when you walk in. They won't custom design; what you see is what you get.)

At 200 West Superior Street is an extraordinarily artful collection of furniture and furnishings (half the pieces are Italian; some are designed by the owner/architect) at **Manifesto.** You'll see some Herman Miller pieces (reissues of top '50s designers) if you peruse the two floors; we saw a dining room table, sofas, and benches (from their Austrian company), lounge chairs, vases, lighting, wineracks, and some accessories.

301 West Superior houses **Luminaire,** a 16,000-square-foot showroom that began as a fine lighting emporium and graduated into retail home furnishings. Everything is top-flight here; find the very best international designers, from Philippe Stark to Ingo Maurer (innovative lighting design).

**The Spicuzza Collection,** 415 North Franklin Street, is the showroom for furniture designer and interior architect Martin Spicuzza. You'll find his woods beautiful and adornments (from luxe fabrics to drawer and door pulls) impressive.

**Galleria M,** 313 West Superior, is Chicago's version of the New York–based Dialogica. The hot furniture design collection, by the team of Monique and Sergio Savarese, was brought to the Midwest by owner M. J. Foreman-Daitch. Pieces here are quirkily contemporary (though they'd fit in anywhere) and mostly affordable and unforgettable. Tabletop accessories have been added, and Dialogica also has come out with a lower-priced line called The Saba Collection.

**Lincoln Park/Clybourn Corridor Jayson Home & Garden,** 1915 North Clybourn, has become one of the hottest retail stores in the Lincoln Park area. In two vintage warehouses, you'll find treasures that interestingly combine old and new, domestic and imported. Unusual gifts include heirloom photo albums; opulent sofas, chairs, and ottomans; and Euro bath luxuries. For the garden, there are plants, fresh flowers, and outdoor furniture, among other goodies.

A charming source for antiques and reproduction pine furniture is **Pine & Design,** 511 West North Avenue, with an in-house cabinetry shop and a new gift gallery of accessories called **Christina Belle.** Farther west is one of the top storage and organization leaders in the housewares industry— **The Container Store,** 908 West North. They have everything for storage—every type of shelving from bookcases to entertainment centers and storage containers for kitchens, bathrooms, and every room in the house, including closets. They also have stores in Schaumburg, Northbrook, and Oak Brook.

An absolute standout is **Fortunate Discoveries,** 1022 West Armitage Avenue. The owner has a marvelous eye for international treasures, such as handwoven kilim ("flatly woven") rugs from the Middle East using various weaving techniques, or old windows from the Swat Valley (Pakistan). Here, too, are one-of-a-kind pillows and furnishings from Africa, Afghanistan, and Indonesia, including benches, armoires, side tables, and multiple accessories.

At 1925 North Clybourn Avenue is a store with a therapeutic aim: **Relax the Back.** It's bent on relief of back pain, thanks to such things as the "new Panasonic Zero Gravity Massage Recliner" and Relax the Back executive office chairs. Farther north on Clybourn at 2418 is **Interior Design Concepts,** where Daryl Michaels's helpful showroom focuses on home safety concepts for the elderly and disabled, such as tubs with doors for people who can't lift their legs over the edge. At Market Square, 2121 North Clybourn Avenue, is **Elegant Bath Accents,** a spacious store housing everything you always wanted in towels, soaps, toiletries, and other bath goodies.

Popular florist **A New Leaf** has opened **A New Leaf Studio & Garden,** 1818 North Wells Street, where shoppers can find antique Mexican curio cabinets, antique armoires, tables, everything from pottery and candles to ceramics, plus dried flowers and potted plants.

A haven for artisans and craftsmen is **Motif,** 1101 West Webster, where we could hardly tear ourselves away from the work of local and national artists, including such jewelry designers as Giselle Minoli and her exquisite sterling silver flowers (calla lilies, roses, and such—these are also carried at **Art Effect** on Armitage and at **Isis,** 900 North Michigan). Here, too, are Alessi products, Nambe pieces, and a selection of children's clothes, shoes, and booties, as well as everything from stuffed animals, soaps, and picture frames to Asian-influenced teapots.

**On Halsted, Clark, and Lincoln**   Halsted has so much to offer, not the least of which are galleries full of decorative furnishings. One of the best is **Gallimaufry** at 3345 North Halsted Street.

At 3647 North Halsted, **Homebodies** is fun to visit because this eclectic specialty shop has thousands of items, from lamps to picture frames to furniture to wind chimes to slipcovers. We even found strings of party lights and dried flowers. To the south is a store that sets the style for sleepyheads: **Bedside Manor Ltd.,** 2056 North Halsted, has beautiful bedding.

On Clark Street at 3336 is the **Wrigleyville Antique Mall.** It's an unlikely setting, but a good place to shop (though there are as many vintage items—'50s and '60s—as antiques).

At 2244 North Broadway, the store that caters to your budget is **Cost Plus World Market.** Some of the items here are truly junque, but in between are necessities that can save you a bundle. At the other end of the spectrum, an outstanding source for fine antique furnishings is **Ile de France,** 2009 North Fremont. Here are international (but mostly French nineteenth-century) antiques, as well as art deco and art nouveau furniture. Mirrors, tables, chairs, and clocks are here, as well as art (paintings, prints). They also have a warehouse for restoration of furniture and decoration (gilding, etc.) at 2222 North Elston and have recently opened in suburban Highland Park.

**In Wicker Park**   At **Eclectic Junction,** 1630 North Damen Avenue, Erika Judd shows a permanent collection of furniture and one-of-a-kind pieces by other artisans. Her wares, she says, are "functional, affordable, traditional installations, as well as usables and wearables."

**Whiz Bang,** 1959 West Cortland, is for the adventurous. They also have furniture—"odd things, and then they re-do 'em," says one who knows. And you may want to look into the '50s–'70s goods on tap at **Modern Times,** 1538 North Milwaukee Avenue.

**Off the Beaten Path**   Discover **Vintage Pine,** a 13,000-square-foot showroom overflowing with current custom, antique, and vintage looks in both furniture and accessories. The address is 904 West Blackhawk, which translates into two blocks south of North Avenue and two blocks west of Clybourn Avenue. The goods here range from shipments of English pine armoires, farm tables, chairs, and silver pieces to items sold by galleries on the premises who deal in antiques and more contemporary housewares.

At 3729 North Southport Avenue is a small shop called **P.O.S.H.** with such interesting items as the kind of vintage water carafes found in French bistros and other unusual tableware. If you continue north, you'll arrive at **Architectural Artifacts, Inc.,** an extraordinary outlet for furniture and decorative items from around the world. It's located in a huge warehouse at 4325 North Ravenswood. Find everything here from garden furniture to old (but sometimes beautiful) fireplace mantels.

## JEWELRY

**In the Loop**  A big Loop attraction for those who must have baubles, bangles, and beads is a series of jewelers (both wholesale and retail) at the renovated **Jewelers' Center at the Maller's Building,** 5 South Wabash Avenue. It's worth a look just to see how beautifully one of the oldest buildings in the Loop has been redesigned, and there will no doubt be one or more jewelry stores on the premises to entice you. **Wabash Jewelers Mall,** street level at 21 North Wabash Avenue on Jewelers Row, also entices with good values.

**On Michigan Avenue**  One of Chicago's most exciting new stores is the Midwest's only **Bulgari,** a gorgeous outpost of the Roman designer at 909 North Michigan. All of the contemporary classics recognizable to fashionables are here, from *tubogas* (hand-wrapped flexible band) designs to the double-stone ring called *Doppio Buccellato.* Here, too: the famed Bulgari fragrances for men and women (some with green tea), scarves, handbags, and sunglasses.

The Drake Hotel houses **Georg Jensen,** 959 North Michigan, a mélange of gorgeous jewelry and tabletop items. Note a Danish artist (actually, all the designers featured here seem to be Danish) named Viviana Torun, who does super silversmithing. Folks who know of Jensen's New York fame find this store one of Chicago's pleasures.

**On Oak Street**  Jewelry here is in the capable hands of two longtime Chicago favorites, one the province of a single master designer, **Lester Lampert,** at 57 East Oak. The other, **Trabert & Hoeffer,** has operated since 1937, most of that time on Michigan Avenue, but currently at 111 East Oak. Fine gemstones and custom designs are the rule here; you're not bombarded by lots of jewelry cases; they bring items to you, somewhat in the style of an extra-*haute* fashion house. But don't be intimidated. Gems *are* expensive, but the staff here can make buying them pleasant.

The newly expanded **Great Lakes Jewelry** (at 104 East Oak, basement level) happens to be a manufacturer-run bargain haven, with good deals on tons of silver (and some gold) jewelry. OK, diamonds are a girl's best friend, but if you're looking for a rhinestone pin that spells out "Chicago," this could be nirvana.

**Off the Beaten Path**  Out west (but still in Chicago), if you're up for driving a distance, you'll come to the showroom/studio of **Annie Afshar,** nationally known as a jeweler who works exclusively with beads. Her Blazing Beads are sold at many leading boutiques, and even in the Neiman Marcus catalog. You'll save money by buying directly from her at 3223 West Altgeld. To make an appointment, call her at (773) 645-8922.

**In Evanston**   Custom-designed jewelry is on tap at **Eve J. Alfille,** 623 Grove Street, where they love nature's images, and at **Peggie Robinson Designs,** 1514 Sherman Avenue (one customer here has been wearing different versions of her hand-hammered silver hoops for 30 years).

## LUGGAGE

**In the Loop**   **Emporium Luggage,** 128 North LaSalle Street. Find Tumi, Atlantic, Impulse, Dakota, and Hartmann luggage, fine attaché cases, briefcases and brief bags, computer cases, garment bags, and writing instruments. The same owners provide more value-oriented products at **Chicago Luggage,** 12 South Wabash. Leather goods, luggage, and accessories are also carried here, but geared toward more mainstream budgets.

   **Deutsch Luggage Shop,** 39 West Van Buren and 40 West Lake, is another family-owned business and a source for fine luggage, leather goods, and business cases. Among brand names are Delsey, Hartmann, Bringgs, Riley, Schlesinger, and Gloria Chavel cosmetic bags for travel. (They also have a store in Skokie.)

**Lincoln Park/Clybourn Corridor**   The former **Kaehler Luggage** is now **Travelworks,** and has moved to 2070 North Clybourn Avenue. The store specializes in luggage, leather goods, and gifts, and there are some terrific buys here. Most major luggage lines are discounted. (They also have a store in Evanston.)

## MARINE SPECIALTY ITEMS

**Lincoln Park/Clybourn Corridor**   An unusual store in this area is **West Marine** at 627 West North Avenue, the last word in supplies, books, and gifts for those who love the sea and ships. Find everything here for the boater but the boat, from personal flotation devices (alias life jackets) to books on boat safety.

## MISCELLANEOUS

When it comes to unusual items, **Diva Collectables** has just about everyone beat. This store, at 2908 North Broadway, features movie memorabilia, out-of-print soundtrack LPs, original and reproduction posters, and (ta-da) a huge selection of Barbra Streisand souvenirs.

## MUSICAL INSTRUMENTS AND RECORDED MUSIC

**In the Loop**   If you are looking for music, you'll find plenty at the **Chicago Music Mart** at DePaul Center, 333 South State Street (park at Crosstown Auto Park, 328 South Wabash Avenue). Here are stores that can supply everything from drums (**Chicago Percussion Center**) to karaoke tapes and pop sheet music (**Carl Fischer Music**). Among a plethora of stores that carry instruments and every kind of music accessory, **Crow's Nest** offers CDs and tapes, and you can buy candy, cards, and gifts at **Intermission Shoppe.** Pick up wonderful souvenirs of musical Chicago at **Accent Chicago.** There are many outposts of the latter, including one at O'Hare Airport, which specialize in nonjunky items that represent (and accent) Chicago products and arts.

*Program note:* Look for free daily performances at the Mart's **Tunes At Noon,** with outdoor performances in the summer at the DePaul Center Plaza.

Our friends at the main store for **Carl Fischer of Chicago,** 312 South Wabash, which has been a local musicians' mecca since 1909 (purveying band, choral, handbell, piano, vocal, guitar, and popular sheet music) also offers music accessories, from sweaters, tote bags, key chains, umbrellas, and bookends (all with musical images) to metronomes and colored guitar straps. They gave us some great tips. For one thing, at a super used bookstore at 3510 North Broadway, **Selected Works,** Keith Peterson sells used sheet music (some vintage); he's open noon–9 p.m. daily. Speaking of vintage, **Pedals, Pumpers & Rolls** restores and repairs old pianos and other automatic musical instruments (player pianos, nickelodeons, reproducing grands, music boxes, etc.), but they're far west of the city (relocated near the Joliet area). By appointment only; call (630) 879-5555 for information.

**On Michigan Avenue**   Another recommendation is **Sherry-Brener,** 226 South Michigan Avenue, selling violins and other stringed instruments, bagpipes and pan pipes, mandolins, guitars handmade in Spain, used guitars, and more. There's also a Sherry-Brener store at 3145 West 63rd Street on Chicago's South Side (Zone 6).

It's fun to look into the futuristic **Sony Gallery,** 663 North Michigan, even though it's pretty touristy. But how else can you check out state-of-the-art electronics?

**On Oak Street**   **Bang & Olufsen** at 15 East Oak features Danish music and video systems.

**Near North**   A block south of Grand Avenue at the edge of The Loop, and a must-see if you're feelin' groovy, is **Jazz Record Mart,** 444 North Wabash Avenue, which bills itself as the world's largest jazz and blues shop.

## ORIENTAL RUGS

**On Halsted, Clark, and Lincoln**   Check out **Peerless Rug Co.,** 3033 North Lincoln. Riches include Oriental rugs and unusual European tapestries, skillful reproductions of centuries-old designs. The motto here is "It's worth the trip," and if you're looking for carpets, indeed it is. For kilim rugs, **Fortunate Discoveries,** 1022 West Armitage Avenue (see Home Furnishings, page 207) is the place to go.

**In Evanston**   A name to note is **Oscar Isberian,** 1028 Chicago Avenue.

## OUTDOOR GEAR

**On Michigan Avenue**   **The North Face** at 875 North (in the John Hancock Building) is newsworthy, with great skiwear and ski equipment, as well as climbing and other outdoor gear. There are also suburban stores (Oak Brook Center and Woodfield in Schaumberg).

**On Halsted, Clark, and Lincoln**   What started as a discount army-navy surplus store has graduated to a sporting goods, camping, and travel emporium where you can pick up anything from a pea coat to mountain climbing gear. The name of it is **Uncle Dan's,** 2440 North Lincoln Avenue, and it's nothing fancy, but is very service-minded. (They're also located in Evanston and Highland Park.)

## SPORTS CARS AND VINTAGE AUTOMOBILES

A day trip to the northern suburbs (Zone 11) takes you to two sources for vintage cars and other antique car collectibles, which may be why some international shoppers find the Chicago area a hub for these auto prizes.

**Chicago Car Exchange, Inc.** is in Libertyville (take I-94 to Route 176 east) at 14085 West Rockland Road (phone (847) 680-1950). Philip J. Kuhn III and his father Philip Kuhn Sr. run the family business, featuring vintage sports cars, classic cars from the '20s, and racy "muscle" cars with big engines from the '60s. One hundred and fifty cars are gathered in an indoor showroom and sold worldwide. "New cars depreciate in value," says Phil Kuhn. "These cars are viewed as an investment to drive." There is a small admission charge of $3.

Not far from there is the **Volo Antique Auto Museum** on 30 wooded acres (27582 Volo Village Road, near Routes 12 and 120). Here are over 200 pre– and post–World War II collector cars and trucks in a multi-million-dollar collection housed in four showroom buildings. All cars are for sale (values range from $7,000–$750,000). Official collector classifications include antique, brass-era, classic, milestone, muscle, exotic and sports cars, domestic and foreign, from the early 1900s through the 1980s.

The museum is owned and operated by the second- and third-generation Grams family (Greg Grams and sons Jay and Brian, and Greg's brother Bill), and the museum is a guest exhibitor at the annual Chicago Auto Show every February. There are other sources for collector cars, but this is the largest. The American Classics Gift and Book Shop (museum building one) has '50s and '60s auto-related gifts; building four has investment-quality, auto-related art and artifacts. There are also three separate but connected (*not* auto-related) antiques malls representing over 300 established antiques dealers. The museum and malls are open daily 10 a.m.–5 p.m.

## TOBACCO

The reemergence of cigars has caused some minor interest in this category, but the following sources are the most interesting:

**The Up Down Tobacco Shop,** a smoker's paradise at 1550 North Wells Street, is an old-timer (and one of the original few) dedicated to smokers who cherish the art of enjoying and buying fine cigars. Up Down goes the same ways, but perseveres mightily. They claim to have the largest selection of premium cigars in Chicago.

The **Blue Havana Smoke Gallery,** 856 West Belmont Avenue, features a "blue" smoking room, a walk-in humidor filled with 200 varieties of cigars, and various cigar guides and accessories. The theme here is Chicago blues, and there are studio portraits of Chicago blues greats (for sale).

On the upscale side, cigars and humidors are classic and impressive at **Dunhill,** Mezzanine, Water Tower Place, 835 North Michigan Avenue.

## TOYS, GAMES, AND GIFTS FOR CHILDREN

**The Loop**   It's a chain store, but the stuff for kids is varied, and they have just about everything that's ever advertised, in case your little darling saw it on TV. It's none other than **Toys R Us,** based at 10 South State Street.

**On Michigan Avenue**   After **FAO Schwarz,** 840 North Michigan, the others often play follow the leader. Sugarplums here include everything from books and art supplies (we found an "art studio" for kids with 14 watercolors, 36 pastel crayons, 36 colored pencils, and 2 brushes in a portable wooden case, $45) to dolls, including a limited edition Barbie for $250.

**On Halsted, Clark, and Lincoln**   At 2146 North Halsted Street is one of the city's most charming stores for children's toys, books, and games: **Saturday's Child** is the name, but it's been a longtime favorite of children born every day of the week. At 2314 North Clark Street is a nifty, intimate, but fully stocked toy store called **Building Blocks.** Finally, at 2911 North Broadway is an adventurous toy store and bookstore called **Toyscape.**

Adventurous because you won't find TV-advertised stuff, but unique toys that even collectors covet.

**In Evanston   Rosie** is recommended for children's toys, books, and games at 620 Grove Street. Everything here looks hand selected, and the service is good.

## Western Goods, Boots, and Saddles

At 1000 West Armitage Avenue is **Out of the West,** a stunning western lifestyle store that's a cross between a luxe ranch and an old-fashioned general store. Savvy buying is obvious in the various categories of goods: Navajo rugs, silver jewelry, silver buckles and handmade belts, a wall of boots, racks of urban-focused sportswear, saddles, home decor, lamps, and tableware. The store deserves cheers for succeeding in establishing the ambience it seeks.

## Glaring Omissions

There are some rather glaring omissions here, so before someone says, "What about **Cartier?**" (630 North Michigan Avenue) or, "What about **Tiffany & Co.?**" (730 North Michigan Avenue), let us hasten to say they are very much alive and glowing, and you'll never see more beautiful stores, *ever.* (You know whether or not you can afford the goods there, don't you?) You also have heard of **Enzo Angiolini Shoes** (701 North Michigan), **Joan & David Shoes** (717 North Michigan), **Victoria's Secret,** and other appealing chain stores, but that's enough about chains.

# Suburban Shopping Centers and Discount Malls

Some Chicago area malls are musts (mostly downtown), a few are recommended if you happen to be in the area, and some don't warrant a visit, even if you're visiting relatives in that suburb.

Most shoppers—whether they're from Lucca in Tuscany or Las Vegas, Nevada—know that a Gap store is a Gap store, Saks Fifth Avenue is SFA, Osco is Osco, and a rose is a rose. Sometimes, however, a mall store will surprise; those are the ones you want to hear about.

If you're driving past the beautiful Baha'i House of Worship on Sheridan Road into Wilmette, you may want to stop at the second-oldest shopping center in the United States, **Plaza Del Lago.** The distinctive style of a romantic Spanish courtyard serves as a backdrop for 30 stores—everything from **Artisan Shop** and **Crate & Barrel** to a fine fish store called

**Burhop's** (they not only sell fish and basic, as well as gourmet, foods, but they make wonderful soups, too). With so many places to shop here, you'll get hungry, so stop at **Convito Italiano** or **Betise** for lunch. Convito features Italian foods (their take-out counter and retail food and wine counters are always packed), and Betise has a French bistro flavor.

One of the newsiest shopping centers on the north shore is **Old Orchard,** Skokie Boulevard and Old Orchard Road, Skokie. Always one of the prettiest outdoor malls in the area, OO was entirely renovated at the time of the entrance of **Nordstrom.** This is a beautiful store, as is **Marshall Field's. Saks Fifth Avenue** is another anchor store, and so are **Lord & Taylor** and **Bloomingdale's.** There are also about 125 more stores, from **FAO Schwarz** to **Warner Bros.** and **The Disney Store. Learningsmith** (games, books, and unique educational items for kids and their parents), **Williams-Sonoma** (housewares and gifts), and **Papyrus** (papers and cards) add to the fun.

**Oakbrook Center** (Zone 9) in Oak Brook is what they call premier shopping and what you'd call first-run in the performance lineup of shopping centers. **Saks** anchors here, along with **Nordstrom** (this was the first in the Midwest), **Neiman Marcus, Marshall Field's, Lord & Taylor,** and **Sears.** Stores here also include **Tiffany & Co., Tommy Hilfiger,** the **Eddie Bauer** (prototype) home store, one of the best museum shops of the **Art Institute, FAO Schwarz, Crate & Barrel, Camille Et Famille** (gifts and artsy home accessories), **Mario Tricoci Hair Salon and Day Spa,** and some 146 others. The **Williams-Sonoma** store has expanded here to become **Williams-Sonoma Grande Cuisine** (lots of product demonstrations here).

**Woodfield Shopping Center** (Zone 10) in Schaumberg (about 40 minutes northwest of Chicago and not far from O'Hare) has been joined by a handful of other shopping centers in the area. Add the Barrington Ice House in Barrington, the folksy charm of Long Grove Shopping Village, and several small malls in Schaumberg to Woodfield, and you've got *Greater* Woodfield's four million square feet of retail (and what we last heard was nearly 500 stores). Whew.

Woodfield Shopping Center also is one of the largest of its kind in the United States, so wear comfy shoes to walk its miles of indoor track. **Nordstrom, Lord & Taylor, Marshall Field's, Sears, J.C. Penney,** and some 230 more are here. Nifty stores vary from **Abercrombie & Fitch** to "learning" stores such as **WTTW Store of Knowledge, Discovery Channel Store, Rand McNally,** and **Imaginarium** (great toys that are educational and fun). Another fun place is **Mary Engelbreit** (products from a nifty designer who invents phrases such as "Let's put the fun back in dysfunctional" and puts 'em on coffee cups. Take the kids to **The Rainforest Cafe**—it's like dining in a faux Disney-esque rainforest.

While we're on the subject of day-tripping, the following destinations may add further incentive to get behind the wheel, shopping bags poised to be filled. All are an hour or two from the city (one-way), so allot enough time. In many cases, however, the savings can be sky-high.

**Gurnee Mills Mall,** the Midwest's largest value retail and manufacturer outlet mall at the intersection of I-94 and Grand Avenue (Illinois Route 132, Gurnee) is bigger than Soldier Field and attracts more visitors than Graceland. Among the 200 stores are the **Off 5th Saks Fifth Avenue Outlet, J.C. Penney Outlet, Bigsby & Kruthers Outlet, Ann Taylor Outlet, Planet Hollywood, Gap Outlet, Nautica,** and **Lord & Taylor Clearance Center.** For more information, call their tourism department at (800) 937-7467.

The new name for **Factory Outlet Center** (take I-94 and Highway 50 to exit 344 in Kenosha, Wisconsin) is **Original Outlet Mall:** 110 outlet stores include **Sony, Eddie Bauer, Carter's** (the kidswear is great), **Oneida, Libbey Glass, Casio, Hush Puppies Factory Direct, Rubbermaid, Bugle Boy,** and **General Nutrition Center.**

**Prime Outlets at Kenosha** (I-94, exit 347 in Kenosha): More chic names are found here than at the other centers. Their big draws are seldom attached to the word *outlet:* **Donna Karan, Ralph Lauren, Tommy Hilfiger,** and **J. Crew.** They're joined by other unexpected outlet names, such as **Nordic Trak, Geoffrey Beene, Liz Claiborne, Nike, Jones New York & Co.,** and **Sara Lee Bakery** among others. Call the center at (414) 857-2101.

And more bargains are available from the Huntly stores at 11800 Factory Shop Boulevard, way out west in Huntley, Illinois. Find **The Gap, Izod, Reebok, Rockport, Casual Corner,** and **Jones N. Y. Factory Finale.**

And to all a good buy.

# Part Ten

# Sight-Seeing Tips and Tours

## Touring Chicago

Visitors to Chicago have a wealth of sight-seeing options to choose from. Consider: Not only does Chicago offer a wide selection of world-class museums, the city is a museum. The Loop and the lakefront encompass the world's largest collection of outdoor modern architecture. Turn any corner in the Loop and you're confronted with yet another structural, aesthetic, or technical innovation in building design.

There's more. Tourists, business people, and residents clog Chicago's downtown streets year-round to savor its stunning skyline, lakefront, art, history, shopping, cultural attractions, and festivals. Inevitably, out-of-towners rub shoulders with the city's outspoken—and often humorous—natives, most of whom are remarkably friendly to visitors. Here are tips to help first-time visitors discover this sprawling, dynamic city.

### TAKING AN ORIENTATION TOUR

Visitors to Chicago can't help but notice the regular procession of open-air tour buses—"motorized trolleys" is probably a more accurate term—that prowl Michigan Avenue, the Loop, and the museums and attractions along the lakeshore. **The Chicago Trolley Co.** and **Chicago Motor Coach Company** offer regularly scheduled shuttle buses that drop off and pick up paying customers along a route that includes the town's most popular attractions. Between stops, passengers listen to a tour guide talk about the city's cataclysmic fire of 1871, machine gun–toting gangsters, and spectacular architecture.

The guides also suggest good places to eat and drop tidbits of interesting—and often funny—Chicago trivia. Examples you're likely to hear include why Chicago was branded "The Windy City" by New York newspapers (because of blowhard politicians bragging about the city) and the best places to go for an Oprah sighting (her studio and the Crate & Barrel on Michigan Avenue).

Our advice: If this is your first visit to Chicago, take one of the tours early in your trip. Here's why: Seen from the air, Chicago is surprisingly contained. The city's towers rise up from the lakeside with a stunning vertical thrust, but then give way to the prairie flatness that characterizes the Midwest. Yet once on the ground, visitors discover that the city is too vast to get a quick handle on—and that includes its downtown. While it's possible to embark on a walking tour that includes River North, the Magnificent Mile, the Loop, Grant Park, and Chicago's major museums, you'll murder your feet—and your enthusiasm for touring—in the process.

Think of the narrated Chicago shuttle-bus tours as an educational system that not only gets you to the most well-known attractions but also provides a timely education on the city's history and scope. (There's a downside to the narrator's spiel, too: a confusing litany of the skyscraper architects' names and a few too many references to the Roaring Twenties gangsters.)

The money you pay for your ticket allows unlimited reboarding privileges for that day, so you can get off at any scheduled stop to tour, eat, shop, or explore, and reboard a later bus. You can also determine which sights may warrant another day of exploration. Tour buses run about every 20 minutes or so and boarding locations include the city's most popular downtown attractions. You can board at any stop along the route and pay the driver.

## Chicago Trolley

Both of the guided tours that operate on a regular route in and around the Loop are good values. **Chicago Trolley** features San Francisco–style "trolleys" and a tour guide; the complete tour lasts about an hour and 20 minutes. Heated in the winter and open air in the summer, the trolleys operate rain or shine from 9:30 a.m. to 5 p.m. daily (hours are longer in the summer).

The tour buses make 12 stops: Sears Tower, Marshall Field's, the Chicago Art Institute, Field Museum, Adler Planetarium, the Museum of Science and Industry, Navy Pier, the Historic Water Tower, Michigan Avenue, Wacker Drive, Hard Rock Cafe, and Planet Hollywood. Hint: If you didn't drive to Chicago and don't have a car, make this your chance to visit the popular Museum of Science and Industry; it's *way* off the beaten track and isn't near a train line. Getting off now can save on cab fare or navigating Chicago's bus system.

Chicago Trolley tickets are $15 for adults, $12 for seniors, and $8 for children ages 3–11. Seniors and youngsters can use their ticket to ride the trolley for free the next day; a two-day ticket for adults is $18 (Sunday–Thursday only). Our advice: If you don't have a car, go for the two-day ticket and use it to get to the Museum of Science and Industry, a massive place that can eat up most of a day. Adults who only wish to tour without reboarding privileges can purchase a "city tour" ticket for $12. For more information, call (312) 663-0260.

### Double-Decker Buses

**Chicago Motor Coach Company** treats visitors to narrated city tours with a view. On days when Chicago's weather is warm enough to drive with the top down, you can't beat the open-air, red double-decker buses for viewing Chicago's downtown architecture (enclosed buses run in winter). The buses stop at Sears Tower, the Chicago Art Institute, Field Museum, Navy Pier, North Pier, the Historic Water Tower, Mercury Boats (at the Michigan Avenue Bridge), and Michael Jordan's Restaurant (in River North).

Tours last an hour and a half, and hours of operation are daily 9:30 a.m. to 5 p.m. in the summer and 10 a.m. to 4 p.m. in the spring and fall; no bus tours run in the winter. Tickets are $12 for adults, $10 for seniors, and $8 for children. For more information, call (312) 666-1000.

## ARCHITECTURE AND BOAT TOURS

It's often said that in Chicago, architecture is a spectator sport. While an introductory bus tour of downtown Chicago gives first-time visitors a sense of the city's layout and a quick glimpse of Chicago architecture, things look different from the Chicago River. During the warmer months, river boats glide down the Chicago River for a dockside view of downtown architecture and historical sites. And the Loop takes on a whole new perspective after taking an eye-opening walking tour with a docent pointing out and explaining the modern architectural trends on display in Chicago's downtown.

### Boat Tours

Once scorned as a sewage canal, today the Chicago River offers visitors stunning views of the city's best buildings, including the Sears Tower, the Civic Opera Building on Wacker Drive, the IBM Building (Mies van der Rohe's last major Chicago structure), and the 1989 NBC Tower.

On downtown boat tours, tour guides weave history and technology as they tell the story of the Great Chicago Fire of 1871 and the role of the structural iron frame in rebuilding the city. The result was the skyscraper and a truly modern style unencumbered by any allegiance to the past.

## Chicago Architecture Foundation Tours

The Chicago Architecture Foundation offers 57 different tours by foot, bus, and boat. Each tour is led by a volunteer from an army of about 400 docents (tour guides). The tour leaders are witty, incredibly informed, and contagiously enthusiastic about Chicago architecture. Our advice: Go on at least one Foundation tour during your visit. Better yet, take a walking tour of the Loop *and* an architectural boat tour. You won't regret it.

**By Boat**   *Chicago's First Lady* pushes off from the southwest corner of Michigan Avenue and Wacker Drive for the CAF Architecture River Cruise. The yacht, which offers outside seating on the upper deck and air-conditioned interior seating, departs four times daily June through October for 90-minute tours; twice daily in May and October (three times daily on weekends); tickets are $18. In addition to a unique river perspective on Chicago architecture, you'll see the riverside railway that delivers newsprint to the *Sun-Times* and get a boater's-eye perspective of the city's bridges. For more information and reservations, call (312) 922-TOUR.

**By Foot**   Two-hour walking tours of the Loop and bus excursions to Chicago's neighborhoods start at the Foundation's headquarters and gift shop, 224 South Michigan Avenue (across from the Chicago Art Institute). The two-hour Loop walking tours excellently complement the boat tour, allowing you to see the buildings from street level, as well as letting you ogle some lobbies that are every bit as spectacular as the buildings' exteriors. Tours cost $10 per person and are offered daily on a varying schedule throughout the year; call (312) 922-TOUR for more information.

**More CAF Tours**   In addition to Loop walking tours and boat cruises, CAF offers the three-and-one-half-hour Chicago Architecture Highlights by Bus tour (March through November, every Saturday at 9:30 a.m.; $25 per person) and Frank Lloyd Wright by Bus tours (May through October, the first Saturday of the month at 10 a.m.; $25). For more information and reservations, call (312) 922-TOUR.

## Historical and Architectural Lake and River Cruises from North Pier

Boat tours depart from North Pier daily May through September for cruises on the Chicago River and Lake Michigan. On the historical cruise, visitors pass the spot where du Sable first established a trading post among the local native Americans and where Fort Dearborn stood to protect the community. The tour also passes through the heart of the city, where the fire of 1871 reduced buildings to ash at a rate of 65 acres an hour.

On Lake Michigan the boat passes Buckingham Fountain, where the Columbian Exposition of 1893 left its legacy of Field Museum, Shedd Aquarium, Adler Planetarium, and the Museum of Science and Industry. But the highlight of the cruise is a view of the magnificent skyline of Chicago, a profile recognized around the world.

Architectural cruises take visitors downtown for up-close views of Chicago's most famous buildings, including the Tribune Tower, the Merchandise Mart, Lake Point Tower, and, of course, the Sears Tower, the third-tallest office building in the world. Visitors also see the spot near the Kinzie Street Bridge where the Chicago River flooded an old railroad freight tunnel in April 1992, shutting down the Loop and causing hundreds of millions of dollars in damage.

The 90-minute cruises leave North Pier daily on the hour from 10 a.m. to 4 p.m. May through September and on a reduced schedule in October. Multilingual tours are offered on Saturdays and Sundays. Prices are $18 for adults, $16 for seniors, and $12 for children and students ages 9–18. For more information and reservations (recommended), call (312) 527-1977.

## Other Boat Cruises

**Mercury Tours** offers architectural, historical, and maritime sights tours May through September from the lower level and southwest corner of the Michigan Avenue Bridge over the Chicago River (at Wacker Drive). Cruises range from one hour to two hours in length, each with continuous commentary. Tours depart throughout the day from morning to late evening; prices range from $10 to $14 for adults and $5 to $7 for children. For more information, call (312) 332-1353.

**Wendella Sightseeing Boats** offers cruises on the Chicago River and along the lakefront mid-April through mid-October. Lake-only tours lasting an hour are $11 for adults and $5.50 for children age 11 and under, and 90-minute lake and river tours cost $13 for adults and $6.50 for children. Two-hour river and lake tours in the evening feature a color light show at Buckingham Fountain; prices are $15 for adults and $7.50 for children. Tours leave throughout the day and evening from the base of the Wrigley Building at the northwest corner of the Michigan Avenue Bridge over the Chicago River. For more information, call (312) 337-1446.

## SPECIALIZED TOURS

**American Sightseeing** offers several general-interest tours around the city and special tours on architecture highlights and specific areas (such as the two-hour North Side Tour; $16 for adults and $8 for children ages 5–14).

The Grand Tour takes visitors to most of Chicago's parks and most scenic locations, as well as the Loop, the Magnificent Mile, Wrigley Field, Lincoln Park Conservatory, the Adler Planetarium, the University of Chicago campus, and the Museum of Science and Industry. The cost of the four-hour tour is $26 for adults and $13 for children.

American Sightseeing bus tours start at 55 East Monroe Street, in the Loop. Unlike the hard benches on the "trolley" tours, the buses feature comfortable reclining seats, overhead lights, and air conditioning. For schedules, hotel pickup, and more information, call (312) 251-3100.

## Gangsters and Ghosts

Would-be ghostbusters can explore Chicago's spooky sights on **Supernatural Tours.** The narrated bus tours highlight the city's heritage of ghost stories and folklore, weird tales, murder sites, cemeteries, gangsters, pubs, and restaurants. Tours are scheduled on weekends from noon to 5 p.m. and 7 p.m. to midnight; the cost is $30 per person and reservations are required. The trips depart from the Goose Island Brewery Restaurant in River North; for more information and schedules, call (708) 499-0300.

While some may consider it inappropriate to emphasize Chicago's gangster past, the folks at **Untouchable Tours** say baloney. Two guys in pinstripe suits and fedoras escort visitors on a two-hour bus tour of Chicago's notorious yesteryear, including the site of Al Capone's former headquarters, the Biograph Theater on Lincoln Avenue (where Dillinger was shot), and the site of the St. Valentine's Day Massacre on Clark Street. The popular tour, led by actor-guides, is both historically correct and a crowd pleaser, especially for youngsters.

Tours are scheduled Monday through Saturday at 10 a.m., as well as Friday evenings at 7:30 p.m., Saturdays at 5 p.m., and Sundays at 11 a.m. and 2 p.m. Tours depart from 610 North Clark Street, near the Rock 'n' Roll McDonald's in River North. The cost is $22 for adults and $16 for children and reservations are required; call (773) 881-1195.

## Airplanes and a Yacht

For a bird's-eye view of the city, head toward Meigs Field (south of Grant Park on Lake Michigan) and book a flight on **Chicago By Air.** Thirty-minute aero tours of Chicago in a single-engine Cessna 172 start at $165 for two. For reservations, call (708) 524-1172 between 6 a.m. and 10 p.m. daily.

While not strictly speaking a guided tour, Lake Michigan cruises on the **Odyssey** feature fine dining, live music, dancing, and breathtaking views of Chicago's skyline. Our local experts report cruising on the sleek and elegant yacht is a great way to see the city and the operation is first-rate. Best bet: a sunset dinner cruise. The chef, by the way, owns the boat. Three-hour dinner cruises start at $73 per person (not including tax and gratuity) and two-hour lunch cruises start at $34; children under age 11 pay half-price. Odyssey departs from Navy Pier throughout the year. For more information and reservations, call (630) 990-0800.

## CARRIAGE RIDES

An easy and fun way to see downtown Chicago is by horse and buggy. **The Noble Horse** at the southwest corner of Michigan Avenue and Chicago Street provides horse-drawn carriage rides April through December, weekdays from 10 a.m. to 3:30 p.m. and 7 p.m. to midnight; weekends from 10 a.m. to 1 a.m. January through April, rides are offered 7 p.m. to midnight on weekdays and 11 a.m. to midnight on weekends. The cost is $30 per half hour for up to four adults and $35 per half hour for five or six adults. Reservations aren't necessary; call (312) 266-7878 for more information.

**The Antique Coach & Carriage Company** offers rides daily from the southeast corner of Michigan Avenue and Huron Street. Hours are 6:30 p.m. to 1 a.m. Monday through Thursday; 6:30 p.m. to 2 a.m. Fridays; 1 p.m. to 2 a.m. Saturdays; and 1 p.m. to 1 a.m. Sundays. The cost is $35 per half-hour. For more information, call (773) 735-9400.

## TOURING ON YOUR OWN: OUR FAVORITE ITINERARIES

If your time is limited and you want to experience the best of Chicago in a day or two, here are some suggested itineraries. The schedules assume you're staying at a downtown hotel, have already eaten breakfast, and are ready to go by around 9 a.m.

### Day One

1. Tour downtown on one of the open-air shuttle bus services with unlimited reboarding privileges for the day. If the weather's clear, get off at the Sears Tower and check out the view. Then catch the next shuttle.

2. Pick one: Explore the Shedd Aquarium or the Adler Planetarium (they're close together). Then back on the bus.

3. Next stop is Navy Pier and lunch at the Navy Pier Beer Garden or Charlie's Ale House (featuring 38 different types of beer).

4. Next, climb aboard for a scenic cruise on Lake Michigan that leaves Navy Pier every half hour in warm weather.

5. After the boat ride, take the shuttle bus to the Historic Water Tower on North Michigan Avenue. Explore the shops along North Michigan Avenue (one of the world's great shopping streets) and stop at the Terra Museum of American Art or the new Museum of Contemporary Art.

6. Dinner at a restaurant in River North. Afterwards, listen to the real thing at Blue Chicago (937 North State Street), a blues bar with a roster of the city's finest musicians.

7. Finish the evening with a visit to the John Hancock Center Observatory for a knockout view of the city and beyond.

### Day Two

1. Sleep in—but not too late. You don't want to miss the 10 a.m. Architecture Foundation walking tour of the Loop.

2. For lunch, sample the Wienerschnitzel at the Berghoff Restaurant (17 West Adams Street), a Chicago institution. Then jump on the Ravenswood El for a ride around the Loop; take it north past the Merchandise Mart and catch the next train back for some terrific views of the city.

3. Explore the Art Institute of Chicago. Try to catch the free tour that begins daily at 2 p.m. near the Grand Staircase.

4. Reward the kids with a trip to the Chicago Children's Museum at Navy Pier. Or explore the other attractions—including a knockout view of the skyline—from this recently renovated Chicago landmark.

5. Dinner in a restaurant at Navy Pier. Two of the best are Riva and Widow Newton's Tavern.

6. An evening of improvisational comedy at The Second City (1616 North Wells Street).

### If You've Got More Time . . .

If you're spending more than two days in town or if this is not your first visit, consider some of these options for an in-depth Chicago experience.

1. Explore one of Chicago's many neighborhoods beyond the Loop.

Suggestions: Hyde Park has the University of Chicago and several museums; shop and eat lunch in Chinatown; Andersonville features an eclectic mix of Swedish and Middle Eastern shops, and inexpensive ethnic restaurants.

2. Oak Park, just west of the city line, boasts two famous native sons: architect Frank Lloyd Wright and Nobel-winning novelist Ernest Hemingway. Spend a morning or afternoon learning more about them.

3. Two Chicago museums are so large that each requires nearly a full day: the Field Museum and the Museum of Science and Industry.

4. Stretch your legs along the Gold Coast, where Chicago's wealthiest residents have made their homes for 100 years; it's just north of the Magnificent Mile. Or rent a bike and ride the path along Lake Michigan.

5. Go to a play. Chicago boasts more than 100 active theater companies.

6. Kick back and enjoy a summer festival in Grant Park.

7. Spend a few hours browsing the art galleries in River North.

8. Check out Marshall Field's on State Street.

9. Attend a concert by the Chicago Symphony Orchestra, consistently rated one of the best orchestras in the world.

10. Root for the Cubs at Wrigley Field, the White Sox at Comiskey Park, or the Bulls or Blackhawks at the new United Center.

# Exploring Chicago's Neighborhoods

Chicago is a big city, the country's third largest, America's Third Coast. You will hear again and again that it is a city of neighborhoods and, in truth, it is. The city's enviable vitality, rich architectural history, and cultural diversity are all found in the wide variety of ethnic enclaves—some mixed and some not—called neighborhoods.

What follows is not a comprehensive guide to Chicago's many neighborhoods, since the city officially claims 77 community areas, but our suggestions for dipping in and sampling the remarkably diverse array of architecture, cuisine, history, and culture that defines Chicago.

Taking an extended ride on the Ravenswood El, for instance, permits you to survey the spectacle of Chicago's neighborhoods—and back porches and rooftop graffiti—without getting your feet wet. (For route and fare information on CTA and Metra, call (312) 836-7000.) But apart from a bike ride along the lakefront, Chicago is a city best explored on foot. You can use the El, the bus system, or a car to get there, but in almost every case, we'd recommend stepping out for a stroll to get the feel and flavor of these neighborhoods.

Our sampling tour of Chicago neighborhoods starts in the north and generally flows south along the lake with several excursions to the northwest and southwest.

## Andersonville (Zone 1)

You may register shock at the notion of "Swede-town" in Chicago, but amble north along Clark Street from Foster and you'll see Swedish flags flying, find the **Swedish American Museum** (5211 North Clark Street), and be tempted to savor excellent coffee cakes and pastries at the **Swedish Bakery** (5348 North Clark) or Swedish pancakes and limpa bread at **Svea Restaurant** (5236 North Clark). The cinnamon rolls from **Ann Sather's Restaurant** (5207 North Clark) are known to be addictive. At least you can buy a boxed dozen to take home.

Yet Andersonville, like most Chicago neighborhoods, is a mixing and melting pot. The well-kept red brick two-flats on the streets fanning east from Clark have become a new mecca for gays and lesbians, and the Clark Street strip features a number of feminist stores and shops, such as **Women & Children First Bookstore** (5233 North Clark), with its wide selection of books by women. Along Clark, you'll also find several thrift shops patronized by veteran deal-finders and **Reza's**, a Persian/Mediterranean restaurant (5255 North Clark).

To get there: Take the CTA Red Line (Howard) to the Berwyn station and then walk west on Foster about four blocks or transfer to the #92 Foster bus at the station.

By car from the Loop, drive north on Lake Shore Drive to the Foster exit and head west to Clark Street. There's metered parking along Clark or free parking on the side streets.

## Devon Avenue (Zone 1)

On a Friday night along Devon Avenue you're likely to see Orthodox Jews in dark suits and black hats heading home from synagogue on the same sidewalks as Indians in bright, flowing saris. Mixed among the kosher butchers and Pakistani groceries on the stretch from Western (2400 West Devon

Avenue) to the north branch of the Chicago River (3200 West Devon Avenue) is a newer sprinkling of Thai and Korean shops and restaurants. Truly, this is where the melting pot flows from *challah* to *naan* to *satay beef.*

You can visit **Rosenblum's World of Judaica** (2906 West Devon) for a treatise on Jewish life, or **Taj Sari Palace** (2553 West Devon) for saris of all colors and styles. **Gitel's Kosher Pastry Shop** (2745 West Devon) and **Tel-Aviv Kosher Bakery** (2944 West Devon) sell the traditional Sabbath challah. For decent kosher restaurants, try **Mi Tsu Yun** (3010 West Devon) or **Jerusalem Kosher Restaurant** (3014 West Devon). **Viceroy of India** (2518 West Devon) comes highly rated for its curries and breads, and **Udupi Palace** (2543 West Devon) serves up South Indian vegetarian meals. Newer on the block is **Tiffin, the Indian Kitchen** (2536 West Devon).

Keep in mind that many stores close early on Friday night and remain closed on Saturday for the Jewish Sabbath.

To get there: Take the CTA Red Line (Howard) north to Loyola, then transfer to a westbound #155 Devon Avenue bus.

By car from the Loop, drive north on Lake Shore Drive. At its northern end, take Ridge (west) to Devon and turn left (west); or take the Kennedy Expressway (I-90/94) north, then merge onto the Edens Expressway (I-94), exit at Petersen heading east and turn north (left) on Kedzie to Devon.

## Uptown (Zone 1)

One of Chicago's newer melting pots, Uptown, stretches north from Irving Park Road to Foster and west from the lakefront to Ashland. Though it has a decidedly seedy appearance in some places where once-magnificent homes have been neglected and allowed to deteriorate, other parts of Uptown bubble with vitality. Pockets of elegance remain in the huge homes that line Hutchinson Street and Castlewood Terrace. The community near Broadway and Argyle, often called New Chinatown, is in fact a brimming mix of Vietnamese, Laotian, Chinese, Cambodian, and Thai immigrants. You'll find Asian groceries, bakeries, and gift shops, barbecued ducks hanging in shop windows, and a profusion of restaurants. Try **Ha Mien** (4920 North Sheridan Road) for excellent Vietnamese fare or **Furama** (4936 North Broadway) for dim sum.

The **Green Mill Lounge** (4802 North Broadway) offers jazz and Sunday night poetry slams of national renown each week.

Stray from the Broadway/Argyle axis and you'll quickly see the grubbier parts of Uptown; don't try it alone or on foot after dark.

To get there: The CTA Red Line (Howard) stops at Argyle Street, where there's a $100,000 pagoda over the station.

By car from the Loop, drive north along Lake Shore Drive, exit at Lawrence (4800 North), head west to Broadway, then north to Argyle.

## Lincoln Square (Zone 1)

Illinois is Lincoln land, as the city's five outdoor "Abe" statues and numerous place names attest. Here, in the area known as Lincoln Square, his statue stands where Lincoln, Lawrence, and Western avenues converge. The centerpiece of Lincoln Square is the small shopping area—virtually a pedestrian mall—along the 4700 block of Lincoln Avenue. Stores featuring Tirolean clothes and **Meyer's Delicatessen,** where the first language is often German, give the place a decided European feel. Stop in at **Merz Apothecary** (4716 North Lincoln Avenue) for imported soaps or any homeopathic remedies you might need. The light, airy space of **Cafe Selmarie,** just off the square, is a favorite place for locals to relax with coffee and pastries to threaten any waistline. Check out the wonderful Louis Sullivan facade of the **Kelmscott Building** (4611 North Lincoln Avenue) and the periodicals section—and modern design—of the **Conrad Sulzer Library** (4455 North Lincoln). **Fine Wine Brokers** (4621 North Lincoln) bills itself as a European-style wine merchant. The large wall mural at 4662 North Lincoln depicts scenes from the German countryside.

Lincoln Square's German residents are nestled against new Greektown west of the mall along Lawrence Avenue between Talman and Maplewood. St. Demetrios Orthodox Church, a 1928 basilica-style structure at 2727 West Winona serves the Greek community. St. Matthias, an 1887 German church, is at 2310 West Ainslie.

To get there: Take the CTA Brown Line (Ravenswood) to the Western Avenue stop (Monday–Saturday until mid-evening; on Sunday, take the Red Line to Belmont and transfer to the Brown Line there) or the #11 bus, which connects the Loop with Lincoln Square, though the ride takes several months. . . .

By car, take Lake Shore Drive north, exit at Lawrence Avenue (4800 North) and head west to Western Avenue (2400 West). There's metered parking on Lincoln Avenue or a lot at Leland next to the El station.

## Lakeview/Wrigleyville (Zone 1)

Elderly Jews ensconced in lakefront condos, yuppies renovating graystones, gays and lesbians congregating at bars and bookstores—you name it, Lakeview's got vitality, history, espresso galore. Even the ivy-walled home of the ever-hapless, ardently supported Chicago Cubs—Wrigley Field— is a real neighborhood ballpark where fans stream in from the Addison El stop and those in the know watch from the roofs of nearby three-flats. (Don't be afraid to try for day-of-game tickets at the window.)

The remaining mansions along Hawthorne Place (a one-way street heading east between Broadway and Sheridan) give a sense of stately lakeside grandeur. The facing rows of townhouses on Alta Vista Terrace (1054 West between Byron and Grace Streets north of Wrigley Field) are mirror images.

Locals flock to **Ann Sather's Restaurant** (929 West Belmont Avenue, a branch of the one in Andersonville), drawn by the irresistible lure of addictive cinnamon rolls and well-prepared, moderately priced food. You'll find thrift shops, hip shops, bookstores, and espresso on nearly every corner, including the pungent smell of beans roasting at the **Coffee & Tea Exchange** (3311 North Broadway), one of the city's finest purveyors of coffee and equipment. **Unabridged Books** (3251 North Broadway) is one of the staunch independents holding out against the invasion of Borders and Barnes & Noble. You'll find the city's largest cluster of gay bars along Halsted and Broadway between Belmont and Addison and an eclectic variety of stores selling things antique to antic along the commercial strips of Belmont, Diversey, Broadway, Halsted, and Clark. (P.S., Lakeview is fine for solo strolling in the day, but at night it's best to go with a buddy.)

To get there: From the Loop, take the CTA Red Line (Howard) or Brown Line (Ravenswood) to Belmont or the #151 bus along Michigan Avenue north to Belmont and then walk west. The #22 Clark Street bus, a quicker option, also puts you in the heart of Lakeview.

By car, drive north on Lake Shore Drive to the Belmont exit and head west on Belmont. Wrigley Field is located at Addison and Clark, about five blocks north of Belmont. (There's a CTA Red Line stop at Addison right near the ballpark.)

## Milwaukee Avenue (Zone 2)

The locus of Chicago's Polish community, once situated at Milwaukee and Division, has angled north to the neighborhood called Avondale, although Milwaukee Avenue, especially between Central Park and Pulaski, remains the primary Polish corridor. On weekend afternoons, this section teems with shoppers and diners, all gossiping—in Polish—and debating the latest shifts in Eastern European alliances.

Your best bet is to stroll along the avenue, taking in the sights and sounds, stepping into **Andy's Deli** (3055 North Milwaukee Avenue) to gape at the 25 varieties of sausage lining the back wall and choose among packaged pierogi, gulasz, and Polish comic books. At the Polish department store, **Syrena** (3004 North Milwaukee), you can snap up that missing tuxedo for your children in white or black.

For a sit-down meal from which you'll struggle to rise, consider the buffet at **Red Apple** (3123 North Milwaukee) or the Polish specials at **Home Bakery & Restaurant** (2931 North Milwaukee).

**St. Hyacinth's Roman Catholic Church** (3636 West Wolfram) looms over the tidy bungalows and two-flats wedged on the side streets angling off Milwaukee. The church, built in ornate Renaissance Revival style, draws up to 1,000 people at a time for Polish-language masses.

To get there: The CTA #56 Milwaukee Avenue bus takes the s-l-o-w, scenic route through some of Chicago's oldest—and now graying—immigrant communities. Board at Randolph and Michigan (southbound) or along Madison (westbound) in the Loop. For a quicker ride, take the CTA Blue Line (O'Hare) to Logan Square and transfer to a northbound #56 Milwaukee Avenue bus.

By car from the Loop, take the Kennedy Expressway (I-90/94) north to the Kimball (Belmont) or Addison exits and head west (left) to Milwaukee Avenue.

## Wicker Park and Bucktown (Zone 2)

If you want to see the hip, new Chicago where Generation X-ers congregate to hear pop artists such as Liz Phair and bands such as Urge Overkill and Smashing Pumpkins—if you want to hang out where slacker attitude prevails—then head for Wicker Park and Bucktown. Adjoining neighborhoods stretching from Division on the south to Fullerton on the north, between the Kennedy Expressway and Western Avenue, these formerly Polish, currently Puerto Rican communities have seen significant incursions by artists and yuppies of all stripes. Near Wicker Park itself, a small triangle at Schiller and Damen, are the late 1800s stone mansions of beer barons lining Pierce, Hoyne, Oakley, and Damen. Chicago author Nelson Algren once lived along here, which is why Evergreen Avenue is also Nelson Algren Avenue. Note the gingerbread house at 2137 West Pierce.

Ground zero for the flourishing arts scene is the **Coyote Building** at 1600 North Milwaukee Avenue and its across-the-street landmark counterpart, the **Flatiron Building** (1579 North Milwaukee). Each year in September the galleries and studios hold a celebratory open house called Around the Coyote. In one corner you'll find **Bella Bello** (1600 North Milwaukee), a charming store filled with flowers, linens, cards, and nifty perfume bottles. Nearby is **Pentimento** (1629 North Milwaukee) featuring clothes by local designers. Damen Avenue has become a mecca for small bistros, such as chef-owned **Le Bouchon** (1958 North Damen Avenue). Neighborhood stalwart **The Northside** (1635 North Damen) has an outdoor patio and a lively crowd.

Steep yourself in the late-night music scene at **The Double Door** (1572 North Milwaukee) or the supreme funk parlor known as **Red Dog** (1958 West North).

To get there: From the Loop, take the CTA Blue Line (O'Hare) to the Damen Avenue stop, which places you right at the confluence of Damen, North, and Milwaukee avenues in the heart of Bucktown. The #56 Milwaukee Avenue bus also takes you through Wicker Park and Bucktown.

By car from the Loop, drive north on the Kennedy Expressway (I-90/94) to the Division Street or North Avenue exits and head west.

## Gold Coast and Old Town (Zone 3)

Behind the high-rises stretching north of Michigan Avenue along Lake Shore Drive are some of the most elegant townhouses and stately mansions in Chicago. It costs a fortune to live here—apropos the name, Gold Coast—but strolling along Astor Street or its neighbors from Division to North Avenue costs not a cent. Along the way, imagine life in the former Patterson-McCormick Mansion (20 East Burton), which has since been divided into condominiums, or count the chimneys at the official residence of Chicago's Catholic Archbishop (1555 North State Parkway). Consider treating yourself to lunch at the **Pump Room** in the Ambassador East Hotel (1301 North State Parkway), where you may see children in their dressed-up best dining with grandmother in her mink.

Old Town, which stretches west along North Avenue, was once a Bohemian center for folkies and artists. Now the rehabbed townhomes and coach houses have made it quieter (and costlier), with upscale boutiques and trendy shops along Wells. Many children of the city's blueblood families enroll at the private Latin School (59 West North Avenue). Conversely, you'll find a young beery crowd at some of the bars along Division. For picnic provisions, you'll want to browse among the many imported specialties at the **Treasure Island** grocery store (1639 North Wells Avenue), within walking distance of Lincoln Park.

To get there: Street parking is at such a premium on the Gold Coast, you might consider walking north from Michigan Avenue or taking the #151 bus and getting off anywhere between Oak Street and North Avenue. Walk west one block. For Old Town, there's a large parking garage next to the Piper's Alley theaters on North Avenue, or the #22 or #36 buses heading north (board downtown along Dearborn) put you in the heart of Old Town.

## Chinatown (Zone 5)

Chicago's traditional Chinatown is a crowded, bustling area along the Wentworth Avenue corridor, its formal entrance marked by the ornate Oriental arch at Wentworth and Cermak. Walk south along Wentworth and note the temple-like On Leong Building (2216 South Wentworth), cornerstone of the commercial district where immigrant bachelors in years past rented space in apartments on the second floor. (Plans call for the building to be converted into a youth center.) Wentworth offers a lively, teeming mix of restaurants, shops, groceries, and even a wholesale noodle company. The Chinatown branch of the public library (2353 South Wentworth) circulates more books and cassettes—many in Chinese—than any other in the city. Newer shopping areas have spilled out across Cermak and Archer Avenues and newer Chinese and Asian neighborhoods have evolved on the far north side near Argyle Street, but for the sights and smells most of us expect in Chinatown, this is where you'll find them.

To get there: From the Loop, take the CTA southbound Red Line (Dan Ryan) from State Street to the Cermak/Chinatown stop. The #24 Wentworth bus heads south from Clark and Randolph in the Loop, and the #62 Archer Avenue bus travels south along State Street (exit at Cermak and Archer and walk one block east).

By car from the Loop, drive south on Michigan Avenue to 22nd Street (Cermak Road), turn right and drive five blocks to a public parking lot at Wentworth and Cermak; or drive south on the Dan Ryan Expressway and take the 22nd Street/Canalport turnoff, which leads to Chinatown.

## Taylor Street (Zone 6)

Once the heart of Italian Chicago, this neighborhood was severely altered by the construction of the University of Illinois campus in the early 1960s, which displaced thousands of residents. Still, the Taylor Street area has undergone a renaissance with new townhouses being built and coffeehouses and fern bars offering proximity to the Loop with the lure of the university. Combine a tour of the area with a visit to the **Jane Addams Hull House** (800 South Halsted Street; see Part Eleven: Zone 4 on page 272).

For a taste of Taylor, try **Al's No. 1 Italian Beef** (1079 West Taylor Street)—so famous that tour buses stop here—followed by an Italian ice at **Mario's Lemonade Stand** on Taylor between Aberdeen and Carpenter. (Open only in summer; you'll have to wait in line or wind your way through cars parked three abreast.) For Italian provisions, don't miss **Conte di Savoia** (1438 West Taylor) or the **Ferrara Original, Inc. Bakery** (2210 West Taylor). A real neighborhood joint is **Tufano's Restaurant,** also known as the **Vernon Park Tap** (1073 West Vernon Park).

On Polk Street between Laflin and Loomis you can see some turn-of-the-century buildings, including two wooden replicas of the style prevalent before the Great Fire of 1871. Bishop Street between Taylor and Polk, and Ada Street between Flournoy and Columbus Park also give a great feel to the neighborhood. St. Basil Greek Orthodox Church at Ashland and Polk bears witness to the neighborhood's transformation from a Jewish community to Greek to Italian—the church was once a synagogue and a Hebrew inscription is still visible on the exterior.

The new "Little Italy" is now along Harlem Avenue on the far western edge of the city between North Avenue and Irving Park.

To get there: Take any CTA Blue Line train heading west to the UIC/Halsted stop or the Racine stop. During the week you can take the #37 bus southbound on Wells through the Loop.

By car from the Loop, drive west on the Eisenhower Expressway (290) to the Ashland exit and head south to Taylor Street.

### Pilsen/Little Village (Zone 6)

Call these Chicago's barrios—home to the largest population of Mexican Americans in the Midwest—where the signs are Spanish and the smells are enticing. Pilsen lies principally along 18th Street between Canal and Damen. Little Village, considered somewhat more prosperous and stable, opens with its own pink stucco gateway arch at 26th Street and Albany and stretches in boisterous fashion west along 26th to Kostner.

Once the province of Bohemians and Poles, Pilsen is now the port of entry for thousands of Mexicans. It has a thriving artists' colony and is home to the **Mexican Fine Arts Center Museum** (1852 West 19th Street). The museum, which opened in 1987 in the converted Harrison Park Boat Craft Shop, strives to showcase the wealth and breadth of Mexican art in its exhibitions. You may want to survey some of the 20 handpainted murals depicting various cultural, religious, and political themes scattered throughout Pilsen (at 1305 West 18th Street, 18th and Racine, 18th and Wood, and lining the concrete wall along the tracks at 16th and Allport). When you visit, note the elaborate cornices and roofs of some of the nineteenth-century storefronts and two-flats along 18th west of Halsted. The Providence of God Church (717 West 18th Street) is the focal point for many celebrations, including a powerful Via Crucis (Way of the Cross) procession on Good Friday.

If the profusion of taquerías, bakeries, and taverns whets your appetite, try **Panaderia Nuevo Leon** (1634 West 18th Street) for sweets, **Carnitas Uruapan** (1725 West 18th) for barbecued pork and spicy salsa, or **Chicago's Original Bishop's Famous Chili** (1958 West 18th at Damen) for a simple bowl of hearty chili con carne served with locally brewed Filbert's root beer.

Little Village has its own colorful wall murals, such as the "Broken Wall Mural" in the back of Los Comales Restaurant next to McDonald's (26th Street and Kedzie). You'll find others at 26th and Homan, 25th and St. Louis, and 25th and Pulaski. Here, too, the neighborhood pulses along the commercial strip of 26th. Consider taking home a piñata selected from the many styles found at **La Justicia Grocery** (Millard and 26th). Watch the cooks grill Mexico City–style fast food at **Chon y Chano** (3901 West 26th), or try the dependable Mexican fare at **La Lo's** (3515 West 26th).

To get there: For Pilsen: Board the westbound CTA Blue Line (54th and Cermak) at Dearborn in the Loop and get off at the 18th Street stop right in the heart of Pilsen. By car, drive south on the Dan Ryan Expressway (I-90/94), exit at 18th Street, and head west.

For Little Village: By public transport, board the #60 Blue Island/ 26th Street bus westbound on Adams in the Loop.

By car from Pilsen, continue west along 18th to Western, go south (left) to 26th Street, and proceed west past the Cook County Courthouse and the turrets marking the perimeter of the Cook County Jail to the arch at Albany.

### Bridgeport (Zone 6)

Bridgeport is the historic political centerpiece of Chicago for, despite a brief interregnum from 1979 to 1989, this working-class neighborhood has supplied the city with its mayors, including the present mayor, Richard M. Daley. In a city where politics are played at Super Bowl level, the political shrines are as you would expect: Mom's house, the neighborhood pub, and the ward organization office (or, in an earlier era, what might have irreverently been called the Machine Shop).

First stop on the pilgrimage, then, is Mom's house—home of "Sis" Daley, the late Richard J. Daley's widow and the current mayor's mom—at 3536 South Lowe, a modest red brick bungalow distinguished only by the flagpole and police officer stationed in an unmarked squad car out front. At the end of the block—big surprise—is a police station whose handy placement was arranged by the late, great mayor. A few blocks to the west and south, you'll find the other two shrines right across the street from each other at 37th Street and Halsted: the 11th Ward Democratic Organization headquarters and **Schaller's Pump,** where the mediocre food is far surpassed by the atmosphere.

Stroll north along Halsted to sample the changing flavor of Bridgeport. You'll see Chinese, Mexican, Italian, and Lithuanian establishments all within a few blocks. Above all, don't miss **Healthy Food Restaurant** (3236 South Halsted Street), where slim waitresses in flowing skirts dish out ample portions of hearty Lithuanian food to the music of Tchaikovsky.

To get there: Take the CTA Red Line (Dan Ryan) to the 35th Street stop at Comiskey Park (from there it's a long hike to Halsted or to transfer to a #35 bus westbound), or board a #44 bus southbound on State Street in the Loop (weekdays only).

By car, drive south on Lake Shore Drive to the 31st Street exit and then west to Halsted; or drive south on the Dan Ryan Expressway to the 35th Street exit and then west to Halsted.

## Hyde Park/Kenwood (Zone 7)

This is the place for big homes, big ideas, and a great cluster of cultural institutions. Drive along Ellis, Greenwood, and Woodlawn between 47th and East Hyde Park Boulevard (5100 South) and you'll marvel at the number of grand mansions on large lots. Years ago they were homes of titans of industry; today more than likely they harbor Nobel laureates on the faculty of the nearby University of Chicago, which anchors Hyde Park with its cerebral gray presence between 57th Street and the Midway Plaisance, a wide, grassy boulevard created for the 1893 Columbian Exposition. Descend the stairs to the **Seminary Co-op Bookstore** (5757 South University) and you can't help but feel like a scholar yourself—or survey the eternal student scene at Hutchinson Commons in the Reynolds Club at 57th Street and University from behind one of the nouveau 'zines free for the taking.

Hyde Park, too, is one of the city's more integrated communities. The late Mayor Harold Washington used to live here, and the 5th Ward is considered one of the city's most liberal. K.A.M. Isaiah Israel (1100 East Hyde Park Boulevard) is the Midwest's oldest Jewish congregation. There are bustling commercial strips along 53rd and 57th Streets and in Harper Court at 52nd and South Harper. You'll certainly shed the tourist label if you tip back a brew at **Woodlawn Tap** (1172 East 55th Street) or eat at **Valois** (1518 East 53rd Street), a cafeteria hang-out for cops, cabbies, and students of urban life where the motto is See Your Food.

To get there: Be prepared for a lot of walking (not recommended after dark), or plan to tour the avenues by car. By public transportation, you can take the #6 Jeffrey express bus (25 cent surcharge) southbound from State Street to 57th and walk to the University of Chicago or the slower #1 Indiana/Hyde Park bus east on Jackson from Union Station, then south on Michigan to East Hyde Park Boulevard for a tour of Kenwood.

Metra electric trains also serve Hyde Park. Board underground at Randolph and Michigan or at Van Buren and Michigan and exit at either the 53rd and Lake Park stop, the combined 55th/56th/57th Street stop, or the University of Chicago stop at 59th Street and Harper. (The fare is $1.75 one-way.)

By car from the Loop, drive south on Lake Shore Drive to the 57th Street exit. Pass in front of the Museum of Science and Industry and follow signs for the University of Chicago. Or take the 47th Street exit, drive west, and then turn south on Woodlawn or Greenwood for a look at the mansions.

The Chicago Architecture Foundation offers two-hour walking tours of Kenwood in May, June, September, and October. Call (312) 922-3432.

## South Shore (Zone 7)

Located between 67th and 79th and reaching from Lake Michigan on the east to Stony Island Avenue on the west, South Shore has been home to Chicagoans for more than 100 years. Today, many of the affluent African Americans who remain in Chicago dwell in some of the large, elegant homes lining South Euclid, Constance, and Bennett Streets between East 67th and East 71st at Jeffrey. Though the commercial strip along East 71st has suffered, the South Shore Bank (71st and Jeffrey) has become a national leader in innovative financing for community development projects.

The South Shore Country Club at the intersection of 71st Street and South Shore remains a gem. Once the site of elite South Side society gatherings, the stucco, Spanish-style structure and club fell on hard times until the Chicago Park District purchased the site 20 years ago. Now restored and open to the public, the Club has a golf course, stables for the Chicago Police Department horses, and up-close lakefront views. In the winter you'll see a few solitary cross-country skiers; in the summer, there's picnicking and lakeside play.

The massive Church of St. Philip Neri (2132 East 72nd Street), one of Chicago's largest, has an exquisite sequence of mosaics depicting the Stations of the Cross. What was once the largest Greek Orthodox church in North America has become an Islamic mosque, the Masjid Honorable Elijah Muhammad (7351 South Stony Island Avenue).

For local cuisine, you may want to try **Army & Lou's** for soul food (422 East 75th Street) or **Alexander's Steak House and Cocktail Lounge** (3010 East 79th Street), where they've been dishing out prime rib and jazz at night for more than 50 years. **Salaam Restaurant & Bakery** (700 West 79th) is a showcase community investment by the Nation of Islam.

To get there: The CTA #6 Jeffrey express bus southbound on State Street will take you to 71st Street and Jeffrey (25 cent surcharge). A quicker option is the Metra electric train from Randolph and Michigan—the station is underground—which stops at Bryn Mawr (71st Street and Jeffrey; the fare is $1.75 one-way).

By car from the Loop, drive south along Lake Shore Drive through Jackson Park to South Shore.

## Other Neighborhoods of Interest

**Rogers Park (Zone 1)**    The city's northernmost conglomeration of cultures and styles, Rogers Park mixes well-preserved lakeside condos with '60s hippie holdovers and ethnic groups ranging from Russian to Jamaican to Pakistani. Visit the **Heartland Cafe** (7000 North Glenwood) for vegetarian food–*cum*–radical politics. Sip espresso at **No Exit Cafe** (6970 North Glenwood) or at **Ennui** (6981 North Sheridan Road).

Rogers Park sprawls pretty far, and it's probably best not to wander alone or travel on foot after dark.

To get there: The CTA Red Line (Howard) stops at Morse, right near the Heartland Cafe, and at Loyola.

By car from the Loop, drive north to the end of Lake Shore Drive and continue north along Sheridan Road. Once you've curved around the buildings of Loyola University, you can turn right on any of the streets off Sheridan Road to view the older condos or continue up Sheridan to the city's border with Evanston.

**Lincoln Park/DePaul (Zone 1)**    This section, sandwiched between Old Town and Lakeview, may have the largest concentration of young urban white professionals in the city—or at least the most visible. Students at DePaul University, the large Catholic institution renowned for its Blue Demons basketball team, probably can't afford to live here after graduation unless they double up in one of the two- or three-flats along Bissell or Sheffield whose back porches face the El tracks.

Still, it's fun to roam the pleasant, tree-lined streets and gawk at the gentrified townhomes. The big ones line Fullerton Parkway as you head west from the lake, but a walk along any of the side streets, such as Hudson, Cleveland, Belden, or Fremont, will provide ample viewing pleasure.

Oz Park at Webster and Orchard is a favorite playground for kids and adults. The shops, galleries, boutiques, and restaurants clustered along Halsted, Armitage, and Clark are fun for browsing and spending.

Should you want to test the widely held theory that the best food in Chicago is to be found under the El tracks, stop by **Demon Dogs** at Fullerton Avenue near Sheffield for a hot dog and fries—you'll feel like a native.

To get there: The CTA Brown Line (Ravenswood) stops at Armitage or Fullerton and the Red Line (Howard) also goes to Fullerton (the stop closest to DePaul). The #151 bus travels through Lincoln Park; the #22 or #36 buses (board north along Dearborn) put you closer to the shopping district.

By car, drive north on Lake Shore Drive to the Fullerton exit and then head west. Or take the North Avenue exit to Stockton and drive through Lincoln Park.

**Ukrainian Village (Zone 2)**    A small pocket south of Wicker Park, Ukrainian Village has plenty of sustenance for body and soul. Note the gingerbread cutouts and stained glass on many of the tidy homes in this neighborhood, which stretches west along Chicago Avenue between Ashland and Western and north to Division. Stop in at the **Ukrainian National Museum** (721 North Oakley Boulevard, Thursday through Sunday 11 a.m.– 4 p.m.) or the **Ukrainian Books and Gift Shop** (2315 West Chicago Avenue) for an Easter egg coloring kit, embroidered suits, or a wooden candelabra. Towering over the intersection of Oakley and Rice Streets you'll see the 13 copper-clad domes of St. Nicholas Ukrainian Catholic Church, modeled after the Basilica of St. Sophia in Kiev. But the real jewel is the much smaller Russian Orthodox Holy Trinity Cathedral (1121 North Leavitt at Haddon Street), designed by Louis Sullivan in 1901 and bearing his characteristic stenciling and ornamentation. **Ann's Bakery** (2158 West Chicago) is a social center as well as a source for great sweet rolls and plum cake.

To get there: By public transportation, take the CTA Blue Line (O'Hare) northbound to Chicago Avenue (not open on weekends), transfer to a westbound #66 bus, and travel to Damen or Ashland. Or you can get the #66 bus westbound right near Water Tower Place at Chicago and Michigan.

By car from the Loop, drive north on Michigan Avenue to Chicago Avenue. Turn left (west) and continue to Ukrainian Village.

**Humboldt Park/Logan Square (Zone 2)**    Originally settled by Polish and Russian Jews, then by Scandinavians, Ukrainians, and Eastern Europeans, Humboldt Park and Logan Square are now home to large numbers of Hispanic residents. A tour here opens a window onto an earlier era of residential gentility as the grand boulevards of Humboldt, Palmer, Kedzie, and Logan—one of the city's widest—are the site of many elegant graystones. Logan Square has Chicago's most unusual intersection—a traffic circle with a massive marble column commemorating the centennial of Illinois statehood. Much of the area off the boulevards has deteriorated; be careful here.

To get there: The CTA Blue Line (O'Hare) stops at Logan Square.

By car, drive west along North Avenue to Humboldt Boulevard and then north to Palmer Square.

**Pullman (Zone 7)**    Once a company town built by George Pullman to house workers at his Pullman Palace Car Works, Pullman is now a historic district with more than 80% of the original 1,800 buildings still standing. Start your tour at the **Historic Pullman Foundation,** housed in the Florence Hotel (named for Pullman's daughter) at 11111 South Forrestville Avenue. The neighborhood harbors architecturally unique mansions—the executives' houses—and far more modest two-story attached row houses in muted Queen Anne style.

To get there: Pullman is on the far southwest side of Chicago, almost at the city's southern boundary. Via public transport, take the Metra Electric train ($2.75 one-way) from the station under Randolph and Michigan to the Pullman stop at 111th and Cottage Grove (it's one block to the Florence Hotel) or to the Kensington stop at 115th, which has more frequent service.

By car, drive south on the Dan Ryan Expressway (I-90/94) and continue south on the Calumet Expressway (I-94) and exit at 111th Street. Head west a few blocks to South Forrestville.

### Final Note

As rich as Chicago is in architecture, history, culture, and ethnic diversity, it *is* a major American city—which is to say, it is grappling with grave problems of unemployment, decaying infrastructure, crime, and besieged public schools. One recent study found that Chicago had four of the five poorest neighborhoods in the country—all located in the sprawling public housing projects that comprise today's ghettos. Many areas of the city's West Side still have not recovered from the fires and looting that followed the assassination of Dr. Martin Luther King Jr. in 1968. You need only drive west along 47th Street after touring the mansions of Kenwood to see the once stately buildings on Drexel Boulevard, now boarded up and barren. Or glance across the Dan Ryan Expressway from the gleaming new Comiskey Park to the forlorn hulks of Stateway Gardens and the Robert Taylor Homes (the largest public housing unit in the world) and in such juxtapositions of wealth and poverty you will recognize the challenges facing Chicago.

# Chicago for Children

*Question:* After taking the kids on the requisite trip to the top of the Sears Tower, what else can a parent do to entertain kids on a Chicago vacation?

*Answer:* A lot. Chicago offers plenty of fun-filled places to visit and things to do that will satisfy the most curious—and fidgety—kids. Their folks will have fun, too.

The *Unofficial Guide* rating system for attractions includes an "appeal to different age groups" category indicating a range of appeal from one star (★), don't bother, to five stars (★★★★★), not to be missed. To get you started, we have provided a list of attractions in and around Chicago most likely to appeal to children.

## More Things to Do with Children

Chicago has more for kids to enjoy than museums, zoos, and tall buildings. Some ideas: Swimming in Lake Michigan at **Oak Street Beach** and **North Avenue Beach,** roller skating at **United Skates of America** (Rainbow Entertainment Center, 4836 North Clark Street, phone (773) 271-6200), browsing at **Nike Town** (a high-tech shoe store at 669 North Michigan Avenue, phone (312) 642-6363) and **FAO Schwarz** (a giant toy store at 840 North Michigan Avenue, phone (312) 587-5000), and spotting the stones pirated from famous and ancient monuments worldwide (including the Parthenon, Notre Dame, and the Pyramids) embedded at street level in the **Tribune Tower** (435 North Michigan Avenue).

## Virtual Reality and Paint Ball

Kids and adults with itchy trigger fingers can play laser tag and "virtual reality" games at **Time Out** (phone (312) 527-3002) and **Virtual World Battletech Center** ("Adventure, Exploration, Pulverization"; phone (312) 836-5977); both are located in North Pier (435 East Illinois Street). Teens age 13 and older can relieve stress at the **Chicago Paint Ball Factory** (1001 West Van Buren Street—west of the Loop; phone (312) 563-1777); rates start at $18 an hour per person.

## Pro Sports and a Really Big Amusement Park

Depending on the season and ticket availability, take the gang to a **Bears, Blackhawks, Bulls, Cubs,** or **White Sox** game. In the summer, don't forget **Buckingham Fountain** in Grant Park: computer-controlled water displays send 14,000 gallons of water a minute through 133 jets. Color displays can be seen nightly from 9 to 11 p.m.

Farther afield (if you've got a car), take a drive to **Six Flags' Great America,** a monster amusement park north of Chicago with more than 100 rides (including eight roller coasters), shops, stage shows, and special theme sections representing different eras in American history. The park is open from May through October with varying hours; admission is $34 for adults, $29 for children ages 3–10, and $16 for seniors. With prices like these, plan on spending the day. More advice: Avoid weekends (the place gets packed) and go early in the day. For more information and directions, call (847) 249-INFO.

Other neat activities kids will enjoy: **bicycling** or **Rollerblading** on the bike path along Lake Michigan, taking the **Untouchable Tour** and exploring the old haunts of Chicago's gangsters (phone (773) 881-1195), and watching airplanes take off and land at the **Meigs Airfield observation deck** (15th Street and Lake Shore Drive, phone (312) 922-5454; it's free).

# Helpful Hints for Tourists

## WHEN THE ADMISSION IS FREE

Many Chicago museums that usually charge admission open their doors for free one day a week. If you'd like to save a few bucks during your visit, use our list when planning your touring itinerary.

In addition, a few worthy attractions around town are free to the public all the time. Here's the list:

- Chicago Board of Trade Visitor Center
- Chicago Botanic Garden ($5 parking on weekdays, $6 on weekends)
- Chicago Cultural Center
- Chicago Mercantile Exchange
- Garfield Park Conservatory
- Harold Washington Library Center
- International Museum of Surgical Science ($2 donation requested)
- Jane Addams Hull House Museum
- Lincoln Park Conservatory
- Lincoln Park Zoo
- Mexican Fine Arts Center Museum
- Museum of Broadcast Communications
- Oriental Institute Museum
- Polish Museum of America ($2 donation requested)
- Smart Museum of Art

## SCENIC CAR DRIVES

While we recommend that visitors to Chicago forego driving and rely on airport vans, taxis, and public transportation when in town, not everyone will heed our advice. In addition, rental cars are plentiful in Chicago, and traffic gets downright manageable on weekends. If you've got access to a set of wheels and feel the urge to roam, here are a few ideas to get you on your way.

### Around Town

The best views of the city are revealed anywhere along **Lake Shore Drive.** (For safety's sake, don't get too distracted by the scenery as you navigate this busy highway.) For an urban exploration beyond the lakefront, tour **Chicago's boulevards and greenways,** a series of wide streets laid out in the nineteenth century that link seven parks along what once was the city's western border.

## Heading North

For a quick and scenic escape from the city, head north on Lake Shore Drive until it becomes **Sheridan Road.** This pleasant drive meanders along the lakeshore and passes through affluent neighborhoods full of gorgeous homes and mansions. In Evanston it skirts the beautiful campus of Northwestern University and, in Wilmette, the breathtaking Baha'i House of Worship.

| Free Admission Days |
|---|
| **Monday**<br>Balzekas Museum of Lithuanian Culture<br>Chicago Historical Society |
| **Tuesday**<br>Adler Planetarium<br>Art Institute of Chicago<br>Brookfield Zoo (October through March; $4 parking)<br>Museum of Contemporary Art (first Tuesday of the month only)<br>Terra Museum of American Art (and first Sunday of the month) |
| **Wednesday**<br>Field Museum of Natural History |
| **Thursday**<br>Brookfield Zoo (October through March; $4 parking)<br>Chicago Children's Museum (evenings)<br>Museum of Science and Industry<br>Shedd Aquarium |
| **Friday**<br>Spertus Museum |
| **Sunday**<br>DuSable Museum of African-American History |

Farther north along Sheridan Road in Glencoe is the **Chicago Botanic Garden**—worth a stop in any season—and, in Highland Park, the **Ravinia Festival,** where evening summertime performances range from Joan Baez to the Chicago Symphony Orchestra. Note: A drive along Sheridan Road is especially popular with Chicagoans in the fall when the leaves change; to avoid the worst of the traffic, go early in the day.

## GREAT VIEWS

Nobody comes to the Midwest for the views, right? Wrong—at least, in Chicago. Here's a list of ten great spots that offer breathtaking vistas of skyline, Lake Michigan, and the city stretching toward the horizon.

1. The observation decks atop the **Sears Tower** and the **John Hancock Center** offer stupendous vistas from vantage points over 1,000 feet high. Go on a clear day; better yet, go at night. Our preference is the Hancock Center, which is closer to the lake and usually not very crowded.

2. **Lake Shore Drive** offers dramatic views of the Chicago skyline and the lake all along its length. We especially like the vantage point looking north where the Stevenson Expressway joins Lake Shore Drive (at McCormick Place).

3. **Grant Park** is a great place to walk and look up at Chicago's downtown. Note: Unless there is a summer festival going on, consider the park unsafe at night.

4. The view of downtown from the **Shedd Aquarium** is a knockout, especially at dusk as the lights begin to wink on.

5. **The Michigan Avenue Bridge** over the Chicago River offers a heart-stopping view of downtown buildings, especially at night: the Wrigley Building and Tribune Tower are both illuminated.

6. Starting around Thanksgiving, the **Festival of Lights** along North Michigan Avenue features more than 300,000 white lights for the holidays.

7. The **Ravenswood El** features surprises around every corner as it encircles the Loop. Don't get off; take it north, then grab the next train toward downtown for more views of the city.

8. **Montrose Harbor** offers a spectacular view of the Chicago skyline, especially at night. You'll need a car: It's located near the northern end of Lincoln Park on a finger of land jutting out into

Lake Michigan; get there from Lake Shore Drive.

9. As a lot of Chicago runners and bicyclists know, a stunning sunrise is a frequent reward on an early morning jaunt on the **Lakefront Trail** along Lake Michigan.

10. Or try this not-to-be-forgotten scene from anywhere on the lakefront (if the heavens cooperate on your trip): **moonrise over Lake Michigan.**

## GETTING INTO "OPRAH"

Wanna be on national TV? Or would you just like to be in the audience at a taping of your favorite talk show? You've come to the right place—Chicago is home to three of America's most popular TV talk shows.

Numero uno, of course, is Oprah, a figure so well known that no more identification is needed. For audience reservations to **The Oprah Winfrey Show,** call (312) 591-9222 at least one month prior to your visit. There's no charge and reservations are accepted for up to four people (who must be age 18 or older). Harpo Studios (that's Oprah spelled backwards), where the shows are taped twice daily (early and late morning) on Tuesdays, Wednesdays, and Thursdays, is located at 1058 West Washington Street, a couple of blocks west of the Loop. The show goes on vacation from late June to late August and again from mid-December through mid-January.

To get into **The Jenny Jones Show,** call (312) 836-9485 at least six weeks before your trip to Chicago. Shows are taped on Mondays, Wednesdays, and Fridays at the NBC Tower, 454 North Columbus Drive, and it's free. Reservations are accepted for up to four people.

For **The Jerry Springer Show,** call (312) 321-5365 at least one month in advance. Tickets are free, parties are limited to six people, and shows are usually taped at 10 a.m. and 1 p.m. on Mondays, Tuesdays, and Wednesdays, and on Wednesday evenings at 6 and 8 p.m. No shows are taped in July. The studios are in the NBC Tower, 454 North Columbus Drive, north of the Loop.

# Part Eleven

# Attractions in Chicago

## The Loop ... and Beyond

Chicago is a sports town, a shopping town, a culinary grab bag of cuisines, a jumble of intriguing ethnic neighborhoods, a glimmering jewel by the lake that takes your breath away at night.

But that's not all. The nation's third-largest city offers visitors a potpourri of attractions that show off its fascinating—and often notorious—past. Visitors can also explore majestic art galleries crammed with world-class collections of paintings and sculpture, gigantic museums dedicated to natural history and technology, the world's largest indoor aquarium, the country's oldest planetarium, a financial district where visitors view frantic commodities trading, a polyglot of ethnic museums . . . and lots more.

The following zone descriptions provide you with a comprehensive guide to Chicago's top attractions, along with listing a few we think you should avoid. We give you enough information so that you can choose the places you want to see, based on your own interests. Each attraction includes a zone number so you can plan your visit logically without spending a lot of valuable time crisscrossing the city.

### A TIME-SAVING CHART

Because of the wide range of attractions in and around Chicago—from an unparalleled collection of French Impressionist paintings in the Art Institute to America's tallest building—we've provided the following chart to help you prioritize your touring at a glance. In it, you'll find the zone, location, authors' rating from one star (skip it) to five stars (not to be missed), and a brief description of the attraction. Some attractions, usually art galleries without permanent collections, weren't rated because exhibits change. Each attraction is individually profiled later in this section.

| Attraction | Description | Author's Rating |
|---|---|---|
| **Zone 1—The North Side** | | |
| Chicago Historical Society | Chicago, U.S. history | ★★½ |
| Lincoln Park Zoo | urban animal park | ★★★ |
| Swedish-American Museum | Swedish immigrant story | ★★½ |
| **Zone 2—North Central/O'Hare** | | |
| Hemingway Museum | writer's memorabilia | ★★ |
| Wright Home and Studio | famous architect's house | ★★★★ |
| Garfield Conservatory | botanical gardens | ★★★ |
| Hemingway's Birthplace | Victorian house | ★½ |
| Museum of Holography | 3D photo gallery | ★★½ |
| Polish Museum | ethnic art and history | ★★½ |
| Ukrainian National Museum | folk art | ★ |
| **Zone 3—Near North** | | |
| Chicago Children's Museum | high-tech playground | ★ |
| International Museum of Surgical Science | history of surgery | ★★½ |
| Hancock Observatory | 94th-floor view | ★★★★★ |
| Museum of Contemporary Art | avant-garde art | ★★★★½ |
| Navy Pier | all-purpose tourist mecca | ★★★★ |
| Peace Museum | exhibits on nonviolence | unrated |
| Terra Museum | American paintings and art | ★★★★ |
| **Zone 4—The Loop** | | |
| Art Institute of Chicago | highbrow art palace | ★★★★★ |
| Chicago Athenaeum | for architecture buffs | ★★½ |
| Chicago Board of Trade | mayhem in the trading pits | ★★ |
| Chicago Cultural Center | art, architecture, tourist info | ★★★½ |
| Chicago Mercantile Exchange | frantic commodity trading | ★★ |
| Hull House Museum | birthplace of social work | ★★½ |
| Museum of Broadcast Communications | TV and radio memorabilia | ★★½ |
| Sears Tower Skydeck | view from America's tallest building | ★★★★★ |
| Spertus Museum | Jewish culture and history | ★★★ |
| Washington Library Center | largest library in U.S., art | ★★★ |

| Attraction | Description | Author's Rating |
|---|---|---|
| **Zone 5—South Loop** | | |
| Adler Planetarium | star show and space exhibits | ★★½ |
| American Police Museum | cop stuff | ★½ |
| Field Museum | nine acres of natural history | ★★★★★ |
| National Vietnam Veterans Art Museum | gut-wrenching art | ★★★ |
| Shedd Aquarium | largest indoor fish emporium | ★★★★★ |
| **Zone 6—South Central/Midway** | | |
| Balzekas Museum | Lithuanian culture and history | ★★ |
| Mexican Fine Arts Center | Mexican art and culture | unrated |
| **Zone 7—South Side** | | |
| DuSable Museum | African American art and culture | ★★★½ |
| Museum of Science and Industry | technology, hands-on exhibits | ★★★★★ |
| Oriental Institute | Near East archaeology | ★★★★ |
| Smart Museum of Art | highbrow art gallery | ★★★ |
| **Zone 8—Southern Suburbs** | | |
| Brookfield Zoo | campus-like animal park | ★★★½ |
| **Zone 9—Western Suburbs** | | |
| Morton Arboretum | 1,500 acres of trees, shrubs | ★★★½ |
| **Zone 11—Northern Suburbs** | | |
| Chicago Botanic Garden | formal, elegant gardens | ★★★★ |

# Sights: Zone 1—The North Side

## Chicago Historical Society

*Type of Attraction:*  A spacious museum highlighting Chicago history, from early frontier days to the present. A self-guided tour.

*Location:*  Clark Street at North Avenue, Chicago, IL 60614

*Admission:*  $5 for adults, $3 for seniors and students age 17–22 with ID, and $1 for children age 6–17. Admission is free on Mondays.

*Hours:*  9:30 a.m. to 4:30 p.m., Monday through Saturday; noon to 5 p.m. on Sundays.

*Phone:*  (312) 642-4600

*When to Go:*  On weekdays during the school year, plan your visit in the afternoon after the school field trips are over.

*Special Comments:*  Parking for disabled visitors is provided in the adjacent lot. There's also a metered lot a block north on Clark Street and a parking garage two blocks west on North Avenue.

*Overall Appeal by Age Group:*

| Pre-school | Grade School | Teens | Young Adults | Over 30 | Senior Citizens |
|---|---|---|---|---|---|
| ★ | ★★½ | ★★½ | ★★★ | ★★★ | ★★★ |

*Authors' Rating:*  There's a lot of neat stuff here, but it's also a bit austere . . . and a little boring. ★★½

*How Much Time to Allow:*  Two hours.

*Description and Comments*   The original entrance, which faces east, features a columned portico and a broad stairway stretching down to the broad lawn facing Lincoln Park and Lake Michigan. Today, the entrance is in the annex facing Clark Street, where large expanses of gridded glass welcome visitors to this large museum that showcases Chicago's history. The clean and modern interior features high ceilings and plenty of elbow room for visitors perusing the many exhibits.

Inside you'll find galleries hung with paintings, glass cases filled with artifacts, and a seemingly endless procession of static displays explaining the city's past. Livelier exhibitions feature a real steam locomotive, an interactive gallery for hands-on fun, and eight miniature scenes depicting Chicago's rapid growth in the nineteenth century.

*Touring Tips*   On the first floor, the Illinois Pioneer Life Gallery offers a fascinating glimpse of the state's early days, including a display of farm implements familiar to early settlers; test your ingenuity by guessing how they were used (answers are provided). The second floor's best exhibit is Chicago History, with a steam locomotive you can climb aboard. The American History Wing is less interesting, but Civil War buffs won't want to miss "A House Divided: America in the Age of Lincoln." Neither exhibit, however, focuses on Chicago. Hungry? The Big Shoulders Cafe on the first floor gets rave reviews from local diners.

*Other Things To Do Nearby*   The Lincoln Park Zoo is within easy walking distance. Head west on North Avenue to find a selection of restaurants and fast-food restaurants. Or take the pedestrian bridge over Lake Shore Drive for views of Lake Michigan.

## Lincoln Park Zoo

*Type of Attraction:* The most visited zoo in the nation, featuring more than 1,600 animals, birds, and reptiles. A self-guided tour.

*Location:* 2200 North Cannon Drive (Lincoln Park, off Lake Shore Drive at Fullerton Avenue north of the Magnificent Mile), Chicago, IL 60614

*Admission:* Free.

*Hours:* 9 a.m. to 5 p.m. daily.

*Phone:* (312) 742-2000

*When to Go:* Any time, except weekday mornings from mid-April to mid-June, when as many as 100 school buses converge on the zoo; by 1:30 p.m., the hordes of youngsters are gone. Weekend afternoons during the summer also attract big crowds.

*Special Comments:* Don't rule out a visit on a rainy or cold day: a lot of the animals are housed indoors. Interestingly enough, neighbors residing in nearby high-rises report they can hear wolves howling on warm summer nights.

*Overall Appeal by Age Group:*

| Pre-school | Grade School | Teens | Young Adults | Over 30 | Senior Citizens |
|---|---|---|---|---|---|
| ★★★★★ | ★★★★★ | ★★★★½ | ★★★½ | ★★★ | ★★★ |

*Authors' Rating:* Alas, this stately, old-fashioned zoo isn't in the same league as newer animal parks springing up around the nation. But it's still a refreshing oasis in the heart of bustling Chicago. ★★★

*How Much Time to Allow:* Two hours.

*Description and Comments*   Beautifully landscaped grounds, Lake Michigan, nearby high-rises, and the Chicago skyline in the distance are the hallmarks of this venerable, but smallish, park. Plus, the stately old buildings that house many of the zoo's inhabitants lend a Victorian elegance. Adults and especially children won't want to miss the Farm-in-the-Zoo (a farm featuring chickens, horses, and cows) and a children's zoo where the kids can enjoy a collection of small animals at eye level.

*Touring Tips*   If you're pressed for time, the most popular exhibits at the zoo are the polar bear, elephants, and (hold your nose) the Primate House, where great apes cavort behind thick panes of glass. Before or after your visit, stop by the Lincoln Park Conservatory, three acres of Victorian greenhouses built in 1891 that provide a lush rainforest setting for flora and fauna from around the world. Seasonally, the Christmas poinsettias and Easter lilies draw huge crowds.

The conservatory is just outside the zoo's northwest entrance (near the elephants)—and it's free. The recently restored Cafe Brauer serves salads and sandwiches; the Penguin Palace Ice Cream Shoppe dishes up ice cream during the summer.

*Other Things To Do Nearby*   The Chicago Historical Society (and its acclaimed cafe) is an easy stroll from the zoo. A walk west for a block or two leads to a number of fast-food restaurants. Or take the pedestrian bridge across Lake Shore Drive and watch the waves crash against the Lake Michigan shoreline.

## Swedish American Museum Center

*Type of Attraction:*  An attractive store-front museum highlighting Swedish culture and the Swedish immigrant experience. A self-guided tour.

*Location:*  5211 North Clark Street, Chicago, IL 60640

*Admission:*  $4 for adults, $2 for seniors, $1 for children.

*Hours:*  10 a.m. to 4 p.m., Tuesday through Friday; 10 a.m. to 3 p.m., weekends. Closed Mondays.

*Phone:*  (773) 728-8111

*When to Go:*  Any time.

*Special Comments:*  All the exhibits are located on the ground floor.

*Overall Appeal by Age Group:*

| Pre-school | Grade School | Teens | Young Adults | Over 30 | Senior Citizens |
|---|---|---|---|---|---|
| ★ | ★★ | ★★½ | ★★½ | ★★½ | ★★½ |

*Authors' Rating:*  Small, but attractive and interesting—and located in a great ethnic neighborhood. ★★½

*How Much Time to Allow:* 30 minutes to an hour.

*Description and Comments* Swedes were a major immigrant group in nineteenth-century Chicago and this museum provides insight into Swedish history and culture and the life of early immigrants. Items on display include jewelry from Lapland, old family bibles, nineteenth-century hand tools, and a recreation of a typical Swedish American home from the early twentieth century.

The gallery also exhibits fascinating black-and-white photos, including old pictures of the departed laid out in their coffins before burial: "Death was present everywhere, in a different way than it is today, and the local photographer would often be asked to immortalize deceased persons, both old and young." How things change.

*Touring Tips* The well-stocked and attractive museum shop features a wide range of items such as Swedish videos (including several films directed by Ingmar Bergman), books, road maps of Scandinavia, audio crash courses in Swedish, and traditional handicrafts from the Old Country.

*Other Things To Do Nearby* Explore Andersonville, the last ethnic stronghold of Swedes in Chicago. It's a fascinating neighborhood—an unusual mix of Swedish and Middle Eastern—full of interesting shops and inexpensive ethnic restaurants. (See page 230 for more information.)

# Sights: Zone 2—North Central/O'Hare

## Ernest Hemingway Museum

*Type of Attraction:* A small collection of exhibits featuring rare photos of the Nobel laureate, his childhood diary, letters, early writing, and other memorabilia focusing on the writer's Oak Park years. A self-guided tour.

*Location:* In the Oak Park Arts Center, 200 North Oak Park Avenue, Oak Park, IL 60302

*Admission:* $4 for adults, $3 for seniors and students, free for children under age 12 with an adult. Combined tickets for both the museum and Hemingway's Birthplace are $6 for adults and $4.50 for seniors and students.

*Hours:* 1 p.m. to 5 p.m., Thursdays, Fridays, and Sundays; 10 a.m. to 5 p.m., Saturdays. Closed Monday through Wednesday.

*Phone:* (708) 848-2222

*When to Go:* Any time.

*Special Comments:* Hemingway's Birthplace is about a block and a half away on the other side of Oak Park Avenue.

*Overall Appeal by Age Group:*

| Pre-school | Grade School | Teens | Young Adults | Over 30 | Senior Citizens |
|---|---|---|---|---|---|
| ★ | ★ | ★½ | ★★ | ★★ | ★★ |

*Authors' Rating:* A *very* narrow slice of the great writer's life that will be best appreciated by hard-core fans. ★★

*How Much Time to Allow:* 30 minutes.

*Description and Comments* A handful of display cases in the basement of a former church house this small collection of Hemingway memorabilia. Artifacts on view range from photos, diaries, and family items to a violin and typewriter once owned by the writer, whom many critics consider the greatest U.S. author. A six-minute video recalls Hemingway's upper-middle-class high school years . . . but doesn't mention that he left town for good at age 20 and, unlike most famous writers from Chicago, wrote very little about his hometown.

*Touring Tips* There's one gem to be found in this smallish collection: the "Dear John" letter Hemingway received from Agnes Von Kurowsky, the nurse who tended his wounds in Italy after he was wounded while serving as a volunteer ambulance driver during World War I. "For the rest of his life Hemingway was marked by his scars from battle and by an abiding distrust of women," the exhibit notes. Hem got his revenge, though; check out the ending of *A Farewell to Arms*—the beautiful nurse who tended the wounded hero croaks in the last chapter. What you *won't* find is any reference to his alleged remark that Oak Park is a town of "broad lawns and narrow minds."

*Other Things To Do Nearby* The Frank Lloyd Wright Home and Studio is only a few blocks away. Unity Temple, a National Historic Landmark designed by Wright in 1905, is located at 875 Lake Street; it's considered a masterpiece and is open weekdays 1 to 4 p.m. for self-guided tours ($4 for adults and $3 for seniors and children under age 18), and on weekends for guided tours at 1, 2, and 3 p.m. Guided tours are $6 for adults and $4 for seniors and children under age 18. Downtown Oak Park has a selection of dining and fast-food options. Brookfield Zoo is a few miles west off the Eisenhower Expressway (take Route 171 south).

## Frank Lloyd Wright Home and Studio

*Type of Attraction:* The Oak Park home of famed architect Frank Lloyd Wright and the birthplace of the Prairie School of architecture. Guided and self-guided tours.

*Location:* 951 Chicago Avenue, Oak Park, IL 60302. If you drive, park in the garage next to the Oak Park Visitor Center at 158 Forest Avenue. The center is open daily from 10 a.m. to 5 p.m. and centrally located, within easy walking distance to all the Wright and Hemingway attractions in town; purchase your tickets and pick up a map and more information inside. The visitor center is closed Thanksgiving, Christmas, and New Year's Day. Parking in the garage is free on weekends.

*Admission:* $8 for adults and $6 for seniors and children under age 18. Forest Avenue walking tours (self-guided by audio cassette) are $8 plus a deposit; guided Forest Avenue walking tours are $8 for adults and $6 for seniors and children. Both guided tours (house and walking) are $14 for adults and $10 for seniors and children.

*Hours:* 45-minute guided home and studio tours begin at 11 a.m., 1 p.m., and 3 p.m. Monday through Friday and about every 15 minutes from 11 a.m. and 3:30 p.m. on weekends; closed Thanksgiving, Christmas, and New Year's Day. Self-guided audio cassette tours of the exteriors of 13 Wright-designed houses along nearby Forest Avenue are available from 10 a.m. to 3:30 p.m. daily. Guided walking tours of the neighborhood are at 10:30 a.m., 11 a.m., noon, 1 p.m., 2 p.m., 3 p.m., and 4 p.m. daily.

*Phone:* (708) 848-1976

*When to Go:* Any time. For the walking tours, bring an umbrella if rain has been forecasted.

*Special Comments:* The house tour involves climbing and descending a flight of stairs.

*Overall Appeal by Age Group:*

| Pre-school | Grade School | Teens | Young Adults | Over 30 | Senior Citizens |
|---|---|---|---|---|---|
| ★ | ★½ | ★★ | ★★★ | ★★★★ | ★★★★ |

*Authors' Rating:* A fascinating glimpse into the life of America's greatest architect. ★★★★

*How Much Time to Allow:* One hour.

*Description and Comments*  Between 1889 and 1909 this house with prominent gables, window bays, and dark, shingled surfaces served as home, studio, and architectural laboratory for young Chicago architect Frank Lloyd Wright. Today it offers a permanent visual record of the beginnings of his continuous exploration of the relationship of light, form, and space. This is where Wright established the principles that guided his life work and launched a revolution that changed the architectural landscape of the twentieth century. Yet this house Wright built with $5,000 borrowed from his employer doesn't reflect his Prairie School of design, the first distinctly American style of architecture featuring low, earth-hugging dwellings. That would come later.

*Touring Tips*   What's fascinating about the tour—and what you should watch out for—are glimpses of early examples of elements that would become hallmarks of a Wright-designed home: large rooms that flow together, unity of design, minimal form, functionality, and the fusion of art and design elements. The tour guides do a good job of pointing them out.

The studio, which ends the tour and was added to the house by Wright in 1898, is a stunner, with walls supported by chains and a two-story octagonal drafting room. Here, working with 15 apprentices, Wright completed about 150 commissions and refined his Prairie School principles.

*Other Things To Do Nearby*   The Ernest Hemingway Museum and the Hemingway Birthplace are only a few blocks away; both destinations are pleasant walks when the weather is nice. Unity Temple, a National Historic Landmark designed by Wright in 1905, is located at 875 Lake Street; it's considered a masterpiece and is open weekdays 1 to 4 p.m. for self-guided tours ($4 for adults and $3 for seniors and children under age 18), and on weekends for guided tours at 1, 2, and 3 p.m. Guided tours are $6 for adults and $4 for seniors and children under age 18. Downtown Oak Park offers several places to grab something to eat.

## Garfield Park Conservatory

*Type of Attraction:*  Four-and-a-half acres of grounds and 5,000 species and varieties of plants, most of them housed under the glass of a landmark 1907 structure. Self-guided tours.

*Location:*  300 North Central Park Boulevard, Chicago, IL 60624

*Admission:*  Free.

*Hours:*  9 a.m. to 5 p.m. daily; 10 a.m. to 5 p.m. during major flower shows.

*Phone:*  (312) 746-5100

*When to Go:*  Any time.

*Special Comments:*  Garfield Park is located in a high-crime area. But stick close to the Conservatory and you'll be okay; the free parking lot is only a few steps away from the entrance.

*Overall Appeal by Age Group:*

| Pre-school | Grade School | Teens | Young Adults | Over 30 | Senior Citizens |
|---|---|---|---|---|---|
| ★★½ | ★★½ | ★★½ | ★★½ | ★★½ | ★★★ |

*Authors' Rating:*  Some really big plants (many dating from 1907) and plenty of interior space promote a feeling of serenity. ★★★

*How Much Time to Allow:* One hour (or longer if you've got a green thumb).

*Description and Comments* Four times larger than the conservatory in Lincoln Park, the Garfield Park Conservatory offers a world-class collection of botanical gardens for visitors to enjoy. The Palm House displays a variety of graceful palms, while the Cactus House encloses one of the nation's finest cactus displays (including giant saguaro) arranged in a typical Southwestern desert motif. A quiet visit here is soothing after a hectic morning of shopping on the Magnificent Mile or sight-seeing in the Loop.

*Touring Tips* Horticulture hounds and home gardeners can quiz the trained personnel that staff the conservatory about house plants and gardening in general. If you can't make it in person, call in your questions at (312) 746-5100. The conservatory hosts major flower shows throughout the year; see the Calendar of Special Events starting on page 49.

*Other Things To Do Nearby* Nothing in the immediate area (which isn't safe for visitors, especially after dark). Garfield Park is one of the areas of green linked by the city's network of boulevards.

## Hemingway's Birthplace

*Type of Attraction:* The partially restored, upper-middle-class Victorian house where Nobel Prize–winner Ernest Hemingway was born in 1899. A guided tour.

*Location:* 339 North Oak Park Avenue, Oak Park, IL 60302

*Admission:* $4 for adults, $3 for seniors and students, free for children under age 12 with an adult. Combined tickets for both Hemingway's Birthplace and the Ernest Hemingway Museum are $6 for adults and $4.50 for seniors and students.

*Hours:* 1 to 5 p.m., Thursday, Friday, and Sunday; 10 a.m. to 5 p.m., Saturday.

*Phone:* (708) 848-2222

*When to Go:* Any time.

*Special Comments:* One short, but rather steep, flight of stairs leads to the second floor.

*Overall Appeal by Age Group:*

| Pre-school | Grade School | Teens | Young Adults | Over 30 | Senior Citizens |
|---|---|---|---|---|---|
| ★ | ★ | ★½ | ★½ | ★½ | ★★ |

*Authors' Rating:* Strictly for die-hard Hemingway fans. ★½

*How Much Time to Allow:* 45 minutes.

*Description and Comments*   Open since the fall of 1993, this fine Victorian house has a long way to go before it becomes fully restored—and even then, it will only interest folks seeking a glimpse of upper-middle-class life in turn-of-the-century Oak Park. Hemingway lived here for five years as a child and only a few of the items on display are original. Upstairs, visitors can look into (but can't enter) the lavishly restored room where the writer was born.

*Touring Tips*   Look for the embalmed muskrats (at least, that's what the docent and I guessed they are) that Hemingway and his doctor father stuffed when the great writer was a boy. Unfortunately, visitors are subjected to a much-too-long video (15 minutes, actually) that tells them more than they'll ever want to know about the Nobel Prize winner's grandparents. Unless you've got an abiding interest in Hemingway's genealogy, plead a tight schedule and try to skip the film.

*Other Things To Do Nearby*   The Ernest Hemingway Museum is down the street; the Frank Lloyd Wright Home and Studio is only a few blocks away. Unity Temple, a National Historic Landmark designed by Wright in 1905, is located at 875 Lake Street; it's considered a masterpiece and is open weekdays 1 to 4 p.m. for self-guided tours ($4 for adults and $3 for seniors and children under age 18), and on weekends for guided tours at 1, 2, and 3 p.m. Guided tours are $6 for adults and $4 for seniors and children under age 18. Downtown Oak Park offers several dining and fast-food options. Brookfield Zoo is a few miles west, off I-290.

## Museum of Holography

*Type of Attraction:*  A small gallery exhibiting holograms, laser-produced photographic images that are three-dimensional and often feature movement, color change, and image layering. A self-guided tour.

*Location:*  1134 West Washington Boulevard, Chicago, IL 60607

*Admission:*  $2.50 per person; under age 6 free.

*Hours:*  12:30 to 5 p.m., Wednesday through Sunday; closed Monday and Tuesday.

*Phone:*  (312) 226-1007

*When to Go:*  Any time.

*Special Comments:*  Located just west of the Loop in an otherwise drab neighborhood of warehouses; one flight of stairs. Images are at adult eye level, so small fry will need a lift to get the full effect.

*Overall Appeal by Age Group:*

| Pre-school | Grade School | Teens | Young Adults | Over 30 | Senior Citizens |
|---|---|---|---|---|---|
| ★½ | ★★ | ★★½ | ★★½ | ★★½ | ★★½ |

*Authors' Rating:*  Not high art, but fascinating—sometimes startling—images. ★★½

*How Much Time to Allow:*  30 minutes to an hour.

*Description and Comments*  It would probably take a physics degree to really understand how holograms are created, but the results are fascinating just the same. The museum, the only one of its kind in the United States, features stunning 3D images such as a microscope that leaps off the surface; when you look into the "eye piece" you're rewarded with the sight of a bug frozen in amber! Other holograms produce a motion-picture effect as you move your head from left to right in front of the image. While the museum is small—it's essentially two small galleries and a gift shop—the stuff on display is unusual, to say the least.

*Touring Tips*  The gift shop offers a wide array of holograms for sale, ranging from bookmarks and cards to framed images. Prices range from a few bucks to several hundred dollars for large, framed holograms. Most, however, are four-inch by six-inch images that start at $60 (including the frame). Note: Before purchasing a hologram, keep in mind that to get the full effect at home, it needs to be illuminated by an unfrosted incandescent bulb mounted at a 45-degree angle to the image.

*Other Things To Do Nearby*  Nothing within walking distance. But the Loop is only a few blocks to the east.

## Polish Museum of America

*Type of Attraction:*  One of the largest and oldest ethnic museums in the United States, featuring Polish and Polish American paintings, sculptures, drawings, and lithographs. A self-guided tour.

*Location:*  984 North Milwaukee Avenue, Chicago, IL 60622

*Admission:*  Free; $2 donation per adult requested.

*Hours:*  11 a.m. to 4 p.m. daily.

*Phone:*  (773) 384-3352

*When to Go:*  Any time.

*Special Comments:*  The museum is located on the second and third floors; visitors must climb two flights of stairs.

*Overall Appeal by Age Group:*

| Pre-school | Grade School | Teens | Young Adults | Over 30 | Senior Citizens |
|------------|--------------|-------|--------------|---------|-----------------|
| ★½ | ★★ | ★★½ | ★★½ | ★★½ | ★★★ |

*Authors' Rating:* An eclectic collection of high-quality art, colorful crafts, and historical items ranging from seventeenth-century armor to modern paintings. ★★½

*How Much Time to Allow:* One hour.

*Description and Comments*   Located in the heart of Chicago's first Polish neighborhood, the Polish Museum emphasizes the art and history of an ethnic group that maintains a strong national identity; famous Poles include Paderewski, Pulaski, Kosciuszko, Copernicus, Madame Curie, and Chopin. Interesting items on display include a one-horse open sleigh carved from a single log in 1703 that a Polish king gave to his daughter, Princess Maria, who married Louis XV of France.

Other stuff on display here—much of it colorful and reflecting a high degree of craftsmanship—include Polish folk costumes, exquisite hand-decorated Easter eggs, wood sculpture, prints, and paintings. It's not a very large place, but there's a lot to see.

*Touring Tips*   The third floor contains an attractive, well-lighted art gallery featuring modern graphic art, paintings, and busts. Check out the stairwell and you'll find a Picasso lithograph and a Chagall etching.

*Other Things To Do Nearby*   Walk a few blocks north on Milwaukee Avenue to explore the old Polish neighborhood, which still has a few shops and restaurants with signs written in Polish; there's an El station at Ashland and Milwaukee avenues.

## Ukrainian National Museum

*Type of Attraction:* A collection of Ukrainian folk art, embroidery, wood carvings, ceramics, beadwork, and painted Easter eggs. A self-guided tour.

*Location:* 721 North Oakley Boulevard, Chicago, IL 60612

*Admission:* Free.

*Hours:* 11 a.m. to 4 p.m., Thursday through Sunday; by appointment only, Monday through Wednesday.

*Phone:* (312) 421-8020

*When to go:* Any time.

*Special Comments:* Visitors must climb a set of stairs to reach the museum entrance.

*Overall Appeal by Age Group:*

| Pre-school | Grade School | Teens | Young Adults | Over 30 | Senior Citizens |
|---|---|---|---|---|---|
| ★ | ★½ | ★½ | ★½ | ★½ | ★★ |

*Authors' Rating:* While some beautiful objects are on display here, this museum is too small and out of the way to recommend a special trip. ★

*How Much Time to Allow:* 30 minutes to an hour.

*Description and Comments* The Ukraine, a nation of 52 million people that was once part of the former Soviet Union and an independent state since 1991, is the second-largest country in Europe. Crammed into this tiny, but bright museum is a wide variety of folk art, including linens, colorful costumes, exquisitely detailed painted Easter eggs, musical instruments, wood models of native Ukrainian houses, swords, and paintings (including a portrait of a fearsome looking Volodymyr the Great, king of the Ukraine from 979 to 1015).

*Touring Tips* Make this a stop on an ethnic exploration of Chicago; see our write-up on the Ukrainian Village on page 241 in "Exploring Chicago's Neighborhoods."

*Other Things To Do Nearby* Next door is Sts. Volodymyr and Olha Ukrainian Catholic Church, topped by three gold domes and decorated by rich mosaics over the door. Around the corner on Chicago Avenue are several Ukrainian eateries and bakeries.

# Sights: Zone 3—Near North

## Chicago Children's Museum

*Type of Attraction:* A high-tech playground and engaging interactive exhibits for children up to age 12. A self-guided tour.

*Location:* Navy Pier, 700 East Grand Avenue, Chicago, IL 60611 (just north of the Chicago River on the lakefront)

*Admission:* $6; free for infants under age 1; free on Thursday evenings after 5 p.m.

*Hours:* 10 a.m. to 5 p.m., Tuesday through Sunday; closed Mondays except Memorial Day through Labor Day (and some school holidays). Open until 8 p.m. on Thursdays.

*Phone:* (312) 527-1000

*When to go:* During the summer, on weekends, and on school holidays, arrive when the museum opens at 10 a.m. During the school year, come in the afternoon to avoid school groups that arrive in the morning.

*Special Comments:*  This isn't a baby-sitting service. While all activities are supervised by the museum staff, all children must be accompanied by someone age 16 or older.

*Overall Appeal by Age Group:*

| Pre-school | Grade School | Teens | Young Adults | Over 30 | Senior Citizens |
|---|---|---|---|---|---|
| ★★★★★ | ★★★★★ | ★ | ★ | ★ | ★ |

*Authors' Rating:*  Nirvana for youngsters through age 12. ★
*How Much Time to Allow:*  Half a day.

*Description and Comments*   This new, $14.5 million, 60,000-square-foot "museum"—it's really a high-tech playground for ankle biters and children through the fifth grade—provides an active play and learning environment spread across three levels of Navy Pier. A dozen exhibits provide a range of age-appropriate activities that captivates toddlers as well as older children. One of the most popular is Waterways, where kids don raincoats (provided) and pump, squirt, and manipulate water (they can shoot a stream of water 50 feet into the air). In The Inventing Lab, children can build and launch gliders from a 50-foot tower. In Treehouse Trails and PlayMaze, toddlers can explore an indoor "nature park" (featuring a hiking trail, pond, waterfall, trees, log cabin, and animal homes) and play in a working bakery, service station, and construction site.

*Touring Tips*   Start a visit with the Climbing Schooner, a three-story replica of a sailing ship that lets kids burn off energy by climbing the rigging up 35 feet to the crow's nest—and then sliding down a ladder. Then explore the rest of the museum.

*Other Things To Do Nearby*   Make a day of it by exploring Navy Pier. Take a scenic cruise on Lake Michigan, relax in the IMAX theater, ride the Ferris wheel and carousel, eat lunch in the food court, or simply take a stroll to enjoy the Chicago skyline and Lake Michigan stretching out to the horizon.

## International Museum of Surgical Science

*Type of Attraction:*  Exhibits from around the world trace the history of surgery and related sciences. A self-guided tour.

*Location:*  1524 North Lake Shore Drive, Chicago, IL 60610

*Admission:*  Free; a donation of $5 for adults and $3 for seniors and students is requested.

*Hours:* 10 a.m. to 4 p.m., Tuesday through Saturday; Closed on Sunday and Monday.

*Phone:* (888) 875-VIEW

*When to Go:* Any time.

*Special Comments:* While the truly squeamish should avoid this place like the plague, there's actually very little on display that's overtly gory or upsetting. The museum is located on the #151 bus route, and limited parking is available in a small lot behind the building; additional parking is located in Lincoln Park and at North Avenue Beach. It's a short, pleasant stroll away from North Michigan Avenue.

*Overall Appeal by Age Group:*

| Pre-school | Grade School | Teens | Young Adults | Over 30 | Senior Citizens |
|------------|--------------|-------|--------------|---------|-----------------|
| ★ | ★½ | ★★ | ★★½ | ★★½ | ★★½ |

*Authors' Rating:* A must-see for folks in the medical field; otherwise, it's a nice fill-in spot when exploring the Gold Coast on foot. ★★½

*How Much Time to Allow:* One hour for most folks; half a day for those with a keen interest in medical science.

*Description and Comments* The mysteries, breakthroughs, failures, and historic milestones of surgical science are on display in this unusual museum housed in an elegant mansion facing Lake Michigan. Implements on display range from the truly horrifying—2,000-year-old skulls with holes bored into them and tin-and-wood enema syringes from the 1800s—to the quaint (such as an X-ray shoe fitter from the early 1950s). The first floor features a recreation of a nineteenth-century pharmacy and an early-twentieth-century dentist's office.

*Touring Tips* Start on the first floor and explore displays of antique medical instruments, then work your way up to the fourth floor. The second floor's Hall of Immortals features 12 eight-foot statues representing great medical figures in history, while the third floor includes an exhibit of antique microscopes and early X-ray equipment. Look for Napoleon's original death mask and more ancient medical instruments on the fourth floor.

*Other Things To Do Nearby* Explore Chicago's opulent Gold Coast neighborhood on foot. It's only a few blocks south to the Magnificent Mile, which features expensive shops, malls, department stores, and a knock-your-socks-off view from the 94th-floor observatory in the John Hancock Center (when it's not raining).

## John Hancock Center Observatory

*Type of Attraction:* A 39-second elevator ride leading to a spectacular, 94th-floor view of Chicago. A self-guided tour.

*Location:* 875 North Michigan Avenue, Chicago, IL 60611

*Admission:* $8 for adults, $6 for seniors and children ages 5–17, and free for children under age 5.

*Hours:* 9 a.m. to midnight daily.

*Phone:* (888) 875-VIEW

*When to Go:* Any time.

*Special Comments:* This is an excellent alternative to the Sears Tower Skydeck, where the lines can be very long. In fact, most Chicagoans say the view is better. If the top of the building is hidden in clouds, come back another day.

*Overall Appeal by Age Group:*

| Pre-school | Grade School | Teens | Young Adults | Over 30 | Senior Citizens |
|---|---|---|---|---|---|
| ★★★★★ | ★★★★★ | ★★★★★ | ★★★★★ | ★★★★★ | ★★★★★ |

*Authors' Rating:* A stunning view, especially at sunset or at night. ★★★★★

*How Much Time to Allow:* 30 minutes.

*Description and Comments*  This distinctive building with the X-shaped exterior crossbracing is the tenth-highest office building in the world. Although the 94th-floor observatory is nine floors lower than the Sears Tower Skydeck, some folks say the view is better here, perhaps due to its proximity to Lake Michigan.

*Touring Tips*  The ideal way to enjoy the vista (you're 1,030 feet above Michigan Avenue) is to arrive just before sunset. As the sun sinks lower in the west, slowly the city lights blink on—and a whole new view appears.

*Other Things To Do Nearby*  The 95th and 96th floors of the John Hancock Center house the highest restaurant and lounge in the city. (You can relax with a drink for about the same cost as visiting the observatory, but there's no guarantee you'll get a seat with a view.) Or return to street level and shop till you drop along chichi North Michigan Avenue; the Water Tower Place shopping mall is next door.

## Museum of Contemporary Art

*Type of Attraction:* An art museum dedicated to the avant garde in all media. A self-guided tour.

*Location:* 220 East Chicago Avenue, Chicago, IL 60611

*Admission:* $6.50 for adults; $4 for students and seniors with ID; free for children age 12 and under; free general admission on the first Tuesday of the month.

*Hours:* 11 a.m. to 6 p.m., Tuesday, Thursday, and Friday; 11 a.m. to 8 p.m., Wednesdays; 10 a.m. to 6 p.m., weekends; closed on Mondays; closed on Thanksgiving, Christmas, and New Year's Day.

*Phone:* (312) 280-2660

*When to go:* Any time.

*Special Comments:* Paid parking is available in the museum's parking garage. The MCA has wheelchair-accessible entrances, elevators, and rest rooms.

*Overall Appeal by Age Group:*

| Pre-school | Grade School | Teens | Young Adults | Over 30 | Senior Citizens |
|------------|--------------|-------|--------------|---------|-----------------|
| ★★½ | ★★★ | ★★★ | ★★★½ | ★★★★½ | ★★★★ |

*Authors' Rating:* Chicago's spanking-new venue for modern art is bright, cheerful, and filled with paintings and sculpture, as well as some other difficult-to-categorize art works. A not-to-be-missed destination for anyone who enjoys art that's both beautiful and challenging. ★★★★½

*How Much Time to Allow:* One to two hours. Dyed-in-the-wool culture vultures should figure on at least half a day.

*Description and Comments*   This new (opened late 1996) five-story art museum provides a major world-class showcase for the MCA's permanent collection of late-twentieth-century art. Bright and airy on the inside, the new building doesn't overwhelm visitors like, say, the huge Art Institute. Most of the art is displayed on the fourth floor, with two smaller galleries on the second floor dedicated to special and traveling exhibitions. With lots of seating, carpeting, and sunlight streaming in through large windows, the MCA is an easy place to visit.

The permanent exhibit shows off paintings, sculpture, prints, and a wide variety of art utilizing a mind-boggling range of materials: acrylics, video, sound, neon, an inflatable raft, flashing lights. . . . Kids, perhaps unsaddled with preconceptions of what defines "art," seem to especially enjoy the MCA's eclectic offerings. Artists represented include Andy Warhol, Roy Lichtenstein, Robert Rauschenberg, Alexander Calder, Marcel Duchamp, Franz Kline, Rene Magritte, and Willem de Kooning.

*Touring Tips*   From either the ground floor entrance or the second floor entrance at the top of the stairs facing Michigan Avenue, take the elevator to the fourth floor. Free 45-minute tours depart from the second floor at 1 p.m. on Tuesdays through Fridays; at 11:15 a.m., 12:15 p.m., and 2 p.m. on weekends; and also at 7 p.m. on Wednesdays. The bilevel book and gift shop features a wide selection of art books and kids' stuff such as games, stuffed animals, T-shirts, and toys. The high-ceilinged cafe, which overlooks the outdoor sculpture garden and Lake Michigan, is comfortable and offers a European-style menu with prices in the $5–8 range. Rest rooms are located on the ground floor near the entrance.

*Other Things To Do Nearby*   The MCA is only a block off the Magnificent Mile, Chicago's shopping mecca; the Water Tower Place shopping mall (and its huge food court) is only a stone's throw away. The John Hancock Observatory, the Terra Museum of American Art, and a wide array of restaurants are all within easy walking distance. Children will enjoy Nike Town at 669 North Michigan Avenue, which features an actual basketball court on the second floor and a 22-foot-long aquarium.

## Navy Pier

*Type of Attraction:*  A recently renovated landmark on Lake Michigan with over 50 acres of parks, gardens, shops, restaurants, a 150-foot Ferris wheel, an IMAX theater, a convention center, a children's museum, and other attractions. A self-guided tour.

*Location:*  700 East Grand Avenue, Chicago, IL 60611 (just north of the Chicago River on the lakefront)

*Admission:*  Free; some attractions such as the Chicago Children's Museum, the Ferris wheel, cruise boats, and the IMAX theater have separate admission charges.

*Hours:*  Memorial Day through Labor Day: 10 a.m. to 10 p.m., Sunday through Thursday; 10 a.m. to midnight, Friday and Saturday. Fall through spring: 10 a.m. to 8 p.m., Monday and Thursday; 10 a.m. to 10 p.m., Friday and Saturday; 10 a.m. to 7 p.m., Sunday. Restaurants are open later throughout the year.

*Phone:*  (312) 595-PIER, (800) 595-PIER (outside the 312 area code), and (312) 595-5100 (administrative offices)

*When to go:*  Attracting five million visitors a year, Navy Pier has catapulted past the Lincoln Park Zoo to become Chicago's number-one attraction—and during warm weather the place is jammed. Try to arrive before 11 a.m., especially if you're driving and on weekends.

*Special Comments:*  While a new 700-space, $19 million parking garage helps, finding a place to put the family car remains a problem at this very popular attraction. Arrive early—or, better yet, take public transportation (the Nos. 29, 56, 65, 66, 120, and 121 buses stop at the entrance) or a cab.

*Overall Appeal by Age Group:*

| Pre-school | Grade School | Teens | Young Adults | Over 30 | Senior Citizens |
|---|---|---|---|---|---|
| ★★★★★ | ★★★★★ | ★★★★★ | ★★★★ | ★★★★ | ★★★★ |

*Authors' Rating:* The view of Chicago's skyline alone makes this a must-see destination. The ultimate is dinner at a window table at Riva or an evening dinner cruise on the *Odyssey.* ★★★★

*How Much Time to Allow:* Depending on the weather, anywhere from an hour to half a day—or longer if a festival or concert is taking place during your visit.

*Description and Comments*    A former U.S. Navy training facility and a campus of the University of Illinois, Navy Pier reopened in 1995 after a $196 million facelift as Chicago's premier visitor attraction. There's something for everyone: a children's museum; a shopping mall and food court; a huge Ferris wheel and a carousel; a six-story-high, 80-foot-wide IMAX theater screen; scenic and dinner cruises on Lake Michigan; a convention center; a beer garden; a concert venue; ice skating in the winter . . . the list goes on.

Here's the scoop on Navy Pier's most popular attractions: The Ferris wheel is open from May through December and costs $3 for adults and $2 for children; it's a 7½-minute ride. Long waits in line aren't a problem because it rotates nonstop at a slow speed that lets visitors load and unload almost continuously. The IMAX theater is located near the entrance of the Family Pavilion shopping mall; tickets for the shows are $8.50 for adults, $7 for seniors, and $5.50 for children. Crystal Gardens (a one-acre indoor tropical garden with fountains and public seating), Festival Hall, Skyline Stage, and the Grand Ballroom feature performances of jazz, blues, rock, theater, and dance, as well as special events such as consumer trade shows, art festivals, miniature golf, and ethnic festivals; most charge admission. For more information on the popular, 50,000-square-foot Chicago Children's Museum, see page 263. Cruise boats depart from Navy Pier's south dock, as does the Shoreline Shuttle, a sight-seeing boat that departs every 30 minutes for the Shedd Aquarium.

*Touring Tips*    Unless your visit to Navy Pier is midweek during the winter, avoid the hassles and expense of parking (more than $5 an hour) by arriving via bus or cab. And try to pick a nice day: the Ferris wheel shuts down in the rain and the view of Chicago's magnificent skyline is what separates this shopping, restaurant, and festival venue from all the others. If you're taking the kids to the Chicago Children's Museum, either arrive when it opens in the morning (when school is out) or in the afternoon during the school year (to avoid school groups that often arrive in the mornings). Before leaving home call Navy Pier for a schedule of special events taking place during your visit.

*Other Things To Do Nearby*   North Pier Festival Market is about two blocks west, offering more shopping and another food court. Kids will enjoy the Battle Tech Center and Virtuality Center game rooms on the third level. You can also stroll the Lakefront Trail or, better yet, rent a bike or inline skates at Bike Chicago (in Navy Pier).

## Peace Museum

*Type of Attraction:*  A museum promoting peace and nonviolence through the arts. A self-guided tour.

*Location:*  314 West Institute Place, Chicago, IL 60610

*Admission:*  Suggested donation of $3.50 for adults, and $2 for children, students, and seniors.

*Hours:*  11 a.m. to 5 p.m., Tuesday through Saturday. Closed Sunday and Monday.

*Phone:*  (312) 440-1860

*When to Go:*  Any time.

*Special Comments:*  Take the elevator directly across from the building entrance to the fourth floor and turn right.

*Overall Appeal by Age Group:*  The Peace Museum hosts temporary exhibits, so it's not possible to rate it by age group.

*Authors' Rating:*  Because it doesn't have a permanent collection, it's not possible to rate the museum; exhibits change about four times a year.

*How Much Time to Allow:*  30 minutes to an hour.

*Description and Comments*   This essentially one-room exhibit space may be the only museum in the world dedicated to world peace. On our visit the exhibit was "A Piece of the Peace: Poetry for the Walls," which examined the role of language in making and breaking peace. Some of the original manuscripts on display were by Joan Baez, Bono (from U2), and '60s protest singer Phil Ochs.

*Touring Tips*   To find out what's on display during your visit, pick up a copy of the Chicago *Reader.*

*Other Things To Do Nearby*   The Merchandise Mart and the Loop are a few blocks south on LaSalle Street.

## Terra Museum of American Art

*Type of Attraction:*  A recently refurbished gallery on the Magnificent Mile (North Michigan Avenue) featuring nineteenth- and twentieth-century American art. A self-guided tour.

*Location:*  666 North Michigan Avenue, Chicago, IL 60611

*Admission:*  Suggested donations are $5 for adults, $2.50 for seniors, and $1.50 for students with ID; free for children under age 14, teachers, and to the public on Tuesdays and first the Sunday of the month.

*Hours:*  10 a.m. to 7 p.m., Tuesday through Saturday; noon to 5 p.m., Sunday ; Closed Mondays.

*Phone:*  (312) 664-3939

*When to Go:*  Any time.

*Special Comments:*  The five-floor museum is wheelchair accessible.

*Overall Appeal by Age Group:*

| Pre-school | Grade School | Teens | Young Adults | Over 30 | Senior Citizens |
|---|---|---|---|---|---|
| ★ | ★★ | ★★½ | ★★★ | ★★★★ | ★★★★ |

*Authors' Rating:*  Elegant, quiet, modern; an oasis of quiet and beauty on bustling North Michigan Avenue. ★★★★

*How Much Time to Allow:*  One to two hours.

*Description and Comments*   The Terra's permanent collection of nineteenth- and twentieth-century art relies heavily on Impressionists. But you'll also find paintings by Homer, Whistler, and other American masters, as well as changing exhibitions of American art. The museum is elegant, wide, and comfortable—a pleasant surprise for folks visiting this highly commercial area for the first time.

*Touring Tips*   Take the (huge) elevator to the fourth floor to begin the tour. After walking up to the fifth-floor gallery, work your way down to the first-floor lobby.

*Other Things To Do Nearby*   The Historic Water Tower is three blocks north on Michigan Avenue, and the Magnificent Mile is primo shopping territory. Kids will enjoy Nike Town, a high-tech shoe store at 669 North Michigan Avenue. For more art, try the Museum of Contemporary Art on East Chicago Street (a block east of the Water Tower).

# Sights: Zone 4—The Loop

## Art Institute of Chicago

*Type of Attraction:* Internationally acclaimed collections of paintings and sculptures housed in a complex of neoclassical buildings erected for the World's Columbian Exposition of 1893. Guided and self-guided tours.

*Location:* 111 South Michigan Avenue, Chicago, IL 60603

*Admission:* $7 for adults; $3.50 for children, students, and seniors; free admission on Tuesday.

*Hours:* 10:30 a.m. to 4:30 p.m., Monday, Wednesday, Thursday, and Friday; 10:30 a.m. to 8 p.m., Tuesday; 10 a.m. to 5 p.m., Saturday; and noon to 5 p.m., Sunday and holidays. Closed Christmas and Thanksgiving days.

*Phone:* (312) 443-3600

*When to Go:* During the school year, the museum is often besieged by groups of school children on field trips in the mornings; afternoons are usually less crowded. Because admission is free on Tuesdays, the museum is almost always packed.

*Special Comments:* The first floor is the only level that connects the three buildings that comprise the Art Institute. It also provides access to Michigan Avenue (west) and Columbus Drive (east), food, rest rooms, and water fountains. Handicapped access is at the Columbus Drive entrance.

*Overall Appeal by Age Group:*

| Pre-school | Grade School | Teens | Young Adults | Over 30 | Senior Citizens |
|---|---|---|---|---|---|
| ★ | ★★½ | ★★★ | ★★★★ | ★★★★★ | ★★★★★ |

*Authors' Rating:* The best of a handful of attractions that elevate Chicago to world-class status. Not to be missed. ★★★★★

*How Much Time to Allow:* At least two hours for a brief run through, all day for art lovers. Better yet, try to visit the Art Institute more than once—the place is huge.

*Description and Comments*  The massive, classical/Renaissance-style home of the Art Institute of Chicago was completed in 1892, just in time for the 1893 World's Columbian Exposition. Located on the edge of Grant Park near the Loop, the museum is easily identified by the two bronze lions standing guard on Michigan Avenue.

It's a world-class museum especially renowned for its Impressionist collection, which includes five of the paintings in Monet's haystack series, Caillebotte's *Paris, a Rainy Day,* and, perhaps the museum's best-known painting, Seurat's pointillist masterpiece *Sunday Afternoon on the Island of La Grande Jatte.* The large museum shop features calendars, books, cards, gifts (mugs, scarves, posters, CDs), and a huge collection of art books (some at reduced prices).

*Touring Tips*   The second-floor gallery of European art is arranged chronologically from late medieval to post-Impressionist, with paintings and sculptures arranged in skylight-brightened rooms; prints and drawings are hung in corridor galleries. By taking a free tour, you'll get an overview of the place and see how various works are related.

For example, my guide linked different eras by explaining the evolution of paint—from egg and pigment used in the late Middle Ages to the stuff Jackson Pollock splattered on canvas with a stick. Fascinating. Tours start daily at 2 p.m. in Gallery 150, on the first floor near the Grand Staircase and the main entrance.

*Other Things To Do Nearby*   The Loop is a block west; Grant Park and Lake Michigan are behind the Art Institute. Walking tours of downtown Chicago start across the street at the Chicago Architecture Foundation; no visit to the Windy City is complete until you've taken at least one. For lunch, Michigan Avenue has several fast-food places nearby, or try the Eurodeli next to the Chicago Architecture Foundation shop.

## The Chicago Athenaeum:  The Museum of Architecture and Design

*Type of Attraction:*  A museum featuring displays on architecture, industrial and product design, graphics, and urban planning. A self-guided tour.

*Location:*  6 North Michigan Avenue, Chicago, IL 60602

*Admission:*  $3 for adults, $2 for students and seniors, free for children under age 5.

*Hours:*  11 a.m. to 6 p.m., Tuesday through Saturday; noon to 5 p.m., Sunday. Closed Mondays.

*Phone:*  (312) 251-0175

*When to go:*  Any time.

*Special Comments:*  The museum is fully accessible to handicapped visitors. Rest rooms are located on the 15th floor; to get on the elevator, ask the person selling tickets for the access code.

*Overall Appeal by Age Group:*

| Pre-school | Grade School | Teens | Young Adults | Over 30 | Senior Citizens |
|---|---|---|---|---|---|
| ★ | ★½ | ★★ | ★★½ | ★★½ | ★★½ |

*Authors' Rating:* For those who just can't get enough about Chicago architecture. ★★½

*How Much Time to Allow:* One hour.

*Description and Comments* Essentially a loft museum for architecture and design buffs, the Chicago Athenaeum provides some behind-the-scenes glimpses of the evolution of the city's famed skyline and the various schools of architecture that developed here. On hand in the second-floor Landmark Chicago exhibit are computer-generated pictures of unbuilt high-rise projects, photos of the John Hancock Center under construction in 1969, and side-by-side tabletop models of downtown Chicago in 1940 and 1990 (built by first-year architecture students). The museum also displays art deco furniture designed by Frank Lloyd Wright (such as a trilevel desk and matching chair from the Johnson Wax Administration Building, circa 1936) and sections of cast-iron grillwork and stair ballisters rescued from various downtown buildings. Think of this museum as icing on the cake for architecture fiends.

*Touring Tips* Much of the space in this small downtown museum is reserved for temporary shows, but don't overlook the permanent display on appliance design on the first floor. Ellen Manderfield, an industrial designer with roots in Chicago, worked for 50 years designing radios, phonographs, kitchen equipment, televisions, and silverware that reflects the range of popular tastes in the '40s, '50s, and '60s. Her renderings and sketches are both nostalgic and fun to look at—especially for those old enough to remember a period when styles ranged from art deco to Danish modern. The museum shop includes an eclectic collection of books and magazines on design and architecture, cutlery, coffee mugs, pure silk pillows, aerodynamic bicycle helmets, unusual household items, Greek leather bags— all selected for their good design.

*Other Things To Do Nearby* The Art Institute of Chicago and the Loop are both nearby, as is the Spertus Museum. Grant Park is a block to the east; the Chicago Cultural Center is an oasis of tranquility along hectic Michigan Avenue. If you haven't taken a Loop walking tour yet, stop by the Chicago Architecture Foundation Shop and Tour Center at 224 South Michigan Avenue and buy tickets.

## Chicago Board of Trade Visitor Center

*Type of Attraction:* Bedlam in the trading pits at the world's oldest and largest futures market. A self-guided tour.

*Location:* 141 West Jackson Boulevard, Chicago, IL 60604

*Admission:* Free.

*Hours:* 8 a.m. to 2 p.m., Monday through Friday. Closed Saturdays and Sundays and on legal holidays.

*Phone:* (312) 435-3590

*When to Go:* Any time.

*Special Comments:* From the lobby, take the escalators to the fifth floor.

*Overall Appeal by Age Group:*

| Pre-school | Grade School | Teens | Young Adults | Over 30 | Senior Citizens |
|---|---|---|---|---|---|
| ★ | ★½ | ★★½ | ★★½ | ★★½ | ★★★ |

*Authors' Rating:* Unrestrained free enterprise isn't always pretty. ★★

*How Much Time to Allow:* Anywhere from 5 to 30 minutes.

*Description and Comments*   The three trading floors of the Chicago Board of Trade are housed in a 45-story art deco skyscraper that's topped with a 31-foot statue of Ceres, the Roman goddess of grain and harvest. Standing in tiered octagonal wooden pits, traders use the "open outcry" method of buying and selling. The result is a controlled form of chaos as traders shout, gesture, jump, and signal. Is this any way to run an economy? Then again, who can argue with success?

In February 1997, the Board of Trade unveiled its new 60,000-square-foot, $182 million financial trading floor. A new visitor center opened in mid-1997, allowing visitors to see the new center for trading bonds and notes. It should be worth a peek: it's large enough to house a 747 jetliner.

*Touring Tips*   A 16-minute film shown in the visitor center theater helps take some of the mystery out of the mayhem. It's informative—and the seats are comfortable. While the action here isn't quite as frantic as what goes on at the Chicago Mercantile Exchange, legend has it that once the action got so crazy in the soybean pit that a trader's leg was broken—and no one noticed until the closing bell ended trading for the day!

*Other Things To Do Nearby*   The Sears Tower is a few blocks west on Jackson Boulevard; the Mies van der Rohe–designed Federal Center and a famous, untitled sculpture by Picasso are a block east and a block north.

## Chicago Cultural Center

*Type of Attraction:*  A huge neoclassical structure containing the Museum of Broadcast Communications, eclectic art, and a free visitor information center; a downtown refuge for weary tourists. A self-guided tour.

*Location:*  78 East Washington Street, Chicago, IL 60602

*Admission:*  Free.

*Hours:*  10 a.m. to 7 p.m., Monday through Wednesday; 10 a.m. to 8 p.m., Thursday; 10 a.m. to 6 p.m., Friday; 10 a.m. to 5 p.m., Saturday; and noon to 5 p.m., Sunday. Closed on holidays.

*Phone:*  (312) 346-3278

*When to Go:*  Any time.

*Special Comments:*  Free building tours are offered on Tuesday and Wednesday at 1:30 p.m. and Saturday at 2 p.m.

*Overall Appeal by Age Group:*

| Pre-school | Grade School | Teens | Young Adults | Over 30 | Senior Citizens |
|---|---|---|---|---|---|
| ★½ | ★★ | ★★½ | ★★★½ | ★★★½ | ★★★★ |

*Authors' Rating:*  An impressive building with a little bit of everything. ★★★½

*How Much Time to Allow:*  One hour for a quick run through. Because of its convenient location and free admission, plan to stop here throughout your visit.

*Description and Comments*    The nation's first free municipal cultural center served as Chicago's central library for nearly 100 years. Today it dispenses culture the way it once loaned books. Highlights of the building are spectacular stained-glass domes located in the north and south wings, which originally served as skylights. They were later enclosed in copper and backlighted to fully reveal and protect their beauty; the 38-foot dome in Preston Hall is thought to be the world's largest Tiffany dome, with a value estimated at $38 million. Preston Bradley Hall was renovated in the '70s into a performance hall and hosts free weekly classical music concerts; the G.A.R. Rotunda and Memorial Hall will intrigue Civil War buffs.

First-time visitors to Chicago should take advantage of the Visitor Information Center in the main lobby and the Welcome Center, which provides orientation to the city and downtown. The coffee bar can inject a caffeine boost and is a place to give respite to weary feet; a number of nearby corridors serve as art galleries showcasing established and emerging artists.

The Grand Staircase features multicolored mosaics set in the balustrades, while the fourth floor of the Cultural Center boasts nearly 13,000 square feet of art exhibition space. The Museum of Broadcast Communications is located on the Washington Street side of the building (see page 282).

*Touring Tips*   Plan to stop at this prime example of nineteenth-century beaux arts architecture early in your visit; the Visitor Information Center in the lobby dispenses free information and touring advice. Then head up the Grand Staircase to view the Tiffany stained-glass dome on the third floor. From there, walk to the fourth-floor exhibition hall to see what's on display. Then take a peek into Preston Bradley Hall; it's a beautiful room.

*Other Things To Do Nearby*   The Art Institute of Chicago is two blocks south on Michigan Avenue; the Loop is a block to the west. Directly across from the Art Institute on South Michigan Avenue is the Chicago Architecture Foundation, the starting point of not-to-be-missed daily walking tours of the Loop. For a great view, walk three blocks north to the Michigan Avenue Bridge and look up.

## Chicago Mercantile Exchange

*Type of Attraction:*   Uninhibited capitalism as traders shout and gesticulate to buy and sell futures and options contracts. A self-guided tour.

*Location:*   30 South Wacker Drive, Chicago, IL 60606

*Admission:*   Free.

*Hours:*   Lower (fourth-floor) trading floor: 8 a.m. to 3:15 p.m., Monday through Friday. Upper (eighth-floor) trading floor: 7:15 a.m. to 2 p.m., Monday through Friday. Closed Saturdays and Sundays and on major holidays.

*Phone:*   (312) 930-8249

*When to Go:*   Any time.

*Special Comments:*   The fourth-floor visitors gallery features an array of interactive videos that give budding futures traders insight into the trading frenzy.

*Overall Appeal by Age Group:*

| Pre-school | Grade School | Teens | Young Adults | Over 30 | Senior Citizens |
|---|---|---|---|---|---|
| ★ | ★½ | ★★ | ★★½ | ★★½ | ★★½ |

*Authors' Rating:*   Bizarre—and strangely fascinating. ★★

*How Much Time to Allow:*   Depending on your appetite for watching unrestrained capitalism in action, anywhere from 5 to 30 minutes.

*Description and Comments*   This is where agricultural commodities (such as pork bellies), foreign currency, interest rates, stock market indices, and gold are traded in separate pits by traders using the "open outcry" method: otherwise normal-looking men and women jump, shout, and wave their arms to get a seller's attention. Visitors see it all through plate-glass windows that overlook the trading floor. Frantic? You bet. More than a million contracts are traded daily at the Merc, which bills itself as "the world's largest marketplace."

*Touring Tips*   Go to the fourth-floor (lower) gallery first, where you can get an explanation of what's going on down on the trading floor; the upper gallery on the eighth floor provides more of an eye-level view of the action. Visitors entering the lobby from Wacker Drive will find the elevators to the visitor galleries to the right.

*Other Things To Do Nearby*   The Sears Tower Skydeck is a block south and 1,300 feet above Wacker Drive. The ground floor of the Merc has a food court; if the weather's nice, grab a table outside and eat lunch overlooking the Chicago River. Wave to the schoolchildren as the tour boats glide by and watch the trains across the river pulling in and out of Union Station. Oddly enough, the tracks are *below* Canal Street on the opposite shore; Chicago streets are elevated.

## Harold Washington Library Center

*Type of Attraction:*  The world's second-largest public library (after the British Library in London). Guided and self-guided tours.

*Location:*  400 South State Street, Chicago, IL 60605

*Admission:*  Free.

*Hours:*  9 a.m. to 7 p.m., Mondays; 11 a.m. to 7 p.m., Tuesday and Thursday; 9 a.m. to 5 p.m., Wednesday, Friday, and Saturday; 1 to 5 p.m., Sunday.

*Phone:*  (312) 747-4999

*When to Go:*  Any time.

*Special Comments:*  The library isn't very visitor-friendly: From the enclosed lobby on the first floor, take the escalators to the third floor, which serves as the main entrance to the library proper. From there, elevators and escalators provide access to the other seven levels. Conversely, to leave the building you must return to the third floor and take the escalators down to the exit level (elevators are available for handicapped folks). What a pain.

*Overall Appeal by Age Group:*

| Pre-school | Grade School | Teens | Young Adults | Over 30 | Senior Citizens |
|------------|--------------|-------|--------------|---------|-----------------|
| ★ | ★★ | ★★ | ★★½ | ★★½ | ★★½ |

*Authors' Rating:* While a trip to the library isn't on most travel itineraries, consider making an exception in Chicago. It's definitely worth a stop. ★★★

*How Much Time to Allow:* One hour; consider joining a free public tour beginning at noon or 2 p.m., Monday through Saturday. The guided tour lasts an hour and starts in the third-floor Orientation Theater.

*Description and Comments* This neoclassical building with elements of beaux arts, classical, and modern ornamentation opened in 1991 and cost $144 million. Named after the late Chicago mayor (a notorious book-worm), the 750,000-square-foot Harold Washington Library Center serves as the Loop's southern gateway.

Inside are housed more than two million volumes; an electronic directory system that displays floor layouts, book locations, and upcoming events; a computerized reference system; more than 70 miles of shelving; banks of computers and printers; a permanent collection of art spread over ten floors; and lots of nooks for curling up with a book.

*Touring Tips* Several not-to-be-missed attractions include the ninth-floor, glass-enclosed Winter Garden; the Harold Washington Collection (an exhibit located next to the Winter Garden); and the Jazz, Blues, Gospel Hall of Fame (eighth floor).

Folks with the time and interest should visit the eighth-floor Listening/Viewing Center, where patrons can watch videos and listen to music from the collection's 100,000 78 rpm records, LPs, and compact discs. Selections are particularly plentiful in popular music, jazz, and blues. Hours are noon to 4 p.m., Monday and Saturday; noon to 6 p.m., Tuesday and Thursday; 10 a.m. to 4 p.m., Wednesday and Friday; closed Sundays. You don't have to be a Chicago resident to take advantage of the free service, although all patrons are limited to one session per day; there is a one-hour time limit if other people are waiting. Since the Center relies on a large array of electronics, it's often closed for maintenance; call (312) 747-4850 before going.

In addition, the library presents a wide range of special events throughout the year, including films, dance programs, lectures, storytelling sessions for children, concerts, special programs for children, art exhibits, and more. See the Chicago *Reader* (a free "alternative" paper) to find out what's happening during your visit.

*Other Things To Do Nearby*   The Loop is a block to the north; hang a right to head toward Grant Park and the Art Institute of Chicago. Turn left at the elevated tracks to reach the Chicago Board of Trade and the Sears Tower. Eating and shopping establishments abound throughout the heart of downtown.

## Hellenic Museum

*Type of Attraction:*  A small museum highlighting the history and contributions of Greek immigrants to American life and culture. A self-guided tour.

*Location:*  National Bank of Greece Building, 168 North Michigan Avenue, Fourth Floor, Chicago, IL 60601

*Admission:*  $3

*Hours:*  10 a.m. to 4 p.m., Tuesday through Friday; other times by prior appointment.

*Phone:*  (312) 726-1234

*When to Go:*  Any time.

*Special Comments:*  Long-term plans are to relocate the museum to larger quarters in Greektown, west of the Loop on Halsted Street.

*Author's Rating:*  Interesting, if narrow, slice of American immigrant history and culture. Worth a peek. ★★

*How Much Time to Allow:*  30 minutes to an hour.

*Description and Comments*   Greece is the major source of Western culture—and Greek immigrants' contributions to American life are the focus of this one-room museum located on North Michigan Avenue. The museum features temporary shows, such as a recent exhibit on Greek American soldiers who fought for their country from the Spanish-American War to the Gulf War.

*Touring Tips*   The small bookstore has a wide array of books on Greek history and culture.

*Other Things to Do Nearby*   The Art Institute of Chicago and the Loop are close, as is the Spertus Museum. Grant Park is a block east and the Chicago Cultural Center offers art and touring information, as well as a coffee shop.

## Jane Addams Hull House Museum

*Type of Attraction:* The restored 1856 country home that became the nucleus of the world-famous settlement house complex founded by Jane Addams (a Nobel Peace Prize winner) at the end of the nineteenth century. A self-guided tour.

*Location:* 800 South Halsted Street, on the campus of the University of Illinois at Chicago.

*Admission:* Free.

*Hours:* 10 a.m. to 4 p.m. weekdays; noon to 5 p.m., Sunday. Closed Saturdays.

*Phone:* (312) 413-5353

*When to Go:* Any time.

*Special Comments:* Park across the street in the University of Illinois parking lot.

*Overall Appeal by Age Group:*

| Pre-school | Grade School | Teens | Young Adults | Over 30 | Senior Citizens |
|---|---|---|---|---|---|
| ★ | ★★ | ★★½ | ★★½ | ★★½ | ★★★ |

*Authors' Rating:* An oasis of dignity, this restored museum is all that remains of a once-vibrant ethnic melting pot once served by the Nobel Peace Prize winner. ★★½

*How Much Time to Allow:* One hour.

*Description and Comments*   This square, brick, nineteenth-century house in the shadow of the University of Illinois at Chicago is where Jane Addams and Ellen Gates Starr began the settlement work that helped give immigrants a better shot at the American dream. The lush Victorian interior includes Addams's desk, an old Oliver typewriter, photos of the staff, and several rooms of rich furnishings.

*Touring Tips*   Start your tour upstairs in the Residents' Dining Hall with the 15-minute slide show on the settlement house movement. The tour ends in the restored mansion.

*Other Things To Do Nearby*   Sample some pasta in Little Italy, southwest of the University of Illinois campus. Greektown and more great ethnic dining is north on Halsted, just past the Eisenhower Expressway. The Loop is a few blocks to the northeast.

## Museum of Broadcast Communications

*Type of Attraction:* A look at American culture through broadcasting memorabilia, hands-on exhibits, and public archives of more than 60,000 radio and television programs and commercials. A self-guided tour.

*Location:* In the Chicago Cultural Center, 78 East Washington Street, Chicago, IL 60602 (Washington Street entrance)

*Admission:* Free.

*Hours:* 10 a.m. to 4:30 p.m., Monday through Saturday; noon to 5 p.m., Sunday. Closed on state and national holidays.

*Phone:* (312) 629-6000

*When to Go:* Any time.

*Special Comments:* Hour-long group tours are offered Monday through Friday at 10:30 a.m. and 2:30 p.m. The charge is $2 per person and tours must be scheduled in advance; call (312) 629-6017.

*Overall Appeal by Age Group:*

| Pre-school | Grade School | Teens | Young Adults | Over 30 | Senior Citizens |
|------------|--------------|-------|--------------|---------|-----------------|
| ★★½ | ★★★ | ★★★ | ★★★ | ★★★ | ★★★★½ |

*Authors' Rating:* A small, attractive museum that's heavy on nostalgia. ★★½

*How Much Time to Allow:* 30 minutes to an hour; folks old enough to remember "Fibber McGee and Molly" may want to spend half a day.

*Description and Comments* Chicago hosts a number of national talk shows, so it's only natural it should be home to this small, modern museum dedicated to TV and radio. Among the attractions are a TV exhibit gallery with changing video presentations, a news center that lets visitors play news anchor, two mini-theaters presenting award-winning TV commercials, and the Radio Hall of Fame (with a comprehensive collection of vintage radio sets).

*Touring Tips* In the A.C. Nielsen Jr. Research Center, visitors can see and hear TV and radio programs from the past. The museum's public archives contain 6,000 TV shows, 49,000 radio shows, and 8,000 commercials accessible for screening in 26 study suites (fee charged).

*Other Things To Do Nearby* Explore the rest of the Chicago Cultural Center or stroll down Michigan Avenue to the Art Institute of Chicago. The Loop, featuring plenty of skyscraper gazing, places to eat and shop, and unlimited people-watching, is a block west. Sign up for a Chicago

Architecture Foundation walking tour of the Loop in their shop across from the Art Institute.

## Sears Tower Skydeck

*Type of Attraction:* Spectacular views into four states from the world's third-tallest office building. A self-guided tour with continuous taped narration.

*Location:* 233 South Wacker Drive (enter at Jackson Boulevard)

*Admission:* $8 for adults, $5 for children ages 5–12, $6 for seniors, $20 for families (two adults, three children), and free for military personnel in uniform and children under age 5.

*Hours:* March through September, daily 9 a.m. to 11 p.m.; October through February, daily 9 a.m. to 10 p.m.

*Phone:* (312) 875-9696

*When to Go:* Early or late on weekends and holidays March through November; waits in line for the elevator ride to the top can exceed two hours on busy afternoons. On hot days, go after 6:30 p.m. to avoid the heat and to see the city in sunset or at night. Skip it in inclement weather or when clouds obscure the top of the building.

*Special Comments:* Don't enter the main lobby of the building facing South Wacker Drive; go to the Skydeck entrance on Jackson Boulevard. If the line is long, consider this alternative: the John Hancock Center on North Michigan Avenue. While not quite as high (it's only the *tenth*-highest office building in the world), some people say the view is better . . . and long waits are rare.

*Overall Appeal by Age Group:*

| Pre-school | Grade School | Teens | Young Adults | Over 30 | Senior Citizens |
|---|---|---|---|---|---|
| ★★★★★ | ★★★★★ | ★★★★★ | ★★★★★ | ★★★★★ | ★★★★★ |

*Authors' Rating:* Incredible. Part of the fun is looking down on all those other skyscrapers. ★★★★★

*How Much Time to Allow:* At least 30 minutes once you reach the viewing deck; signs posted at various points in the waiting area in the basement tell you how long you'll stand in line before boarding an elevator.

*Description and Comments*  The distinctive, 110-story Sears Tower (easily identified by its black aluminum skin, towering height, and twin antenna towers) reaches 1,454 feet; the Skydeck on the 103rd floor is 1,353 feet above the ground. It's a 70-second elevator ride to the broad, wide-windowed viewing area, where you're treated to a magnificent 360-degree view of Chicago, Lake Michigan, and the distant horizon.

*Touring Tips*   Enter the building at the Skydeck entrance on Jackson Boulevard; take the elevator *down* to purchase a ticket. Try to visit the tower on a clear day; better yet, go at night when the crowds are thinner and a carpet of sparkling lights spreads into the distance.

*Other Things To Do Nearby*   The Chicago Mercantile Exchange is around the corner on Wacker Drive; after watching the frenzy in the trading pits, go downstairs for something to eat from a wide array of eateries. To view more unrestrained capitalism in action, head south toward the Sears Tower, then east on Jackson Boulevard to the Chicago Board of Trade.

## Spertus Museum of Judaica

*Type of Attraction:* 3,500 years of Jewish history on display, from ceremonial treasures to the Zell Holocaust Memorial. A self-guided tour.

*Location:* 618 South Michigan Avenue, Chicago, IL 60605

*Admission:* $4 for adults; $2 for seniors, children, and students; and $9 for families; free admission on Friday.

*Hours:* 10 a.m. to 5 p.m., Sunday through Thursday; 10 a.m. to 3 p.m., Friday. Closed Saturdays.

*Phone:* (312) 922-9012

*When to Go:* Any time.

*Special Comments:* The permanent collection is located on one floor.

*Overall Appeal by Age Group:*

| Pre-school | Grade School | Teens | Young Adults | Over 30 | Senior Citizens |
|---|---|---|---|---|---|
| ★★ | ★★½ | ★★½ | ★★★ | ★★★ | ★★★½ |

*Authors' Rating:* Small, tasteful, and full of beautiful objects artfully displayed in a modern setting. ★★★

*How Much Time to Allow:* One hour.

*Description and Comments*   The theme of this museum is the survival of the Jewish people as embodied in their art, including Torahs, Torah arks, ceremonial coats, parchment manuscripts, Hanukkah lamps, and tableware, just to name a few of the beautiful items on display. On a more somber note, the Zell Holocaust Memorial recalls the horrors of the concentration camps with heaps of clothing, piles of buttons, and video monitors slowly scrolling through the names of victims.

The Artifact Center, a level down from the museum, is a place where children through age 12 can play archaeologist by digging on a model tel, a mound built up over time by layers of successive human settlement. Other hands-on activities are available in The Marketplace, a group of market stalls where kids can examine objects from ancient Israel. All activities are supervised, so parents can leave the kids for an hour or so and view the permanent exhibits and special shows in the museum. Hours are 1 to 4:30 p.m.

*Touring Tips*    Check at the admission desk to find out what's on display in the second-floor, temporary-exhibit galleries.

*Other Things To Do Nearby*    The Loop, the Art Institute of Chicago, and the Chicago Architecture Foundation are all close.

# Sights: Zone 5—South Loop

## Adler Planetarium

*Type of Attraction:* Narrative Sky Shows in a domed theater, a slide presentation, and exhibits on astronomy and space exploration. A self-guided tour.

*Location:* 1300 South Lake Shore Drive, Chicago, IL 60605

*Admission:* $3 for adults, and $2 for seniors and children ages 4–17; free admission on Tuesdays; $3 for sky show exhibits (all ages).

*Hours:* 9 a.m. to 5 p.m., Monday through Thursday; open until 9 p.m. on Fridays; and open until 6 p.m. on weekends and holidays. Closed Thanksgiving and Christmas Days.

*Phone:* (312) 322-0300

*When to Go:* Any time.

*Special Comments:* The comfortable, high-backed seats in the theater almost guarantee you won't get a stiff neck from watching the star show on the domed ceiling.

*Overall Appeal by Age Group:*

| Pre-school | Grade School | Teens | Young Adults | Over 30 | Senior Citizens |
|---|---|---|---|---|---|
| ★ | ★★★★ | ★★★ | ★★½ | ★★½ | ★★½ |

*Authors' Rating:* Some fascinating stuff on display, but the low-key planetarium show is geared to younger viewers and hard-core space cadets. ★★½

*How Much Time to Allow:*  40 minutes for the show and at least half an hour to view the exhibits.

*Description and Comments*   The Adler Planetarium was the first in the country when it opened in 1930. The 12-sided pink granite building that houses the Sky Theater was funded by a Sears, Roebuck & Company executive who had the Zeiss projector imported from Germany. In addition to the narrated Sky Shows (which change throughout the year), visitors can explore a wide range of exhibits on topics that include telescopes, the planets, man-made satellites, the moon, optics, and navigation. It's a modern, informative place that will delight youngsters and adults who read Carl Sagan. Good news for astronomy buffs: In early 1997 the Adler embarked on a $40 million expansion and renovation program that will add 60,000 square feet of new space. The project is scheduled for completion in 1999.

*Touring Tips*   Enter the building through the glass building that faces the planetarium, not the granite steps. On Friday nights (when the planetarium is open until 9 p.m.) visitors can tour the Doane Observatory and see its 20-inch telescope. Visit the planetarium late in a day of hard sight-seeing; relaxing in a comfortable, high-backed chair for 40 minutes is nirvana, even if you don't give a hoot about the cosmos. The view of the city skyline on the promontory leading to the building is spectacular, especially at sunset when the skyscrapers begin to light up.

*Other Things To Do Nearby*   The John G. Shedd Aquarium and the Field Museum of Natural History are both within easy walking distance on the new, traffic-free Museum Campus. The half-mile promontory is a great place to watch planes taking off from Meigs Field; it's also a popular make-out spot for Chicago couples. Bad news if you're hungry: Getting something to eat beyond a hot dog requires flagging a cab or grabbing a bus downtown.

## American Police Center & Museum

*Type of Attraction:*  A one-room collection of cop memorabilia, equipment, photos, a police memorial, and educational displays. A self-guided tour.

*Location:*  1717 South State Street, Chicago, IL 60616

*Admission:*  $4.50 for adults, $3.50 for seniors, $3 for children ages 3–11.

*Hours:*  9:30 a.m. to 4:30 p.m., Monday through Friday. Closed Saturdays and Sundays.

*Phone:*  (312) 431-0005

*When to Go:*  Any time.

*Special Comments:* While many of the exhibits are geared for younger visitors, some photos of dead criminals and crime victims are gruesome. To get there, take the #29 State Street bus south from the Loop; the museum is on the left.

*Overall Appeal by Age Group:*

| Pre-school | Grade School | Teens | Young Adults | Over 30 | Senior Citizens |
|---|---|---|---|---|---|
| ★★ | ★★★★ | ★★★½ | ★★ | ★★ | ★★ |

*Authors' Rating:* Kids may not care, but the whole place looks run down and tacky. ★½

*How Much Time to Allow:* One hour.

*Description and Comments*   Yes, that's Batman and his pal Superman in the rafters surveying the neighborhood for bad guys. Other, uh, interesting items on display in this large, concrete-block room with a linoleum floor include the seat John Dillinger sat in before his fateful exit from Chicago's Biograph Theater, an electric chair ("The Texas Thunderbolt") actually used to execute criminals in the '20s and '30s, and plenty of grainy black-and-white photos of stiffs. Less interesting—but more upbeat—items include mannequins in cop uniforms, police vehicles, mug shots, drug paraphernalia displays, and a firefighter display.

*Touring Tips*   Don't be shy: take a seat in the electric chair located outside "Gangster Alley," the gangster-era exhibit. (Boy, cops sure like capital punishment.) Folks old enough to remember won't want to miss the propagandistic display on the Yippie-led "Days of Rage" that took place during the 1968 Democratic National Convention. Needless to say, there's no mention of the "police riot" that horrified the world and scared off future conventions for nearly 30 years (the Dems returned in '96).

*Other Things To Do Nearby*   Nothing recommended. The #29 bus will return you to the Loop.

## Field Museum of Natural History

*Type of Attraction:* One of the largest public museums in the United States, with more than nine acres of exhibits. A self-guided tour.

*Location:* East Roosevelt Road at Lake Shore Drive (in Grant Park)

*Admission:* $7 for adults; $4 for seniors, children ages 3–17, and students with ID; Combined admission to "Life over Time" is $2 for adults and $1 for children, in addition to general admission. Free general admission on Wednesdays (but not to the special shows).

*Hours:* 9 a.m. to 5 p.m. daily. Closed Christmas and New Year's Day.

*Phone:* (312) 922-9410

*When to Go:* Any time. "Life over Time," the Field's newest permanent exhibit, gets crowded on summer and weekend afternoons.

*Special Comments:* No rest rooms are available in the "Life over Time" exhibit; the nearest facilities are at the north and south ends of the second floor. If someone in your party needs to make a pit stop while touring the special exhibits, go to the Dinosaur Hall exit and speak to a Visitor Services Representative (in a red jacket).

*Overall Appeal by Age Group:*

| Pre-school | Grade School | Teens | Young Adults | Over 30 | Senior Citizens |
|------------|--------------|-------|--------------|---------|-----------------|
| ★★★★★ | ★★★★★ | ★★★★★ | ★★★★★ | ★★★★★ | ★★★★★ |

*Authors' Rating:* This world-renowned institution draws on more than 20 million artifacts and specimens to fill its exhibits. If you can't find something you like here, it's time to get out of Chicago. ★★★★★

*How Much Time to Allow:* Two hours for a brief run through; all day for a more leisurely exploration—but even then, you won't see it all.

*Descriptions and Comments*    Founded in 1893 to create a permanent home for the natural history collections gathered in Chicago for the World's Columbian Exposition, the Field Museum today is one of the great institutions of its kind in the world, focusing on public learning and scientific study of the world's environments and cultures. For visitors, it's a chance to explore a mind-boggling assortment of the world's wonders.

While much of the museum reflects the Victorian mania for collecting—aisle after aisle of wood-and-glass display cases and dioramas are filled with items from around the world—much of what you find here includes newer, more dynamic exhibits. Many emphasize hands-on fun and thematic exhibits, such as "Africa," "Inside Ancient Egypt," "Into the Wild," "Gems," "Traveling the Pacific," and "Life over Time," a high-tech journey that takes visitors through 3.8 billion years of the history of life.

"Life over Time" is the newest permanent exhibit and picks up where the dinosaur show leaves off. Fossils, dioramas, a nine-foot-tall walk-in reproduction of a hut built of mammoth bones, and videos in the 7,000-square-foot exhibit explore climatic change and mammal evolution during the Ice Age.

*Touring Tips*    Folks with youngsters in tow or with a strong interest in dinosaurs should make their way to the second level to explore "Life over Time." (If it's crowded and you're told to wait until the entry time stamped on your ticket, don't stand in line: explore the rest of the museum and come back.) It's a kid-oriented exhibit that's heavy on education, hands-on science stuff, and TV monitors showing "newscasts" by suit-clad anchors "reporting" on the beginning of life a billion years ago. It all ends up in a huge hall filled with dinosaur fossils and reconstructed skeletons. It's pure bliss for the Barney crowd.

After exploring the world of dinosaurs and mammoths, check your map and pick something of interest. Here's some help: Tots will enjoy the play area on the second floor, while older folks can check out exhibits of gems and jades also on the second floor. The popular Egyptian tomb (complete with mummies) is on the first floor, as are exhibits on Native Americans, Africa, birds, reptiles, a re-creation of a wilderness, and a "nature" walk. The ground floor features places to grab a bite to eat and exhibits on bushmen, sea mammals, prehistoric people, and ancient Egypt.

*Other Things To Do Nearby*   The Shedd Aquarium and Adler Planetarium are both within easy walking distance on the new, traffic-free Museum Campus. Fast food is available inside the museum, but anything else requires taking a cab or bus downtown.

## John G. Shedd Aquarium

*Type of Attraction:*  The world's largest indoor aquarium; the Oceanarium, the world's largest indoor marine mammal facility, re-creates a Pacific Northwest coastline. A self-guided tour.

*Location:*  1200 South Lake Shore Drive

*Admission:*  Aquarium and Oceanarium: $11 for adults, $9 for seniors and children ages 3–11. Aquarium only: $5 for adults, $4 for children and seniors. Aquarium is free on Thursday.

*Hours:*  9 a.m. to 5 p.m., Monday through Friday (till 6 p.m. in the summer); 9 a.m. to 6 p.m., Saturday and Sunday. Closed Christmas and New Year's Day.

*Phone:*  (312) 939-2438

*When to Go:*  Before noon during the summer and on major holidays. A time-ticket system is in effect for visitors to the extremely popular Oceanarium and tickets are often sold out by 3 p.m.; if you get a ticket, waits of two to three hours are not uncommon on busy days. (If you're waiting, you may tour the aquarium or other nearby attractions.) Try to time your visit to coincide with the aquarium's coral reef feedings—a diver enters the circular 90,000-gallon exhibit and hand-feeds an assortment of tropical fishes; kids love it. Feeding times are 11 a.m. and 2 p.m. weekdays, and 11 a.m., 2 p.m., and 3 p.m. weekends and during the summer.

*Special Comments:*  Three continuous nature slide shows lasting about 30 minutes are featured in the Phelps Auditorium. The seats are comfortable, and it's a great place to chill out when crowds are heavy.

*Overall Appeal by Age Group:*

| Pre-school | Grade School | Teens | Young Adults | Over 30 | Senior Citizens |
|---|---|---|---|---|---|
| ★★★★★ | ★★★★★ | ★★★★★ | ★★★★★ | ★★★★★ | ★★★★★ |

*Authors' Rating:*  Whales breaching the surface with Lake Michigan in the background is an unforgettable sight. ★★★★★

*How Much Time to Allow:*  Two hours.

*Description and Comments*  Not only does the Shedd Aquarium house more than 6,000 aquatic animals, the building itself is an architectural marvel, featuring majestic doorways, colorful mosaics, and wave and shell patterns on the walls. For most folks, however, the highlight of a visit is the Oceanarium, which treats visitors to a wide array of sea mammals—both from the surface and underwater through glass windows. The huge exhibit, which features a Lake Michigan backdrop, is new and spiffy.

In the aquarium, cool and dark rooms are lined with tanks filled with a wide assortment of creatures, including a huge alligator snapping turtle, electric eels, piranhas, and an especially creepy-looking green moray eel (which, we're sad to report, is actually blue; its skin appears green because it's coated with thick yellow mucus—yuck).

*Touring Tips*  Purchase a ticket that includes admission to the Oceanarium; from the foyer, head left around the circular Coral Reef Exhibit to the entrance. After touring both levels of the sea mammal emporium, return to the aquarium for a leisurely stroll past the many tanks; don't forget about the feedings in the coral reef (see above for times).

*Other Things To Do Nearby*  The Adler Planetarium and the Field Museum of Natural History are both within walking distance on the new, traffic-free Museum Campus. If it's late in the afternoon and the sun's about to set, stick around; the Chicago skyline is about to do its nighttime thing. It's a view you won't soon forget. For something to eat beyond a hot dog, grab a taxi or bus to downtown.

## National Vietnam Veterans Art Museum

*Type of Attraction:*  An art museum featuring more than 500 works of art (paintings, sculpture, and photographs) created by combat veterans from all nations that fought in the Vietnam War. A self-guided tour.

*Location:* 1801 South Indiana Avenue, Chicago, IL 60616 (in the Prairie Avenue Historic District)

*Admission:* $4 for adults, $2 for children under age 16.

*Hours:* 11 a.m. to 6 p.m., Tuesday, Thursday, and Friday; 11 a.m. to 9 p.m., Wednesday; 10 a.m. to 5 p.m., Saturday; noon to 5 p.m., Sunday. Closed Mondays and major holidays.

*Phone:* (312) 326-0270

*When to go:* Any time.

*Special Comments:* The museum is off the beaten tourist path; if you don't have a car, consider public transportation. From Michigan Avenue, take the #3 or #4 bus south to 18th Street, then walk a block east (toward Lake Michigan) to the museum.

*Overall Appeal by Age Group:*

| Pre-school | Grade School | Teens | Young Adults | Over 30 | Senior Citizens |
|------------|--------------|-------|--------------|---------|-----------------|
| ★ | ★ | ★½ | ★★ | ★★★ | ★★★ |

*Authors' Rating:* Spartan and grim—and a potentially wrenching experience for anyone who served in Vietnam, lost a friend or relative in the war, or is old enough to remember the conflict. ★★★

*How Much Time to Allow:* One to two hours.

*Description and Comments*    Opened in a renovated industrial space in August 1996, this museum—the only one of its kind—is filled with disturbing images of a conflict many Americans would rather forget. But the 95 artists who created the 500 works on display can't forget; they all pulled combat duty in Vietnam, and their work is visceral and gut-wrenching. Images of death and dying are a recurrent theme, as are shredded American flags, bombs with dollar bills as fins, a painting of LBJ with an American flag shirt and tie, a GI strung to a post by barbed wire (titled "Waiting for Kissinger"), and a wide array of weapons and artillery displayed as works of art (including a Viet Cong 122mm rocket launcher sitting in front of a painting titled "Rocket Attack"). The bare concrete floors and exposed piping and air ducts add to the no-nonsense, serious tenor of the gallery.

*Touring Tips*    Be warned: A visit to this museum is no stroll in the park— it's relentlessly grim and powerful. A good way to start a tour is in the small multimedia theater on the first floor, which continuously shows slide images of the war through the eyes of the soldiers. Many of the images reappear later in the art on display.

*Other Things To Do Nearby*    Next door are the Prairie Avenue House Museums, two historic houses that provide visitors a glimpse into Chicago's prairie heritage and later Victorian splendor. Docent-guided tours are offered Wednesday through Sunday, noon to 4 p.m.; the cost is $8 for adults and $6 for students and seniors. For more information call (312) 326-1480.

# Sights: Zone 6—South Central/Midway

## Balzekas Museum of Lithuanian Culture

*Type of Attraction:* An eclectic collection of exhibits on Lithuanian history and culture. A self-guided tour.

*Location:* 6500 South Pulaski Road, Chicago, IL 60629

*Admission:* $4 for adults, $3 for seniors and students, and $1 for children; free admission on Mondays.

*Hours:* 10 a.m. to 4 p.m. daily; open until 8 p.m. Friday. Closed Thanksgiving, Christmas, and New Year's Day.

*Phone:* (312) 582-6500

*When to Go:* Any time.

*Special Comments:* Call in advance for information on special exhibits and programs. All exhibits are located on the ground floor.

*Overall Appeal by Age Group:*

| Pre-school | Grade School | Teens | Young Adults | Over 30 | Senior Citizens |
|---|---|---|---|---|---|
| ★½ | ★★ | ★★ | ★★ | ★★ | ★★½ |

*Authors' Rating:* Although there's some interesting stuff here, it's a small museum that lacks coherence. ★★

*How Much Time to Allow:* 30 minutes to an hour.

*Description and Comments*  Inside this small museum you'll find items ranging from a suit of armor to press clippings from World War II—and everything in between: old photos of immigrants, folk art (including dolls, toys, leather items, wooden household utensils), photos of rural Lithuania, genealogical information, a playroom for children (with a poster depicting the ancient kings of Lithuania), glass cases full of old prayer books, swords, rare books, jewelry, native costumes, coins, stamps. . . . There's a lot on display here, but it's all in a jumble.

*Touring Tips*  Visitors can watch a short video about Lithuania that primes them for a tour of the museum.

*Other Things To Do Nearby*  Not much. If you're flying in or out of Midway, it's only a few blocks away. Oak Park, the hometown of Frank Lloyd

Wright and Ernest Hemingway, is about five miles to the north, just off the Eisenhower Expressway (I-290).

## Mexican Fine Arts Center Museum

*Type of Attraction:* The only Mexican museum in the Midwest features temporary exhibits by local, national, and international artists. A self-guided tour.

*Location:* 1852 West 19th Street, Chicago, IL 60608

*Admission:* Free.

*Hours:* 10 a.m. to 5 p.m., Tuesday through Sunday. Closed Mondays.

*Phone:* (312) 738-1503

*When to Go:* Any time.

*Special Comments:* All the exhibition space is on one level.

*Overall Appeal by Age Group:* All the exhibits are temporary, so it's not possible to rate the museum by age group.

*Authors' Rating:* Because the museum only displays temporary exhibits, it's not possible to give a rating. The galleries are attractive and well lighted; the Day of the Dead exhibit shown during my visit was an entertaining collection of colorful, funny, and bizarre folk art.

*How Much Time to Allow:* One hour.

*Description and Comments* In addition to changing exhibits by Hispanic artists, the Mexican Fine Arts Center Museum presents an ongoing series of readings, performances, and lectures. To see what's going on during your visit, pick up a free copy of the Chicago *Reader.*

*Touring Tips* The large gift shop offers an extensive selection of Mexican items such as handicrafts, posters, toys, and books.

*Other Things To Do Nearby* Pilsen, located along 18th Street between Canal and Damen Streets, is a thriving Hispanic neighborhood with signs in Spanish and lots of spicy smells (good ethnic eateries, too). The Jane Addams Hull House Museum is about two miles northeast of the museum on Halsted Street (at the University of Illinois at Chicago).

# Sights: Zone 7—South Side

## DuSable Museum of African-American History

*Type of Attraction:* A collection of artifacts, paintings, and photos that trace the black experience in the United States. A self-guided tour.

*Location:* 740 East 56th Place (57th Street and Cottage Avenue near the eastern edge of the University of Chicago), Chicago, IL 60637

*Admission:* $3 for adults, $2 for students, $1 for children ages 6–12; free admission on Sunday.

*Hours:* 10 a.m. to 5 p.m., Monday through Saturday; noon to 5 p.m., Sunday.

*Phone:* (773) 947-0600

*When to Go:* Any time.

*Special Comments:* The large main-floor gallery hosts temporary exhibits; check the Chicago *Reader* or call before visiting to find out what's on display.

*Overall Appeal by Age Group:*

| Pre-school | Grade School | Teens | Young Adults | Over 30 | Senior Citizens |
|------------|--------------|-------|--------------|---------|-----------------|
| ★½ | ★★½ | ★★★ | ★★★½ | ★★★★ | ★★★★ |

*Authors' Rating:* Fascinating stuff, including, on my visit, an eye-opening show on the everyday lives of slaves in the antebellum South. ★★★½

*How Much Time to Allow:* One to two hours.

*Description and Comments*　This museum, which once served as a park administration building and a police lockup, is named after Jean Baptist Pointe du Sable, a Haitian of mixed African and European descent who was Chicago's first permanent settler in the late eighteenth century. Exhibits include paintings by African Americans, displays that vividly portray the lives of blacks in pre–Civil War days, and a room dedicated to black hero Joe Louis.

*Touring Tips*　Paintings are located on the lower level, while temporary exhibits are displayed upstairs along with two small permanent exhibits on segregation (look for the sign, "For White Passengers") and on boxing champ Joe Louis. Avoid weekday mornings, when large school groups schedule visits; Thursdays, when admission is free, are also crowded. The gift shop features jewelry, fabrics, and arts and crafts created by African Americans.

*Other Things To Do Nearby*　Outside the DuSable Museum the beautiful lawns of Washington Park beckon in nice weather. The nearby University of Chicago campus is a great place to stroll; places to visit include the Oriental Institute Museum and the Smart Museum of Art. The immense Museum of Science and Industry is on 57th Street. Valois, a cafeteria where locals hang out, is located at 1518 East 53rd Street. Don't venture too far from the campus, though; it's only a marginally safe neighborhood.

## Museum of Science and Industry

*Type of Attraction:* 14 acres of museum space housing more than 2,000 wide-ranging exhibits (many of them hands-on), an Omnimax Theater, the Henry Crown Space Center, and a replica of a coal mine. A self-guided tour.

*Location:* 57th Street and Lake Shore Drive, Chicago, IL 60637

*Admission:* Museum only: $7 for adults, $6 for seniors, and $3.50 for children ages 3–11. Combination tickets for the museum and the Omnimax Theater are $11 for adults, $9 for seniors, and $6.50 for children. Tickets for the Omnimax only are $7 for adults, $6 for seniors, and $5 for children. Admission to the museum (but not the Omnimax Theater) is free on Thursdays.

*Hours:* 9:30 a.m. to 5:30 p.m. daily from Memorial Day through Labor Day and during holidays; 9:30 a.m. to 4 p.m., Monday through Friday, and 9:30 a.m. to 5:30 p.m. on weekends and holidays the rest of the year. Closed Christmas Day.

*Phone:* (773) 684-1414

*When to Go:* Monday through Wednesday are the least crowded days, while Thursday, when admission is free, attracts the most visitors. Weekends are usually packed, but Sundays are generally less crowded than Saturdays.

*Special Comments:* Expect to get lost (well, disoriented) while exploring this immense—and often bewildering—museum. The public address system, by the way, is reserved for summoning the parents of lost children.

*Overall Appeal by Age Group:*

| Pre-school | Grade School | Teens | Young Adults | Over 30 | Senior Citizens |
|---|---|---|---|---|---|
| ★★★★★ | ★★★★★ | ★★★★★ | ★★★★★ | ★★★★★ | ★★★★★ |

*Authors' Rating:* Can there be too much of a good thing? Probably not, but this huge place comes close. Anyway, you'll find one full-sized wonder after another, plus plenty of hands-on fun that makes other museums seem boring by comparison. ★★★★★

*How Much Time to Allow:* Even a full day isn't enough time to explore the museum in depth. First-time visitors should figure on spending at least half a day and plan to come back.

*Description and Comments*   It might be easier to catalog what you *won't* find in this mega-museum, which once held the distinction of being the second-most-visited museum in the world (after the National Air and Space Museum in Washington, D.C.) before it started charging admission in 1991. Even with its rather steep admission price, the place still attracts nearly two million visitors a year.

Full-size exhibits include a real Boeing 727 jetliner, a Coast Guard helicopter, World War II German fighter planes—all suspended from the ceiling; the Apollo 8 command module that circled the moon in 1968; a mock-up of a human heart you can walk through; exhibits on basic science and, of all things, plumbing; and re-creations of nineteenth-century living rooms. Visitors can also thrill to a film in the domed Omnimax Theater, which boasts a five-story, 76-foot diameter screen and a 72-speaker, 20,000-watt sound system. It's like nothing at your local mall.

*Touring Tips*    Unless you've got all day and feet of steel, do some homework. Grab a map at the entrance and make a short list of must-see attractions. Just make sure you walk past the information booth to the Rotunda and the eye-popping view of that 727 docked at the balcony overlooking the main floor.

To get to the Henry Crown Space Center and the Omnimax Theater, walk through the Food for Life exhibit near the main entrance and descend to the ground floor near the U.S. Navy exhibit. The space exhibit features lunar modules, moon rocks, and a mock-up of a space shuttle. Nearby is U-505, a German submarine captured on June 4, 1944; on busy days the wait to tour the interior can last an hour.

At "Navy: Technology at Sea," kids can man the helm of a war ship. Other exhibits include antique cars, bicycles, historic locomotives, computers, an energy lab, dolls, architecture. . . . The list goes on and on and on.

*Other Things To Do Nearby*    The University of Chicago campus is full of beautiful buildings and interesting museums that offer a nice contrast to the hectic—and sometimes confusing—Museum of Science and Industry. It's a short walk from the museum. For a bite to eat, join the locals at Valois (1518 East 53rd Street), a cafeteria frequented by cops, cab drivers, and students.

## Oriental Institute Museum

*Type of Attraction:*  A showcase for the history, art, and archaeology of the ancient Near East. A self-guided tour.

*Location:*  1155 East 58th Street (on the campus of the University of Chicago), Chicago, IL 60637

*Admission:*  Free.

*Hours:* 10 a.m. to 4 p.m., Tuesday, Thursday, Friday, and Saturday; open until 8:30 p.m., Wednesday; noon to 4 p.m., Sunday. Closed Mondays, Independence Day, Thanksgiving, Christmas, and New Year's Day.

*Phone:* (773) 702-9521

*When to Go:* Any time.

*Special Comments:* As we go to press, the Oriental Institute Museum is closed and undergoing an $11 million renovation. New exhibits will include artifacts from the Nile Valley and the ancient Near East, as well as a reconstruction of part of the palace of an Assyrian king dominated by a 40-ton winged bull. Other new goodies on display when the museum reopens include a 17-foot-tall statue of King Tut and a jar and fragment of the Dead Sea Scrolls. Note: The Suq, the museum's gift shop, remains open while renovations are underway.

*Overall Appeal by Age Group:*

| Pre-school | Grade School | Teens | Young Adults | Over 30 | Senior Citizens |
|---|---|---|---|---|---|
| ★★ | ★★★ | ★★★★ | ★★★★ | ★★★★ | ★★★★ |

*Authors' Rating:* An often-overlooked gem that shouldn't be missed.
★★★★

*How Much Time to Allow:* One to two hours.

*Description and Comments*   Most of the artifacts displayed in this stunning collection are treasures recovered from expeditions to Iraq (Mesopotamia), Iran (Persia), Turkey, Syria, and Palestine. The University of Chicago's Oriental Institute has conducted research and archaeological digs in the Near East since 1919 and since 1931 has displayed much of its collection in this impressive building. Items date from 9000 B.C. to the tenth century A.D. and include papyrus scrolls, mummies, everyday items from the ancient past, and gigantic stone edifices.

*Touring Tips*   Not-to-be-missed artifacts on display include a cast of the Rosetta Stone (195 B.C.), which provided the key for unlocking the meaning of Egyptian hieroglyphics; huge, wall-sized Assyrian reliefs; a striding lion from ancient Babylon that once decorated a gateway; a colossal, ten-ton bull's head from Persepolis (a Persian city destroyed by Alexander the Great in 331 B.C.), and a 13-foot-high statue of King Tut. The museum is a real find for archaeology buffs and anyone interested in ancient history. It's safe to say the current renovation will make it even better.

*Other Things To Do Nearby*   The Du Sable Museum, the Smart Museum of Art, and the rest of the University of Chicago campus are all close—and well worth exploring. The huge Museum of Science and Industry is on 57th Street. For lunch, try Valois, a cafeteria hangout for local gendarmes and residents located at 1518 East 53rd Street.

## David and Alfred Smart Museum of Art

*Type of Attraction:*  A collection of art objects spanning five millennia, including works by Albrecht Dürer, August Rodin, Frank Lloyd Wright, Walker Evans, and Mark Rothko. A self-guided tour.

*Location:*  5550 South Greenwood Avenue (on the University of Chicago campus), Chicago, IL 60637

*Admission:*  Free.

*Hours:*  10 a.m. to 4 p.m., Tuesday through Friday; noon to 6 p.m. on weekends. Closed Mondays and holidays.

*Phone:*  (312) 702-0200

*When to Go:*  Any time.

*Special Comments:*  All the galleries are on one level and are wheelchair accessible. Free parking is available in the lot on the corner of 55th Street and Greenwood Avenue on weekends.

*Overall Appeal by Age Group:*

| Pre-school | Grade School | Teens | Young Adults | Over 30 | Senior Citizens |
|---|---|---|---|---|---|
| ★ | ★★ | ★★½ | ★★★ | ★★★ | ★★★ |

*Authors' Rating:*  A sparkling white series of rooms featuring an eclectic array of art; you're sure to find something you like. ★★★

*How Much Time to Allow:*  One to two hours.

*Description and Comments*   The art on display in this recently renovated gallery ranges from the ancient Greek to outrageous modern works culled from its permanent collection of more than 7,000 objects. In addition, the museum schedules eight special exhibitions each year. The feel of the place, like the campus around it, is serious, cerebral, and highbrow.

*Touring Tips*   Don't miss the furniture on display designed by Frank Lloyd Wright, "Dining Table and Six Chairs," a prime example of the Chicago architect's spare, modern style. (And you thought the Wizard of Oak Park only designed houses you can't afford.) The Smart, a museum named for the founders of *Esquire* magazine, is a compact and easy gallery to explore. The bookstore features art books, posters, cards, children's books, and jewelry.

*Other Things To Do Nearby*  The Oriental Institute Museum and the Du-Sable Museum are close. If the weather is nice, stroll the beautiful University of Chicago campus; look for the Henry Moore sculpture (placed on the site of the first self-sustaining nuclear reaction on December 2, 1942) across from the Enrico Fermi Institute. The massive Museum of Science and Industry is on 57th Street. Join the locals for lunch at Valois, located at 1518 East 53rd Street.

# Sights: Zone 8—Southern Suburbs

## Brookfield Zoo

*Type of Attraction:*  A zoo featuring 2,500 animals and more than 400 species spread throughout 215 acres of naturalistic habitat. A self-guided tour.

*Location:*  First Avenue and 31st Street in Brookfield (14 miles west of the Loop). By car, take I-55 (Stevenson Expressway), I-290 (Eisenhower Expressway), or I-294 (Tri-State Tollway) and watch for signs. By train, take the Burlington/Metra Northern Line to the Zoo Stop at the Hollywood Station. For information on reaching the zoo by bus, call (312) 836-7000 (city) or (800) 972-7000 (suburbs).

*Admission:*  $6 for adults and $3 for seniors and children ages 3–11. Parking is $4. Admission is half-price on Tuesday and Thursday during April through September, and free on Tuesday and Thursday during October through March; parking remains the same price.

*Hours:*  9:30 a.m. to 5:30 p.m., Memorial Day through Labor Day; 10 a.m. to 4:30 p.m. the rest of the year.

*Phone:*  (708) 485-0263

*When to Go:*  On weekdays in the spring and fall, come after 1:30 p.m. to avoid large school groups.

*Special Comments:*  Telecommunications devices for the deaf (TDD) are available in the administration building.

*Overall Appeal by Age Group:*

| Pre-school | Grade School | Teens | Young Adults | Over 30 | Senior Citizens |
|---|---|---|---|---|---|
| ★★★★★ | ★★★★★ | ★★★★ | ★★★★ | ★★★½ | ★★★½ |

*Authors' Rating:*  Widely separated buildings, well-landscaped grounds, and a campus-like setting make for a pleasant (not spectacular) zoo. ★★★½

*How Much Time to Allow:*  Two hours to half a day.

*Description and Comments*   Attractions at this lush, wooded park include bottlenosed dolphins, walruses, re-creations of steamy rainforests featuring exotic animals, and an "African waterhole" populated by giraffes, zebras, and topi antelope. More traditional sights include lions, tigers, snow leopards, reptiles, and elephants. The Australia House features a variety of unusual animals from Down Under.

Although the zoo is spread out, visitors don't necessarily have to hoof it from exhibit to exhibit. Motor Safari, an open-air tram that operates from late spring to early fall, lets you get off and reboard four times along its route; the trams run every 5 to 15 minutes. The fee is $2.50 for adults and $1.50 for seniors and children ages 3–11. In the winter, the deal gets better: The Snowball Express is a free, heated mini-bus that circulates throughout the zoo; flag it down any time and hop aboard.

*Touring Tips*   The most popular exhibits at Brookfield Zoo are the dolphin show at the 2,000-seat Seven Seas Panorama ($2 for adults, $1.50 for children; for show times, check at zoo kiosks or the Seven Seas ticket booth; it's free anytime to watch the sea mammals underwater through plate glass windows), Tropic World (a huge indoor rainforest containing gorillas, monkeys, free-flying tropical birds, waterfalls, rocky streams, and big trees), Habitat Africa (a five-acre savannah that opened in 1993), "The Swamp" (a replica of a Southern cypress swamp), and summertime elephant demos.

First-time visitors can catch a free slide presentation at the Discovery Center that runs every 15 minutes (longer intervals in the winter). Finally, keep a few things in mind when planning a visit to the zoo: the most pleasant weather occurs in the spring and fall, animals are most active in the mornings and late afternoons, and the zoo is least crowded on rainy, chilly days.

*Other Things To Do Nearby*   Oak Park, hometown of Ernest Hemingway and Frank Lloyd Wright, is a few miles east of the Brookfield Zoo on the Eisenhower Expressway. Take I-290 east to Harlem Avenue (Route 43 north), then turn right on Lake Avenue to Forest Avenue and the visitor center. In addition to snack bars in the zoo, fast-food restaurants are on the road linking the zoo and the Eisenhower Expressway.

# Sights: Zone 9—Western Suburbs

## Morton Arboretum

*Type of Attraction:* A 1,500-acre, landscaped outdoor "museum" featuring more than 3,000 kinds of trees, shrubs, and vines from around the world. Guided and self-guided tours.

*Location:* Route 53 (just off I-88) in Lisle, IL (25 miles west of the Loop)

*Admission:* $7 per car; $3 per car on Wednesdays only.

*Hours:* Gates open at 7 a.m. daily and close at 7 p.m. during daylight savings time (or sunset in the winter). On major holidays, the grounds are open, but the buildings are closed.

*Phone:* (630) 719-2400 and (630) 719-2465

*When to Go:* Spring and fall are the most beautiful seasons to visit, although the arboretum is worth a look year-round. May and October weekends are the busiest; come in the morning to avoid the heaviest crowds.

*Special Comments:* If throngs are packing the arboretum during your visit, head for the trails in Maple Woods at the east side of the park; most visitors don't venture far from the visitor center.

*Overall Appeal by Age Group:*

| Pre-school | Grade School | Teens | Young Adults | Over 30 | Senior Citizens |
|---|---|---|---|---|---|
| ★★½ | ★★★ | ★★★ | ★★★½ | ★★★½ | ★★★★ |

*Authors' Rating:* You don't have to be a tree hugger to appreciate this unusual—and beautiful—park. ★★★½

*How Much Time to Allow:* One hour for a scenic drive to half a day to explore by foot.

*Description and Comments*    In 1922 Joy Morton, the man who started the Morton Salt Company, founded this arboretum, a large park honeycombed with 25 miles of trails and 12 miles of one-way roads for car touring. Terrains here include native woodlands, wetlands, and prairie. The visitor center provides information on tours, trails, and places of special interest such as the Plant Clinic, and houses a free library with books and magazines on trees, gardening, landscaping, nature, and other plant-related subjects.

The park, approximately four miles long and a mile wide, is divided into two segments bisected by Route 53; the visitor center is located on the east side. By car or on foot, visitors can explore a wide range of woodlands ranging from Northern Illinois and Western North American forests to collections of trees from Japan, China, the Balkans, and Northeast Asia. Interspersed between the woods are gently rolling hills and lakes.

*Touring Tips*    Driving the 12 miles of roadway takes about 45 minutes without stopping. Good places to park the car and stretch your legs include Lake Marmo on the west side (park in lot P24) and the Maple Woods on the east side (lot P14). Foot trails range from pavement to wood chips, mowed paths, and gravel.

One-hour, open-air tram tours of the grounds are offered spring through fall from the visitor center. In May and October, the busiest months, tours start at 10:45 a.m., noon, 1:15 p.m., and 2:30 p.m. on weekends, and at noon, 1:15 p.m., and 2:30 p.m. weekdays. In June, July, and August, tours are offered at noon and 1:15 p.m. on weekends and Wednesdays. Tickets are $2 per person.

*Other Things To Do Nearby*   Argonne National Laboratory, one of the nation's largest centers of energy research, is about five miles south of the Morton Arboretum. Saturday tours are available and advanced reservations are required; call (630) 252-5562. If you're heading back to Chicago on I-88 to I-290 (the Eisenhower Expressway), both the Brookfield Zoo and Oak Park are convenient stopping-off points.

# Sights: Zone 11—Northern Suburbs

## Chicago Botanic Garden

*Type of Attraction:*  18 formal gardens featuring collections showcasing plants of the Midwest (including plants being tested for their performance in the Chicago area) and native and endangered flora of Illinois. Guided and self-guided tours.

*Location:*  1000 Lake-Cook Road, Glencoe, IL 60022. From Chicago, take Sheridan Road north along Lake Michigan, or I-94 (the Edens Expressway) to Lake-Cook Road. The gardens are about 15 miles north of the Loop.

*Admission:*  Free. Parking is $5 per car on weekdays and $6 on weekends.

*Hours:*  8 a.m. to sunset daily. Closed Christmas Day.

*Phone:*  (847) 835-5440

*When to Go:*  June through August to see the most flowering plants in bloom. Yet staffers say the gardens are gorgeous year-round—and especially after a heavy snowfall. Avoid summer afternoons on weekends, when crowds are at their heaviest; come in the morning and leave by 1 p.m. to miss the worst crowds.

*Special Comments:*  Prohibited activities include bicycling (except on designated bike routes), inline skating, or other sports activities such as Frisbee throwing, skiing, fishing, or skating; collecting plants and flowers; climbing on trees and shrubs; standing or walking in garden beds; and feeding wildlife. No pets are allowed except guide and hearing dogs.

*Overall Appeal by Age Group:*

| Pre-school | Grade School | Teens | Young Adults | Over 30 | Senior Citizens |
|---|---|---|---|---|---|
| ★★★ | ★★★ | ★★★ | ★★★½ | ★★★★ | ★★★★½ |

*Authors' Rating:* A stunning collection of beautifully designed gardens, pathways, ponds and pools, and outdoor sculpture. ★★★★

*How Much Time to Allow:* Half a day.

*Description and Comments*   This living museum is a 300-acre park of gently rolling terrain and water that contains 18 garden areas brimming with plants. Other collections include an herbarium of 5,000 dried plants, rare books, and an art collection of plant-related prints, drawings, sculpture, and decorative objects.

Among the most popular areas are the Japanese, English Walled, Naturalistic, Prairie, and Rose gardens. Linking the formal gardens are paths that wander past lakes, ponds, and greens that are meticulously groomed and provide impressive views. The Orientation Center near the parking lots features an audiovisual presentation, exhibit panels, computers, and a wall map to help visitors plan their visit. Food is available in the Gateway Center, and a picnic area is located between parking lots 1 and 2.

*Touring Tips*   Narrated tram tours lasting 45 minutes are offered year-round. From April through October, the tours depart daily every 30 minutes from 10 a.m. to 3 p.m.; November through March, tours leave at 11 a.m., noon, 1 p.m., and 2 p.m. on weekends only. Tickets are $4 for adults, $3 for seniors, and $2 for children ages 3–15.

If you're short on time and want to see the garden's highlights, cross the footbridge from the Gateway Center and turn left at the Heritage Garden. Then visit the Rose, English Walled, Waterfall, and Japanese gardens.

Combine a visit with a workout: The North Branch Bicycle Trail starts at Caldwell and Devon avenues in Chicago and continues north 20 miles along the North Branch of the Chicago River to the Chicago Botanic Garden. Bring a lunch and eat it at the picnic area between parking lots 1 and 2.

*Other Things To Do Nearby*   Ravinia, the summer home of the Chicago Symphony Orchestra, is on Sheridan Road; it's only a few minutes away. Sheridan Road follows Lake Michigan and is one of the best scenic drives around Chicago. Take a left onto Lake-Cook Road; it becomes Sheridan Road at the third traffic light.

# Part Twelve

# Dining and Restaurants

## Dining in Chicago

Chicago, in my opinion, is the dining mecca of the United States—certainly in terms of ethnic diversity. It's no longer the "Second City." Even a well-known New York critic wrote several years ago that "Chicago was the most exciting city for dining." Most experts agree that it is one of the best places for quality and a wide variety of cuisines. New York, still deemed number one by many, excels in ethnic cuisine as well; however, dining in Chicago is less of a hassle—not as crowded and certainly less costly. This heartland city has not only caught up, but has surpassed most other key cities in the dining arena.

O'Hare International Airport, the busiest airport in the world, provides a port of entry for the best fresh seafood and other products to be flown in regularly from around the globe. In fact, Chicago has a wider assortment of fresh seafood than many coastal cities, although it's in the Midwest. And because Chicago is a key convention town, it features lots of restaurants and hotels for diners demanding the best quality.

At last count, Chicago had just under 6,000 restaurants in the city, and 2,000 of those have liquor licenses. Including Chicago, Cook County has 9,000 food service establishments, according to the Illinois Restaurant Association. No one can give a specific count of restaurants in this vast suburbia. To select just over 90 or so of the best of these was no easy task. The restaurants profiled reflect a balance of cuisines, styles, geographic locations (although most are centrally located), price, and the popular as well as the hidden gems. Numerous fine restaurants are not included here, but that doesn't mean they are unworthy. Some are quite new and need a chance to settle in; others were in the process of change at press time; some will be covered in subsequent editions of this book.

## BURGEONING NEIGHBORHOODS

Particularly hot neighborhoods for new restaurants include:

- River North, with its art galleries and antique shops (**Michael Jordan's Restaurant, Brasserie Jo,** and **Wildfire** are three here)

- the gentrified diagonal Near North Clybourn Corridor (**Goose Island Brewing,** 1800 North Clybourn Avenue, phone (312) 915-0071, makes great seasonal beers and serves appropriate fare). **Bistro Ultra,** 2239 N. Clybourn, phone (773) 529-3300, which opened in 1997, is intimate (55 seats), smartly decorated with fine art Belle Epoque posters on exposed brick walls, and serves some exceptional fare, including bay scallops Provençale, Lake Superior grilled whitefish, and Don Juan's Rack (of lamb). Prices are modest, service is professional, and it's worth seeking out.

- Randolph Market (**Vivo Italian,** phone (312) 733-3379), **Marché** (French/American brasserie, phone (312) 226-8399), and the latest operated by the same owners, **Red Light** (Pan-Asian, especially Chinese and Thai with Malaysian and Vietnamese elements, phone (312) 733-8880), provide a good dining mix. Newer places include **Millenium** (steakhouse with nice outdoor area, phone (312) 455-1400), **Toque** (New American, phone (312) 666-1100, and **Bluepoint** (seafood, phone (312) 207-1222).

- the booming Near West, incorporating the Randolph and Fulton Markets and River West neighborhoods, from Ogden and the United Center stadium anchoring the west to Canal on the east, Madison on the south border and up north to Grand Avenue. Two new hotspots: **Thyme** (French regional/Mediterranean-influenced, phone (312) 226-4300) and **Blackbird** (New American/Country French-influenced, phone (312) 715-0708). **Madison's,** an Italian steakhouse (1330 West Madison Street, phone (312) 455-0099), also has good seafood and a comprehensive wine list.

- Navy Pier's grand opening was in 1995 (**Riva's,** (312) 644-RIVA, the original anchor restaurant there). Several other places have opened since to offer a variety of food choices. In 1997, **Joe's B-Bop Cafe & Jazz Emporium** opened (barbecue-style foods, see profile). In 1998, **Bubba Gump Shrimp Co. Restaurant & Market** (phone (312) 595-5500, specializing in shrimp dishes) opened, fashioned after the hit film *Forrest Gump.*

- Wicker Park/Bucktown, one of the top three artist communities in the United States. One newcomer is **ConFusion,** 1620 North Damen Avenue, phone (773) 772-7100, serving fusion cuisine and offering lovely outdoor garden dining. **Soul Kitchen,** 1576 North Milwaukee Avenue, Bucktown, phone (773) 342-9742, features a fine mix of Soul, Southwestern, Creole, and Caribbean cuisines.

Halsted Street, which was called First Street in earlier times, continues to be "restaurant row" with several good dining spots on the same block, especially north from North Avenue. Printer's Row in the south downtown area developed several years ago and seems well anchored with some stable restaurants. Some restaurants recently opened in Chinatown, and several years ago Greektown got a few new faces. The "Little Saigon" or "New Asia" area at North Argyle Street and Sheridan Road is home to a few good storefront restaurants and ethnic shops. And West Devon Avenue has several special street signs designating its diverse ethnicity: some of the best Indian restaurants are found from 2300–2600 West Devon Avenue, and new ones keep popping up.

The southwest Naperville suburban area has developed in the past several years, and a lot of restaurant activity has recently occurred in the west, north, and northwest suburbs. Except for the bastions of old Italian neighborhoods such as the Heart of Italy (near Midway Airport—see profiles of **Bruna's Ristorante**) and Taylor Street, and several fine restaurants here and there, the South Side is sparse as a dining zone. There are great Italian shops and restaurants on West Harlem Avenue. Highwood (in the North Shore), anchored by generations-old Italian establishments, has diversified (**Gabriel's, Froggy's, Del Rio, Pappagallo's,** and the new **The Bistro** in Highwood) and now supposedly boasts more restaurants per capita than almost any other suburb in the country.

The Rosemont area near O'Hare offers a good assortment of restaurants since many conventions and business meetings are held there. The Westin Hotel O'Hare (6100 North River Road; phone (847) 698-6000) has two good restaurants: **The Benchmark** (bistro-style atmosphere with French influence in dishes) and **The Bakery Cafe** (American cuisine, casual). The Hotel Sofitel (5550 North River Road; phone (847) 678-4488) also has two restaurants: **Chez Colette** (charming French brasserie with a fireplace) and the fine dining **Le Cafe de Paris** (which offers a unique très-French menu with waiter and maître d' speaking only French on Thursday and Friday evenings; reservations requested, (847) 928-6950). For other noteworthy restaurants in this area, see profiles of **Carlucci** (Rosemont) and **Pazzo's Cucina Italiana.** And connoisseurs with cars seeking unusual places with exceptional wine lists will not mind the 30- or 45-minute trips to **1776** in Crystal Lake (take Northwest Tollway to Randall Exchange; phone (815) 356-1776) for unusual regional American food, including Midwestern (lots of game). Also worth the drive are **302 West** in Geneva (phone (630) 232-9302), which features a creative single-page menu and 13-page wine list; **D & J Bistro** (phone (847) 438-8001) in Lake Zurich (mostly French fare); and **Bistro Banlieue** (phone (630) 629-6560) in Lombard (for French/American cuisine). And certainly the well established **Le Vichyssois** (phone (815) 385-8221) in Lakemoor; **Montparnasse** (phone (630) 961-8203) in Naperville; **Carlos'** (phone (847) 432-0770) in Highland Park; and **Le Titi de Paris** (phone (847) 506-0222) in Arlington Heights are four of the best suburban French restaurants. **Tallgrass** (phone (815) 838-5566) in Lockport is a great destination for New French cuisine (two prix fixe menus).

Downtown Chicago amazingly continues to build and develop areas such as Cityfront, Navy Pier, and the North Pier Terminal. Just east of Swissôtel Chicago is a new golf course, Illinois Center Golf, with a cafe. The newly relocated **The Palm,** now in the Swissôtel Chicago, has one of the best views of Navy Pier.

## HOTEL DINING

Hotel dining is better than ever; executive chefs allot large budgets for the best ingredients and can concentrate on their kitchens, unlike the owner-chefs running independent places. Also, since hotels must attract a local clientele to survive and competition is fierce, they've really improved their dining act in the past several years. Hotel dining has become a destination, and it's often complemented by live music in a nearby lounge. In the past several years, many hotels have made their restaurants more casual and affordable.

Examples of luxury hotels with top-notch dining options are The Ritz-Carlton (see profile of **The Dining Room** and **The Cafe**), Four Seasons Hotel (see profile of **Seasons**), The Drake Hotel (see profile of **Cape Cod Room**), The Fairmont Hotel at Grant Park (see profile of **Entre Nous**), and Westin Hotel River North (formerly Hotel Nikko) on the Chicago River (**Celebrity Cafe**). Swissôtel Chicago (phone (312) 565-0565) has a charming **Konditorei** (bakery) and **Cafe Suisse** (serving daily buffet breakfasts and lunches). I also recommend the cuisine at the Omni Ambassador East (see profile of **Pump Room**) and the Hyatt on Printer's Row (see profile of **Prairie**). The Hotel Inter-Continental (phone (312) 944-4100) features the award-winning **Boulevard Restaurant** and the casual **Cafe 525.** The Westin Hotel recently underwent a $6.5 million renovation and enlarged and combined the previous restaurant and bar into **The Chelsea Restaurant and Bar,** an American bistro with innovative American cuisine.

Other noteworthy hotel dining: The Regal Knickerbocker Hotel's new **NIX** (serving fusion cuisine—here it's Asian/American with some southwestern influences); Sutton Place Hotel (see profile of **Brasserie Bellevue**); Midland Hotel (**Ticker Tape Bar & Bistro**); the Palmer House Hilton (**French Quarter** and **The Big Downtown**); Chicago Hilton and Towers (see profile of **Kitty O'Shea's**); Chicago Marriott Downtown (**Allie's Bakery** and **JW's** are being merged into a new bistro interior); Sheraton Chicago Hotel and Towers (**Streeterville**); The Tremont Hotel (**Iron Mike's Grille**); and across the street, the Whitehall Hotel (**Whitehall Place Restaurant**—a bistro with multicultural cuisines and a nice Sunday brunch, and Claridge Hotel (**Foreign Affairs**). And this list is not comprehensive!

## CELEBRITY RESTAURANTS

This is a big sports city, so naturally a few athletes, coaches, and announcers own restaurants. Some, like Ditka's (which was overpriced) and Red Kerr's (which was good), have closed. Others, such as **Harry Caray's** and **Michael Jordan's,** offer good food and service (see profiles). Former Bears Coach Mike Ditka (now in New Orleans) just combined forces with restaurateur Joe Carlucci and opened **Iron Mike's Grille** in The Tremont Hotel (see profile). There are numerous restaurant hangouts around the ballparks, and some of the food service within the parks is noteworthy. Food service at both Comiskey Park, home of the Chicago White Sox, and Wrigley Field, home of the Chicago Cubs, is managed by the Levy Restaurants and is excellent. Entertainment celebrities, political figures, and other VIPs have their favored haunts as well, and many are included in this guide. **The Pump Room, Cape Cod Room,** and **Spiaggia** are just three examples. A longtime standby is **Eli's, The Place for Steak** (see profile).

## NEW-AGE CUISINE

Food is more enlightened today—lighter, with flavoring coming from fresh herbs, spices, infused oils, vinaigrettes, and wines, and from healthful cooking methods like grilling, flattop grilling, and roasting in woodburning ovens. Sure, restaurant icons still offer some old-guard, flourthickened sauces with cream and butter, but they are usually enjoyed only occasionally. Most day-to-day eating is geared to feeling fine, and that means lower fat (less meat and fried fare), higher carbohydrates (grains, veggies, and fruit), and less sodium and sugar. New-age cuisine leans in the direction of natural foods, chemical-free ingredients, and more vegetarian fare. Chefs proudly promote vegetarian specialties and menus, and more business men and women are ordering these items for lunch with mineral water instead of the steaks and martinis they downed years ago. However, history repeats itself, and we're seeing a comeback of steak places and martini bars, touting their special flavors and concoctions that sell for a whopping $6–9 a drink!

## NEW-AGE DINING STYLE

There is a tendency for restaurant interiors to be casual and homey these days, bringing some comfort and a nurturing environment to our dining-out experiences—much needed in our fast-paced, high-stress lives. Food at such places is appropriately simple and home-style.

Smoking recently has become a more important health and social issue, and in Chicago all restaurants must set aside a minimum of 30% of their active dining room for nonsmokers. Restaurants that wish to establish larger nonsmoking sections have the option of certifying a minimum of 50% of their space as nonsmoking. Once a minimum is decided upon, it must be maintained until the next license renewal. Establishments may also select to be 100% smoke-free, and several enlightened owners have banned smoke from their places. The designated nonsmoking area must be contiguous. Bars and meeting rooms for private functions are exempt. Sign postings with specific wording designated by the city are required.

## TRENDS

Stir-fry and flattop grill places are a rage and spreading like wildfire in both the city and suburbs. The magical formula tends to be: the customer selects items from a vast raw buffet of vegetables, meats, poultry, seafood, and sauces, and combines them in a bowl. The contents of the coded bowl are then cooked by the staff for all to watch, and within minutes the dish is ready to eat. A combination of self-serve and service, and the number of bowlfuls, may vary with the restaurant, but the elemental concept is the same. The food is fresh, tends to be healthful, and is served quickly.

Cuisines that are hot: Spanish cuisine made a splash here as a result of 1992, Spain's legendary year commemorating the 500th anniversary of the discovery of America, the Barcelona Summer Olympics, and Expo '92 in Seville. Spain's tapas and the sampling or "tasting" style has spread from the host cuisine to others, so we now see American and eclectic tapas. Mediterranean and Italian cuisines continue in popularity. Recently more French bistros and brasseries, Louisiana, Latin, and fusion restaurants have appeared. And two completely new cuisines recently hit the scene on North Sheridan Road, just south of L'Olive. One is **Tibetan Cafe** and next to it is a Nigerian place called **Suya African Grill.**

Restaurants are giving customers more options, and many offer half-portions when possible. Some places even offer half glasses of wine so people can do more tastings (see Profile of **Hudson Club**).

We've seen a glut of bagel shops, and it undoubtedly will be the survival of the fittest. And after all our new coffee houses, some predict that soon we will be seeing more tea cafes and houses.

In the heartland, chefs take pride in seeking out small, quality purveyors and changing their menus to utilize the freshest of seasonal ingredients. Wine lists have improved dramatically, and many have become user-friendly, with more options by the glass and half bottle. More wine bars have sprung up and more restaurants are adding "wine bar" to their name. One example is **Cyrano's Bistro & Wine Bar,** 546 North Wells; phone (312) 467-0546.

## TOURISTY PLACES

There are many places that tourists, for one reason or another, have heard about and want to try. Some, like the Pump Room, Michael Jordan's, and Iron Mike's Grill are excellent or very good. Others are less so, and many are overpriced. Some of the following may offer good food and unique atmosphere, but overall they do not merit full profiles:

### Dick's Last Resort
435 East Illinois Street
This North Pier spot attracts tourists who shop in the building and see the riverfront. It's OK for simple American fare, but not as a dining destination.

### Ed Debevic's Short Order Deluxe
640 North Wells Street
Typical American diner food in a fun atmosphere.

### Gene & Georgetti
500 North Franklin Street
Considered by many steak-lovers to be a great place, but inconsistent food and service, crowded conditions, and dated decor prevent a recommendation.

### Greek Islands Restaurant
200 South Halsted Street
A popular, large Greektown favorite that is attractive and serves decent Greek food. Unfortunately, much of it is kept on a steam table. Several other nearby restaurants are profiled in this guide.

### The Hard Rock Cafe
63 West Ontario Street
Good American/ethnic food and glitzy presentations; decibel level has been lowered to a comfortable level.

### Planet Hollywood
633 North Wells Street
Flashy decor and mediocre American fare.

### Three Happiness
2130 South Wentworth Avenue, Chinatown
Bustling, popular Cantonese and dim sum place; good, authentic food, if you don't mind crowds. Reservations accepted weekdays.

| New and Changing Restaurants | |
| --- | --- |
| **Restaurant** | **Cuisine** |
| A La Turka | Turkish |
| Aubriot | French |
| Ben Pao | Chinese |
| The Bistro in Highwood | American Bistro |
| Bistrot Zinc/ Café Zinc | French |
| Bricks | Pizza and Beer |
| Cafe Matou | French |
| Cafe Spiaggia | Italian |
| The Capital Grille (imported from the East Coast; Gold Coast) | New York–style steakhouse |
| Cheesecake Factory (John Hancock Building) | Eclectic American |
| Chez Delphonse | Caribbean |
| Club Macanudo | New American |
| ConFusion | Fusion |
| Cyrano's | French Bistro |
| Elaine's (Streeterville) | American (breakfast all day) |
| erwin, an american cafe & bar | New American |
| Flat Top Grill (locations in city and Evanston) | Asian grilling on flattop |
| Green Dolphin Street (with jazz club) | Contemporary |
| Le Français | French |
| Lans Bistro Pacific | Pan-Asian |
| M-Cafe (Museum of Contemporary Art) | Eclectic |

| New and Changing Restaurants (*continued*) | |
| --- | --- |
| **Restaurant** | **Cuisine** |
| Madam B | Pacific Rim |
| McCormick's & Schnick's | Seafood |
| Mas | Nuevo Latino |
| mk | New American |
| Mongolian Barbecue | Stir-fry with Asian slant |
| Mossant | French Bistro |
| Nacional 27 | Nuevo Latino |
| Nick & Tony's | Home-style Italian |
| Nix (Regal Knickerbocker Hotel) | Fusion |
| Palette's | American (+ entertainment) |
| Phoenix (Chinatown) | Chinese |
| Red Light (Randolph Market) | Pan-Asian |
| The Shark Bar Restaurant | Southern |
| Savarin | New Classic French |
| Smith & Wollensky | Steak and seafood |
| Southern Roots | Southern |
| Tapas Barcelona | Spanish tapas |
| Tavern on Rush | American steakhouse |
| Trattoria Parma (formerly Mare) | Regional Italian |
| Triple Crown Seafood (Chinatown) | Cantonese/seafood |
| Vegetarian Garden (Chinatown) | Vegetarian Chinese |
| Zarrosta Grill | California and Italian |

# The Restaurants

## OUR FAVORITE CHICAGO RESTAURANTS: EXPLAINING THE RATINGS

We have developed detailed profiles for what we consider the best restaurants in town. Each profile features an easy-to-scan heading which allows you to check out the restaurant's name, cuisine, star rating, cost, quality rating, and value rating very quickly.

**Star Rating**   The star rating is an overall rating which encompasses the entire dining experience, including style, service, and ambience in addition to the taste, presentation, and quality of the food. Five stars is the highest rating possible and connotes the best of everything. Four-star restaurants are exceptional and three-star restaurants are well above average. Two-star restaurants are good. One star is used to connote an average restaurant which demonstrates an unusual capability in some area of specialization, for example, an otherwise unmemorable place which has great barbecued chicken.

**Cost**   To the right of the star rating is an expense description which provides a comparative sense of how much a complete meal will cost. A complete meal for our purposes consists of an entree with vegetable or side dish, and choice of soup or salad. Appetizers, desserts, drinks, and tips are excluded.

| | |
|---|---|
| Inexpensive | $16 and less per person |
| Moderate | $17–29 per person |
| Expensive | $30–40 per person |
| Very Expensive | Over $40 per person |

**Quality Rating**   To the right of the cost rating appears a number and a letter. The number is a quality rating based on a scale of 0–100, with 100 being the highest (best) rating attainable. The quality rating is based expressly on the taste, freshness of ingredients, preparation, presentation, and creativity of food served. There is no consideration of price. If you are a person who wants the best food available, and cost is not an issue, you need look no further than the quality ratings.

**Value Rating**   If on the other hand you are looking for both quality and value, then you should check the value rating, expressed in letters. The value ratings are defined as follows:

| | |
|---|---|
| A | Exceptional value, a real bargain |
| B | Good value |
| C | Fair value, you get exactly what you pay for |
| D | Somewhat overpriced |
| F | Significantly overpriced |

**Location**   Just below the restaurant address and phone number is a designation for geographic zone. This zone description will give you a general idea of where the restaurant described is located. For ease of use, we divide Chicago into 11 geographic zones.

| | |
|---|---|
| Zone 1. | North Side |
| Zone 2. | North Central/O'Hare |
| Zone 3. | Near North |
| Zone 4. | The Loop |
| Zone 5. | South Loop |
| Zone 6. | South Central/Midway |
| Zone 7. | South Side |
| Zone 8. | Southern Suburbs |
| Zone 9. | Western Suburbs |
| Zone 10. | Northwest Suburbs |
| Zone 11. | Northern Suburbs |

If you are in The Loop area and intend to walk or take a cab to dinner, you may want to choose a restaurant from among those located in Zone 4.

If you have a car, you might include restaurants from contiguous zones in your consideration. (See pages 10–32 for detailed zone maps.)

## OUR PICK OF THE BEST CHICAGO RESTAURANTS

Because restaurants are opening and closing all the time in Chicago, we have tried to confine our list to establishments—or chefs—with a proven track record over a fairly long period of time. Newer or changed establishments that demonstrate staying power and consistency will be profiled in subsequent editions.

The list is highly selective. Non-inclusion of a particular place does not necessarily indicate that the restaurant is not good, but only that it was not ranked among the best or most consistent in its genre. Detailed profiles of each restaurant follow in alphabetical order at the end of this chapter. Also, we've listed the types of payment accepted at each restaurant using the following codes:

| | |
|---|---|
| AMEX | American Express |
| CB | Carte Blanche |
| D | Discover |
| DC | Diners Club |
| MC | MasterCard |
| VISA | VISA |

| The Best Chicago Restaurants | | | | | |
|---|---|---|---|---|---|
| Name | Star Rating | Price Rating | Quality Rating | Value Rating | Zone |
| **American** (see also New American) | | | | | |
| Seasons Restaurant | ★★★★½ | Mod/Exp | 97 | C | 3 |
| Spago | ★★★★½ | Mod/Exp | 94 | B | 3 |
| Mango | ★★★★ | Inexp/Mod | 92 | B | 3 |
| The Pump Room | ★★★★ | Exp | 92 | C | 3 |
| The Cafe | ★★★½ | Mod | 90 | C | 3 |
| Iron Mike's Grille | ★★★½ | Mod/Exp | 90 | C | 3 |
| **American** (continued) | | | | | |
| House of Blues | ★★★½ | Inexp/Mod | 89 | B | 3 |
| The Mity Nice Grill | ★★★½ | Inexp/Mod | 86 | C | 3 |
| Harry Caray's | ★★★½ | Mod/Exp | 86 | C | 4 |
| foodlife | ★★★ | Inexp | 82 | C | 3 |
| **Bakery Cafe** | | | | | |
| Corner Bakery | ★★★½ | Inexp/Mod | 90 | B | 4 |

## The Best Chicago Restaurants (continued)

| Name | Star Rating | Price Rating | Quality Rating | Value Rating | Zone |
|---|---|---|---|---|---|
| **Barbecue/Southern** | | | | | |
| Joe's B-Bop Cafe | ★★★½ | Inexp/Mod | 90 | B | 3 |
| **Cajun/Creole** | | | | | |
| Louisiana Kitchen | ★★★½ | Mod | 91 | B | 1 |
| Heaven on Seven | ★★★½ | Inexp | 86 | B | 4 |
| **Chinese** | | | | | |
| Szechwan East | ★★★★ | Mod | 92 | C | 3 |
| Mandar Inn | ★★★½ | Inexp/Mod | 88 | C | 5 |
| **Continental** | | | | | |
| Cité | ★★★★ | Exp/Very Exp | 89 | D | 1 |
| Zum Deutschen Eck | ★★★½ | Inexp/Mod | 88 | C | 1 |
| **Ethiopian** | | | | | |
| Mama Desta's Red Sea Ethiopian Restaurant | ★★★ | Inexp | 86 | B | 1 |
| **Fondue** | | | | | |
| Geja's Cafe | ★★★½ | Exp | 90 | B | 1 |
| **French** (see also New French) | | | | | |
| Everest | ★★★★★ | Exp | 98 | C | 4 |
| Toulouse on the Park | ★★★★½ | Mod | 94 | B | 1 |
| Kiki's Bistro | ★★★★ | Inexp/Mod | 94 | C | 3 |
| Mon Ami Gabi | ★★★★ | Mod | 92 | C | 1 |
| Brasserie Jo | ★★★★ | Inexp/Mod | 92 | B | 3 |
| Entre Nous | ★★★★ | Mod/Exp | 90 | C | 4 |
| Bistro 110 | ★★★½ | Mod | 86 | C | 3 |
| **French/Vietnamese** | | | | | |
| Le Colonial | ★★★½ | Mod | 88 | C | 1 |
| **Fusion** | | | | | |
| Trio | ★★★★★ | Exp/Very Exp | 98 | C | 11 |
| **German/American** | | | | | |
| Golden Ox | ★★★★ | Mod | 90 | C | 1 |
| The Berghoff | ★★★½ | Inexp | 88 | B | 4 |
| **Greek** | | | | | |
| The Parthenon | ★★★★½ | Inexp/Mod | 95 | B | 4 |
| Papagus Greek Taverna | ★★★★ | Mod | 90 | C | 3, 6 |

## The Best Chicago Restaurants (continued)

| Name | Star Rating | Price Rating | Quality Rating | Value Rating | Zone |
|------|------------|-------------|---------------|-------------|------|
| **Healthy Dining** | | | | | |
| Earth | ★★★½ | Mod/Exp | 89 | B | 3 |
| **Indian** | | | | | |
| Klay Oven | ★★★★ | Mod | 94 | B | 4 |
| Bukara | ★★★½ | Mod | 80 | C | 3 |
| **Irish Pub** | | | | | |
| Kitty O'Shea's | ★★★ | Inexp | 81 | B | 5 |
| **Italian** (see also New Italian) | | | | | |
| Vivere (Italian Village) | ★★★★½ | Mod | 95 | C | 4 |
| Spiaggia | ★★★★ | Mod/Exp | 93 | C | 3 |
| Coco Pazzo | ★★★★ | Mod | 91 | C | 4 |
| Pane Caldo | ★★★½ | Inexp/Mod | 89 | C | 3 |
| Cafe Luciano | ★★★½ | Inexp/Mod | 88 | B | 3, 11 |
| Carlucci | ★★★½ | Mod | 88 | C | 2 |
| La Strada | ★★★½ | Mod/Exp | 87 | C | 4 |
| Bruna's Ristorante | ★★★ | Inexp/Mod | 80 | B | 5 |
| **Italian/Mediterranean** | | | | | |
| Cuisines | ★★★½ | Inexp/Mod | 89 | B | 4 |
| **Japanese** | | | | | |
| Sai Cafe | ★★★½ | Inexp/Mod | 91 | B | 1 |
| **Korean** | | | | | |
| Woo Lae Oak | ★★★★ | Inexp | 94 | C | 3 |
| **Mediterraean** | | | | | |
| Mantuano Mediterraean Table | ★★★★ | Inexp/Mod | 91 | C | 3 |
| **Mexican** | | | | | |
| Topolobampo | ★★★★½ | Mod | 95 | C | 4 |
| Frontera Grill | ★★★★ | Inexp | 93 | B | 4 |
| ¡Salpicón!, A Taste of Mexico | ★★★½ | Inexp/Mod | 85 | C | 3 |
| **Middle Eastern** | | | | | |
| Uncle Tutunji's | ★★★ | Inexp | 85 | B | 3 |
| **Midwestern** | | | | | |
| Prairie | ★★★★½ | Mod/Exp | 95 | C | 5 |

## The Best Chicago Restaurants (continued)

| Name | Star Rating | Price Rating | Quality Rating | Value Rating | Zone |
|------|-------------|--------------|----------------|--------------|------|
| **Moroccan/Mediterranean** | | | | | |
| L'Olive | ★★★½ | Inexp | 91 | A | 1 |
| **New American** | | | | | |
| Charlie Trotter's | ★★★★★ | Very Exp | 98 | C | 1 |
| Printer's Row | ★★★★½ | Mod | 95 | B | 5 |
| Spruce | ★★★★½ | Inexp/Mod | 94 | B | 3 |
| Park Avenue Cafe | ★★★★ | Mod/Exp | 94 | C | 3 |
| Gordon | ★★★★ | Exp | 93 | C | 4 |
| North Pond Cafe | ★★★★ | Mod | 92 | B | 1 |
| one sixtyblue | ★★★★ | Mod/Exp | 92 | C | 2 |
| Hudson Club | ★★★★ | Mod | 91 | B | 1 |
| The Signature Room at the Ninety-Fifth | ★★★★ | Mod/Exp | 91 | C | 3 |
| Crofton on Wells | ★★★½ | Mod | 91 | B | 3 |
| Jack's | ★★★½ | Mod | 90 | B | 1 |
| **New French** | | | | | |
| The Dining Room | ★★★★½ | Mod/Exp | 95 | C | 3 |
| Yoshi's Cafe | ★★★★ | Inexp/Mod | 94 | B | 1 |
| Ambria | ★★★★ | Mod/Exp | 93 | C | 1 |
| Yvette | ★★★½ | Inexp/Mod | 85 | C | 3 |
| Yvette Wintergarden | ★★★½ | Inexp/Mod | 85 | C | 4 |
| **New Italian** | | | | | |
| Bella Vista | ★★★½ | Inexp/Mod | 86 | C | 1 |
| Pazzo's Cucina Italiana | ★★½ | Inexp/Mod | 79 | B | 2, 8 |
| **Persian** | | | | | |
| Reza's | ★★★½ | Inexp/Mod | 90 | C | 1, 3 |
| Pars Cove | ★★★½ | Inexp/Mod | 89 | C | 1 |
| **Polish** | | | | | |
| Lutnia Continental Cafe | ★★★½ | Mod/Inexp | 87 | C | 2 |
| Pierogi Inn | ★★½ | Inexp | 79 | B | 2 |
| **Prime Rib** | | | | | |
| Lawry's The Prime Rib | ★★★★ | Mod | 90 | B | 3 |
| **Russian** | | | | | |
| Russian Tea Time | ★★★★ | Mod | 93 | C | 4 |
| **Seafood** | | | | | |
| Shaw's Crab House and The Blue Crab Lounge | ★★★★½ | Mod | 95 | C | 4 |

## The Best Chicago Restaurants (continued)

| Name | Star Rating | Price Rating | Quality Rating | Value Rating | Zone |
|------|-------------|--------------|----------------|--------------|------|
| **Seafood (continued)** | | | | | |
| Cape Cod Room | ★★★★ | Mod/Exp | 95 | C | 3 |
| Nick's Fishmarket | ★★★★ | Mod/Exp | 95 | D | 2,4 |
| Riva | ★★★½ | Mod/Exp | 90 | C | 3 |
| **Southwestern** | | | | | |
| Blue Mesa | ★★★★ | Inexp/Mod | 89 | B | 1 |
| **Spanish/Tapas** | | | | | |
| Emilio's Tapas Bar Restaurant | ★★★★ | Mod | 91 | C | 1 |
| Cafe Iberico Tapas Bar | ★★★½ | Inexp/Mod | 87 | B | 3 |
| **Steak** | | | | | |
| Gibson's Steakhouse | ★★★★½ | Mod/Very Exp | 94 | C | 3 |
| Chicago Chop House | ★★★★ | Mod | 94 | C | 3 |
| Ruth's Chris Steakhouse | ★★★★ | Mod/Exp | 93 | B | 4 |
| Morton's of Chicago | ★★★★ | Exp | 92 | C | 2, 3, 8 |
| Palm Restaurant | ★★★★ | Mod/Exp | 92 | C | 4 |
| Eli's, The Place for Steak | ★★★½ | Mod/Exp | 88 | C | 3 |
| **Thai** | | | | | |
| Arun's | ★★★★½ | Mod/Exp | 95 | C | 1 |
| Thai Borrahn | ★★★★ | Inexp/Mod | 90 | B | 3 |
| **Vegetarian** | | | | | |
| Seasons Restaurant | ★★★★½ | Mod/Exp | 97 | C | 3 |
| Reza's | ★★★½ | Inexp/Mod | 90 | C | 1, 3 |
| **Vietnamese** | | | | | |
| Pasteur | ★★★★ | Inexp/Mod | 92 | B | 1 |

## MORE RECOMMENDATIONS

Here are a few quick recommendations for special-interest groups:

### The Best Bagels

**Einstein Bagels**    44 East Walton (Gold Coast) (312) 943-9888

About 30 locations in the city and suburbs and growing. Bagels are made on the premises; favorite flavors include cinnamon-raisin, blueberry, spinach-herb, and sun-dried tomato. Sandwiches and spreads are also sold.

**Jacob's Brothers**    53 West Jackson Boulevard (312) 922-2245

**Kaufman's Bagel and Delicatessen**   4905 Dempster Street, Skokie (847) 677-9880
   Old-style Jewish bagels that have a following.

## The Best Bakeries

**Ambrosia Euro-American Patisserie**   710 West Northwest Highway, Barrington (847) 304-8278

**Blind Faith Cafe and Bakery**   525 Dempster Street, Evanston (847) 328-6875; a new city location (773) 871-3820

**Bread with Appeal**   1009 West Armitage Avenue (773) 244-2700
   Excellent breads and baked items; they also serve sandwiches, salads, soups, and box lunches. Dine in or carry out; catering is available.

**The Corner Bakery**   516 North Clark Street (312) 644-8100;   Union Station, Adams Street Concourse, 210 South Canal Street (312) 441-0821; Water Tower Place, foodlife, 835 North Michigan Avenue (312) 335-3663; Sante Fe Building, 224 South Michigan Avenue (at Jackson Boulevard) (630) 431-7600; 240 Oakbrook Center (in the mall), Oak Brook (630) 368-0505; 1901 East Woodfield Road, Schaumburg (847) 240-1111. New locations opening frequently.

**Foodstuffs**   2106 Central Avenue, Evanston (847) 328-7704; 338 Park Avenue, Glencoe (847) 835-5105

**Great Harvest Bread Co.**   846 West Armitage Avenue (773) 528-6211
   Check for other suburban locations, including Evanston.

**Konditorei**   Swissôtel Chicago, 323 East Wacker Drive (312) 565-0565

## The Best Barbecue and Ribs

**Bones**   7110 North Lincoln Avenue, Lincolnwood (847) 677-3350

**Gayle Street Inn**   4914 North Milwaukee Avenue (773) 725-1300
   Baby backs.

**Hecky's BBQ**   1902 Green Bay Road, Evanston (847) 492-1182
   Rib tips, chicken wings.

**Joe's B-Bop**   Navy Pier, 600 East Grand Avenue, (312) 595-5299

**Leon's Bar-B-Q**   8259 South Cottage Grove Avenue (773) 488-4556; 1158 West 59th Street (773) 778-7828; 1640 East 79th Street (773) 731-1454

**Miller's Pub**   134 South Wabash Avenue (312) 645-5377

**N. N. Smokehouse**   1465-67 West Irving Park Road (773) TNT-4700

**Robinson's No. 1 Ribs**   655 West Armitage Avenue (312) 337-1399
   Ribs and chicken.

**Smoke Daddy**    1804 West Division Street (773) 772-MOJO

Three kinds of ribs; a rib combo sampler; smoked sweet potato; live blues, jazz, and mambo music.

**Twin Anchors Restaurant and Tavern**    1655 North Sedgwick Street (312) 266-1616

In business for over 60 years.

## The Best Beer Lists

**Big Bar**    Hyatt Regency, 151 East Wacker Drive (312) 565-1234

**Cork & Carry**    10614 South Western Avenue (773) 445-2675

Seventy varieties, 12 on tap.

**Goose Island Brewing Company**    1800 North Clybourn Avenue (312) 915-0071

**Hopcats Brew Club**    2354 North Clyourne Avenue (773) 868-4461

**Jameson's Tavern**    118 South Clinton Street (312) 876-0016

**Joe Bailly's**    10854 South Western Avenue (773) 238-1313

**Millrose Brewing Company**    45 South Barrington Road, South Barrington (847) 382-7673

**Ranalli's**    1925 North Lincoln Avenue (312) 642-4700

**Red Lion Pub**    2446 North Lincoln Avenue (773) 348-2695

One of the best selections of English beers.

**Resi's Bierstube**    2034 West Irving Park Road (773) 472-1749

Perhaps the oldest beergarden in the city—over 30 years at press time; 60 imports and 6 on tap.

## The Best Breakfasts

**Ann Sather's**    929 West Belmont Avenue (773) 348-2378; 5207 North Clark Street, Andersonville (773) 271-6677

**Army & Lou's**    422 East 75th Street (773) 483-3100

**The Corner Bakery**    (See p. 319, The Best Bakeries.)

**Egg Harbor Cafe**    512 North Western Avenue, Lake Forest (847) 295-3449

**Elaine's (formerly Elaine's & Ina's Kitchen)**    Ontario Center Building, 448 East Ontario Street (312) 337-6700

**Heaven on Seven**    111 North Wabash Avenue (312) 263-6443

**Iron Mike's Grille**    100 East Chestnut (312) 587-8989
Hearty football-style breakfasts.

**Lou Mitchell's**    565 West Jackson Boulevard (312) 939-3111

**Mrs. Park's Tavern**    198 East Delaware Place (312) 280-8882

**The Pump Room**    Omni Ambassador East Hotel, 1301 North State Parkway (312) 266-0360

**Seasons Restaurant**    The Four Seasons Hotel, 120 East Delaware Place (312) 280-8800, Ext. 2134

**3rd Coast**    29 East Delaware Place (312) 664-7225; 1260 North Dearborn Street (312) 649-0730
The Dearborn location is the original; open 24 hours. Owned by brothers, but are separate businesses, however similar.

**Voila!**    33 West Monroe Street (312) 580-9500

## The Best Brunches

**Bistro 110**    110 East Pearson Street (312) 266-3110
New Orleans–style jazz brunch on Sunday.

**Blue Mesa**    1729 North Halsted Street (312) 944-5990
New Mexican cuisine, Sunday brunch.

**Celebrity Cafe**    Westin Hotel River North, 320 North Dearborn Street (312) 744-1900

**Cité**    Top of Lake Point Tower (world's tallest residential building) 70th floor, 505 North Lake Shore Drive (312) 644-4050
Sunday champagne brunch.

**The Dining Room**    The Ritz-Carlton Chicago, 160 East Pearson Street (312) 266-1000
Exquisite and extensive Sunday buffet brunch.

**Four Farthings Tavern & Grill**    2060 North Cleveland Avenue (773) 935-2060
Newly expanded Sunday buffet brunch.

**Hong Min**    221 West Cermak Road, Chinatown (312) 842-5026
Saturday and Sunday brunch.

**House of Blues**    329 North Dearborn Street (312) 527-2583
Sunday gospel brunch, with seatings at 10 a.m., 12:15 p.m., and 2:30 p.m.

**Joe's B-Bop**    Navy Pier, 600 East Grand Avenue, (312) 595-5299
Sunday jazz brunch.

**Louisiana Kitchen**   2666 North Halsted Street (773) 529-1666
Sunday jazz brunch.

**The Pump Room**   Omni Ambassador East Hotel, 1301 North State
Parkway (312) 266-0360
Sunday brunch.

**Seasons Restaurant**   Four Seasons Hotel, 120 East Delaware Place
(312) 280-8800
Sunday brunch.

**The Signature Room at the Ninety-Fifth**   John Hancock Center, 95th
floor, 875 North Michigan Avenue (312) 787-9596
Elegant Sunday buffet champagne brunch with live music.


## The Best Burgers and Sandwiches

**Abbey Pub**   4320 West Grace (772) 463-5808

**Arturo Express/Turano Baking Co.**   919 North Michigan Avenue (312)
251-2250; 980 North Michigan Avenue (312) 222-1525

**Billy Goat Tavern**   430 North Michigan Avenue (312) 922-6847

**Ed Debevic's**   66 North Wells (312) 664-1707

**Hackney's**   1514 East Lake Avenue, Glenview (847) 724-7171; 1241
Harms Road, Glenview (847) 724-5577
Known for burgers and fried onion loaf; other suburban locations:
Wheeling, LaGrange, and Lake Zurich.

**Iron Mike's Grille**   100 East Chestnut (312) 587-8989

**John Barleycorn Memorial Pub, Inc.**   658 West Belden Avenue (773)
348-8899
Bar food, good burgers and sandwiches, salads; classical music and art
slides. Nice garden.

**Kasia's Deli & Catering**   2101 West Chicago Avenue (773) 486-6163
Polish fare.

**Kitty O'Shea's**   Chicago Hilton & Towers, 720 South Michigan Avenue
(312) 922-4400

**Magnum's Steak & Lobster**   225 West Ontario (312) 337-8080

**Moody's**   5910 North Broadway (773) 275-2696
Specialties include the Moody Burger with various cheeses. Great garden.

## The Best Coffee and Dessert Places

**Cafe Express**   615 Dempster Street, Evanston (847) 864-1868

**Cafe Express South**   500 Main Street, Evanston (847) 328-7940

**The Corner Bakery**   (See p. 319, The Best Bakeries.)

**Eli's Cafe**   inside **Eli's, The Place for Steak,** 215 East Chicago Avenue (312) 642-1393; another Cafe inside **Eli's Bakery,** 6701 West Forest Preserve Drive (773) 736-3417

**Jillian's Coffee House and Bistro**   674-West Diversey (773) 529-7012

**Lutz's Continental Cafe and Pastry Shop**   2458 West Montrose Avenue (773) 478-7785

## The Best Cornbread

**Bandera**   535 North Michigan Avenue (312) 644-FLAG
It's made in an iron skillet and browned around the edges.

**Joe's B-Bop**   Navy Pier, 600 East Grand Avenue, (312) 595-5299

**Louisiana Kitchen**   2666 North Halsted Street (773) 529-1666

**Redfish and the Voodoo Lounge**   400 North State Street (312) 467-1600

## The Best Delis

**Bagel Restaurant and Deli**   3107 North Broadway (773) 477-0300; 50 Old Orchard Shopping Center, Skokie (847) 677-0100

**Manny's Coffee Shop and Deli**   1141 South Jefferson (312) 939-2855
Since 1942. Great corned beef and pastrami sandwiches.

## The Best Hot Dogs

**Gold Coast Dogs**   418 North State Street (312) 527-1222; 2100 North Clark Street (773) 327-8887
Vienna beef dogs; friendly, accommodating service, including curbside; also great burgers and other sandwiches. Call about other locations such as Northwestern Atrium, (312) 879-0447, or Union Station, (312) 258-8585.

**Portillo's Hot Dogs**   100 West Ontario Street (312) 587-8910
Steamed Vienna beef dogs served Chicago style in poppyseed buns.

## The Best Picnic Meals

**Ann Sather**   929 West Belmont Avenue (773) 348-2378; 5207 North Clark Street, Andersonville (773) 271-6677

Box lunches created from choice of sandwiches, salads, and desserts (some Swedish specialties). Open daily. 24-hour advance notice required.

**Mitchell Cobey Cuisine**   100 East Walton (312) 944-3411

Mostly French cuisine with international influences. Numbered box lunches can be customized. Open Monday–Saturday; same-day service for small orders; 24-hour advance notice required for large orders.

**Sopraffina**   10 North Dearborn Street (312) 984-0044

Italian. Create your own menu. 24-hour notice required.

**Tutto Pronto**   401 East Ontario Street (312) 587-7700

Italian food and wine shop with deli. Wicker baskets and totes available.

## The Best Pizza

**Bacino's**   Several locations; 2204 North Lincoln Avenue (773) 472-7400

Good stuffed and heart-healthy pizza.

**Bertucci's Brick Oven Pizza**   675 North LaSalle Street (312) 266-3400

Three other new locations in suburbs. More thick-crust pizza pie.

**California Pizza Kitchen**   414 North Orleans Street (312) 222-9030

Call about other locations. Thin-crust/gourmet.

**Edwardo's Natural Pizza Restaurant**   1212 North Dearborn Street (312) 337-4490; 521 South Dearborn Street (312) 939-3366

Call for other locations in the city and suburbs. Some stuffed pizza versions are recommended; Edwardo's grows its own basil.

**Father & Son Pizza**   645 West North Avenue (312) 654-2550; 2475 North Milwaukee (773) 252-2620

**Giovanni's Pizza**   6823 West Roosevelt Road, Berwyn (708) 795-7171

**Lou Malnati's**   439 North Wells Street (312) 828-9800; 6649 North Lincoln Avenue, Lincolnwood (847) 673-0800

Gourmet deep-dish and thin-crust.

**O Famé**   750 West Webster Avenue (773) 929-5111

Good thin-crust, pan, or Chicago-style pizzas. They also have a full menu.

**The Original Gino's East**   1321 West Golf Road, Rolling Meadows (847) 364-6644

Award-winning pizza, rated Number One in the nation by *People* magazine editors.

**Pat's Pizzeria & Ristorante**   3114 North Sheffield Avenue (773) 248-0168; 211 North Stetson (312) 946-0732

Pat's has been named the Number One thin crust pizza by the *Chicago Tribune* and the *Chicago Sun-Times*.

**Pizzeria Uno**   29 East Ohio Street (312) 321-1000

**Pizzeria Due**   619 North Wabash Avenue (312) 943-2400

Both Uno and Due serve Chicago-style, deep-dish pizza.

**Suparossa**   7309 West Lawrence Avenue, Harwood Heights (flagship) (847) 867-4641

Newest locations at press time: 210 East Ohio Street and in Woodridge. Call for other locations in the city and suburbs. Original stuffed pizza—the award-winning lasagna pizza stuffed with ricotta and spinach is a favorite. The new wood-fired oven pizzas are great appetizers.


## The Best Wine Bars

**Espial Bistro & Bar**   948 West Armitage Avenue (773) 871-8123

French/Italian food; international wines.

**Geja's Cafe**   340 West Armitage Avenue (773) 281-9101

This fondue cafe was the city's first wine bar. It's very romantic with live guitar.

**Madison's (Italian Steakhouse)**   1330 West Madison Street, in United Center area (312) 455-0099

More than 20 wines by the glass. Good wine list.

**Meritage Cafe and Wine Bar**   2118 North Damen Avenue (773) 235-6434

Sophisticated; great international wine list with many by the glass, including three-ounce tastes. Appropriate food, informed staff. Large tented year-round garden.

**Narcisse**   710 North Clark Street (312) 787-2675

Sexy, sensuous interior; chic crowd. Great champagne and caviar bar with light fare. Savvy staff. New room downstairs called **Boudoir.**

**Pops for Champagne**   2934 North Sheffield Avenue (773) 472-1000

The first champagne bar here; lovely space with outdoor garden. Knowledgeable staff; jazz. Adjacent **Star Bar** does monthly tastings; call (773) 472-7272. North Shore location opening soon.

**Webster's Wine Bar**   1480 West Webster Avenue (773) 868-0608

Living room–like interior. Long list of wines by the glass or two-ounce tastes; complementary, healthful, simple foods.

## AMBRIA ★★★★

| | | QUALITY |
|---|---|---|
| New French | Moderate/Expensive | 93 |
| | | VALUE |
| | | C |

Beldon Stratford Hotel, 2300 North Lincoln Park West;
   (773) 472-0076
Zone 1   North Side

Reservations: Required
When to go: Early on weeknights; late on weekends
Entree range: $19.50–29.95
Payment: All major credit cards
Service rating: ★★★★
Friendliness rating: ★★★★
Parking: Valet, $6
Bar: Full-service, dining bar for customers only
Wine selection: Award-winning list of 570 international wines; $15–1,500 per bottle; 5 by the glass, $8–12. Sommelier is skilled at suggesting appropriate wines to go with the food and personal tastes.
Dress: Dressy; jacket required, tie optional—no denim or sneakers
Disabled access: Wheelchair accessible; call ahead for special accommodations
Customers: Sophisticated, selective clientele; international and upscale local

**Dinner:** Monday–Thursday, 6–9:30 p.m.; Friday and Saturday, 6–10:30 p.m. Sunday, closed.

**Setting & atmosphere:** Deep-toned woods, ultra suede banquettes and crystalline-etched glass with art nouveau architectural touches; tiny shaded lamps on each table; massive flower-filled urns. This place resembles an old mansion or club from the 1900s; murals and elegant fixtures; fashionable decor and ambience.

**House specialties:** Roasted New York State foie gras with caramelized apples; loin of lamb with sweet mini-peppers and rosemary infusion; fillet of Casco Bay cod in rice paper with lobster-paprika sauce; mango parfait with berries.

**Other recommendations:** Baby pheasant, foie gras, wild mushrooms, and thyme broth; a symphony of market vegatables and grains; soufflé du jour.

**Summary & comments:** Well-established (17-plus years) crème de la crème of French restaurants and one of the top-shelf places within the Lettuce Entertain You Enterprises group. Longtime chef-owner Gabino Sotelino maintains fine quality here, using his solid culinary skills to produce French cuisine légère with Italian and Spanish influences. The menu has been simplified over the years. Lovely presentations. Some minor flaws occasionally in food and service, but overall, a very reliable place.

**(Ambria)**

**Honors & awards:** Four-star rating from *Chicago* magazine, *Chicago Tribune,* and *Mobil Travel Guide;* five diamonds from AAA; Award of Excellence for its wine cellar from *Wine Spectator.*

| ARUN'S | | ★★★★½ |
|---|---|---|
| Thai | Moderate/Expensive | **QUALITY** 95 |
| 4156 North Kedzie Avenue; (773) 539-1909 Zone 1 North Side | | **VALUE** C |

Reservations: Recommended
When to go: Dinner
Entree range: $13.95–23.95
Payment: Major credit cards
Service rating: ★★★★½
Friendliness rating: ★★★★½
Parking: Street
Bar: Full service, including Thai and Japanese beers

Wine selection: International— about 2 dozen Austrian, French, Italian, and Californian wines; bottles, $18–46; by the glass, $5
Dress: Casual
Disabled access: Yes
Customers: Local and out-of-town, business, couples

**Dinner:** Tuesday–Saturday, 5–10 p.m.; Sunday, 5–9 p.m.; Monday, closed.

**Setting & atmosphere:** Colorful exterior. Beautifully appointed, multi-level interior with a small, museum-like front alcove devoted to antiques and exquisite art. The narrow upper dining area has open windows with a view into the lower dining room. Colorful authentic art and other Thai artifacts adorn the intimate rooms. The kitchen has recently been enlarged. Owner's brother, an artist/architect, did much of the work, and the owner's paintings decorate the rest rooms.

**House specialties:** Khao kriab (steamed rice dumplings filled with Dungeness crabmeat, shrimp, chicken, peanuts, garlic, and a tangy sweet-sour vinaigrette); picturesque golden baskets (flower-shaped, bite-sized pastries filled with a mixture of shrimp, chicken, sweet corn, and shiitake mushrooms, garnished with intricately carved vegetable baskets); three-flavored red snapper (crisply fried whole fish with traditional Bangkok-style three-flavored tamarind sauce: spicy, sweet, and sour); three-combination curry (country-style yellow curry with shrimp quenelle, chicken, squash, and fuzzy melon in a sauce that's hot, spicy, and peppery).

**Other recommendations:** Hoy tord (crusty golden mussel pancake topped with bean sprouts, garlic chive, and hot chile and sweet chile-garlic

**(Arun's)**

sauces); Siamese dumplings (delicate rice dumplings with minced shrimp, chicken, sweet daikon turnips, peanuts, chopped chiles, cilantro, and lettuce); chicken coconut soup; summer salad (seasonal) with mint, sprouts, and fish cake slices; gingery veal with lemongrass and miso (no veal in Thai history—the owner created this); meefun delight (soft-fried noodles with shrimp, chicken, and scallion). Desserts are delightful: seven-layer rice custard (alternating colors of white, pink, and pale green) steamed from a mixture of rice flour and coconut milk. And while poetic license was employed with the next, it's great nonetheless: poached pear in red wine with bite-sized chocolate cakes and strawberry-ginger sauce. End with a wonderful elixir of lemongrass, water, and tiny fruit balls, which is purifying and serves as a digestive.

**Summary & comments:** This magnificently decorated restaurant serves appropriately exquisite food. Chef-owner Arun Sampanthavivat has refined traditional Thai cuisine and elevated Thai cooking to a new fine dining plateau. The menu reveals the use of chiles, but the food doesn't cause burns and tears if you're cautious about eating the peppers. The flavor nuances are more herbal, spicy, sweet, and sour. Arun loves to carve the intricate vegetable baskets that garnish plates, and spends about two hours daily on this task. To be able to spend more time managing the business, he's appointed a Thai chef, Rang San Sutzharit, to run the kitchen. The higher prices here are understandable once you taste the results of this labor-intensive cuisine.

**Honors & awards:** Four stars from *Mobil Travel Guide,* 1997; chef was named Best Chef in the Midwest, 1997, by the James Beard Foundation.

| **BELLA VISTA** | | ★★★½ |
|---|---|---|

| New Italian | Inexpensive/Moderate | QUALITY |
|---|---|---|
| | | 86 |
| 1001 West Belmont Avenue; (773) 404-0111 | | VALUE |
| Zone 1   North Side | | C |

| | |
|---|---|
| Reservations: Recommended | Parking: Valet, $5 |
| When to go: Weeknights | Bar: Yes |
| Entree range: $8–18 | Wine selection: 300 international |
| Payment: All major credit cards | selections, $19–150; substantial |
| Service rating: ★★★½ | Italian; 10 by the glass, |
| Friendliness rating: ★★★★ | $4.50–6.50 |

## (Bella Vista)

**Dress:** Casual
**Disabled access:** Yes
**Customers:** Younger professional, affluent, couples, families with young children

**Lunch:** Monday–Saturday, 11:30 a.m.–5 p.m.

**Dinner:** Monday–Thursday, 5–11 p.m.; Friday and Saturday, 5 p.m.–2 a.m.; Sunday, 5–10 p.m.

**Setting & atmosphere:** The name "beautiful view" says it well—a stunning interior and elegant, award-winning architecture in the former Belmont Trust and Savings Bank from 1929, a historic landmark building; beaux-arts motif with exquisite hand-painted walls, walk-through wine cellar, inlaid Italian marble floor, and wood-fire stove; copper- and glass-enclosed pizza kitchen; 30-foot ceiling. Seats 300 on 5 levels. Every table has a good view.

**House specialties:** Antipasto del Giorno with seasonal oak-roasted vegetables, seafood salad, oak-roasted potato salad, and two other selections; gourmet wood-fire pizzas (e.g., fresh basil pesto, tomatoes, pine nuts, and fresh mozzarella; or roasted potato, grilled eggplant, olives, spicy tomato sauce, and fresh Parmesan); black pepper linguini with shiitake and portobello mushrooms, and baby artichokes in a mushroom-rosemary broth; free-form lamb and potato torta (grilled loin of lamb layered with potato "sheets," bacon, spinach, caramelized onions, and fresh mint).

**Other recommendations:** Oak-roasted calamari marinated in lemon and fresh rosemary with plum tomatoes and wilted arugula; Gorgonzola salad with endive, watercress, pears, peppered pecans, and red wine vinaigrette.

**Entertainment & amenities:** Architectural tours of the restaurant are a must. The restaurant holds special dinners around winemakers and menus from films, such as *Big Night.*

**Summary & comments:** The architecture and interior design are a feast for the eyes, and the dishes are colorful and intricately presented. A former chef created food to outshine the decor, and at times it was confusing to the palate. There was a lot happening on most plates—a panoply of garnishes and little sides; however, the flavors tended to complement the main ingredients. A new chef simplified presentations and the food today continues in that style. The Bella Vista Cafe, a more casual bar room, serves the same menu as the dining room.

## THE BERGHOFF                                    ★★★½

| German/American | Inexpensive | QUALITY |
|---|---|---|
| | | 88 |

17 West Adams Street; (312) 427-3170

Zone 4    The Loop

| VALUE |
|---|
| B |

**Reservations:** Recommended for 5 or more

**When to go:** Busy at lunchtime and the early dinner hour, so avoid if you're in a rush; generally fast service

**Entree range:** Lunch, average $8–12; dinner, $9–17

**Payment:** VISA, MC, AMEX, DC

**Service rating:** ★★★½

**Friendliness rating:** ★★★★

**Parking:** Discount in nearby garages after 4 p.m.

**Bar:** Full service; the Berghoff's own regular and dark beer is available on tap

**Wine selection:** Extensive German, French, American, and Italian; inexpensive house wines available by the glass, half and full liter

**Dress:** Summer, casual; winter tends to be dressier (more suits and ties, although ties are not required)

**Disabled access:** Yes, including rest rooms

**Customers:** Local, including a loyal German clientele; some tourists

**Lunch/Dinner:** Monday–Thursday, 11 a.m.– 9 p.m.; Friday, 11 a.m.– 9:30 p.m.; Saturday, 11 a.m.– 10 p.m.

**Setting & atmosphere:** Turn-of-the-century building; old paintings; lots of wood in the spacious dining room, which is decorated with traditional dried flowers and branches. Rathskeller downstairs serves lunch.

**House specialties:** Good traditional German specialties: sauerbrauten and Wiener schnitzel; seafood such as fillet of sole with roasted almonds and lemon-parsley butter. Daily specials include some German items, such as schlacht-platte (a combination of bratwurst, "Kasseler Rippchen," and smoked Thuringer with kraut). Creamed herring and chilled smoked salmon are two nice appetizers.

**Other recommendations:** Seafood de Jonghe; veal medallions in mushroom-sherry wine sauce; chicken schnitzel; broiled swordfish steak; Black Forest torte.

**Summary & comments:** The menu proudly states, "family operated since 1898," when Herman Joseph Berghoff opened his cafe as a showcase for his celebrated dormunder-style beer. In a day when restaurants' life spans are shorter, this longevity is quite an achievement. The Berghoff, which turned 100 in April 1998, is a Chicago landmark due to the good quality German traditional food and many other dishes, fine Berghoff beer and

**(The Berghoff)**

Berghoff bourbon, low prices, old-world atmosphere, and efficient service. The management has modernized the menu to satisfy current desires — lighter fare, including seafood, salads, and light entrees. There are just a few standard German dishes on the regular menu, and several appear among the substantial number of specials each weekday along with American (e.g., Southwestern-style salmon) and even Italian entrees (e.g., linguini with angry shrimp). Seasonal dishes are also served, such as duck or goose around Christmas. The delicious, textured bread here is made from the brewery side-products (hops, etc.), and loaves are sold to carry home. Accomodating waiters wear old-world black trousers, white shirts, and aprons. This place is a great success story, serving 2,000 a day in the street-level dining room and downstairs for lunch. Private parties and catering are available.

| BISTRO 110 | | ★★★½ |
|---|---|---|
| French Bistro | Moderate | QUALITY<br>86 |
| 110 East Pearson Street; (312) 266-3110<br>Zone 3　Near North | | VALUE<br>C |

**Reservations:** Recommended for 5 or more

**When to go:** Any time

**Entree range:** $10–26

**Payment:** All major credit cards

**Service rating:** ★★★½

**Friendliness rating:** ★★★★½

**Parking:** Valet

**Bar:** Full service

**Wine selection:** Extensive French and domestic

**Dress:** Casual

**Disabled access:** Yes

**Customers:** Neighborhood, local, business, tourist, shoppers, hip urbanites

**Brunch:** Outdoor seating for Sunday jazz brunch, 11 a.m.–4 p.m.

**Lunch/Dinner:** Monday–Thursday, 11:30 a.m.–11 p.m.; Friday and Saturday, 11:30 a.m.–midnight; Sunday, 11 a.m.–10 p.m.

**Setting & atmosphere:** Sidewalk cafe is great in summer; attractive bar area with tables near the window for the great view; colorful murals; some recent renovations; inside seats 135 in the dining room, 56 in the cafe.

**House specialties:** Oven-roasted whole garlic served with fresh crusty French bread; wood-roasted chicken, snapper, and other fish specials usually served with an array of roasted vegetables; onion soup; creative pastas (e.g., linguini with rock shrimp).

**(Bistro 110)**

**Other recommendations:** Clafoutis "tutti frutti" berries; chocolate mousse; crème brûlée.

**Entertainment & amenities:** Sunday New Orleans–style à la carte jazz brunch featuring the Grady Johnson Jazz Trio. Occasional French promotions with exchange chefs from France.

**Summary & comments:** Very alive, energetic bistro that is like a scene out of Paris. One of the loveliest views of the Historic Water Tower. The chef, Dominique Toligne, oversees a menu with an emphasis on the bistro classics. The food is well-prepared and especially flavorful and healthful from the wood oven. Pastries for savory and sweet tarts are flaky and very French in nature. This place can reach high decibels on a bustling night.

| BLUE MESA No longer open. | ★★★★ | |
|---|---|---|
| | QUALITY | |
| Southwestern       Inexpensive/Moderate | 89 | |
| | VALUE | |
| 1729 North Halsted Street; (312) 944-5990 | B | |
| Zone 1    North Side | | |

Reservations: Accepted
When to go: Any time
Entree range: $8–13
Payment: VISA, MC, AMEX, D, DC
Service rating: ★★★½
Friendliness rating: ★★★★½

Parking: Valet, $5
Bar: Full service
Wine selection: Limited Spanish and American
Dress: Casual
Disabled access: Yes
Customers: Mixed

**Brunch:** Sunday, 11 a.m.–3 p.m.

**Dinner:** Monday–Thursday, 5–10:30 p.m.; Friday and Saturday, 5–11:30 p.m.

**Setting & atmosphere:** Recently renovated authentic adobe restaurant. Kiva fireplace in the bar, redesigned to increase seating; window benches with pillows line front area. Rounded rooms in vibrant tones of stone blue, brick red, and moss decorated with dried chiles and New Mexican artwork. Native American drawings are painted on the walls. Year-round tented patio and indoor patio (9 months of year) adds a casual outdoor feel.

**House specialties:** Santa Fe appetizer sampler: ancho quesadillas, filled with New Mexican chiles and asadero cheese; wild mushroom sopes (filled corn masa boats). Enchilada del Mar, a blend of shrimp, scallops, fish,

**(Blue Mesa)**

corn, mushrooms, and leeks in a lobster chipotle sauce, between two blue corn tortillas and topped with cheese; some of the best chicken and steak fajitas around (choices also offered, grilled vegetables and salmon); lamb en Colorado (the chef's pride: grilled baby chops marinated with fresh oregano and garlic in a red bricks Colordao sauce); planked salmon, brushed with ancho glaze, roasted on cedar plank, topped with mango salsa. Complimentary jalapeño corn bread with honey butter. Dessert specials include the signatures white chocolate quesadilla (white chocolate mousse served in a crispy cinnamon tortilla with honey-raspberry sauce) and adobe pie (coffee and chocolate Häagen-Dazs layered with fudge on an Oreo crust), served with toasted pecans and caramel sauce.

**Other recommendations:** Fire roasted tamale (made in a pan, not rolled in corn husks, but same flavor). Pork tenderloin Amarillo, in guajillo sauce, with corn dumplings; grilled vegetable burrito; chicken enchilada; chile rellenos with two cheeses on red and green chile sauces. Jicama tostada (not on menu) was great. Tres leches cake, flan of day, Margarita sorbet.

**Summary & comments:** This authentic adobe restaurant is devoted to the unique cuisine of New Mexico, with some creative license. The cooking and atmosphere pay tribute to Santa Fe culture, which is an exciting blend of Indian and Spanish traditions. Mexican chef Dudley Nieto, former owner of highly acclaimed Chapulin, took over the kitchen here in 1998. Passionate about traditional Southwestern and Mexican cooking and with impressive credentials, including a cookbook he co-authored, Nieto updated the menu while keeping its original focus. Enjoy a drink at the lovely bar and then move to the dining room for a meal that gives a taste of historical Santa Fe right in Chicago.

---

| **BRASSERIE JO** | | ★★★★ |
|---|---|---|
| Alsatian French | Inexpensive/Moderate | **QUALITY** 92 |
| 59 West Hubbard; (312) 595-0800 Zone 3 Near North | | **VALUE** B |

Reservations: Accepted
When to go: Avoid peak meal times
  unless you have a reservation
Entree range: $10–18
Payment: All major credit cards
Service rating: ★★★★

Friendliness rating: ★★★½
Parking: Valet
Bar: Full service, including Hopla
  (slang in French for "fun"), an Alsatian beer made exclusively for the
  restaurant by Baderbrau Brewery

## (Brasserie Joe)

| | |
|---|---|
| Wine selection: Extensive, moderately priced regional French wine list, including some fine Alsatian selections | Dress: Casual<br>Disabled access: Yes<br>Customers: Business, international travelers, tourists, couples |

**Lunch:** Monday–Friday, 11:30 a.m.–4 p.m.

**Dinner:** Monday–Thursday, 5–10 p.m.; Friday and Saturday, 5–11 p.m.; Sunday, 4–10 p.m.

**Setting & atmosphere:** Parisian Sam Lopata has created an authentic, comfortable brasserie with a 1940s look: marble, large mirrors, rich cherry wood, French furniture, and a custom-designed chandelier. For an exotic feel, there is also a 25-foot, glass-enclosed wintergarden with palm trees and wicker furniture.

**House specialties:** Onion soup gratinée in crock; croques monsieur with mesclun (baby lettuce mix) and frites (french fries); warm pretzel baguette with smoked chicken, Brie, and mesclun; Alsace cheesy sausage salad; crêpes with spinach, baked ham, blue cheese, mushrooms, and cheese; fish du jour; pâté en croute Strasbourgeoise; house salad Brasserie Jo; Brasserie steak with pommes frites; onion tart Uncle Hansi; mussels in white wine; steak tartare with pommes frites; escalope of salmon with lentils.

**Other recommendations:** Cod brandade; chicken ravioli; mussels in parchment; Les Plats du Jour de Jo (such as couscous, beef Wellington, duck a l'orange, or sautéed rabbit in mustard sauce); fruit tarts; homemade ice creams.

**Summary & comments:** Master chef-owner Jean Joho, well known for his upscale Everest (see page 358), is from France's Alsace region, and he injects his heritage into this brasserie. Legend has it that Alsatians introduced to Paris the concept of the "brasserie," literally "brewery," but also a place for people to relax, socialize, dine, and drink into the wee hours. Thanks to Joho's dedication to authenticity and fresh ingredients, Chicagoans now have their own real brasserie, too. Brasserie Jo serves traditionally hearty food and drink. A unique touch that reflects Joho's culinary breadth is Les Plats du Jour, entree specials that change daily; many of these are traditional, complex dishes rarely seen on menus, such as cassoulet, beef Wellington, and bouillabaisse, and overall they are executed deliciously. The melt-in-the-mouth onion tart was named after his Uncle Hansi, who gave him the recipe. Managing partner Robert Vick of Lettuce Entertain You Enterprises operates the restaurant along with Joho.

**Honors & awards:** "Best New Restaurant" in 1995 by the James Beard Foundation; chef Joho won the 1995 Perrier-Jouet Best American Midwest Chef Award at the Fifth Annual James Beard Awards.

## BRUNA'S RISTORANTE ★★★

| | | |
|---|---|---|
| Italian | Inexpensive/Moderate | **QUALITY** 80 |
| 2424 South Oakley Avenue; (773) 254-5550 Zone 5  South Loop | | **VALUE** B |

**Reservations:** Recommended
**When to go:** Any time for lunch or dinner
**Entree range:** $8.95– 16.95
**Payment:** VISA, MC, AMEX, DC, CB, D
**Service rating:** ★★★½
**Friendliness rating:** ★★★★½
**Parking:** Street; valet on Friday and Saturday evenings
**Bar:** Full service
**Wine selection:** Mostly Italian, including restaurant's private label imported from Italy (Vino Nobile di Montepulciano and chianti); some excellent selections, $15.50–95 per bottle; some great choices by the glass, $3.50–4.50
**Dress:** Casual
**Disabled access:** No, but staff will assist those in wheelchairs up the two steps
**Customers:** Diverse, business, especially for lunch; couples and family, especially for dinner

**Lunch/Dinner:** Monday–Thursday, 11 a.m.–10 p.m.; Friday and Saturday, 11 a.m.–11 p.m.; Sunday, 1–10 p.m.

**Setting & atmosphere:** Old-world style with original, oil-painted murals; ceramics; casual, warm look.

**House specialties:** Pastas (e.g., Luciano's fusilli, various ravioli, tortellini alla Bolognese); Bruna's veal scaloppine; shrimp fra diavolo; chicken limone.

**Other recommendations:** Desserts including tiramisu and fruit tart.

**Summary & comments:** Owner Luciano Silvestri is on hand to direct the operation and has a keen pride in his wine cellar and the recipes he brings back from his biannual trips to Italy. He and his wife, Ilona, bought this restaurant from the original owner in 1981; it has been open since 1933— it's the oldest restaurant in the Heart of Italy, a close-knit Italian community on the near southwest side. The cooking here is full flavored, well prepared, and served with style.

## BUKARA ★★★½

| | | QUALITY |
|---|---|---|
| Indian | Moderate | **80** |

| | VALUE |
|---|---|
| 2 East Ontario Street; (312) 943-0188 | **C** |
| Zone 3   Near North | |

| | |
|---|---|
| Reservations: Recommended | Bar: Full service, including Taj Mahal beer |
| When to go: Any time | |
| Entree range: $8–25 | Wine selection: Fairly extensive; mixed |
| Payment: All major credit cards | |
| Service rating: ★★★★ | Dress: Moderately casual, business |
| Friendliness rating: ★★★½ | Disabled access: Yes, including rest rooms |
| Parking: Discount with validation at garage at 10 East Ontario | Customers: Diverse, business |

**Lunch:**  Monday–Friday (buffet available for $7.95), 11:30 a.m.–2:15 p.m.; Saturday and Sunday, noon–2:45 p.m.

**Dinner:**  Sunday–Thursday, 5:30–9:30 p.m.; Friday and Saturday, 5:30–10:30 p.m.

**Setting & atmosphere:**  Handsomely appointed, classy interior with visible tandoor kitchen. Newly built, comfortable Uncle Phil's Global Bar features 42 beers from 22 nations and international music.

**House specialties:**  Marinated fresh seafood, poultry, and meats roasted in tandoors; sikandari raan (whole leg of lamb); tiger prawns Bukara; dal Bukara (black lentils); and roti (whole-wheat bread).

**Other recommendations:**  Spiced cottage cheese–stuffed bread; roomali (plain wheat bread); shish kebab (skewered, charcoal-grilled, cumin-flavored, minced lamb); flavorful kulfi gulabi dessert, an exotic pudding of dates, almonds, and milk.

**Summary & comments:**  The ancient nomad cooking of the Indian subcontinent was introduced at this restaurant several years ago. To be authentic, no utensils are used. Eating with your hands as the nomads did is sensuous and fun, although they weren't seated in such an elegant atmosphere. There's an Indian saying, "Eating with utensils is like making love through an interpreter." Sauces are well spiced, and, although some tandoori meats can be on the dry side, most are delectable. Catering is available.

## THE CAFE ★★★½

| American/International | Moderate | QUALITY |
|---|---|---|
| | | **90** |

The Ritz-Carlton, Chicago, 160 East Pearson Street; (312) 266-1000
Zone 3   Near North

| | VALUE |
|---|---|
| | **C** |

**Reservations:** Recommended
**When to go:** Weekends are the busiest
**Entree range:** $11–28; most lunch entrees $14–19.50
**Payment:** All major credit cards
**Service rating:** ★★★★½
**Friendliness rating:** ★★★★★
**Parking:** Ask about reduced parking
**Bar:** Beer and wine selections

**Wine selection:** Extensive selections of Californian, French, and Italian wines by bottle or by glass
**Dress:** Casual to dressy
**Disabled access:** Yes, entrance and main floor seating
**Customers:** Business, locals, and hotel guests, including many celebrities

**Open:** Monday–Thursday, Sunday, 6:30 a.m.–midnight; Friday and Saturday, 6:30 a.m.–1 a.m.

**Setting & atmosphere:** In an open alcove of the spectacular 12th-floor hotel lobby. Marble-topped oak cafe tables, botanical Wedgwood china, glistening sterling silver flatware, and fresh flowers; colorful art on walls.

**House specialties:** "Heartland Breakfast" that includes juice, two eggs over easy, homemade chicken or country sausage, Mom's hash browns, toasted bread, and coffee ($15.50). For lunch and dinner, specialties include chilled, grilled vegetable antipasto mozzarella di bufala, French onion soup gratinee, triple-decker turkey club sandwich, and dairy-free vegetarian lasagna. Signature dessert: varying flavored crème brûlée.

**Other recommendations:** Daily specials: a wonderful corn chowder or grilled salmon entree with vegetables. Caesar salad comes as an appetizer, entree, and with grilled chicken breast. Pumpkin risotto with porcini mushrooms. Hearty side orders: mashed Idaho potatoes and roasted garlic and Parmesan bread. Desserts rotate; the peach cobbler is noteworthy.

**Summary & comments:** This cafe offers a fine dining experience with china and silver, top-quality food and service, and beautiful surroundings for the price. Special menus occasionally celebrate a Chicago Art Institute exhibit, such as "Michelangelo and His Influence"; for that occasion, Michelangelo-inspired Italian recipes by cookbook author Giuliano Bugialli were featured.

**Honors & awards:** See profile of The Dining Room.

## CAFE IBERICO TAPAS BAR ★★★½

| | | QUALITY |
|---|---|---|
| Spanish/Tapas | Inexpensive/Moderate | 87 |
| | | VALUE |
| 739 North LaSalle Street; (312) 573-1510 | | B |
| Zone 3   Near North | | |

**Reservations:** Recommended for 9 or more

**When to go:** Before 6:30 p.m. or after 8:30 p.m.

**Entree range:** $7.50–17.95; tapas, $3.50–4

**Payment:** VISA, MC, D, AMEX

**Service rating:** ★★★½

**Friendliness rating:** ★★★½

**Parking:** Valet

**Bar:** Full service

**Wine selection:** Spanish; some nice selections, including sangria

**Dress:** Casual

**Disabled access:** Yes, including rest rooms

**Customers:** Diverse, many Latin Americans and Europeans

**Lunch/Dinner:** Monday–Thursday, 11 a.m.–11 p.m.; Friday and Saturday, 11 a.m.–1 a.m.; Sunday, noon–1:30 a.m.

**Setting & atmosphere:** Authentic touch of Spain: a tapas bar that has been recently expanded with 85 extra seats; a dining room with checkered table cloths, wall murals, and wine bottles on ceiling racks; the rustic bodega (wine cellar room) downstairs; and a newly built deli and ceramics shop.

**House specialties:** Paella estilo Iberico; gazpacho Andaluz. Tapas include grilled octopus with potatoes and olive oil; Spanish cured ham, Manchego cheese, and toasted tomato bread; tortilla Española. Specials include hard-to-find fish cheeks with baby eels. Poached pears with wine and ice cream.

**Other recommendations:** Shrimp with wine and garlic sauce; croquetas de pollo (chicken croquettes), a home-style dish; stuffed eggplant with goat cheese; crema Catalana for dessert.

**Summary & comments:** Just north of downtown, this popular place has expanded by adding a bodega complete with wood-burning oven. Authentic atmosphere, cuisine, and wines make this one of the best tapas places in the city, especially for the prices. Spanish food conveys passionate regionalism and culinary traditions, and it's possible to experience a good sampling of that here.

## CAFE LUCIANO ★★★½

| Italian | Inexpensive/Moderate | QUALITY |
|---|---|---|
| | | 88 |
| | | VALUE |
| | | B |

871 North Rush Street; (312) 266-1414
Zone 3   Near North
2676 Green Bay Road, Evanston; (847) 864-6060
Zone 11   Northern Suburbs

**Reservations:** Recommended (Chicago); only for large groups on Friday and Saturday (Evanston)
**When to go:** Before 7 p.m. (Chicago); before 5 p.m. (Evanston)
**Entree range:** $10–16.95 (Evanston); $10–18.95 (Chicago)
**Payment:** All major credit cards (AMEX *not* accepted at Evanston location)
**Service rating:** ★★★★

**Friendliness rating:** ★★★★½
**Parking:** Street or city lots, valet after 5 p.m. (Chicago); free valet (Evanston)
**Bar:** Full service
**Wine selection:** Moderate, mostly Italian
**Dress:** Casual
**Disabled access:** Yes (Evanston); No (Chicago)
**Customers:** Mostly local

**Lunch/Dinner:** *Chicago:* Monday–Thursday, 11:30 a.m.–10 p.m.; Friday and Saturday, 11:30 a.m.–11 p.m.; Sunday, noon–10 p.m.

**Dinner:** *Evanston:* Sunday–Thursday, 5–10 p.m.; Friday and Saturday, 5–11 p.m.

**Setting & atmosphere:** Homestyle Italian bistro setting; rustic walls and wooden floors; very colorful vines, paintings, and trims on marbled beige walls. Outdoor seating in Chicago; desserts displayed in Evanston location, which is also smoke-free.

**House specialties:** Rigatoni country-style; giambotta (hearty mix of chicken, sweet sausage, onions, sweet peppers, mushrooms, and potatoes sautéed in light olive oil and white wine sauce); eggplant Parmigiana alla Luciano. Appetizers: roasted peppers; polenta con funghi; mussels alla Luciano.

**Other recommendations:** Farfalle alla Stefano (porcini mushrooms, asparagus, peas, and onions in a light tomato sauce with a touch of cream, tossed with bowtie pasta); seafood pomodoro (in zesty marinara sauce over linguini); desserts (change often; many homemade).

**Entertainment & amenities:** *Chicago:* piano in evenings from 7 p.m. to closing.

**(Cafe Luciano)**

**Summary & comments:**  The classic Italian cooking here has bold, lively flavors and is presented beautifully. The chef has a good sense of marrying ingredients properly. Menu has "Luciano Lite" offerings—lower in calories, fat, and sodium. Hearty portions, a good wine selection, a casual atmosphere, and friendly and efficient service combine to make the Evanston location so successful that it expanded within one year. Menus and decor similar at other locations. Owning company Café Concepts substituted Cucina Roma, an Italian bistro, for Cafe Luciano in Westmont, and opened another in Naperville.

| **CAPE COD ROOM** | | ★★★★ |
|---|---|---|
| | | **QUALITY** |
| Seafood | Moderate/Expensive | **95** |
| | | **VALUE** |
| The Drake Hotel, 140 East Walton Place; (312) 787-2200 | | **C** |
| Zone 3   Near North | | |

**Reservations:** Recommended
**When to go:** Monday, Tuesday, or Wednesday
**Entree range:** $21–43, served with potato and vegetables
**Payment:** All major credit cards
**Service rating:** ★★★★
**Friendliness rating:** ★★★★½
**Parking:** Valet for hotel guests
**Bar:** Full service
**Wine selection:** Good assortment of champagnes and sparkling wines; imported and domestic whites and reds chosen for the seafood menu. House wines—several by the glass; imports include French, German, and Italian; bottles range from $23–100. The hotel's extensive reserve list also available.
**Dress:** Business casual
**Disabled access:** Yes, including rest rooms
**Customers:** Diverse, travelers, loyal regulars, locals, business, single diners and couples, celebrities including Steve Lawrence, Eydie Gorme, Jane Meadows, and Paul Newman, and politicos such as Mayor Richard Daley

**Lunch/Dinner:**  Every day, noon–11 p.m.

**Setting & atmosphere:**  Very authentic-looking rustic Cape Cod setting with nautical decor. Charming and intimate.

**House specialties:**  The Cape Cod's famous Bookbinder red snapper soup with sherry; New England clam chowder; bouillabaisse (with a variety of freshwater fish and seafood); raw bar; oysters Rockefeller; halibut papillote (fillet in parchment with lobster, mushrooms, and red wine sauce); imported Dover sole and turbot; New England scrod.

**(Cape Cod Room)**

**Other recommendations:** Smoked salmon; oyster stew; Drake stew; crabmeat à la Newburg; shrimp à la Drake (casserole with shallots and Newburg sauce, glazed with Parmesan). Desserts include key lime pie and strawberry rhubarb crumble with vanilla ice cream.

**Entertainment & amenities:** Sitting at the bar to see the initials carved by celebrities who've dined here over the years. Longtime manager Patrick Bredin will gladly help interpret them.

**Summary & comments:** This seaworthy legend has been sailing full tilt since 1933, and at "60-something" is the city's oldest seafood restaurant. Before Shaw's Crab House, Nick's Fishmarket, and several other excellent seafood restaurants opened, the Cape Cod Room was synonymous with Chicago seafood dining. Located on the main floor of one of the city's finest hotels, it has long been a premier place for imported Dover sole and turbot, broiled New England scrod, bouillabaisse, and the famous Bookbinder red snapper soup. The raw bar continues to be a reliable source for oysters or clams on the shell and a great socializing spot for single travelers. Categorized by type of seafood as well as seafood salads, vegetables, and desserts, the menu also has a section, "From Our Broiler," offering four items from the land—steaks and lamb chops are a few alternatives to the array of items from the waters. There are the old classic lobster preparations (e.g., lobster Thermidor and à la Newburg) as well as the best—simply broiled or steamed. Other period pieces are shrimp de Jonghe, oysters Rockefeller, and clams casino.

**Honors & awards:** Travel Holiday Award for 40 years; Fine Dining Hall of Fame by *Nations Restaurant News;* Ivy Award by *Restaurants & Institutions Magazine.*

## CARLUCCI ★★★½

| Tuscan Italian | Moderate | QUALITY |
| | | 88 |
| | | VALUE |
| | | C |

6111 North River Road, Rosemont; (847) 518-0990
Zone 2   North Central/O'Hare

**Reservations:** Recommended
**When to go:** Any time
**Entree range:** $11.95–30
**Payment:** All major credit cards
**Service rating:** ★★★★
**Friendliness rating:** ★★★★
**Parking:** Free valet and lot
**Bar:** Full service

**Wine selection:** Extensive Italian; selected for the rustic food; several by the glass; fairly priced
**Dress:** Well-dressed, business attire preferable
**Disabled access:** Yes
**Customers:** Business, travelers, couples especially in the evenings

**(Carlucci)**

**Lunch:** Monday–Friday, 11 a.m.–2.30 p.m.

**Dinner:** Monday–Thursday, 5–10 p.m.; Friday and Saturday, 5–11 p.m.;
Sunday, 4:30– 9 p.m.

**Setting & atmosphere:** Open kitchen with rotisserie; handsome bar area;
exquisite doorways, frescoes, and tiles.

**House specialties:** Roasted quail; roasted pork loin; wood-fired pizzas;
black olive pasta with sea scallops; chianti-poached pears.

**Other recommendations:** Antipasto; Tuscan seafood soup.

**Summary & comments:** This, the second of the Carlucci restaurants,
has served excellent Tuscan cuisine since it opened several years ago and
is a great place for dinner before going to, or returning from, O'Hare
International Airport. The space is beautifully designed with a lovely bar
area and a welcoming open kitchen with a rotisserie in the main dining
room. There's lots of bustle, especially on weekends, and showmanship
with grappa carts displaying the liquor infused with fruits. Well managed
by the Carlucci family and partners, who train their staff well, including
in the art of proper Italian wine and dish pronunciation. The first Carlucci on Halsted closed in early 1997 to reopen in the House of Blues
Hotel.

| CHARLIE TROTTER'S | | ★★★★★ | |
|---|---|---|---|
| New American | Very Expensive | **QUALITY** | |
| | | 98 | |
| 816 West Armitage Avenue; (773) 248-6228 | | **VALUE** | |
| Zone 1   North Side | | C | |

**Reservations:** Required
**When to go:** Wednesdays seem to be
the least crowded
**Entree range:** Prix fixe tasting menu,
$100
**Payment:** VISA, MC, AMEX, CB,
DC
**Service rating:** ★★★★★
**Friendliness rating:** ★★★★½
**Parking:** Valet
**Bar:** Wine only
**Wine selection:** Extensive, award-
winning, international list with
1,000 different wines including
French, Californian, and Italian.
Rich in Burgundies and Bordeaux,
$40–1,000 per bottle. Choices by
the glass, $9–16, change daily
with the menu. Sommelier will
assist customers with ordering.
**Dress:** Business; jackets requested,
not required
**Disabled access:** Yes
**Customers:** Local, tourist, business

**(Charlie Trotter's)**

**Dinner:** Tuesday–Thursday, 6–10 p.m.; Friday and Saturday, 5:15–10 p.m. (closing hours depend on business; last seating is at 10 p.m.; occasionally open on Sunday and Monday)

**Setting & atmosphere:** Upscale, understated elegance in a renovated townhouse built in the 1880s. Quietly elegant contemporary dining rooms on two floors. Burgundy carpeting, cream wall covering, white linen tablecloths, china and crystal setting.

**House specialties:** Menu changes daily according to the season and market availability. Examples are smoked Atlantic salmon, Maine lobster, and Oestra caviar with daikon, jicama, blended horseradish, and spicy herb sauce; the unusual peeky toe crab and black striped bass with braised cardoon, spring peas, and curry emulsion; California pigeon breast with crispy polenta, braised red cabbage, shiitakes, and cumin-infused broth; Iowa lamb loin with caramelized rutabaga, braised legumes, and meat juices. Vegetarian tasting menus include dishes along the likes of warm goat cheese with bleeding heart radishes, artichokes, and roasted hickory nuts; ragout of early spring morels, fava beans, haricots verts, and baby leeks in their own juices. Some items flavored with chef's infused oils.

**Other recommendations:** Vanilla-yogurt, pineapple, and pink guava sorbets with lemongrass broth; desserts vary daily along with the menu.

**Summary & comments:** Chef-owner Charlie Trotter is extremely gifted (he's been termed a culinary genius) in creating dishes in a new realm with sometimes disparate ingredients and eclectic foreign influences. Classic dish foundations are often given an element of surprise and become unexpected pleasures. Trotter's cooking is difficult to define since it has long had French underpinnings, uses 95% American ingredients, and is influenced by numerous foreign cuisines. It began more as experimental contemporary French and recently turned in the direction of contemporary American, and is usually wonderful. His menu reflects the produce market availability and his creative use of lesser-known and -used vegetables. The fixed degustation menu limits the diners' choices, however, and is not everyone's favored way of dining. There's no à la carte, but call ahead to request any special food for dietary restrictions. Trotter had his kitchen redesigned to include state-of-the art equipment. Available for special parties.

**Honors & awards:** AAA five diamonds; five stars from *Mobil Travel Guide*; Relais Gourmand member; *Wine Spectator* readers voted it "Best Restaurant in the U.S." and Charlie Trotter "Best Chef in the U.S."

## CHICAGO CHOP HOUSE ★★★★

| | QUALITY |
|---|---|
| Steak                    Moderate | 94 |

| | VALUE |
|---|---|
| 60 West Ontario Street; (312) 787-7100 | C |

Zone 3   Near North

Reservations: Recommended
When to go: Before 7 p.m. or after
   10 p.m.; lunch is less busy
Entree range: $16–30
Payment: All major credit cards
Service rating: ★★★★½
Friendliness rating: ★★★★½
Parking: Valet, $6 lunch, $7 dinner

Bar: Full service
Wine selection: International, exten-
   sive (has own warehouse)
Dress: Business casual
Disabled access: No, but managers
   are willing to assist
Customers: Business, VIPs, lots of
   celebrities

**Lunch/Dinner:** Monday–Thursday, 11:30 a.m.–11 p.m.; Friday, 11:30 a.m.–11:30 p.m.

**Dinner:** Saturday, 4–11:30 p.m.; Sunday, 4–11 p.m.

**Setting & atmosphere:** Century-old brownstone with three floors of dining rooms and more than 1,400 historical Chicago pictures. Every chicago mayor is on the wall—not even City Hall has that!

**House specialties:** U.S. prime aged steaks and prime rib; Chop House char-broiled New York strip steak, either 16- or 24-ounce; T-bone steak, 24-ounce; namesake potato pancake.

**Other recommendations:** Spring lamb chops; roast loin of pork chops; broiled Lake Superior whitefish with lemon butter; Russ's American fries; creamed spinach.

**Entertainment & amenities:** Pianist on Monday–Friday, 5–11 p.m.; Saturday and Sunday, 6–11 p.m.

**Summary & comments:** One of Chicago's best restaurants for quality steaks and chops, founded by the late well-known restaurateur, Henry Norton. It has a loyal following, especially with certain celebrities. A place to see VIPs. Menu is traditional steak house–style, featuring steaks and chops, a couple of chicken items, several seafood preparations, a handful of appetizers (all seafood), and some sides. Food is kept simple and properly prepared.

**Honors & awards:** *Knife and Fork* Club '91–'95. In '94 voted Number Two steak house in the United States by Tom Horan's America's Top 10 Clubs. Listed by *Gourmet* as one of top five steakhouses in Chicago. *Wine Spectator* Award for Excellence '94–'98. Zagat Award, '97 and '98.

## CITÉ ★★★★

| Continental | Expensive/Very Expensive | QUALITY |
|---|---|---|
| | | **89** |

Top of Lake Point Tower, 505 North Lake Shore Drive;
(312) 644-4050
Zone 1   North Side

| | VALUE |
|---|---|
| | **D** |

**Reservations:** Required (weekends book up fast; plan ahead)
**When to go:** It's easier to get a reservation on weeknights
**Entree range:** $23–48
**Payment:** Major credit cards
**Service rating:** ★★★★½
**Friendliness rating:** ★★★★
**Parking:** Valet in building garage
**Bar:** Full service

**Wine selection:** Extensive; American and European wines, ranging from $40–140 per bottle; four available by the glass
**Dress:** Jackets required for men
**Disabled access:** Yes
**Customers:** Business, tourists, couples, guests of special events, such as weddings or birthday celebrations

**Lunch:** Monday–Friday, noon–3 p.m.; Sunday brunch, 11 a.m.–3 p.m.

**Dinner:** Sunday–Thursday, 5–9:30 p.m.; Friday and Saturday, 5–10:30 p.m.

**Setting & atmosphere:** The panoramic, 70th-floor view of Chicago's skyline and lakefront fosters a heady, romantic atmsophere at Cité. Though the view alone is spectacular, Cité enhances the intimate scene with fresh flower arrangements on every table. The circular dining room with a marble floor is positively elegant.

**House specialties:** Appetizers: sautéed wild mushrooms in puff pastry; Mediterranean tapas with tastes from Spain, Greece, and France; shrimp coriander. Entrees (include Cité salad): grilled Norwegian salmon fillet, with raspberry champagne sauce; roast rack of spring lamb, with sweet Dijon, fresh rosemary, and pecans; fresh seafood according to availability: baked red snapper Mediterranean in crust of aromatic vegetables. Grand Marnier soufflé and several desserts prepared tableside: crêpes Suzette, bananas Foster, cherries jubilee.

**Other recommendations:** Pasta primavera; classic steak Diane, flambéed tableside; daily selections from pastry trolley.

**Entertainment & amenities:** The spectacular panoramic view of Chicago's skyline and lakefront. Piano music nightly. Live music/entertainment at Le Cabaret at Cité, Wednesday–Sunday evenings ($25 cover); dinner/show package available.

**Summary & comments:** As the restaurant's postcard states: "Let the skyline surround you," and indeed it does here. This is one of the greatest

**(Cité)**

views of Chicago, and it's 25 floors closer to earth than The Signature Room at the Ninety-Fifth. The restaurant has had its ups and downs over the years, but lately has seemed reliable in its commitment to fine dining. A new manager has made changes, such as opening Le Cabaret at Cité, a new venue with live entertainment. Singer and actress Karen Mason opened Le Cabaret at Cité in 1997. A great restaurant for a special occasion: birthday guests see their name in a frame at the table.

| COCO PAZZO | | ★★★★ |
|---|---|---|

| Northern Italian | Moderate | QUALITY |
|---|---|---|
| | | 91 |

| 300 West Hubbard Street; (312) 836-0900 | VALUE |
|---|---|
| Zone 4   The Loop | C |

Reservations: Highly recommended, especially on weekends
When to go: During the week
Entree range: $13–30
Payment: V, MC, AMEX, D
Service rating: ★★★★
Friendliness rating: ★★★★
Parking: Valet; city garages nearby
Bar: Full service, including grappa selection

Wine selection: 85 Italian selections, some French champagne, some sparkling wines from California; prices from $20–225 per bottle
Dress: Casual to upscale, no jackets required
Disabled access: Yes
Customers: Mostly local, professional, couples, business (especially at lunch)

**Lunch:** Monday–Friday, 11 a.m.–2:30 p.m.

**Dinner:** Monday–Thursday, 5:30–10:30 p.m.; Friday and Saturday, 5:30–11:30 p.m.; Sunday, 5–10 p.m.

**Setting & atmosphere:** Open kitchen with wood-burning oven and rotisserie produces a warm, inviting interior. Rustic decor: brick walls; wooden floors, beams, and chairs; and track lighting and columns. Sophisticated blue velvet drapes enhance the room along with white linen-covered tables spaced for privacy; elegant bar.

**House specialties:** Rotisserie special of the day (e.g., lamb); tagliata alla fiorentina (grilled rib-eye steak); baked vegetables and roasted butterflied trout; ravioli filled with baby artichokes; sea bass braised with tomato, black olives, capers, garlic, and white wine over spinach. Signature dessert is cioccolato fondente con gelato cappuccino—flourless chocolate cake with a warm mousse center and cappuccino ice cream.

**(Coco Pazzo)**

**Other recommendations:** Risotto del Giorno (chef's special Arborio rice of the day); coscia di agnello al giarrosto (leg of lamb seasoned with fresh herbs, slowly cooked on the rotisserie, thinly sliced, and served with potatoes); osso buco (veal shank); vegetali al forno (assorted thinly-sliced seasonal vegetables with extra virgin olive oil, baked in a wood-burning oven).

**Summary & comments:** The young star executive chef, Gregorio Stephenson, prepares creative, hearty Tuscan-style dishes; specialties change every day. The pastry chef bakes bread and wonderful simple, flavorful desserts such as torta di limone (lemon tart) and budino (white chocolate bread pudding). This restaurant and Il Toscanaccio (66 North St. Clair; phone (312) 664-2777) are restaurateur Pino Luongo's only Chicago entries of his successful group of New York–based dining establishments.

**Honors & awards:** *Mobil Travel Guide* Award; AAA four diamonds; DiRoNA Award.

| **CORNER BAKERY** | | ★★★½ |
|---|---|---|
| Bakery Cafe | Inexpensive/Moderate | **QUALITY** |
| | | **90** |
| 516 North Clark Street; (312) 644-8100 | | **VALUE** |
| Zone 4 The Loop | | **B** |

Sante Fe Building, 224 South Michigan Avenue (at Jackson Boulevard) (312) 431-7600   Zone 4 The Loop

**Reservations:** Not accepted
**When to go:** Any time; busiest at peak breakfast and lunch hours
**Entree range:** Loaves, $1.50–6; sandwiches and soups, $1.95–5.25
**Payment:** All major credit cards
**Service rating:** ★★★★ (since self-serve, pertains to clerks)
**Friendliness rating:** ★★★★½

**Parking:** Street or nearby garages or lots
**Bar:** None
**Wine selection:** None
**Dress:** Casual
**Disabled access:** Yes; call first
**Customers:** Varied, professionals (before and after work and for lunch)

**Open:** Monday–Friday, 6:30 a.m.–9 p.m.; Saturday and Sunday, 7:30 a.m.–9 p.m. Call individual locations for hours since some vary.

**Setting & atmosphere:** The original Clark Street location is a small, cozy shop with several tables near windows; hearth bakery; great aromas. The

**(Corner Bakery)**

Santa Fe Building is historic, and the 80-seat bakery is about the largest of the ten locations; the sidewalk cafe on Michigan Avenue is open in the summer. Other locations are slightly different, but the basic concept is the same.

**House specialties:** A variety of about 25 breads baked fresh daily, including baguettes, country loaves, and specialty breads such as kalamata olive, chocolate-cherry, multi-grains, and ryes. Lunch items: focaccia and various sandwiches such as chicken pesto with tomato and arugula on a baguette or tuna salad with sweet red onion and sprouts on an olive baguette; roasted vegetable salad; Oriental pasta salad; rope pasta salad with butternut squash, goat cheese, and spinach tossed in sherry vinaigrette with rosemary.

**Other recommendations:** Raisin-nut bread; kugelhopf (seasonal); mushroom pizza (oyster, shiitake, and white cap mushooms with mozzarella and Asiago cheeses); cheese bread; tomato flatbread (thin, crackerlike); variety of muffins (good blueberry); bars (try lemon and apricot); cookies (pecan chocolate chip); mini Bundt cakes; hot chocolate; juices; cappuccino.

**Summary & comments:** This bakery concept, originated by Lettuce Entertain You Enterprises and chef Jean Joho in 1991, produces some of the finest hearth-cooked, European-style breads and rolls anywhere; therefore, their sandwiches are excellent. An assortment of about 25 freshly baked loaves are available daily. The number of locations is growing: bakeries are now in the Water Tower Place, Union Station, Oak Brook, Old Orchard, and Schaumburg, and adjacent to some Maggiano's Little Italy restaurants. The success of this place proves that people have been starving for great bread and baked items. The staff of life is very alive here.

---

| **CROFTON ON WELLS** | | ★★★½ |
|---|---|---|
| New American | Moderate | **QUALITY**<br>91 |
| 535 N. Wells; (312) 755-1790<br>Zone 3    Near North | | **VALUE**<br>B |

Reservations: Recommended; often necessary three weeks in advance for weekends
When to go: Weeknights
Entree range: $16–35
Payment: All major credit cards
Service rating: ★★★½
Friendliness rating: ★★★

Parking: Valet, lunch and dinner, $6
Bar: Full
Wine selection: Fairly extensive international list, from $6–$12
Dress: Casual
Disabled access: Yes
Customers: Mixed, all ages; mostly professionals and locals; Crofton fans

## (Crofton On Wells)

**Lunch:** Monday–Friday, 11:30 a.m.–2:30 p.m.

**Dinner:** Monday–Thursday, 5–10 p.m., Friday–Saturday, 5–11 p.m.

**Setting & atmosphere:** Contemporary intimate space with classical accents and tones of river stone, beige, and silver was designed by chef-owner Crofton. Sophisticated, serene and rather austere with unadorned light gray walls (no paintings). Attractive bar surrounded by glass votives. Curvaceous gilt mirror on back wall; sheer drapes artistically divide the dining room from the kitchen area.

**House specialties:** Soup: sweet corn garbure (cabbage, chicken stock, bacon) with cilantro pesto; appetizer crabcake of jumbo lump crabmeat, bound by shrimp mousse, with sweet red peppers, chives, served with piquant Creole mustard sauce (a must). Entrées: sublime roast Atlantic salmon, roasted baby cauliflower, sweet pea emulsion, white truffle oil; succulent pan-roasted diver scallops with a Mediterranean touch of ratatouille, saffron-mussel sauce, basil oil. Made-to-order desserts: indulge in the warm macaronnade of extra bittersweet chocolate, a soufflé-like cake with a runny center, with raspberries and crème fraîche; crème brulée, "Jean Banchet," a tribute to the master chef, with candied orange zest and Grand Marnier.

**Other recommendations:** Appetizer timbale of grilled vegetables & goat cheese, grilled wild scallion broth; sauté of wild mushrooms, bacon, cracked peppercorn cream in fried leek basket. Entrée: herb-roasted poussin (French, young chicken), champagne grapes, vegetable couscous, verjus reduction. Dessert: warm feuilleté of peach and raspberry, caramel sauce, Poire William cream.

**Entertainment & amenities:** Special menus and celebrations.

**Summary & comments:** Crofton's background in classical French cuisine is evident in her American seasonal cooking, which she finds more creative since she can experiment with a broad range of ingredients. She had experience at Le Francais with Jean Banchet, at Montparnasses in Naperville with owner Jean-Paul Eskenazi, a Parisian, and then worked at the former Cassis. This is her first restaurant, and her signature is imprinted here from the interior to the food. The moderate prices belie the labor intensity of this exciting cuisine.

**Honors & awards:** 3 stars from both *Chicago Sun-Times* and *Chicago Tribune;* 4 gavels, *Chicago Lawyer.*

| CUISINES | | ★★★½ |
| --- | --- | --- |
| | | QUALITY |
| Italian/Mediterranean | Inexpensive/Moderate | 89 |
| | | VALUE |
| Renaissance Chicago Hotel, One West Wacker Drive; | | B |
| (312) 795-3330 | | |

Zone 4    The Loop

**Reservations:** Requested and suggested
**When to go:** Weekdays
**Entree range:** $8.95–29; one item at $32.95
**Payment:** VISA, MC, AMEX, D, DC, CB, JCB
**Service rating:** ★★★★½
**Friendliness rating:** ★★★★★
**Parking:** Valet
**Bar:** Full service
**Wine selection:** Extensive. Over 220 bottles with focus on French, Italian, and Californian; many nice vertical cabernet sauvignon tasting possibilities; 8-page list and 1-page wines-by-the-glass list.
**Dress:** Tastefully casual (no shorts or T-shirts); dressier on Friday and Saturday evenings
**Disabled access:** Yes
**Customers:** Tourist, hotel guests, locals, theatergoers

**Lunch:**  Monday–Friday, 11:30 a.m.–2 p.m.

**Dinner:**  Every day, 5:30–10:30 p.m.

**Setting & atmosphere:**  The decor is not the airy and light Mediterranean style popular some places—this is more opulent: plush, romantic, elegant with comfortable banquettes; wood and marble; open kitchen with wood-burning oven.

**House specialties:**  Starters of grilled octopus with warm Spanish potato salad; snapper Napoleon with spinach, tomato, and cabernet-butter sauce; lobster bisque; crabmeat and scallop lasagna; grilled tuna, French beans, and tomato, caper, and olive relish. Desserts: apple phyllo basket (warm diced and thinly sliced apples in phyllo with a sweet caramel sauce and white chocolate ice cream) and chocolate cigar (this is an outstanding presentation of Cointreau white chocolate mousse wrapped in dark chocolate with darling cocolate matches on a plate dusted with cocoa in a harlequin pattern).

**Other recommendations:**  Robust, grilled small pizza with dried tomato and fontina; appetizer of crabmeat and shiitake mushrooms in phyllo; grilled swordfish (ordered with accompaniments from red snapper—ragout of artichokes, leeks, tomato, and muscat wine); three-layer chocolate torte; papaya compote; ethereal tiramisu.

**(Cuisines)**

**Summary & comments:** Start with the nine-page wine list here, then look at the one-page menu for dishes to match your bottle selection. The menu leans toward Italian with many French, some American, and a few Middle Eastern choices. There's a Mediterranean influence, and overall the cooking has bold flavors from herbs, sun-dried items, and olives. There's an element of surprise (e.g., a salad of field greens with quail eggs and prosciutto cracklings) and a comfort zone with standards like minestrone. The risotto here is cooked to a softer consistency than usual. Only one item sampled could have been better: a grilled veal flank special was chewy, although flavorful; it was accompanied by a host of items, including an apricot chutney and fresh rosemary. There have been some changes since the hotel became the Renaissance Chicago: A 50% menu change recently occurred, but many house specialties remained the same. And a refreshing complimentary fruit plate arrives at the end of the meal—a very thoughtful touch. The value here is excellent considering the food, wine, and hospitality.

**Honors & awards:** *Wine Spectator* Award of Excellence, 1992–1998.

## THE DINING ROOM ★★★★½

| New French | Moderate/Expensive | QUALITY |
|---|---|---|
| | | 95 |

The Ritz-Carlton Hotel, 160 East Pearson Street;

| | | VALUE |
|---|---|---|
| | | C |

(312) 266-1000, ext. 4223
Zone 3   Near North

**Reservations:** Strongly recommended, especially for weekends and holidays; call one week ahead for Sunday and holidays, and midweek for weekends

**When to go:** Weekends are busiest; business depends on conventions in the hotel and Chicago events

**Entree range:** $30–36

**Payment:** VISA, MC, AMEX, DC, CB

**Service rating:** ★★★★★

**Friendliness rating:** ★★★★★

**Parking:** 3 hours free with validation at restaurant; car parked by valet at hotel entrance

**Bar:** Full service, 2 bars in hotel

**Wine selection:** Extensive 50-page list with about 500 selections; more than 20,000 bottles in temperature-controlled cellars; from $30–2,200 per bottle; mostly French Burgundy and Bordeaux with a fair number of American wines

**Dress:** Jacket required, tie optional; brunch, casual—no cutoffs or tank tops

**Disabled access:** Yes, entrance and rest room

**Customers:** Many business, hotel guests, and local; not touristy; families and couples, honeymooners and anniversary celebrators

## (The Dining Room)

**Brunch:** Sunday, 2 seatings for buffet brunch at 10:30 a.m. and 1 p.m.

**Dinner:** Monday–Saturday, 6–11 p.m.; Sunday, 6–10 p.m.

**Setting & atmosphere:** Luxurious Edwardian-style two-level room with carved French pine, beveled mirrors, crystal, and Louis XV chairs at tables in the central area. Quiet, cozy niches; large tables for families; intimate banquettes in raised tier for couples. Sunday brunch served on outdoor terrace.

**House specialties:** Maine lobster with couscous and stuffed zucchini blossom filled with seafood mousseline, with shellfish-chive jus; applewood home-smoked salmon with traditional garnishes; Beluga caviar parfait with corn cake; chilled terrine of artichokes, baby spinach, and oven-dried tomatoes, and French green bean salad; veal chop with spring morel mushrooms and asparagus–Italian parsley salad; four to five items change daily; always five meat entrees and five seasonal fish; verbal special of the day.

**Other recommendations:** Shrimp cake with an assortment of Kingsfield green beans and honey-thyme vinaigrette; Colorado rack of lamb glazed with thyme and honey, artichoke hearts, and lamb shank and braised fennel gratin; sautéed swordfish with portobello mushroom and tomato Provençale, in a mustard–red wine vinaigrette; six-course vegetarian degustation menu, $50; set pre-theater menu from 6–7 p.m.; six-course degustation menu, $60.

**Entertainment & amenities:** Pianist (classical, contemporary, and requests) during dining hours.

**Summary & comments:** Voted by readers of several magazines to be the best hotel dining room in Chicago, and every visit here proves why. Top-flight, progressive French cuisine, opulent atmosphere, and professionally friendly—never intimidating—service. This is a stellar dining experience at one of the finest hotels anywhere. Sarah Stegner became the chef of the Dining Room in 1991 and has won numerous awards since. Her inspirational cooking is predominantly light, incorporating low-fat alternative cuisine dishes and featuring an abundance of vegetables, herbs, and strong flavors, while stressing simplicity in presentation.

**Honors & awards:** Chef Sarah Stegner won New York's James Beard Award for upcoming chefs; *Gourmet* magazine, "Best Restaurant in Chicago," 1996; *Bon Appetit* magazine, "One of the Top 13 Hotel Dining Rooms in the United States," 1996; wine list received the *Wine Spectator* Grand Award for 12 years in succession.

## EARTH ★★★½

| | | |
|---|---|---|
| Healthy/clean cuisine | Moderate/Expensive | **QUALITY** 89 |
| 738 N. Wells St.; (312) 335-5475 | | **VALUE** B |
| Zone 3 Near North | | |

Reservations: Dinner only, strongly recommended

When to go: Anytime; weeknights usually less busy

Entree range: $14.95–18.95

Payment: AMEX, D, DC, MC, VISA

Service rating: ★★★½

Friendliness rating: ★★★★

Parking: Valet at dinnertime, $6

Bar: Several good organic beers; one organic vodka.

Wine selection: Carefully selected list of domestic and imported eco-friendly wines, including organi-cally grown Storybook Mountain, 1990 Napa Valley Zinfandel, one of my favorites; several from insecticide-free vineyards. Almost all available by the glass $4.95–7.95; bottles $22–60.

Dress: Casual

Disabled access: Yes, but one step in front; staff will assist. Ramp in back; call first

Customers: Sophisticated; mostly professionals of all ages, especially 35–50; also the health-and environment-conscious

**Lunch:** Monday–Saturday 11:30 a.m.–2:30 p.m.

**Dinner:** Tuesday–Thursday 5:30 p.m.–9 p.m.; Fri., Sat 5:30 p.m.–10 p.m.

**Setting & atmosphere:** Pristine storefront interior is bright and elegant in its simplicity. Attractive lighting; an artistic row of glass block vases with seasonal flowers accent white walls. The restaurant was constructed from natural materials and non-toxic substances. Wooden tables and bar. Beautiful hickory floor the result of an environmental project to use wood that usually is made into sawdust.

**House specialties:** Creative soups of the day, such as corn and sweet potato soup with chiles and cilantro; the signature mussels steamed in fresh apple cider, plump and flavorful. Great salads: spring shoot salad with mesclun greens & pink peppercorn yogurt dressing; Earth salad with house honey-mustard dressing. Entrees: vegetable strudel with or without shrimp; roasted monkfish with Indian pesto fettuccine and curry sauce; sea bass fillet topped with Swiss chard; slightly sweet-spicy jungle curry with tofu, colorful vegetables and brown rice (chef does creative things with tofu here). From the substantial dessert menu, a delicious semisweet and milk chocolate mousse; individual lemon tart with fresh fruit; rosemary-

**(Earth)**

scented crème brûlée; fresh fruit sorbets in exotic flavors such as guanabana and passionfruit (dairy-free, fat-free, no refined sugar).

**Other recommendations:** Sautéed sea scallops with jicama and endive in citrus sauce; naturally smoked salmon with fresh herbed goat cheese and chive oil. Entrée: marinated seitan (wheat protein) changes with season, such as with lotus root, soba noodles, vegetables and eggplant caviar in seaweed broth (vegan, indicated by "V"). Dessert: Ginger, coconut and lemongrass tapioca pudding in a phyllo cup.

**Entertainment & amenities:** Special events to increase environmental awareness, such as Harvest Moon festival in October, which promotes Midwestern organic produce.

**Summary & comments:**   Earth is a profound name for a restaurant, and this River North place lives up to the high standards and expectations of the environment- and health-conscious. Owner Barry Bursak, who is committed to the environmental cause, has made his restaurant as pure as possible while offering exciting cuisine in a fine dining atmosphere. The flavorful, clean fare here is prepared by classically-trained Chef Charles Warshawsky, who elevates low-fat, healthful cooking from the commonplace to an upscale gastronomic landscape. He creatively blends together Asian, French and Mexican ingredients that result in robust, flavor-packed, seasonal dishes that have gained him a following. This is not a vegetarian restaurant, but there are many vegetarian items, and those that are vegan are indicated by a "V."

**Honors & awards:** Three-star review in *Chicago Tribune;* "Hot Spot" feature in *Chicago Sun-Times.;* named one of the "best new restaurants of the year" by *Chicago* magazine; one of six healthful restaurants in the United States, *Bon Appetit* (September, 1998); and featured on the Television Food Network.

| ELI'S, THE PLACE FOR STEAK | ★★★½ |
|---|---|

| Steak | Moderate/Expensive | QUALITY |
|---|---|---|
| | | **88** |

| 215 East Chicago Avenue; (312) 642-1393 | VALUE |
|---|---|
| Zone 3   Near North | **C** |

Reservations: Accepted
When to go: Early or late for both lunch and dinner
Entree range: $17.50–32
Payment: All major credit cards

Service rating: ★★★½
Friendliness rating: ★★★★
Parking: $5 with validation at garage next door
Bar: Full service

## (Eli's, The Place for Steak)

Wine selection: Mostly American, with some French and Italian selections, ranging from $16–260 (the highest for Roederer Cristal Champagne) per bottle; most in the $20–42 range.

Dress: Casual

Disabled access: Yes

Customers: Mixed, business (especially at lunch), tourists, locals

**Lunch:** Monday–Friday, 11 a.m.–3 p.m.

**Dinner:** Sunday–Thursday, 5–10:30 p.m.; Friday and Saturday, 5–11 p.m.

**Setting & atmosphere:** Photo gallery of celebrities who have dined here with the late founder Eli Shulman and his son Mark, now the owner; comfortable carpeted dining room with white tablecloths, candle lamps, and paintings; a charming enclosed sidewalk cafe with half curtains on doors that open in the summer.

**House specialties:** Complimentary iced relishes, chopped liver, and breads; Eli's special New York sirloin steak, seasoned with crushed black peppercorns and served with onion, red-and-green-pepper relish, and a choice of cottage or steak fries or a baked potato; Eli's house salad (lettuce, tomatoes, beets, croutons) with good creamy garlic dressing; Eli's Famous Garbage Salad (garden vegetables served over mixed salad greens tossed in Eli's dressing).

**Other recommendations:** Soup of the day: good creamy tomato-based seafood chowder. Eli's famous potato pancakes, served with applesauce and sour cream; Eli's chicken and matzo ball soup; Eli's Caesar salad; calf's liver Eli, sautéed with onions, green peppers, and mushrooms. Eli's cheesecake (usually about a dozen varieties on the dessert tray; try key lime, cappuccino hazelnut, mint chocolate chip, toffee top, peanut butter blast, or praline). If you're not fond of cheesecake, Eli's bakery also makes carrot cake, apple tart, and "Midnight sensation" chocolate cake.

**Summary & comments:** You'll never forget where you are dining, since Eli's name is reinforced throughout the menu. In addition, when I asked our waiter to recommend several items for dinner, he repeated three times, "Eli's is the place for steak." We got the message. Naturally, we ordered the special New York sirloin steak with crushed black peppercorns, and it was delicious and properly prepared to a medium-rare, as ordered. I also ordered salmon fillet pesto, and they cook fish well here, too. Although Eli's is expensive, at least you get relishes, chopped liver, delicious bread, and potato included in the entree price here, unlike some steak houses.

## EMILIO'S TAPAS CHICAGO ★★★★

| | | QUALITY |
|---|---|---|
| Spanish/Tapas/Paella | Moderate | **91** |

444 West Fullerton Avenue; (773) 327-5100

| | VALUE |
|---|---|
| | **C** |

Zone 1   North Side

**Reservations:** Accepted
  Monday–Thursday and Saturday
**When to go:** Weekdays
**Entree range:** $13–14; tapas, $2–12
**Payment:** VISA, MC, AMEX, DC
**Service rating:** ★★★½
**Friendliness rating:** ★★★★
**Parking:** Valet; nearby garages
**Bar:** Full service

**Wine selection:** Mostly Spanish,
  including sherries and sangria;
  good range of types and prices,
  beginning at $15 a bottle; a few
  Californian
**Dress:** Casual
**Disabled access:** Yes
**Customers:** Diverse

**Lunch/Dinner:** Sunday–Thursday, 11:30 a.m.–10 p.m.; Friday and Saturday, 11:30 a.m.–11 p.m.

**Setting & atmosphere:** Colorful ceramic decor complements the setting, which has the feel of Andalucia, the Spanish province from which Emilio hails.

**House specialties:** Paella de mariscos (seafood); patatas con aïoli (potato salad with garlic mayonaise); tortilla española (a Spanish omelette with onions and potatoes); salpicon de Burgos (marinated shrimp, scallops, and monkfish with tri-colored peppers, leeks, olive oil, and sherry vinaigrette); pan con tomate, jamon, y queso (tomato bread topped with Serrano ham and Manchego cheese); ensalada de verduras templadas (grilled seasonal vegetables with sherry vinaigrette); gambas a la plancha (grilled shrimp brochette served in garlic butter); pincho de pollo al mojo picon (grilled and marinated chicken brochette served with cumin mayonnaise); datiles con bacon (dates wrapped in bacon with roasted red pepper–butter sauce).

**Other recommendations:** Empanada de cordero con curri (puff pastry filled with lamb, chorizo, and curry, served with tomato–basil sauce); cazuela de judias con almejas (casserole of lima beans, Manila clams, and shallots, served in a spicy tomato broth); mejillones al ajillo (black mussels served with garlic, parsley, and white wine); lomo de cerdo al ajillo (pork tenderloin medallions served in a garlic sauce with Spanish potatoes).

**Entertainment & amenities:** Flamenco on occasion.

**Summary & comments:** Known as the King of Tapas, Emilio Gervilla brought the Spanish tapas concept to Chicago more than a decade ago. He

**(Emilio's Tapas Chicago)**

opened Emilio's Tapas Bar Restaurant in Hillside in 1988, the first of his own restaurants. Since then he's expanded to several more, mostly in the western suburbs. The latest is this one on the mid-North Side of the city. Emilio is from Granada, knows his cuisine well, and is a hands-on restaurateur. This place offers an authentic, delicious trip to Spain.

| ENTRE NOUS | ★★★★ |
|---|---|

| French | Moderate/Expensive | QUALITY |
|---|---|---|
| | | 90 |

| Fairmont Hotel, 200 North Columbus Drive; (312) 565-7997 | VALUE |
|---|---|
| Zone 4   The Loop | C |

Reservations: Recommended
When to go: Early evenings
Entree range: Dinner, $19–34
Payment: All major credit cards
Service rating: ★★★★½
Friendliness rating: ★★★★★
Parking: Hotel garage, validated; valet, $12
Bar: Full service

Wine selection: Award-winning, extensive, international, world-class collection; lovely wine library in the dining room
Dress: Moderately upscale
Disabled access: Yes
Customers: Mostly local, a few tourists

**Dinner:** Tuesday–Saturday, 5:30–10 p.m.

**Setting & atmosphere:** Elegant, plush, and sophisticated. Large table with flowers and display of some dishes is the central focus of dining room, and one wall is a wine library.

**House specialties:** Specialties change daily. Dinner appetizer: pan-fried Chesapeake crab cakes (with sautéed arugula and lobster sauce). Dinner entrees: pot-au-feu of grouper and prawns with root vegetables and basil; roast rack of Sonoma lamb with mustard-herb crust and rosemary lentils. Weekly table d'hôte four-course dinner menu, $29; $44 with wine.

**Other recommendations:** Lobster bisque; applewood smoked chicken breast with caraway cabbage and fire-roasted chestnuts. Dessert tray holds several light, layered pastries; almond cheesecake; chocolate raspberry torte.

**Entertainment & amenities:** Jazz in the Metropole; ask about dinner-jazz package in Entre Nous.

**Summary & comments:** Entre Nous (between us) is an intimate French phrase and charming name for this romantic hotel dining room. The creative cuisine has many innovative touches (the marrow melted over herbed

**(Entre Nous)**

tenderloin, for example). New chef Matthew Koury works with Fairmont executive chef Norbert Bumm to produce seasonal promotions and menus. The service is gracious and accommodating and, overall, dining here is distinctive.

**Honors & awards:** Wine collection has received the Award of Excellence from *Wine Spectator* for three consecutive years; four stars from *Mobil Travel Guide;* DiRoNA Award.

| EVEREST | | ★★★★★ |
|---|---|---|

| French | Expensive | QUALITY<br>98 |
|---|---|---|
| 440 South LaSalle Street (One Financial Place, 40th Floor);<br>(312) 663-8920 | | VALUE<br>C |

Zone 4   The Loop

**Reservations:** Required
**When to go:** Varies; call before you go
**Entree range:** À la carte, $26.50–32.50; pre-theater menu, $44; evening tasting menu, $79
**Payment:** All major credit cards, plus JCB
**Service rating:** ★★★★★
**Friendliness rating:** ★★★★½
**Parking:** Complimentary valet in building garage
**Bar:** Full service

**Wine selection:** Extensive award-winning list with 650 international wines, mostly French, Alsatian, and American; $39+ per bottle; 10–12 selections by the glass
**Dress:** Jacket and tie suggested
**Disabled access:** Wheelchair accessible; call ahead for special accommodations
**Customers:** Upscale, business, couples

**Dinner:** Tuesday–Thursday, 5:30–9:30 p.m.; Friday and Saturday, 5:30–10 p.m.; Sunday and Monday, closed.

**Setting & atmosphere:** Softly lit, romantic, simple elegance; flowers and candlelight; 75-seat dining room separated into an atrium level for a private atmosphere and a spectacular western view of Chicago; tuxedo-clad waiters. Six private dining rooms for parties of eight or more are open every day for breakfast, lunch, and dinner (reservations must be made in advance for these rooms).

**House specialties:** Smoked salmon served with warm oatmeal blinis (cold appetizer); creamless navy bean soup and confit of rabbit; terrine of pheasant, partridge, and squab marbled with wild herbs and vegetables; Maine lobster roasted with Alsace Gewurtztraminer and ginger.

**(Everest)**

**Other recommendations:** Ballotine of wild Atlantic salmon and marinated cabbage, Alsace-style; double lamb consommé, mini–goat cheese ravioli; New York State foie gras; saddle of Millbrook venison, wild huckleberries, Alsace Wassertriwella; ballotine of skate stuffed with mushrooms and wrapped around non-sour Alsatian sauerkraut in a light Riesling juniper berry sauce. Pre-theater dinner menu that changes monthly with seatings at 5:30 p.m., $39; degustation menu, $69 per person.

**Entertainment & amenities:** The spectacular western view of Chicago.

**Summary & comments:** Mount Everest was climbed first by Sir Edmund Hillary, and chef Jean Joho has succeeded in making his Everest the pinnacle of French gastronomy in Chicago—in fact it's one of the country's premier restaurants. In partnership with Lettuce Entertain You Enterprises, Joho is a protégé of Paul Haeberlin of the acclaimed L'Auberge de L'Ill in Alsace, France. He began training at 13 as an apprentice. His education continued in French, Italian, and Swiss kitchens, and at age 23, he became sous-chef of a Michelin two-star restaurant with the command of a staff of 35. His French cuisine is masterful, with much use of his beloved Alsatian homeland's ingredients; each dish is a work of art to behold. Dining here is truly tops for food, service, and view of the city.

**Honors & awards:** Four-star reviews from the *Chicago Tribune,* the *Chicago Sun-Times, Chicago* magazine; featured in *Playboy* and *Esquire;* winner of Ivy Award and Gault Millau honors; chef-owner Jean Joho won the James Beard Award for Best Chef in Midwest and *Food and Wine* magazine's Top Chef of the Year Award; he's been inducted into Nation's Restaurant News' Fine Dining Hall of Fame and received the *Wine Spectator* Award of Excellence, 1992, 1997–98. Reba Mandari Culinary Award of Excellence, 1998.

| FOODLIFE | | ★★★ |
|---|---|---|

| American | Inexpensive | QUALITY |
|---|---|---|
| | | **82** |
| 835 North Michigan Avenue, Water Tower Place; (312) 335-3663 | | **VALUE** |
| Zone 3   Near North | | **C** |

**Reservations:** Parties of 6 or more only

**When to go:** Steer away from peak lunchtime and rush hour business

**Entree range:** $6.95–9.95

**Payment:** All major credit cards

**Service rating:** ★★★ (largely self-serve)

**Friendliness rating:** ★★★★

**Parking:** Water Tower underground garage

**Bar:** Wine, beer, and sangria only

**(foodlife)**

Wine selection: Wine by the glass
  only
Dress: Casual

Disabled access: Yes
Customers: Professionals, shoppers,
  tourists, families, couples

**Open:**  Juice, espresso, and Corner Bakery: every day 7:30 a.m.–9 p.m. All other kiosks: Monday–Thursday, 11 a.m.–9 p.m.; Friday and Saturday, 11 a.m.–10 p.m.; Sunday, 11 a.m.–9 p.m.

**Setting & atmosphere:**  Attractive food court that resembles an outdoor cafe with trees. Environment-friendly atmosphere. Credo is "Be kind; eat true; it's now." Large variety of food stations; all food is displayed in an appealing manner.

**House specialties:**  Thirteen food stations: juice bar, grains, burgers, Mexican, greens, pizza, pasta, hot stuffs (stuffed potatoes), rotisserie chicken, stir-fry heaven, desserts, sacred grounds (espresso, candy, cakes, cookies), and Corner Bakery. Mediterranean rice dishes; grilled, marinated vegetables; "enlightened" Caesar; vegetarian pizza with multi-grain crust; pot stickers; rotisserie chicken; homemade pies and cookies.

**Other recommendations:**  Cold and hot bean salads; health burgers; salsa bar; stir-frys with Pan-Asian influences; yogurt-fruit shakes and power drinks.

**Summary & comments:**  This food court concept drew great press upon opening in 1993. It is one of the most innovative food concepts by Rich Melman of Lettuce Entertain You Enterprises. He explains, "We have a social life, a business life, a family life, and a love life. Now there is an environment dedicated to your food life. It's about choices." Whatever your craving, you can eat healthfully, indulge, or compromise a bit in between. The freshest ingredients, without preservatives, are used. Customers are given a sensor card to use at each station. The card tracks the meal cost, you give the card to the cashier before you exit, and the total cost is tallied. Convenient and fast. It's largely self-service, but the staff at each kiosk assists. A new adjacent foodlife market offers freshly prepared foods for carryout. Call (312) 335-3663.

## FRONTERA GRILL ★★★★

| | | QUALITY |
|---|---|---|
| Mexican | Inexpensive | 93 |

445 North Clark Street; (312) 661-1434
Zone 4   The Loop

| | VALUE |
|---|---|
| | B |

**Reservations:** Only for parties of 5–10
**When to go:** Tuesday, Wednesday, or Thursday; early or late
**Entree range:** $8–17
**Payment:** All major credit cards
**Service rating:** ★★★½
**Friendliness rating:** ★★½
**Parking:** Valet, $7; public lots; street.

**Bar:** Shares a common bar with Topolobampo; good tequila and Mexican beer list
**Wine selection:** Quite extensive; very international
**Dress:** Casual
**Disabled access:** Yes
**Customers:** Mixed, locals and travelers, business, couples

**Lunch:** Tuesday–Friday, 11:30 a.m.–2:30 p.m.; Saturday, 10:30–2:30.

**Dinner:** Tuesday–Thursday, 5:20–10 p.m.; Friday and Saturday, 5–11 p.m.

**Setting & atmosphere:** Casual and rustic; attractive Mexican art and touches; sidewalk cafe.

**House specialties:** Menu changes every two weeks. Examples include: tacos al carbón (beef, poultry, or fish grilled over a wood fire, with roasted pepper rajas, salsas, other accompaniments, and homemade tortillas); wood-grilled fish and meats such as pork tenderloin marinated in red chili–apricot mole sauce, and black tiger shrimp in green pumpkin seed mole with roasted chayote and zucchini. Good desserts, such as special ice cream and cooked plantains.

**Other recommendations:** Tortilla soup; jicama salad; pollo en crema poblana. Various types of chiles are used in sauces that range from mild and earthy to hot and spicy.

**Summary & comments:** The menu offers a great variety of some rarely known dishes from regional Mexican cuisine. Owners Rick Bayless (chef) and wife Deanne (manager) lived in Mexico and co-authored a cookbook, *Authentic Mexican,* which was published about the time this restaurant opened several years ago. Both the book and restaurant received good reviews. Many reports from diners and one personal experience indicate that service could be friendlier and more accommodating, especially at the entrance regarding seating.

**Honors & awards:** *London Herald* and *New York Times* reviews. Recognized as the best-researched Mexican restaurant offering regional dishes.

## GEJA'S CAFE                                          ★★★½

| Fondue | Expensive | QUALITY |
|---|---|---|
| | | 90 |

340 West Armitage Avenue; (773) 281-9101

Zone 1    North Side

| | VALUE |
|---|---|
| | B |

**Reservations:** Accepted Sunday–Thursday; on Friday and Saturday first seating at 5 p.m.

**When to go:** Weeknights, early in evening

**Entree range:** $75 dinner for 2 includes appetizer, wine, entree, and dessert

**Payment:** Major credit cards

**Service rating:** ★★★★

**Friendliness rating:** ★★★★½

**Parking:** Valet, $6

**Bar:** Full service

**Wine selection:** 250 international selections; 30 by the glass

**Dress:** Upscale casual to formal

**Disabled access:** Stairs; no access

**Customers:** Couples, business, yuppie, all ages

**Dinner:** Monday–Thursday, 5–10:30 p.m.; Friday, 5 p.m.–midnight; Saturday, 5 p.m.–12:30 a.m.; Sunday, 4:30–10 p.m.

**Setting & atmosphere:** Intimate and charming, with secluded booths and tables; wine bottle decor; dimly lit and romantic.

**House specialties:** Classic cheese fondue; seafood, chicken, steak, and combo fondues; chocolate fondue served with fruit and cake.

**Other recommendations:** Sausage and cheese platter with salad.

**Entertainment & amenities:** Nightly flamenco or classical guitarist.

**Summary & comments:** Walk down a few steps into a romantic oasis in Lincoln Park and enter a sensual culinary experience that was created over three decades ago by visionary and wine lover John Davis. Fondue is a communal way of dining, and it's alive and thriving at Geja's. Order à la carte or the complete dinners. For a taste of Switzerland, try the classic cheese fondue made with Gruyère and kirschwasser, served with bread and crisp apple wedges for dipping. Flaming chocolate fondue is flambéed with orange liqueur and served with fruit and pound cake for dipping.

**Honors & awards:** Voted "most romantic restaurant" many times by *Chicago* magazine and other publications.

## GIBSON'S STEAKHOUSE ★★★★½

| | | QUALITY |
|---|---|---|
| Steak | Moderate/Very Expensive | **94** |

| | VALUE |
|---|---|
| 1028 North Rush Street; (312) 266-8999 | **C** |
| Zone 3  Near North | |

Reservations: Recommended
When to go: Crowded most
  evenings; go early
Entree range: $20–25; colossal surf
  and turf, $85
Payment: All major credit cards
Service rating: ★★★★½
Friendliness rating: ★★★★½
Parking: Valet
Bar: Full service; the signature drink
is the Gibson (large martini)
Wine selection: International; mostly
  Californian and French
Dress: Business, dressy—tuxedos
  are not unusual
Disabled access: Yes
Customers: Diverse, masculine group
  spanning various backgrounds;
  mostly locals ages 20–60; lots of
  local and international celebs

**Dinner:** Monday–Saturday, 5 p.m.–midnight; Sunday, 4 p.m.–midnight; bar remains open every day, 12 p.m.–12:30 a.m.

**Setting & atmosphere:** 1940s clubby wooden art deco; looks old (but not worn) with antiques and dated photos; comfortable.

**House specialties:** Steaks are prime aged. Bone-in sirloin (also known as Kansas City strip); Chicago cut (huge rib-eye steak with fat trimmed); snow and stone crab claws appetizer.

**Other recommendations:** Lobster tail; planked whitefish; chargrilled swordfish; 1¼-lb. baked potatoes; carrot cake.

**Entertainment & amenities:** Live piano every evening; lively bar.

**Summary & comments:** Recognized by steak aficionados as one of the city's top places for prime cuts, with prices to match. All the quality steakhouses are expensive, so this one is competitive with the herd. Food is elegantly served by polite waiters in attractive, comfortable surroundings.

## GOLDEN OX ★★★★

| German/American | Moderate | QUALITY |
|---|---|---|
| | | **90** |

| | | VALUE |
|---|---|---|
| 1578 North Clybourn Avenue; (312) 664-0780 | | **C** |
| Zone 1   North Side | | |

**Reservations:** Recommended
**When to go:** Any time
**Entree range:** $11.50–25
**Payment:** All major credit cards
**Service rating:** ★★★
**Friendliness rating:** ★★★½
**Parking:** Free valet
**Bar:** Full service

**Wine selection:** Substantial international list; French, Spanish, German, domestics
**Dress:** Casual to formal
**Disabled access:** Yes
**Customers:** Diverse, local, travelers, couples, business, family

**Lunch/Dinner:** Monday–Saturday, 11 a.m.–11 p.m.; Sunday, 3–9 p.m.

**Setting & atmosphere:** Magnificent and very comfortable. Intricate decoration with shiny brown shellacked walls, paintings, murals depicting classics (the Ziegfield and Brunhilde story), cuckoo clocks, ornate beer steins. Looks like an ancient castle or museum. Carpeted; red ceiling with black beams; fireplace; brown leather chairs; gold tablecloths with white covers; dirndl-clad waitresses.

**House specialties:** Bavarian-style bratwurst; smoked Thuringer; potato pancakes; Wiener schnitzel; sauerbraten; paprika rahm schnitzel; crisp half roasted duckling; fresh seafood (e.g., imported Dover sole, broiled walleyed pike). Entrees are served with choice of spaetzle, potato, or butter noodles.

**Other recommendations:** Hasenpfeffer (in season—imported rabbit, marinated and stewed); sausage plate; fresh chopped chicken liver; oyster à la Golden Ox; kalte kartoffel (cold potato) suppe; tortes.

**Entertainment & amenities:** Zither player on Saturday evenings; strolling musician on Friday evenings. Browsing through the spectacularly decorated rooms.

**Summary & comments:** Pricier than most German restaurants, but Golden Ox has a fuller traditional German menu—well-prepared—and an exquisite atmosphere. It is the best German restaurant I know of. Quality has been maintained over the years, but service can be slow and occasionally uninformed in the wine area. Overall, friendly and accommodating.

**Honors & awards:** *Food Industry News* award for Best German Restaurant.

## GORDON ★★★★

| | |
|---|---|
| | QUALITY |
| | 93 |

New American          Expensive

| | |
|---|---|
| | VALUE |
| | C |

500 North Clark Street; (312) 467-9780
Zone 4   The Loop

**Reservations:** Recommended
**When to go:** Major destination dining—corporate and special occasions
**Entree range:** $19–28; five-course degustation menu, $59, paired with wines, $79
**Payment:** All major credit cards
**Service rating:** ★★★★
**Friendliness rating:** ★★★★
**Parking:** Valet, street, and nearby lot
**Bar:** Full service; specializes in single malt scotches

**Wine selection:** In depth American and French; some German; many nice choices by the glass and half bottle; about 10 available by the glass for $7–12
**Dress:** Jackets requested, tie optional; mostly business attire; tends to be dressier in evenings
**Disabled access:** Yes
**Customers:** Corporate executives and business, movie and TV personalities; couples, especially weekend evenings

**Lunch:** Tuesday–Friday, 11:30 a.m.–2 p.m.

**Dinner:** Sunday–Thursday, 5:30–8:30 p.m.; Friday and Saturday, 5:30 p.m.–11:30 p.m.

**Setting & atmosphere:** Attractive bar entry; divided dining space includes one elevated section. Eclectic and ornate; slightly surreal contemporary art with colorful, amusing avant-garde murals. Large vases of flowers.

**House specialties:** Menu changes seasonally, but some dishes remain. Examples include the signature original Gordon artichoke fritter with béarnaise sauce; sautéed foie gras with braised beef brisket, endive, Napa cabbage, and tomato puree; smoked salmon Napoleon with beets, crème fraîche, Ostra caviar, and two infused oils; grilled strip steak with black beans and basil, homemade Worcestershire sauce, and caramelized onions. Desserts: butterscotch-ginger brûlée with Mother Sinclair's Scottish shortbread and candied ginger; hot chocolate ganache cake with candied clementines, orange-caramel sauce, and Earl Grey–infused chocolate ice cream.

**Other recommendations:** Roasted rack of lamb with couscous, crawfish, and a most unusual Kahlua sauce; grilled duck breast and spring roll with braised daikon and plum sauce; nice salads, with organically grown lettuces and tomatoes from Gordon's farm. Desserts: gianduja mousse with toffee, pecans, bananas, and coconut sorbet; chilled Bing cherry soup with almond panna cotta and chocolate almond biscotti.

**(Gordon)**

**Entertainment & amenities:** Live mellow jazz (usually a trio) and dancing on Friday and Saturday nights.

**Summary & comments:** Shortly after Gordon celebrated its 20th anniversary in 1996, Don Yamauchi (formerly of Carlos') joined owner Gordon Sinclair's team as executive chef, aiming to continue the restaurant's renowned "highly creative approach" to dining. He is constantly changing the menu, incorporating available ingredients and his creative whims. When Sinclair started this business, the neighborhood was still derelict. It has since blossomed into a thriving restaurant, antique shop, and gallery district called River North. His flamboyant style, ability to maintain high standards despite rotating chefs (about one per year), and occasional promotional events make this a rather eccentric place of quality with distinctive character. The menu includes quotes such as, "Sex is good, but not as good as fresh sweet corn" (Garrison Keillor). Complimentary appetizers are served, such as marinated shrimp in puff pastry. Sinclair recently decided to offer only half portions of entrees, which doubles your sampling pleasure. For those who want more of a good dish, double portions are available at double the price minus $2. Sinclair enjoys working on his farm in Harvard, Illinois; certain days, his produce appears on the menu. Celebrators who call ahead can see their names on the menu.

**Honors & awards:** *Mobil Travel Guide,* four stars; *Wine Spectator* Award of Excellence. Chef Yamauchi: *Food and Wine's* 10 Best Chefs in America, 1993; nominated for Best Chef in Midwest by the James Beard Foundation in 1992.

---

## HARRY CARAY'S ★★★½

| American/Italian | Moderate/Expensive | QUALITY |
|---|---|---|
| | | 86 |
| 33 West Kinzie Avenue; (773) 465-9269 | | VALUE |
| Zone 4   The Loop | | C |

**Reservations:** Lunch, recommended; dinner, recommended for 8 or more

**When to go:** Any time

**Entree range:** $8.95–39.95; pastas average $9.95; steaks average $28.95

**Payment:** Major credit cards

**Service rating:** ★★★★

**Friendliness rating:** ★★★★

**Parking:** Valet

**Bar:** Full service; bar is 60 feet, 6 inches long, which is the same distance from home plate to the pitcher's mound; American and imported beers, featuring Bud beers, of course; a caricature of Harry on the menu states, "I'm a Cub fan, I'm a Bud man!"

**(Harry Caray's)**

Wine selection: Extensive Italian and American, as well as several champagnes. Table wines start at an affordable $13 per bottle with many in the $20s–30s; several by the glass

Dress: Casual; you'll see a good share of Cubs wear

Disabled access: Yes, including rest rooms

Customers: Diverse, local, business, baseball fans, couples

**Lunch:** Monday–Friday, 11:30 a.m.–3 p.m., appetizers and sandwiches served in the bar daily

**Dinner:** Monday–Friday 5–10:30 p.m.; Friday and Saturday, 5–11 p.m.; Sunday, 4–10 p.m.

**Setting & atmosphere:** Located in a historic red brick building. Pictures, memorabilia of the famous sportscaster; active bar/lounge; comfortable—usually busy—dining room. Private rooms upstairs.

**House specialties:** Chef Abraham's calamari; steamed mussels, red or white sauce; chicken Vesuvio with terrific potatoes (can be ordered with all white meat for $3 extra); grilled New York sirloin steak (16 ounces) with peppercorns or Vesuvio style.

**Other recommendations:** Harry's Italian salad; cheese ravioli with marinara sauce; grilled fresh fish (marinated tuna, lightly crumbed, seasoned with rosemary, shines); trio of double lamb chops oreganato. Desserts include a great carrot cake and small ice cream profiteroles with hot fudge and crème anglaise.

**Entertainment & amenities:** Browsing through the Harry Caray memorabilia. Gift shop with line of Harrywear and souvenirs.

**Summary & comments:** You can't miss the Chicago restaurant because Harry Caray's favorite exclamation, "Holy Cow!", is emblazoned on an outside wall. Named for the late Cubs' announcer, Harry Caray's is a splendid dining experience from the masterful opening pitch all the way through. Unlike many celebrity sports-figure places, this one takes the restaurant business seriously. Harry Caray loved Italian fare, so it's on the menu, from salads to pastas and chicken Vesuvio (really a Chicago invention—not Italian). All the fish is fresh and grilled or otherwise cooked to perfection. Fresh herbs season much of the food. Weekend lunch-goers might try the sandwich cart. Good Italian desserts and wines.

## HEAVEN ON SEVEN                                    ★★★½

| Cajun/Creole | Inexpensive | QUALITY |
| --- | --- | --- |
| | | 86 |
| | | VALUE |
| | | B |

111 North Wabash Avenue; (312) 263-6443
Zone 4   The Loop

Reservations: Not accepted

When to go: Breakfast, 7 a.m.; lunch, 11:30 a.m.; before the lines or after lunchtime

Entree range: $3.50–9.95

Payment: Cash only

Service rating: ★★★½

Friendliness rating: ★★★★

Parking: Garage

Bar: None

Wine selection: Some Californian, Chilean, French, and Italian wines; $15–75 by the bottle, $4.50–6.50 by the glass

Dress: Casual

Disabled access: Yes

Customers: Diverse, business, professional, shoppers

**Breakfast/Lunch:** Monday–Friday, 8:30 a.m.–4:30 p.m.; Saturday, 10 a.m.–3 p.m.

**Dinner:** Every third Friday of the month, 5:30–9:30 p.m.; and on Fat Tuesday with a live New Orleans jazz band.

**Setting & atmosphere:** Upbeat; brown tables, each with several bottles of hot sauce. Wooden floor, red plantation plants, big hot-sauce collection, New Orleans art.

**House specialties:** Southern fried chicken salad; soft-shell poboys; pasta shrimp angry, pasta shrimp voodoo; crayfish tamales; jambalaya; Louisiana soul.

**Other recommendations:** Crab cakes; chicken-fried steak; rabbit with mushroom étouffée.

**Summary & comments:** Funky place on the seventh floor of the Garland building in the Loop, which began as the Garland Restaurant and Coffee Shop. The Bannos family–owned place still serves regular breakfast, but has made its reputation on the great Creole and Cajun fare (including the Creole and Cajun breakfast), every bit as delicious as in Louisiana. Long lines at lunch move quickly. Those who love food with a burn will have a field day trying the various hot sauces on the table. After a meal here, you'll think you've gone to Cajun heaven. A new location at 600 North Michigan Avenue, (312) 280-7774, serves lunch and dinner.

**Honors & awards:** Recommended by various local publications, *Newsweek,* and *National Geographic.*

## HOUSE OF BLUES ★★★½

| | | |
|---|---|---|
| American/Southern | Inexpensive/Moderate | **QUALITY**<br>89 |
| 329 North Dearborn Street; (312) 527-2583<br>Zone 3   Near North | | **VALUE**<br>B |

**Reservations:** Recommended
**When to go:** Any time; Sunday gospel brunch (if you want hand-clapping, joyful, uplifting participation entertainment with your buffet brunch); Music Hall: whenever there is a concert you want to attend
**Entree range:** $8.50–12.95
**Payment:** All major credit cards
**Service rating:** ★★★½
**Friendliness rating:** ★★★½
**Parking:** Valet
**Bar:** Full service, including imported and domestic beers at both Foundation Room and restaurants
**Wine selection:** House of Blues restaurant: mostly domestic, some international; several selections by the glass; Foundation Room: international list
**Dress:** Casual
**Disabled access:** Yes
**Customers:** Varied from tourists to all types of locals, especially those who enjoy blues, country, jazz, and other featured music and southern fare

**Open:** Every day, 11:30 a.m.–1 or 1:30 a.m., depending on entertainment.

**Setting & atmosphere:** Spectacular, with every inch painted and somehow covered with art. House of Blues supposedly has the largest Delta folk art collection anywhere, and it's evident here in the halls and on the walls and ceiling. Even the bathrooms are worth seeing. Three dining rooms, incuding the Chicago Room (dedicated to this city's blues legends) and the Delta Room (dedicated to Delta blues greats), are alive with ceiling panels of bas-relief portraits of blues icons. With the feeling of a southern "juke joint," the restaurant also showcases a B.B. Blues Bar and stage.

**House specialties:** Appetizers: Mississippi cat bites (tender farm-raised catfish, lightly floured, fried, and served with slightly spicy Cajun tartar sauce); shrimp rémoulade, with capers, chopped egg, and black olives; New Orleans–style chicken and sausage gumbo. Entrees: étouffée (fresh crawfish and gulf shrimp with rich, medium-spiced sauce, with rice); jambalaya ("The Big Easy" shrimp, tender chicken, smokehouse ham, and Andouille sausage tossed in Creole sauce, Cajun rice).

**Other recommendations:** Crawfish cheesecake appetizer; Memphis barbecue chicken; mesquite-grilled veggie sandwich; sides of cornbread with maple butter and turnip greens; pecan tasty (a tart made of homemade cream cheese pastry crust with Southern roasted pecans, sugar cane, and

**(House of Blues)**

caramel filling) with ice cream. Gospel brunch (with eggs, sausage, jambalaya, bread pudding), so popular there are now three seatings at 10 a.m., 12:15 p.m., and 2:30 p.m.

**Summary & comments:** This largest of the House of Blues locations is one of those places that must be seen and experienced to be believed. It defies description, since there is so much soul, care, and money invested in this music sanctuary—you'll be transported when you step inside. Founder Isaac Tigrett said this HOB opening (November 1996) was the most important one he'll ever do, since Chicago is the living home of the blues. This multimedia restaurant accommodates over 300 in its three dining areas, and the menu offers good Southern specialties by executive chef Samuel McCord, who had the same post at HOB in New Orleans. "Help Ever—Hurt Never" is one of the mottos here, typifying the HOB mission statement that celebrates the diversity and brotherhood of world culture and promotes racial and spiritual harmony through love, peace, truth, righteousness, and nonviolence. Just getting that message makes everyone feel accepted and respected.

---

## HUDSON CLUB ★★★★

| New American | Moderate | QUALITY |
|---|---|---|
| | | 91 |

504 North Wells; (312) 467-1947

| | VALUE |
|---|---|
| | B |

Zone 1    North Side

**Reservations:** Yes

**When to go:** Well after dark, to see the interior in the night light and to experience the evening energy.

**Entree range:** $13.95–24.95

**Payment:** All major credit cards

**Service rating:** ★★★★½

**Friendliness rating:** ★★★★½

**Parking:** Valet, $7

**Bar:** Complete with an aggressive, user-friendly program; extensive beer list, with a trio of beer flights

**Wine selection:** Extraordinary! 24 flights (tastings of four related wines) and an amazing 175-plus selections by the glass

**Dress:** Chic casual to business and dressy

**Disabled access:** Complete

**Customers:** Sophisticated food and wine lovers and the hip but uninitiated eager to learn about wine in an unpretentious atmosphere; mostly professionals; Gen-X-ers; all ages. Locals and travelers.

**(Hudson Club)**

**Dinner:** Monday–Thursday, 5:30–10 p.m.; Friday & Saturday, 5:30–11 p.m.

**Setting & atmosphere:** Sleek, sensuous, spacious, resembling a luxury liner and a jet airliner merged with a swank 1940's supper club with an elongated bar. Hudson Club was based on the aerodynamic flourishes of the Hudson Hornet automobile. Luxurious materials used include polished mahogany, brushed aluminum and wine-colored velvet.

**House specialties:** Cold appetizers of home smoked salmon with potato pancakes and creme fraiche; spinach salad with crispy fried oysters, Maytag blue cheese, warm balsamic vinaigrette. Entrées: portobello mushroom Wellington; pan-seared sea scallops, pistachio-crusted with Belgian endive, French beans, Citron vodka-vanilla syrup; pan-roasted striped bass, sautéed greens and Anna potatoes. Desserts (changing menu): chef's cheese flight; crème brûlée with fresh fruit; chocolate hazelnut truffle torte with bittersweet chocolate sauce and Frangelico cream.

**Other recommendations:** Curried tuna tartare; hot lobster martini; corn flake-crusted shrimp. Entrée: wood-roasted monkfish, corn and bacon risotto with chanterelle mushrooms, red wine reduction. Dessert: chocolate bourbon pecan tart, warm with Jack Daniels ice cream, caramel sauce.

**Entertainment & amenities:** Trying wine or beer flights; taking off on a fantasy flight while being swept away by the interior design.

**Summary & comments:** Hudson Club is sophisticated yet casual and never snobbish about its extraordinary bar and educational wine and beer program. Key players here are Howard Natinsky and Steve Soble, Chicagoans with a vision who hung up their business suits, changed careers and opened a classy neighborhood pool hall, Corner Pocket. Now their company, Spare Time, Inc., owns several properties, and Hudson Club is their first restaurant. They brought in a professional team to develop the place, including managing partner Larry Dwyer (from an advertising career); wine expert Curt Burns, whose card says "wine guy," showing his down-to-earth style; executive chef Paul Larson (La Tour, Plaza Hotel in Basel, Switzerland, the Art Institute, and Winnetka Grill), and pastry chef Jeanne Kraus (Blind Faith Cafe & Bakery, Evanston, and Winnetka Grill).

**Honors & awards:** *Chicago* magazine, "Best New Restaurants", May, 1997.

| IRON MIKE'S GRILLE | ★★★½ |
| --- | --- |

| | QUALITY |
| --- | --- |
| Classic American Bistro     Moderate/Expensive | 90 |
| | VALUE |
| 100 East Chestnut; (312) 587-8989 | C |
| Zone 3    Near North | |

Reservations: Recommended
When to go: Avoid peak meal times
  unless you have a reservation
Entree range: $9.89–28.89
Payment: VISA, MC, DC, D
Service rating: ★★★★½
Friendliness rating: ★★★★½
Parking: Valet, $6
Bar: Full service
Wine selection: International, with

largest selection from California
and Northwest America; a good
selection of French and Italian; a
couple of Australian selections
Dress: Upscale, dressy
Disabled access: Yes
Customers: Football fans, Italian
food lovers, professionals, couples,
tourists

**Open:** Sunday–Thursday, 7 a.m.–11 p.m. (bar open until 2 a.m.); Friday and Saturday, 7 a.m.–midnight (bar open until 3 a.m.).

**Setting & atmosphere:** Located in the charming Tremont Hotel, the main floor includes a traditional, mahogany bar with split-level seating and a handsome dining room with golden globe ceiling fixtures, gold-and-green-striped drapes, white tablecloths, and glass-enclosed displays of the omnipresent sports memorabilia. Upstairs you'll find the cigar parlor in a denlike, couch-filled setting, and a dining room with leather-upholstered booths, beamed ceilings, and a fireplace.

**House specialties:** Ditka's favorite—pork chops with grilled pancetta and honey–green peppercorn sauce; "Black and blue" tuna putannesca (richly flavored with olives and red peppers); "duck cigar," a crêpe filled with braised duck (shredded to resemble tobacco!) and caramelized onions, served (believe it or not) on a wooden cigar box; Grabowski sausage cassoulet (grilled pheasant and duck sausage with white beans); Grille (house) salad with sherry vinaigrette.

**Other recommendations:** Breakfast: "The Midwesterner" (Ditka's famous French toast or pancakes with maple syrup and cinnamon whipped cream, bacon or sausage, juice, and morning beverage), "The Training Meal" (beef filet, eggs, potatoes, juice, bread, and beverage), and several other options, including "Hall of Fame Omelette." Lunch is similar to dinner, with lighter items. Fridge Burger is available for both lunch and dinner. Angel hair with pesto and oven-dried tomatoes; linguini with shrimp, calamari, scallops, mussels, and spicy sauce; crispy cayenne-crusted oysters with balsamic-

**(Iron Mike's Grille)**

jalapeño mayonnaise (a touch of New Orleans, reflecting Ditka's current job as coach for the Saints); Superbowl salad (a huge football player's size) of mixed greens, arugula, French beans, red peppers, walnuts, avocado, smoked bacon, artichoke chips, kalamata olives, and Parmesan.

**Summary & comments:** Over 2,000 people, including many VIPs, attended the grand opening in 1997, making big news everywhere. Da Coach himself, Mike Ditka, was there to greet wellwishers, as were the Carlucci brothers, Joe and Charlie, who are partners with Ditka in this venture. Located in the beautiful Tremont Hotel, site of the former Crickets and then Cafe Gordon, this refurbished space has been handsomely appointed to exude a masculine ambience. The menu features Ditka's favorites, including the famous pork chops (among the best!), as well as Carlucci's Italian specialties and some New Orleans items (because of Ditka's latest coaching job). The prices end in numbers reflecting important years for Da Coach, such as side dish prices of $3.20–4.20, symbolizing Super Bowl XX, when he coached the Bears to the national championship.

| JACK'S | | ★★★½ |
|---|---|---|
| New American | Moderate | **QUALITY** |
| | | **90** |
| 3201 North Halsted; (773) 244-9191 | | **VALUE** |
| Zone 1   North Side | | **B** |

Reservations: Yes; strongly recommended on weekends

When to go: Weeknights less busy

Entree range: $14.95–19.95

Payment: All major credit cards

Service rating: ★★★★

Friendliness rating: ★★★★½

Parking: Valet, $6

Bar: Full

Wine selection: International with mostly west coast domestic; from $19–58; some half bottles; glasses from $4.75–6.50, about 14 selections available

Dress: Casual

Disabled access: Yes

Customers: Mixed, all ages; mostly professionals; those seeking flavorful food and moderate prices

**Brunch:** Sunday, 11 a.m.–2:30 p.m.

**Dinner:** Monday–Thursday, 5:30 p.m.–10:30 p.m.; Friday & Saturday, 5 p.m.–11:30 p.m.

**Setting & atmosphere:** Rehabbed corner storefront with large windows, attractive bar in left corner of L-shaped space; banquettes and tables

**(Jack's)**

spaced comfortably. Unusual industrial-type lighting with beams. Comfortable and cozy.

**House specialties:** Starters of quesadillas with smoked chicken, wild mushrooms, sweet onions, pepper Jack and goat cheese, tomato avocado salsa; grilled calamari over black linguini in spicy tomato basil sauce. Main courses: perfectly grilled Norwegian salmon with mango mustard glaze, sundried tomato mushroom risotto cake and ratatouille; the very "in" seared ahi tuna with coriander crust over bok choy with wasabi mashed potatoes and stir-fried vegetables, sweet sake ginger lime sauce. Desserts: Jack's chocolate kahlua cake with coffee ice cream (lusty); New Orleans-style bread pudding with Jack Daniels caramel sauce.

**Other recommendations:** Starter of seafood ravioli with basil-lemon cream sauce. Main course: pesto grilled chicken over pasta with roasted vegetables and blackened tomato sauce. Dessert: chocolate raspberry terrine with raspberry sauce, coffee ice cream; Door County cherry pie with slivered almonds and vanilla ice cream.

**Entertainment & amenities:** Special menus, such as one that celebrates the solstice, June 20-July 4.

**Summary & comments:** Jack's is a hidden gem that is well worth the trip, even from a distant location. Jack Jones, the eponym here, renders cooking so outstanding for the modest cost that even with taxi fare from downtown factored in, the bill will be less than most tabs at comparable downtown restaurants. Friendly service and a savvy wine list are bonuses. After graduating culinary school in 1987, Jones worked in several fine restaurants before opening his first bistro, Daniel J's (Daniel is his middle name), in 1993. Now that Daniel J's is closing, his fans come here to satisfy their cravings for his cooking.

**Honors & awards:** Named one of the 20 best new restaurants in the city by *Chicago* magazine.

## JOE'S B-BOP CAFE ★★★½

| | | QUALITY |
|---|---|---|
| BBQ and Southern | Inexpensive/Moderate | **90** |

| |
|---|
| 1 Navy Pier, 600 E. Grand Ave.; (312) 595-5299 |
| Zone 3    Near North |

**VALUE**
**B**

**Reservations:** Only parties of 6 or more

**When to go:** Lunch if walking around the pier during the day; evenings for music and dinner; Sunday jazz brunch if you desire a buffet.

**Entree range:** $10.95–17.95 or market price of fish; Sunday brunch buffet $16.95; kids 5–12 $5.95; kids under 5 free

**Payment:** All major credit cards

**Service rating:** ★★★★½

**Friendliness rating:** ★★★★½

**Parking:** Validated lot on Navy Pier; valet weekends at Pier entrance

**Bar:** Full; good selection of beers; at Sunday brunch, Joe's Fabulous Bloody Mary Bar

**Wine selection:** Limited, six American selections, all available by the glass, from $5–6.25; bottles $20–26

**Dress:** Casual and very casual

**Disabled access:** Yes

**Customers:** Mix of locals and tourists, families and singles, people of all ages who enjoy jazz.

**Brunch:** Sunday, 10:30 a.m.–2 p.m.

**Lunch/Dinner:** Monday–Thursday, 10:30 a.m.–8 p.m.; Friday & Saturday, 10:30 a.m.–10 p.m.; Sunday, 10:30 a.m.–7 p.m.

**Setting & atmosphere:** Casual, energetic, fun. Entryway features a juice bar and gift shop with a plank floor; focus in the spacious 190-seat dining room is a monumental, 135-foot-long colorful mural, History of Jazz, on a serpentine wall above the perimeter banquette seats. Bandstand on far end in front of windows opens out onto the patio on the pier and the lake beyond.

**House specialties:** Appetizers: Crunchy sweet potato chips with a dynamite honey-mustard dip; jalapeno poppers (red ones that are not fiery), cheese-filled, crunchy, homemade salsa with a kick; smoked chicken quesadillas with salsa. Main courses: B-Bop BBQ™ combos: King Oliver (baby back ribs and half a Yardbird™ chicken); Duke Ellington (ribs and pulled pork), or Count Basie (ribs and 24-hour brisket). Pulled-pork bun (Memphis-style with mustard slaw on top, with Carolina-style Hot Five Sauce on the side). Fats' Cornbread™. "Last licks:" Sumpin' choclit (recommended—luscious enough to satisfy any chocolate lover's craving); fudgey layered cake with a rich sauce.

**(Joe's B-Bop Cafe)**

**Other recommendations:** Barbecued rib tips and buffalo wings as appetizers; shrimp & sausage filé gumbo. Main courses: Separate BBQ items (include each of the above, ribs, chicken and brisket, plus rib tips and center cut boneless pork chops). Homemade fruit cobbler, with or without ice cream; Eli's cheesecake.

**Entertainment & amenities:** Live jazz nightly; weeknights usually 6–9:30 p.m., until 10:30 p.m. in summer; weekends 7–11 p.m.(call for information); no cover charge. Juice bar. Outdoor patio with 115 seats, depending on weather.

**Summary & comments:** This Navy Pier restaurant is an energetic mix of good BBQ and groovy, live jazz. The place swings, especially later in the evening. Wayne Segal (who operated Jazzz Showcase, founded over 50 years ago by his father Joe) and the Chicago Restaurant Corp. teamed up to open this place in 1997. The chef who gets credit for the spicy Southern cooking is Joe Biniwewicz, and the pitmaster is Irving Vance, who turns out some satisfying, soulful Memphis Tennessee BBQ using a dry rub.

**Honors & awards:** *Chicago Daily Herald,* "Pick of the Week."

---

| KIKI'S BISTRO | | ★★★★ |
|---|---|---|
| French Bistro | Inexpensive/Moderate | QUALITY **94** |
| 900 North Franklin Street; (312) 335-5454 Zone 3   Near North | | VALUE **C** |

**Reservations:** Recommended for lunch and dinner
**When to go:** Any time
**Entree range:** Lunch, $8.50–12; dinner, $13–22
**Payment:** All major credit cards
**Service rating:** ★★★★
**Friendliness rating:** ★★★★
**Parking:** Free valet
**Bar:** Full service; bar/lounge separate from dining room
**Wine selection:** 20 French and 15 American (Californian) white wines; over 30 reds; wines, $20–60; 8 champagnes, $35–100; 12 wines by the glass, $4.50
**Dress:** Informal; no athletic wear
**Disabled access:** Yes, entrance and rest rooms
**Customers:** International, celebrities (Prince Albert), business, families, couples

**Lunch:** Monday–Friday, 11 a.m.–2 p.m.

**(Kiki's Bistro)**

**Dinner:** Monday–Thursday, 5–9:45 p.m.; Friday and Saturday, 5–10:45 p.m.; Sunday, closed.

**Setting & atmosphere:** Resembles a French inn; lovely cottage-style woodwork and rustic decor; romantic and intimate. Noise level can be high with a full house.

**House specialties:** Duck pâté with pistachio; Roquefort terrine with frisée and green apple salad, port wine reduction; tarte de Provence (ratatouille and goat cheese in a light pastry). Sautéed breast of duck on wild rice with corn sauce and red pepper; daily fish (Bouillabaisse a la Marseillaise; honey-glazed wild striped bass; pan-roasted Atlantic flounder with crispy polenta; or grilled Alaskan halibut with artichoke broth). One lunch special was fine: flounder on a bed of spinach with an unusual cranberry sauce. Steak au poivre with cognac cream sauce. Chef's new creations include Oriental lobster salad, wasabi caviar; ragout of assorted mushrooms with escargots in phyllo, shallot port wine sauce; roast guinea hen with wild rice, Swiss chard and vegetables with natural jus and figs, and cassoulet Toulousain with duck confit, lamb and garlic sausage. Desserts: chocolate terrine in a crust and another rich chocolate creation topped with glazed sliced bananas with several sauces.

**Other recommendations:** Onion soup gratinée; poulet roti (roast chicken marinated in olive oil, herbs de Provence, and garlic in natural jus, with mashed potatoes); steak pommes frites; soup, pasta, and pizza du jour; seared quail with red cabbage and mixed greens; crème brûlée; croustade de poire (pear in pastry with caramel sauce); crème caramel; sautéed bing cherries with goat cheese ice cream.

**Summary & comments:** Many of the French bistro standards—steak pommes frites, onion soup gratinée, and poulet roti—are standouts, prepared expertly by new chef Jose Calzada. Owner Georges Cousances (Kiki) is an experienced restaurateur who makes certain the place runs smoothly. Service, food, wine, and charming atmosphere combine to make this a quintessential bistro without the claustrophobic closeness of many others.

## KITTY O'SHEA'S ★★★

| | | QUALITY |
|---|---|---|
| Irish Pub | Inexpensive | 81 |

| | VALUE |
|---|---|
| | B |

Chicago Hilton and Towers, 720 South Michigan Avenue;
(312) 922-4400
Zone 5   South Loop

Reservations: No
When to go: Evenings
Entree range: $7.25–12.75
Payment: All major credit cards
Service rating: ★★★
Friendliness rating: ★★★½
Parking: Street and valet

Bar: Full service, including Guinness, Harp, and various Irish items and local microbrews
Wine selection: American
Dress: Casual
Disabled access: Yes
Customers: Local, convention

**Open:**  Every day, 11 a.m.–1:30 a.m.

**Setting & atmosphere:**  Dimly lit, Dublin-style pub with authentic antiques, including the beer taps.

**House specialties:**  Potato and leek soup; Irish lamb stew; shepherd's pie; Blarney Burger Deluxe with Irish cheese and O'Shea's fries; Biddy Mulligan's fish and chips.

**Other recommendations:**  Dublin wings; Kitty's corned beef and cabbage; Brannigan's bread pudding.

**Entertainment & amenities:**  Monday–Saturday, 9 p.m.–1 a.m., live performances of traditional Irish folk music.

**Summary & comments:**  You can't get more Irish than Kitty O'Shea's. Not only is much of the interior imported from Ireland, so is the old sod staff. Guinness and Harp are drawn from antique beer taps (try the layered black and tan), the food is simple pub fare, and the spirited entertainment (some big names) completes the picture. Kilkenny-born manager Eamonn Brady uses his impressive entertainment background to book the lively musical groups here. It's hand-clapping fun!

## KLAY OVEN ★★★★

| | | QUALITY |
|---|---|---|
| Indian | Moderate | 94 |

414 North Orleans Street; (312) 527-3999

| | VALUE |
|---|---|
| | B |

Zone 4  The Loop

Reservations: Highly recommended
When to go: Weekdays less crowded;
 Friday and Saturday very busy
Entree range: $6.95–24.95
Payment: Major credit cards
Service rating: ★★★★ ½
Friendliness rating: ★★★★ ½
Parking: Street and garage nearby
Bar: Full service, including Indian
beer and a large single malt Scotch
 collection
Wine selection: American, French,
 and Italian; pricing very fair
Dress: Moderately casual to upscale
Disabled access: Yes
Customers: International; diverse;
 business, especially at lunch

**Lunch:** Tuesday–Friday, 11:30 a.m.–2:30 p.m.; Saturday and Sunday, noon–3 p.m. (buffet)

**Dinner:** Sunday–Thursday, 5:30–10 p.m.; Friday and Saturday, 5:30–10:30 p.m.

**Setting & atmosphere:** Upscale casual with lots of light wood, white tablecloths, elegantly folded napkins, lovely screen-like wall coverings, and beautiful art. The space is divided nicely into intimate alcoves, some of which are perfect for private parties.

**House specialties:** Appetizers: Matar aloo samosa (triangular pastry stuffed with mixture of peas and potatoes flavored with ginger, coriander leaves and dried mango powder) and keema samosa (lamb in pastry), served with spicy coriander and sweet tamarind-banana chutneys; murg pakora (boneless chicken pieces coated in seasoned chickpea flour and deep-fried). From the tandoori (clay oven): tiger prawns marinated in spiced yogurt; tandoori lobster (seasoned yogurt-marinated lobster tail) From the karahi (Indian wok): Bhuna gosht (boneless lamb cooked with onions, ginger and fresh coriander leaves). Great breads, such as paratha (whole wheat) and piaza kulcha (flatbread with onion filling). A great finale is ras malai, an exquisite dessert pudding of milk, honey, and pistachio, decorated with silver leaf. Masala, the steamed cardamom tea, is settling after a spicy meal and can be a dessert unto itself.

**Other recommendations:** Appetizer: Reshmi kabab (chicken spiced with cumin, cloves and cinnamon); tamatar shorba (spicy classical soup). Main courses: Tandoori mixed grill (combination of boneless lamb, boneless

**(Klay Oven)**

chicken, and prawn, each marinated differently). Gajjar halvah (sweetened finely shredded carrot-almond dessert).

**Summary & comments:**  Klay Oven elevates Indian cuisine to a fine dining experience, from the refined, freshly cooked food to the serene setting and professional service. The centuries-old clay oven (tandoor) and the Indian wok (karahi) are virtually greaseless cooking methods. Prem Khosla, owner since 1995, is a seasoned restaurateur. The menu is well designed and eductional, giving descriptions of dishes and special ingredients.

**Honors & awards:** *Chicago* magazine's "Critic's Choice Top 25 Restaurants"; *Food Industry Guide,* Award of Excellence, 1996–97.

| LA STRADA | | ★★★½ |
|---|---|---|
| Italian | Moderate/Expensive | QUALITY **87** |
| 155 North Michigan Avenue at Randolph Street; (312) 565-2200 Zone 4   The Loop | | VALUE **C** |

**Reservations:** Accepted, especially for lunch

**When to go:** Any time; can be busy at lunch

**Entree range:** Lunch, $10–15; dinner, $20–30

**Payment:** All major credit cards

**Service rating:** ★★★★½

**Friendliness rating:** ★★★★½

**Parking:** Lunch, street or garage; dinner, valet

**Bar:** Full line of all spirits, grappas, cognacs, ports, beers, and cordials

**Wine selection:** Over 200 selections from Italy, France, Spain, and California; several nice choices by the glass

**Dress:** Business, semiformal, no shorts

**Disabled access:** Glass elevator, rest rooms accesible

**Customers:** Diverse, business, professional, traveler, and celebrities (mayor, other politicians)

**Lunch:** Monday–Friday, 11:30 a.m.–4 p.m.

**Dinner:** Monday–Thursday, 4–10 p.m.; Friday, 4–11 p.m.; Saturday, 5–11 p.m.; Sunday, closed.

**Setting & atmosphere:** Crystal chandeliers, elegant tabletops, large booths and spacious tables for privacy; Renaissance frescoes; recently renovated.

**(La Strada)**

**House specialties:** Wild mushroom torte (layers of mushrooms with fontina cheese crepes, tomato sauce); potato and sea scallops cannelloni; sweet corn and pancetta risotto; salmon tartare. Prime provimi veal chops with thick polenta fries, shredded sweet potato fries and roasted three onion butter; potato crusted salmon; artichoke and gaeta olive crusted lamb rack with assorted creative vegetables; young organic greens, roasted baby leeks, pickled cucumber, egg, crisp prosciutto, garlic crostini, herbed vinaigrette. Dolci: torte Midici (flourless chocolate cake, warm Chambord raspberry compote, melted white chocolate) and fruit lasagna (seasonal fruit compote layered with phyllo and Frangelico whipped cream.

**Other recommendations:** Ravioli del giorno; carpaccio della Strada. Vegetarian Prix Fixe luncheon. Homemade fettucini with shelled Maine lobster, tomato confit, basil relish, chive infused olive oil (was a bit bland with a thick sauce); Dover sole Meunier or grilled; whole fish of day, oven-roasted with clams, mussels and shrimp, both carved tableside. La Strada tiramisu; tableside zabaglione (for two) over fresh berries; floating island surprise.

**Entertainment & amenities:** Every night, cocktail lounge; Thursday through Saturday nights, live piano entertainment.

**Summary & comments:** This downtown Michigan Avenue restaurant always exudes a special feeling of fine dining, and it's one of the few places to find classical Italian regional cuisine with emphasis on the Northern area. The menu was changed considerably in 1998 by new Executive Chef Marc Rosen (Remi Ristorante and Russian Tea Room, New York City; Palm Aire Resort and Spa, Pompano Beach, Florida). His colorful food is served in sumptuously comfortable, private surroundings with attentive service that borders on lavish. It comes as no surprise that this is one of Mayor Richard Daley's favorite places, and that it has cultivated its followers over 18-plus years in business. The restaurant's adjacent casual eatery is J. Randolph's Bar & Grill (phone (312) 565-2203), serving breakfast, lunch, and dinner; it features historical Chicago photos, sports memorabilia, and televised sporting events. Owners' new location is Cafe La Strada in the Hotel Moraine, Highwood, Illinois (847) 433-0065.

**Honors & awards:** *Travel Holiday* for 12 years; DiRoNA founding member; *Chicago Sun-Times,* three stars.

## LAWRY'S THE PRIME RIB ★★★★

| | | QUALITY |
|---|---|---|
| Prime Rib | Moderate | **90** |

| | VALUE |
|---|---|
| 100 East Ontario Street; (312) 787-5000 | **B** |

Zone 3   Near North

**Reservations:** Highly recommended

**When to go:** Weekday lunch or dinner usually less crowded

**Entree range:** Lunch, $5.95–10.95; dinner, $18.95–25.95

**Payment:** All major credit cards

**Service rating:** ★★★★

**Friendliness rating:** ★★★★

**Parking:** Valet during dinner ($6 per car)

**Bar:** Full service

**Wine selection:** Very good; mostly American, some French; featured wines; several by the glass

**Dress:** Lunch, business; dinner, casual to dressy

**Disabled access:** No

**Customers:** Business, conventioneers, families, couples

**Lunch:** Monday–Friday, 11:30 a.m.–2 p.m.

**Dinner:** Monday–Thursday, 5–10:30 p.m.; Friday and Saturday, 5–11:30 p.m.; Sunday, 3–9:30 p.m.

**Setting & atmosphere:** Housed in the stately century-old McCormick family mansion on the Gold Coast, with stunning winding staircases, splendid woodwork, and fireplaces. From the 1890s, when it was a setting for receptions for foreign dignitaries, the mansion changed hands several times until Richard N. Frank, CEO of Lawry's, bought and renovated it and opened the doors to become the second Lawry's in 1974. The original Lawry's The Prime Rib opened in 1938 in Beverly Hills, California.

**House specialties:** This is the reason for coming here: roast prime ribs of beef, available in four cuts: California (smaller), English (thinner slices), Lawry (traditional, generous), and Chicago (extra-thick with rib bone). Original spinning bowl salad; Yorkshire pudding; mashed potatoes and whipped cream horseradish come with prime rib; à la carte Lawry's baked potato is almost a meal itself—share it.

**Other recommendations:** Dinner fish special, such as grilled marlin with roast tomato vinaigrette or grilled ahi tuna served with ginger soy sauce; à la carte creamed spinach. Lunch: prime rib of beef; turkey, pastrami, and corned beef sandwiches; Lawry's Cobb salad; English trifle.

**Summary & comments:** The name says it all—prime rib is the menu here. The tradition of over 50 years is a magical formula that works

**(Lawry's The Prime Rib)**

because of the restaurant's commitment to the finest prime, dry-aged beef and other quality ingredients prepared to perfection. The general consensus is that Lawry's can't be beat on prime rib. Wine list includes Lawry's private selection and two featured wines. Attention to detail and service is impressive, and the elegance of the mansion setting gilds the lily. They've broadened their menu with fish specials; the quick "ale and sandwich bar"offers an affordable, casual lunch in a majestic mansion — a rare treat. Since Jackie Shen was appointed executive chef (formerly of Jackie's), diners can continue to enjoy her signature dessert: chocolate bag filled with white chocolate mousse, strawberries, and kiwi, with raspberry sauce.

**Honors & awards:** *North Shore* magazine, "Best Prime Rib."

---

## LE COLONIAL ★★★½

| French/Vietnamese | Moderate | QUALITY |
|---|---|---|
| | | 88 |
| 937 North Rush Street; (312) 255-0088 | | VALUE |
| Zone 1   North Side | | C |

Reservations: Recommended

When to go: Avoid peak meal times unless you have a reservation

Entree range: $12.50–19

Payment: VISA, MC, AMEX, DC

Service rating: ★★★★

Friendliness rating: ★★★★

Parking: Valet, $7

Bar: Full service

Wine selection: French and American wines, including dessert wines, ranging from $18–225; four each of red and white, as well as two Champagnes and several ports, available by the glass, $5–16

Dress: Business casual

Disabled access: Yes, also rest rooms

Customers: Chic professionals; business; couples, especially weekends

**Lunch:** Monday–Saturday, noon–2:30 p.m.

**Dinner:** Monday–Friday, 5–11 p.m.; Saturday, 5 p.m.–midnight; Sunday, 5–10 p.m.

**Setting & atmosphere:** The interior design by Greg Jordan, who was inspired by the film *Indochine,* offers patrons a choice of two atmospheres: the bar and tranquil dining room downstairs with rattan chairs and louvered shutters; and the romantic lounge upstairs with overstuffed sofas and chairs, and a terrace (weather permitting). The decor transports diners to the 1920s era of French-colonial Southeast Asia. Potted palms, fans

## (Le Colonial)

whirring overhead, louvered shutters, and rattan furniture sustain the Pacific tone set by Le Colonial's exotic, fresh cuisine.

**House specialties:** Chao tom (grilled shrimp wrapped around sugarcane with angel hair noodles); steamed dumplings with chicken and mushrooms; spicy beef salad with lemongrass and basil; crisp-seared whole red snapper with a spicy sour sauce; sautéed jumbo shrimp with eggplant in curried coconut sauce; banana tapioca pudding; tropical fruit sorbets.

**Other recommendations:** Pho (hearty oxtail soup with rice noodles, beef, and herbs); spring rolls made with shrimp, pork, and mushrooms; oven-roasted chicken with lemongrass and lime dipping sauce; ginger-marinated roast duck with tamarind dipping sauce; grilled eggplant in a spicy basil lime sauce; stir-fried rice with lemongrass, shrimp, and toasted sesame seeds.

**Summary & comments:** You won't miss Le Colonial from Rush Street, since the dove gray vintage townhouse with its lovely balcony, ceiling fans, columns, and cast-iron railing are clearly from another era and place. When you enter downtown Chicago's first French-Vietnamese fine dining restaurant, you get lost in an Asian time warp from the early 20th century, when the French-colonial period was at its peak in Vietnam. Ceiling fans stir the banana trees and palms. Taking the stairway to the lounge gives a wonderful view of the attractive main floor dining room. Photos of life in Saigon during the 1920s dot the walls. Le Colonial is owned by Jean Goutal and Rick Wahlstedt, who are partners in Le Colonial in Manhattan; there is a third location in Los Angeles owned by the other two New York partners.

## L'OLIVE CAFE  ★★★½

| Moroccan/Mediterranean | Inexpensive | QUALITY |
|---|---|---|
| | | 91 |

3915 North Sheridan Road; (773) 472-2400

| | VALUE |
|---|---|
| | A |

Zone 1   North Side

**Reservations:** Recommended for 5 or more

**When to go:** Any time

**Entree range:** $10.95–15.95

**Payment:** VISA, MC, DC, D

**Service rating:** ★★★

**Friendliness rating:** ★★★★½

**Parking:** Street

**Bar:** None

**Wine selection:** BYOB with $1.50 per person corkage fee; limited French, Spanish, and Italian list available at nearby shop

**Dress:** Casual

**Disabled access:** Yes, except rest room

**Customers:** Local, international, Moroccan, French, politicians

**Dinner:** Tuesday–Sunday, 5–11 p.m.; Monday, closed.

**Setting & atmosphere:** Intimate and homey former diner with olive silhouettes on windows, renovated for double-door entryway. Decorated with ceiling fans, mirrors, wall border murals, colorful rugs, Moroccan tagines (conical clay vessels), jars of preserved lemons and olives, and strings of garlic. Glass tops over tablecloths; mix-matched chairs.

**House specialties:** Bastilla (traditional flaky pigeon pie), here with chicken, almonds, and rose water; merguez (spicy Moroccan lamb sausage); warm fig salad with ginger and honey-spiced spinach. Several versions of the national dish, couscous (steamed semolina grains): vegetarian with saffron broth; calamari; grilled chicken breast; lamb; royal (meat, chicken, and merguez sausage) with spicy harissa sauce. Tagines (oven-braised dishes cooked in conical clay pots), deliciously moist with lamb or chicken (on menu), dried fruits, or preserved lemons and olives; specials might be seafood, poultry, or meat. Signature dish is lamb tagine, with cinnamon, dried apricots, and raisins.

**Other recommendations:** Appetizers: goat cheese hummus; Moroccan olives with harissa; zaalouk (roasted eggplant and roasted garlic dip); shrimp peel with spinach and chickpeas; sautéed fresh sardines stuffed with roasted peppers and tomatoes; Moroccan combination salad with roasted carrots, peppers, and eggplant. Daily specials include some seafood and another specialty. Desserts: warm, flaky apple tart with caramel sauce; proverbial Moroccan mint tea.

**(L'Olive Cafe)**

**Summary & comments:** L'Olive (pronounced "low leave" in French) is aptly named, since the olive is a key Mediterranean ingredient and paramount to Morocco, the North African homeland of chef/owner Mohamed Ben Mchabcheb. He introduced Moroccan cuisine to Chicago in 1988. His French cuisine training and passion for his native cuisine show in his exquisite versions of bastilla, couscous, and tagines. He does Mediterranean Moroccan cuisine with his own creative touches. This is the only place in the city for this cuisine beyond couscous; it even exceeds some of the food I tried in Morocco on several visits. With the many appetizers offered, it's fun to share several as openers. Daily specials provide a forum for the chef's creativity. Chef does catering, private parties, and carryout. Definitely worth going out of your way for a meal here. Excellent value.

**Honors & awards:** Rated among top ten restaurants in Chicago by WBBM; three stars from *Chicago Tribune*.

---

## LOUISIANA KITCHEN                                    ★★★½

| | QUALITY |
|---|---|
| Louisiana Creole and Cajun    Inexpensive/Moderate | 91 |
| 2666 North Halsted St.; (773) 529-1666 | VALUE |
| Zone 1    North Side | B |

Reservations: Parties of 6 or more
When to go: Weekend evenings for the liveliest atmosphere; Sunday brunch for a great jazz experience
Entree range: $9.95–17.95
Payment: All major credit cards
Service rating: ★★★★
Friendliness rating: ★★★★½
Parking: Valet, $4
Bar: Full, with good selection of beers; specialty drinks

Wine selection: About two dozen international selections and several domestics from California; gently priced from $20–35/bottle, and from $4–6/glass for the dozen so offered
Dress: Casual; very casual in garden
Disabled access: Yes
Customers: Mixed, all ages; jazz lovers; aficionados of Louisiana cuisine.

**Brunch:** Saturday, 11 a.m.–3 p.m.; Sunday jazz brunch (served, not buffet), 11 a.m.–3 p.m.

**Lunch/Dinner:** Saturday, 3 p.m.–midnight; Sunday, 3–10 p.m.

**Dinner:** Tuesday & Wednesday, 5–10 p.m.; Thursday, 5–11p.m.; Friday, 5 p.m.–midnight

## (Louisiana Kitchen)

**Setting & atmosphere:** Interior is intimate with white tablecloths and blue-cushioned chairs; casual mood with wooden floors and lower half wall and enlarged portrait photos of jazz greats. Lively and electric; music loud but not offensively so. Lovely outdoor garden reminiscent of Bayou country with brick patio floor, wrought iron fence and gate, and a large central tree illuminated by tiny lights.

**House specialties:** Appetizers: fried alligator, crispy bite-size nuggets, delicious with Creole honey mustard sauce (some of the best, per New Orleans customers); Louisiana's seafood gumbo (thick, slightly spicy). Entrées under "Lagniappe" (a little something extra): Sautéed shrimp and blackened catfish Acadienne, with garlic, tomatoes, green onions, herbs and white wine; catfish seasoned with Mama Bazzell's Cajun Seasoning, with seasoned rice and blackened vegetables. Desserts: Louisiana bread pudding, warm and sweet with butter-rum sauce; bourbon pecan torte (pie-like); mocha hazelnut truffle (dense cake cut into wedges).

**Other recommendations:** Appetizers: Blackened shrimp with house seasoning mix; fried oysters and lobster (tail). French Quarter specialties: Louisiana jambalaya, a robustly flavored rice combination with chicken and smoked sausage (shrimp option too). Desserts: Mississippi mud pie with chocolate sauce; variety of cheesecakes.

**Entertainment & amenities:** Live jazz for Sunday brunch, which is served. Fine quality taped jazz other times. Mardi Gras celebration.

**Summary & comments:** A fourth-generation French Creole/Cajun cook, owner John Moultrie grew up in Chicago and learned his culinary secrets from his grandmother, who told him stories about her parents' Florida restaurant, Bazzell's, which opened in 1910. Moultrie's first solo venture was the popular Jazz Oasis in River North, and then Bazell's French Quarter Bistro in Old Town, which he closed and plans to relocate. Louisiana Kitchen is the only city restaurant I know of specializing in authentic Louisiana fare in a relaxed, fine dining jazz-oriented setting.

**Honors & awards:** 1998 Silver Platter Award.

## LUTNIA CONTINENTAL CAFE ★★★½

| Polish | Moderate/Inexpensive | QUALITY |
|---|---|---|
| | | 87 |

5532 West Belmont Avenue; (773) 282-5335

Zone 2   North Central/O'Hare

| | VALUE |
|---|---|
| | C |

Reservations: Recommended
When to go: Any time
Entree range: $8.95–20
Payment: Major credit cards
Service rating: ★★★★
Friendliness rating: ★★★★
Parking: City garage
Bar: Full service, including Polish

vodka
Wine selection: International,
   including Hungarian
Dress: Casual and dressy, depending
   on occasion
Disabled access: Yes
Customers: Local, some European,
   business, couples

**Lunch/Dinner:** Saturday and Sunday, 1–11 p.m.

**Dinner:** Tuesday–Friday, 5–11 p.m.

**Setting & atmosphere:** Elegant and romantic: candlelabras, red carpet, and musical instruments and paintings on walls; white tablecloths with fresh roses and candles; some intimate tables; white baby grand piano.

**House specialties:** Duck breast flambé in orange sauce; stroganoff tenderloin flambé served in pastry shell; stuffed boneless quail with cranberry sauce. Besides flambéed dishes, there is tableside service of certain salads, such as Caesar (for two). Traditional Polish dishes all get high marks: potato pancakes, pierogi (stuffed dumplings), and bigos (hunter's stew).

**Other recommendations:** Mushrooms stuffed with escargots and scallops; white borscht (tart, with sour cream and sausage); cucumber salad; spinach salad. Homemade apple cake and flambéed blintzes; Polish old-fashioned coffee with honey liqueur.

**Entertainment & amenities:** Live piano nightly playing romantic music, such as Chopin.

**Summary & comments:** Gracious Polish couple, Chris and Evana Ruban, are owners; the recipes served here are Chris's. Dinner includes an appetizer, bread, soup, and a vegetable. The upscale food is very good, served on fine china by an attentive staff with European flair.

**Honors & awards:** *North Shore* magazine, "Best Eastern European Restaurant."

## MAMA DESTA'S RED SEA ETHIOPIAN RESTAURANT ★★★

| Ethiopian | Inexpensive | QUALITY |
|---|---|---|
| | | 86 |

| 3216 North Clark Street; (773) 935-7561 | VALUE |
|---|---|
| Zone 1   North Side | B |

**Reservations:** Recommended for 4 or more
**When to go:** Weekdays after 7 p.m.
**Entree range:** $6–8.50
**Payment:** Major credit cards
**Service rating:** ★★★★
**Friendliness rating:** ★★★★
**Parking:** Public lots nearby

**Bar:** Full service
**Wine selection:** Mixed; mostly African and American
**Dress:** Casual
**Disabled access:** Yes
**Customers:** Diverse, local, international, usually the 20–30-something age group

**Lunch:** Friday–Sunday, 11:30 a.m.–3 p.m.

**Dinner:** Monday–Thursday, 3–11 p.m.; Friday–Sunday, 3 p.m.–midnight

**Setting & atmosphere:** Two cozy, candlelit rooms. Diners can sit at tables and in booths in one room or at mesobes (large woven baskets that serve as tables; no chairs) in another room. The decor is simple but tasteful: white tablecloths, red carnations, and candles.

**House specialties:** Lentil-vegetable soup; vegetable dishes: yemisir wat (spiced green lentils, pureed until very smooth, unlike other versions which are more textured); kosta (chard cooked with onions, garlic, coriander, and green peppers); gomen (green vegetables sautéed with garlic, cumin, and green peppers, garnished with homemade cheese); chicken dishes: doro wat (chicken simmered with garlic and onions in spicy berbere sauce, including coriander, cumin, garlic, and cardamom); doro tibs (boneless chicken sautéed with onions, green pepper, tomato, and awaze, a mixture of spices and herbs with red pepper base); zizil wat (beef simmered in mildy spiced berbere sauce); yasa tibs (mildly spicy boneless, fish—great sautéed catfish —with onions, green peppers, spices, and herbs). Dessert: Red Sea cream (pudding of sweet and sour creams, brown sugar, raspberry puree, garnished with crème de cacao).

**Other recommendations:** Yebeg tibs (lamb cubes sautéed with peppers, onions, spices, berbere sauce). Try the Ethiopian wine, Tej. It's made of honey and is sweet, spicy, and smooth; sounds strange for a table wine, but it's actually good with the piquant food.

**Summary & comments:** The saucy dishes are hearty, wholesome, and colorful, and are served family style on classic injera, a tart sourdough pan-

**(Mama Desta's Red Sea Ethiopian Restaurant)**

cakelike bread made from teff (milletlike grain). The injera is placed on a large metal platter. To eat Ethiopian style, pick up one type of food with a piece of torn bread and eat them together. Ethiopians do not use knives and forks. The bread is both a plate and spoon.

**Honors & awards:** *Chicago Tribune,* three stars.

| MANDAR INN | | ★★★½ |
|---|---|---|
| Chinese | Inexpensive/Moderate | QUALITY 88 |
| 2249 South Wentworth Avenue, Chinatown; (312) 842-4014 Zone 5   South Loop | | VALUE C |

Reservations: Accepted; recom-
mended for weekends
When to go: Any time
Entree range: $6.50–28
Payment: VISA, MC, AMEX, DC
Service rating: ★★★★
Friendliness rating: ★★★★★
Parking: Community Chinatown lot offers 2 hours free with restaurant validation

Bar: Full service
Wine selection: Mostly Californian, some French (including Wan Fu), Asian; inexpensive; 8 by the glass
Dress: Casual, some dressy
Disabled access: No
Customers: Locals, some families, suburbanites, tourists, mix of Asian and non-Asian patrons

**Open:** Sunday–Thursday, 11:30 a.m.–9:30 p.m.; Friday and Saturday, 11:30 a.m.–10:30 p.m.

**Setting & atmosphere:** Decorated in shades of rose and maroon with comfortable green banquettes. Attractive 95-seat dining space; pretty linen napkins and artistic touches.

**House specialties:** Flaming appetizers (for two), including shrimp toast, egg roll, ribs, and barbecue pork; kwoh-te (freshly made pot stickers); empress chicken; Szechuan green beans (great texture and flavor); Szechuan eggplant; lobster and scallops volcano (seafood with pea pods and mushrooms in wine and oyster sauce, dramatically served on a sizzling hot platter).

**Other recommendations:** Orange chicken; moo shi pork; Peking duck (one day's advance notice; compared to most other places and downtown prices, it's a bargain); beef in a nest.

**Summary & comments:** You can get more than Mandarin cuisine at this respected Chinatown restaurant, which has been in this location for over

**(Mandar Inn)**

13 years after moving from a previous address. Szechuan, Hunan, and Cantonese cuisines are also offered on the extensive menu. If you're dining with a group, consider the fixed-price Mandar dinners listed for parties of two to eight; the larger the group, the more dishes can be sampled. Owner Sharolyn Jay develops the recipes and oversees the operation, and her daughter assists with the front of the house. Their graciousness prevails, and customers feel very welcome.

**Honors & awards:** Three stars from *Mobil Travel Guide*.

| MANGO | | ★★★★ |
|---|---|---|

| American Bistro | Inexpensive/Moderate | QUALITY |
|---|---|---|
| | | 92 |

| 712 North Clark Street; (312) 337-5440 | VALUE |
|---|---|
| Zone 3   Near North | B |

Reservations: Recommended
When to go: Early (around 5 p.m.) or late
Entree range: $11–18
Payment: Major credit cards
Service rating: ★★★★½
Friendliness rating: ★★★★½
Parking: Lot next door; valet
Bar: Full service

Wine selection: Fairly extensive list of French, American, and Italian; about 13 by the glass, most $4–5.50; affordable
Dress: Casual, chic, business
Disabled access: Yes
Customers: Business by day, a blend of all kinds by night

**Lunch:** Monday–Friday, 11:30 a.m.–2 p.m.

**Dinner:** Monday–Thursday, 5–11 p.m.; Friday and Saturday, 5 p.m.–midnight; Sunday, 5–10 p.m.

**Setting & atmosphere:** There are two dining rooms: the main level room is open and airy, sporting clean lines and mango-shaped and -hued lights; the one downstairs is an intimate wine cellar with Mexican tile and brick features. The restaurant is smoke-free. Private rustic room upstairs with a fireplace upstairs, adjacent to the cooking school kitchen.

**House specialties:** Mediterranean fish soup with fennel and leek in a saffron broth; risotto with asparagus, Parmesan, and olive oil; pork chops with northern beans; duck prosciutto with mango, mâche lettuce, and chive dressing; chicken and walnut tart with caramelized pear, baby field greens, and red onion compote; freshwater shrimp wrapped in potato with spinach and wasabi; tower of smoked salmon with sundried tomatoes, black olives, and red pepper coulis; Chiappetti's lamb shank glazed in

**(Mango)**

molasses with country vegetables and lentils; roasted pork chop with northern white beans, caramelized onions, and sweet mustard sauce.

**Other recommendations:** Goat cheese "brick" with roasted peppers and basil; fresh tomato-cucumber salad; Amish-raised chicken with garlic potatoes and lemon-rosemary sauce. Save room for Mango's luscious desserts, such as Wright's flourless chocolate cake with hazelnut brittle; banana chocolate mousse cake with crisp wafer; honey-glazed pear in orange juice–glazed phyllo dough crust with frozen passion fruit parfait. (The chefs here love phyllo and use it often throughout the menu, from appetizer through dessert.)

**Summary & comments:** Talented chef Steven Chiappetti and his manager-partner George Guggeis opened this casual American bistro in late 1995, and immediately received favorable media attention. The atmosphere in the 55-seat main dining room is warm and welcoming, the prices are affordable, the cooking is refined, and the dishes are visually pleasing. Chiappetti's family owns the four-generations-old Chiappetti Lamb Packing, the only remaining company from the Stockyard Pavilion. So it's not surprising that the finest quality of lamb, pork, and beef are found on his menu, and that he prepares them expertly. But fish and poultry don't take a back seat here, and creative vegetarian items please nonmeat eaters. Be sure to allow for desserts, which are both fun and delicious here. A most enjoyable dining experience made even better without the guilt of breaking the budget. The chef has started a weekend cooking school upstairs in a home-style kitchen and conducts corporate class-and-dinner events in his private adjacent room.

**Honors & awards:** In 1996, chef-owner Steven Chiapetti won the national competition required to earn him the privilege of being the only eligible American chef to compete for the prestigious Bocuse d'Or, an international "chef cook-off" held annually in Lyon, France. He ranked in the top ten of his peers, the best chefs from around the world.

## MANTUANO MEDITERRANEAN TABLE ★★★★

| | | QUALITY |
|---|---|---|
| Mediterranean | Inexpensive/Moderate | **91** |

| | VALUE |
|---|---|
| 455 City Front Plaza, NBC Tower; (312) 832-2600 | **C** |
| Zone 3   Near North | |

Reservations: Recommended
When to go: Any time; off-meal times for light fare and wine
Entree range: $13.95–26.95
Payment: All major credit cards except D
Service rating: ★★★★
Friendliness rating: ★★★★½
Parking: Valet, $7

Bar: Full service
Wine selection: Fairly extensive, especially Mediterranean; wine tastings; many by the glass
Dress: Moderately casual, business
Disabled access: Yes
Customers: Couples, young professionals, tourists, families

**Lunch:**  Monday–Friday, 11:30 a.m.–2 p.m.

**Dinner:**  Monday–Thursday, 5–10 p.m.; Friday & Saturday, 5–11 p.m.

**Setting & atmosphere:**  Spacious hallway with several cafe tables leads to a colorful retail market. Two artistic dining rooms available for private parties; the bar room with a view is more bustling than the romantic inner room.

**House specialties:**  Flaming ouzo shrimp; grilled portobello with manchego, marinated tomatoes; Casbah platter; rotisserie half-chicken; Portuguese seafood Cataplana (shrimp, lobster, clams, mussels, calamari, octopus); Moroccan vegetable tagine; double-cut Greek lamb chops; gnocchi with mushrooms and Romano; double-decker garlic mushroom pizza. Flourless chocolate cake; gelatos and sorbets.

**Other recommendations:**  Greektown grilled calamari and octopus; real San Daniele prosciutto; Mediterranean Caesar. Large herbaceous seafood ravioli with asparagus and cremini (special); baccalà alla Calabrese (southern Italian–style cod); brick oven–roasted salmon. Warm raisin and cinnamon bread pudding with walnut gelato and caramel sauce.

**Entertainment & amenities:**  Retail market; views of Chicago's architecture.

**Summary & comments:**  Chef Tony Mantuano and his wife, Cathy, who organizes the wine list, outgrew their location at Tuttaposto on North Franklin Street and moved downtown in 1997 in a joint venture with Taste America Restaurants, Inc. Although lamb is the meat of the Mediterranean, there is more beef on this menu. The chef adds unique creative touches and his food is boldly flavored.

## THE MITY NICE GRILL ★★★½

| | | QUALITY |
|---|---|---|
| American | Inexpensive/Moderate | 86 |

| VALUE |
|---|
| C |

835 North Michigan Avenue, Water Tower Place, Mezzanine;
(312) 335-4745
Zone 3   Near North

**Reservations:** Recommended
**When to go:** Any time
**Entree range:** Lunch, $11–13; dinner, $13–18
**Payment:** All major credit cards
**Service rating:** ★★★½
**Friendliness rating:** ★★★★½
**Parking:** Water Tower underground garage (discount after 5 p.m.)

**Bar:** Full service
**Wine selection:** Good selection; several by the glass
**Dress:** Casual
**Disabled access:** Yes
**Customers:** Professionals, business, couples, families, shoppers, tourists

**Lunch/Dinner:** Monday–Saturday, 11 a.m.–10 p.m.; Sunday, 11 a.m.–9 p.m.

**Setting & atmosphere:** Casual, neighborhood-style spot downtown. Classic bar for people-watching; comfortable 180-seat restaurant, simply decorated. A 1940s-style decor with a 1990s grill.

**House specialties:** Grilled flatbreads; turkey steak; chicken, fish, and special roasts of the day; steaks; abundant salads; pastas; great homemade crumble-topped apple pie.

**Other recommendations:** "Minute Chicken Terri D.," a loyal customer's favorite dish named for her; weekly specials based on seafood, etc., in season.

**Summary & comments:** Rich Melman, founder of Lettuce Entertain You Enterprises, says, "Today, more than ever, we need to be nice to each other. That's why I decided to call it 'Mity Nice Grill.'" It's a great concept for a restaurant in our increasingly stressful world. The staff is mity nice here, and so is the food.

## MON AMI GABI                                    ★★★★

| French Bistro | Moderate | QUALITY |
|---|---|---|
| | | 92 |

2300 North Lincoln Park West; (773) 348-8886
Zone 1   North Side

| | VALUE |
|---|---|
| | C |

**Reservations:** Accepted and recommended

**When to go:** Early weeknights; late weekends

**Entree range:** Appetizers, $3.95–9.95; Entrées, $12.95–23.95

**Payment:** All major credit cards

**Service rating:** ★★★★

**Friendliness rating:** ★★★½

**Parking:** Valet, $6

**Bar:** Full service; turn-of-the-century Parisian bar

**Wine selection:** All French, more than 100 selections, from $15–$139 a bottle; selection of 8 regional wines by the glass ($4.95–6.75) from wine cart

**Dress:** Casual

**Disabled access:** Wheelchair accessible; call ahead for special accommodations

**Customers:** Casual, chic crowd; local, media; all ages; low-key after opera and art gallery crowd

**Dinner:** Monday–Thursday, 5:30–10:30 p.m.; Friday and Saturday, 5:30–11 p.m.; Sunday, 5–9 p.m.

**Setting & atmosphere:** Refurbished and reopened in 1998, the former Un Grand Cafe room was made more intimate with an authentic replica of a turn-of-the-century Parisian bar with a list of shellfish whimsically priced in francs. Feels like a bistro on the West Bank of Paris; chic; intimate outdoor garden; view of Lincoln Park Conservatory and gardens.

**House specialties:** First courses:  Onion soup au gratin; a fine rendition of rich baked oysters Florentine; steamed mussels mariniere (also a main course). Entrées: steak frites four ways, from classique (plain) to au poivre, Roquefort and Bordelaise; I was impressed with this last version (steak is pounded thin, cooked as ordered medium-rare and served with caramelized onions and perfect, crispy pommes frites). Paillarde of halibut with sauce gribiche is exemplary. Roast chicken with pearl onions, mushrooms, au jus and frites;  Chilean sea bass en papillote, julienne vegetables; Plats du jour listed on rotating basis (check blackboard).  Desserts shine here; try tarte tatin; cherry clafouti; lemon pudding.

**Other recommendations:** Plateaux de fruit de mer (coquilles Gabi; succulent mussels a la Claude served with slivers of red bell peppers. Entrées: paillarde of lamb, herb jus; beef Wellington, sauce Perigeaux; shrimp

**(Mon Ami Gabi)**

Provençale with egg noodles, roasted tomatoes, garlic, herbs. Tomato salad with haricot vert, Roquefort, marinated onions, vinaigrette (seasonal). Strawberry Briand (refreshing sour cream milk ice with sliced berries).

**Entertainment & amenities:** Taking in the stately architecture and charming atmosphere, including the Lincoln Park Conservatory across the street and the lovely garden open for summer dinner service down a few steps.

**Summary & comments:** The former Un Grand Cafe concept gave way to Mon Ami Gabi when Richard Melman, CEO of Lettuce Entertain You Enterprises, Inc. and managing partner-chef Gabino Sotelino were planning to merely freshen up this 17-year-old bistro. They changed the menu to emphasize seafood, including a fresh shellfish bar, and steak frites, now offered four ways. The wine list was expanded and made exclusively French. New chef de cuisine is Claude Gaty. Expect some innovative dishes amidst the culinary anchors.

**Honors & awards:** 1997 Gold Cup Award.

| MORTON'S OF CHICAGO | | ★★★★ |
|---|---|---|
| Steak | Expensive | **QUALITY**<br>92 |
| 1050 North State Street; (312) 266-4820<br>Zone 3    Near North | | **VALUE**<br>C |

One Westbrook Corporate Center; 22nd Street and Wolf Road, Westchester
(708) 562-7000
Zone 8    Southern Suburbs

9525 West Bryn Mawr Avenue, Rosemont (847) 678-5155
Zone 2    North Central/O'Hare

**Reservations:** Suggested
**When to go:** Any time
**Entree range:** $17–30
**Payment:** All major credit cards
**Service rating:** ★★★★½
**Friendliness rating:** ★★★★½
**Parking:** Free (Rosemont and West-chester); call other places for details
**Bar:** Full service; 40 varieties of martinis
**Wine selection:** Extensive; several selections by the glass
**Dress:** Jacket preferred, tie optional (but flexible)
**Disabled access:** Yes, for all locations
**Customers:** Diverse, local, business, couples, travelers; downtown location also gets celebrities

**(Morton's of Chicago)**

**Lunch:** *(Westchester only)* Monday–Friday, 11:30 a.m.–2:30 p.m.

**Dinner:** Monday–Saturday, 5:30–11 p.m.; Sunday, 5–10 p.m.

**Setting & atmosphere:** Comfortable, well appointed. Suburban places are quieter and more intimate; downtown is bigger and more crowded.

**House specialties:** 24-oz. porterhouse steak, also available as a 3-lb. double; whole baked Maine lobsters; special-fed, farm-raised salmon; black bean soup; steamed asparagus with hollandaise.

**Other recommendations:** Sicilian veal chop; domestic rib lamb chops; fresh Cockenoe oysters on the half shell to start; Caesar salad; sautéed fresh spinach and mushrooms; baked Idaho potato; Godiva hot chocolate cake; soufflé for two—chocolate, Grand Marnier, or lemon.

**Entertainment & amenities:** Watching the "show and tell" performance by the waiters with the display cart of huge cuts of steaks, chops, live lobsters, and other raw ingredients.

**Summary & comments:** Many steak connoisseurs stake their claim in Morton's as their favorite place for porterhouse or certain other cuts. The management is a stickler for quality, and the kitchen prepares the meat properly to order. The diner pays dearly for this high quality. The $29 steak gets only a garnish; everything must be ordered à la carte, as is the case in many steak restaurants. Clockwork service makes everything move along at a great pace. Needs are anticipated by the professional servers. The downtown place is the most bustling and noisiest of the three locations. The two suburban siblings with similar menus cover the territory fairly well.

## NICK'S FISHMARKET                                     ★★★★½

| Seafood | Moderate/Expensive | QUALITY |
|---|---|---|
| | | 95 |

| One First National Bank Plaza, Monroe Street at Dearborn Street; (312) 621-0200 | VALUE |
|---|---|
| | D |

Zone 4   The Loop

10275 West Higgins Road, O'Hare International Center, Rosemont; (847) 298-8200
Zone 2   North Central/O'Hare

**Reservations:** Recommended
**When to go:** Weekdays
**Entree range:** Lunch $14–25; Dinner $18–47 (Maine lobster top price)
**Payment:** All major credit cards

**Service rating:** ★★★★½
**Friendliness rating:** ★★★★½
**Parking:** Valet, validated self-parking in First National garage (Downtown); Lot (Rosemont)

**(Nick's Fishmarket)**

Bar: Full service

Wine selection: Extensive (over 100) international; French, Italian, domestic, $20–200 a bottle; about 18 choices by the glass, $4.95 and up

Dress: Jacket suggested; collared shirt or sweater required

Disabled access: Yes

Customers: Largely businesspeople, professionals, couples

**Lunch:** *Downtown:* Monday–Friday, 11:30 a.m.–3 p.m.

**Dinner:** *Downtown:* Monday–Thursday, 5:30–11 p.m.; Friday and Saturday, 5:30 p.m.–midnight. *Rosemont:* Sunday–Thursday, 6–10 p.m.; Friday and Saturday, 6–11 p.m.

**Setting & atmosphere:** Downtown, the new location across the plaza from the original space, overlooks the Marc Chagall mosaic and the lively fountain. Ambience of a 1930s oceanliner with art deco-inspired carpeting, window treatments, furnishings and art with a contemporary touch. New entryway from sidewalk leads to Nick's Bar & Grill with scaled down prices, a chic bar and 90 seats. The escalator takes diners down to plaza level to the new comfortable fine dining room with 150 seats and tuxedoed waiters. Rosemont has lovely aquariums and plush, comfortable club-like setting; tuxedoed waiters; private room seats 35. Lavish interior exudes posh and pizazz.

**House specialties:** Appetizers such as seared black and blue ahi, with baby bok choy; jumbo lump crabcake with spinach sauté, pineapple rémoulade and sweet soy wasabi; outstanding seafood crepes topped with lobster and vermouth sauce. Entrees: Chef's favorite Dover sole, boned tableside with an exquisite caviar vermouth sauce; grilled or sautéed Hawaiian or other fresh fish, such as the uliehu (Hawaiian bluenose snapper) special with carved potato "mushrooms," snowpea pods and carrots; linguini with black trumpet mushrooms, rosemary cream; peanut-crusted breast of capon with pocket of roasted artichoke mousseline; New York strip steak with mushroom sauté, light peppercorn sauce. Classic house salad (à la carte) topped with tiny shrimp. Desserts: Towers of Chicago (a construction of a quartet of mousses with raspberry sauce); excellent tart Key lime pie.

**Other recommendations:** Lobster bisque with lobster ravioli and sherry finish; cold appetizers of smoked salmon Napoleon with Roquefort and caper Bavarian and roasted chicken and goat cheese terrine with sun-dried tomato couscous. Entrees: Alaskan halibut, fennel salad, caviar chardonnay sauce and marinated shrimp; roasted Maine lobster clam bake; Holland turbot fillet, chanterelle and asparagus sauté, mustard and summer truffles

**(Nick's Fishmarket)**

(in season); California abalone specials if you can afford them (chef's cost is $64/pound!). Desserts: chocolate gateau; white chocolate crème brûlée.

**Entertainment & amenities:** Live music at both places; call for specifics.

**Summary & comments:** Top-quality seafood place with pristinely fresh catches, many from Hawaiian waters. Well-known owner/founder Nick Nicholas owns several restaurants in Boca Raton, Florida, Washington D.C., Philadelphia and Las Vegas besides here, and he brings seafood in fresh to Chicago. He has a savvy staff with a penchant for serving seafood properly. Service is proficient and gracious, geared to expense-account business clientele. Steer toward the simpler preparations, such as roasted Maine lobster rather than the Thermidor with the classic but rich Mornay sauce. New chef André Halston has created a new menu with some exciting dishes accented by unusual accompaniments (e.g. spinach and eggplant cake with dates and mint jus for rack of lamb) while keeping the signature items and longtime favorites.

**Honors & awards:** DiRoNA 1994-1997; Mobil 4-Star AAA Award 1977-1997; *Gourmet* Magazine, Top 20 Restaurants in Chicago—Readers' Poll 1996, 1997; *Wine Spectator,* Award of Excellence, 1997.

| NORTH POND CAFE | | ★★★★ |
|---|---|---|
| New American Midwestern Organic Moderate | | **QUALITY** 92 |
| 2610 N. Cannon Drive; (773)-477-5845 Zone 1 North Side | | **VALUE** B |

Reservations: Recommended

When to go: Depends on whether you prefer lunch in daylight by the pond, especially outdoors, or indoors for dinner

Entree range: $16–23.

Payment:VISA, MC, AMEX

Service rating: ★★★★

Friendliness rating:★★★★

Parking: Street

Bar: Full

Wine selection: International; about 70 selections, $14–95; about 14 by the glass, from $4.50–8

Dress: Casual

Disabled access: Yes

Customers: Mixed; all ages; families with children; couples; singles; mostly locals

**Brunch:** Sunday, 11 a.m.

**Lunch:** Tuesday–Saturday, 11 a.m.–2:30 p.m.

**Dinner:** Tuesday–Sunday, 5–9:30 p.m.

**(North Pond Cafe)**

**Setting & atmosphere:**  Lovely setting in a beautiful part of Lincoln Park on North Pond; idyllic; removed from the traffic and city noise. Interior pond mural around ceiling reprises the beautiful exterior pondscape. Attractive posters of Midwestern activities.

**House specialties:**  Appetizers such as excellent house-cured salmon with fingerling potatoes, lemon "gem" dressing; Lou Polley's summer squash soup with crab succotash. Entrées: roasted halibut and salmon fish cakes, bacon and orange mash potatoes, Tabasco butter sauce (spicy-hot!); citrus-marinated salmon with roasted spring vegetables, mustard cream sauce; pepita toasted Amish chicken with tortilla stuffing, fava beans and cauliflower, mole sauce. Desserts: Selection of cheese from Capriole Farms, Greenville, Indiana; Pies of all kinds, such as blueberry, sweet potato and peach crumble; Champagne sorbet.

**Other recommendations:**  Appetizer: Cornmeal-crusted oysters with oyster mushrooms, arugula and corn, Tabasco butter sauce. Entrées: Vegetarian menu, a three-course menu selected daily; sumac berry crusted turkey breast with saffron potatoes, natural jus, tarragon butter. Dessert:  sorbets, such as lemon with almond tuille.

**Entertainment & amenities:**  Viewing the North Pond with ducks and surrounding nature.

**Summary & comments:**  Chef-owner Mary Ellen Diaz, formerly of Printer's Row, has been inspired by the turn-of-the-century Arts and Crafts movement, which reasserted the link between art and function and emphasized an appreciation for nature. She cooks with organic ingredients, which underscore her philosophy that life's essence is in the natural connections of the environment. The location in a former warming shed, situated on the pond, seems perfectly suited to Diaz's style.

**Honors & awards:**  *Chicago Sun-Times* feature, and three-star review April 17, 1998.

## ONE SIXTYBLUE ★★★★

| | | QUALITY |
|---|---|---|
| New American | Moderate/Expensive | **92** |

| | VALUE |
|---|---|
| | **C** |

160 N. Loomis; (312)-850-0303
Zone 2  North Central/O'Hare

Reservations: Yes
When to go: Anytime
Entree range: $20–29
Payment: VISA, MC, AMEX, DC
Service rating: ★★★★ ½
Friendliness rating: ★★★★ ½
Parking: Valet, $6
Bar: Full
Wine selection: International, wine

organized by varietals on list;
about 100 selections, from $200
up; several by the glass
Dress: Chic casual
Disabled access: Complete
Customers: Mixed; mostly sophisticated professionals; including
Michael Jordan who frequents this
place

**Dinner:** Sunday-Thursday, 5–10 p.m.; Friday and Saturday, 5–11 p.m.

**Setting & atmosphere:** Cohesive amalgam of contemporary materials; incredibly spacious with wonderful lighting; linear shapes; curved, brushed stainless steel lighting fixtures and paper-covered shades over chocolate brown light boxes; zinc-topped bar. Adam Tihany, perhaps the most recognized name in restaurant design, is the designer of one sixtyblue.

**House specialties:** "Two begin:" wood-roasted kataifi-wrapped asparagus with parma ham, red bell pepper coulis and sweet lemon pulp; mixed wild mushroom sauté with mascarpone polenta, fresh herbs and mushroom juices. "Four dinner": low roasted lemon verbena salmon with warmed spinach, potato brandade and summer truffle; roast loin of monkfish with overnight tomato, chanterelles and a shellfish, crème fraîche nage; macadamia-nut crusted sturgeon with a salad of braised onion, watercress and a fresh crab emulsion vinaigrette. Desserts: chocolate soufflé; almond-based spongecake.

**Other recommendations:** "Two begin": Peeky toe crab sandwich with roasted tomato vinaigrette and basil oil; salad of baby greens and fresh herbs turned in a hazelnut vinaigrette. "Four dinner": pan-seared sea scallops with melted leeks, grilled oyster mushrooms and a sauce of orange and rosemary; prime-aged delmonico steak with portobello mushroom, shipped yukon gold potato and a light sauce of balsamic vinegar and ginger.

**Summary & comments:** For a top-dollar restaurant in a burgeoning real estate area, one sixtyblue offers a wonderfully generous amount of per-diner space, which, coupled with the lustrous lighting on white walls, gives

**(one sixtyblue)**

a sense of freedom and ease. The Michael Jordan mystique is so closely coupled with one sixtyblue that it has been the subject of controversy related to his namesake restaurant. People come here mainly for the wonderful food prepared by talented chef Patrick Robertson (from well known restaurants in New York, France and Italy), not necessarily to see Jordan, but the fact that he frequents this place makes it more exciting.

| PALM RESTAURANT | ★★★★ | |
|---|---|---|
| | | **QUALITY** |
| Steak/Seafood | Moderate/Expensive | **92** |
| | | **VALUE** |
| Swissôtel Chicago, 323 East Wacker Drive; (312) 616-1000 | | **C** |
| Zone 4   The Loop | | |

| | |
|---|---|
| Reservations: Recommended | Bar: Full service; handsome bar area |
| When to go: Any time, but can be busy at peak lunch and dinner hours | Wine selection: Fairly extensive with 92 by the bottle ($21–210) and another 12 by the glass; mostly |
| Entree range: Lunch, $8–14; dinner, $18–36 | American with several French and Italian and a couple of Australian |
| Payment: VISA, MC, AMEX, DC | selections |
| Service rating: ★★★★½ | Dress: Casual to dressy |
| Friendliness rating: ★★★★½ | Disabled access: Yes |
| Parking: Valet ($5), street, and nearby lot | Customers: Diverse, locals, tourists, celebrities |

**Lunch/Dinner:** Every day, 11:30 a.m.–11 p.m.

**Setting & atmosphere:** The new, spacious setting at the Swissôtel offers several dining areas with comfortable tables and booths, some with views of the city lakefront. The rooms are beautifully decorated in forest green and dark wood with white tablecloths. The highlight is the Palm's traditional "Wall of Fame," featuring caricatures of about 250 VIPs and Chicago's movers and shakers (many of them are personally signed). Take advantage of great views of Navy Pier from the second level, including the rest rooms. Outdoor patio dining with a lake view is available in summer.

**House specialties:** Jumbo Nova Scotia lobsters, three pounds and more; a variety of steaks: prime-aged New York Sirloin, filet mignon, porterhouse, and prime rib; Gigi salad (shrimp, lettuce, tomato, green beans, radicchio, chopped egg, and bacon); good selection of sides, such as creamed and leaf spinach, hash browns, and cottage fries. One lunch spe-

**(Palm Restaurant)**

cial is a lobster club, a towering layered bun sandwich of lobster salad with bacon, tomato, red onion, lettuce, and fries. New Chef Paul Principato's creativity is expressed in daily specials, such as spicy lobster fra diablo (cooked with garlic, crushed red pepper, plum tomatoes, white wine and basil, served over linguine) and crab cakes ( jumbo lump crab, celery, onion and pimento). Excellent desserts include Key lime pie and rich chocolate pecan pie.

**Other recommendations:** Linguini with red or white clam sauce; pasta of the day; veal in different styles, including Milanese, Marsala, and Piccata; Caesar and other salads. Daily lunch specials might be grilled amberjack and asparagus Ferrara, named after a waiter (served with fresh tomato, marinara sauce, and melted Gruyere) and grilled or steamed vegetable platter. They are best-known for New York cheesecake (which, unfortunately, was once served still slightly frozen); another good dessert is the deep dish apple cobbler.

**Entertainment & amenities:** Reading the "Wall of Fame."

**Summary & comments:** The luxury Swissôtel Chicago became the new site of the Palm in the fall of 1996, after a 14-month hiatus. Formerly at the Mayfair Regent Hotel for 15 years, the restaurant was forced to move when the hotel was sold and the building converted into a residential property. With a more beautiful setting overlooking the lakefront and almost double the space on two levels, the new Palm retained its menu and veteran staff. Known for its spirited service, this restaurant is also fun and entertaining because of the caricatures on the walls and characters at the tables. John Ganzi and Pio Bozzi started their Palm Restaurant in 1926 in an Italian neighborhood on Second Avenue in New York City. Wally Ganzi, Jr., and Bruce Bozzi, third-generation owners, expanded the original Palm and, in the early 1970s, began opening Palms in other cities, beginning with Washington, D.C. The menu is standard across the United States. Today other locations include Los Angeles, Houston, Atlanta, Boston, and Mexico City. The Palm's secret for success seems to be consistency in its nonfussy, quality food with professional service in an upbeat, comfortable setting.

## PANE CALDO                                              ★★★½

| | QUALITY |
|---|---|
| Northern Italian        Inexpensive/Moderate | **89** |
| 72 East Walton Street; (312) 649-0055 | **VALUE** |
| Zone 3    Near North | **C** |

**Reservations:** Highly recommended

**When to go:** At lunch or early dinner, between 5–6 p.m.

**Entree range:** Pastas, $9.50–16.50; meat, chicken, and fish dishes, $13.50–19.95

**Payment:** VISA, MC, AMEX

**Service rating:** ★★★★

**Friendliness rating:** ★★★★

**Parking:** Reduced-rate parking next door

**Bar:** Full service, with about 16 grappas and several sambuca selections

**Wine selection:** Fairly extensive (about 67; 8 by the glass), mostly Italian with several Californian and several French champagnes; small riserva list

**Dress:** Casual

**Disabled access:** Yes

**Customers:** Diverse, business, couples, Gold Coast shoppers and tourists

**Lunch:** Every day, 11:30 a.m.–2:30 p.m., when lunch menu (sandwiches, salads, pizza, pasta) and regular dinner menu are available

**Dinner:** Sunday–Thursday, 5–10:30 p.m.; Friday and Saturday, 5–11:30 p.m.

**Setting & atmosphere:** Intimate trattoria-style setting. Sophisticated, soft lighting; burnt gold walls, decorated with original paintings; attractive floral arrangements. Dining room seats 78; bar seats 10; cozy private room seats 20; new private party room seats 100.

**House specialties:** Tortelloni di zucchini al Parmigiano (homemade, stuffed with acorn squash in light Parmesan cheese sauce); ravioli stuffed with lobster in creamy saffron sauce. Antipasti: grilled, marinated calamari with scampi in aromatic olive oil; the unusual mille foglie di pollo (layers of chicken, prosciutto, spinach, and mozzarella in wine mushroom sauce).

**Other recommendations:** Antipasti: duck and chicken dumplings, "Polpettine di anatra e pollo" with onion confit marmalade; porcini mushroom risotto. Great grilled double lamb chops with garlic, rosemary, and mustard sauce. Roasted veal chop stuffed with Gorgonzola cheese (a special). Daily "Progressive Sampling" menu, $45 per person, and a vegetarian version, $39 per person, minimum 2 people. Also daily specials, including antipasti, fish, pasta, risotto, and other secondi.

**(Pane Caldo)**

**Entertainment & amenities:** On-premise bakery that supplies delicious "warm bread," as the restaurant's name suggests.

**Summary & comments:** Pane Caldo, "warm bread," is an appropriate name since there's an on-premise bakery that makes warm bread for tables—delicious focaccia and rosemary bread, as examples—with the complimentary olive tapenade and cheecha (dried pomodoro dip: tomato-parsley-balsamic vinaigrette) at the start. Additional bonuses include an intermezzo apple-Armagnac sorbetto and chocolate truffles and sweets at the finish. Menu changes monthly and includes many unusual items, such as the mille foglie di pollo mentioned. Chef Maurice Bonhomme produces at least six vegetarian menu items using organic ingredients. The patissiere offers a "Dolci" menu with more than a dozen temptations, including homemade sorbettos, Tarte D'Opera (chocolate cake with hazelnut-coffee mousse, raspberry sauce), and warm almond tart with fresh pears in a vanilla-rhubarb sauce. Owner Antoine Cedicci, who started Pane Caldo in 1992, also owns La Borsa, 375 North Morgan Street.

**Honors & awards:** Voted best salmon in Chicago by *New York Times* in 1993; voted most authentic Italian cuisine by *Chicago* magazine in 1994.

| PAPAGUS GREEK TAVERNA | ★★★★ |
|---|---|

| Greek | Moderate | QUALITY |
|---|---|---|
| | | 90 |

Embassy Suites Hotel, 620 North State Street; (312) 642-8450  
Zone 3   Near North

**VALUE**  
**C**

270 Oakbrook Center, Oakbrook; (630) 472-9800  
Zone 6   South Central/Midway

**Reservations:** Recommended  
**When to go:** Any time for mezedes (little plates), lunch, or dinner  
**Entree range:** $7–25  
**Payment:** Major credit cards  
**Service rating:** ★★★★  
**Friendliness rating:** ★★★½  
**Parking:** Valet, $6 for 3 hours; validated parking in Embassy Suites

underground lot (Monday–Friday); free mall lot at Oakbrook  
**Bar:** Full service  
**Wine selection:** Expansive; mostly Greek  
**Dress:** Casual to dressy  
**Disabled access:** Yes  
**Customers:** Mixed, local, travelers, business

**Lunch/Dinner:** Monday–Thursday, 11:30 a.m.–10 p.m.; Friday, 11:30 a.m.–midnight; Saturday, noon–midnight; Sunday, noon–10 p.m.

**(Papagus Greek Taverna)**

**Setting & atmosphere:** Comfortable, rustic old-world-style taverna.

**House specialties:** Mezedes (appetizers) are the centerpiece here: taramosalata (cod or lobster roe salad); spanikopita (spinach pie); saganaki (flambéed cheese); grilled garlic-marinated shrimp. Main courses: Greek roast chicken; spicy lamb and beef meatballs; braised lamb with orzo.

**Other recommendations:** Roasted eggplant spread; marinated char-grilled octopus; olive bread salad; char-grilled skewer of swordfish.

**Summary & comments:** Some of the best light renditions of traditional Greek cuisine, served in a colorful, rustic setting. Chef uses a creative license on many items. This may not be in Greektown, but it has brought a good taste of Greece to the downtown area. Even the earlier skeptics have conceded that this place knows its stuff. Greek family-style feast is available.

**Honors & awards:** *Chicago Tribune's* "the best Greek restaurant in Chicago."

| PARK AVENUE CAFE | | ★★★★ |
|---|---|---|
| New American | Moderate/Expensive | QUALITY 94 |
| 199 East Walton Place; (312) 944-4414 Zone 3   Near North | | VALUE C |

**Reservations:** Recommended

**When to go:** Avoid peak meal times unless you have a reservation

**Entree range:** $18–29; tasting menu, $52

**Payment:** AMEX, VISA, MC, D, DC

**Service rating:** ★★★★ ½

**Friendliness rating:** ★★★★H

**Parking:** Valet

**Bar:** Full service with full list of single malts and cognacs

**Wine selection:** Ambitious list, mostly American; some French and Italian; $18–392 per bottle; extensive list of ports.

**Dress:** Casual; no T-shirts or cutoffs

**Disabled access:** Yes

**Customers:** Locals, travelers, business, professional, couples, singles; families, especially at brunch

**Brunch:** Sunday, 10:30 a.m.–2 p.m., $30; children, $11.

**Dinner:** Monday–Saturday, 5–11 p.m.; Sunday, 5–10 p.m.

**Setting & atmosphere:** Country contemporary design with wood floors, open kitchen, and bake shop; several interconnected dining areas are separated by niches decorated with American folk sculpture, some of it whim-

**(Park Avenue Cafe)**

sical; tubs of floral and wheat arrangements; warm lighting from forest green shades suspended over seating.

**House specialties:** Menu changes daily according to freshest possible seasonal ingredients. An example is Chef David Burke's trademarked Smoked Pastrami Salmon, an appetizer of thin slices of the peppered fish complemented by a corn blini. Entrées: slow-roasted honey-glazed duck that melts in the mouth and might include cranberry in the glaze and a wild rice pancake on the side; oven-roasted pork with shellfish "paella;" lemon roasted chicken with prawns and linguini; Burke's trademarked Swordfish Chop (a fillet of swordfish cleverly molded around a chop bone) offered as a special. For dessert, try the restaurant's classics, including The Chocolate Cube, a unique firm chocolate shell that hides chocolate mousse surrounding more white mousse. Another whimsical dessert is The Park Avenue Park Bench, a sculptured replica made of dark chocolate and a luscious praline mousse, a dark chocolate lamp pole with a flourless chocolate cake base and a white chocolate truffle globe.

**Other recommendations:** Appetizers such as chestnut bisque with duck confit; country salad with walnuts & goat cheese fondue. Entrees with creative twists such as seared duck with bleu cheese-stuffed pear and caramelized endive; miso-glazed sea bass with shrimp tortellini. Desserts range from fanciful, such as poached pear financier with white wine ice cream and pumpkin crème brûlée to basic American favorites like warm blueberry cobbler with ice cream.

**Summary & comments:** This fine dining restaurant on the second level of the DoubleTree Guest Suites Chicago opened here in 1995, and its contemporary American cuisine quickly received high praise. New Chef de Cuisine Jason Handelman, who was executive sous chef, took over the kitchen in 1998 and added some new items. The wonders he works with American cuisine, combining excellence and whimsy, would make any American diner feel patriotic. Pastry chef Delfina Perez Najera also has a magic touch, both in her creation of edible sculptures and in producing traditional full-flavored desserts. Just downstairs from the restaurant, at street level, is Mrs. Park's Tavern, a more casual, less expensive cafe (main courses, $10–24; sandwiches from $9; phone (312) 280-8882). Both restaurants hold frequent wine promotions to showcase their varied, extensive lists. Park Avenue Cafe introduced the first American dim sum brunch, with more than 50 tasting portions of the restaurant's specialties along with Asian items, served traditionally from rolling carts.

**Honors & awards:** AAA, four diamonds; *Chicago Tribune,* three stars.

| **PARS COVE** | ★★★½ |
|---|---|

|  |  | QUALITY |
|---|---|---|
| Persian | Inexpensive | **89** |
|  |  | VALUE |
| 435 West Diversey Parkway; (773) 549-1515 | | **C** |
| Zone 1   North Side | | |

Reservations: Recommended
When to go: Any time
Entree range: $5.95–9.95
Payment: All major credit cards
Service rating: ★★★½
Friendliness rating: ★★★★½
Parking: Limited parking behind
   restaurant, street, and nearby
   garage

Bar: Full service
Wine selection: International; several
   by the glass
Dress: Varied; can range from casual
   to formal
Disabled access: No, but willing to
   help; 4 steps down
Customers: Diverse, professional,
   business, ethnic, couples

**Open:** Monday–Thursday, 4–11 p.m.; Friday, 4 p.m.–midnight;
Saturday, 11 a.m.–midnight; Sunday, 11 a.m.–11 p.m.

**Setting & atmosphere:** The decor is attractive and cozy, especially the
front non-smoking room. The restaurant features nice Persian decorative
touches and plants in window alcoves by the stairs. It's dimly lit; romantic.

**House specialties:** Chicken fessenjan, a very popular Persian dish of chicken
breast simmered with pomegranate and walnut sauce; charbroiled kebabs of
lamb, beef, or filet mignon; variety of seasonal fresh fish, including salmon,
whitefish, swordfish, trout, and red snapper. Seafood degustation for two or
more, $12.95 each, includes appetizers, baked shrimp, scallops, lobster, fish
with vegetables, couscous, and rice. Vegetarian specialties such as veggie
Mediterranean (in split pea–tomato-lime sauce) and veggie fessenjan.

**Other recommendations:** Appetizers, including baba gannoujh, dolmeh,
tabbouleh, and herb yogurt served with Persian bread. Lentil soup; Pars
salad (tomato, cucumber, and onion with lemon dressing). Zolobia, a fried
Persian dessert with yogurt and honey.

**Summary & comments:** This place has had a following since the owner
had his first restaurant in a different location. The fish and seafood have
always been its strength, but chicken, meat, and vegetarian items are
equally savory and somewhat exotic. Persian cooking uses lots of herbs, citrus marinades, and pomegranate juice, so sauces tend to be fragrant and
slightly sweet-tart. Most entrees come with fluffy Persian rice pilaf. Portions are generous, and service is gracious.

**Honors & awards:** *Chicago Tribune* and *Chicago* magazine, four stars.

## THE PARTHENON ★★★★½

| | | |
|---|---|---|
| Greek | Inexpensive/Moderate | **QUALITY** |
| | | **95** |

314 South Halsted Street, Greektown; (312) 726-2407

Zone 4   The Loop

**VALUE**
**B**

| | |
|---|---|
| Reservations: Recommended | Wine selection: Extensive, mostly |
| When to go: Weekdays usually less | Greek; house wines available by |
| busy | the glass, carafe, and bottle |
| Entree range: $6–10 | Dress: Casual |
| Payment: Major credit cards | Disabled access: Wheelchair access, |
| Service rating: ★★★★½ | rest rooms |
| Friendliness rating: ★★★★★ | Customers: Greek-American, diverse |
| Parking: Free valet | American |
| Bar: Full service | |

**Lunch/Dinner:** Sunday–Friday, 11 a.m.– 1 a.m.; Saturday, 11 a.m.–2 a.m.

**Setting & atmosphere:** Barbecuing lamb on a spit and gyros in the window; enter through the original bar area. New chic, contemporary bar and lounge with tables was recently added in the space next door. Several cozy dining rooms, some with lovely murals; lively Greek setting with waiters' shouts of "Oopa!" as they flambé saganaki with brandy. Everyone seems to have an enjoyable time here, but it's quiet enough to have a private conversation over a meal.

**House specialties:** Flaming saganaki (kasseri used instead of the saltier kefalotiri) and succulent homemade gyros—both introduced to Chicago here. Great assortment of mezedes (substantial appetizers) such as spinach-feta pies, mini chicken breast shish kebabs, braised octopus, tzatziki, and homemade sausage; a special assortment platter with about 11 items and pita for two or more, $10.95 per person. Entrees: meatballs à la Smyrna (Tuesdays and Wednesdays); Greek-style broiled whole red snapper or sea bass, filleted tableside if desired; top-quality lamb prepared in various ways: rotisserie-roasted, extra thick prime chops, broiled to order, and fork-tender with artichokes avgolemono; and (more unusual) tigania (pork tenderloin chunks marinated in wine sauce). Succulent Athenian broiled chicken and a new item, chicken breast spanaki (skinless breast stuffed with spinach and feta and served with rice pilaf).

**Other recommendations:** Kotopitakia (chicken and vegetable phyllo pie); dolmades (herbed rice- or meat-stuffed vine leaves); broiled octopus; vegetarian moussaka (layered eggplant and potato dish); lamb sweetbreads;

**(The Parthenon)**

shrimp flambée; Aegean platter (panfried scallops, codfish, baby squid, and smelt, with skordalia—garlic potato dip). Desserts: galaktobouriko (phyllo filled with custard and baked in syrup); crispy walnut-rich baklava; homemade yogurt with walnuts; rice pudding and assorted traditional cookies.

**Summary & comments:**  The Parthenon is the oldest restaurant in Greektown, having celebrated its 30th anniversary in July 1998 (the former first Greektown restaurant has closed). Of all the Greek restaurants in the Chicago area, this reliable establishment, appropriately named for the majestic structure on the acropolis of Athens, has remained tops for the most comprehensive menu, consistent quality of food, and gracious service. The name carries a deep responsibility for excellence, and the Liakouras family never takes that lightly. Chris Liakouras, who started this second restaurant in Greektown in 1968 with his brother Bill, now runs it with his daughter, Joanna. She is the only woman manager of a Greek restaurant and is now a partner, along with chef Sotiris Stasinos, and her father, who remains the main partner. John, one of the managers, has been an anchor for many years, and much of the staff is loyal and stable. Here, new dishes are always being added to the ambitious menu, which is in English and Greek, and there are daily dinner specials. The family-style dinner is large and complete ($13.50). Many items are à la carte, "so ordering is more flexible," according to Chris. Most of the mezedes on the menu are offered in two portion sizes. This basic concept is ideally suited to the Greeks' cultural sense of filoxenia (hospitality) and the centuries-old tradition of getting together with friends to eat several little dishes, drink wine, and talk. You couldn't find a better place than here. Everyone has fun. Returning to the Parthenon after just one visit is like coming home. Kaly orczi! (Good appetite!)

**Honors & awards:**  Much continuing great press over the years, including *Chicago* magazine, the *Chicago Tribune,* the *Chicago Sun-Times,* and various television and radio stations.

## PASTEUR ★★★★

| | | |
|---|---|---|
| Vietnamese | Inexpensive/Moderate | QUALITY 92 |
| | | VALUE B |

5525 North Broadway; (773) 878-1061
Zone 1   North Side

Reservations: Accepted
When to go: Early dinner
Entree range: $8.95–13.50; market price
Payment: All major credit cards
Service rating: ★★★
Friendliness rating: ★★★★
Parking: Street; church lot across street

Bar: Full service
Wine selection: Limited; affordable; bottles, $18–69; by the glass, $4–5.50
Dress: Casual
Disabled access: Yes
Customers: Mixed

**Lunch/Dinner:** Wednesday–Sunday, noon–10 p.m.; Friday and Saturday, noon–11 p.m.

**Dinner:** Monday and Tuesday, 4 p.m.–10 p.m.

**Setting & atmosphere:** Spectacular split-level interior; large palm trees, ceiling fans. Beautiful private dining room upstairs and charming, cozy bar area. Sidewalk cafe.

**House specialties:** Appetizers: goi cuon (spring roll of shrimp, vegetables, noodles); banh tom co ngu (traditional Hanoi dish of shrimp, yams, and bananas, lightly fried); pho (Hanoi soup specialty: aromatic beef broth over rice noodles and beef strips). Entrées: tom sa-te (sautéed jumbo shrimp); ga kho gung (clay pot chicken); scallop kao me (with sesame seeds, grilled). Mango mousse cake.

**Other recommendations:** Appetizers: bo tai chanh (spicy charbroiled beef strips); chao tom (shrimp paste wrapped around fresh sugarcane, grilled). Entrées: bo cuon la lot (grilled beef rolls stuffed with chicken and shrimp); bo luc lac (sautéed marinated beef chunks); ca-ry ga (Saigon specialty of delicate curry broth with chicken slices).

**Summary & comments:** Pasteur has been reborn in a new location, and is a truly upscale Vietnamese fine-dining establishment at affordable prices. Ingredients mingle well in various specialties here, and there is a profusion of fresh herbs. It's more fun to dine with three or four for a better sampling. Pasteur also offers full-blown services for banquets, catering, carryout, and delivery. It's definitely a destination Vietnamese dining experience.

## PAZZO'S CUCINA ITALIANA                                ★★½

| | QUALITY |
|---|---|
| New Italian          Inexpensive/Moderate | **79** |
| | VALUE |
| 8725 West Higgins Road; (773) 714-0077 | **B** |

Zone 2    North Central/O'Hare

Three Westbrook Corporate Center, 22nd and Wolf Road, Westchester;
   (708) 531-1112 or (708) 531-TOGO
Zone 8    Southern Suburbs

| | |
|---|---|
| Reservations: Accepted | Bar: Full service |
| When to go: Off-peak times | Wine selection: Extensive; bottles of |
| Entree range: Most items around | Pazzo's chianti placed on tables |
| $10 | (using the honor system), $3.75 a |
| Payment: VISA, MC, AMEX, DC | glass |
| Service rating: ★★★ | Dress: Casual |
| Friendliness rating: ★★★★★ | Disabled access: Yes |
| Parking: Building lots, street, free | Customers: Business, local, family |
| garage | |

**Lunch/Dinner:** Monday–Thursday, 11 a.m.–10 p.m.; Friday, 11 a.m.–
11 p.m.; Saturday, 4:30–11 p.m.

**Setting & atmosphere:** Contemporary, casual, and spacious with an open
kitchen. Private rooms are available at each location for parties.

**House specialties:** Brick-oven pizza selection; Pazzo's Caesar with mixed
greens, herb croutons, shaved Parmigiano, and Pazzo's creamy Caesar dressing; insalatina di gamberetti (marinated shrimp on butter lettuce, radicchio,
cucumbers, with lemon caper dressing); polenta cup filled with basil pesto
and ragout of vegetables, black olives, and spicy tomato sauce. Fresh pastas:
zebra panzottini (striped semolina pasta filled with ricotta and spinach in
pepper cream sauce); mushroom-filled tortelloni with prosciutto, mushrooms, and tomatoes in a Parmesan cream sauce; pollo rigatoni (square rigatoni with chicken, roasted peppers, black olives, and spinach in a white
cream sauce). Veal chop Milanese, breaded, sautéed, and baked with garlic
mashed potatoes; Pazzo's strip steak; Pollo Della Casa (panfried breast, seasoned in homemade breadcrumbs, with lemon, capers, and mushrooms).
Dolci: chocolate raspberry cake; homemade tiramisu; gelato.

**Other recommendations:** Oriental lime chicken salad with mixed greens,
peanuts, sesame seeds, and crispy noodles in a mustard vinaigrette; Mediterranean salad of romaine lettuce, cucumbers, bell peppers, tomatoes, and
onions, tossed with kalamata olive oil and feta.

**(Pazzo's Cucina Italiana)**

**Summary & comments:** Fun and delicious Italian cuisine, colorful presentations, generous portions, low prices, and friendly staff—these are the key buzz words that spell success for this California-based chain. The first Chicago location debuted in 1993 under the former name, Milano's Italian Kitchen. The name change for only the Chicago restaurants occurred in 1994; the eight other locations around the country will keep the Milano's name. It's not surprising that this place wins over first-time customers. Diners get a bonus at the new Westchester location—live entertainment by singing servers.

**Honors & awards:** *Chicago Sun-Times'* "Top 3 Caesar Salad in the City" award.

---

| **PIEROGI INN** | | ★★½ |
|---|---|---|

| Polish | Inexpensive | QUALITY<br>79 |
|---|---|---|
| | | VALUE<br>B |

4801 N. Milwaukee Ave. at corner of Lawrence Avenue
  (773) 736-4815
Zone 2  North Central/O'Hare

| | |
|---|---|
| **Reservations:** Recommended for large parties and for weekends | **Bar:** Full |
| | **Wine selection:** Good |
| **When to go:** Any time | **Dress:** Casual |
| **Entree range:** $4.95–9.95 | **Disabled access:** Yes, including rest rooms |
| **Payment:** All major credit cards | |
| **Service rating:** ★★★½ | **Customers:** Polish-Americans, including radio celebrities, and other locals |
| **Friendliness rating:** ★★★★½ | |
| **Parking:** Street | |

**Lunch/Dinner:** Every day, 10 a.m.–10 p.m.

**Setting & atmosphere:** Recently merged with owner's new restaurant, Chopin Mon Ami, a contemporary Polish bistro with a French twist that pays tribute to the great Polish composer, Frederic Chopin. Pierogi Inn, one side of the space, is a comfortable, homey setting with a carryout counter, several tables with red checked tablecloths and a blackboard menu. Decorated with Polish artifacts, including traditional colorful paper cuttings, wooden birds, and costumed figurines.

**House specialties:** Pierogi (dumplings filled with the traditional mushrooms, cabbage, potato and cheese, and with creative items such as shrimp, whitefish, strawberries, and other seasonal fruits); great soups, especially

**(Pierogi Inn)**

mushroom, barley, and barszcz with uszka (red beet soup with wild mushroom dumplings).

**Other recommendations:**  Roast duck; chicken or beef goulash; veal cutlet with sauerkraut; golabki (stuffed cabbage rolls); uszka with tomatomushroom sauce; nalesniki (cheese blintzes).

**Summary & comments:**  Pierogi Inn began as a small storefront with a large carryout business, and now it shares the dining room space with the chef-owner's new Chopin Mon Ami, several doors away from the original location. It remains simple with a blackboard menu and has loads of charm, reflecting its owner.  This little gem is popular because the Polish cooking is authentic, flavorful, and a good value. Chef Ryszard Anton Zawadzki's mother, Aleksandra Bielska, is usually in the kitchen and makes all the delicious, time-consuming pierogis—the main attraction here. Catering and carryout. Smacznego!

**Honors & awards:** Silver Platter, 1994–1996. Much local press. Zawadzki has had a regular television cooking show on Chicago Cable channel 25.

---

| **PRAIRIE** | ★★★★½ |
|---|---|

| Midwestern | Moderate/Expensive | QUALITY |
|---|---|---|
| | | **95** |

| 500 South Dearborn Street; (312) 663-1143 | VALUE |
|---|---|
| Zone 5   South Loop | **C** |

**Reservations:** Recommended
**When to go:** Monday is the slowest day, but any time is fine
**Entree range:** Lunch, $9.75–18.25; dinner à la carte, $16–27
**Payment:** All major credit cards
**Service rating:** ★★★★
**Friendliness rating:** ★★★★½
**Parking:** Valet ($5, day; $8, evening)
**Bar:** Full service
**Wine selection:** Mostly Californian; some from Oregon and Washington; seven available in smaller

bottles; about 11 available by-the-glass.
**Dress:** Summer, casual to formal; winter, business and dressy (suits and ties optional)
**Disabled access:** Yes, including rest rooms
**Customers:** Local business clientele, theatergoers, couples, Bears football fans on Sunday morning, some foreign and domestic tourists

**Breakfast:** Monday–Friday, 6:30–10 a.m.; Saturday and Sunday, 7–10 a.m.

**(Prairie)**

**Brunch:** Saturday and Sunday, 11 a.m.–2 p.m.

**Lunch:** Monday–Friday, 11:30 a.m.–2 p.m.; Saturday, 11 a.m.–2 p.m.

**Dinner:** Monday–Saturday, 5–10 p.m.; Sunday, 5–9 p.m.

**Setting & atmosphere:** Striking split-level space with tall windows and honey-colored oak cathedral ceiling. The interior is patently a Frank Lloyd Wright design—a fine example of the Prairie School of Architecture. Attractive display case, open kitchen, and comfortable lounge area.

**House specialties:** Midwestern duck, local corn, Illinois and Wisconsin cheeses, and other heartland products are prepared in seasonal ways (e.g., Wisconsin Cheddar and dark ale soup; appetizer: sauté of wild mushrooms in a crispy sweet potato basket with sour cream and corn purée—beautiful presentation); farm-raised coho salmon, poached with leeks, pea cakes and sundried tomato jus, topped with daikon sprouts; Wisconsin honey-coated duck breast, stuffed pear in Frangelico berry sauce; sweet onion crusted pork (boneless chop with roasted corn vegetable slaw); black bean and cilantro-encrusted whitefish with cucumber onion relish, carrot jus; warm strawberry-rhubarb tart with apple-cinnamon ice cream (in spring).

**Other recommendations:** Appetizer: Prairie duck breast (spice-rubbed with white Cheddar rice and honey malt demi. Entrées: Dried mushroom filet of beef, herb-crusted tart with wild mushrooms, marscapone cheese; domestic lamb rack, stuffed with apple sausage, Yukon potato leek salad, and BBQ chili oil; breast of chicken, stuffed with asparagus and endive wrapped in prosciutto with plum fig compote.

**Summary & comments:** New Executive Chef André Bienvenu succeeds original Chef Stephen Langlois, who opened this restaurant after avidly combing old heartland cookbooks and unearthing authentic recipes from farm cooks, then imaginatively incorporating seasonal ingredients into his stunningly visual creations. Bienvenu carries on that tradition, adding his own twist, such as adding a flavorful crust of herbs, onion or dried fruit to meats, fish and a mushroom tart. The only restaurant here devoted exclusively to Midwestern cuisine.

**Honors & awards:** DiRoNA Award, 1996–1997.

| PRINTER'S ROW | ★★★★½ |
|---|---|

| New American | Moderate | QUALITY |
|---|---|---|
| | | 95 |

| 550 South Dearborn Street; (312) 461-0780 | VALUE |
|---|---|
| Zone 5    South Loop | B |

**Reservations:** Recommended
**When to go:** Any time; weekdays usually less busy
**Entree range:** Lunch, $8.50–12.95; dinner, $16.95–22.95
**Payment:** VISA, MC, AMEX, D
**Service rating:** ★★★★½
**Friendliness rating:** ★★★★
**Parking:** Street or lots nearby
**Bar:** Full service
**Wine selection:** Big American wine list; numerous fine choices by the glass, bottle, or half bottle; 120–130 bottles
**Dress:** Casual; comfortable for after work, pre-theater, or business lunch
**Disabled access:** Yes
**Customers:** Blend of neighborhood, business, travel, professional, and suburban

**Lunch:** Monday–Friday, 11:30 a.m.–2:30 p.m.

**Dinner:** Monday–Thursday, 5–10 p.m.; Friday and Saturday, 5–11 p.m.

**Setting & atmosphere:** In the historic Printer's Row area, this establishment is both sophisticated and comfortable. Cozy banquettes, warm lighting, artistic fish tiles on a central pillar, and beautiful tableware on white tablecloths create warmth and intimacy. Seats up to 120 in 3 rooms; great private party location.

**House specialties:** Grilled duck breast with smoked tomato sauce, smooth polenta, and balsamic vinegar; menu features shellfish or wild and farm-raised fish and seasonal game (e.g., venison chop with an American-Italian sun-dried blueberry-grappa sauce). Tuna seared with Chinese molasses (not sweet), cucumber, and chile vinaigrette is an example of an Asian influence here. Vegetable paella, mildly spicy with saffron rice, herbs, and a garden variety of veggies, satisfies any Spanish cravings.

**Other recommendations:** Grilled salmon with prosciutto-pasta cake and whole grain mustard butter; roasted, custom-cut pork chop; desserts such as homemade ice cream (honey walnut or black currant); coffee crème brûlée (flavors change weekly); pear tart with lemon ice cream.

**Summary & comments:** Chef-owner Michael Foley opened this restaurant about 20 years ago, when the Printer's Row area was not yet renovated. This pioneer soon received recognition and awards for his innova-

**(Printer's Row)**

tive, modern American cooking, which is committed to healthful preparations based on fresh, local products, many of them organic, and influenced by his travels. A third-generation restaurateur, Foley has much experience, and his unwavering dedication over the years has produced consistent quality here. His cooking sometimes gives a twist to common items. The menus change five times a year and focus on servicing daily diners through à la carte items. One of Chicago's best dining experiences. Can accommodate private functions from 15–120.

**Honors & awards:** Among the host of local, regional, national, and international awards are *Travel Holiday Magazine* Good Value Dining Award, 1992–96; *Wine Spectator*'s Award of Excellence, 1988–1996; DiRoNA Award, 1996.

---

## THE PUMP ROOM ★★★★

| French-inspired American | Expensive | QUALITY 93 |
|---|---|---|

| Omni Ambassador East Hotel, 1301 North State Parkway; (312) 266-0360 | VALUE C |
|---|---|

Zone 3   Near North

**Reservations:** Recommended
**When to go:** Friday or Saturday evenings for the full experience with music; weeknights for a quiet dinner
**Entree range:** Breakfast, $7.95–14; lunch, $10.50–16; dinner, $21–34; pre-theatre three-course meal, $44 served until 7 p.m.
**Payment:** All major credit cards
**Service rating:** ★★★ ½
**Friendliness rating:** ★★★★ ½
**Parking:** Valet, $11; nearby self-park garage
**Bar:** Full service; a list of cognacs, sherries, single-malt scotches, and ports is available for after-dinner sipping
**Wine selection:** Extensive international list of about 120 selections; several fine selections available by the glass
**Dress:** Days, business, no jeans or tennis shoes; evenings, dressy; gentlemen required to wear jackets after 4 p.m.
**Disabled access:** No
**Customers:** Professionals mostly aged 30-plus, many celebrities, stylish couples and singles

**Breakfast:** Monday–Saturday, 6:30–11 a.m.
**Brunch:** Sunday, 11:15 a.m.–2:30 p.m.

## (The Pump Room)

**Lunch:** Monday–Friday, 11:30 a.m.–2:30 p.m.

**Dinner:** Monday–Thursday, 6–9:45 p.m.; Friday and Saturday, 6–11 p.m.; Sunday, 5–10 p.m.

**Setting & atmosphere:** This legendary place reopened in 1998, after a seven-month, $2 million restoration. It returned to its original colors of blue and gold, and now tables are graced with Bernardaud Limoges china and the original flatware pattern. The formal, elegant, split-level dining room still features Booth One and the intimate Green Booth. Sparkling split-level dining room is lavishly appointed with stunning crystal chandeliers, lush floral arrangements, and sheer ceiling drapes. This atmosphere and the restaurant's six-decade history still cast a spell.

**House specialties:** Appetizers: Smoked salmon terrine with cucumber salad, Tobiko caviar; crunchy Maryland crab cakes with Savoy cabbage cole slaw and basil oil. Entrées: Excellent American red snapper with saffron pearl pasta, crawfish and lobster sauce; perfectly seasoned and cooked-to-order Colorado rack of lamb with riso pasta, ratatouille and roasted garlic sauce; dry-aged prime New York steak with potato gratin, French beans and roasted shallot sauce. Desserts are delicious and beautiful: pistachio parfait with macadamia nougatine and coffee creme Anglaise; hot chocolate cake with mango coulis; porcupine with chocolate meringue—great presentation!

**Other recommendations:** Appetizer: Crispy sweetbread with enoki mushrooms and Italian parsley. Entrées: Norwegian salmon with asparagus crust and ragout of morel mushrooms; roasted Amish chicken breast with baby artichokes and chicken jus. Desserts: Mango Bavarian with galonga jus; fruit tart with fig puree.

**Entertainment & amenities:** Live entertainment nightly in lounge with dancing.

**Summary & comments:** "Booth One" is a legend made famous by this Chicago landmark, a premier celebrity gathering place since 1938. Have an aperitif in the lounge, then browse through the "who's who in entertainment" photo exhibit before dining. New owners hired Executive Chef Martial Noguier, a talented Parisian who worked with top chefs in France. He has revamped the menu, which is now French-inspired American. A special place for business meals, celebrity sightings, and romantic dinners with dancing. Phil Collins got turned away because of no jacket, and then entitled his 1987 album, "No Jacket Required."

**Honors & awards:** AAA four diamonds; *Chicago Tribune,* Best Brunch.

## REZA'S                                    ★★★½

| Persian/Vegetarian          Inexpensive/Moderate | QUALITY |
|---|---|
| | **90** |

5255 North Clark Street; (773) 561-1898

Zone 1   North Side

| | VALUE |
|---|---|
| | **C** |

432 West Ontario Street; (312) 664-4500

Zone 3   Near North

**Reservations:** Recommended on
Thursday, Friday, and weekends

**When to go:** Avoid end of week and
weekends

**Entree range:** $6.95–14.95

**Payment:** VISA, MC, AMEX, DC,
D

**Service rating:** ★★★½

**Friendliness rating:** ★★★★½

**Parking:** Valet (downtown); free lot
(Clark Street)

**Bar:** Full service

**Wine selection:** Extensive; international; fairly priced; several by the
glass

**Dress:** Moderately casual

**Disabled access:** Yes, including rest
rooms, elevators

**Customers:** Diverse; more local at
Clark Street; more business downtown

**Lunch/Dinner:** Every day, 11 a.m.–midnight

**Setting & atmosphere:** Clark Street location is modern Persian; spacious,
casual look—attractive and comfortable. Ontario location is site of a former working brewery, so the vats are visible; very attractive, spacious room
with exposed brick walls and wood trim.

**House specialties:** Vegetarian samplers and seafood dishes Persian-style;
eggplant steak appetizer (thick eggplant slice broiled in robust herbed
sauce of onion, garlic, and tomatoes); grilled mushrooms (trio of skewered
charbroiled mushrooms with tart marinade that tastes of lemon juice);
Reza's salad (mixed lettuce with radish, tomato, black olives, feta, green
pepper, and croutons); kebabs: lamb and chicken combo with grilled
vegetables and Persian dill rice; shrimp and filet with veggies.

**Other recommendations:** Variety of appetizers such as dolmeh felfel
(stuffed green pepper), baba gannoujh, tabbouleh, hummus; Reza's special
chicken (two strips of marinated boneless breast, with grilled veggies and
Persian dill rice); duck breast with sweet and sour pomegranate sauce and
walnuts; marinated charbroiled quail.

**Entertainment & amenities:** Wednesday, guitar; other weeknights,
piano. Call first. Downtown location has nightly music and a free shuttle
bus for lunch to and from Merchandise Mart and other locations.

**(Reza's)**

**Summary & comments:** The original Reza's has expanded several times and does a brisk business. The huge, newer place on the west side of downtown is in the former Sieben's Brewery, which then became Berghoff Brewery and Restaurant. It's a great place for casual business lunches. Both are large and bustling, with a regular following. They promote their vegetarian dishes. Knowledgeable and accommodating servers.

| RIVA | ★★★½ |
|---|---|

| | | QUALITY |
|---|---|---|
| Seafood/Steak/Pasta | Moderate/Expensive | **90** |
| | | VALUE |
| Navy Pier, 700 East Grand Avenue; (312) 644-7482 | | **C** |
| Zone 3   Near North | | |

Reservations: Recommended
When to go: Avoid peak meal times unless you have a reservation
Entree range: Lunch, average $14; dinner, $10.95–24.95
Payment: Major credit cards
Service rating: ★★★½
Friendliness rating: ★★★½
Parking: Sheltered valet parking, $7
Bar: Full service

Wine selection: Lengthy international list that leans toward Californian and Italian; reserve list; a good selection of wines by the glass
Dress: Casual to dressy
Disabled access: Yes, elevator available
Customers: Tourists, locals, celebrities, politicians

**Lunch/Dinner:** Sunday–Thursday, 11 a.m.–10:30 p.m.; Friday and Saturday, 11 a.m.–11:30 p.m.

**Setting & atmosphere:** Beautiful restaurant with expansive windows offering a premier view of Navy Pier, Monroe Harbor, and Chicago's downtown skyline. Spacious main dining room with exposed brick walls, mahogany trim, brass chandeliers and ceiling fans, and a lobster tank in center; colorful decor; 40-foot-long display kitchen with upper-wall mural depicting Navy Pier's history; welcoming bar area; three private dining rooms.

**House specialties:** Crab cakes with jalapeño tartar sauce and radicchio cole slaw; baby spinach salad; fillet mignon of tuna, marinated, grilled, and served over horseradish mashed potatoes in roasted shallot sauce; grandmother's cake (lemon custard tart with almonds, pine nuts, and confectioners' sugar).

**(Riva)**

**Other recommendations:** Swordfish and other seafood; chocolate truffle torte; atomic cake (three layers of banana, vanilla chiffon, and chocolate chiffon cakes with fruit and custards, whipped cream filling); bindi Italian sorbets.

**Summary & comments:** President and Mrs. Clinton were here, and there's a photo to prove it. The city's politicians and other dignitaries have visited, as well, and there has been a steady flow of locals and tourists since the grand opening in 1995. Riva is Italian for "shoreline," and restaurateur Phil Stefani's newest place is aptly named since it has one of the most breathtaking views of Chicago's Lake Michigan shore. While some have reported uncaring service here, other experiences have been favorable. Definitely a destination restaurant. Riva Cafe, on the first floor downstairs, is more informal and serves light fare; it opens onto an outdoor dining area in warm weather.

## RUSSIAN TEA TIME ★★★★

| Russian | Moderate | QUALITY |
|---|---|---|
| | | **93** |
| | | VALUE |
| | | **C** |

77 East Adams Street; (312) 360-0000
Zone 4   The Loop

**Reservations:** Highly recommended
**When to go:** Quieter time 2–5 p.m.
**Entree range:** $10–26
**Payment:** Major credit cards
**Service rating:** ★★★★
**Friendliness rating:** ★★★★½
**Parking:** Lots nearby
**Bar:** Full service, including Russian vodkas and caviar
**Wine selection:** Two dozen selections; mainly French, Italian, California, and Washington wines; several by the glass
**Dress:** Casual to moderately upscale and dressy
**Disabled access:** Yes; menus available in braille
**Customers:** Diverse, Russian-American, symphony and opera crowd, talk-show hosts and guests from television and radio stations nearby

**Lunch/Dinner:** Monday, 11 a.m.–9 p.m.; Tuesday–Thursday, 11 a.m.–11 p.m.; Friday and Saturday, 11 a.m.–midnight; Sunday, 11 a.m.–9 p.m.

**Setting & atmosphere:** Cozy, old-world atmosphere with a great deal of woodwork, Russian urns, pots, and tablecloths; well-spaced booths and tables; dessert display case.

## (Russian Tea Time)

**House specialties:** Blini with top-quality Russian caviar; borscht; goriachaya zakuska (appetizer platter for two-plus including chicken dumplings, stuffed cabbage, and beets); wild game (e.g., stuffed quails with pomegranate sauce); vegetarian dishes (e.g., jumbo stuffed mushrooms with spinach, onion, and cheese); hot farmer's cheese blintzes.

**Other recommendations:** Elaborate kulebiaka (meat pie) filled with ground beef, cabbage, and onions; blinchiki (crêpes—the beef stroganoff are great; also salmon and cheese); roast pheasant "Erevan" with Armenian brandy, walnut and pomegranate sauce, and brandied prunes; Tashkent carrot salad (named for hometown of owners; à la carte or comes with entrees); chicken croquettes; hearty homemade apricot-plum strudel is the thick-crusted Russian version; Russian tea (blend of three, including black currant).

**Summary & comments:** The only serious Russian restaurant in town (the Russian Palace opened nearby), this exquisite cafe received rave reviews within the first several months of opening in fall 1993. The Chicago Symphony bought the building the cafe was originally in, and the conductor, former conductor, symphonygoers, and operagoers all dine here before or after events. The cafe also expanded its vegetarian options recently; the *Chicago Sun-Times* has named Russia Tea Time as one of the city's Top 10 vegetarian-friendly spots. Owner Vadim Muchnik is the gracious host and kisses ladies' hands, while his mother, Klara, heads the kitchen. The ambitious menu is about as long as Tolstoy's *War and Peace,* and the menu describes customs and a bit of historical background of dishes and their famous namesakes. This is a fine ethnic experience.

**Honors & awards:** *Vegetarian Journal* voted it among the ten best restaurants in North America.

## RUTH'S CHRIS STEAKHOUSE    ★★★★

| Steak | Moderate/Expensive | QUALITY |
|---|---|---|
| | | 93 |

| | | VALUE |
|---|---|---|
| | | B |

431 North Dearborn Street; (312) 321-2725
Zone 4   The Loop

**Reservations:** Recommended
**When to go:** Avoid peak times, 6–8 p.m. weekends
**Entree range:** $10–27
**Payment:** All major credit cards
**Service rating:** ★★★½
**Friendliness rating:** ★★★★
**Parking:** Free valet
**Bar:** Full service

**Wine selection:** International, especially American, French, and Italian; heavy California bent; several by the glass
**Dress:** Casual to dressy
**Disabled access:** Yes
**Customers:** Very local; have a following

**Lunch/Dinner:** Monday–Friday, 11:30 a.m.–11 p.m.; Saturday, 4:30–11 p.m.; Sunday, closed.

**Setting & atmosphere:** Clubby; plaid carpet; lots of sports memorabilia.

**House specialties:** All prime cuts here: New York strip steak, 16–18 ounces; 20-ounce T-bone; petite filet of beef tenderloin, 8-ounce; provimi veal chop. Veal sweetbreads; barbecued shrimp Orleans; three classic sauces offered with entrees and sides.

**Other recommendations:** Fish of the day; live Maine lobster; porterhouse for two; Prince Edward's mashed potatoes with garlic; turtle soup served with sherry; gumbo Louisiane; bread pudding with Jack Daniel's whiskey sauce; pecan pie.

**Summary & comments:** This New Orleans franchise spot arrived on the Chicago dining scene several years ago and is most successful. It was the #1 Ruth's Chris Steakhouse worldwide in 1996 for the greatest number of steaks sold. The menu pays tribute to its roots with several New Orleans touches. Steaks sizzle appealingly because they get a coating of butter. Juices are sealed into steaks on the hottest 1,800° F grill. One of a fast-growing chain with a good reputation.

| SAI CAFE | ★★★½ |
|---|---|

| Japanese | Inexpensive/Moderate | QUALITY |
|---|---|---|
| | | 91 |

2010 N. Sheffield; (773) 472-8080
Zone I    North Side

| | VALUE |
|---|---|
| | B |

**Reservations:** Yes
**When to go:** Weeknights less busy; weekends if you prefer bustling atmosphere
**Entree range:** $9.95–22.95
**Payment:** VISA, MC, AMEX
**Service rating:** ★★★ ½
**Friendliness rating:** ★★★★ ½
**Parking:** Valet

**Bar:** Full; Southeast Asian beers (Sapporo, Kirin)
**Wine selection:** Limited; specialty wines (Kinsen plum wine; Sho chiku bai sake; cold sakes)
**Dress:** Casual
**Disabled access:**
**Customers:** Mixed ethnic and American; all ages; Japanese sushi lovers

**Dinner:** Monday–Thursday, 4:30–10 p.m.; Friday and Saturday, 4:30 p.m.–midnight; Sunday, 2:30–10 p.m.

**Setting & atmosphere:** Cheerful, light wood; several rooms. Attractive sushi bar where diners can order anything from the menu while watching the sushi chefs perpare the colorful specialty served on wooden boards. Cozy nonsmoking back dining room with tables rather close together is decorated with sake aging drums and other artifacts.

**House specialties:** Appetizers: Pan-fried scallops with a flavorful house sauce; Gyo-za (Japanese pan-fried dumplings, 6 pieces); kani-su (Alaskan King crab with cucumber marinated in vinegar sauce). Main courses: À la carte sushi, selected from a list of about 32; I loved the maguro (tuna), hamachi (yellow tail) and namesake (fresh salmon, as opposed to smoked). Ethereal vegetable tempura (nice variety of vegetables with a lacy coating, fried crisp, served with a flavorful dipping sauce; shrimp and combo available). Some entrees come with soup and rice, others with soup only. Complimentary dessert of orange segments in orange shell baskets; red bean or green tea ice cream.

**Other recommendations:** Appetizers: ikura oroshi (salmon roe with sliced cucumber; sashimi (variety of raw fish). Main courses: "Chef Special Hand-rolled" including regular or spicy scallop rolls. Cooked dishes include sukiyaki (sliced beef, bean curd, mushroom, napa, yam noodles, green onion cooked in broth) and teriyaki (charcoal broiled chicken, beef or fish with teriyaki sauce).

**(Sai Cafe)**

**Entertainment & amenities:** Watching the sushi chefs perform their magic and turning out the beautiful orders of sushi and maki (hand rolls).

**Summary & comments:** From the first call, I realized this restaurant had a friendly and helpful attitude, and it carries through from owner James Bel, who is usually on hand to greet guests and oversee his operation. Our waitress was always smiling and accommodating, and the service was well paced. This hospitality plus the top-quality fish and seafood and the attractive presentations encourage diners to return—why this spot is usually crowded.

| ¡SALPICÓN!, A TASTE OF MEXICO | | ★★★½ |
|---|---|---|

| Mexican | Inexpensive/Moderate | QUALITY |
|---|---|---|
| | | 85 |
| 1252 North Wells; (312) 988-7811 | | VALUE |
| Zone 3   Near North | | C |

**Reservations:** Recommended
**When to go:** Dinner; less crowded weekdays
**Entree range:** $12.95–22.95
**Payment:** All major credit cards
**Service rating:** ★★★★½
**Friendliness rating:** ★★★★½
**Parking:** Street or nearby garages
**Bar:** Full service; super- and ultra-premium tequilas; tequila flights (1 ounce of 4); ¡Salpicón! Margarita; Mexican and microbrew beers
**Wine selection:** Extensive; several by the glass, $6–13.50; bottles, $21–295; reserve list
**Dress:** Casual
**Disabled access:** Yes
**Customers:** Locals, professionals, theater and opera crowd

**Brunch:** Sunday, 11 a.m.–2:30 p.m.

**Dinner:** Wednesday–Monday, 5–10 p.m.; set-price early menu before 6:30 p.m.

**Setting & atmosphere:** Brightly painted storefront; colorful art by renowned Mexican artist Alejandro Romero. Recently expanded to include a dining area behind the bar.

**House specialties:** Jalapeños rellenos de queso capeados ( jalapeños stuffed with Chihuahua cheese, dipped in a light egg batter, sautéed); Chiapas-style tamale with chicken and a sweet-seasoned pork picadillo with a classic mole poblano; ensalada de espinaca con queso de cabra (fresh spinach salad with goat cheese, toasted sesame seeds, and caramelized red onions in

**(¡Salpicón!, A Taste of Mexico)**

a spicy chipotle-honey dressing); codornices en salsa de chile ancho con miel (garlic-marinated and grilled Manchester Farm quail served in a sauce of ancho chiles, garlic, caramelized onions, and honey with cilantro, potato, and queso anejo cakes); flan de caramelo (classic egg custard with a rich caramel sauce); arroz con leche (traditional rice pudding); pastel tres leches (light orange-flavored cake soaked in a trio of milks, served with fresh fruit sauce).

**Other recommendations:** Tostaditas de Tinga (crispy small tortillas mounded with shredded pork and chorizo in a roasted tomato-chipotle sauce); jaibas al mojo de ajo (summer special: Chesapeake Bay soft-shell crabs sautéed); and cinnamon crêpes stuffed with mango and fresh raspberries under a house-made goat's milk caramel (special).

**Summary & comments:** Salpicón translates as a "splash," and owners Vincent and Priscila Satkoff truly bring a splash of Mexico to Chicago with their Old Town restaurant. Mexican-born chef Priscilla Satkoff's expert culinary skills and passion for food were inspired and developed by her grandmother and mother, who were gourmet cooks but didn't know it. Only high-quality seafood and meats are used, and plate presentations are just as festive as the restaurant interior. All salsas and sauces are prepared fresh daily and everything is homemade, including tortillas (here usually a smaller size) and totopos (chips). The service staff is exceptionally friendly and well informed.

**Honors & awards:** *Wine Spectator* Award of Excellence, 1996; three stars from both the *Chicago Tribune* and the *Chicago Sun-Times*. *Chicago* magazine named it one of the top ten new restaurants of 1995.

| SEASONS RESTAURANT | | ★★★★½ | |
|---|---|---|---|
| | | QUALITY | |
| American | Moderate/Expensive | 97 | |
| The Four Seasons Hotel, 120 East Delaware Place | | VALUE | |
| at Michigan Avenue; (312) 280-8800, Ext. 2134 | | C | |
| Zone 3   Near North | | | |

Reservations: Recommended
When to go: Any time
Entree range: $22–34
Payment: VISA, MC, AMEX, DC, D
Service rating: ★★★★★

Friendliness rating: ★★★★★
Parking: Valet at the hotel entrance or self-parking on Rush or Walton streets with covered access to hotel's seventh-floor lobby; parking is discounted with validation

**(Seasons Restaurant)**

Bar: Full service

Wine selection: 320 selections of domestic and imported wines including California sparkling wines and French champagnes;

many fine selections by the glass

Dress: Jacket required for men; upscale casual; dressy

Disabled access: Yes

Customers: Traveler, business, local

**Breakfast:** *Seasons Restaurant:* Monday–Saturday, 6:30–10:30 a.m.; Sunday, 6:30–10 a.m. *Seasons Cafe:* Sunday–Thursday, 8–11:30 a.m.; Friday and Saturday, 8 a.m.–12:30 p.m.

**Brunch:** Sunday, 10:30 a.m.–1:30 p.m.

**Lunch:** Monday–Saturday, 11:30 a.m.–1:30 p.m.

**Dinner:** Daily, 6–10 p.m.

**Setting & atmosphere:** Opulent carpeted dining room with drapes, crystal sconces, and white tablecloths; lovely floral arrangements; elegant; artwork on walls; nice view from tables near windows. The adjacent cafe is also swank with a more casual approach.

**House specialties:** Menu changes each season. Some examples: grilled portobello mushroom with foie gras and balsamic syrup; organic field greens, raspberry vinaigrette, and goat cheese crouton; naturally farmed veal chop, pickled corn relish, and arugula whipped potatoes. Specials such as pan-seared Gulf snapper with basil oil; vegetable-potato Napoleon; and Japanese buckwheat noodles. Desserts such as warm fig and blueberry compote; orange-Drambuie ice cream with wild honey–cabernet sauce; Seasons chocolate marjolaine.

**Other recommendations:** Lunch: Maine lobster salad with Southwestern flavors; seared ahi tuna salad with cooling papaya-ginger relish; steamed Atlantic salmon fillet on cucumber semolina; beef vinaigrette; scaloppine of chicken on fennel-potato pancake with spring morel-port wine sauce; grilled prime minute steak, Dijon mustard béarnaise, and shoestring fries. Dinner: Roast Casco cod fillet with smoked cod-scallop hash; roasted free-range chicken and pearl barley–sweet corn pilaf; prime rib-eye steak, rustic onion baked potato, and garlic-mustard and rosemary grits; Atlantic salmon fillet braised in chardonnay with fennel-herb risotto and shallot-wine reduction.

**Entertainment & amenities:** Jazz from the adjacent Seasons Lounge Friday and Saturday evenings can be heard in the dining room.

**Summary & comments:** Seasons specializes in innovative American cuisine made from fresh—often unusual—regional ingredients served in a

**(Seasons Restaurant)**

simple style. Executive chef Mark Baker, who is from Boston, loves working with New England seafood, and it shows. He completely changes the menu the first day of spring, summer, and autumn, and changes it partially mid-winter to utilize the freshest local products. Seasons has worked with the Department of Agriculture in several different states to hand pick the highest caliber regional suppliers. The restaurant also offers alternative cuisine which is low in calories and cholesterol. Baker's cooking overall avoids rich sauces; his creations evolve with richness of flavor from prime ingredients cooked together and from reductions and vinaigrettes. One of the most splendid hotel dining rooms anywhere. Try Seasons Cafe for lighter fare for any meal at lower prices.

**Honors & awards:** Three and a half stars from *Chicago* magazine; three stars from *Chicago Tribune*; recently recognized by *Food and Wine* and *Forbes* magazines.

---

## SHAW'S CRAB HOUSE AND THE BLUE CRAB LOUNGE ★★★★½

| Seafood | Moderate | QUALITY |
|---------|----------|---------|
| | | **95** |

| | | VALUE |
|--|--|--|
| | | **C** |

21 East Hubbard Street; (312) 527-2722
Zone 4   The Loop

**Reservations:** Main dining room, highly recommended; Blue Crab Lounge, not accepted
**When to go:** Any time
**Entree range:** $16–36; Blue Crab Lounge, blackboard items à la carte and a bit cheaper
**Payment:** All major credit cards
**Service rating:** ★★★★
**Friendliness rating:** ★★★★
**Parking:** Valet, $6

**Bar:** Full service
**Wine selection:** Largely Californian, several international; good selection by the glass; list chosen to be seafood-friendly
**Dress:** Dining room, business casual; lounge, casual
**Disabled access:** Wheelchair acces
**Customers:** Business, travelers, couples, singles

**Lunch:** *Main dining room:* Monday–Friday, 11:30 a.m.–2 p.m.

**Lunch/Dinner:** *Blue Crab Lounge:* Monday–Thursday, 11:30 a.m.–10 p.m.; Friday, 11:30 a.m.–11 p.m.; Saturday, 11:30 a.m.–11 p.m.

**Dinner:** *Main dining room:* Monday–Thursday, 5:30–10 p.m.; Friday and Saturday, 5–11 p.m.; Sunday, 5–10 p.m.

**(Shaw's Crab House/Blue Crab Lounge)**

**Setting & atmosphere:** Two restaurants in one, with the main dining room (325 seats) reminiscent of an old New England seafood house, and the Blue Crab Lounge essentially a raw bar with high tables and stools, also serving the full menu from the dining room.

**House specialties:** Shaw's crab cakes; a great variety of oysters; sautéed sea scallops; Shaw's seafood platter.

**Other recommendations:** Lobster bisque; fresh seasonal specialties such as Maryland soft-shell crabs, Dungeness crab, stone crab, and other seafood. Daily desserts: popular refreshing key lime pie, fruit cobblers, crème brûlée, and pecan pie.

**Entertainment & amenities:** Blue Crab Lounge, jazz or blues, Tuesday and Thursday, 7–10 p.m.

**Summary & comments:** Pristinely fresh products, a variety of preparations, an extensive list of seafood-friendly wines, and knowledgeable service make Shaw's one of the best seafood places around. An on-staff seafood buyer constantly monitors products and storage temperatures. Oyster, Swedish crayfish, and other promotions keep the crowds coming. Overall, simple preparations fare better than the more elaborate dishes. Chef Yves Roubaud's crab cakes rate as the best. The bread basket items are addictive.

**Honors & awards:** *Forbes* magazine voted it among top six oyster bars in the country; *Chicago Tribune,* three stars.

## THE SIGNATURE ROOM AT THE NINETY-FIFTH ★★★★

| New American | Moderate/Expensive | QUALITY |
| --- | --- | --- |
| | | 91 |
| 875 North Michigan Avenue, atop the John | | VALUE |
| Hancock Center; (312) 787-9596 | | C |
| Zone 3  Near North | | |

**Reservations:** Recommended
**When to go:** Any time
**Entree range:** $21–30; Sunday brunch buffet, $29.95
**Payment:** All major credit cards
**Service rating:** ★★★★½
**Friendliness rating:** ★★★★½
**Parking:** Self-park garage
**Bar:** Full service
**Wine selection:** Award-winning, all-American list with 155 selections; most are moderately priced, from $25 a bottle to expensive vintages at $250 a bottle; several good selections by the glass
**Dress:** Chic casual, business, semi-formal to dressy; at dinner, jackets suggested but not required
**Disabled access:** Yes
**Customers:** Locals, business, couples, tourists

**(The Signature Room at the Ninety-Fifth)**

**Brunch:** Sunday, 10:30 a.m.–2:30 p.m.; extensive buffet of hot and cold foods, large assortment of desserts

**Lunch:** Monday–Saturday, 11 a.m.–2:30 p.m.; cold and hot buffet available for $8.95

**Dinner:** Sunday–Thursday, 5–10 p.m.; Friday and Saturday, 5–11 p.m.

**Setting & atmosphere:** The view from the top of the city on the 95th floor of the John Hancock Center is spectacular on a clear day. The breathtaking panorama is a beautiful, majestic backdrop for dining. Elegant, contemporary, sleek interior with wrap-around windows and a wrap-around mural depicting Chicago through the eyes of artists. The large chandeliers have been removed for a more modern look.

**House specialties:** Cured salmon appetizer; signature soup; roasted vegetable antipasti; honey-and-ginger-glazed salmon with napa cabbage, shiitake mushroom, and daikon salad, with ginger-lime vinaigrette; sautéed linguini with rock shrimp and bay scallops, mushrooms, spinach, roasted tomatoes, garlic, and herb-infused olive oil; roasted Colorado lamb chops; homemade ice cream.

**Other recommendations:** Appetizers: Roasted portobello mushroom glazed with goat cheese, sun-dried tomatoes, and black olives, with basil pesto; chilled Gulf shrimp with avocado-tomato salsa and gazpacho sauce. Signature tiramisu cake; chocolate crêpe cannoli.

**Entertainment & amenities:** Live music (often piano, violin, or saxophone) Saturday, 7–11 p.m.; Sunday, 11 a.m.–2 p.m. and 7–10 p.m.

**Summary & comments:** Healthful, contemporary American cuisine based on organically grown produce and chemical-free ingredients overall. The light cuisine is flavored a great deal with infused oils. The greatest 360-degree panoramic view of Chicago and its lakefront is from this restaurant, atop the John Hancock Center. The management, in its vision statement on the menu, makes its commitment to excellence in products, service, and atmosphere with an environmental conscience. It donates 10% of profits to a chosen charity each month.

**Honors & awards:** Silver Platter Award; Top Ten Most Distinguished Restaurants in North America; Restaurant of the Year by Food and Beverage Equipment Executives, 1996; *North Shore* magazine, Most Romantic Restaurant.

## SPAGO ★★★★½

| | | QUALITY |
|---|---|---|
| American | Moderate/Expensive | 94 |

520 North Dearborn at Grand Avenue; (312) 527-3700

Zone 3   Near North

| | VALUE |
|---|---|
| | B |

**Reservations:** Required
**When to go:** Avoid peak meal times unless you have a reservation
**Entree range:** Lunch, $12.50–18.75; dinner, $15.50–25.50
**Payment:** VISA, MC, AMEX, CB, Optima, D, DC
**Service rating:** ★★★★½
**Friendliness rating:** ★★★★½
**Parking:** Valet, $6

**Bar:** Full service
**Wine selection:** Mostly American and European, with some representations from other countries; good selection by the glass, but a bit pricey starting at $6
**Dress:** Jackets and ties preferred
**Disabled access:** Yes
**Customers:** Locals and travelers; mixed couples, families

**Lunch:** *Grill:* Every day, 11:30 a.m.–2:30 p.m.

**Dinner:** *Dining Room:* Sunday–Thursday, 5–10:30 p.m.; Friday and Saturday, 5–11 p.m. *Grill:* Monday–Thursday, 5–10:30 p.m.; Friday and Saturday, 5 p.m.–midnight; Sunday, 5–9:30 p.m. Bar open every day, 11:30 a.m.–2 a.m.

**Setting & atmosphere:** This $5-plus-million, 20,000-square-foot multi-level space in River North was designed by Adam D.Tihany of New York (who also did Spago locations in Las Vegas and Mexico City). This location has a clubby look, with fluid design, and features a casual grill and a dining room, both with open kitchens. The sophisticated nonsmoking dining room, with a huge vase of flowers at the entry, is decorated with patterned carpet and upholstery and subdued colors and lighting. The curved staircase leads to the second floor club room bar and lounge with a fireplace and leather couches and chairs. The top level has three private party rooms with views of the skyline. The custom-made look includes lovely wood, terrazzo, and intricate lighting. Robert Rauschenberg paintings are here, plus local artists' works.

**House specialties:** Menu changes seasonally. Pizzas baked in wood-burning ovens; homemade pastas; mesquite-grilled fish and meats; Spago homemade charcuterie plate. Examples: stir-fried spicy lamb with garlic, chile, cilantro, and ginger-sesame glaze, served with radicchio leaves; tuna tatki with marinated seaweed and cucumber salad; leek and artichoke ravioli with sautéed black bass and young garlic-porcini sauce. Granny Smith

**(Spago)**

apple tart with cinnamon ice cream; chocolate tart with vanilla ice cream and orange glaze.

**Other recommendations:** Sautéed foie gras with sweet potato chips and apple chutney; Maine scallops with pad thai noodles and spicy coconut sauce; roasted Cantonese duck with star anise, grapefruit, and a sesame bun; almond butter crunch tart (not much crunch, however) with maple-walnut ice cream.

**Summary & comments:** After several delays, Spago finally opened in autumn 1996, and immediately received a lot of media attention. Chicagoans are glad that this Spago has been tailored to them. Superstar, Austrian-born chef Wolfgang Puck, who is credited with recreating California cuisine with his Spago on Sunset Strip (1982), said in a private interview that all his restaurants are like children; each is individual. He loves Chicago and is very pleased to be here. Wolfgang's brother Klaus and wife Amanda, with degrees from the Cornell School of Hotel Administration, are co–general managers. Managing partner Tom Kaplan has spent the past 14 years involved with Spago restaurants in Los Angeles, Tokyo, Las Vegas, and Mexico City. Executive chef François Kwaku-Dongo headed the kitchen at Spago in West Hollywood for five years before coming here to serve American cuisine with European and Asian influences and many Midwestern ingredients. Puck gives his executive chef a lot of flexibility, and the food has been innovative and flavorful on all visits. Some of the signature dishes have been transplanted, but there are many new items in the repertoire. The Grill and bar area have a separate menu.

---

| SPIAGGIA | | ★★★★ |
|---|---|---|

| Italian | Moderate/Expensive | QUALITY |
|---|---|---|
| | | 93 |
| | | VALUE |
| | | C |

980 North Michigan Avenue; (312) 280-2750
Zone 3   Near North

**Reservations:** Recommended
**When to go:** Any time
**Entree range:** $8.95–29.95; per person total, $50–60
**Payment:** All major credit cards
**Service rating:** ★★★★
**Friendliness rating:** ★★★½

**Parking:** Valet, underground city facility on Walton
**Bar:** Full service
**Wine selection:** Extensive, Italian, $25–125 a bottle
**Dress:** Business, some semiformal and formal

## (Spiaggia)

Disabled access: Yes

Customers: Local, national, international, business travelers, North Shore, northwest, and other suburbanites, celebrities from entertainment and political arenas (The Rolling Stones, Placido Domingo, Elton John, Robert Duvall, Norman Mailer, Alice Cooper, Dustin Hoffman, former Illinois Governor James Thompson, Mayor Richard Daley, Robert De Niro, Paul Newman, Itzhak Pearlman, Zubin Mehta, and Daniel Barenboim)

**Lunch:** Monday–Saturday, 11:30 a.m.–2 p.m.

**Dinner:** Monday–Thursday, 5:30–9:30 p.m.; Friday and Saturday, 5:30–10:30 p.m.; Sunday, 5:30–9 p.m.

**Setting & atmosphere:** Contemporary, rather formal dining setting overlooking Lake Michigan and Oak Street Beach. *Note:* Spiaggia was about to undergo remodeling at press time.

**House specialties:** Rags of fresh pasta with mushrooms; ricotta ravioli filled with sweet Tuscan pecorino cheese; seafood risotto; wood-roasted veal chop with smoked pancetta and vodka-cream sauce; fillet of salmon with asparagus, basil, and white wine sauce; wood-roasted guinea hen with Savoy cabbage, pancetta, and porcini mushrooms.

**Other recommendations:** Mascarpone torte; homemade ice creams.

**Entertainment & amenities:** Piano every evening at 6 p.m.

**Summary & comments:** Named because it's possible to see Oak Street Beach from the restaurant's windows, this very chic restaurant, one of the Levy Restaurants, has had ups and downs. Under the talented direction of chef Paul Bartolotta, the food has been elevated to a new plateau. He's rescued it from the earlier experimental and creative Italian fare and brought it back to regional roots. And the sometimes inconsistent, reserved service appears to have gotten on track. The casual Cafe Spiaggia next door offers a recently expanded menu of excellent light fare for lower prices, (phone (312) 280-2764).

**Honors & awards:** Chef Paul Bartolotta is the recipient of the James Beard Award; *Chicago* magazine's Critics Choice Award; Insegna del Ristorante Italiano del Mundo (for overseas Italian restaurants showing superior culinary achievement), June 1997.

## SPRUCE                                    ★★★★½

| | | QUALITY |
|---|---|---|
| New American | Inexpensive/Moderate | 94 |
| | | VALUE |
| 238 East Ontario; (312) 642-3757 | | B |
| Zone 3   Near North | | |

Reservations: Recommended

When to go: Early or late, Monday through Thursday

Entree range: Three course prix fixe menu $45, with $28 à la carte entrees; five course prix fixe menu $85; paired with wines, $115

Payment: MC, VISA, AMEX, DC, D

Service rating: ★★★★½

Friendliness rating: ★★★★★

Parking: Valet, dinner; self-park

Bar: Full service, but no seating

Wine selection: Extensive, intelligent list of American, French and Italian wines, $25–100 per bottle; 20 by the glass, $7–14

Dress: Business casual to dressy

Disabled access: Yes

Customers: Business, downtown shoppers, travelers staying at nearby hotels

**Dinner:** Monday–Thursday, 5:30–10 p.m.; Friday and Saturday, 5:30–11 p.m., Sunday 5–9 p.m.

**Setting & atmosphere:** The action takes place in a large dining room that some see as "very New York;" hardwood floors, fresh flowers, warm lighting, and original art lend an intimate feel that enhances Spruce's casual elegance. A private room partitioned off the main dining area can seat parties of up to 45 guests. Several steps down from street level with windows.

**House specialties:** Menu changes to reflect what's seasonally available. The three course prix fixe menu features starters such as succulent crisp sweetbreads, earthy with wild mushrooms, cranberry beans and garlic chips. Entrees to try: tender pepper seared venison striploin with salsify, dried pears, balsamic vinegar with green beans and a wrap filled with fruit; pan roasted pheasant enhanced with black currants, foie gras sauce, with creamy polenta and hedge hog mushrooms; sautéed striped bass with little neck clams, prosciutto and champagne sauce. Vegetarians will enjoy root vegetable ragout with jasmine rice spring rolls and warm wasabi vinaigrette. Desserts: Spruce bananas, a warm flourless chocolate banana cake (almost a soufflé) with roasted banana ice cream on a slice of banana bread with two sauces; warm pear hazelnut tart with Earl Grey ice cream.

**Other recommendations:** Appetizer of pan roasted quail with dried cranberries in port vinaigrette. Dishes on earlier visits have included herbed

**(Spruce)**

rabbit "chops" on crisp risotto cake with baba gannoujh and chipotle oil (somewhat spicy). For dessert, seasonal offerings such as citrus Napoleon; papaya and lime consomme with tropical fruit sorbets; house-made brioche bread pudding with roasted mango and Tahitian vanilla bean ice cream.

**Summary & comments:** This is one of the most exciting fine dining restaurants in downtown Chicago for the sheer pleasure of the food. One professional from Vancouver Island said, "My lunch was one of the ten best meals I've had in the United States, including New York and San Francisco." (Sadly, Spruce no longer serves lunch.) Executive Chef Jeffrey Constance took over the kitchen in 1998. Constance hails from the Belleville, Illinois/St. Louis area, where he returned to develop his personal, bold-flavored style after working in some of New York's finest restaraunts. Managing partner Dan Sachs also brings great credentials to this restaurant (Spiaggia, New York's Tribeca Grill, and London's Kensington Palace). The food here is innovative, flavorful, and made from great ingredients, such as heirloom tomatoes, veggie chips, and artisan cheeses.

**Honors & awards:** *North Shore* magazine, #1 Readers' Favorite, 1997; AAA four diamonds, 1994–1996; *Esquire* magazine, Best New Restaurant, 1996.

---

| SZECHWAN EAST | | ★★★★ |
|---|---|---|
| Chinese | Moderate | **QUALITY** 92 |
| 340 East Ohio Street; (312) 255-9200 Zone 3   Near North | | **VALUE** C |

Reservations: Recommended

When to go: Any time

Entree range: $7.95–13.95; $24.95 per person for Imperial dinner or $31.95 per person for Emperor's dinner (2 person minimum for both)

Payment: All major credit cards

Service rating: ★★★★

Friendliness rating: ★★★★★

Parking: Validated adjacent McClurg Court Garage (indoor walkway)

Bar: Full service, incuding Man-

darin cocktails and imported beers

Wine selection: Regular list: about 24 international selections, including Harvest Moon chardonnay private label and several Oriental choices; mostly affordable; most bottles, $12–22, with several in $30s, and Dom Perignon for $120; several by the glass

Dress: Casual

Disabled access: Yes

Customers: Mixed, business, couples, mainly locals

**(Szechwan East)**

**Brunch:** Sunday champagne buffet, 11:30 a.m.–2 p.m., $15.95

**Lunch:** Monday–Saturday, 11:30 a.m.–2 p.m.; 30-item lunch buffet, $8.95

**Dinner:** Every day, 5–10 p.m.

**Setting & atmosphere:** Attractive, spacious dining room in tasteful Chinese decor divided into sections; recently renovated and expanded to include a second bar and indoor cafe and outdoor sidewalk cafe in summer.

**House specialties:** Appetizers: Fire pot satay beef; crab claws stuffed with minced shrimp and water chestnuts; Shanghai pot stickers filled with chicken and cabbage. Entrees: Governor's Chicken (chicken sautéed with sliced bell peppers, minced ginger, and garlic), a best-seller; steamed fillet of Chilean black sea bass with ginger root and scallions; black bean salmon (fillets); steamed fish (fillet—the orange roughy is great!) with rice and wine-ginger–black bean sauce; Peking duck (now available in half-duck portions, enough for two entrees; no advance order required). Vegetable dishes: Szechuan string beans; festival of mushrooms; steamed vegetable delight with tofu and garlic dipping sauce. Other items include three delicacies in a nest (scallops, escargot, and filet mignon chunks with Chinese vegetables, in a potato bird's nest); vegetable tempura; Hwa Shee Jeer Surprise (chicken and escargot in spicy hot sauce with mushrooms and vegetables); walnut chicken. Expanded lunch/brunch buffet, including fried wonton and calamari-peapod salad.

**Other recommendations:** Assorted hot appetizers, including the daily special vegetarian and the Suchow potstickers; Taiwanese escargot rice (healthier than fried rice); moo shi crêpes with chicken, vegetables, shrimp, beef, pork, or duck; dim sum trio (shrimp, pork, chicken dumplings in mini steamer). Desserts: rich Chinese crêpes with dates; banana in flaming rum; light almond tofu; Chinese cakes.

**Summary & comments:** This is the reincarnation of one of Chicago's longtime top Chinese restaurants (considering current owner Alfred Hsu managed the predecessor Szechwan House at its previous Michigan Avenue location since 1981). While managing Szechwan House, Hsu, together with the legendary restaurateur Austin Koo, opened 17 other Chinese restaurants. When Szechwan House had to relocate in 1995 because the building was razed, Hsu opened Szechwan East on his own with the same staff and actually improved an already excellent restaurant. He and his master chef Hu Xiao Jun, a Szechuan native, expanded the comprehensive, 120-item menu and increased the dining options, including half orders of most entrees. There is a trio of "healthy options" (steamed vege-

**(Szechwan East)**

tables solo or with chicken or shrimp) and vegetarian dishes, "Chef's Specials," and multi-course set-price dinners. The restaurant is capable of turning out some impressive banquets. Excellent cooking and attentive service from the friendly staff continue. The food is exciting and the ever-changing menu tempts return visits. Carryout, dinner delivery, lunch boxes, and catering are available.

## THAI BORRAHN ★★★★

| Thai | Inexpensive/Moderate | QUALITY |
|---|---|---|
| | | **90** |

| 16 East Huron Street; (312) 440-6003 | VALUE |
|---|---|
| Zone 3    Near North | **B** |

**Reservations:** Lunch, only for large groups; dinner, recommended
**When to go:** Any time
**Entree range:** $6.25–18
**Payment:** VISA, MC, AMEX, DC
**Service rating:** ★★★★
**Friendliness rating:** ★★★★½
**Parking:** Street
**Bar:** Full service, including Singha, the popular Thai beer

**Wine selection:** Limited international, including Japanese saké, plum wine, and selections from Brazil, France, and Italy; mostly American; 11 by the glass, affordable
**Dress:** Business casual to dressy
**Disabled access:** No; restaurant on second floor—no elevator
**Customers:** Local

**Open:** Monday–Thursday, 11 a.m.–10 p.m.; Friday, 11 a.m.–10:30 p.m.; Saturday, 4–10:30 p.m.; Sunday, 4–10 p.m.

**Setting & atmosphere:** "Borrahn" in Thai means "ancient times," and this restaurant's attractive decor with some antiques underscores this theme. Traditionally carved statues and puppets grace the walls, which feature a geometric-style wood paneling popular in Thailand. Classically patterned blue-and-white china, as well as authentic footed rice bowls, also help conjure the image of a pleasant eatery in Bangkok, the hometown of chef and co-owner Chanpen Ratana.

**House specialties:** The famous pad thai (thin rice noodles, sweet turnip, bean sprouts, tofu, and egg stir-fried in sweet-sour tamarind sauce with a choice of meat or vegetables); tom yum chicken (hot and sour soup with lemongrass, cilantro, lime, chile, and mint); on request, Thai Borrahn jan ront (sesame beef in a hot plate with oyster sauce and vegetables).

**Other recommendations:** Borrahn spring roll (unusual with avocado, cream cheese, and more); seaweed spring roll; house garden salad with mild

**(Thai Borrahn)**

curry peanut sauce; pad talay (seafood combination in sauce with vegetables, basil, and ginger); catfish red curry.

**Summary & comments:** This upscale downtown restaurant offers affordable gourmet Thai cuisine from Bangkok, with some regional specialties as well. In its new home on the second floor of an East Huron building, Thai Borrahn continues its tradition of authentic recipes from chef Ratana's family. Her husband Vallop Ratana is her partner and her sister, Suvana Sook Dee, is general manager. There's a seafood focus to the newly expanded, varied menu, and several vegetarian items and options are offered. The food is artfully presented and decorated with fruit and vegetable carvings, a signature trait on which Thai chefs pride themselves. A great place for Thai food when you're in the North Michigan Avenue area—or make it a destination.

| TOPOLOBAMPO | | ★★★★½ |
|---|---|---|
| | | **QUALITY** |
| Mexican | Moderate | **95** |
| | | **VALUE** |
| 445 North Clark Street; (312) 661-1434 | | **C** |
| Zone 4   The Loop | | |

Reservations: Required
When to go: Tuesday, Wednesday, or Thursday
Entree range: $14–25
Payment: All major credit cards
Service rating: ★★★½
Friendliness rating: ★★½
Parking: Valet, $7; street; public lots
Bar: Shares a common bar with

Frontera Grill; good tequila and Mexican beer list
Wine selection: Quite extensive; very international
Dress: Tastefully casual, no sneakers or jeans
Disabled access: Yes
Customers: Mixed, local and traveler, business, couples

**Lunch:** Tuesday–Friday, 11:30 a.m.–2 p.m.

**Dinner:** Tuesday–Thursday, 5:30–9:30 p.m.; Friday and Saturday, 5:30–10:30 p.m.

**Setting & atmosphere:** Formal and elegant; comfortable.

**House specialties:** Menu changes every two weeks. Cooking is refined at Topolobampo. Appetizer samplers might offer crispy, smoky-flavored pork carnitas, guacamole with tomatillos, cactus salad, and more. Fish gets unusual treatment, such as succulent pan-roasted sea bass with roasted gar-

**(Topolobampo)**

lic, sweet plantains, toasted pecans, wine-marinated prunes, and olive oil, with red chile rice. Another sampler plate might offer chicken enchiladas in green pumpkin seed mole; griddle-baked quesadilla of cheese, duck, and peppers; tostada of marinated cactus salad and black beans. Good desserts, such as special ice cream and cooked plantains.

**Other recommendations:** Sopa Azteca with chicken breast, avocado, and cheese; cod empanadas; tamale of fresh masa with pheasant; roasted capon breast stuffed with squash blossoms and wild greens.

**Summary & comments:** The menu offers a great variety of some rarely known dishes from regional Mexican cuisine. Owners Rick Bayless (chef) and wife Deanne (manager) lived in Mexico and co-authored a cookbook, *Authentic Mexican,* which was published about the time their Frontera Grill restaurant opened several years ago. Both the book and restaurant received good reviews. Many reports from diners and one personal experience indicate that service could be friendlier and more accommodating, especially at the entrance regarding seating.

**Honors & awards:** *London Herald* and *New York Times* reviews. Recognized as the best-researched Mexican restaurant offering regional dishes; chef Rick Bayless won Best Chef of the Midwest in 1994 and the International Chef of the Year Award, James Beard Foundation 1995. Julia Child Best Cookbook of the Year, 1996.

---

## TOULOUSE ON THE PARK ★★★★½

| Light French-American | Moderate | QUALITY |
|---|---|---|
| | | 94 |

| 2140 North Lincoln Park West; (773) 665-9071 | VALUE |
|---|---|
| Zone 1    North Side | B |

Reservations: Recommended

When to go: Any time with reservation; less busy on weeknights

Entree range: $15.50–22; some specials $24.95

Payment: VISA, MC, AMEX, DC

Service rating: ★★★★½

Friendliness rating: ★★★★

Parking: Valet, $6

Bar: Full service. Outstanding cognac selection. Exquisite

Toulouse Cognac Bar across the hall from dining room, (773) 665-9073.

Wine selection: More than 50 American, French, and Italian, 8 half bottles, 7 by the glass, $6

Dress: Formal to business

Disabled access: Yes

Customers: More upscale, all ages; business; romantic couples

**(Toulouse on the Park)**

**Dinner:** Monday–Thursday, 5:30–10:30 p.m.; Friday and Saturday, 5:30–11:30 p.m.; Sunday, closed.

**Bar:** Monday–Thursday, 6 p.m.–1 a.m.; Friday, 6 p.m.–1 a.m.; Saturday, 6 p.m.–2 a.m.

**Setting & atmosphere:** Owner Bob Djahanguiri has designed all of his restaurants, and this one was inspired by the grand Versailles style. The stunning 75-seat interior is a shimmering jewel box, divided into three spaces and decorated and furnished in the opulent Louis XV style. Mirrors reflect the hand-painted ceiling and walls and give *en trompe l'oeil* ("to fool the eye") effect of a much larger space. The Toulouse Cognac Bar is romantic and plush with Baroque-designed ceiling and crimson walls with a large portrait of the namesake artist Henri de Toulouse-Lautrec.

**House specialties:** Seasonal changing menus. Soup, fish, and game du jour specials, such as cream of onion soup, or pan-roasted Australian prawn and red trout sauté with lemon pasta and beet vinaigrette. From the menu: grilled salmon with lobster oil vinaigrette; noisette of sautéed veal with wild mushrooms and batonet of vegetables; roasted rack of lamb with natural juices, fresh herbs; roasted duck breast with green peppercorn sauce. Appetizers: grilled portobello mushroom with romaine and concassee; sautéed sea scallops in saffron sauce.

**Other recommendations:** House pâtés; sautéed chicken breast with saffron broth. Daily desserts are presented with spun sugar decorations that are about as spectacular as the interior. Recommended: raspberry and passion fruit mousse, Napoleon (chocolate and vanilla on raspberry ice cream), and chef's trio: petit fondant, petit brûlée, and orange ice cream.

**Summary & comment:** This is one of the best fine dining restaurants in the city, especially because it is surprisingly affordable for the fine French cuisine in opulent surroundings. Chef Thomas Cicero meets the challenge of creating menus with delicious, upscale dishes that would seem to be higher priced. Dining here is a sumptuous bargain.

**Honors & awards:** *Esquire* magazine, Most Romantic Restaurant in the United States.

## TRIO                                            ★★★★★

| Fusion | Expensive/Very Expensive | QUALITY |
|---|---|---|
| | | 98 |

| | VALUE |
|---|---|
| 1625 Hinman Avenue, Evanston; (847) 733-8746 | C |
| Zone 11    Northern Suburbs | |

**Reservations:** Highly suggested; weekends often booked weeks in advance; accepted up to 3 months in advance

**When to go:** Tuesday–Thursday

**Entree range:** $17–30; some specialties are higher; 8- to 10-course degustation, $75; vegetarian version, $65

**Payment:** VISA, MC, AMEX, D, DC

**Service rating:** ★★★★★

**Friendliness rating:** ★★★★★

**Parking:** Valet, $5

**Bar:** Full service; international beers; extensive single malt scotches; infused grappas

**Wine selection:** Fairly extensive; French, American, Italian, and several other international; French and Italian listed by region; many smaller wineries' vintage quality wines; good range of style and price, from $30 a bottle; slanted toward seafood-friendly choices; 10–12 by the glass; wine flight tastings (e.g., 4 half-glasses); willing to open almost any bottle to serve a glass; reserve list, sommelier to assist

**Dress:** Jackets suggested; dressy overall

**Disabled access:** Yes; need assistance up 2 steps for rest rooms

**Customers:** All types, all ages, except children (a few); business, couples

**Lunch:** Friday, seating noon–1 p.m.; four-course prix fixe ($26).

**Dinner:** Tuesday–Thursday, 5:30–9:30 p.m.; Friday and Saturday, 5:30–10:30 p.m.; Sunday, 5–9 p.m.

**Setting & atmosphere:** Housed in The Homestead, a hotel designed in Williamsburg Inn style. Country estate–type living room is a waiting lounge. Welcoming entryway with display of kitchen-made specialty items; wine rack room dividers. Comfortable, warm main dining room and a brighter, more intimate porch room overlooking a garden. A subtle, rustic courtyard decor with antique weathered wood paneling and carved alabaster wall sconces, with earthy purples and greens and dried flowers. The kitchen, with one table in an alcove, is a bit more than half of the 3,500 square feet of restaurant space.

**House specialties:** Appetizers: porcini (roasted winter corn) "cappuccino" with Parmesan tuille; wild mushroom and Parmesan risotto with white truffle oil; mirrored mosaic (fish changes: one example was great ginger-

**(Trio)**

cured gravlax, Pacific oyster, and Szechuan tuna sashimi); caviar service on a painter's palette (domestic); seared Hudson Valley foie gras (used lavishly here) with mango, or with roasted Granny Smith apple, black lentils, vanilla, and saké-infused veal reduction. Main courses: potato-crusted Columbia River sturgeon, Mt. Walden smoked trout, and lobster bordelaise; pomegranate-glazed pheasant breast, caramelized salsify, and swiss chard in a bittersweet tangerine sauce. Specials such as lobster bisque; grilled veal chop and crispy sweetbreads with three-bean ragout, escarole, and pearl onions, in a rosemary-infused veal reduction. Desserts: lemon tart Nico with white pepper ice cream, blackberry compote, dried apricots, and golden raisins; the Great Pumpkin Crème Caramel; and Valrhona chocolate bliss (Della's decadent mélange that once included a chocolate hazelnut tart, a spun sugar cup holding chocolate mousse, a chocolate meringue cookie dipped in pistachios with fudge sorbet, berries, and more).

**Other recommendations:** Circle Ranch buffalo carpaccio, tempura tiger shrimp, and horseradish aïoli; hazelnut- and herb-crusted rack of lamb with foie gras hummus, ratatouille, roasted garlic, and black and green olives; the "Vegetarian" is a daily celebration of seasonal market vegetables and grains; crème brûlée; box of Trio's truffles to take home.

**Summary & comments:** By far, one of the finest, most spectacular restaurants to open here in some time. It made culinary waves immediately after opening in 1993. Shawn McClain, sous-chef since then, was promoted to executive chef when the original "trio" split in 1995. Trio was named for the three cuisines the restaurant represents and for the original talented partnership of ongoing proprietor Henry Adaniya, executive chef Rick Tramonto, and his wife, pastry chef Gale Gand. The husband-wife chef team left to open the larger, more casual Brasserie-T in Northfield. Current pastry chef Della Gossett creates desserts as delicious as they are beautiful. The cooking is built on classic French and Italian foundations with Asian influences, and the finished dishes are avant garde. McClain's style is more delicate and subtle than his predecessors; in one instance, a wonderful pomegranate-glazed pheasant breast was a bit short on sauce. Stunning presentations—some whimsical—are arranged on unusual surfaces such as marble, granite, and mirrors. One whimsical example is warm lobster martini, which fell short of the usual high standards here, but was attractive. A complimentary sorbet arrives as an intermezzo during dinner. An entire dinner parade of such spectacular menu items is definitely culinary theater. There are those who prefer the sub-

**(Trio)**

tleties of dining and consider this theatrical display a bit ostentatious. However, there's no disagreement on the culinary expertise here and the passion and energy exhibited on every level. Informed servers anticipate diners' needs, but are never doting. The joy of cooking here has rejuvenated even the most jaded, worldly diner. The degustation menu is a great spontaneous tasting opportunity. Kitchen table must be reserved weeks in advance.

**Honors & awards:** *Chicago Tribune* and *Chicago Sun-Times,* four stars, 1996; *Gourmet* magazine rated it among the nation's top restaurants, 1996; *North Shore* magazine, Top 30 in the City, 1996.

| UNCLE TUTUNJI'S | | ★★★ |
|---|---|---|
| | | QUALITY |
| Middle Eastern | Inexpensive | 85 |
| 615 North Wells Street; (312) 587-0721 | | VALUE |
| Zone 3    Near North | | B |

**Reservations:** Recommended for weekends
**When to go:** Any time
**Entree range:** $5.50–11.95
**Payment:** All major credit cards
**Service rating:** ★★½
**Friendliness rating:** ★★★★
**Parking:** Two hours free; facilities on Erie and Wells, and Franklin and Ohio

**Bar:** Full service
**Wine selection:** Limited; mostly Californian, some Italian and French; $16–28 a bottle; only 3 by the glass
**Dress:** Casual
**Disabled access:** Yes, including rest rooms
**Customers:** 95% local, some Middle Eastern, travelers, business, couples

**Lunch/Dinner:** Monday–Thursday, 11 a.m.–9 p.m.; Friday and Saturday, 11 a.m.–10:30 p.m.; Sunday, closed.

**Setting & atmosphere:** Beautiful Assyrian murals depicting ancient Assyrian life, design circa 800 B.C.; main dining area divided into two sections; white tablecloths covered with paper.

**House specialties:** Dolmeh (stuffed grape leaves with meat or vegetables); kibbeh (fried cracked wheat and meat mixture); tabbouleh (cracked wheat salad); baba gannoujh (eggplant-tahini dip); Tutunji platter: shawerma (gyros), kifta kebab, lamb kebab, and chicken.

**Other recommendations:** Vegetarian entrees, including a combo plate; couscous (meat or vegetarian).

**(Uncle Tutunji's)**

**Summary & comments:** This downtown gem is still one of the best Middle Eastern restaurants around for its charming atmosphere, array of skillfully prepared dishes, and friendly staff. Formerly Ishtar Inn, the restaurant was renamed when a new owner took over. The last visit revealed that lamb kebabs were tough and the service had rough edges. The cuisine is very meat-and-vegetable oriented—no fish. All the dishes sampled were robustly well flavored and fresh; entrees come with salad, rice, and pita bread. The bargain prices are unheard of downtown—a real find!

| VIVERE (ITALIAN VILLAGE) | ★★★★½ |
|---|---|

| Italian | Moderate | QUALITY |
|---|---|---|
| | | **95** |

| 71 West Monroe Street; (312) 332-4040 | VALUE |
|---|---|
| Zone 4    The Loop | **C** |

**Reservations:** Recommended always
**When to go:** Any time
**Entree range:** Lunch, $8.75–12.75; dinner, $11.50–22.50
**Payment:** Major credit cards
**Service rating:** ★★★★★
**Friendliness rating:** ★★★★★
**Parking:** Valet, $6
**Bar:** Full service
**Wine selection:** Regular list, "Current Wine Selections," is extensive and well balanced; mostly Italian; good American and French selection; several German and Portuguese; also, an award-winning, 36-page, 950-selection reserve list
**Dress:** Chic casual, dressy
**Disabled access:** Yes
**Customers:** Diverse, business, couples, operagoers, theatergoers

**Lunch:** Monday–Friday, 11:30 a.m.–2:30 p.m.

**Dinner:** Monday–Thursday, 5–10 p.m.; Friday and Saturday, 5–11 p.m.; Sunday, closed.

**Setting & atmosphere:** Award-winning decor is a unique "modern Italian baroque," a blend of the elements of a Medieval castle with futuristic fantasy—burgundy velvet chairs mix with peach hues and black accents, mirrors, and marble and shell-shaped light fixtures. Intimate open mezzanine area.

**House specialties:** Tortine di funghi misti (garlic-infused mushrooms in an onion-thyme cream sauce); carpaccio, fava beans, truffle oil mayonnaise, and spinach soufflé; roasted butternut squash–filled pasta in Amaretti biscotti-

**(Vivere (Italian Village))**

pear-pecan sauce; braided lobster-filled tomato pasta with a lobster–light cream sauce; duck breast, sliced and fanned on a plate with zucchini puree, crisp leeks and celery root, and a red wine–balsamic vinegar sauce; veal tenderloin in a porcini-pancetta-gin cream sauce with seasonal vegetables. Seafood of the day, such as Atlantic salmon in artichoke tomato sauce (charcoal-grilled or ai ferri—seared on a hot iron griddle).

**Other recommendations:** Pheasant-filled pasta with butter, sage, and Parmesan; eggless pasta with four-cheese filling in cherry tomato–basil sauce; daily risotto; oak-grilled lamb chops; roasted artichokes in white wine-Mandarin-basil sauce. Desserts: mango sorbetti with tuille; gelati; a chocolate-truffle cake creation; panna cotta (timbale of sweet cream, caramel sauce, and nougat).

**Summary & comments:** Vivere means "to live" in Italian, and indeed, this is the way to do it Italian-style. After celebrating its 70th anniversary in 1997, the Italian Village is a city landmark. Vivere is part of a triad of restaurants that make up the Italian Village, launched in 1927 by Alfredo Capitanini and now run by his sons Ray and Franco and Franco's three children. Chef Marcelo Gallegos prepares exciting contemporary, regional Italian food. The wine lists are dazzling and the prices overall spell good value. The heart-of-downtown location makes this a perfect place for an early dinner before the opera or theater. Vivere is on the main floor; the Village, upstairs (a charming recreation of a town in Italy); and Cantina Enoteca (a great Italian seafood restaurant), downstairs. Italian Village holds an annual Garlic Festival in March. The same wine lists are available in all three, and they are organized by co-owner Ray Capitanini and Wine Consultant Robert Rohden.

**Honors & awards:** Wine list has received a *Wine Spectator* "Grand Award" annually since 1984. *Interiors* magazine award for design. In 1997, Vivere tied for second place in *Wine Spectator*'s award for Best Italian Restaurant in the United States.

## WOO LAE OAK ★★★★

| | | |
|---|---|---|
| Korean | Inexpensive | **QUALITY** |
| | | **94** |
| 30 West Hubbard Street; (312) 645-0051 | | **VALUE** |
| Zone 3   Near North | | **C** |

**Reservations:** Accepted
**When to go:** Weekdays (less crowded)
**Entree range:** $8–16
**Payment:** VISA, MC, DC
**Service rating:** ★★★★
**Friendliness rating:** ★★★★
**Parking:** Free valet
**Bar:** Full service; sake; small selec-
tion of beers, including Korean
and Japanese
**Wine selection:** Limited; mostly
domestic and French
**Dress:** Casual; many in business
attire
**Disabled access:** Yes
**Customers:** Businesspeople

**Open:** Every day, 11:30 a.m.–10 p.m.

**Setting & atmosphere:** Upscale decor with tables separated by frosted glass partitions and half walls of natural wood allowing for privacy. Ancient Korean pottery and classical music add to the elegance.

**House specialties:** Goo jul pan (Korean hors d'oeuvres of nine various ingredients wrapped in a pancake); mo doom jun (combination of pan-fried meatballs, shrimp fillet, fish fillet, and green peppers stuffed with ground beef, all coated with egg and flour); bul go ki (thin slices of marinated, grilled tender beef); kal bi (grilled boneless short rib cubes); jun gol (sukiyaki); buh sut jun gol (variety of mushrooms, thin slices of beef, and other vegetables; available without meat); dol sot bi bim bap (grilled, marinated strips of beef and vegetables topped with fried egg, hot paste sauce); su jung gua (sweet ginger-flavored drink).

**Other recommendations:** Se wu tui gim (deep fried battered shrimp and vegetables); dak gui (lightly marinated, grilled boneless sliced chicken); yeon aw gui (fresh broiled salmon); chap chae (vermicelli noodles and vegetables sautéed in specially seasoned sauce); sik hee (sweet rice-flavored Korean punch); guail (seasonal fresh fruits).

**Summary & comments:** Each table has a built-in gas grill so diners can cook their own food. All main courses are served with kim chee (pickled and spiced cabbage), as well as side dishes such as spinach and spicy daikon radish. Opened in 1996, 50 years after the Jang family founded their first restaurant in Seoul, the Chicago venue of Woo Lae Oak is the eighth restaurant opened by Jin Keun Jang. His intention is to introduce Korean culture through high-quality food.

**Honors & awards:** Chosen by *Chicago* magazine as a "Pick of the Week."

## YOSHI'S CAFE ★★★★

| | | QUALITY |
|---|---|---|
| New French | Inexpensive/Moderate | **94** |

3257 Halsted Street; (773) 248-6160

| | VALUE |
|---|---|
| | **B** |

Zone 1   North Side

**Reservations:** Recommended, especially for weekends

**When to go:** Weekend nights are busiest

**Entree range:** $6–18

**Payment:** All major credit cards except DC

**Service rating:** ★★★★½

**Friendliness rating:** ★★★★½

**Parking:** Valet, $6

**Bar:** Full service; bar/lounge adjacent to main dining room

**Wine selection:** About 80 selections, mostly American and French, some international; $25 and up per bottle; 15 available by the glass, $4.50–6

**Dress:** Casual

**Disabled access:** Yes

**Customers:** Diverse, local, visitors, European, couples, business, family

**Dinner:** Tuesday–Thursday, 5–10:30 p.m.; Friday and Saturday, 5–11 p.m.; Sunday, 5–9:30 p.m.; Monday, closed.

**Setting & atmosphere:** Very romantic, airy dining room with peach and beige walls, white linen tablecloths, and lots of silver; recently expanded to seat about 130 patrons, more than double its original size.

**House specialties:** Menu has an emphasis on seafood, with some occasional unusual items, such as domestic fugu (blowfish—the Japanese type is poisonous if not prepared properly, but rest assured that domestic fugu is nonpoisonous). Items change due to availability. Tuna tartare with guacamole and toast; varied Japanese sushi and sashimi (spicy tuna roll; squid with tiny asparagus; rolled salmon with crab meat); salad of tomato, green beans, and cucumber with basil-infused oil vinaigrette; homemade buckwheat pasta (soba) with Oriental vegetables; veal scaloppine with mushroom Calvados sauce and risotto garnish. Specials such as grilled half duck, boned, with fresh persimmon sauce. Homemade desserts are worth the calories: dark chocolate pecan cake; velvety crème brûlée of the day (orange-ginger, coffee); refreshing lemon tart; thin sliced apple tart.

**Other recommendations:** Grilled seared tuna with red wine-garlic-honey sauce; tofu steak with shrimp and shiitake mushrooms, sweet saké, soy sauce, and sesame oil sauce; grilled beef tenderloin with zinfindel sauce; veal with curry port wine sauce; rotisserie of chicken with rosemary au jus and mashed potatoes.

**(Yoshi's Cafe)**

**Entertainment & amenities:**  Viewing the artistic food plate presentations.

**Summary & comments:** Yoshi Katsumura and his wife, Nobuko, have operated their Franco-Japanese fine dining gem on Halsted for more than a decade. In 1995, they renovated and enlarged the dining room to turn it into more of a true cafe; they also revamped the menu and lowered prices dramatically. About a fifth of the menu changes daily, and it changes completely every two months; there are daily specials. While an occasional dish might lack seasoning, Yoshi's French food with Asian influences is still mostly superb in his subtle style and beautifully presented, often on colorful Japanese plates. The professional, accommodating service remains as unwavering as before, but the feeling is more casual, set by the jazz and other musical tapes. A big bonus is that the prices make this affordable fine dining.

**Honors & awards:** DiRoNA Award (distinguished restaurant in North America since 1992, four diamonds); *Chicago Tribune* and *Chicago Sun-Times,* three stars; *Gourmet* magazine's readers' poll, America's Favorite Chicago Restaurant, 1996.

| YVETTE | | ★★★½ |
|---|---|---|
| | | QUALITY |
| New French | Inexpensive/Moderate | 85 |
| | | VALUE |
| 1206 North State Parkway; (312) 280-1700 | | C |
| Zone 3    Near North | | |

**Reservations:** Recommended
**When to go:** Any time; weekdays less busy
**Entree range:** $12–20
**Payment:** VISA, MC, AMEX, DC
**Service rating:** ★★★½
**Friendliness rating:** ★★★★½
**Parking:** City lot across the street (discounted)

**Bar:** Full service
**Wine selection:** American, French, and Italian wines, ranging from $24–150 per bottle
**Dress:** Informal, tastefully casual, some dressy
**Disabled access:** Yes
**Customers:** Upscale, largely professional, couples, all ages

**Brunch:** Saturday and Sunday, 11 a.m.–3 p.m.

**Dinner:** Monday–Thursday, 4:30 p.m.–midnight; Friday and Saturday, 4:30 p.m.–1 a.m.; Sunday, 4:30–11 p.m.; 365 days a year

**Setting & atmosphere:** Sophisticated cabaret ambience in cafe area up front, set to accommodate musicians; dining room in back is comfortable,

**(Yvette)**

with white, paper-covered tables. Chic Gold Coast bistro with an al fresco sidewalk cafe during the warmer months.

**House specialties:** Eggplant Mediterranean with olive oil and tomato; shrimp Provençal with tomato concasse, garlic, and olives, drizzled with extra virgin olive oil; French onion soup au gratin; seared bay scallops with spinach and roasted tomatoes over fusilli and mushrooms; roasted filet of lamb with rosemary couscous, grilled ratatouille and natural jus; salmon Yvette, smoked to order and served over angel hair pasta with vegetables and beurre blanc.

**Other recommendations:** Fruit and cheese plate with glass of port; a daily selection of homemade desserts.

**Entertainment & amenities:** Every night, live music ( jazz, cabaret) and dancing; no cover.

**Summary & comments:** Unique French bistro with a cabaret atmosphere and nightly entertainment and dancing. Owner Bob Djahanguiri's hallmark with all his restaurants is designing them himself and blending live music with good French food and ambiance. In addition to this, he owns Yvette Wintergarden and Toulouse on the Park (see profiles). Yvette is a very romantic place for a special occasion or any time you're yearning for a taste of France.

---

## YVETTE WINTERGARDEN ★★★½

| New French | Inexpensive/Moderate | QUALITY 85 |
|---|---|---|
| | | VALUE C |

311 South Wacker Drive; (312) 408-1242
Zone 4   The Loop

**Reservations:** Recommended
**When to go:** Lunch or for a different ambiance at dinner with music; before theater or opera
**Entree range:** $10.50–16
**Payment:** VISA, MC, AMEX, DC
**Service rating:** ★★★★
**Friendliness rating:** ★★★★
**Parking:** Adjacent lot, $5 after 5 p.m.
**Bar:** Full service

**Wine selection:** 50 from France, America, and Italy; $15–350 a bottle; many in $20–35 range; half bottles, around $8; 6 by the glass
**Dress:** Informal, casual; tends to be dressier in the evening for dancing
**Disabled access:** Yes
**Customers:** Upscale, professional, all ages

**Lunch:** Monday–Friday, 11:30 a.m.–2 p.m.

**(Yvette Wintergarden)**

**Dinner:** Monday–Thurday, 5–9 p.m.; Friday and Saturday, 5–10:30 p.m.; complimentary hors d'oeuvres, Monday–Friday, 5:30–7 p.m.; pre-theater menu, Monday–Saturday, 5–7 p.m.

**Setting & atmosphere:** Spectacular tropical atrium entrance; dining room is intimate and dimly lit; comfortable seating in one dining room designed to view live performances.

**House specialties:** Menu changes seasonally. Lobster and artichoke fritters; baked escargot (snails with blue cheese, garlic butter, and tomato concasse); sautéed striped sea bass served with green olive, pistachio, and arugula pesto, and mushroom and roasted tomato ragout.

**Other recommendations:** Seasonal terrine of the day; salade Niçoise; grilled tenderloin of pork with three-mustard sauce, braised cabbage, and mashed potatoes; freshly made desserts of the day (tarts, mousse).

**Entertainment & amenities:** Monday–Saturday, live music—large dance floor; no cover.

**Summary & comments:** The latest menu deviates from French cuisine to include Italian items such as beef carpaccio and chicken pesto (roasted breast stuffed with basil pesto on capellini pasta with marinara sauce), and a Cajun blackened fillet of fresh tuna. Some items are the same as, and many similar to, those at Yvette. Owner Bob Djahanguiri has a particular talent for creating romantic French bistros, restaurants, and cabarets with appropriate live music. This place developed after his Yvette. It's larger and a great downtown spot for before the theater or opera, or for relaxing with dinner and dancing. Yvette Wintergarden does private parties for 10–1,500.

| ZUM DEUTSCHEN ECK | ★★★½ |
|---|---|

| Continental/German      Inexpensive/Moderate | QUALITY |
|---|---|
| | **88** |

| 2924 North Southport Avenue; (773) 525-8121 | VALUE |
|---|---|
| Zone 1   North Side | **C** |

| | |
|---|---|
| Reservations: Recommended for weekends | Payment: VISA, MC, AMEX, CB, DC, D |
| When to go: Early evenings, 4 p.m. on weekends | Service rating: ★★★½ |
| | Friendliness rating: ★★★½ |
| Entree range: $14.95–18.95 | Parking: Ample parking |

## (Zum Deutschen Eck)

**Bar:** Full service; seats 40 people

**Wine selection:** Fairly extensive selections of American and German

**Dress:** Casual

**Disabled access:** Yes, wheelchair accessible

**Customers:** Some are third-generation customers; a wide range

**Lunch/Dinner:** Monday–Thursday, 11:30 a.m.–10:30 p.m.; Friday, 11:30 a.m.–midnight; Saturday, noon–midnight; Sunday, noon–10 p.m. (Buffet brunches served on Easter, and on Mother's and Father's Days.)

**Setting & atmosphere:** Bavarian chalet–style restaurant with a colorful bar featuring original painted murals and hand-carved booths. Two charming, cozy dining rooms with German woodwork and artifacts. Three banquet rooms with seating from 25 to 400. Warm and welcoming.

**House specialties:** German standards: liver dumpling soup (always available); German schlachtplatte (combo including Thueringer, knackwurst, Kasseler Rippchen/smoked pork loin). Various schnitzels: basic Wiener schnitzel, Dijon, rahmschnitzel (with bacon), schnitzel à la Jaeger (in red wine sauce with vegetables)—most mit buttered noodles. Giant pork shank with sauerkraut; sauerbraten; hasenpfeffer.

**Other recommendations:** Scallop strudel; herring salad; Caesar salad; shrimp de Jonghe; fresh seafood; half roast duckling; homemade pastries.

**Entertainment & amenities:** Live entertainment on weekend evenings. "Mike and Sally, the Spectacular Duo" play a wide variety of instruments performing music and songs from all over Europe.

**Summary & comments:** This place started in a slower era as a neighborhood corner bar in the shadow of the Gothic St. Alphonsus Church. Founded and owned by the Wirth family since 1956, Zum Deutschen Eck has been transformed into a successful restaurant/banquet complex, and the live entertainment with sing-alongs makes weekends quite lively. Entrees come with dumplings, noodles, or potato as well as choice of appetizer and salad. Dining here is a slice of Bavaria sans Lufthansa Airlines.

| Hotel | Room Star Rating | Zone | Street Address |
|---|---|---|---|
| Ambassador West Hotel | ★★★½ | 3 | 1300 North State Parkway Chicago, 60610 |
| Best Western Grant Park Hotel | ★★½ | 5 | 1100 South Michigan Avenue Chicago, 60605 |
| Best Western Inn of Chicago | ★★½ | 3 | 162 East Ohio Street Chicago, 60611 |
| Best Western O'Hare | ★★½ | 2 | 10300 West Higgins Road Rosemont, 60018 |
| Best Western River North | ★★½ | 3 | 125 West Ohio Street Chicago, 60610 |
| The Blackstone Hotel | ★★★ | 5 | 636 South Michigan Avenue Chicago, 60605 |
| The Carleton of Oak Park | ★★★ | 2 | 1110 Pleasant Street Oak Park, 60302 |
| Cass Hotel | ★½ | 3 | 640 North Wabash Avenue Chicago, 60611 |
| Chicago Hilton & Towers | ★★★★ | 5 | 720 South Michigan Avenue Chicago, 60605 |
| Claridge Hotel | ★★★½ | 3 | 1244 North Dearborn Parkway Chicago,60610 |
| Clarion Executive Plaza | ★★★ | 4 | 71 East Wacker Drive Chicago, 60601 |
| Club Hotel by Doubletree | ★★★ | 10 | 1450 East Touhy Avenue Des Plaines, 60018 |
| Comfort Inn Downers Grove | ★★½ | 8 | 3010 Finley Road Downers Grove, 60515 |
| Comfort Inn Lincoln Park | ★★ | 1 | 601 West Diversey Parkway Chicago, 60614 |
| Comfort Inn O'Hare | ★★½ | 2 | 2175 East Touhy Avenue Des Plaines, 60018 |
| Courtyard by Marriott Downtown | ★★★½ | 3 | 30 East Hubbard Street Chicago, 60611 |
| Courtyard by Marriott Oak Brook Terrace | ★★★½ | 8 | 6 Transam Plaza Drive Oak Brook Terrace, 60181 |
| Courtyard by Wood Dale | ★★★½ | 10 | 900 North Wood Dale Road Chicago, 60191 |
| Days Inn Gold Coast | ★★ | 1 | 1816 North Clark Street Chicago, 60614 |

| Local Phone | Fax | Toll Free Reservations | Rack Rate | No. of Rooms | On-site Dining | Pool |
|---|---|---|---|---|---|---|
| (312) 787-3700 | (312) 787-9475 | (800) 300-WEST | $$$$$ | 220 | ✔ | |
| (312) 922-2900 | (312) 922-8812 | (800) GRANT-PK | $$+ | 172 | ✔ | ✔ |
| (312) 787-3100 | (312) 573-3180 | (800) 557-BEST | $$$+ | 357 | ✔ | |
| (847) 296-4471 | (847) 296-4958 | (800) 528-1234 | $$+ | 143 | ✔ | ✔ |
| (312) 467-0800 | (312) 467-1665 | (800) 727-0800 | $$$– | 148 | ✔ | ✔ |
| (312) 427-4300 | (312) 427-4736 | (800) 622-6330 | $$– | 305 | ✔ | |
| (708) 848-5000 | (708) 848-0537 | (888) CARLETON | $$+ | 110 | ✔ | |
| (312) 787-4030 | (312) 787-8544 | (800) 227-7850 | $$– | 175 | ✔ | |
| (312) 922-4400 | (312) 922-5240 | (800) HILTONS | $$$$$ | 1750 | ✔ | ✔ |
| (312) 787-4980 | (312) 266-0978 | (800) 245-1258 | $$$$– | 170 | ✔ | |
| (312) 346-7100 | (312) 346-1721 | (800) 621-4005 | $$$$$– | 420 | ✔ | |
| (847) 296-8866 | (847) 296-8268 | (800) 444-CLUB | $$+ | 245 | ✔ | ✔ |
| (630) 515-1500 | (630) 515-1595 | (800) 228-5150 | $+ | 115 | | ✔ |
| (773) 348-2810 | (773) 348-1912 | (800) 228-5150 | $$ | 75 | | |
| (847) 635-1300 | (847) 635-7572 | (800) 228-5150 | $$– | 148 | ✔ | |
| (312) 329-2500 | (312) 329-0293 | (800) 228-9290 | $$$+ | 336 | ✔ | ✔ |
| (630) 691-1500 | (630) 691-1518 | (800) 228-9290 | $$+ | 147 | | ✔ |
| (630) 766-7775 | (630) 766-7552 | (800) 321-2211 | $$– | 149 | ✔ | ✔ |
| (312) 664-3040 | (312) 664-3048 | (800) DAYS-INN | $$$ | 275 | ✔ | |

| Hotel | Room Star Rating | Zone | Street Address |
|---|---|---|---|
| Days Inn Lakeshore | ★★★ | 3 | 644 North Lakeshore Drive Chicago, 60611 |
| Days Inn Lincoln Park North | ★★★ | 1 | 646 West Diversey Chicago, 60614 |
| Days Inn O'Hare South | ★★½ | 2 | 3801 North Mannheim Road Schiller Park, 60176 |
| Doubletree Guest Suites | ★★★★ | 3 | 198 East Delaware Place Chicago, 60611 |
| The Drake Oak Brook | ★★★ | 8 | 2301 York Road Oak Brook, 60521 |
| The Drake | ★★★★½ | 3 | 140 East Walton Place Chicago, 60611 |
| Embassy Suites Chicago | ★★★★ | 3 | 600 North State Street Chicago, 60610 |
| Essex Inn | ★★½ | 5 | 800 South Michigan Avenue Chicago, 60605 |
| The Fairmont Hotel | ★★★★½ | 4 | 200 North Columbus Drive Chicago, 60601 |
| Four Points Sheraton | ★★★ | 2 | 10249 West Irving Park Road Schiller Park, 60176 |
| Four Seasons Hotel | ★★★★½ | 3 | 120 East Delaware Place Chicago, 60611 |
| Hampton Inn Midway Bedford Park | ★★★ | 6 | 6540 South Cicero Avenue Bedford Park, 60638 |
| Hampton Inn O'Hare | ★★★ | 2 | 3939 North Mannheim Road Schiller Park, 60176 |
| Hilton Suites Oak Brook Terrace | ★★★★ | 8 | 10 Drury Lane Oak Brook Terrace, 60181 |
| Holiday Inn Chicago City Center | ★★★ | 3 | 300 East Ohio Street Chicago, 60611 |
| Holiday Inn Chicago O'Hare | ★★½ | 2 | 8201 Higgins Road Chicago, 60621 |
| Holiday Inn Evanston | ★★½ | 11 | 1501 Sherman Avenue Evanston, 60201 |
| Holiday Inn Express Downers Grove | ★★½ | 8 | 3031 Finley Road Downers Grove, 60515 |
| Holiday Inn Mart Plaza | ★★★ | 3 | 350 North Orleans Street Chicago, 60654 |

| Local Phone | Fax | Toll Free Reservations | Rack Rate | No. of Rooms | On-site Dining | Pool |
|---|---|---|---|---|---|---|
| (312) 943-9200 | (312) 255-4411 | (800) 325-2525 | $$– | 575 | ✔ | ✔ |
| (312) 525-7010 | (312) 525-6998 | (800) 325-2525 | $$– | 128 | | ✔ |
| (847) 678-0670 | (847) 678-0690 | (800) 325-2525 | $$– | 144 | ✔ | ✔ |
| (312) 664-1100 | (312) 664-9881 | (800) 424-2900 | $$$$+ | 345 | ✔ | ✔ |
| (630) 574-5700 | (630) 574-0830 | (800) 334-9805 | $$$– | 170 | ✔ | ✔ |
| (312) 787-2200 | (312) 787-1431 | (800) HILTONS | $$$$ $$– | 535 | ✔ | |
| (312) 943-3800 | (312) 943-7629 | (800) 362-2779 | $$$$+ | 358 | ✔ | ✔ |
| (312) 939-2800 | (312) 922-6153 | (800) 621-6909 | $$+ | 255 | ✔ | ✔ |
| (312) 565-8000 | (312) 856-1032 | (800) 562-1003 | $$$$ $$– | 692 | ✔ | |
| (847) 671-6000 | (847) 671-0371 | (800) 323-1239 | $$$ | 296 | ✔ | ✔ |
| (312) 280-8800 | (312) 280-1748 | (800) 332-3442 | $$$$$ $$$$– | 343 | ✔ | ✔ |
| (708) 496-1900 | (708) 496-1997 | (800) HAMPTON | $$+ | 167 | | |
| (847) 671-1700 | (847) 671-5909 | (800) HAMPTON | $$ | 150 | | ✔ |
| (630) 941-0100 | (630) 941-0299 | (800) HILTONS | $$$+ | 212 | ✔ | ✔ |
| (312) 787-6100 | (312) 787-6259 | (800) HOLIDAY | $$$$+ | 500 | ✔ | ✔ |
| (773) 693-2323 | (773) 693-3771 | (800) 654-2000 | $$$– | 120 | ✔ | ✔ |
| (847) 491-6400 | (847) 328-3090 | (800) EVANSTON | $$$– | 159 | ✔ | ✔ |
| (630) 810-9500 | (630) 810-0059 | (800) HOLIDAY | $$– | 123 | | |
| (312) 836-5000 | (312) 222-9508 | (800) HOLIDAY | $$$$$– | 524 | ✔ | ✔ |

| Hotel | Room Star Rating | Zone | Street Address |
|---|---|---|---|
| Holiday Inn O'Hare International | ★★★ | 2 | 5440 North River Road Rosemont, 60018 |
| Hotel Allegro | ★★★★ | 4 | 171 West Randolph Street Chicago, 60601 |
| Hotel Inter-Continental Chicago | ★★★★ | 3 | 505 North Michigan Avenue Chicago, 60611 |
| Hotel Sofitel Chicago | ★★★★½ | 2 | 5550 North River Road Rosemont, 60018 |
| House of Blues Hotel | ★★★★½ | 3 | 333 North Dearborn Chicago, 60610 |
| Howard Johnson Express O'Hare | ★★½ | 2 | 4101 North Mannheim Road Schiller Park, 60176 |
| Hyatt at University Village | ★★★½ | 6 | 625 South Ashland Avenue Chicago, 60607 |
| Hyatt on Printer's Row Chicago | ★★★★ | 4 | 500 South Dearborn Street Chicago, 60605 |
| Hyatt Regency Chicago in Illinois Center | ★★★★ | 4 | 151 East Wacker Drive Chicago, 60601 |
| Hyatt Regency McCormick Place | ★★★★½ | 5 | 2233 Martin Luther King Drive Chicago, 60616 |
| Hyatt Regency O'Hare | ★★★★ | 2 | 9300 West Bryn Mawr Avenue Chicago, 60018 |
| Hyatt Regency Oak Brook | ★★★½ | 8 | 1909 Spring Road Oak Brook, 60523 |
| La Quinta Motor Inn Oak Brook | ★★½ | 8 | 1 South 666 Midwest Road Oak Brook Terrace, 60181 |
| Lenox House Suites | ★★★ | 3 | 616 North Rush Street Chicago, 60611 |
| Marriott Chicago Downtown | ★★★½ | 3 | 540 North Michigan Avenue Chicago, 60611 |
| Marriott Oak Brook | ★★★½ | 8 | 1401 West 22nd Street Oak Brook, 60523 |
| Marriott Residence Inn Downtown | ★★★★ | 3 | 201 East Walton Street Chicago, 60611 |
| Marriott Suites Downers Grove | ★★★★ | 8 | 1500 Opus Place, Business Corridor Downers Grove, 60559 |
| Marriott Suites O'Hare | ★★★★ | 2 | 6155 North River Road Chicago, 60018 |

| Local Phone | Fax | Toll Free Reservations | Rack Rate | No. of Rooms | On-site Dining | Pool |
|---|---|---|---|---|---|---|
| (847) 671-6350 | (847) 671-5406 | (800) HOLIDAY | $$$$$– | 507 | ✔ | ✔ |
| (312) 236-0123 | (312) 236-0917 | (800) 643-1500 | $$$+ | 483 | ✔ | |
| (312) 944-4100 | (312) 944-3050 | (800) 628-2468 | $$$$ $$+ | 844 | ✔ | ✔ |
| (847) 678-4488 | (847) 678-4244 | (800) 233-5959 | $$$+ | 300 | ✔ | ✔ |
| (312) 245-0333 | (312) 923-2442 | (800) 235-LOEWS | $$$$– | 367 | ✔ | |
| (847) 678-4470 | (847) 678-3837 | (800) 446-4656 | $$– | 67 | | |
| (312) 243-7200 | (312) 243-1289 | (800) 233-1234 | $$$+ | 114 | ✔ | |
| (312) 986-1234 | (312) 939-2468 | (800) 233-1234 | $$$– | 161 | ✔ | |
| (312) 565-1234 | (312) 565-2966 | (800) 233-1234 | $$$+ | 2019 | ✔ | |
| (312) 567-1234 | (312) 528-4000 | (800) 233-1234 | $$$$ $$– | 800 | ✔ | ✔ |
| (847) 696-1234 | (847) 698-0139 | (800) 233-1234 | $$$+ | 1100 | ✔ | ✔ |
| (630) 573-1234 | (630) 573-1133 | (800) 233-1234 | $$$$– | 425 | ✔ | ✔ |
| (630) 495-4600 | (630) 495-2558 | (800) 531-5900 | $$– | 150 | | |
| (312) 337-1000 | (312) 337-7217 | (800) 44-LENOX | $$$+ | 325 | ✔ | |
| (312) 836-0100 | (312) 836-6139 | (800) 228-0265 | $$$$– | 1173 | ✔ | ✔ |
| (630) 573-8555 | (630) 573-1026 | (800) 228-9290 | $$+ | 347 | ✔ | ✔ |
| (312) 943-9800 | (312) 943-8579 | (800) 331-3131 | $$$– | 221 | | |
| (630) 852-1500 | (630) 852-6527 | (800) 228-9290 | $$– | 254 | ✔ | ✔ |
| (847) 696-4400 | (847) 696-2122 | (800) 228-9290 | $$– | 256 | ✔ | ✔ |

| Hotel | Room Star Rating | Zone | Street Address |
|---|---|---|---|
| The Midland Hotel | ★★★ | 4 | 172 West Adams Street Chicago, 60603 |
| Motel 6 Chicago Downtown | ★★½ | 3 | 162 East Ontario Street Chicago, 60611 |
| O'Hare Hilton | ★★★½ | 2 | O'Hare International Airport Chicago, 60666 |
| O'Hare Marriott | ★★★½ | 2 | 8535 West Higgins Road Chicago, 60631 |
| Ohio House Motel | ★★ | 3 | 600 North LaSalle Street Chicago, 60610 |
| Omni Ambassador East | ★★★½ | 3 | 1301 North State Parkway Chicago, 60610 |
| Omni Chicago Hotel | ★★★★★ | 3 | 676 North Michigan Avenue Chicago, 60611 |
| Omni Orrington Hotel Evanston | ★★★ | 11 | 1710 Orrington Avenue Evanston, 60201 |
| Palmer House Hilton | ★★★★ | 4 | 17 East Monroe Street Chicago, 60603 |
| Quality Inn Downtown | ★★½ | 2 | 1 South Halsted Street Chicago, 60661 |
| Radisson Hotel & Suites Chicago | ★★★½ | 3 | 160 East Huron Street Chicago, 60611 |
| Radisson O'Hare | ★★½ | 2 | 6810 North Mannheim Road Rosemont, 60018 |
| Radisson O'Hare | ★★½ | 2 | 6810 North Mannheim Road Rosemont, 60018 |
| Radisson Suites Downers Grove | ★★★★ | 8 | 2111 Butterfield Road Downers Grove, 60515 |
| The Ramada Congress Hotel | ★★½ | 4 | 520 South Michigan Avenue Chicago, 60605 |
| Ramada Plaza Hotel O'Hare | ★★½ | 2 | 6600 North Mannheim Road Rosemont, 60018 |
| The Raphael Chicago | ★★★ | 3 | 201 East Delaware Place Chicago, 60611 |
| Red Roof Inn Downers Grove | ★★ | 8 | 1113 Butterfield Road Downers Grove, 60515 |
| Regal Knicker-bocker Hotel | ★★★½ | 3 | 163 East Walton Place Chicago, 60611 |

| Local Phone | Fax | Toll Free Reservations | Rack Rate | No. of Rooms | On-site Dining | Pool |
|---|---|---|---|---|---|---|
| (312) 332-1200 | (312) 332-5909 | (800) 621-2360 | $$$$ | 256 | ✔ | |
| (312) 787-3580 | (312) 787-1299 | (800) 466-8356 | $$– | 195 | | |
| (773) 686-8000 | (773) 601-2873 | (800) HILTONS | $$$+ | 858 | ✔ | |
| (773) 693-4444 | (773) 693-3164 | (800) 228-9290 | $$$+ | 681 | ✔ | ✔ |
| (312) 943-6000 | (312) 943-6063 | None | $+ | 50 | | |
| (312) 787-7200 | (312) 787-4760 | (800) 843-6664 | $$$$$– | 275 | ✔ | |
| (312) 944-6664 | (312) 266-3015 | (800) 843-6664 | $$$$ $$– | 347 | ✔ | ✔ |
| (847) 866-8700 | (847) 866-8724 | (800) 618-5111 | $$$– | 280 | ✔ | |
| (312) 726-7500 | (312) 917-1707 | (800) HILTONS | $$$$ $$– | 1639 | ✔ | ✔ |
| (312) 829-5000 | (312) 829-8151 | (800) 228-5151 | $$$– | 406 | ✔ | ✔ |
| (312) 787-2900 | (312) 787-5158 | (800) 333-3333 | $$$$$– | 370 | ✔ | ✔ |
| (847) 297-1234 | (847) 297-5287 | (800) 333-3333 | $$+ | 457 | ✔ | ✔ |
| (847) 297-8464 | (847) 297-5287 | (800) 333-3333 | $$+ | 475 | ✔ | ✔ |
| (630) 971-2000 | (630) 971-1021 | (800) 777-7800 | $$$– | 250 | ✔ | ✔ |
| (312) 427-3800 | (312) 427-3972 | (800) 635-1666 | $$– | 842 | ✔ | |
| (847) 827-5131 | (847) 827-5659 | (800) 272-6232 | $$+ | 723 | ✔ | ✔ |
| (312) 943-5000 | (312) 943-9483 | (800) 821-5343 | $$$$$ | 172 | ✔ | |
| (630) 963-4205 | (630) 963-4205 | (800) 843-7663 | $ | 135 | | |
| (312) 751-8100 | (312) 751-0370 | (800) 621-8140 | $$$$$– | 254 | ✔ | |

| Hotel | Room Star Rating | Zone | Street Address |
|---|---|---|---|
| Renaissance Chicago Hotel | ★★★★ | 4 | One West Wacker Drive Chicago, 60601 |
| Renaissance Hotel Oak Brook | ★★★½ | 8 | 2100 Spring Road Oak Brook, 60523 |
| Residence Inn by Marriott | ★★★★ | 2 | 7101 Chestnut Street Rosemont, 60018 |
| Residence Inn by Marriott O'Hare | ★★★½ | 2 | 9450 West Lawrence Avenue Schiller Park, 60176 |
| The Ritz-Carlton Chicago | ★★★★½ | 3 | 160 East Pearson Street Chicago, 60611 |
| Rosemont Suites O'Hare | ★★★½ | 2 | 5500 North River Road Rosemont, 60018 |
| Sheraton Chicago Hotel & Towers | ★★★½ | 3 | 301 East North Water Street Chicago, 60611 |
| Sheraton Gateway Suites O'Hare | ★★★★ | 2 | 6501 North Mannheim Road Rosemont, 60018 |
| Sleep Inn Midway Airport | ★★½ | 6 | 6650 South Cicero Avenue Bedford Park, 60638 |
| Summerfield Suites Chicago | ★★★½ | 3 | 166 East Superior Street Chicago, 60611 |
| Surf Hotel | ★★★ | 1 | 555 West Surf Street Chicago, 60657 |
| The Sutton Place Hotel | ★★★★ | 3 | 21 East Bellevue Place Chicago, 60611 |
| Swissôtel Chicago | ★★★★ | 4 | 323 East Wacker Drive Chicago, 60601 |
| The Talbott Hotel | ★★★ | 3 | 20 East Delaware Place Chicago, 60611 |
| Travelodge Chicago O'Hare | ★★½ | 2 | 3003 Mannheim Road Des Plaines, 60018 |
| The Westin Hotel Chicago | ★★★★ | 3 | 909 North Michigan Avenue Chicago, 60611 |
| The Westin Hotel O'Hare | ★★★★ | 2 | 6100 River Road Rosemont, 60018 |
| The Westin River North Chicago | ★★★★½ | 3 | 320 North Dearborn Street Chicago, 60610 |
| The Whitehall Hotel | ★★★★ | 3 | 105 East Delaware Place Chicago, 60611 |

| Local Phone | Fax | Toll Free Reservations | Rack Rate | No. of Rooms | On-site Dining | Pool |
|---|---|---|---|---|---|---|
| (312) 372-7200 | (312) 372-0834 | (800) HOTELS-1 | $$$$ | 553 | ✔ | ✔ |
| (630) 573-2800 | (630) 573-7134 | (800) HOTELS-1 | $$$+ | 170 | | ✔ |
| (847) 375-9000 | (847) 375-9010 | (800) 331-3131 | $$$– | 192 | | ✔ |
| (847) 725-2210 | (847) 725-2211 | (800) 331-3131 | $$$– | 170 | ✔ | ✔ |
| (312) 266-1000 | (312) 266-1194 | (800) 621-6906 | $$$$ $$$ | 430 | ✔ | ✔ |
| (847) 678-4000 | (847) 928-7659 | (888) 476-7366 | $$$+ | 294 | ✔ | ✔ |
| (312) 464-1000 | (312) 464-9140 | (800) 325-3535 | $$$$– | 1200 | ✔ | ✔ |
| (847) 699-6300 | (847) 699-0391 | (800) 325-3535 | $$$$+ | 297 | ✔ | ✔ |
| (708) 594-0001 | (708) 594-0058 | (800) 627-5337 | $$– | 120 | | |
| (312) 787-6000 | (312) 787-6133 | (800) 833-4353 | $$$$+ | 119 | | ✔ |
| (773) 528-8400 | (773) 528-8483 | (800) 787-3108 | $$+ | 55 | | |
| (312) 266-2100 | (312) 266-2103 | (800) 810-6888 | $$$$ $$– | 246 | ✔ | |
| (312) 565-0565 | (312) 565-0540 | (800) 654-7263 | $$$$$– | 630 | ✔ | ✔ |
| (312) 944-4970 | (312) 944-7241 | (800) TALBOTT | $$$$– | 146 | ✔ | ✔ |
| (847) 296-5541 | (847) 803-1984 | (800) 578-7878 | $+ | 94 | | ✔ |
| (312) 943-7200 | (312) 649-7447 | (800) 228-3000 | $$$$$+ | 750 | ✔ | |
| (847) 698-6000 | (847) 698-3000 | (800) 228-3000 | $$$$+ | 525 | ✔ | ✔ |
| (312) 744-1900 | (312) 527-2650 | (800) 228-3000 | $$$$$ | 424 | ✔ | |
| (312) 944-6300 | (312) 944-8552 | (800) 948-4255 | $$$$– | 221 | ✔ | |

# Index

Addams, Jane, Hull House Museum, 35, 281
Adler Planetarium, 285–86
  disabled visitor access to, 112
Aerobics, facilities for, 162
Aerospace museums, 295–96
African Americans
  events concerning, 50
  history museum, 293–94
  South Shore mansions, 240
Airplane tours, 226
Airport Express, 98–99, 102
Airports, 48
  Midway, 48, 85, 100–102
  O'Hare International, 48, 85, 96–100
  skycap tipping at, 109
  transportation to/from McCormick Place, 85
Alcohol. See also Entertainment and night life
  regulations on, 113
American Police Center & Museum, 286–87
American Sightseeing tours, 225–26
Amoco Building, 42
Amtrak service, 48, 102–3
Amusement parks, 244
  Navy Pier, 268–70
Andersonville
  Midsummer Festival, 51
  sightseeing in, 230
Animals. See Zoos
Antique Coach & Carriage Company, The, 227
Antique shows, 52
Aquariums, 247, 289–90

Aragon Ballroom, 132
Arboretums, 300–302
Archeology museums, 296–98
Architecture, 39–43
  art deco, 40–41
  Carson Pirie Scott, 184–85
  Chicago School, 39–40
  classical, 40
  after fire, 39
  International Style, 41
  mansions
    Gold Coast, 235
    Hawthorne Place, 233
    Hyde Park, 239
    Pullman, 242
    South Shore, 240
    Uptown, 231
    Wicker Park, 234
  museums of, 185, 273–74
  postmodern, 41–42
  Prairie School, 40, 256–58
  skyscrapers, 42
  tours, 43, 50, 223–25. See also Neighborhoods, sightseeing in
  Wright, Frank Lloyd, 40, 50, 163, 224, 256–58
Arie Crown Theater, 85
Arlington International Race Course, 174
Arrival and orientation, 95–120
  by car. See Driving; Parking
  city layout, 104–7
  disabled visitor access, 111–13
  geography, 103–4
  highways, 95–96, 106
  homeless population, 118–20

Arrival and orientation, *(continued)*
  information sources. *See* Information
    sources
  liquor rules, 113
  local customs and protocols, 108–10
  by plane. *See* Airports
  radio stations, 111
  safety tips, 114–20
  sales taxes, 113
  smoking regulations, 113
  telephone service, 113
  time zone, 113
  by train. *See* Trains
  transportation options for, 48–49
Art
  murals, 237
  outdoor sculptures, 43–44
  shopping for, 185–88
Art Chicago, 50
Art deco architecture, 40–41
Art festivals, 51, 52
Art Institute of Chicago, 40
  disabled visitor access to, 111
  shopping in, 186
Art museums
  African–American, 293–94
  American, 186, 271
  Art Institute of Chicago, 40, 111,
    186, 272–73
  contemporary, 186, 266–68
  disabled visitor access to, 111
  eclectic, 298–99
  holography, 260–61
  Jewish, 284–85
  Mexican, 237, 293
  Near East, 296–98
  Oriental, 296–98
  peace, 270–71
  Polish, 261–62
  shopping in, 186
  Ukrainian, 262–63
  Vietnam veterans, 290–92
Art shows, 50
Asian community, 231–32, 235–36
Athenaeum, Chicago, 185, 273–74
Attractions, 249–303
  chart of, 249–51
  Loop, 250, 272–85
  Near North, 250, 263–71

North Central/O'Hare, 250, 255–63
North Side, 250, 252–55
South Central/Midway, 251, 292–93
South Loop, 251, 285–92
South Side, 251, 293–99
Suburbs
  Northern, 251, 302–3
  Southern, 251, 299–300
  Western, 251, 300–302
Auto(s). *See also* Driving; Parking
  shopping for, 216–17
Auto museums, 216–17
Auto shows, 49
Automatic teller machines, at O'Hare
  International Airport, 100

Baby furniture, shopping for, 188–89
Bagels, 318
Bakeries, 318–19
Balzekas Museum of Lithuanian Culture,
  292–93
Banking services, 100
Bars. *See also* Entertainment and night
    life
  tipping in, 109
Baseball, 171–72
Basketball, 171, 173, 174
Bath supplies, shopping for, 207–13
Beaches, 168–69
Bears (football team), 171–73
Beauty items, shopping for, 189
Bed and breakfasts, 61
Beer, 151, 319–20
Bellmen, tipping, 109
Berghoff Oktoberfest, 53
Betting, 174–75
Bicycles, shopping for, 190
Bicycling
  mountain, 167–68
  road, 166–67
Black Harvest Film Festival, 52
Blackhawks (hockey team), 171, 173
Blues Festival, 51
Board of Trade, 275
Boat(s)
  recreation in, 169
  shopping for, 190
  supplies for, shopping for, 214
  tours in, 223–27

Boat shows, 49, 52
Book fairs, 52
Books, shopping for, 191–92, 218, 230, 233, 239, 242
Botanical gardens. *See* Garden(s)
Brach's Kids Holiday Parade, 54
Bridal wear, shopping for, 194
Bridgeport, sightseeing in, 238–39
Broadcast communications museum, 282–83
Brookfield Zoo, 299–300
    disabled visitor access to, 112
    walking in, 164
Buckingham Fountain, 225, 244
Bucktown, sightseeing in, 234–35
Bud Billiken Parade, 52
Buildings. *See* Architecture; *specific buildings*
Bulls (basketball team), 171, 173
Burnham, Daniel H., 36, 40
Buses, 125–26
    to/from McCormick Place, 84
    tours in, 221–23, 226
        architecture, 224
        wheelchair accessible, 112–13
Business Center, McCormick Place, 85, 87
Business travelers. *See also* Conventions and trade shows
    types of, 80
Busse Woods Bicycle Trail, 168
Byrne, Jane, 38

Cabs, 127
    crime avoidance in, 116–17
    to/from McCormick Place, 84–85
    to/from Midway Airport, 102
    to/from O'Hare International Airport, 98–99
    tipping for, 109
    to/from Union Station, 103
Calendars
    convention, 89–91
    special events, 49–54
Cameras, shopping for, 192
Camp Sagawau, 170
Candlelight Tours of Prairie Avenue Houses, 54
Canoes

recreation in, 169
shopping for, 193
Capone, Alphonse, 36–37, 226
Car(s). *See also* Driving; Parking
    shopping for, 216–17
Carjackings, 118
Caroling to the Animals, 54
Carriage rides, 227
Carson Pirie Scott & Company, 40, 184–85
Casinos, riverboat, 174–75
Celebrate on State Street Festival, 51
*Chicago* (magazine), 111
Chicago Air and Water Show, 52
Chicago Architecture Foundation tours, 224
Chicago Athenaeum: The Museum of Architecture and Design, 185, 273–74
Chicago Auto Show, 49
Chicago Blues Festival, 51
Chicago Board of Trade Building, 41
Chicago Boat, Sports, and RV Show, 49
Chicago Botanic Garden, 246, 302–3
    disabled visitor access to, 112
    walking in, 164
Chicago By Air tours, 226
Chicago Children's Museum, 263–64
Chicago Country Music Festival, 51
Chicago Cultural Center, 40, 276–77
    information at, 107
    shopping in, 186
Chicago Fire of 1871, 35–36, 224
    architecture before, 236
Chicago Gospel Festival, 51
Chicago Historical Society, 252–53
    disabled visitor access to, 111–12
Chicago International Film Festival, 53
Chicago Jazz Festival, 51
Chicago Mercantile Exchange, 277–78
Chicago Motor Coach Company tours, 221–23
Chicago Office of Tourism, 47
Chicago Park District
    Azalea Flower Show, 49
    Holiday Flower Show, 49, 54
    Spring Flower Show, 50
    tennis facilities in, 164–65
Chicago Place (shopping center), 179
Chicago River, 104

Chicago River, *(continued)*
  boat tours on, 223–25
  reversal of, 35–36
*Chicago Social*, 111
Chicago String Ensemble, 140
*Chicago Sun–Times*, 110
Chicago Symphony Orchestra, 140
Chicago Transit Authority, 123–26
  airport trains, 99, 102
  disabled visitor services of, 112–13
*Chicago Tribune*, 110
Chicago Trolley Company tours,
  221–23
*Chicago's First Lady* boat tours, 224
Children
  activities for, 243–44
  bookstore for, 191
  clothing stores for, 194–95
  festivals for, 52
  gift shopping for, 217–18
  museums for, 263–64
  parades for, 54
  playgrounds for, at O'Hare Interna-
    tional Airport, 100
China, shopping for, 203–4
Chinatown, 235–36
Chinese New Year Parade, 49
Christmas activities, 54
Chrysanthemum Show, 53
Churches. *See under* Worship, places of
Cinco de Mayo Festival, 50
Circuses, 50
City of Chicago Department on Disability,
  information sources at, 112
Clark Street, shopping in, 177, 230
  children's toys and games, 217
  clothing, 200
  home furnishings, 212
Clothing, shopping for. *See under* Shopping
Clybourn/Lincoln Park Corridor, shopping in, 177
  art, 188
  books, 192
  clothing, 198–99, 202
  crystal and china, 203–4
  food, 205–6
  home furnishings, 210–11
  luggage, 214
  marine specialty items, 214

wines, 206
Coffee places, 322
Collectibles, shopping for, 214
College sports teams, 174
Columbian Exposition of 1893, 35, 225
Columbus Day Parade, 53
Comedy, 134–35
Comiskey Park, 172
Commodities exchanges
  Chicago Board of Trade Visitor Center,
    275
  Chicago Mercantile Exchange, 277–78
Concerts. *See* Music
Condominium rental, 61–62
Congress Parkway, 99
Conrad Sulzer Library, 232
Conventions and trade shows, 79–94
  calendar for, 89–91
  lodging for, 66–67
    at McCormick Place, 84–85
    at Navy Pier, 91, 93
    at Rosemont Convention Center, 94
  lunch alternatives for, 88
  at McCormick Place, 66, 79–88
  at Navy Pier, 89, 90, 91, 93
  problems during, 47
  at Rosemont Convention Center,
    89–90, 92–94
Costumes, shopping for, 201
Country Music Festival, 51
Coyote Building, 234
Crafts, shopping for, 185–88
Crime, 114–20
  lodging security and, 68
  museum of, 286–87
Cross–country skiing, 170–71
Crowds, avoiding, 46–47
Cruises, river and lake, 223–27
Crystal, shopping for, 203–4
Cubs (baseball team), 171–72
Cultural Center, Chicago, 40, 107, 186,
  276–77
Cultural festivals, 50, 52, 53
Currency exchange, at O'Hare Interna-
  tional Airport, 100
Customs, local, 108–10
Cycling
  mountain, 167–68
  road, 166–67

Daley, Richard J., 33, 37–38, 238
Daley, Richard M., 33, 38, 238
Daley Bicentennial Plaza, 165, 170
Dan Ryan Expressway, 95, 106
Dancing, 135–36
David and Alfred Smart Museum of Art, 298–99
Delis, 323
Department stores, 178–80, 182–85
DePaul University
    neighborhood of, 241
    sports teams, 174
Devon Avenue, sightseeing in, 230–31
Dillinger, John, 226, 287
Dining. *See* Restaurants
Dinner cruises, 226–27
Disabled visitors
    access for, 111–13. *See also specific attractions*
    services for, 112–13
        at O'Hare International Airport, 99–100
Discount outlets, 201–3, 220
Doormen, tipping, 109
Dorm programs, 62
Downtown, lodging in, 58–59
Dress recommendations
    for restaurants, 108
    for theater, 139
Driving, 48–49, 121–23. *See also* Parking
    to/from McCormick Place, 82, 84
    to/from Midway Airport, 102
    to/from O'Hare International Airport, 99
    to/from Rosemont Convention Center, 94
    routes for, 95–96
    scenic, 245–47, 300–302
    in subterranean streets, 123
    traffic problems in, 46–47, 106, 121
du Sable, Jean Baptist Point, 32, 224
DuSable Museum of African–American History, 293–94
Duty free shopping, 100

East Building (McCormick Place), 85, 87
East–West Tollway, 95, 96
Eating. *See also* Restaurants
    at conventions, 88
Edens Expressway, 96

Edgar Allan Poe Reading, 53
Eisenhower Expressway, 95–96, 106
El (elevated trains), 123–25
    views from, 247
Eleanor Residence for Women, 62
Empress River Casino, 175
Entertainment and night life, 129–60
    alternative rock, 155–56
    alternative–country music, 151
    American roots music, 146–47
    artists' bars, 157–60
    beer parlors, 151
    blues, 133–34, 142–43, 151, 152–53
    champagne bars, 158–59
    classical music, 140
    comedy, 134–35
    country–western music, 133, 143–44
    dance clubs, 135–36
    folk music, 144–45
    gentlemen's clubs, 137–38, 140–41
    interactive theater, 134–35
    jazz, 132, 147–48
    piano bars, 137
    rock music, 130–32, 149–50
    singles bars, 136–37, 153–54
    sports bars, 141–42, 156–57, 160
    theater, 138–39
    tropical bars, 148–49
Ernest Hemingway Museum, 255–56
Ethnic festivals, 50, 52, 53
Evanston, shopping in, 177
    children's toys and games, 218
    food, 206
    jewelry, 214
    Oriental rugs, 216
Exercise. *See* Recreation

Farmer's Market, 205
Federal Center Complex, 41
Fermi, Enrico, 37
Ferris wheel, at Navy Pier, 269
Festival Hall, at Navy Pier, 91, 93
Festival of Lights, 247
Field Museum of Natural History, 287–89
    disabled visitor access to, 112
57th Street Art Fair, 51
Film festivals, 50, 52, 53
Fire of 1871, 35–36, 224
    architecture before, 236

Fireworks, 51
Fitness centers, 162
Flatiron Building, 234
Flower(s). *See also* Garden(s)
    shopping for, 204–5
Flower shows, 49, 50, 53, 54
Food. *See also* Restaurants
    at conventions, 88
    shopping for, 205–6
Food festivals, 51
Football, 172–74
Foreign visitor services, at O'Hare
    International Airport, 99, 100
Forest Preserve, Palos, 164, 167
Formalwear, shopping for, 206
Fort Dearborn, 32, 33, 224
Fox River Trail, 168
Furniture, baby, shopping for, 188–89
Furs, shopping for, 206–7
Futures markets
    Chicago Board of Trade Visitor Center,
        275
    Chicago Mercantile Exchange, 277–78

Galleries, art
    for shopping, 185–88
    for viewing. *See* Art museums
Gambling, 174–75
Games
    shopping for, 217–18
    virtual reality, 244
Gangsters
    Capone, Al, 36–37, 226
    museums, 226
    tours related to, 226
Garden(s), 51, 246
    Chicago Botanic Garden, 112, 164, 246,
        302–3
    disabled visitor access to, 112
    Garfield Park Conservatory, 258–59
    Lincoln Park Conservatory, 254
    Morton Arboretum, 300–302
Garden supplies, shopping for, 207
Garfield Park Conservatory, 258–59
Gay and Lesbian Pride Parade, 51
Gentlemen's clubs, 137–38, 140–41
Geography, of Chicago, 103–4
German community, 232
Ghost–related tours, 226

Ginza Holiday, 52
Glassware, shopping for, 203–4
Glencoe, shopping in, 201
Gold Coast, 105
    sightseeing in, 235
    walking in, 163
Gold Coast Art Fair, 52
Golf, 165–66
Goodman Theater, 138
Gospel Festival, 51
Grand Concourse, McCormick Place,
    79, 82
Grant Park, 104
    tennis facilities at, 165
    views from, 247
Great America amusement park, 244
Greek community, 232
Greek culture, museum of, 280

Hair salons, 189
Halsted Street, shopping in, 177
    children's toys and games, 217
    clothing, 200, 202
    home furnishings, 212
Handicapped visitors
    access for, 111–13. *See also specific
        attractions*
    services for, 112–13
        at O'Hare International Airport,
            99–100
Harold Washington Library Center, 42,
    278–80
Harrah's riverboat casinos, 175
Hawthorne Race Course, 174
Haymarket Riot, 36
Hearing impaired, telephones for,
    99–100
Hellenic Museum, 280
Hemingway, Ernest
    birthplace of, 259–60
    museum, 255–56
Henry Crown Space Theater, 295–96
Highways, 95–96, 106
    scenic, 245–47
    subterranean, 123
Hispanic community, 237–38, 242
Historic Pullman District tours, 53
Historic Pullman Foundation, 242
History

of Chicago, 31–39
tours related to, 224–25
History museums, 252–53
African American, 293–94
Jewish, 284–85
Lithuanian, 292–93
Near East, 296–98
Oriental, 296–98
Polish, 261–62
Hockey, 171, 173
Holidays, calendar of, 49–54
Hollywood Casino Aurora, 174–75
Holocaust Memorial, Zell, 284–85
Holography museums, 260–61
Home furnishings, shopping for,
207–13
Homeless population, 118–20
Horse racing, 174
Hot Tix program, 139
Hotels. *See* Lodging
House tours
Hemingway birthplace, 259–60
Hull House, 281
Prairie Avenue, 54
Pullman District, 53
Housewares, shopping for, 203–4
Hull House Museum, 35, 281
Humboldt Park, sightseeing in, 242
Hyde Park
shopping in, 192
sightseeing in, 239–40

IBM Building, 41
Ice skating, 170
Illinois Institute of Technology, 41
Illinois Market Place Visitor Information
Center, 108
Illinois River, 104
Immigrants, 32
Independence Day Concert and Fire-
works, 51
Indian community, 230–31
Industrial design museum, 185, 273–74
Industry, history of, 34–35
Industry museums, 295–96
Information sources, 47, 107–8
Chicago Cultural Center, 40, 107,
186, 276–77
disabled visitor services, 112

O'Hare International Airport, 99
publications, 110–11
visitor centers, 47
In-line skating, 166–67
International Museum of Surgical Science,
264–65
Irish festivals, 50, 52
Italian community, 235–36

Jahn, Helmut, 42
Jane Addams Hull House Museum, 281
Japanese festival, 52
Jazz Festival, 53
*Jenny Jones Show*, 248
*Jerry Springer Show*, 248
Jewelry, shopping for, 213–14, 218
Jewish community, 230–31, 239
Jewish history museum, 284–85
John G. Shedd Aquarium, 247, 289–90
John Hancock Center, 42
observatory, 247, 266
Jolliet, Louis, 32
Jones, Jenny, 248
Jordan, Michael, 156–57, 171

Kayaks, shopping for, 193
Kendall College, dorm program of, 62
Kennedy Expressway, 95, 106
Kenwood, sightseeing in, 239–40
Kettle Moraine, 167–68
Kids on the Fly, 100
Kitchen items, shopping for, 203–4

Lake Michigan
beaches, 168–69
boat tours on, 224–27
running along, 164
views of, 247–48
walking along, 163
water sports on, 169–70
Lake Shore Drive, 96, 104–5
scenic drives on, 245
views from, 247
Lake Shore Park, tennis facilities at, 165
Lakefront Trail, 163, 164, 166–67
views from, 248
Lakeside Center (McCormick Place), 85,
87
Lakeview, sightseeing in, 232–33

Landscaping supplies, shopping for, 207
Language services, at O'Hare International Airport, 99
Latino community, 237–38, 242
Latino Film Festival, 50
Libraries
  Conrad Sulzer, 232
  Harold Washington, 278–80
"Life over Time" exhibit, 288–89
Lincoln Avenue, shopping in, 177
  clothing, 201, 203
  home furnishings, 212
  Oriental rugs, 216
  outdoor gear, 216
Lincoln Park, 105
  sightseeing in, 241
  walking in, 163
Lincoln Park Conservatory, 254
Lincoln Park Zoo, 253–54
  Christmas activities, 54
  Halloween event, 53
  special events, 49
Lincoln Park/Clybourn Corridor, shopping in, 177
  art, 188
  books, 192
  clothing, 198–99, 202
  crystal and china, 203–4
  food, 205–6
  home furnishings, 210–11
  luggage, 214
  marine specialty items, 214
  wines, 206
Lincoln Square, 232
Linens, shopping for, 207–13
Liquor. *See also* Entertainment and night life
  regulations on, 113
Lithuanian museums, 292–93
Little Village, sightseeing in, 237–38
Lodging, 55–78
  bed and breakfast, 61
  best deals in, 77–78
  for business travelers, 66–67
  characteristics of, 67–70
  condos, 61–62
  from consolidators, 61
  for conventions, 66–67
    at McCormick Place, 84–85

    at Navy Pier, 91, 93
    at Rosemont Convention Center, 94
  corporate rates for, 57
  costs of, 72–78
    convention rates, 66–67
  discounts for, 56–57, 60–61
  dorm programs, 62
  downtown, 58–59
  fitness facilities in, 161, 162
  good deals in, 56–57, 60–62
  half-price programs for, 57, 60
  package deals in, 62–63
  parking at, 56
  preferred rates for, 60–61
  quality ratings of, 72–78
  rating/ranking of, 67–78
  reservations for, 64
    bed and breakfast, 61
    condominiums, 61–62
    for conventions, 66–67
    services, 61
    telephone numbers for, 65
  restaurants in, 307–8
  safety in, 68–69
  security in, 68
  selection of, 55–56
  tipping in, 109
  top 30, 77–78
  travel agent help with, 63–64
  weekend rates for, 56–57
  from wholesalers, 61
Logan Square, sightseeing in, 242
Loop, The
  area west of, 105–6
  attractions, 250, 272–85
    Art Institute of Chicago, 40, 111, 186, 272–73
    Chicago Athenaeum; The Museum of Architecture and Design, 185, 273–74
    Chicago Board of Trade Visitor Center, 275
    Chicago Cultural Center, 40, 107, 186, 276–77
    Chicago Mercantile Exchange, 277–78
    Harold Washington Library Center, 278–80

Hellenic Museum, 280
Jane Addams Hull House Museum, 35, 281
   Museum of Broadcast Communications, 282–83
   Sears Tower, 283–84
   Spertus Museum of Judaica, 284–85
elevated service in, 125
geography of, 104
map of, 16–17
sculpture in, 43–44
shopping in, 176–77
   art, 185
   children's toys and games, 217
   clothing, 193–94, 201–2
   department stores, 182–85
   food, 205
   jewelry, 213
   luggage, 214
   music–related items, 215
walking tours, 224
Louis, Joe, exhibit on, 294
Loyola University, sports teams, 174
Luggage, shopping for, 214

McCormick Place Convention Center, 79–89
   airport connections with, 85
   Arie Crown Theater, 85
   Business Center, 85, 87
   convention calendar for, 89–91
   drawbacks of, 81–82
   exhibit hall designations, 82
   exhibitor move–in and move–out, 84
   Lakeside Center (East Building), 85, 87
   layout of, 82
   lodging near, 66
   map of, 83, 86
   North Building, 87
   numbering system, 86
   off–site eating alternatives, 88
   overview of, 80–81
   parking at, 82, 84
   South Building, 88
   transportation to/from, 84–85
   union rules for, 81–82
Mace, for self–defense, 117–18
McFetridge Sports Center, tennis facilities at, 165

Madison Street, 106–7
Magnificent Mile. *See* Michigan Avenue
Magnificent Mile Festival of Lights, 54
Malls, 178–81, 218–20
Manderfield, Ellen, 274
Manhattan Project, 37
Maps
   Downtown lodging, 58
   Loop, The, 16–17
   McCormick Place, 83, 86
   Midway Airport, 101
   Midwest, 2
   Near North, 14–15
   North Central/O'Hare, 12–13
   O'Hare International Airport, 97
   Rosemont Convention Center, 92
   South Central/Midway, 20–21
   South Loop, 18–19
   South Side, 22–23
   Suburbs
      Northern, 30
      Northwest, 28–29
      Southern, 24–25
      Western, 26–27
   Zones of Chicago, 8–30
Marine animals, aquariums for, 247, 289–90
Marine weather forecasts, 170
Marshall Field's, 182–83
Meatpacking industry, 34
Medical science museums, 264–65
Medinah Shrine Circus, 50
Meigs Airfield observation deck, 244
Menswear, shopping for, 193, 195, 198–99
Mercury Tours, 225
Mexican community, 237–38
Mexican Fine Arts Museum, 237, 293
Michigan Avenue (Miracle Mile), 105
   bridge on, views from, 247
   parking for, 122
   shopping on. *See under* Shopping
Midsummer Festival in Andersonville, 51
Midway. *See* South Central/Midway
Midway Airport, 48, 100, 102
   map of, 101
   transportation to/from McCormick Place, 85
Mies van der Rohe, Ludwig, 41

Milwaukee Avenue, sightseeing in,
233–34
Miracle Mile. *See* Michigan Avenue
Money services, at O'Hare International
Airport, 100
Montrose Avenue Beach, 169
Montrose Harbor, view from, 247
Moore, Henry, 37
Morton Arboretum, 300–302
walking in, 164
Mosques, 240
Motels. *See* Lodging
Mountain biking, 167–68
Museum(s)
archeology, 296–98
architecture, 185, 273–74
art. *See* Art museums
auto, 216–17
broadcast communications, 282–83
disabled visitor services at, 111–12
free admission to, 245, 246
Hellenic, 280
Hemingway, 255–56
history. *See* History museums
holography, 260–61
Hull House, 281
industrial design, 185, 273–74
industry, 295–96
Lithuanian, 292–93
natural history, 112, 287–89
outdoor, architecture as, 43
peace, 270–71
police, 286–87
Polish, 261–62
science, 287–89, 295–96
space, 295–96
surgical science, 264–65
Swedish, 230, 254–55
Ukrainian, 242, 262–63
Vietnam War, 290–92
Museum Campus, walking in, 163–64
Museum of Contemporary Art, 186,
266–68
Museum of Science and Industry,
295–96
Music, 129
alternative rock, 155–56
alternative–country, 151
American roots, 146–47

baroque, 140
blues, 133–34, 142–43, 151, 152–53
classical, 140
country–western, 51, 133, 143–44
festivals for, 51, 53, 131, 247
folk, 144–45
instruments for, 215
jazz, 132, 147–48
in parks, 51, 52
piano bars, 137
in public library, 279
radio stations for, 111
recordings of, shopping for, 215
rock, 130–32, 149–50
in Wicker Park, 234

National African American History
Month, 50
National Antique Show & Sale, 52
National Vietnam Veterans Art Museum,
290–92
Native Americans, history of, 31–32
Natural history museums, 112, 287–89
Nautilus equipment, 161
Navy Pier, 105, 268–70
Chicago Children's Museum at,
263–64
conventions at, 89, 90, 91, 93
shopping at, 181
NBC Tower, 42
Near North
attractions, 250, 263–71
Chicago Children's Museum,
263–64
International Museum of Surgical
Science, 264–65
John Hancock Center Observatory,
266
Museum of Contemporary Art,
266–68
Navy Pier. *See* Navy Pier
Peace Museum, 270–71
Terra Museum of American Art,
186, 271
map of, 14–15
shopping in. *See under* Shopping
sightseeing in, 235
Neighborhoods. *See also specific
neighborhoods and zones*

crime in, 114–15
sightseeing in
  Andersonville, 230
  Bridgeport, 238–39
  Bucktown, 234–35
  Chinatown, 235–36
  DePaul, 241
  Devon Avenue, 230–31
  Gold Coast, 235
  Humboldt Park, 242
  Hyde Park, 239–40
  Kenwood, 239–40
  Lakeview, 232–33
  Lincoln Park, 241
  Lincoln Square, 232
  Little Village, 237–38
  Logan Square, 242
  Milwaukee Avenue, 233–34
  Near North, 235
  North Central/O'Hare, 233–35,
    241–42
  North Side, 230–33, 240–41
  Old Town, 235
  Pilsen, 237–38
  Pullman, 242–43
  Rogers Park, 240–41
  South Central/Midway, 236–39
  South Loop, 235–36
  South Shore, 240
  South Side, 239–40, 242–43
  Taylor Street, 236–37
  Ukrainian Village, 241–42
  Uptown, 231–32
  Wicker Park, 234–35
  Wrigleyville, 232–33
Neilsen, A.C., Jr., Research Center, 282
Neiman Marcus, 179
Ness, Eliot, 37
*New City*, 110
New East Side ArtWorks Festival, 52
Newberry Consort, 140
Newberry Library Annual Book Fair, 52
Newspapers, 110–11
Night life. *See* Entertainment and night
  life
Noble Horse, The, carriage rides, 227
North Avenue Beach, 168–69
North Branch Bicycle Trail, 168
North Building (McCormick Place), 87

North Central/O'Hare
  attractions, 250, 255–63
    Ernest Hemingway Museum,
      255–56
    Frank Lloyd Wright Home and
      Studio, 256–58
    Garfield Park Conservatory,
      258–59
    Hemingway's Birthplace, 259–60
    Museum of Holography, 260–61
    Polish Museum of America, 261–62
    Ukrainian National Museum,
      262–63
  map of, 12–13
  sightseeing in, 233–35, 241–42
North Pier, cruises from, 225
North Side
  attractions, 250, 252–55
  map of, 10–11
  sightseeing in, 232–33, 240–41
  tours, 225–26
Northbrook, shopping in, 201
Northlight Theater, 139
North–South Tollway, 96
Northwest Tollway, 95
Northwestern University, sports teams,
  174

Oak Park
  Visitor Center, 108
  walking in, 163
  Wright–designed homes in, 163
  Wright home and studio in, 50,
    256–58
Oak Street, shopping in, 177
  clothing, 195–97
  home furnishings, 207–8
  jewelry, 213
  music–related items, 215
  stationery, 191
Oak Street Beach, 168
Observatory, John Hancock Center, 247,
  266
Oceanarium, 247, 289–90
*Odyssey* boat tours, 226–27
Off–track betting, 174–75
O'Hare International Airport, 48,
  96–100
  driving from, 99

O'Hare International Airport (continued)
  layout of, 98
  map of, 97
  parking at, 100
  people mover in, 98
  play area at, 100
  statistics on, 96
  transportation to/from, 98–99
    McCormick Place, 85
  visitor services at, 99–100
O'Hare region. See North
  Central/O'Hare
Oktoberfest, 53
Old Town, sightseeing in, 235
One Mag Mile, 181
Oprah Winfrey Show, 248
Orchestra Hall, 140
Oriental Institute Museum, 296–98
Oriental rugs, shopping for, 216
Orientation tours, 221–23
Outdoor gear, shopping for, 216
Oz Festival, 52

Package deals, for lodging and travel,
  62–63
Paint ball, 244
Palos Forest Preserve District, 164, 167
Parades, 49–54
Parking, 49, 121–22. See also individual
    attractions
  Comiskey Park, 172
  commercial lots and garages for, 122
  lodging, 56
  McCormick Place, 82, 84
  Michigan Avenue (Magnificent Mile),
    122
  O'Hare International Airport, 100
  safety tips for, 117
  tipping for, 109
  Wrigley Field, 172
Parks
  amusement, 244
  Grant Park, 104, 165, 247
  Lake Shore Park, 165
  music in, 51, 52
Peace Museum, 270–71
Pedways, 128
People mover, O'Hare International
  Airport, 98

Pilsen, sightseeing in, 237–38
Pizza, 323–24
Plane travel. See also Airports
  observation deck for, 244
  for sightseeing tours, 226
Planetarium, 285–86
  disabled visitor access to, 112
Playgrounds
  Chicago Children's Museum, 263–64
  at O'Hare International Airport, 100
Plaza Escada, 180
Poe, Edgar Allan, 53
Police museums, 286–87
Polish community, 233–34
Polish Constitution Day Parade, 50
Polish Film Festival in North America,
  53
Polish Museum of America, 261–62
Porters, tipping, 109
Postal services, at O'Hare International
  Airport, 99
Postmodernism, in architecture, 41–42
Power (soccer team), 173
Prairie Avenue, house tours, 54
Prairie School of architecture, 40,
  256–58
Pratt Boulevard Beach, 169
Precipitation, seasonal, 46
Protocols, local, 108–10
Public transportation. See Transportation
Publications, for visitors, 110–11
Pullman, George, 242
Pullman District
  house tours in, 53
  sightseeing in, 242–43
Pullman Strike, 36

Racing, horse, 174
Radio, museum of, 282–83
Radio stations, 111
Rand, Sally, 37
Ravinia Festival, 51, 131, 247
Reader, 110
Records, shopping for, 215
Recreation, 161–75
  aerobics, 162
  baseball, 171–72
  basketball, 171, 173, 174
  bicycling, 166–67

canoeing, 169
for children, 244
college sports teams, 174
fitness centers, 162
football, 172–74
gambling, 174–75
golf, 165–66
hockey, 171, 173
horse racing, 174
ice skating, 170
indoor, 161–62
in–line skating, 166–67
in lodging, 162
mountain biking, 167–68
Nautilus equipment, 161
off–track betting, 174–75
publications for, 111
riverboat casinos, 174–75
running, 164
skiing, 170–71
soccer, 173
spectator sports, 171–75, 244
swimming, 168–69
tennis, 164–65
walking, 127–28, 163–64
weather and, 161
weights, 161
windsurfing, 169–70
Reliance Building, 40
Rental
bikes, 167, 168
canoes, 169
condominiums, 61–62
ice skates, 170
in–line skates, 167
skis, 171
Reservations, for lodging, 64
bed and breakfast, 61
condominiums, 61–62
conventions, 66–67
services, 61
telephone numbers for, 65
Restaurants, 304–451, *See also* Neighborhoods, sightseeing in
bagel, 318–19
bakeries, 318
barbecue, 319–20
beer in, 320
best, 314–18
breakfasts in, 320–21
brunches in, 321–22
burger, 322–23
celebrity, 308
coffee in, 323
cornbread in, 323
deli, 323
dessert, 323
dinner cruises, 226–27
dress recommendations for, 108
hot dogs in, 324
in lodging, 307–8
new, 305–7
new–age, 308–9
picnic meals, 324
pizza, 324–25
profiles of, 326–451
rating of, 312–14
ribs, 319–320
sandwiches in, 322
smoking in, 309
tipping in, 109
touristy, 310–11
trends in, 309–10
wine in, 325
River North, 105
shopping in, 177
art, 187–88
clothing, 198
home furnishings, 208–10
stationery, 192
Riverboat casinos, 174–75
Rogers Park, sightseeing in, 240–41
Rollerblading, 166–67
Rosemont Convention Center, 93–94
calendar for, 89–90
map of, 92
Rosemont Horizon, 131–32
Rugs, Oriental, shopping for, 216
Running, 164

Saddles, shopping for, 218
Safety tips, 114–18
for bicycling, 166–67
for Lakefront Trail, 163
for lodging, 68–69
Sailing craft, shopping for, 190
St. Patrick's Day Parade, 50
St. Valentine's Day Massacre, 226

Sandburg, Carl, 36
Scenic drives, 245–47, 300–302
Science museums, 295–96
   natural history, 287–89
   surgical, 264–65
Sculpture, in the Loop, 43–44
Sears Tower, 42
   views from, 247, 283–84
Seasons to visit, 45–47
Second City, 138–39
Self–defense, 117–18
Settlement house complex, 281
Settlers, 32
*Shear Madness*, 134–35
Shedd Aquarium, 289–90
   views from, 247
Sheffield Garden Walk and Festival, 51
Sheridan Road, scenic drives on, 246
Shoes, shopping for, 194, 195, 218
Shopping, 176–220. *See also* Neighbor-
    hoods, sightseeing in
   Andersonville, 230
   art, 185–88
   autos, 216–17
   baby furniture, 188–89
   bath supplies, 207–13
   beauty items, 189
   bikes, 190
   boats, 190
   books, 191–92, 230, 233, 239, 242
   boots, 218
   cameras, 192
   canoes, 193
   cars, 216–17
   children's gifts, 217–18
   china, 203–4
   Clark Street, 177, 230
    children's toys and games, 217
    clothing, 200
    home furnishings, 212
   clothing, 193–203
    bridal wear, 194
    costumes, 201
    at discount outlets, 201–3
    formalwear, 206
    furs, 206–7
    high–fashion, 196–97
    menswear, 193, 195, 198–99
    Michigan Avenue, 178–81, 194–95
    western, 218

collectibles, 214
crafts, 185–88
crystal, 203–4
department stores, 178–80, 182–85
discount outlets, 220
duty free, 100
East of Michigan Avenue, 181
Evanston, 177
   children's toys and games, 218
   food, 206
   jewelry, 214
   Oriental rugs, 216
flowers, 204–5
food, 205–6
furniture, 188–89
galleries, 185–88
games, 217–18
garden supplies, 207
Glencoe, clothing, 201
Halsted Street, 177
   children's toys and games, 217
   clothing, 200, 202–203
   home furnishings, 212
home furnishings, 207–13
housewares, 203–4
Hyde Park, 192
jewelry, 213–14, 218
kayaks, 193
kitchen items, 203–4
landscaping supplies, 207
Lincoln Avenue, 177
   clothing, 201, 203
   home furnishings, 212
   Oriental rugs, 216
   outdoor gear, 216
Lincoln Park/Clybourn Corridor, 177
   art, 188
   books, 192
   clothing, 198–99, 202
   crystal and china, 203–4
   food, 205–6
   home furnishings, 210–11
   luggage, 214
   marine specialty items, 214
   wines, 206
Lincoln Square, 232
linens, 207–13
Loop, 176–77
   art, 185
   children's toys and games, 217

clothing, 193–94, 201–2
  department stores, 182–85
  food, 205
  jewelry, 213
  luggage, 214
  music–related items, 215
luggage, 214
malls, 178–81, 218–20
marine specialty items, 214
Michigan Avenue (Miracle Mile), 105,
    177
  art, 185–86
  books, 191, 192
  children's toys and games, 217
  clothing, 178–81, 194–95, 202
  crystal and china, 203
  jewelry, 213, 218
  music–related items, 215
  outdoor gear, 216
music recordings, 215
musical instruments, 215
Navy Pier, 268–70
Near North, 177
  art, 186–87
  beauty items, 189
  books, 191
  clothing, 197–98
  crystal and china, 203
  food, 205
  home furnishings, 208
  music–related items, 215
Northbrook, clothing, 201
Oak Street, 177
  clothing, 195–97
  home furnishings, 207–8
  jewelry, 213
  music–related items, 215
  stationery, 191
Oriental rugs, 216
outdoor gear, 216
records, 215
River North, 177
  art, 187–88
  clothing, 198
  home furnishings, 208–10
  stationery, 192
rugs, 216
saddles, 218
sailing craft, 190
shoes, 194, 195, 218

shopping centers, 218–20
sports cars, 216
stationery, 191–92
tobacco, 217
toys, 217–18
western goods, 218
Wicker Park, 177, 234
  art, 188
  clothing, 201
  home furnishings, 212
Wilmette, 204, 206
wines, 206
Winettka, 201
yachts, 190
Shuttles
  to/from McCormick Place, 84, 85
  to/from Midway Airport, 102
  to/from O'Hare International Airport,
    98–99
Sightseeing. See Attractions; Tours
Singles bars, 136–37, 153–54
Six Flags' Great America, 244
Skating
  ice, 170
  in–line, 166–67
Skiing, 170–71
Sky Theater, 285–86
Skybridge Network, 94
Skycaps, tipping, 109
Skydeck, Sears Tower, 247, 283–84
Skyline Stage, 131
Skyscrapers, 42
Slacker territory, 234–35
Smart Museum of Art, 298–99
Smoking
  regulations for, 113
  in restaurants, 309
  supplies for, shopping for, 217
Soccer, 173
Soldier Field, 173
South Building (McCormick Place), 88
South Central/Midway
  attractions, 251, 292–93
  map of, 20–21
  sightseeing in, 237–39
South Loop
  attractions, 251, 285–92
    Adler Planetarium, 285–86
South Loop (continued)
    American Police Center &

Museum, 286–87
Field Museum of Natural History, 112, 287–89
National Vietnam Veterans Art Museum, 290–92
Shedd Aquarium, 247, 289–90
map of, 18–19
sightseeing in, 235–36
South Shore, sightseeing in, 240
South Shore Country Club, 240
South Side
attractions, 251, 293–99
David and Alfred Smart Museum of Art, 298–99
DuSable Museum of African–American History, 293–94
Museum of Science and Industry, 295–96
Oriental Institute Museum, 296–98
map of, 22–23
St. Patrick's Day Parade, 50
sightseeing in, 239–40
Space museums, 295–96
Special events calendar, 49–54
Spertus Museum of Judaica, 284–85
Spooky Zoo Spectacular, 53
Sports. *See also* Recreation
spectator, 171–75
baseball, 171–72
basketball, 171, 173, 174
for children, 244
college teams, 174
football, 172–74
gambling, 174–75
hockey, 171, 173
horse racing, 174
off–track betting, 174–75
riverboat casinos, 174–75
soccer, 173
Sportsman's Park, 174
Springer, Jerry, 248
State of Illinois Center, 42
State Street, 106–7
State Street Festival, 51
Stationery, shopping for, 191–92
Steppenwolf Theater, 138
Stevenson Expressway, 95, 106
Stockyards, 34
Street layout, 106–7

*StreetWise*, 111
Suburbs
Northern
attractions, 251, 302–3
map of, 30
Northwest, map of, 28–29
Southern
attractions, 251, 299–300
map of, 24–25
Western
attractions, 251, 300–302
map of, 26–27
Subways, 123–25
Sullivan, Louis, 184, 242
Supernatural Tours, 226
Surgical science museum, 264–65
Swedish American Museum, 230, 254–55
Swimming, 168–69
Synagogues, 239

Talk show taping, admission to, 248
Taste of Chicago, 51
Taste of Ireland Festival, 52
Taste of River North, 51
Taxes, 113
Taxis. *See* Cabs
Taylor Street, sightseeing in, 236–37
Telephones, 113
for hearing impaired, at airport, 99–100
Television
admission to shows, 248
museum of, 282–83
Temperatures, seasonal, 46
Tennis, 164–65
Terra Museum of American Art, 186, 271
Theater
interactive, 134–35
legitimate, 138–39
Thoroughbred racing, 174
Time zone, 113
Tipping, 109–10
Tobacco shops, 217
*Tony n' Tina's Wedding*, 135
Tours, 221–48. *See also specific attractions*
airplane, 226
Andersonville, 230
architecture, 43, 50, 223–25. *See also*

Neighborhoods, sightseeing in
boat, 223–27
Bridgeport, 238–39
Bucktown, 234–35
carriage, 227
for children, 243–44
Chinatown, 235–36
DePaul, 241
Devon Avenue, 230–31
double–decker buses, 223
driving, 245–47
free admission for, 245, 246
gangster–related, 226
Gold Coast, 235
for great views, 247–48
historical, 224–25
house. *See* House tours
Humboldt Park, 242
Hyde Park, 239–40
in–depth, 228–29
Kenwood, 239–40
Lakeview, 232–33
Lincoln Park, 241
Lincoln Square, 232
Little Village, 237–38
Logan Square, 242
Milwaukee Avenue, 233–34
Near North, 235
North Central/O'Hare, 233–35,
241–42
North Side, 230–33, 240–41
Old Town, 235
orientation, 221–23
Pilsen, 237–38
Pullman, 242–43
Rogers Park, 240–41
South Central/Midway, 236–39
South Loop, 235–36
South Shore, 240
South Side, 239–40, 242–43
specialized, 225–27
supernatural, 226
Taylor Street, 236–37
trolley, 222–23
TV talk show taping, 248
two–day, 227–28
Ukrainian Village, 241–42
Uptown, 231–32
walking, 43, 224
Wicker Park, 234–35

Wrigleyville, 232–33
Toys, shopping for, 217–18
Trade shows. *See* Conventions and trade
shows
Trading pits
Chicago Board of Trade Visitor Center, 275
Chicago Mercantile Exchange,
277–78
Traffic, 46–47, 48–49, 106, 121
Trains
arrival by, 48, 102–3
elevated, 123–25
views from, 247
history of, 33–34
to/from McCormick Place, 84–85
to/from Midway Airport, 102
to/from O'Hare International Airport,
99
Transportation, 48–49
at airports, to/from McCormick Place,
85
Chicago Transit Authority, 123–26
airport trains, 99, 102
disabled visitor services of, 112–13
crime avoidance in, 116–17
for disabled visitors, 112–13
to/from McCormick Place, 84–85
to neighborhoods. *See* Neighborhoods,
sightseeing in
to/from O'Hare International Airport,
98–99
Travel agents, help from, 63–64
Travel packages, 62–63
Tribune Tower, 41
Tri–State Tollway, 95, 106
Trolley tours, 221–23

Ukrainian National Museum, 262–63
Ukrainian Village, 241–42
Union Station, 48, 102–3
Union Stockyards, 34
United Center, 131, 173
University of Chicago
neighborhood of, 239
walking in, 164
University of Illinois
neighborhood of, 235–36
University of Illinois *(continued)*
sports teams, 174

Untouchable Tours, 226
Uptown, tours, 231–32

Venetian Night, 52
Veteran's Day Parade, 54
Vietnam Veterans Art Museum, 290–92
Views, 247–48, 266, 283–84
Virtual reality games, 244
Visitor centers, 47, 107–8
  Chicago Cultural Center, 40, 107, 186,
    276–77
"Viva Chicago" Latin Music Festival, 53

Waiters, tipping, 109
Walking, 163–64
  in city, 163–64
  lakeside, 163
  locations for, 127–28
  on pedways, 128
Walking tours
  architecture, 43, 224
  Loop, 224
Walnut Room, Marshall Field's, 182,
  183
War museums, 290–92
Washington, Harold, 38, 239
  library dedicated to, 278–80
Water sports, 169–70
Water Tower Place, 179–80
Water Tower Welcome Center, 107–8
Waveland, tennis facilities at, 165
Weather, 45–46
  marine, forecasts for, 170
  for recreation, 161
Weight lifting, 161–62
Wendella Sightseeing Boats, 225
Western goods, shopping for, 218
Wheelchairs, accessibility with, 111–13
White Sox (baseball team), 171–72
Wicker Park
  shopping in, 177, 234
    art, 188
    clothing, 201
    home furnishings, 212
  sightseeing in, 234–35
Wilmette, shopping in, 204, 206

Wilmot Mountain, 170
Windsurfing, 169–70
*Windy City Sports*, 111
Wines
  in restaurants, 324–25
  shopping for, 206
Winettka, shopping in, 201
Winfrey, Oprah, 222, 248
World Music Theatre, 131
Worship, places of
  Church of St. Philip Neri, 240
  K.A.M. Isaiah Israel, 239
  Masjid Honorable Elijah Muhammad
    mosque, 240
  Providence of God Church, 237
  Russian Orthodox Holy Trinity
    Cathedral, 242
  St. Basil Greek Orthodox Church,
    236–37
  St. Demetrios Orthodox Church, 232
  St. Hyacinth's Roman Catholic
    Church, 234
  St. Matthias, 232
  St. Nicholas Ukrainian Catholic
    Church, 242
  Unity Temple, 256
Wright, Frank Lloyd
  furniture designed by, 274, 298
  home and studio, 50, 256–58
  Oak Park homes designed by, 163
  Prairie School, 40
  tours, 224
Wright Plus tour, 50
Wrigley Building, 41
Wrigley Field, 171–72, 232
Wrigleyville, sightseeing in, 232–33

Yachts, shopping for, 190

Zell Holocaust Memorial, 284–85
Zones of Chicago, 7
  maps of, 8–30
Zooperbowl Cafe Brauer, 49
Zoos. *See also* Lincoln Park Zoo
  Brookfield, 112, 164, 299–300
  special events at, 49

## *Unofficial Guide* **Reader Survey**

If you would like to express your opinion about Chicago or this guide-book, complete the following survey and mail it to:

> *Unofficial Guide* Reader Survey
> PO Box 43059
> Birmingham AL 35243

Inclusive dates of your visit: _____

*Members of
your party:*     Person 1     Person 2     Person 3     Person 4     Person 5
Gender:          M  F         M  F         M  F         M  F         M  F
Age:             _____

How many times have you been to Chicago?          _____
On your most recent trip, where did you stay?     _____

Concerning your accommodations, on a scale of 100 as best and 0 as worst, how would you rate:

The quality of your room?    _____    The value of your room?            ____
The quietness of your room?  _____    Check-in/check-out efficiency? ____
Shuttle service to the parks? _____   Swimming pool facilities?          ____

Did you rent a car? _____    From whom? _____

Concerning your rental car, on a scale of 100 as best and 0 as worst, how would you rate:

Pick-up processing efficiency? ____    Return processing efficiency?   ____
Condition of the car?          ____    Cleanliness of the car?         ____
Airport shuttle efficiency?    ____

Concerning your dining experiences:

Including fast-food, estimate your meals in restaurants per day? _____
Approximately how much did your party spend on meals per day? _____
Favorite restaurants in Chicago:          _____

_____

Did you buy this guide before leaving? ☐    while on your trip? ☐

How did you hear about this guide? (check all that apply)

Loaned or recommended by a friend ☐   Radio or TV ☐
Newspaper or magazine ☐               Bookstore salesperson ☐
Just picked it out on my own ☐        Library ☐
Internet ☐

What other guidebooks did you use on this trip? _____

_____

_____

_____

On a scale of 100 as best and 0 as worst, how would you rate them?

_____

_____

_____

Using the same scale, how would you rate *The Unofficial Guide(s)?*

_____

Are *Unofficial Guides* readily available at bookstores in your area? _____

Have you used other *Unofficial Guides?* _____

Which one(s)? _____

_____

_____

_____

_____

Comments about your Chicago trip or *The Unofficial Guide(s):*

_____

_____

_____

_____

_____

_____

_____

_____

_____

_____

_____

_____

_____

_____

_____